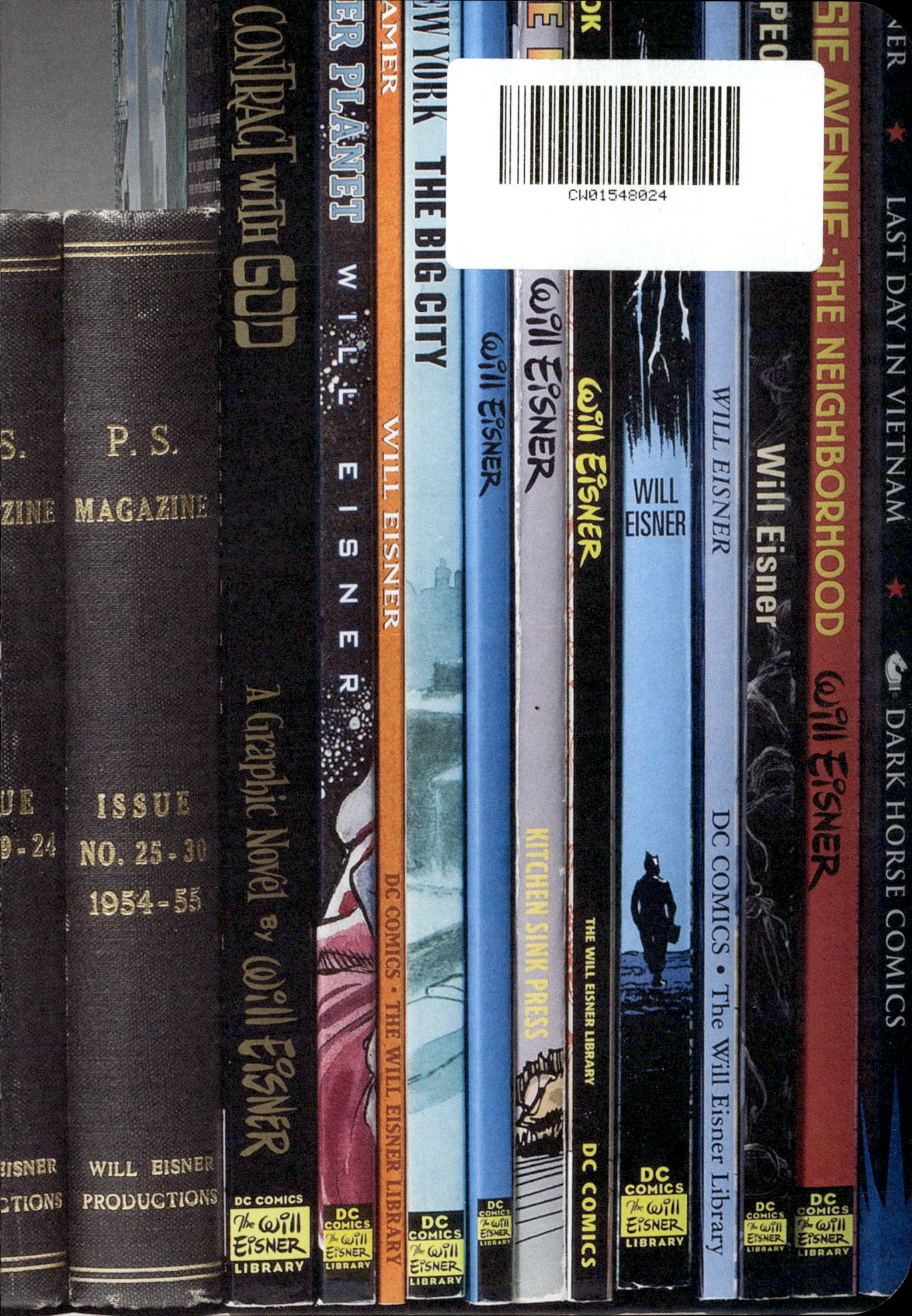
P. S.
MAGAZINE
ISSUE
NO. 25 - 30
1954 - 55
WILL EISNER
PRODUCTIONS
CONTRACT WITH GOD
A Graphic Novel by Will Eisner
DC COMICS
The Will Eisner Library
WILL EISNER
DC COMICS
The Will Eisner Library
WILL EISNER
DC COMICS • THE WILL EISNER LIBRARY
THE BIG CITY
DC COMICS
The Will Eisner Library
Will Eisner
Will Eisner
KITCHEN SINK PRESS
Will Eisner
THE WILL EISNER LIBRARY
DC COMICS
WILL EISNER
DC COMICS
The Will Eisner Library
WILL EISNER
DC COMICS • The Will Eisner Library
Will Eisner
THE NEIGHBORHOOD
Will Eisner
DC COMICS
The Will Eisner Library
LAST DAY IN VIETNAM
DARK HORSE COMICS

PS Magazine

The Best of *The Preventive Maintenance Monthly*

for Will & Ann

P★S MAGAZINE

THE BEST OF THE PREVENTIVE MAINTENANCE MONTHLY

Will Eisner

Introduction by General Peter J. Schoomaker, USA (Ret.)
Preface by Ann Eisner
Selected and with commentary by Eddie Campbell

Abrams ComicArts, New York

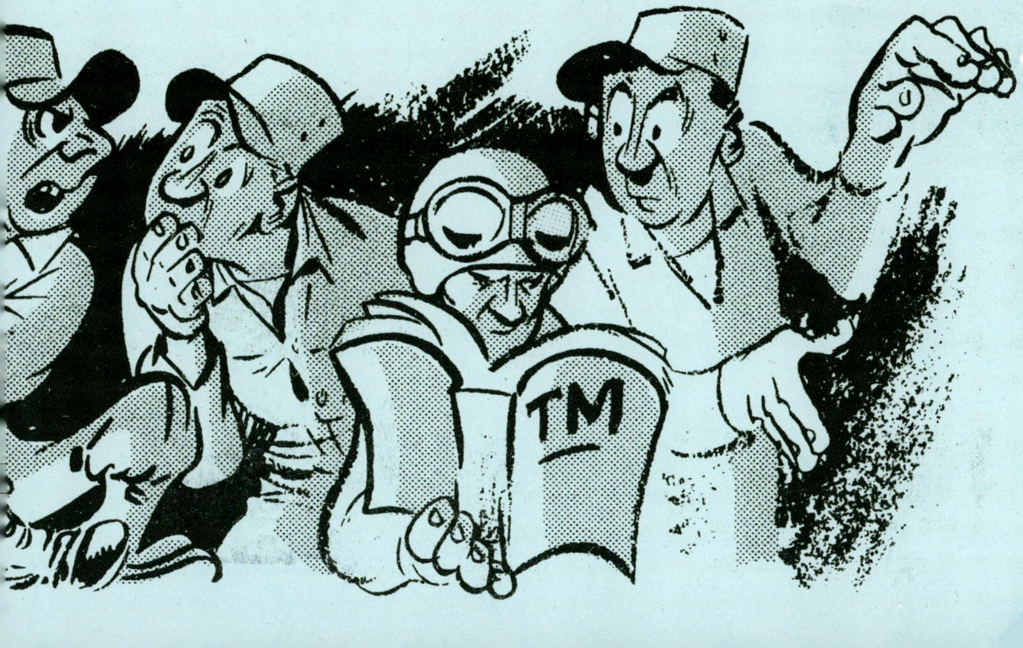
TM

Acknowledgments

The entire run of Eisner's *PS* magazine is available online. Thanks to Virginia Commonwealth University (www.library.vcu.edu) and the VCU Libraries Digital Collections (http://dig.library.vcu.edu/cdm4/index_psm.php?CISOROOT=/psm).

At Abrams ComicArts: Charles Kochman (editorial), Neil Egan (design), Scott Auerbach (managing editorial), and Alison Gervais (production). Thanks also to Jennifer Redding (design assistance).

Special thanks to Eddie Campbell (for taking 227 issues and twenty years and distilling them down to a "best of" 270 images), General Peter J. Schoomaker, and Ann Eisner for providing context for this material. The book would not be the same without your insights.

Thanks to Paul E. Fitzgerald, author of *Will Eisner and PS Magazine*, which he self-published in 2009 (FitzWorld.US).

The Will and Ann Eisner Family Foundation: Carl and Nancy Gropper, and Ann Eisner. Thank you for giving your blessing and support. We could not (would not) have done this book without you.

And last but certainly not least: Thanks to agents Judy Hansen and Denis Kitchen from the Kitchen and Hansen Agency, LLC (for permissions, guidance, and friendship).

About This Book

All of the images were scanned from original printed copies of *PS*. Issues 1 through 30 are from Will Eisner's personal bound volumes, which were generously lent for this project by Ann Eisner and Denis Kitchen (thanks again, Denis!). The balance of the Eisner file copies were provided by Denis Kitchen from his personal collection. Additional issues were purchased from Bud Plant at the San Diego Comic-Con in July 2010. All pages are presented at 100% (the trim size of *PS* varied over the years, but averaged 5 × 7"). Page numbers from the comics were removed at the printer to avoid confusion with the page numbers of this book. All of the articles are in as close to chronological order as possible; allowing for pages that needed to start on either a left- or right-hand page necessitated some shifting.

EDITOR: Charles Kochman
DESIGNER: Neil Egan
PRODUCTION MANAGER: Alison Gervais

Library of Congress Cataloging-in-Publication Data

Eisner, Will.
  PS magazine : the best of the preventive maintenance monthly / by Will Eisner ; selected and with an overview by Eddie Campbell ; preface by Ann Eisner ; introduction by Peter J. Schoomaker.
    p. cm.
  ISBN 978-0-8109-9748-6
  1. Eisner, Will—Themes, motives. I. Campbell, Eddie, 1955– II. PS (United States. Dept. of the Army) III. Title. IV. Title: Best of the Preventive maintenance monthly.
  NC1429.E46A4 2011
  741.5'973—dc22
                        2011012342

Compilation copyright © 2011 Harry N. Abrams, Inc.
The logo and signature of Will Eisner is a registered trademark of Will Eisner Studios, Inc. Used by permission.
Introduction copyright © 2011 General Peter J. Schoomaker
Preface copyright © 2011 Ann Eisner
"A *PS* Briefing" copyright © 2011 Eddie Campbell

Endpaper photograph by Geoff Spear
Photographs and captions on pages 8, 9, 10, 11, 12, and 18 courtesy of the Denis Kitchen Art Agency.

Published in 2011 by Abrams ComicArts, an imprint of ABRAMS. All rights reserved. No portion of this book may be reproduced, stored in a retrieval system, or transmitted in any form or by any means, mechanical, electronic, photocopying, recording, or otherwise, without written permission from the publisher.

Abrams ComicArts is a registered trademark of Harry N. Abrams, Inc., registered in the U.S. Patent and Trademark Office.

Printed and bound in China
10 9 8 7 6 5 4 3 2 1

Abrams ComicArts books are available at special discounts when purchased in quantity for premiums and promotions as well as fundraising or educational use. Special editions can also be created to specification. For details, contact specialsales@abramsbooks.com or the address below.

THE ART OF BOOKS SINCE 1949
115 West 18th Street
New York, NY 10011
www.abramsbooks.com

COVER AND OPPOSITE: no. **40, 1956**
BACK COVER: no. **21, 1954**
TITLE PAGE: no. **28, 1955**

Contents

Introduction — 6
by General Peter J. Schoomaker, USA (Ret.)

Preface — 8
Recollections of Will Eisner and PS Magazine by Ann Eisner

A PS Briefing — 10
by Eddie Campbell

1951–1953 — 20
1954–1959 — 66
1960–1971 — 192

Introduction

An ounce of prevention is worth a pound of cure.
—Benjamin Franklin

Created as a postscript to the standard technical manuals issued by the U.S. Army, PS was conceived as a simple means of communicating to soldiers—in easy-to-comprehend and often humorous cartoons—how to take better care of their equipment. Paul E. Fitzgerald, a former army second lieutenant who was PS magazine's managing editor from 1953 to 1963, succinctly boils down the concept of PS in his book *Will Eisner and PS Magazine*: "In essence, the premise is that it is easier and quicker and cheaper to check an engine's oil-level daily than it is to replace the engine."

PS tries to catch the attention of its readers with a mixture of comic book characters, vivid graphics and color, gags, talking equipment, and informal, no-nonsense writing. The emphasis is on pictures over words, but the combination has proven to be a successful tool in providing soldiers with the best, most up-to-date information available. Throughout my own career, dog-eared copies of PS could to be found in the hands of all ranks—from private to general—in the motor pools, workshops, supply rooms, and offices of literally every organization in the army, at home and abroad. Many copies, I am sure, were carried onto the battlefield and experienced combat.

In the first issue of PS, in 1951, General J. Lawton Collins introduced the magazine with the following note:

> The modern Army of today must possess mobility—and mobility depends to a large degree upon prompt, efficient, and continuing maintenance. Therefore, it is imperative that the men and women who operate and maintain our cars and trucks and tanks and other equipment are kept well informed on better maintenance.
>
> If PS magazine will help to accomplish this mission, it will perform a most valuable service in helping the Army achieve the high degree of ready mobility so essential to victory in modern war.

During my tenure as army chief of staff, my charge was to make the army a force that was better organized, better led, better trained, better equipped, and more strategically agile. And that's the goal of PS magazine: to assist soldiers in adapting to ever-changing environments and conditions, and to help them be knowledgeable of all aspects of their tasks and the tools and equipment around them.

In the pages that follow, readers will find out "How to Load a Truck" (pages 24–31), "How to Start a Stalled Engine" (pages 34–41), and "How to Keep Your Hydra-Matic Happy" (pages 135–37). Soldiers are asked to "Know Your Tools" (pages 128–33) and "Are You Guilty of Overstock?" (page 75). And they will encounter regular features like "Joe's Dope Sheet" and "Question and Answer Department," as well as a cast of recurring characters such as Sgt. Half-Mast McCanick, Sgt. Bull Dozer, Private Fosgnoff, Private Joe Dope, and Connie Rodd. Some of these are quaint lessons by today's standards, but looking back I am taken with their earnestness, intent, and value.

PS was created by renowned artist Will Eisner. Its home office was initially located at Aberdeen Proving Ground, Maryland. In 1955, it was moved to Raritan Arsenal, New Jersey, with subsequent moves to Fort Knox, Kentucky, in 1962; Lexington, Kentucky, in 1973; and its current home at Redstone Arsenal, Alabama, in 1993.

Sixty years after the earliest material in this book was created, our courageous men and women of the U.S. military still use PS to supplement their knowledge of vehicles, aircraft, firepower, electronics, and weapons systems. Clearly PS works, or it wouldn't have lasted over seven hundred issues and continue to be issued on a monthly basis. For a little pamphlet of humorous cartoons, that's a tall order. But as you can see from this collection you hold in your hands, PS accomplishes its mission.

General Peter J. Schoomaker,
   U.S. Army (Retired)
Tampa, Florida
April 2011

GENERAL PETER J. SCHOOMAKER, USA (RET.), was recalled to active duty by President George W. Bush and served from 2003 until 2007 to lead and transform the U.S. Army during the wars in Iraq and Afghanistan as the 35th army chief of staff and a member of the Joint Chiefs of Staff. He served on active duty from 1969 to 2000 in a variety of assignments with conventional units and special operations forces, retiring at the rank of four-star general as commander in chief of the United States Special Operations Command. He participated in numerous combat operations, including Desert One in Iran, Urgent Fury in Grenada, Just Cause in Panama, Desert Shield/Desert Storm in Southwest Asia, and Uphold Democracy in Haiti, and supported various other worldwide joint contingency operations, including those in the Balkans.

ABOVE: **no. 49, 1956**
OPPOSITE: **no. 1, 1951**

Preface
Recollections of Will Eisner and PS Magazine

In 1951, Will acquired a contract from the army to create a monthly magazine instructing enlisted personnel on how to repair and maintain equipment used in the course of their duties. When he came home and told me, I didn't have any mixed feelings; it sounded wonderful. Will could use his talents, as he had with *Army Motors* during World War II, to translate dry technical manuals into graphic, easy-to-understand instructions.

Naively, we never anticipated the aggravation that would follow. I remember twenty years of machinations that went into the annual negotiations regarding whether or not to renew Will's contract—each had to be put out to bid according to government regulations and co...sibly be awarded to another... The decision, to Will's frustra...ould always be made by people who...ad little knowledge of sequential art and who thought the intellectual approach of academia preferable. After tests were conducted that overwhelmingly showed that soldiers better understood technical material when it was presented using Will's graphic approach, opposition grudgingly disappeared.

Opposition also came from a "committee" that would approve or disapprove his interpretations or representations for

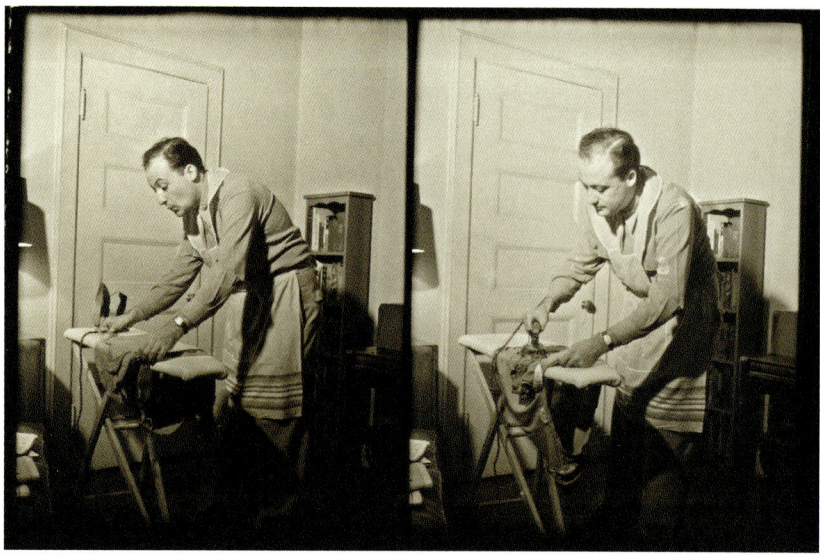

each issue of *PS* magazine. Every month Will would spend a full day with them, arguing his approach on each article. For some of the people on the committee, Will had great respect; for others, quiet, though seething, impatience. The peace of home, a relaxing dinner, and a recital of *my* day's activities would eventually iron out some of the wrinkles from his forehead.

Once the magazine was up and running, Will decided it was important for Will to go into the field" for a few weeks, wherever soldiers were stationed overseas, and get a feel for their lives, their hands-on use of *PS* magazine, and their reaction to the material in the publication as a part of their daily routines. I wasn't at all happy about that. It meant taking Will away from home for up to six weeks at a time annually. He'd pretend distress, but I knew he really looked forward to the trips and enjoyed his adventures. He was a Boy Scout at heart. Will loved the camaraderie, and any primitive conditions he might encounter, which would have horrified me, were completely inconsequential to him. His letters home, with their illustrations, were definitely a source of education and comfort.

Will was very open about where he was going, with the exception of one particular trip. He told me he was heading to Japan and Korea but conveniently omitted the part about Vietnam from his itinerary. The war was in deadly progress at the time, and I'm sure he knew I would have prostrated myself in front of the army plane and yelled, "Over my dead body!" if I had known in advance. It was definitely one of Will's more memorable trips, and it inspired his graphic novel *Last Day in Vietnam* (2000).

I never understood why some people were angry with Will for not discontinuing his work for the army during the Vietnam War. Will shared the same opinion as many, that the war was a mistake. But with *PS* he tried to help the troops—many of whom had been drafted into the conflict against their will—remain safe by instructing them how to best maintain and repair their equipment.

When Will decided to give up *PS* magazine in October 1971 after 227 issues, I saw him once again looking for new worlds to conquer, new barriers to break through. He once said to me that he had a drawer full of ideas and the only problem was which of them to explore first. After *PS* there were a few other ventures and then, eventually, *A Contract with God* was born. He called it a graphic novel.

Ann Eisner
Parkland, Florida
August 2010

RIGHT: **Will and Ann, circa 1980s**

A PS BRIEFING
BY EDDIE CAMPBELL

WILL EISNER WAS A CARTOONIST with a drawing style that is difficult to emulate, and I speak as one who has been called upon to attempt it on a couple of occasions. Eisner mastered a system of exaggerated anatomy, of extremely articulated figures, and within those, extremely articulated individual faces, hands, eyes, and feet, too. Everything appeared to move independently. And among all this, especially in the earlier part of his career, Eisner would integrate the busy multiple-source lighting of the cinema of the period, effects we associate with film noir. And it would all be achieved with a few deft flicks of an ink-loaded brush. As to his subjects, Eisner's female characters, when they were not spoiled brats or overbearing wives, were sexier (and more aggressively so) than any other artist's sexy girls, until the fad for "good girl art" in the late forties gave us a whole wave of specialists in that department. Eisner's heroes were manly, but with an endearing sense of humor (he always said that Cary Grant would be the ideal actor to portray his comic book character the Spirit and, in a later era, James Garner would have been his choice). Eisner's comical characters had a grotesqueness that was once thought essential to humor but was out of fashion in mid-century American culture.

Will Eisner was also an entrepreneur among cartoonists. If he'd been a musician, he'd have been not just a virtuoso soloist but a big band leader as well. Before he was even twenty, Eisner put into action his idea of running a studio to supply the multifarious upstart comic book publishers of the late 1930s with material for their magazines, and was around early enough in this capacity to reject Jerry Siegel and Joe Shuster's Superman when those young hopefuls walked into his office. It was, you may observe, an unpredictable business. Shortly after, in 1940, Eisner was the one to package a comic book insert that at its height appeared in twenty newspapers, and for which he audaciously retained the copyright (unheard of for its time). *The*

RIGHT: **Will Eisner, 1943**
OPPOSITE: Eisner at target practice, most likely at Fort Dix, New Jersey, 1942

Spirit ran weekly from June 2, 1940, until October 5, 1952, and remains a benchmark for sequential art.

The comic book business shrank in the mid-1950s, and a huge number of the artists who had filled the four-color newsprint monthlies found their way into other fields, many of them working anonymously as assistants on long-running daily newspaper strips, or getting out of the drawing line altogether. Most of the characters disappeared too, as did the publishers who conveyed them to us on a monthly and often weekly basis. There are very few threads of continuous connection between the so-called Golden Age of comic books and their Silver Age revival in the late fifties and early sixties. Eisner was absent from this, offstage, having anticipated the changes. Much later we find him packaging and drawing facile joke books such as *Incredible Facts, Amazing Statistics, Monumental Trivia* (1974), and *How to Avoid Death & Taxes . . . and Live Forever* (1975). In 1978, Eisner's *A Contract with God and Other Tenement Stories* was published. This longer, personal comics narrative appeared virtually from out of nowhere and took the community of comics aficionados quite by surprise. It effectively launched his second career as a graphic novelist, with more than twenty new books appearing over the next twenty-seven years. (All of these graphic novels are still in print, in both hard- and softcover.) Eisner differentiated his two careers by having this part of his oeuvre published by a book publisher, as opposed to a *comics* publisher. He had literary ambitions, which demanded, using his own metaphor, that he raise comics out of their cultural ghetto.

Between these two periods of acclaim—*The Spirit* and his later graphic novels—lies a stretch of twenty years in which Eisner's

work was not readily available to the public, and it remains obscure. In 1948, Eisner founded a company, American Visuals, that had become very busy by the time *The Spirit* concluded in 1952. The specialty of American Visuals was the application of comic book art to commercial purposes, and the single largest product of the company was *PS: The Preventive Maintenance Monthly*, a digest-size magazine produced for the U.S. Army. Eisner delivered 227 issues of *PS* from June 1951 to October 1971.

The concept of the magazine didn't arrive whole, and in fact the parts came together a few years earlier, just after the United States entered World War II and Eisner was drafted in May 1942. Always

with an eye toward opportunity, Eisner positioned himself to take over the art department of *Army Motors* magazine and set about effecting a more harmonious balance between its textual and pictorial elements. This publication, which communicated automotive maintenance information to working soldiers, started in April 1940. In the package, Eisner inherited a couple of fictional host characters: Sergeant Half-Mast (as in "half-assed") McCanick and Connie Rodd, a female mechanic invented presumably in response to the same stimulus that made a national icon of Rosie the Riveter (first heard of as the titular heroine of a popular song from 1942). Eisner added another character in the form of Joe Dope, who appeared at first on color pull-out posters. These were often captioned with a limerick, such as this one from circa 1944: "Joe Dope is a guy you can't teach / Here's the way he closes a breech! / When he gets through this chore / On the enemy's shore / They'll spread him all over the beach." Joe Dope is a hypothetical soldier who always screws up. In appearance, he is very much at the grotesque end of Eisner's gallery of types, and this would cause problems with the brass later on.

With the onset of the Korean War in mid-1950, America was once again thrown into a conflict for which it was not completely prepared, with much of its military equipment at least five years old and imperfectly maintained. In addition, a lot of new equipment was rushed into use after a minimum of testing.

There was a move at the office of the chief of ordnance to initiate action to revive the old *Army Motors* magazine, and Will Eisner, with the advantage of his previous experience, found himself negotiating a contract to provide creative art and publication design for a new magazine, this one to be called *PS: The Preventive Maintenance Monthly*. The magazine was given a six-issue trial run, and then it was up and running, though it failed to make a monthly schedule until its fourth year. The first year, 1951, saw seven issues, the second a mere four, and the third another five. The first full year of publication was 1955. In organizing the material for this book, it was useful to think of those initial sixteen issues as the first phase of *PS* since they correspond to the years of the Korean conflict. For the sake of orderliness, we considered the remainder of the fifties as phase two, and the rest, 1960–1971, as phase three. The best of these phases was the first, with the others descending by degrees. The relative numbers of our selections reflect this.

PS (or postscript) was intended as a supplement to the official manual and was full of updates, solutions to problems unforeseen when the manual was issued, field-fixes, and recommendations based on actual experience taken from letters sent in by working soldiers. *PS* tells its readers how to clean a rifle, how to defrost a jeep battery, and the right way to cut down trees, with information provided by military writers and dressed up for the soldiers' edification in lively and humorous typographical settings. Eisner said that his rationale for the magazine was to take the hard, technical information supplied to him by the military writers and present it in a way the regular GIs could understand. In a 1991 comment (*Spirit* no. 85, Kitchen Sink Press), Eisner explained, "Whereas the government issue manuals would say 'Remove all sedimentary deposits from the combustion area,' I would say something like 'Scrape the crud off the engine.'" The same GIs would probably have spent some or much of their youth in the forties reading comic books. For them, Eisner would dress up the material in his cartoon style, and much of this work still holds up. Having studied and loved Eisner's work for many years, I find that the Eisnerian settings humanize the lessons and succeed in removing me to a distant time and place where I start to care about the proper way to fill out an Unsatisfactory Equipment Report (UER form 4G8) and am glad that I learned in time to "stick to the 'block' method of adjusting track tension on the late M48 and T67 (flamethrower) tanks with their tension idler wheels." Humorous drawings also have a long history of use as mnemonic devices, going back to the marginal drawings in medieval illuminated prayer books. Who, having seen the drawing shown below from *PS* no. 59 (1957), could forget to watch out for that badly designed front seat setting? It's the driver wearing a protective catcher's mask that cracks me up.

Eisner's personality is peppered all through the early issues, though inevitably more intensely in some places than in

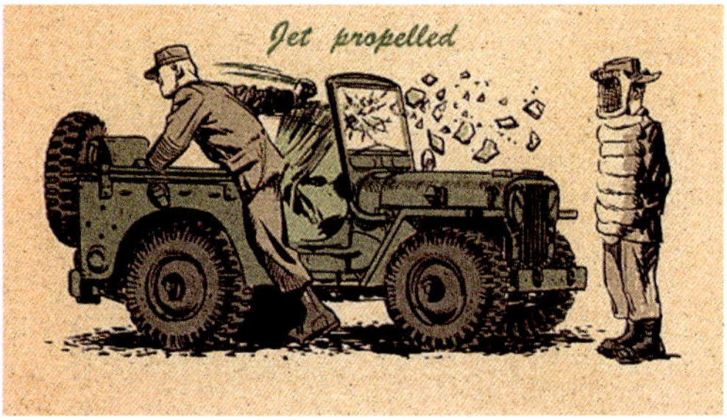
Jet propelled

OPPOSITE: A pre–*PS* magazine Will Eisner (center, more than likely holding a "Private Dogtag" strip for *The Flaming Bomb*, the army newspaper), and unknown military staff. Aberdeen, Maryland, 1942 or 1943
RIGHT: no. 59, 1957

others. There are densely illustrated passages, and also long stretches where you could easily give up if you have not waited as long as I have to see this stuff (the first three or four dozen issues are especially scarce).

In the beginning the whole booklet was printed in full color, but after the first year only a middle eight-page section got the chromatic treatment, with the rest of the magazine limited to black and one other color, which changed from issue to issue from blue to yellow to red to green. At first the covers were printed on newsprint, but after the first year the slicker paper you find on comic book covers was used. By 1960, the whole magazine was printed on better paper (as you can see starting on page 194). In the middle of the central color section of eight pages, there was always a pinup spread titled "Joe's Dope" that functioned like the character's World War II posters, with an obligatory limerick. Furthermore, all the regular features and columns got cartoon headers, and elsewhere spot illustrations, as well as technically accurate renderings of equipment and supplies.

At first Eisner's style looks like a throwback to his work during the *Army Motors* period from the mid-forties, with the later years of *The Spirit* looking more progressive by comparison. However, at the same time, there is a certainty that what we are looking at is more purely Eisner's work than *The Spirit* had been for quite some time, (Eisner employed a team of assistants to work on the weekly supplement). As the monthly issues of *PS* tumble out, you can see the artist finding symbolic images that he reuses to great effect. There is, for example, the supply window seen on pages 52–53, which is attached, as it should be, to the supply room or shed. Later, on pages 120–121, Eisner draws the window detached from its building, hanging around the neck of a supply officer standing "in the field," representing the important concept of supply in a military operation. Eisner finds himself resorting to the techniques of an editorial cartoonist, rather than a narrative artist, reducing complicated ideas to an immediately readable image.

Eisner employed a staff of fifteen, including those making film negatives and color separations. He also needed artists to handle the workload, and by the time *PS* hits its full monthly stride in 1954, other hands besides his become noticeable, though Eisner's is the only signature you'll see in these pages. (Anonymity in the low arts was commonplace in those days. As one wag remarked, "I never cared that my name wasn't on the work, so long as it was on the check.") Eisner's signature, when it is seen, serves more as a trademark than a signature in the normal sense. So those interested, as I am, in the minutiae of who did what, must look elsewhere for clues.

Eisner said that Dan Zolnerowich was good at the serious figures, as well as drawing tanks and such. On pages 152–153, Eisner has signed a "Dope Sheet" in which the two tanks look like the work of another hand, perhaps Dan Zolne (as he elsewhere signed the work). Klaus Nordling was part of the *PS* team too. He had worked with Eisner on the *Spirit* section, mainly drawing *Lady Luck* but also filling in on the Spirit feature itself on occasion. I fancy that's his work on the color story "Seep or Leak" beginning on page 103. Nordling's figures appear less bothered by gravity than Eisner's, and he has given the grotesque characters a touch of sweetness. I've always been fond of his work. Somewhere along the way Chuck Kramer joins the team, working on many of the humorous pages by the 1960s. I

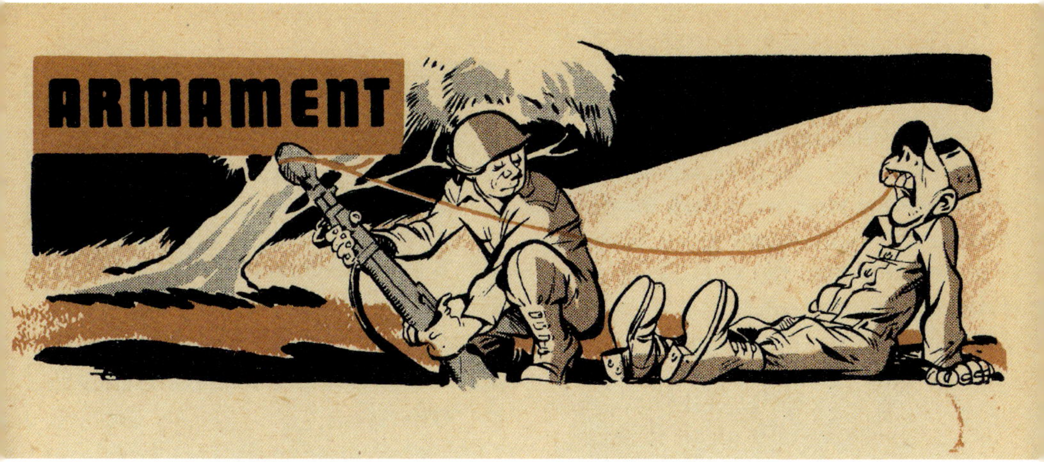
ARMAMENT

have learned over the years never to be too assertive about who ghosted what in old comics, but I'd say with confidence it's Kramer's hand we see in tandem with Eisner's in the later color stories reprinted here, such as the one beginning on page 231. I am sure there are other names we could mention, but it's not the sort of thing of which Eisner's shop kept details.

To convey information most effectively to the soldiers, Eisner lined up a handful of regular characters who most of the time exist only in the banners that run across the first pages of their regular features in the magazine, which change from issue to issue. I find myself acquiring an affection for them, as they seem to exist as much in his imagination as any Eisner character who ever had a proper fleshed-out story life: "Sgt. Half-Mast McCanick's Question and Answer Department" (pages 194 and 220–221), "Windy Winsock's Windstorms," "Connie Rodd's Short 'n Sweet Dept.," sometimes titled "Connie Rodd's Briefs" (pages 125 and 162). There were also Sgt. Bull Dozer (page 217) and Percy the Skunk (page 161), whose area of expertise was chemical weaponry. Joe Dope usually got the color story, and Connie would be in there too, often on the pinup posters. Sometimes it's a good, fun read such as "Lucky Pierre" (pages 54–57) and "Hairnet" (pages 69–75), a spoof of the TV crime series *Dragnet*. But generally the characters would just be explaining some form or piece of equipment; on page 171 we've reprinted a particularly attractive opening page of a story.

Eisner would usually depict all of his characters together on the special covers of the Christmas issues (page 126), which were sometimes wraparounds (pages 160–161).

Eisner gave Private Joe Dope a sidekick, an even more grotesque character named Private Fosgnoff. Joe has two square, protruding teeth at the front; Fosgnoff has them at the sides. The two are seen together in a favorite piece of mine from 1954 beginning on page 96, in which the principle of supply and demand

ABOVE: no. 29, 1955

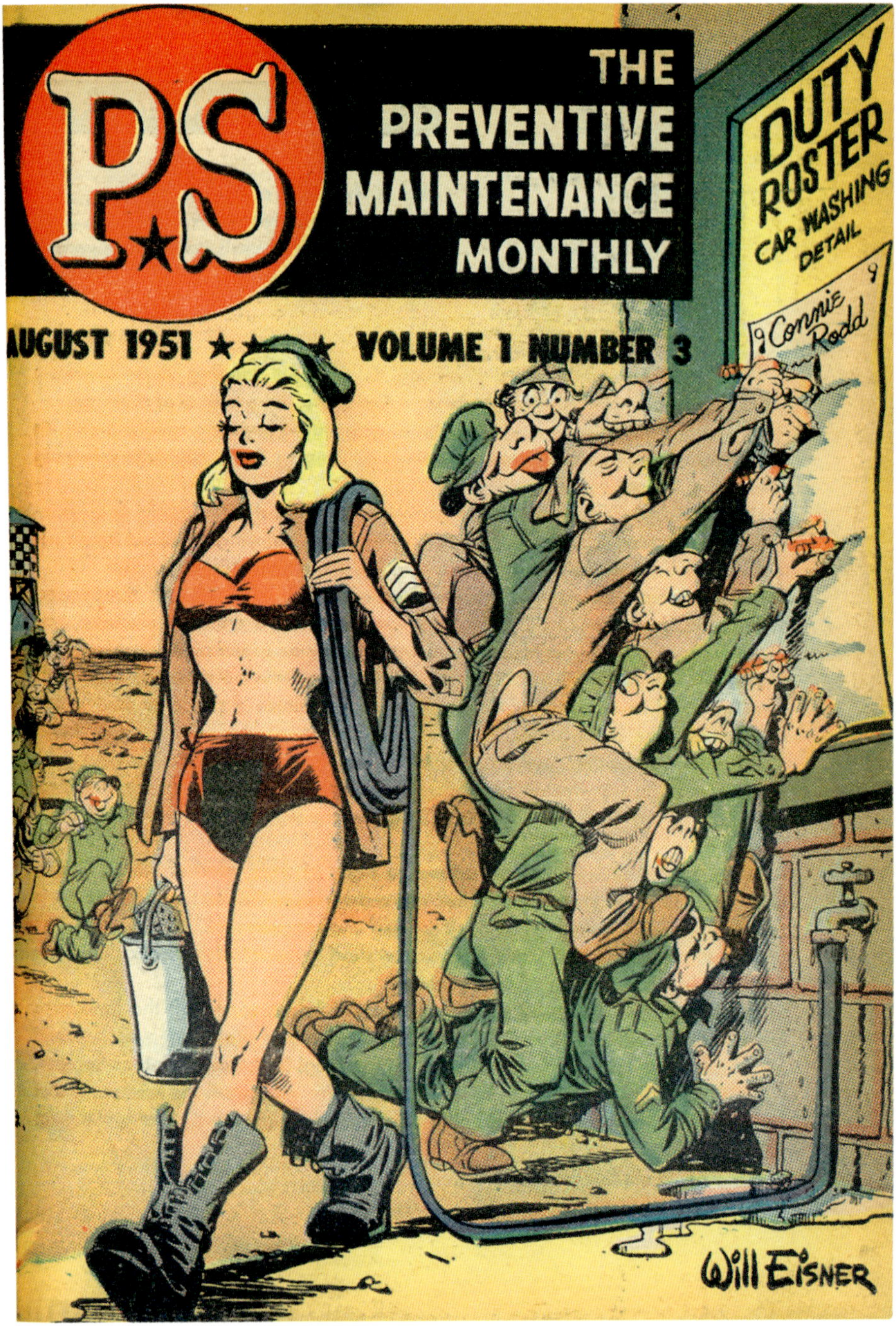
P★S
THE PREVENTIVE MAINTENANCE MONTHLY
AUGUST 1951 ★★★★ VOLUME 1 NUMBER 3
DUTY ROSTER
CAR WASHING DETAIL
Connie Rodd
Will Eisner

is explained using taxi dancers at a ballroom. The madam is indicating a trio of girls lolling indolently on the railing, surplus to needs, a situation that could not have failed to arouse a response among soldiers stuck in a barracks. The whole spread integrates cartoon figures and type in an attractive ensemble that has a hint of narrative progress. It was a delightful effect that didn't happen often in *PS*, and less so as the years advanced.

What did happen was that the brass put pressure on Eisner to get rid of these characters. It was the age of witchhunts and wowsers (to borrow a fine piece of old Australian slang), and the great blandifying of everything. The Pentagon ruled that Joe Dope was considered offensive to the dignity of the American soldier, and Private Fosgnoff was even worse. Fosgnoff was summarily discharged, his departure depicted in a one-page narrative in 1955, shown here on page 123. Joe Dope was turned into an all-American boy, and Eisner saved his own dignity by showing how Joe got that way in the color story "It's Your Life, Bud" in issue no. 47 (pages 141–148), a spoof of the TV show *This Is Your Life*. The reader is advised that this involves a miscalculation of the headspace on a .50-caliber machine gun and consequent plastic surgery. Connie Rodd would be next, though her blandifying would take some time. In the *Army Motors* years Eisner could be spontaneously funny with shower and peephole shenanigans, not unlike on the cover of *PS* no. 3, August 1951 (opposite), with its agglomeration of drooling males forming a veritable erection as they struggle among themselves to ejaculate their names onto the duty roster for car-washing detail. Connie is indeed quite delectable in those loosely strung army boots, denying the passage of sixty years. She inevitably became less sexually charged over the late fifties and the sixties, but it would take the increased presence of women in the army to complete the process, and that was after Eisner left the magazine.

A much larger problem was looming that would plague Eisner for years after his tenure at *PS*: the Vietnam conflict, which expanded rapidly under President Johnson in the mid-1960s. "The differences were like night and day," Eisner said in 1991 about a field trip (*Spirit* no. 81, Kitchen Sink Press). "In Korea we were all John Waynes. In Vietnam there was a feeling of shame; you could tell something wasn't right. You didn't see the flag that much." In later years, after he reentered the public arena, Eisner was often called upon to justify his production of a military magazine at a time when America's involvement in Vietnam attracted a huge amount of serious criticism and anger at home. The truth was, times had changed. Eisner had begun his illustration work with the army back in 1942, when every sane person recognized that the world was under attack by insanity and something had to be done about it. In an era when Joseph Heller's novel *Catch-22* was considered an apt caricature of the U.S. military, the smiley-faced helicopters inside the special Vietnam issue (no. 174, 1967), the cover of which is shown on page 193, look like they belong in *Thomas the Tank Engine* and are mercifully excluded from this collection.

The color story from issue no. 205 (1969) features Santa and his elves. *PS* had started with the notion of talking to soldiers in terms they understood. In the decade when age and youth were more sharply divided than perhaps any other

OPPOSITE: no. 3, August 1951

time in history, some of the cartoony stuff in *PS* looks like Eisner has forgotten he's addressing adults. I recently found this comment on the Internet: "A friend of mine brought one of these [*PS* magazine] home from the army way back when. He said it didn't actually help with the training because it was so lunatic. We all thought of it as being on the pathetic side of funny."

Will Eisner relinquished his *PS* contract as of the October 1971 issue (no. 227). Other editors and artists have since taken it over, and the magazine continues to be published monthly, probably past issue no. 700 by the time this book appears. I expect it does its job and that the people who produce it give it their best and get satisfaction from the work. When I see it on occasion, it doesn't tend to hold my attention, but it's not meant to after all. It's geared to a different generation who were brought up on a different kind of comic book diet. But then, Eisner's run of the magazine wasn't aimed at me either. He was an artist whose best work rises above the period of its making, casting its spell far and wide. I know there are people who collect those old magazines primarily for the technical content, but in the early run there was one, no. 14 (1953), a special issue devoted to a new tank, which for some reason had little cartoon work in it by Eisner and his staff. Perhaps the brass

ABOVE: American Visuals art director Ted Cabarga (standing, with necktie), Will Eisner (seated), and *PS* editor James Kidd (standing, right). Kidd was the editor of *PS* from 1953 to 1982. Early 1960s
OPPOSITE: Detail from no. 22, 1954

were testing whether the foolish pictures were really necessary. For me it had the sterility that Eisner said the official manuals had, and it interests me not.

When Eisner withdrew from *PS* in 1971, I had been aware of his work for four years, since the brief 1967 Harvey Comics reprinting of *The Spirit*. I kind of assumed that Eisner had retired, but he was the same age I am as I write this: fifty-four. At that time *The Spirit* was being revived in monthly comic books using Eisner's archives of original art, and he was providing new covers and commentary. It hardly seemed to be full-time employment. There were the joke books, but who was paying attention to those? And who could have foreseen what lay ahead—that Will Eisner would be one of the leading figures in a new phase of the always interesting and complicated history of comics, with his graphic novels and his books of sequential art instruction? Or that he would be deeply committed to building this body of personal work until the day he died, January 3, 2005, at the age of eighty-seven. Or that I, too young for the Vietnam generation, would get to sit on a few convention panels with him over the years and debate the tricks of our trade. It still is, you may conclude, an unpredictable business.

The final selection on page 272 is a memorial printed in *PS* no. 628 (March 2005), published after Eisner's death, incorporating an illustration he had drawn on an earlier occasion in which he reflected with affection on the characters he had created for *PS* magazine more than fifty years before. It's in his late "dirty water" style, as he liked to call it, after the carefree effects obtained by shading his picture with the water he had been using to clean his brush. I like that he considers the pre-facelift Joe Dope to be the authentic version.

In selecting what we believe to be the best of *PS* magazine, we're grateful to Eisner's widow, Ann, for making available his personal set of bound volumes, enabling us to reproduce the work at the best quality possible.

Eddie Campbell
Brisbane, Australia
2010

EDDIE CAMPBELL is an award-winning comics writer and artist whose work includes *From Hell* (with Alan Moore), *The Fate of the Artist*, the autobiographical *Alec: The Years Have Pants*, and *The Playwright* (with Daren White).

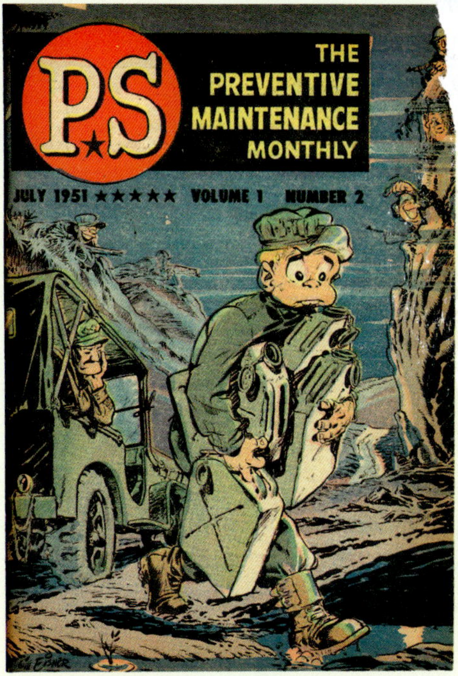
P.S
THE PREVENTIVE MAINTENANCE MONTHLY
JULY 1951 ★★★★★ VOLUME 1 NUMBER 2
Will Eisner

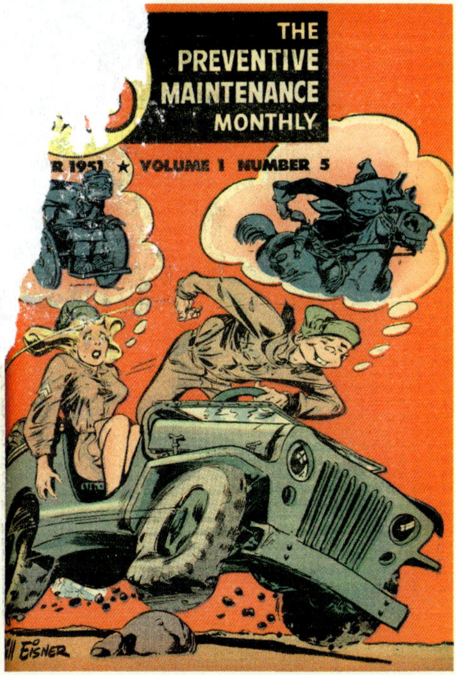
THE PREVENTIVE MAINTENANCE MONTHLY
R 1951 ★ VOLUME 1 NUMBER 5
Will Eisner

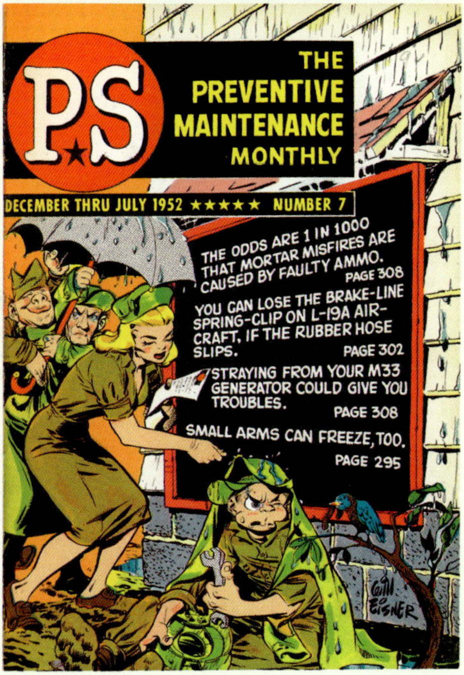
P.S
THE PREVENTIVE MAINTENANCE MONTHLY
DECEMBER THRU JULY 1952 ★★★★★ NUMBER 7
THE ODDS ARE 1 IN 1000 THAT MORTAR MISFIRES ARE CAUSED BY FAULTY AMMO. PAGE 308
YOU CAN LOSE THE BRAKE-LINE SPRING-CLIP ON L-19A AIRCRAFT, IF THE RUBBER HOSE SLIPS. PAGE 302
STRAYING FROM YOUR M33 GENERATOR COULD GIVE YOU TROUBLES. PAGE 308
SMALL ARMS CAN FREEZE, TOO. PAGE 295
Will Eisner

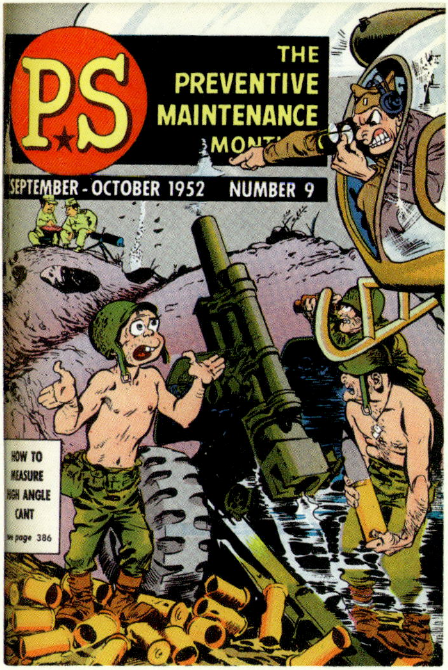
P.S
THE PREVENTIVE MAINTENANCE MONT
SEPTEMBER - OCTOBER 1952 NUMBER 9
HOW TO
MEASURE
IGH ANGLE
CANT
ee page 386

P.S
TH
PREVENTIVE
MAINTENANCE
MONTHLY
OVEMBER 1951 ★★ VOLUME 1 NUMBER 6
Will Eisner

P.S
THE
PREVENTIVE
MAINTENANCE
MONTHL
NUMBER 10
NOVEMBER 1952
RUBBER BANDS
PAPER CLIPS

★★★★

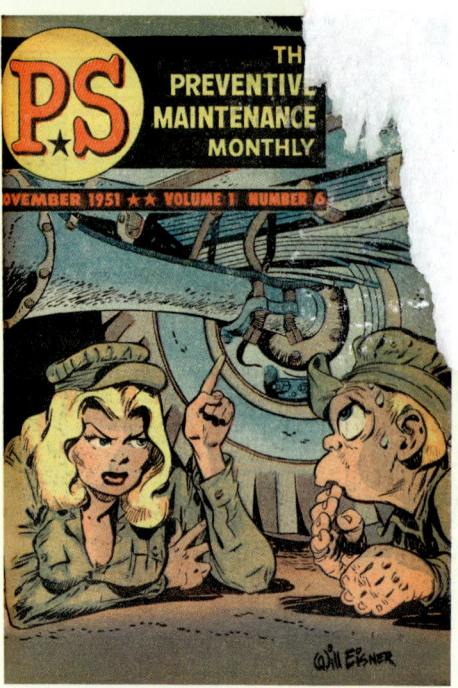

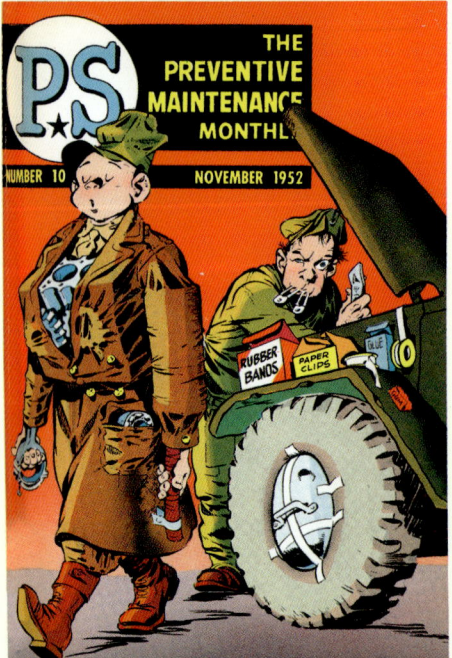

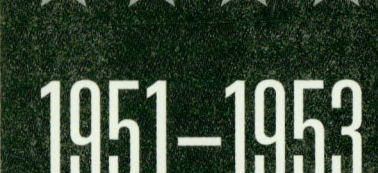

1951–1953

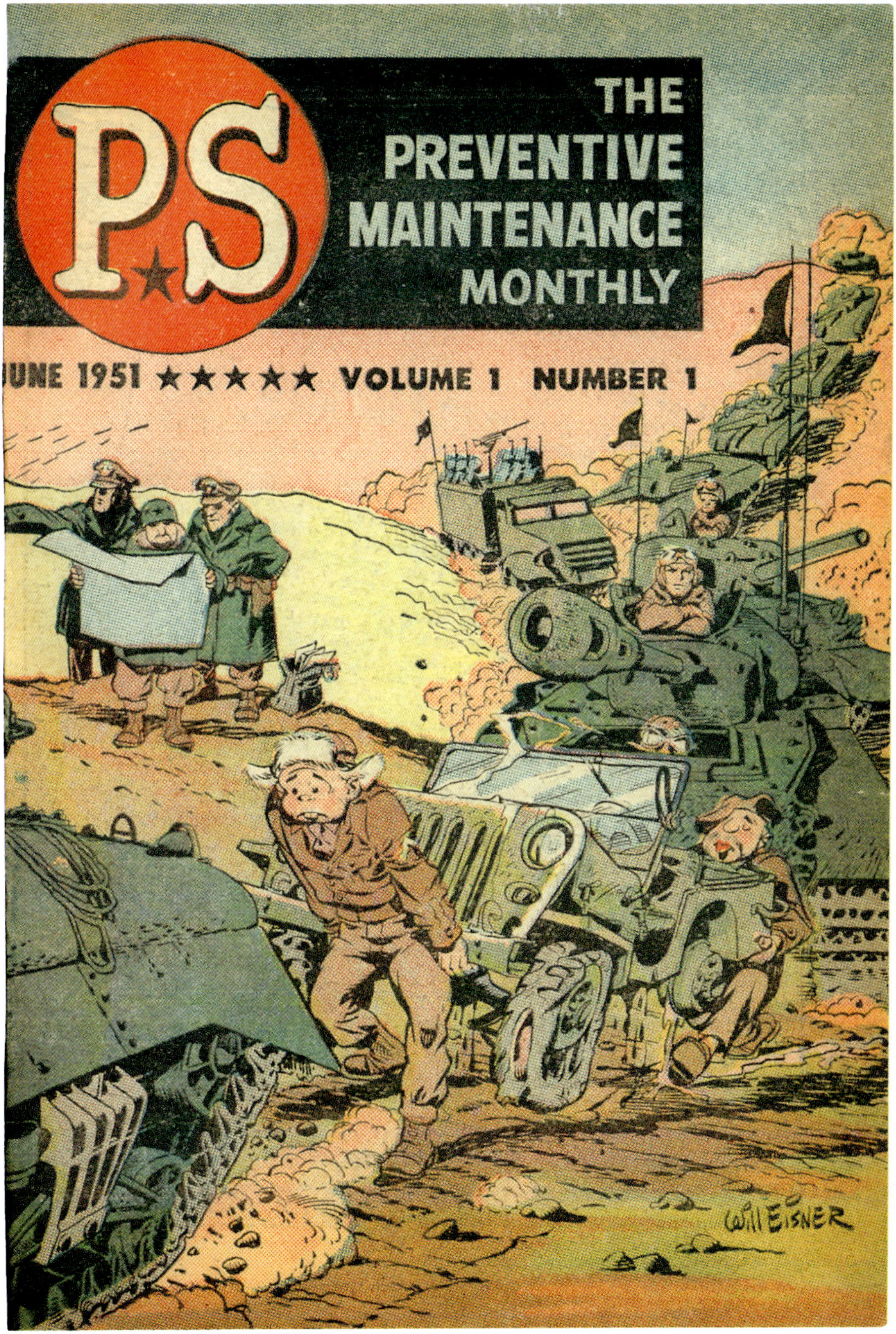
P★S
THE PREVENTIVE MAINTENANCE MONTHLY
UNE 1951 ★★★★★ VOLUME 1 NUMBER 1
WILL EISNER

no. 1, June 1951

REPORTING FOR DUTY

You are now holding in your hand the first issue of "P.S. Magazine"—the magazine of maintenance for trucks and tanks, the nuts-and-bolts digest for anything on wheels or tracks. If you were lucky enough to have worked with or operated vehicles in World War II, you will remember a little clambake called "Army Motors." "P.S." is the successor to "Army Motors," the magazine of fixes and facts, on trucks and tanks. Do you hear strange music in your transfer case? Are you ashamed to face the neighbors because your M46 tank makes little puddles of oil upon the ground? "P.S." will give you the answers, and what to do about it.

Not that we know all the answers! It's just that we are fixed to get you the answers. We are surrounded by people who designed your trucks and tanks and invented all the little gadgets that are on them. We have with us such old timers as Sgt. Half-Mast McCanick, the original answer man. Half-Mast is close enough to the manufacturers' engineers to spit on them. And often does. Send Half-Mast your maintenance problems, your truck and tank troubles. Anybody can write to Half-Mast, in channels or out. Be you high brass, or low brass, or no brass at all, Half-Mast will get you the answers.

Connie Rodd, gal mechanic, is with us too. Connie is the toothsome lass who operates the shop kinks, shortcuts, and cute tricks department. Connie's old man built the original body by Fisher and he didn't do so bad by her either. Connie is famous for her (ahem) internal combustion and for inviting your particular attention to those trouble spots, big and little, on your vehicles and what to do about them.

"P.S." has a "Contributions Dept." Have you dreamed up a special tool to make a hard job easier? Have you unscrewed the inscrutable, or worked out a faster or easier way to change a part or make an adjustment? Write the details to "P.S." MAGAZINE," Aberdeen Proving Ground, Md., we'll publish them and make life easier for the rest of the Army.

For your good ideas, for your questions to Half-Mast which reveal a situation that needs solvin', for any letter from you that uncovers a vehicular or organizational condition that needs correctin', you will receive direct-by-mail, ab-so-lutely free, a one-year personal subscription to "P.S. Magazine."

What else are we givin' away? We are giving away pages and pages of service information which may pull you out of a pinch, or even save your skin when the goin' gets tough. Send no $$$'s, "P.S." is free.

Look for us every month at your favorite motor pool, motor officer or motor sergeant.

The Editors

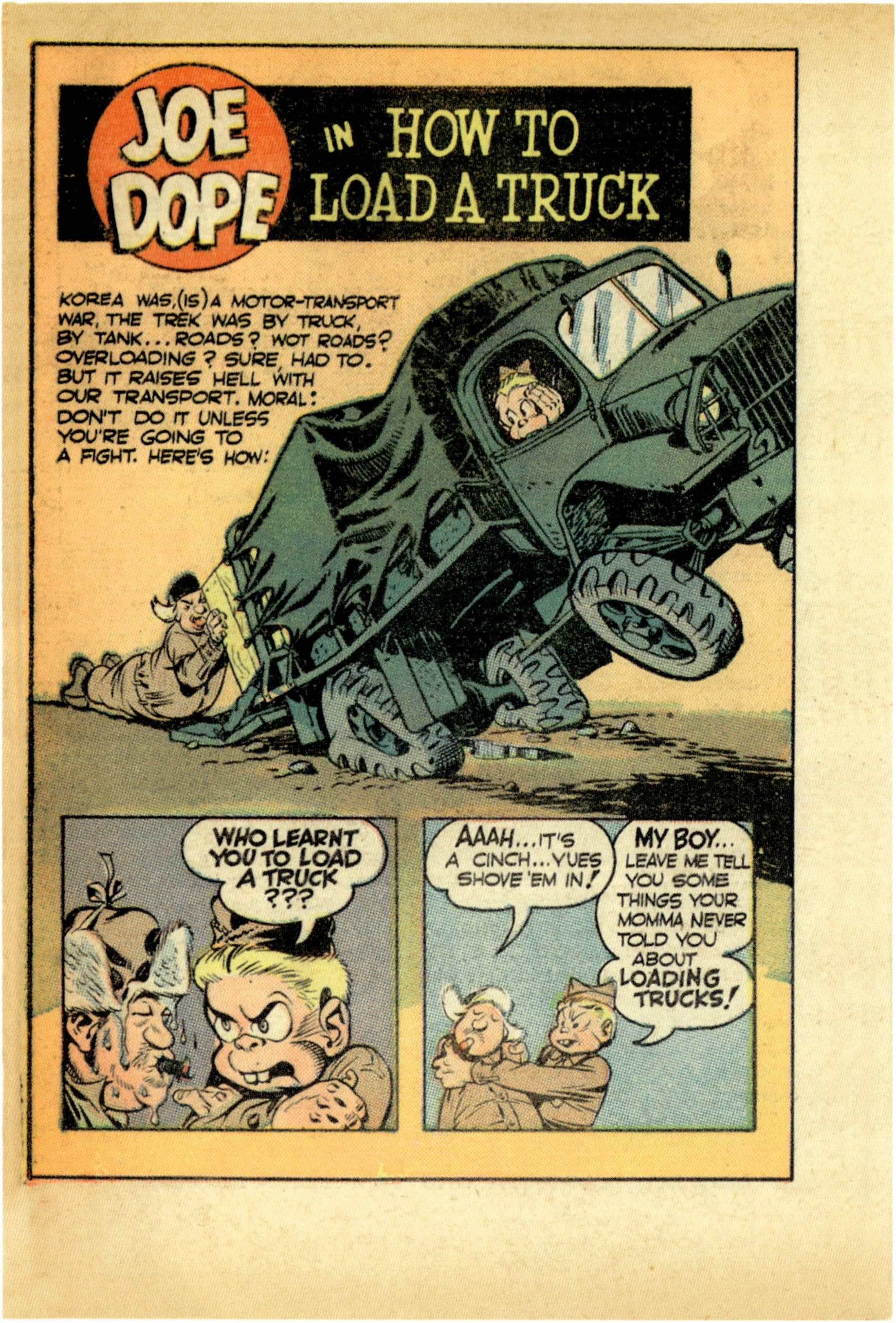
JOE DOPE
IN HOW TO LOAD A TRUCK
KOREA WAS,(IS) A MOTOR-TRANSPORT WAR, THE TREK WAS BY TRUCK, BY TANK... ROADS? WOT ROADS? OVERLOADING? SURE, HAD TO. BUT IT RAISES HELL WITH OUR TRANSPORT. MORAL: DON'T DO IT UNLESS YOU'RE GOING TO A FIGHT. HERE'S HOW:
WHO LEARNT YOU TO LOAD A TRUCK ???
AAAH...IT'S A CINCH...YUES SHOVE 'EM IN!
MY BOY... LEAVE ME TELL YOU SOME THINGS YOUR MOMMA NEVER TOLD YOU ABOUT LOADING TRUCKS!

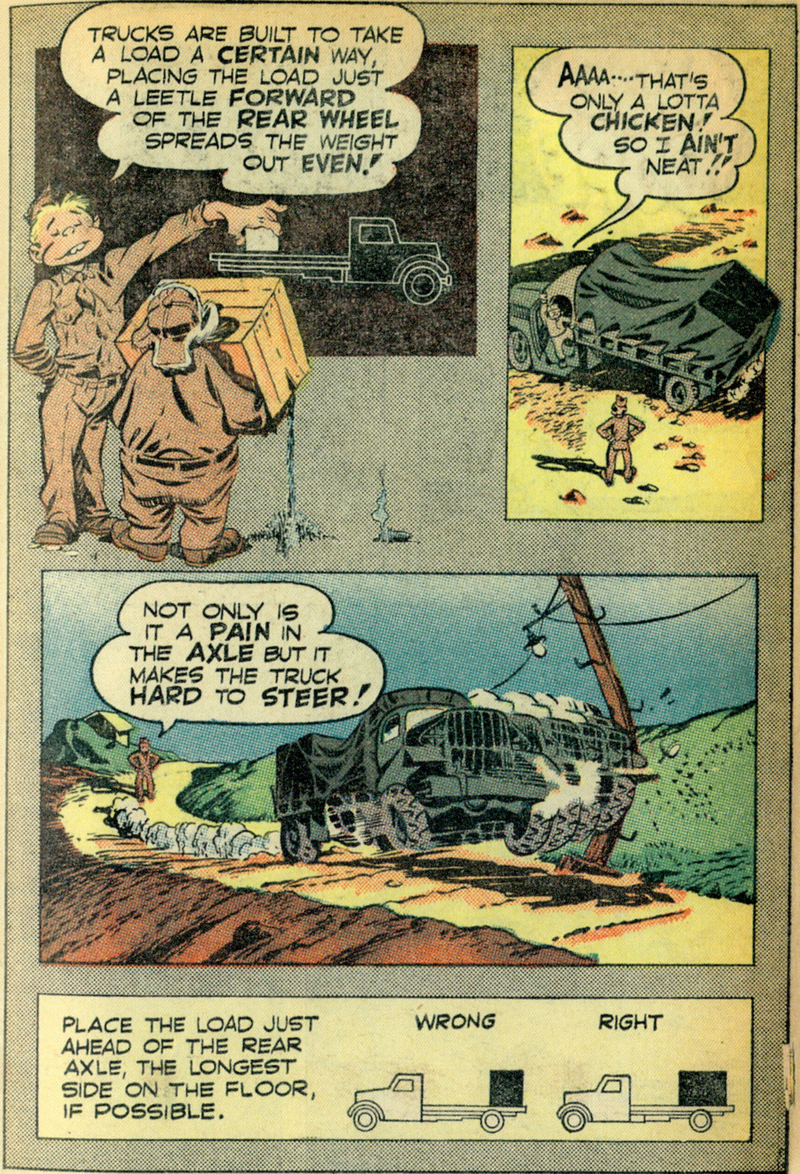
TRUCKS ARE BUILT TO TAKE A LOAD A CERTAIN WAY, PLACING THE LOAD JUST A LEETLE FORWARD OF THE REAR WHEEL SPREADS THE WEIGHT OUT EVEN.!
AAAA....THAT'S ONLY A LOTTA CHICKEN! SO I AIN'T NEAT!!
NOT ONLY IS IT A PAIN IN THE AXLE BUT IT MAKES THE TRUCK HARD TO STEER!
PLACE THE LOAD JUST AHEAD OF THE REAR AXLE, THE LONGEST SIDE ON THE FLOOR, IF POSSIBLE.
WRONG
RIGHT

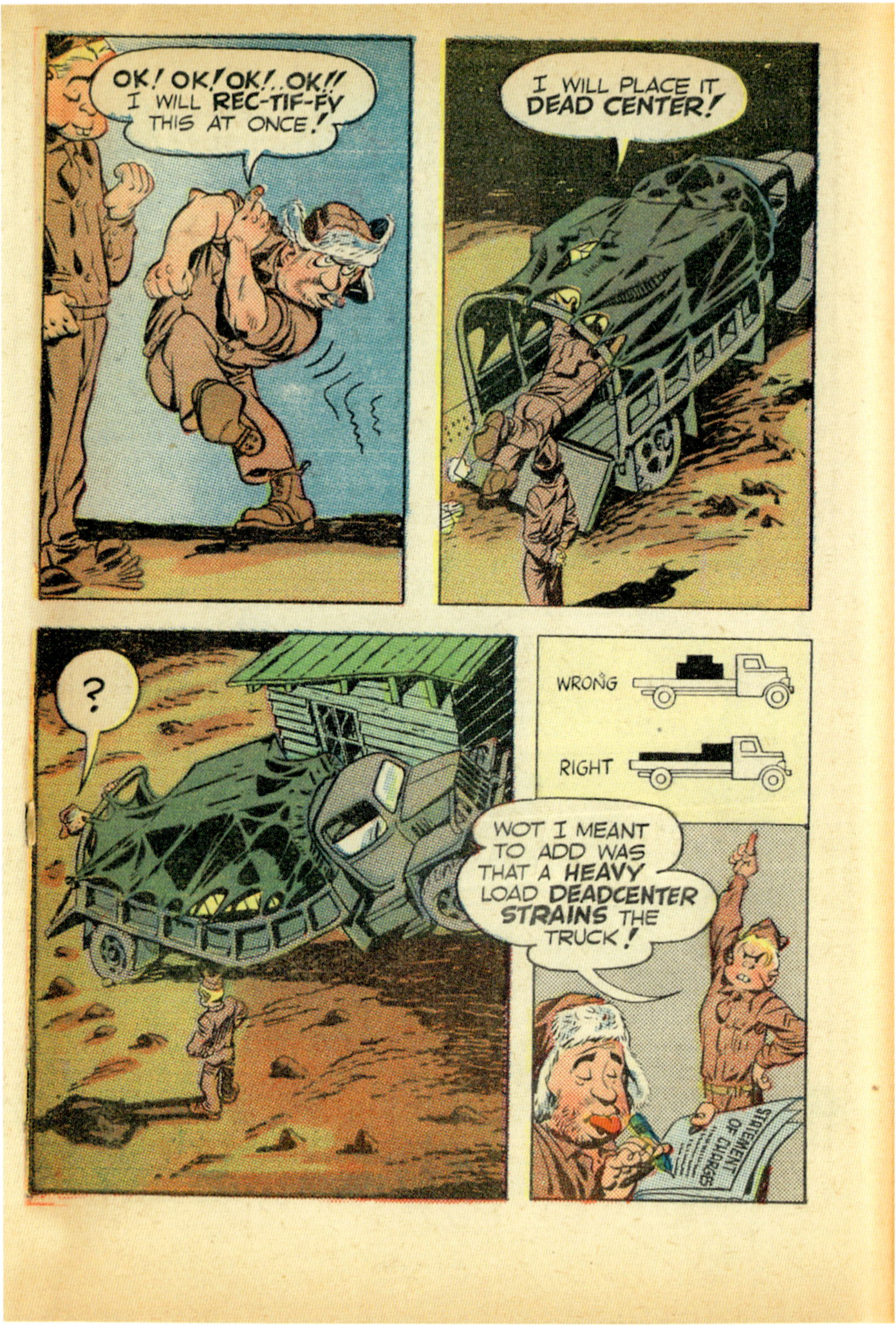
OK! OK! OK!..OK!!
I WILL REC-TIF-FY THIS AT ONCE!
I WILL PLACE IT DEAD CENTER!
?
WRONG
RIGHT
WOT I MEANT TO ADD WAS THAT A HEAVY LOAD DEADCENTER STRAINS THE TRUCK!
STATEMENT OF CHARGES

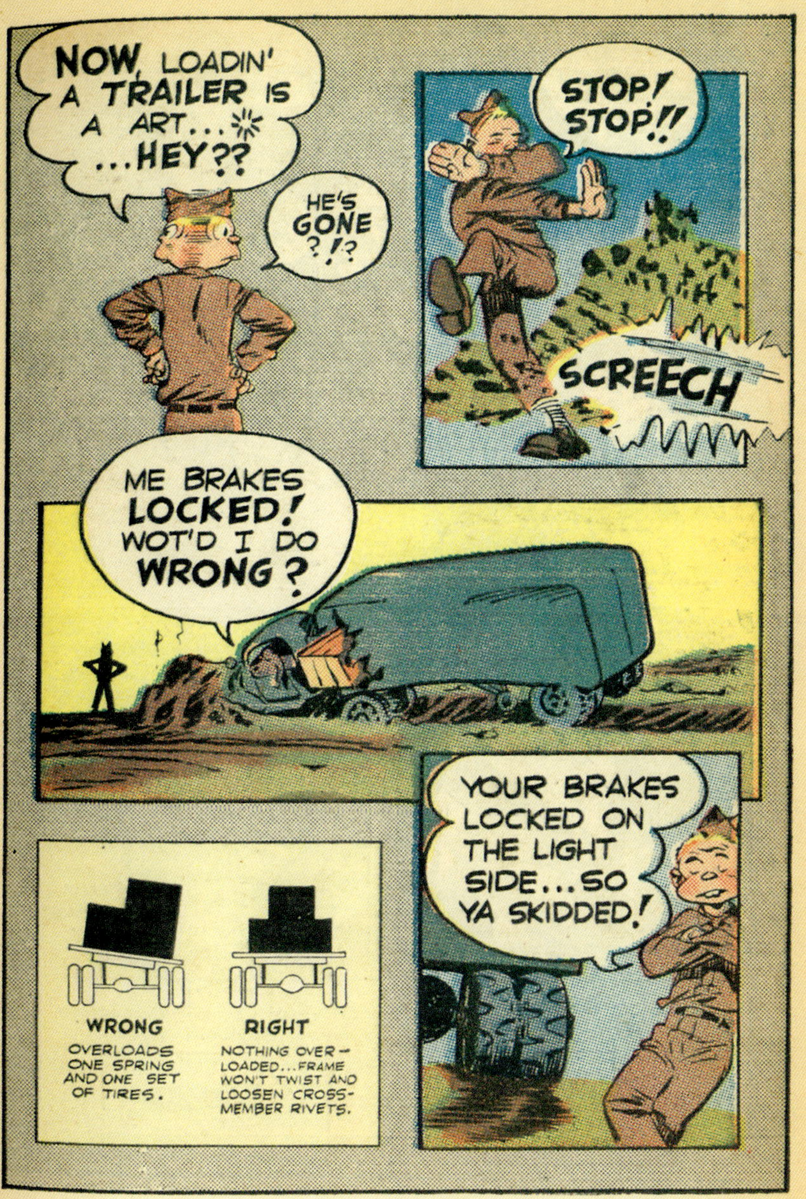
NOW, LOADIN' A TRAILER IS A ART... ...HEY??
HE'S GONE ?!?
STOP! STOP!!
SCREECH
ME BRAKES LOCKED! WOT'D I DO WRONG?
YOUR BRAKES LOCKED ON THE LIGHT SIDE... SO YA SKIDDED!
WRONG
OVERLOADS ONE SPRING AND ONE SET OF TIRES.
RIGHT
NOTHING OVER-LOADED... FRAME WON'T TWIST AND LOOSEN CROSS-MEMBER RIVETS.

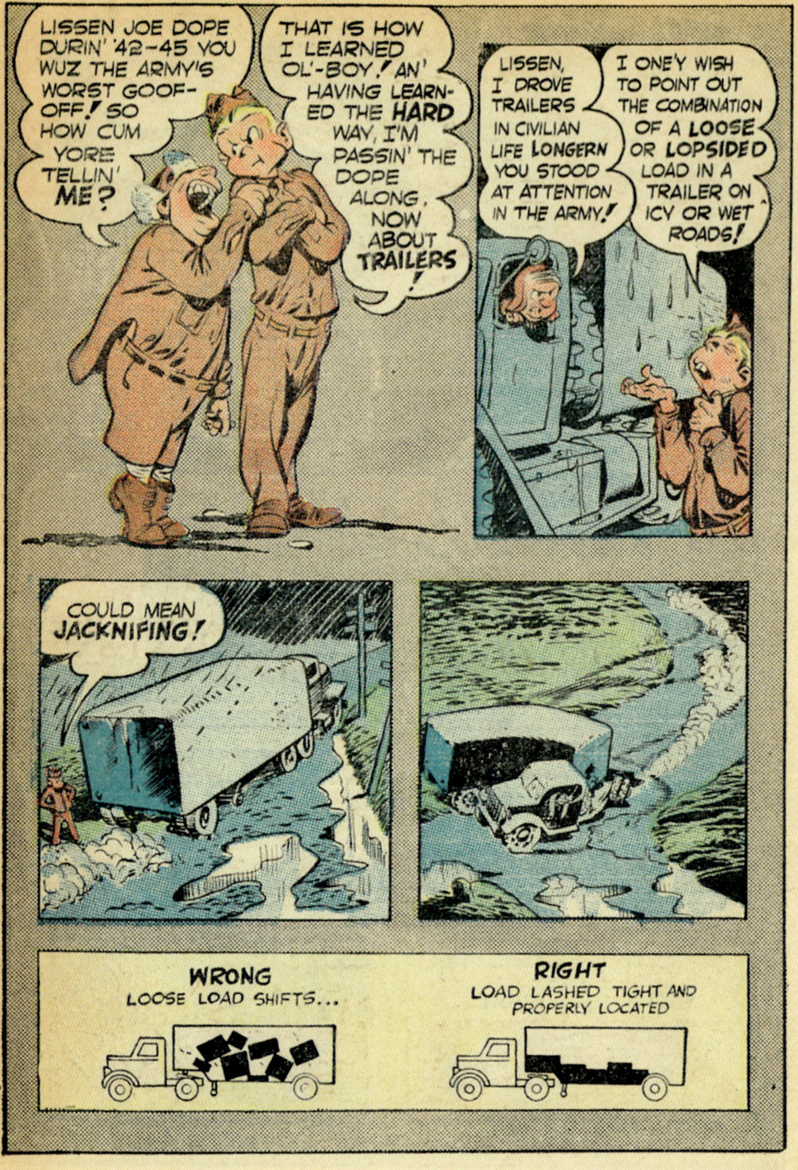
LISSEN JOE DOPE DURIN' '42-45 YOU WUZ THE ARMY'S WORST GOOF-OFF! SO HOW CUM YORE TELLIN' ME?
THAT IS HOW I LEARNED OL'-BOY! AN' HAVING LEARNED THE HARD WAY, I'M PASSIN' THE DOPE ALONG. NOW ABOUT TRAILERS!
LISSEN, I DROVE TRAILERS IN CIVILIAN LIFE LONGERN YOU STOOD AT ATTENTION IN THE ARMY!
I ONE'Y WISH TO POINT OUT THE COMBINATION OF A LOOSE OR LOPSIDED LOAD IN A TRAILER ON ICY OR WET ROADS!
COULD MEAN JACKNIFING!
WRONG
LOOSE LOAD SHIFTS...
RIGHT
LOAD LASHED TIGHT AND PROPERLY LOCATED

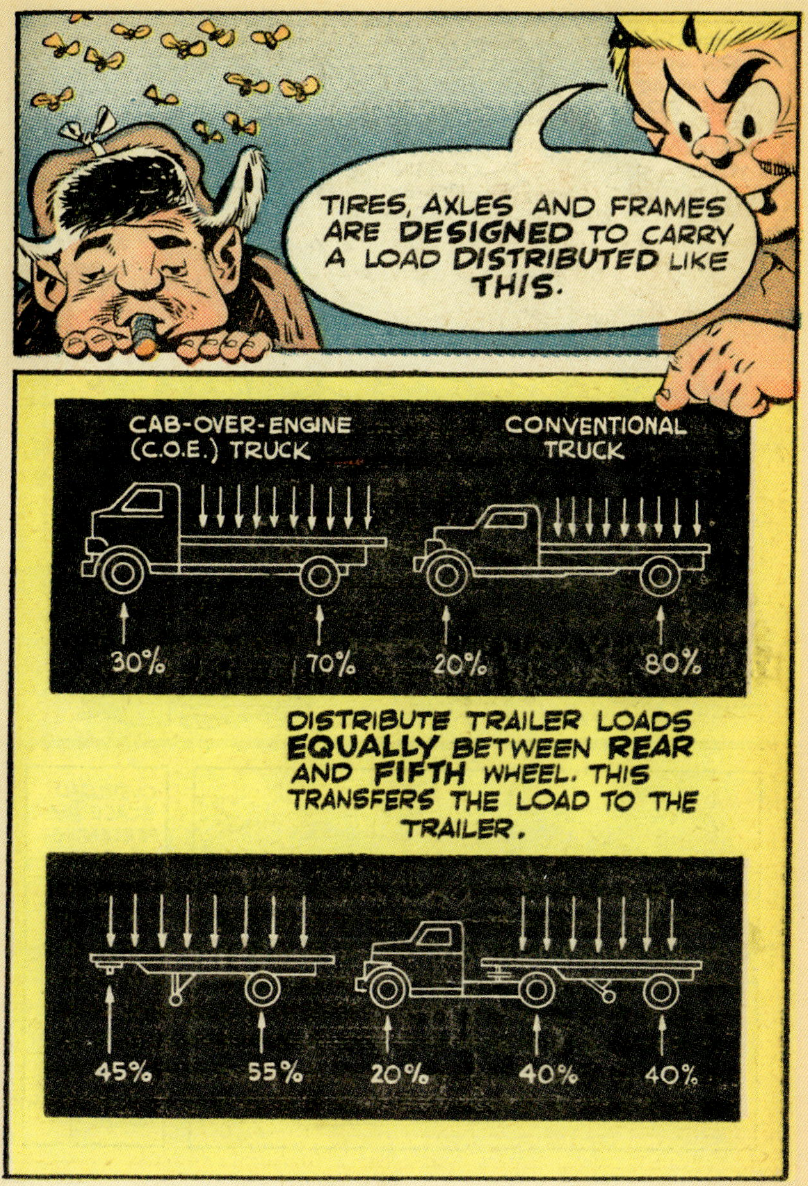
TIRES, AXLES AND FRAMES ARE DESIGNED TO CARRY A LOAD DISTRIBUTED LIKE THIS.
CAB-OVER-ENGINE (C.O.E.) TRUCK
CONVENTIONAL TRUCK
30%
70%
20%
80%
DISTRIBUTE TRAILER LOADS EQUALLY BETWEEN REAR AND FIFTH WHEEL. THIS TRANSFERS THE LOAD TO THE TRAILER.
45%
55%
20%
40%
40%

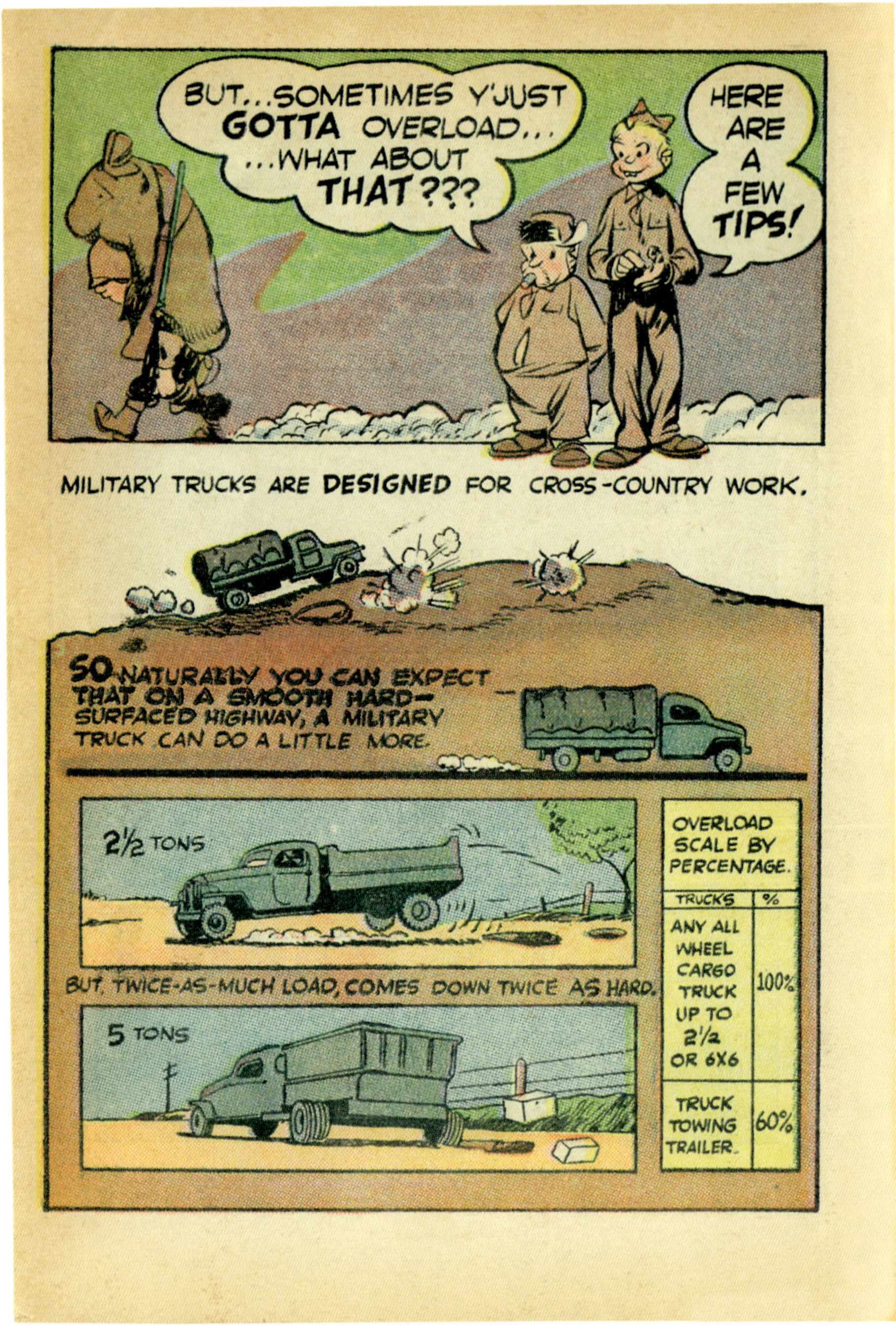
BUT...SOMETIMES Y'JUST GOTTA OVERLOAD... ...WHAT ABOUT THAT???
HERE ARE A FEW TIPS!
MILITARY TRUCKS ARE DESIGNED FOR CROSS-COUNTRY WORK.
SO NATURALLY YOU CAN EXPECT THAT ON A SMOOTH HARD-SURFACED HIGHWAY, A MILITARY TRUCK CAN DO A LITTLE MORE.
2½ TONS
BUT, TWICE-AS-MUCH LOAD, COMES DOWN TWICE AS HARD.
5 TONS
OVERLOAD SCALE BY PERCENTAGE.
TRUCKS
%
ANY ALL WHEEL CARGO TRUCK UP TO 2½ OR 6X6
100%
TRUCK TOWING TRAILER.
60%

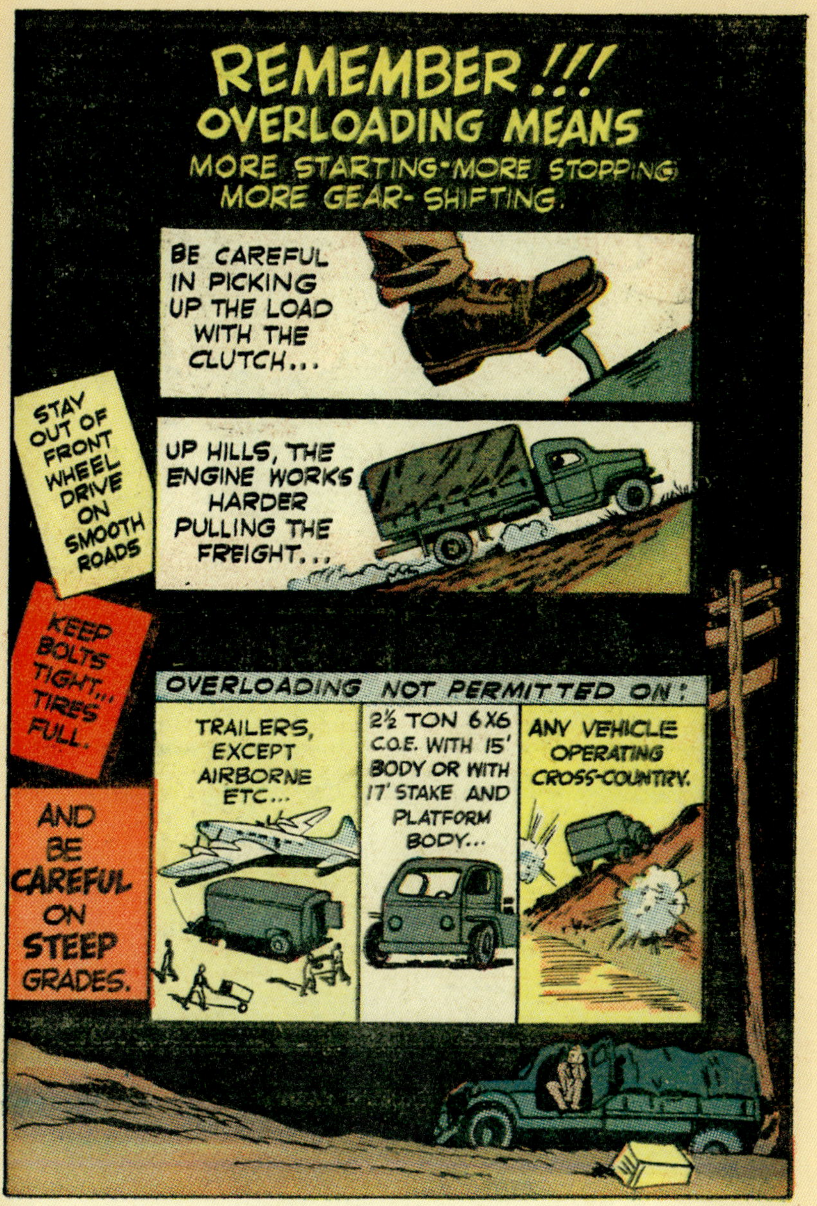
REMEMBER!!!
OVERLOADING MEANS
MORE STARTING-MORE STOPPING
MORE GEAR-SHIFTING.
BE CAREFUL IN PICKING UP THE LOAD WITH THE CLUTCH...
STAY OUT OF FRONT WHEEL DRIVE ON SMOOTH ROADS
UP HILLS, THE ENGINE WORKS HARDER PULLING THE FREIGHT...
KEEP BOLTS TIGHT... TIRES FULL.
OVERLOADING NOT PERMITTED ON:
TRAILERS, EXCEPT AIRBORNE ETC...
2½ TON 6X6 C.O.E. WITH 15' BODY OR WITH 17' STAKE AND PLATFORM BODY...
ANY VEHICLE OPERATING CROSS-COUNTRY.
AND BE CAREFUL ON STEEP GRADES.

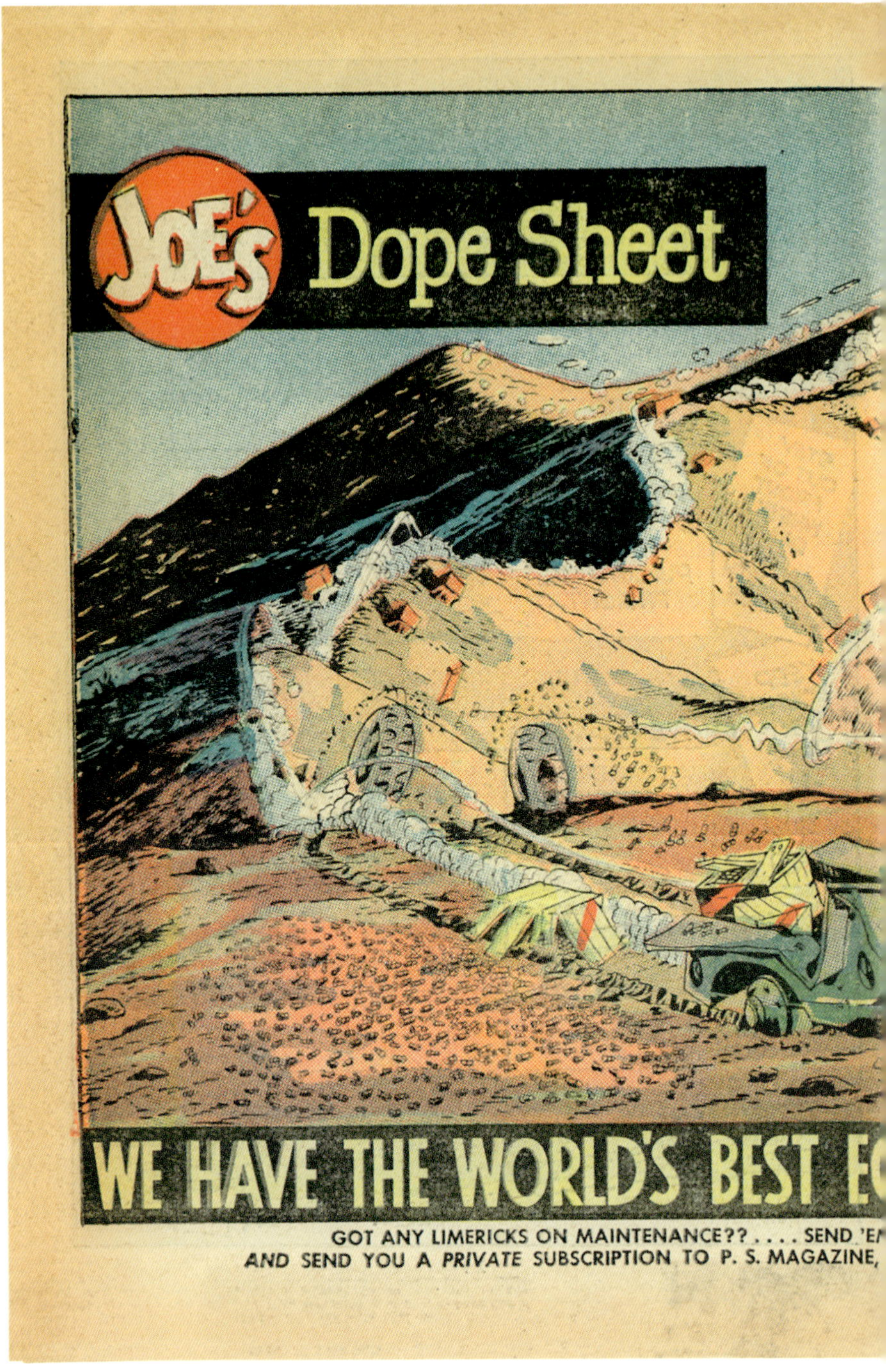
JOE'S Dope Sheet
WE HAVE THE WORLD'S BEST E
GOT ANY LIMERICKS ON MAINTENANCE?? . . . . SEND 'E
AND SEND YOU A PRIVATE SUBSCRIPTION TO P. S. MAGAZINE,

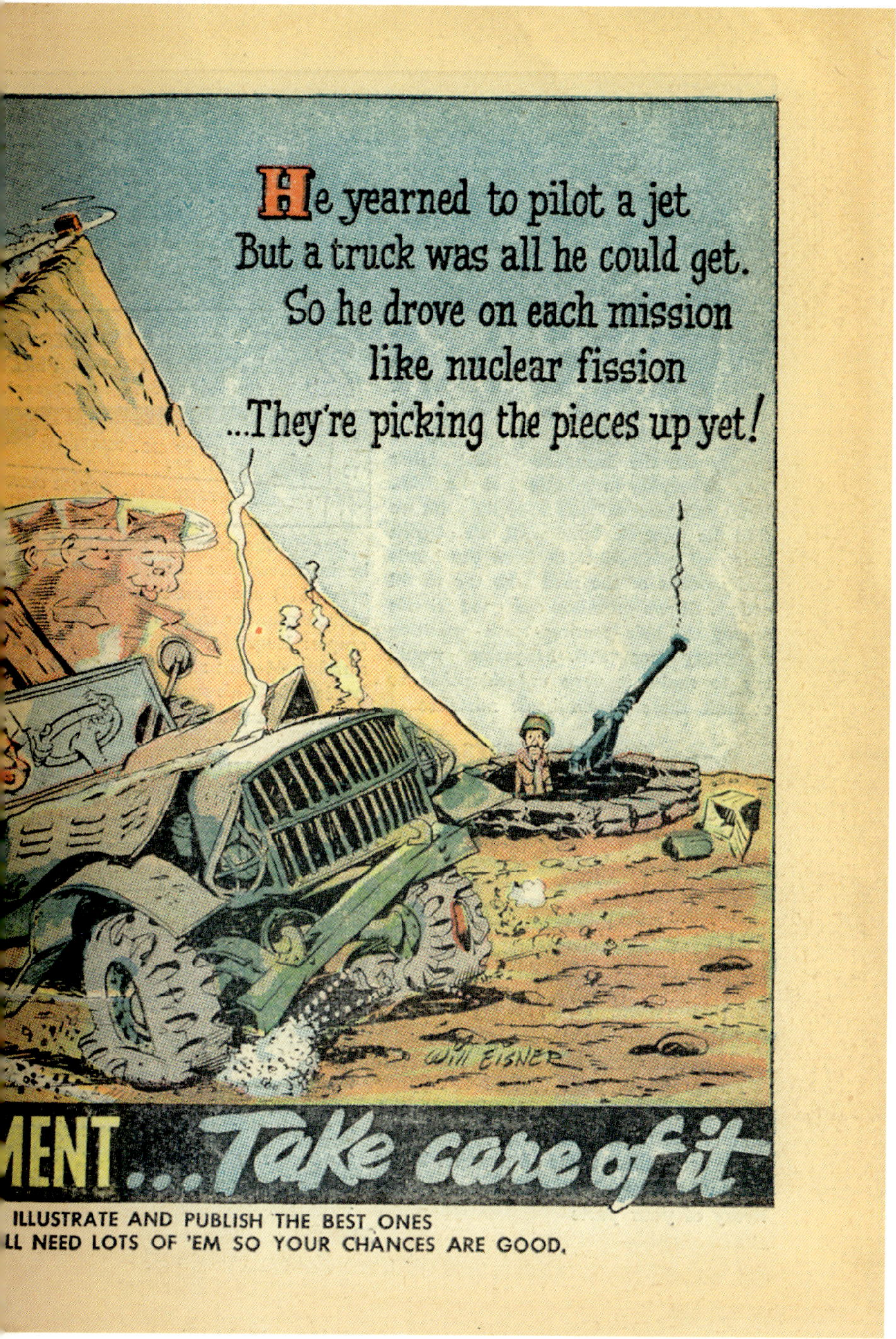
He yearned to pilot a jet
But a truck was all he could get.
So he drove on each mission
like nuclear fission
...They're picking the pieces up yet!
WILL EISNER
MENT ... Take care of it
ILLUSTRATE AND PUBLISH THE BEST ONES
LL NEED LOTS OF 'EM SO YOUR CHANCES ARE GOOD.

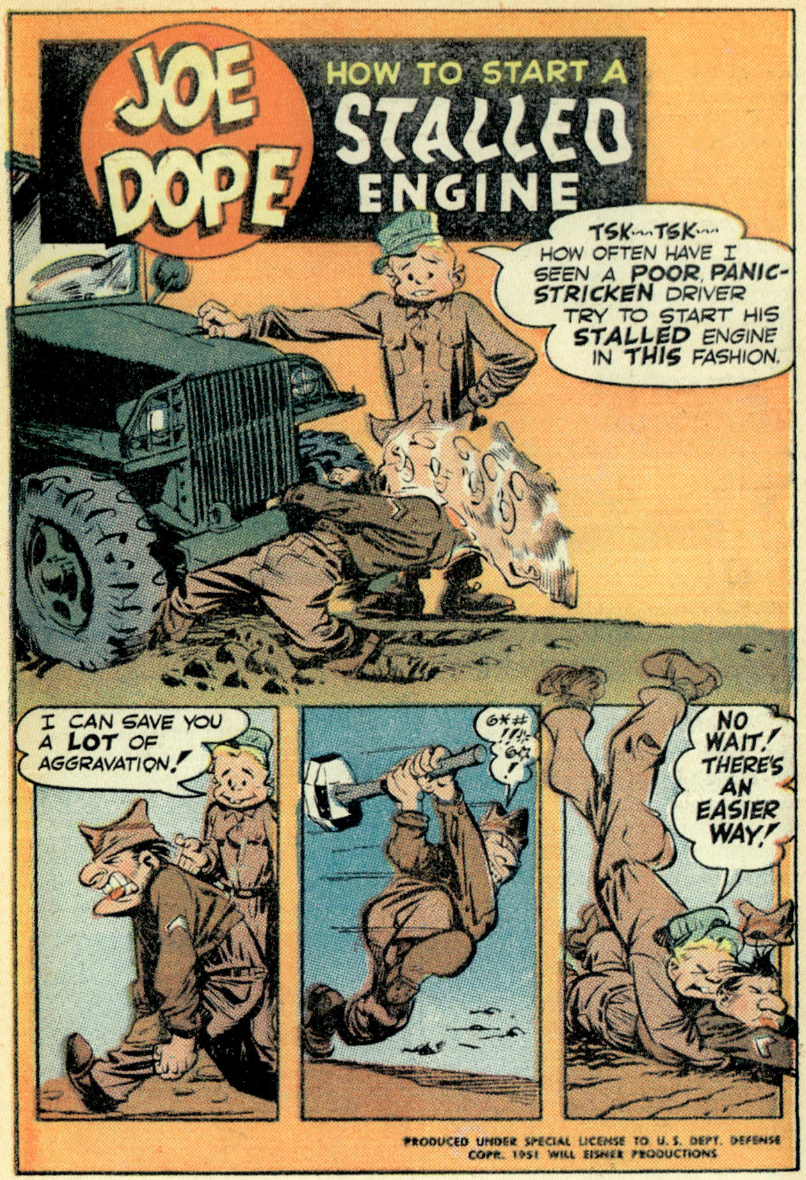
JOE DOPE
HOW TO START A
STALLED
ENGINE
TSK...TSK... HOW OFTEN HAVE I SEEN A POOR, PANIC-STRICKEN DRIVER TRY TO START HIS STALLED ENGINE IN THIS FASHION.
I CAN SAVE YOU A LOT OF AGGRAVATION!
NO WAIT! THERE'S AN EASIER WAY!
PRODUCED UNDER SPECIAL LICENSE TO U.S. DEPT. DEFENSE
COPR. 1951 WILL EISNER PRODUCTIONS

no. 2, July 1951

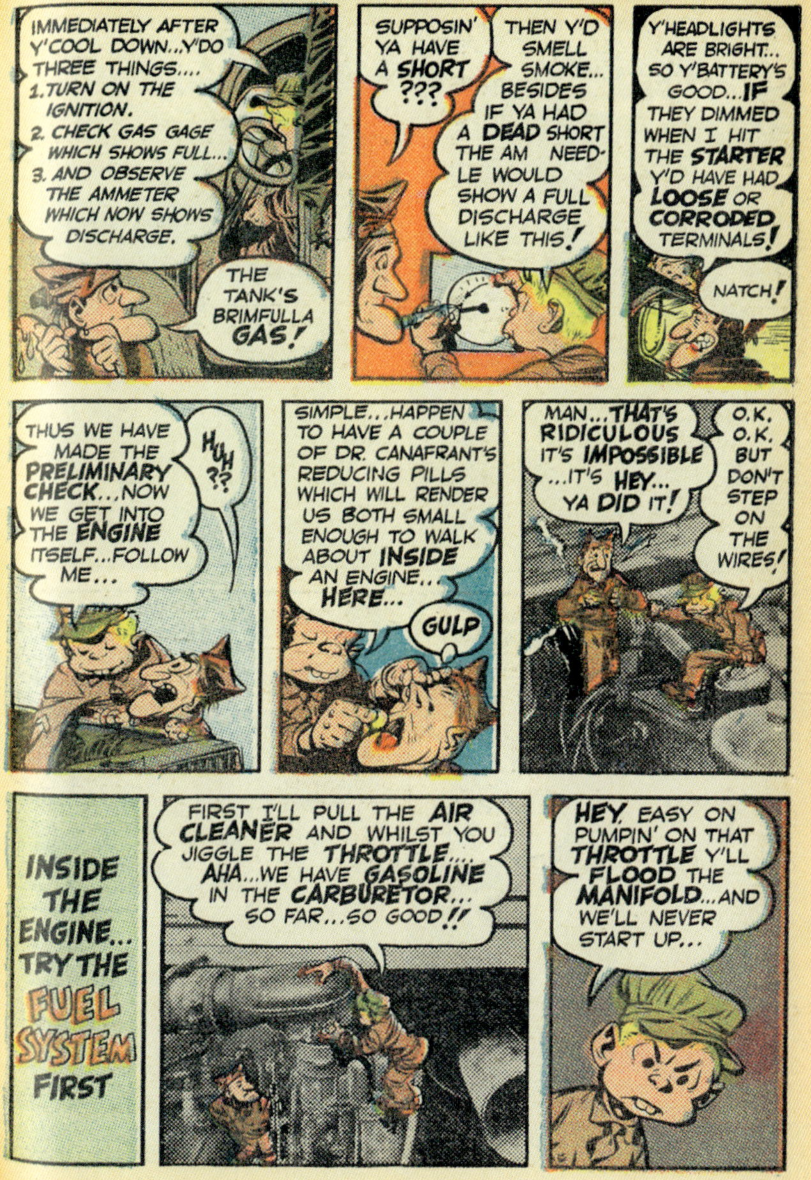
IMMEDIATELY AFTER Y'COOL DOWN...Y'DO THREE THINGS.... 1. TURN ON THE IGNITION. 2. CHECK GAS GAGE WHICH SHOWS FULL... 3. AND OBSERVE THE AMMETER WHICH NOW SHOWS DISCHARGE.
THE TANK'S BRIMFULLA GAS!
SUPPOSIN' YA HAVE A SHORT ???
THEN Y'D SMELL SMOKE... BESIDES IF YA HAD A DEAD SHORT THE AM NEEDLE WOULD SHOW A FULL DISCHARGE LIKE THIS!
Y'HEADLIGHTS ARE BRIGHT... SO Y'BATTERY'S GOOD...IF THEY DIMMED WHEN I HIT THE STARTER Y'D HAVE HAD LOOSE OR CORRODED TERMINALS!
NATCH!
THUS WE HAVE MADE THE PRELIMINARY CHECK...NOW WE GET INTO THE ENGINE ITSELF...FOLLOW ME...
HUH ??
SIMPLE...HAPPEN TO HAVE A COUPLE OF DR. CANAFRANT'S REDUCING PILLS WHICH WILL RENDER US BOTH SMALL ENOUGH TO WALK ABOUT INSIDE AN ENGINE... HERE...
GULP
MAN...THAT'S RIDICULOUS IT'S IMPOSSIBLE ...IT'S HEY... YA DID IT!
O.K. O.K. BUT DON'T STEP ON THE WIRES!
INSIDE THE ENGINE... TRY THE FUEL SYSTEM FIRST
FIRST I'LL PULL THE AIR CLEANER AND WHILST YOU JIGGLE THE THROTTLE.... AHA...WE HAVE GASOLINE IN THE CARBURETOR... SO FAR...SO GOOD!!
HEY, EASY ON PUMPIN' ON THAT THROTTLE Y'LL FLOOD THE MANIFOLD...AND WE'LL NEVER START UP...

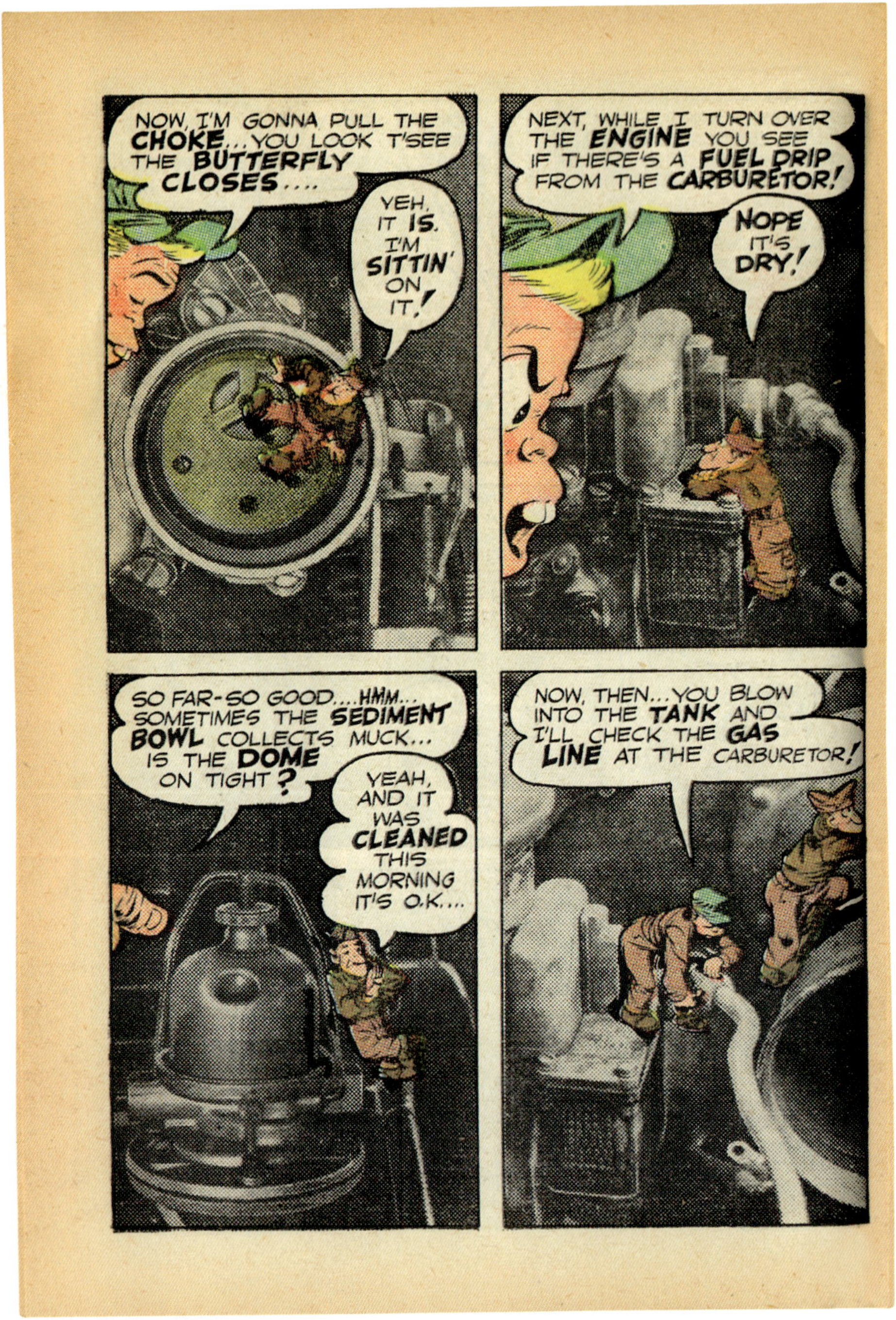
NOW, I'M GONNA PULL THE CHOKE...YOU LOOK T'SEE THE BUTTERFLY CLOSES....
YEH, IT IS. I'M SITTIN' ON IT!
NEXT, WHILE I TURN OVER THE ENGINE YOU SEE IF THERE'S A FUEL DRIP FROM THE CARBURETOR!
NOPE IT'S DRY!
SO FAR-SO GOOD....HMM... SOMETIMES THE SEDIMENT BOWL COLLECTS MUCK... IS THE DOME ON TIGHT?
YEAH, AND IT WAS CLEANED THIS MORNING IT'S O.K....
NOW, THEN...YOU BLOW INTO THE TANK AND I'LL CHECK THE GAS LINE AT THE CARBURETOR!

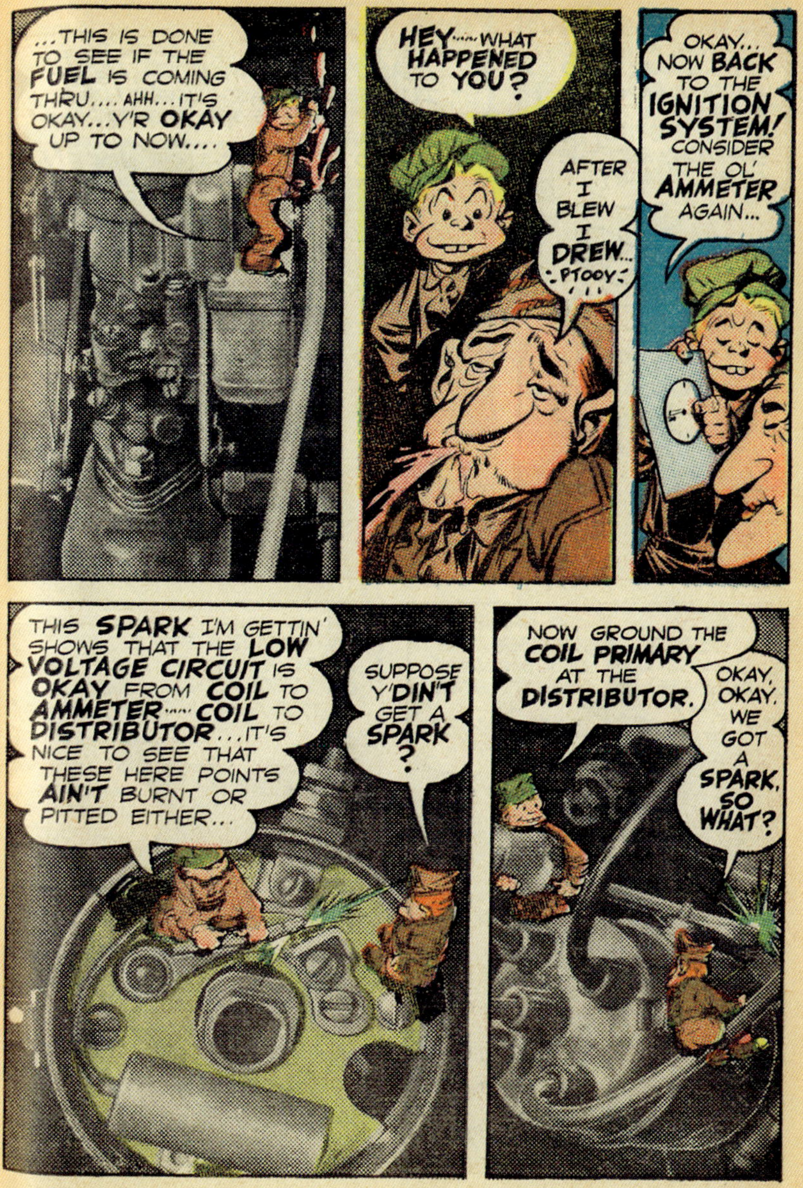
...THIS IS DONE TO SEE IF THE FUEL IS COMING THRU.... AHH...IT'S OKAY...Y'R OKAY UP TO NOW....
HEY.....WHAT HAPPENED TO YOU?
AFTER I BLEW I DREW... PTOOY
OKAY... NOW BACK TO THE IGNITION SYSTEM! CONSIDER THE OL' AMMETER AGAIN...
THIS SPARK I'M GETTIN' SHOWS THAT THE LOW VOLTAGE CIRCUIT IS OKAY FROM COIL TO AMMETER..... COIL TO DISTRIBUTOR...IT'S NICE TO SEE THAT THESE HERE POINTS AIN'T BURNT OR PITTED EITHER...
SUPPOSE Y'DIN'T GET A SPARK?
NOW GROUND THE COIL PRIMARY AT THE DISTRIBUTOR.
OKAY, OKAY. WE GOT A SPARK, SO WHAT?

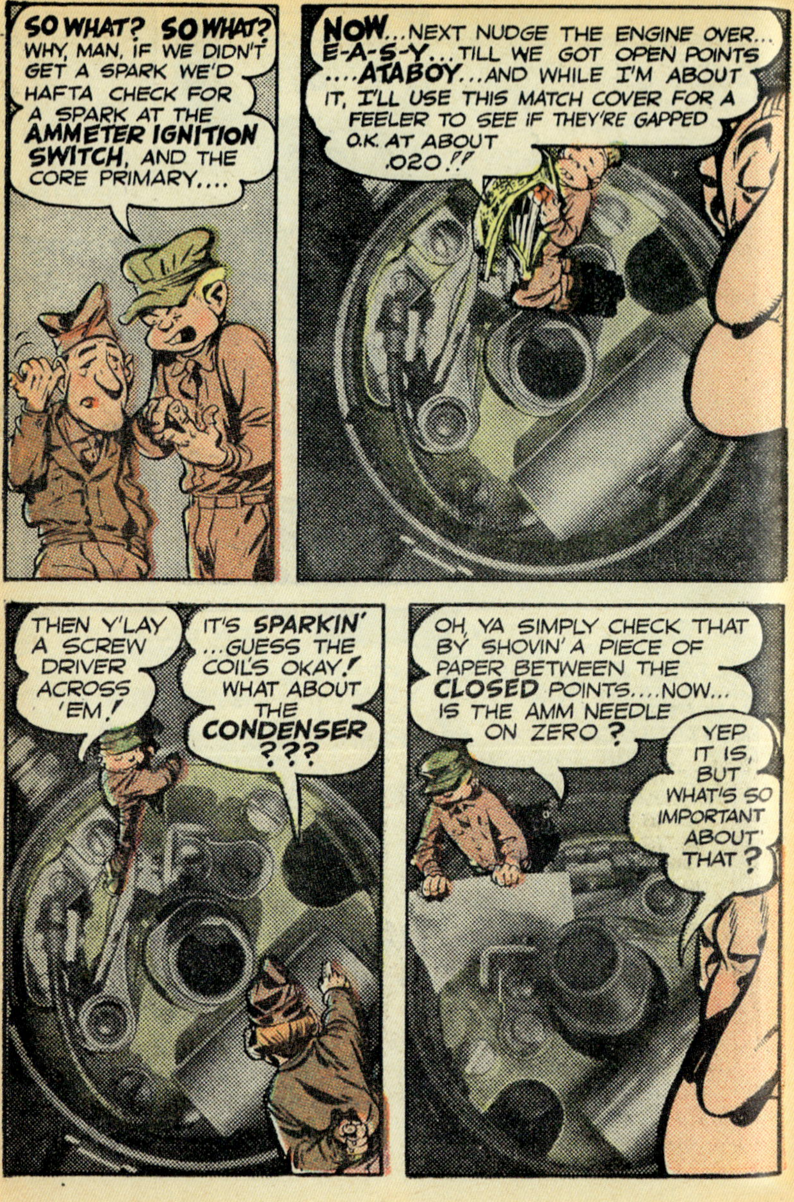
SO WHAT? SO WHAT? WHY, MAN, IF WE DIDN'T GET A SPARK WE'D HAFTA CHECK FOR A SPARK AT THE AMMETER IGNITION SWITCH, AND THE CORE PRIMARY....
NOW...NEXT NUDGE THE ENGINE OVER... E-A-S-Y...TILL WE GOT OPEN POINTS ....ATABOY...AND WHILE I'M ABOUT IT, I'LL USE THIS MATCH COVER FOR A FEELER TO SEE IF THEY'RE GAPPED O.K. AT ABOUT .020 !?
THEN Y'LAY A SCREW DRIVER ACROSS 'EM!
IT'S SPARKIN' ...GUESS THE COIL'S OKAY! WHAT ABOUT THE CONDENSER ???
OH, YA SIMPLY CHECK THAT BY SHOVIN' A PIECE OF PAPER BETWEEN THE CLOSED POINTS....NOW... IS THE AMM NEEDLE ON ZERO ?
YEP IT IS, BUT WHAT'S SO IMPORTANT ABOUT THAT ?

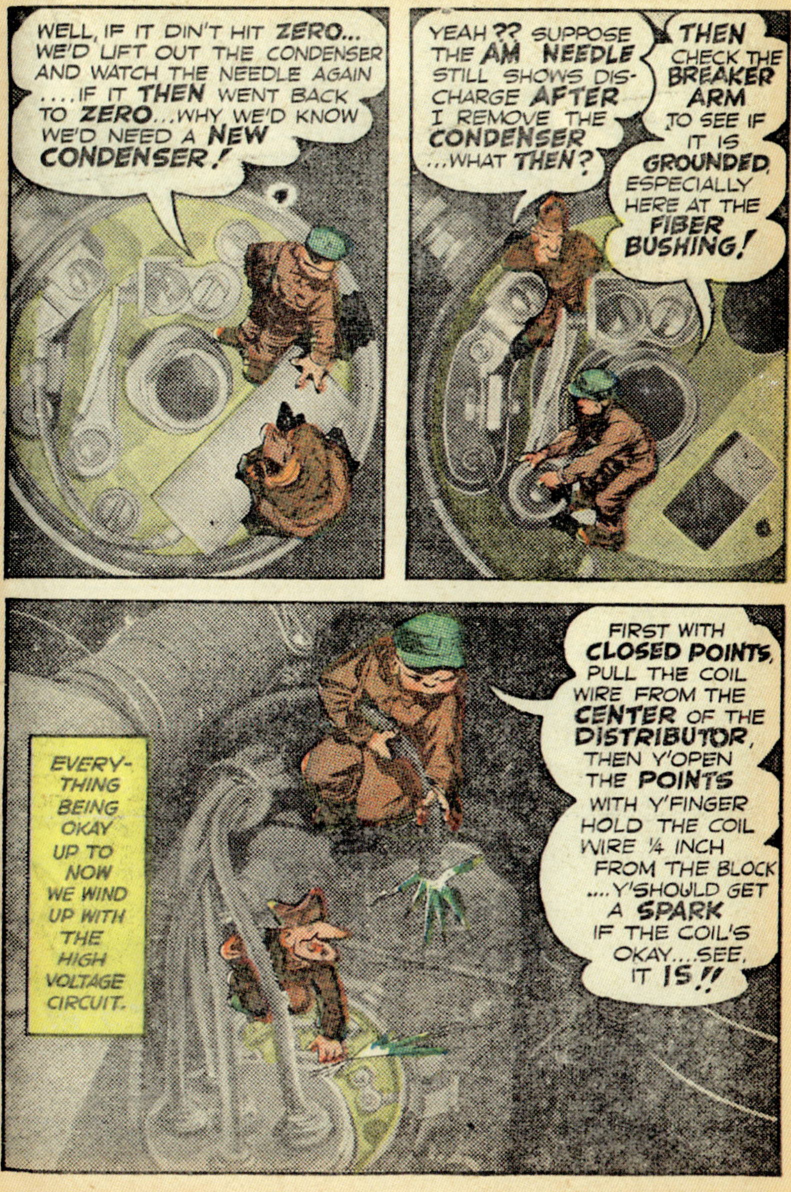
WELL, IF IT DIN'T HIT ZERO... WE'D LIFT OUT THE CONDENSER AND WATCH THE NEEDLE AGAIN ....IF IT THEN WENT BACK TO ZERO...WHY WE'D KNOW WE'D NEED A NEW CONDENSER!
YEAH?? SUPPOSE THE AM NEEDLE STILL SHOWS DISCHARGE AFTER I REMOVE THE CONDENSER ...WHAT THEN?
THEN CHECK THE BREAKER ARM TO SEE IF IT IS GROUNDED, ESPECIALLY HERE AT THE FIBER BUSHING!
EVERYTHING BEING OKAY UP TO NOW WE WIND UP WITH THE HIGH VOLTAGE CIRCUIT.
FIRST WITH CLOSED POINTS, PULL THE COIL WIRE FROM THE CENTER OF THE DISTRIBUTOR, THEN Y'OPEN THE POINTS WITH Y'FINGER HOLD THE COIL WIRE ¼ INCH FROM THE BLOCK ....Y'SHOULD GET A SPARK IF THE COIL'S OKAY....SEE, IT IS!!

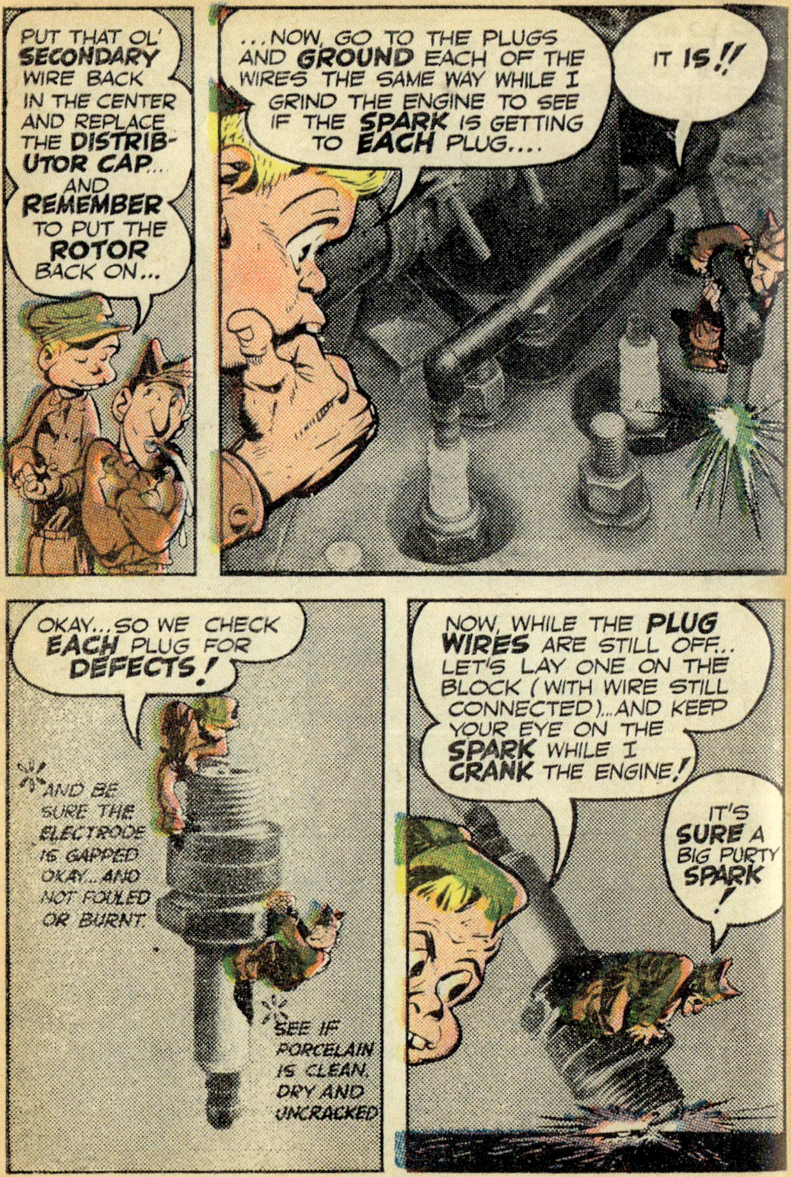
PUT THAT OL' SECONDARY WIRE BACK IN THE CENTER AND REPLACE THE DISTRIB-UTOR CAP... AND REMEMBER TO PUT THE ROTOR BACK ON...
...NOW, GO TO THE PLUGS AND GROUND EACH OF THE WIRES THE SAME WAY WHILE I GRIND THE ENGINE TO SEE IF THE SPARK IS GETTING TO EACH PLUG....
IT IS!!
OKAY...SO WE CHECK EACH PLUG FOR DEFECTS!
AND BE SURE THE ELECTRODE IS GAPPED OKAY...AND NOT FOULED OR BURNT
SEE IF PORCELAIN IS CLEAN, DRY AND UNCRACKED
NOW, WHILE THE PLUG WIRES ARE STILL OFF... LET'S LAY ONE ON THE BLOCK (WITH WIRE STILL CONNECTED)...AND KEEP YOUR EYE ON THE SPARK WHILE I CRANK THE ENGINE!
IT'S SURE A BIG PURTY SPARK!

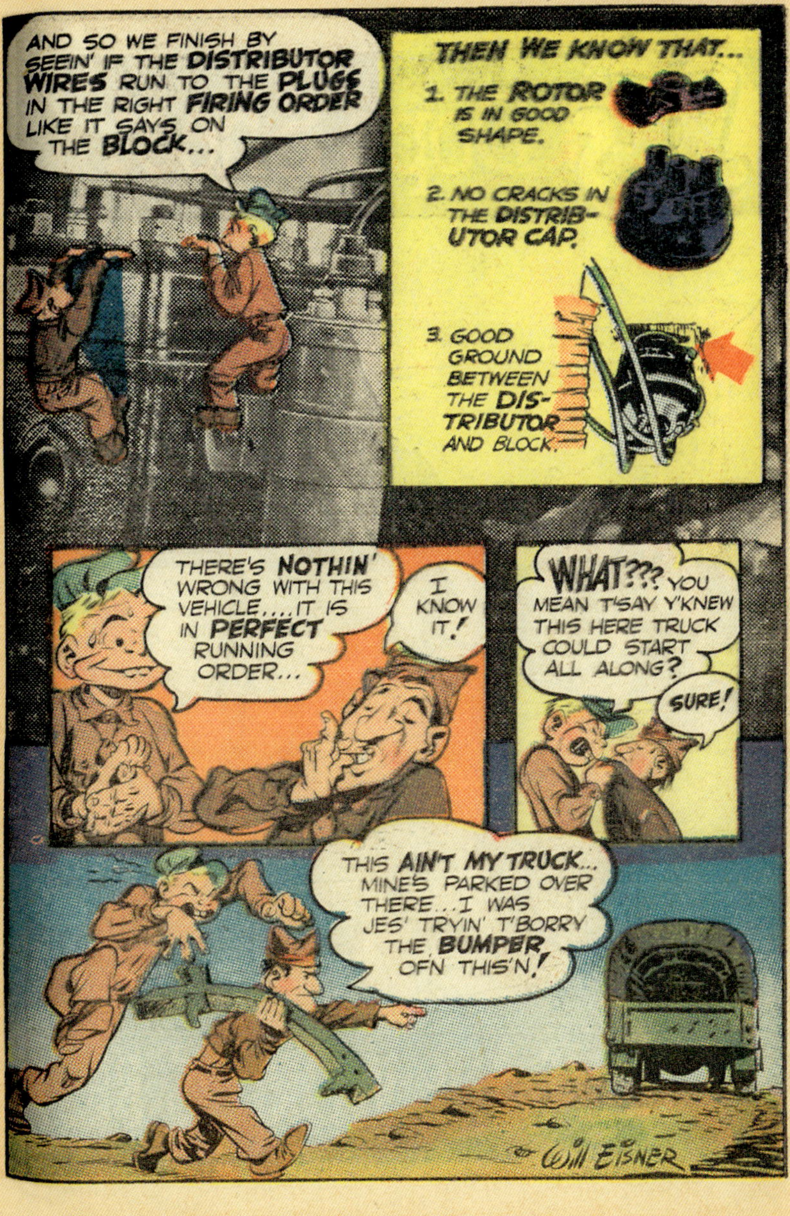
AND SO WE FINISH BY SEEIN' IF THE DISTRIBUTOR WIRES RUN TO THE PLUGS IN THE RIGHT FIRING ORDER LIKE IT SAYS ON THE BLOCK...
THEN WE KNOW THAT...
1. THE ROTOR IS IN GOOD SHAPE.
2. NO CRACKS IN THE DISTRIBUTOR CAP.
3. GOOD GROUND BETWEEN THE DISTRIBUTOR AND BLOCK.
THERE'S NOTHIN' WRONG WITH THIS VEHICLE....IT IS IN PERFECT RUNNING ORDER...
I KNOW IT!
WHAT??? YOU MEAN T'SAY Y'KNEW THIS HERE TRUCK COULD START ALL ALONG?
SURE!
THIS AIN'T MY TRUCK... MINE'S PARKED OVER THERE...I WAS JES' TRYIN' T'BORRY THE BUMPER OFN THIS'N!
Will Eisner

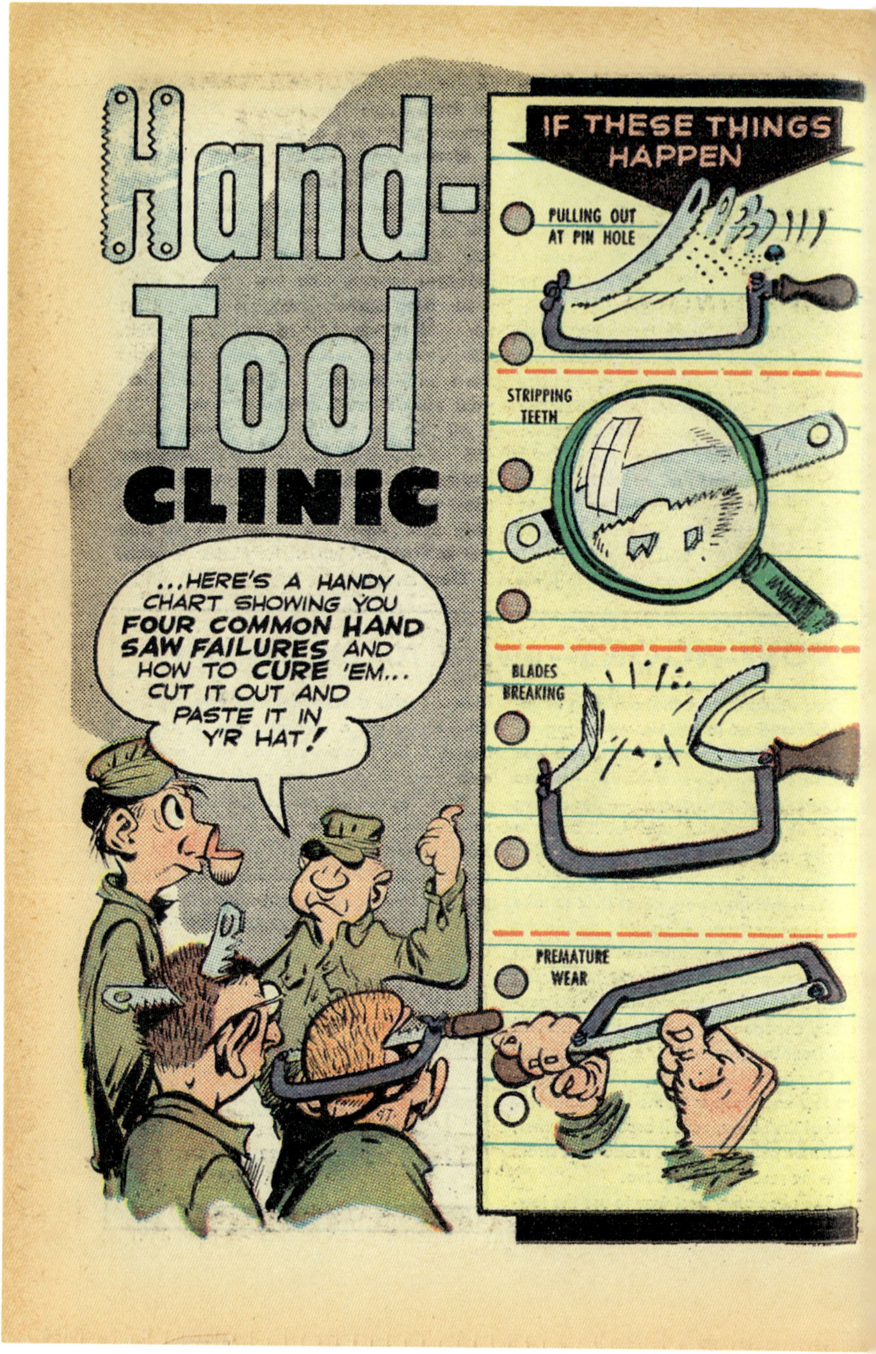
Hand-Tool CLINIC
...HERE'S A HANDY CHART SHOWING YOU FOUR COMMON HAND SAW FAILURES AND HOW TO CURE 'EM... CUT IT OUT AND PASTE IT IN Y'R HAT!
IF THESE THINGS HAPPEN
PULLING OUT AT PIN HOLE
STRIPPING TEETH
BLADES BREAKING
PREMATURE WEAR

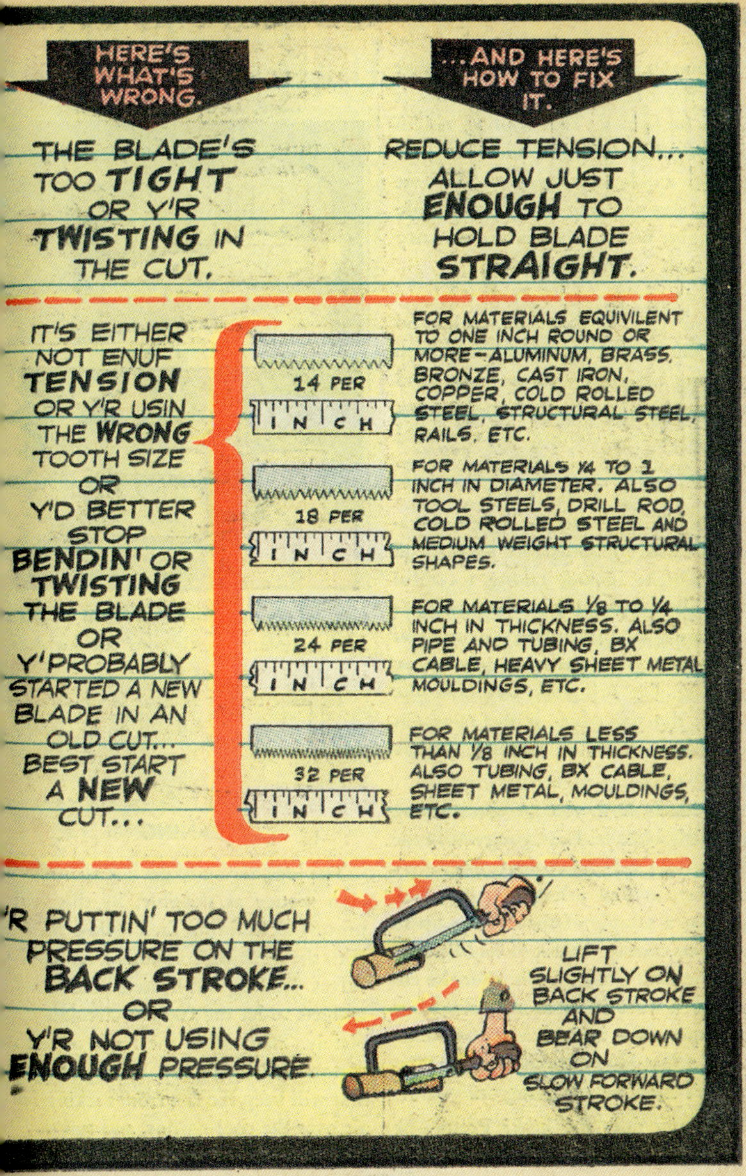
HERE'S WHAT'S WRONG.
...AND HERE'S HOW TO FIX IT.
THE BLADE'S TOO TIGHT OR Y'R TWISTING IN THE CUT.
REDUCE TENSION... ALLOW JUST ENOUGH TO HOLD BLADE STRAIGHT.
IT'S EITHER NOT ENUF TENSION OR Y'R USIN THE WRONG TOOTH SIZE OR Y'D BETTER STOP BENDIN' OR TWISTING THE BLADE OR Y'PROBABLY STARTED A NEW BLADE IN AN OLD CUT... BEST START A NEW CUT...
14 PER INCH
FOR MATERIALS EQUIVILENT TO ONE INCH ROUND OR MORE—ALUMINUM, BRASS, BRONZE, CAST IRON, COPPER, COLD ROLLED STEEL, STRUCTURAL STEEL, RAILS, ETC.
18 PER INCH
FOR MATERIALS 1/4 TO 1 INCH IN DIAMETER. ALSO TOOL STEELS, DRILL ROD, COLD ROLLED STEEL AND MEDIUM WEIGHT STRUCTURAL SHAPES.
24 PER INCH
FOR MATERIALS 1/8 TO 1/4 INCH IN THICKNESS. ALSO PIPE AND TUBING, BX CABLE, HEAVY SHEET METAL MOULDINGS, ETC.
32 PER INCH
FOR MATERIALS LESS THAN 1/8 INCH IN THICKNESS. ALSO TUBING, BX CABLE, SHEET METAL, MOULDINGS, ETC.
'R PUTTIN' TOO MUCH PRESSURE ON THE BACK STROKE... OR Y'R NOT USING ENOUGH PRESSURE.
LIFT SLIGHTLY ON BACK STROKE AND BEAR DOWN ON SLOW FORWARD STROKE.

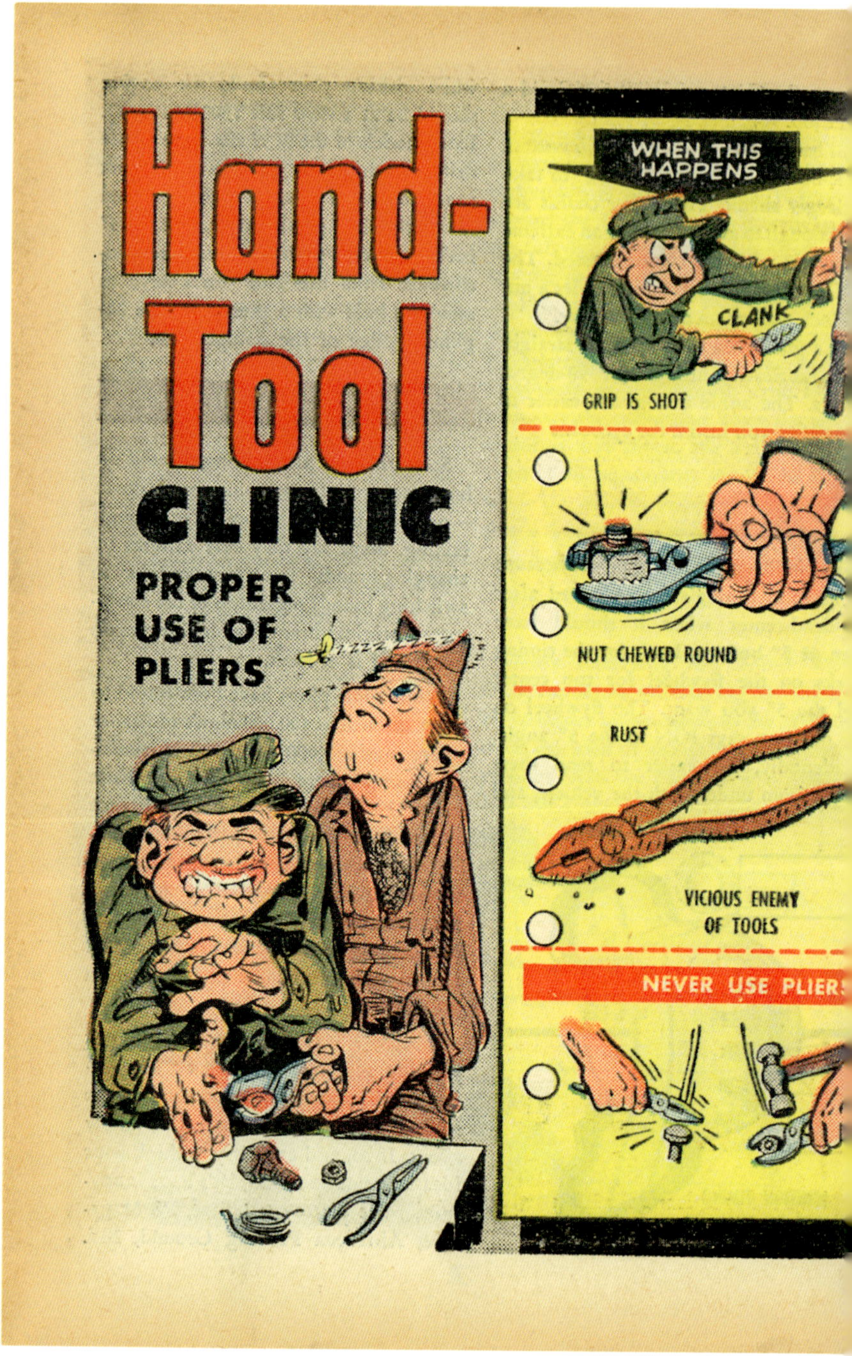
Hand-Tool
CLINIC
PROPER USE OF PLIERS
WHEN THIS HAPPENS
CLANK
GRIP IS SHOT
NUT CHEWED ROUND
RUST
VICIOUS ENEMY OF TOOLS
NEVER USE PLIER

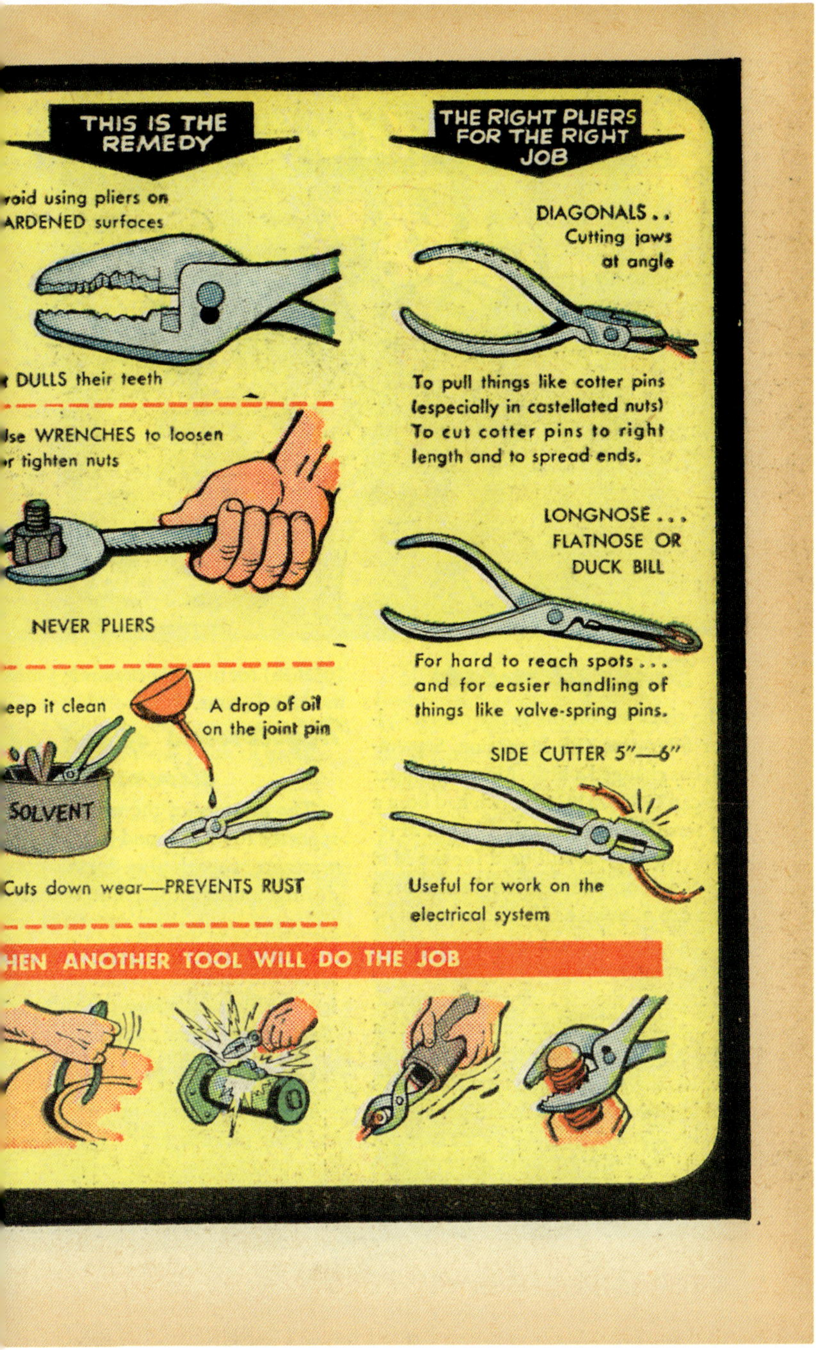

THIS IS THE REMEDY
void using pliers on
ARDENED surfaces
DULLS their teeth
Jse WRENCHES to loosen
r tighten nuts
NEVER PLIERS
eep it clean
A drop of oil
on the joint pin
SOLVENT
Cuts down wear—PREVENTS RUST
HEN ANOTHER TOOL WILL DO THE JOB
THE RIGHT PLIERS FOR THE RIGHT JOB
DIAGONALS . .
Cutting jaws
at angle
To pull things like cotter pins
(especially in castellated nuts)
To cut cotter pins to right
length and to spread ends.
LONGNOSE . . .
FLATNOSE OR
DUCK BILL
For hard to reach spots . . .
and for easier handling of
things like valve-spring pins.
SIDE CUTTER 5"—6"
Useful for work on the
electrical system

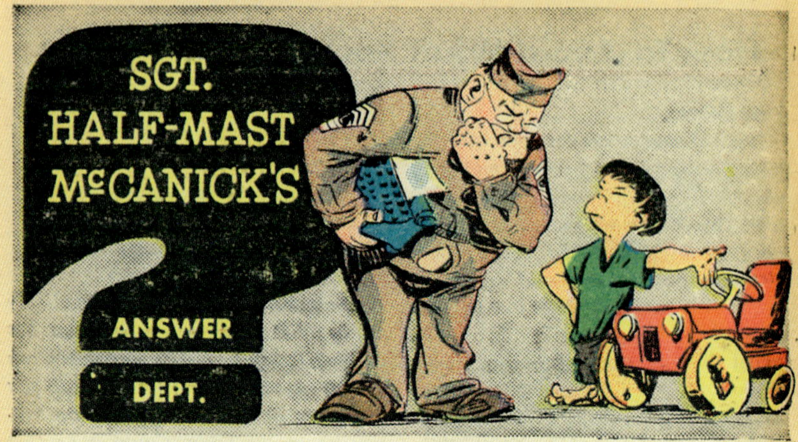
SGT. HALF-MAST McCANICK'S
ANSWER
DEPT.

WINCH-CLUTCH LEVER

Dear Half-Mast,

We are having trouble with the winch clutch levers breaking on the 5-ton M-51 truck. The lever binds on the front grill bracket. It is made of a very poor grade of aluminum. What to do?

Sgt W. L. E.

Dear Sgt W. L. E.,

Granted the lever would be made of poor grade aluminum—there's a trick to operating the clutch to prevent the lever from breaking. Could be that in some cases the operator's been trying to engage the winch-drum clutch with the jaws not in the proper relative position. Crunch-crunch!

Now then, if operating alone, rotate the winch drum by hand, with reasonable pressure on the winch-clutch operating-lever. Apply pressure by hand instead of foot, hammer, or two-foot length of pipe. If you have an assistant driver, while he applies pressure on the winch-drum operating-lever, you can engage the winch drive in reverse position, rotating the winch very cautiously. When the two clutch members are properly matched, they will become engaged — and then there's no reason for breakage.

Half-Mast

JIMMY SYMBOLS

Dear Half-Mast,

On a GMC $2\frac{1}{2}$-ton 6x6 model you find the symbols CCKW353. I know 353 means LWB, but can you tell me what CCKW means? I've checked everywhere.

Sgt K. L. H.
Korea

Dear Sgt K. L. H.,

Don't worry about that CCKW. The only guy that gets anything out of it is the manufacturer. He uses it as a model designation. For you, it's like the farmer who saw his first giraffe—it just didn't exist.

Half-Mast

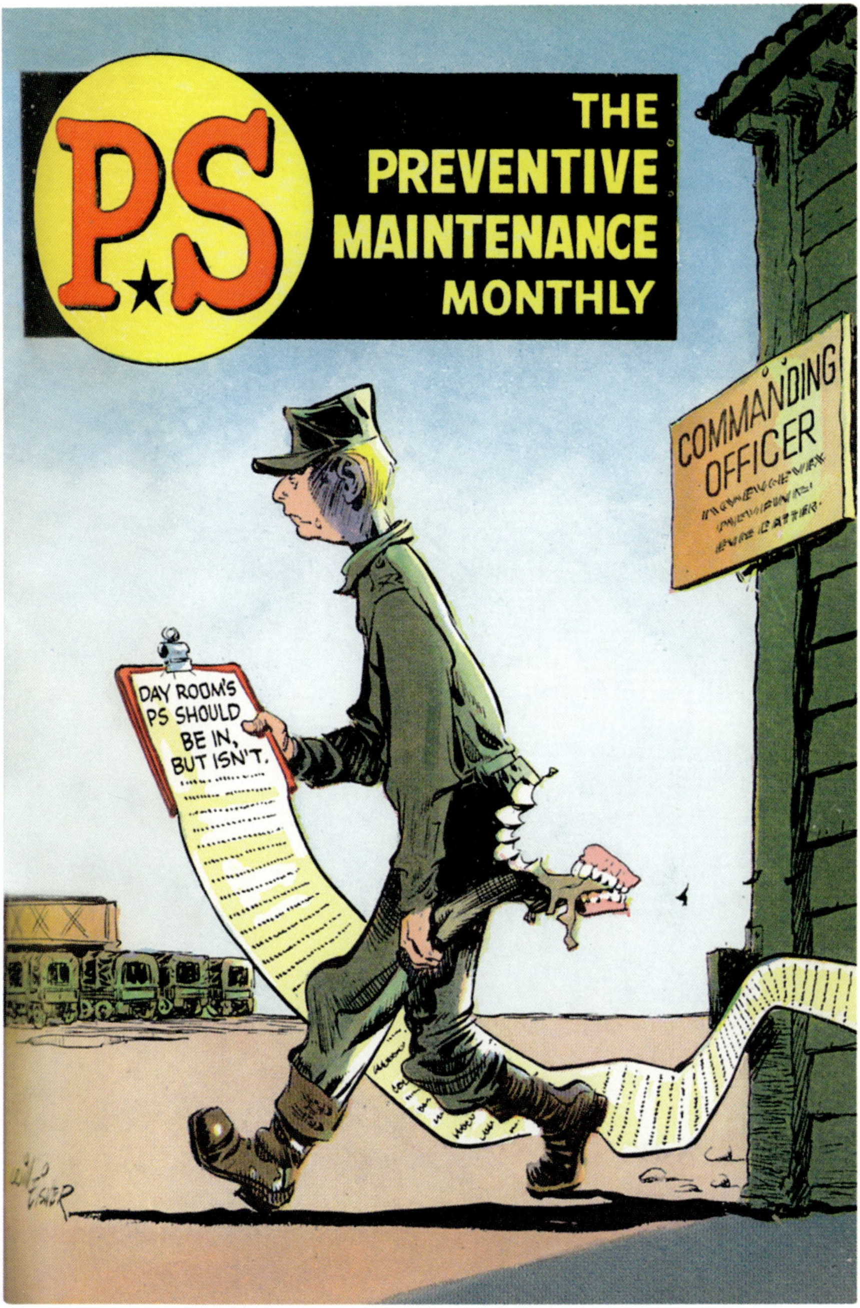
P★S
THE PREVENTIVE MAINTENANCE MONTHLY
COMMANDING OFFICER
DAY ROOM'S PS SHOULD BE IN, BUT ISN'T.

no. 15, 1953

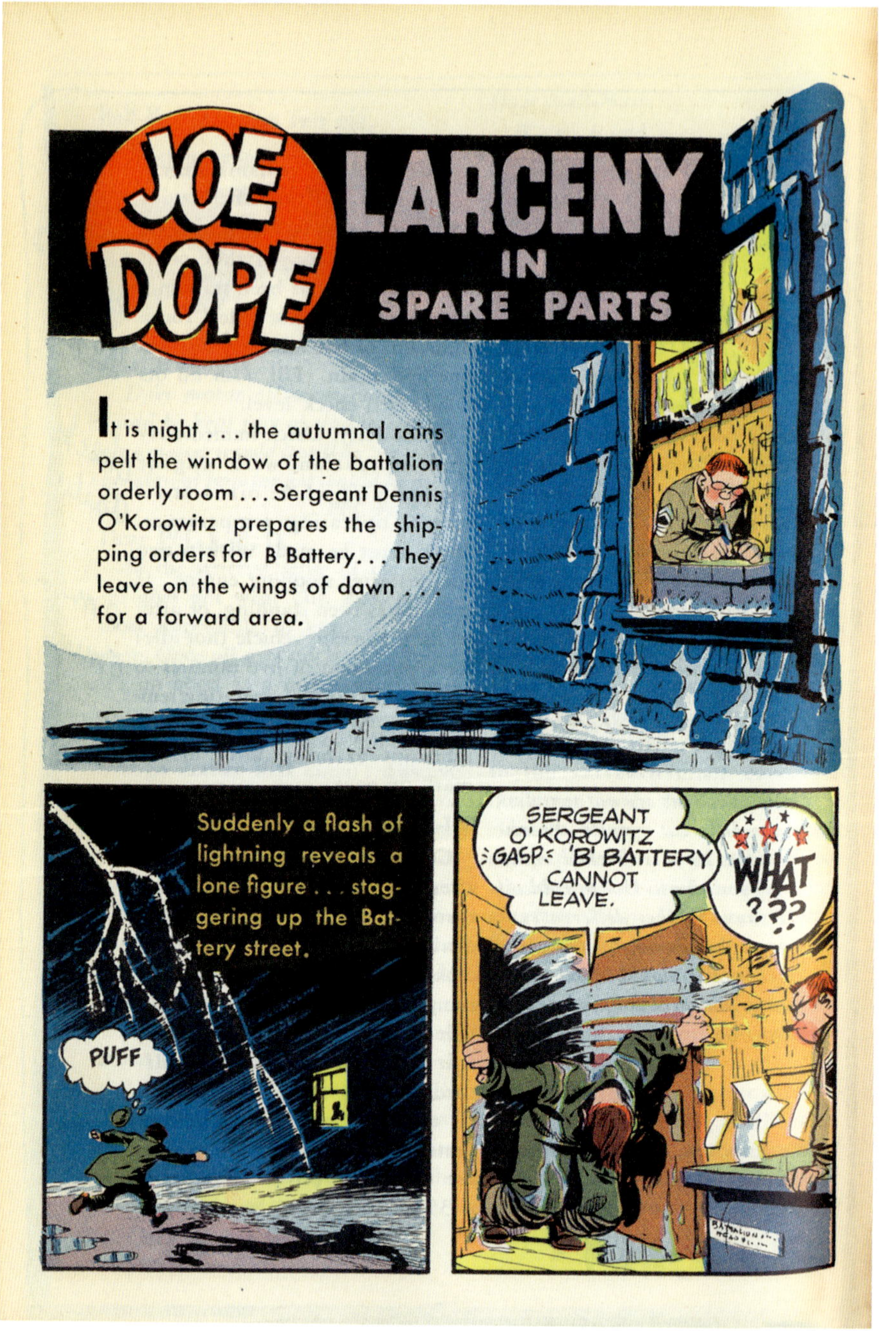
JOE DOPE
LARCENY
IN
SPARE PARTS
It is night . . . the autumnal rains pelt the window of the battalion orderly room . . . Sergeant Dennis O'Korowitz prepares the shipping orders for B Battery. . . They leave on the wings of dawn . . . for a forward area.
Suddenly a flash of lightning reveals a lone figure . . . staggering up the Battery street.
PUFF
SERGEANT O'KOROWITZ GASP 'B' BATTERY CANNOT LEAVE.
WHAT ???

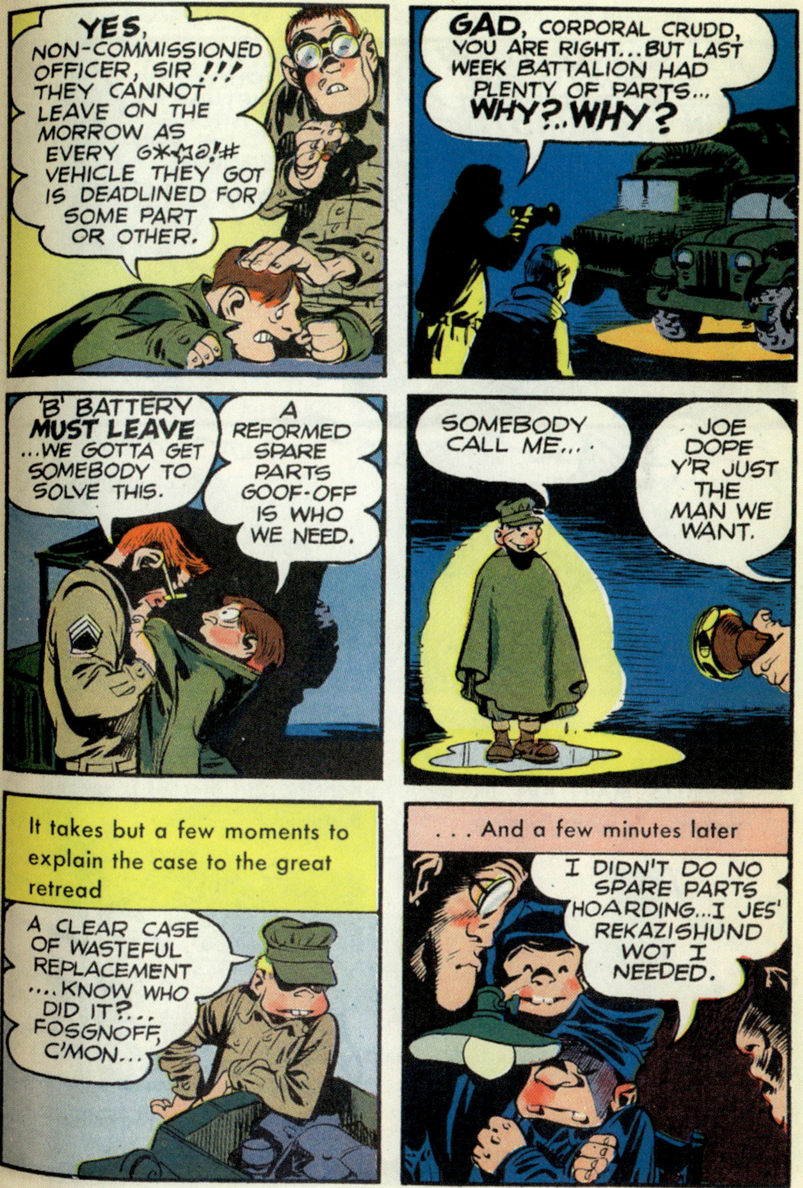

YES, NON-COMMISSIONED OFFICER, SIR !!! THEY CANNOT LEAVE ON THE MORROW AS EVERY G*☆@!# VEHICLE THEY GOT IS DEADLINED FOR SOME PART OR OTHER.
GAD, CORPORAL CRUDD, YOU ARE RIGHT... BUT LAST WEEK BATTALION HAD PLENTY OF PARTS... WHY?..WHY?
'B' BATTERY MUST LEAVE ...WE GOTTA GET SOMEBODY TO SOLVE THIS.
A REFORMED SPARE PARTS GOOF-OFF IS WHO WE NEED.
SOMEBODY CALL ME...
JOE DOPE Y'R JUST THE MAN WE WANT.
It takes but a few moments to explain the case to the great retread
A CLEAR CASE OF WASTEFUL REPLACEMENT ....KNOW WHO DID IT?... FOSGNOFF, C'MON...
. . . And a few minutes later
I DIDN'T DO NO SPARE PARTS HOARDING...I JES' REKAZISHUND WOT I NEEDED.

But what he "needed" depleted stock **WASTEFULLY!**

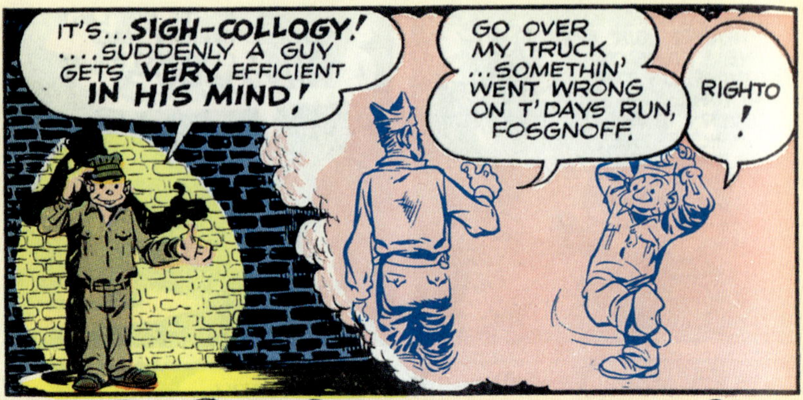
IT'S...SIGH-COLLOGY! ....SUDDENLY A GUY GETS VERY EFFICIENT IN HIS MIND!
GO OVER MY TRUCK ...SOMETHIN' WENT WRONG ON T'DAYS RUN, FOSGNOFF.
RIGHTO !

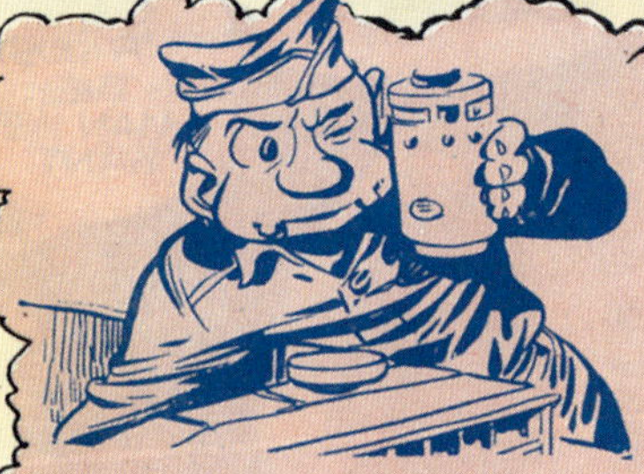

Here's his chance, he thinks, to buck for a promotion . . . He begins to "MAINTAIN" like the dickens . . . by discarding.

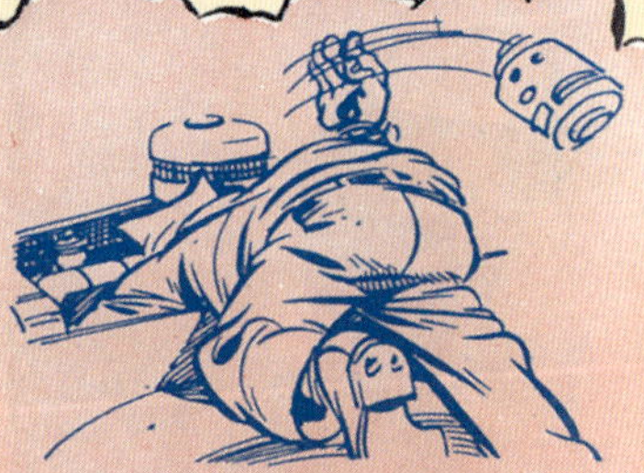

Nothing escapes his careful scrutiny . . . No major component or part thereof is spared a study.

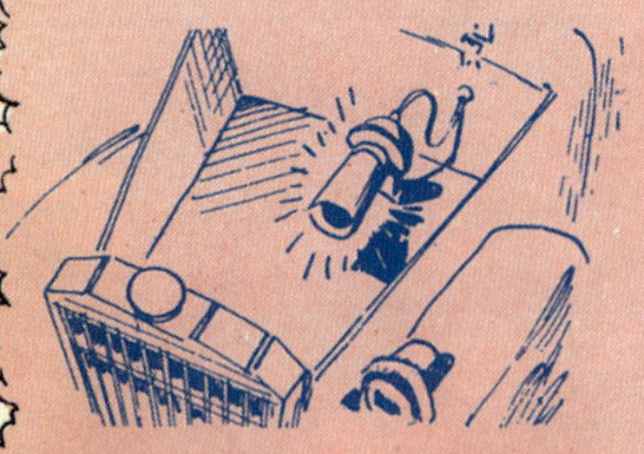

Only those parts that are shiny-new remain. The rest go.

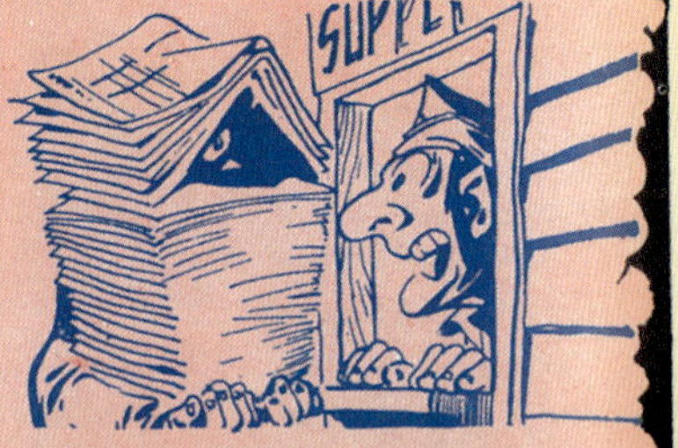

Naturally his parts requisitioning is very considerable . . .

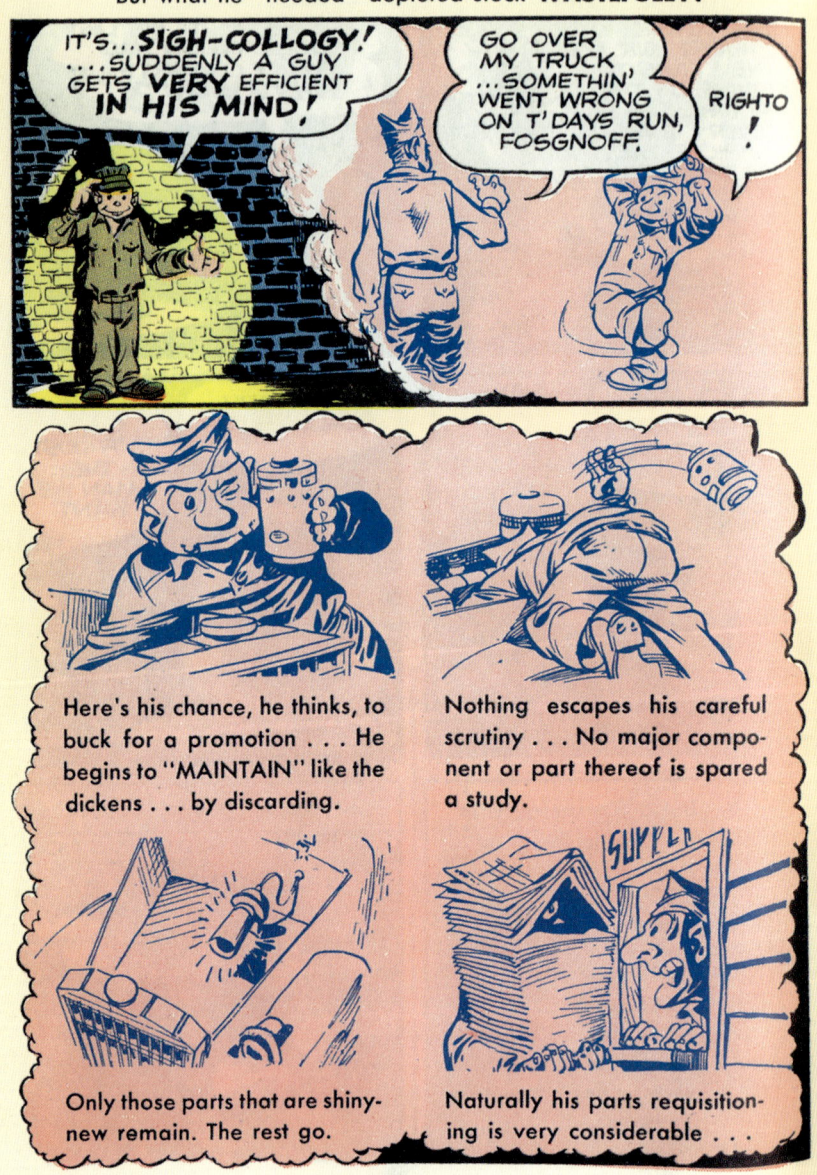

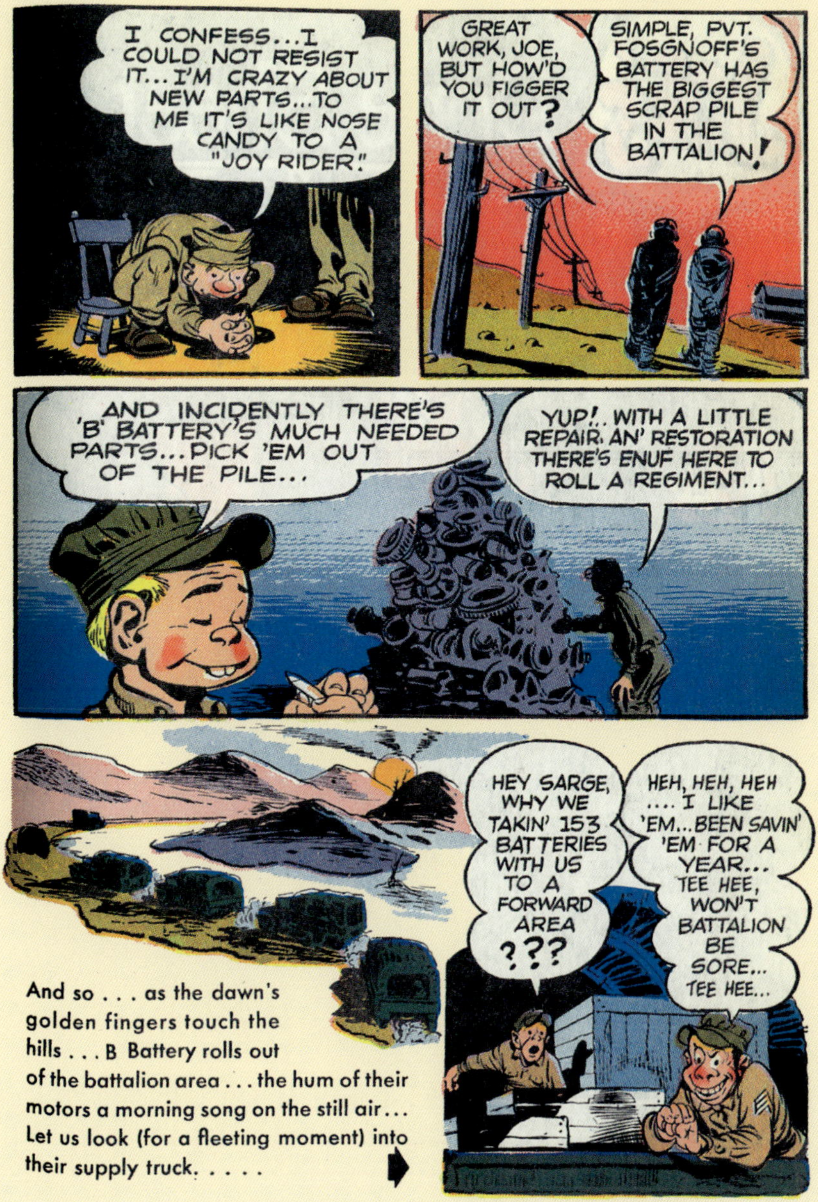
I CONFESS...I COULD NOT RESIST IT...I'M CRAZY ABOUT NEW PARTS...TO ME IT'S LIKE NOSE CANDY TO A "JOY RIDER."
GREAT WORK, JOE, BUT HOW'D YOU FIGGER IT OUT?
SIMPLE, PVT. FOSGNOFF'S BATTERY HAS THE BIGGEST SCRAP PILE IN THE BATTALION!
AND INCIDENTLY THERE'S 'B' BATTERY'S MUCH NEEDED PARTS...PICK 'EM OUT OF THE PILE...
YUP!..WITH A LITTLE REPAIR AN' RESTORATION THERE'S ENUF HERE TO ROLL A REGIMENT...
And so . . . as the dawn's golden fingers touch the hills . . . B Battery rolls out of the battalion area . . . the hum of their motors a morning song on the still air... Let us look (for a fleeting moment) into their supply truck. . . . .
HEY SARGE, WHY WE TAKIN' 153 BATTERIES WITH US TO A FORWARD AREA ???
HEH, HEH, HEH .... I LIKE 'EM...BEEN SAVIN' 'EM FOR A YEAR... TEE HEE, WON'T BATTALION BE SORE... TEE HEE...

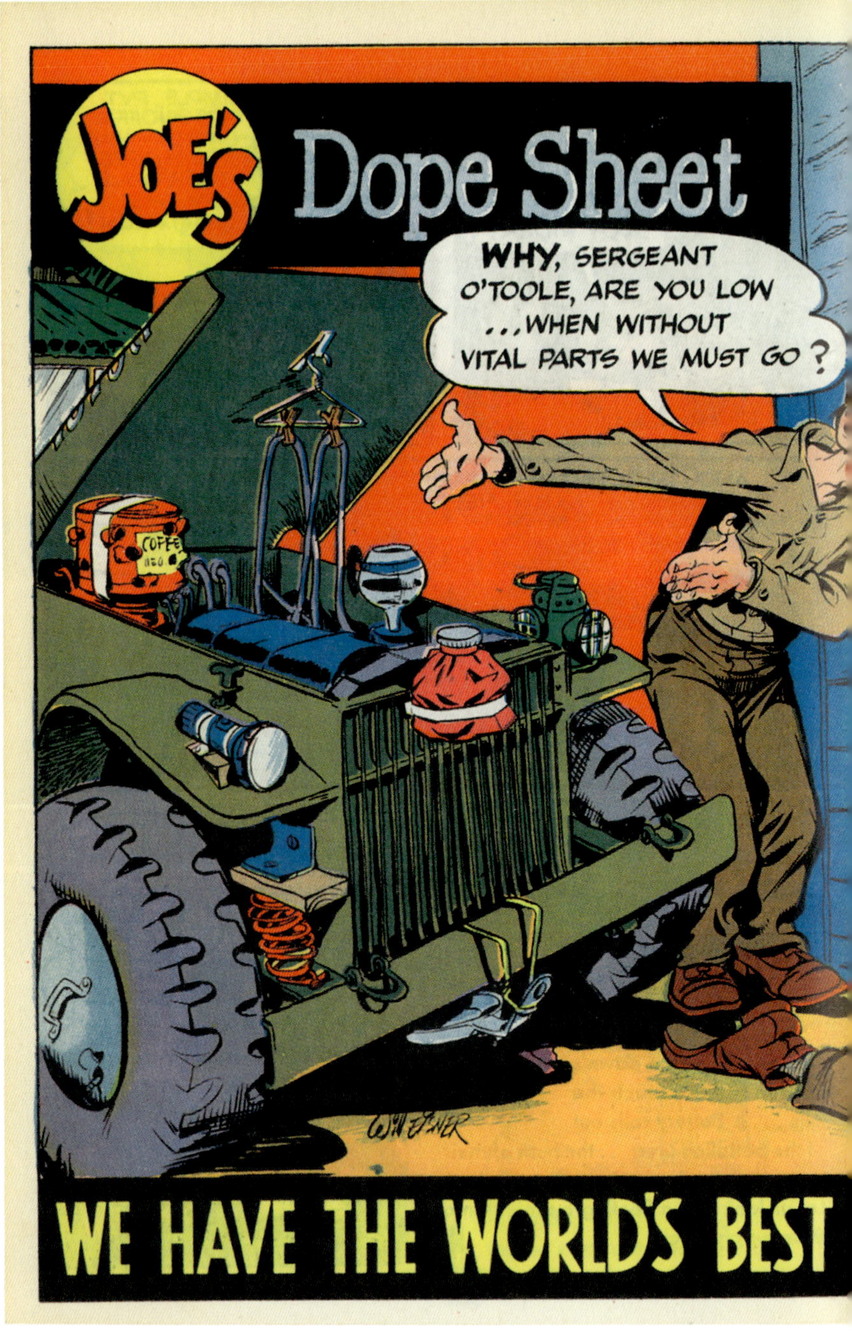
JOE'S Dope Sheet
WHY, SERGEANT O'TOOLE, ARE YOU LOW ...WHEN WITHOUT VITAL PARTS WE MUST GO?
WILL EISNER
WE HAVE THE WORLD'S BEST

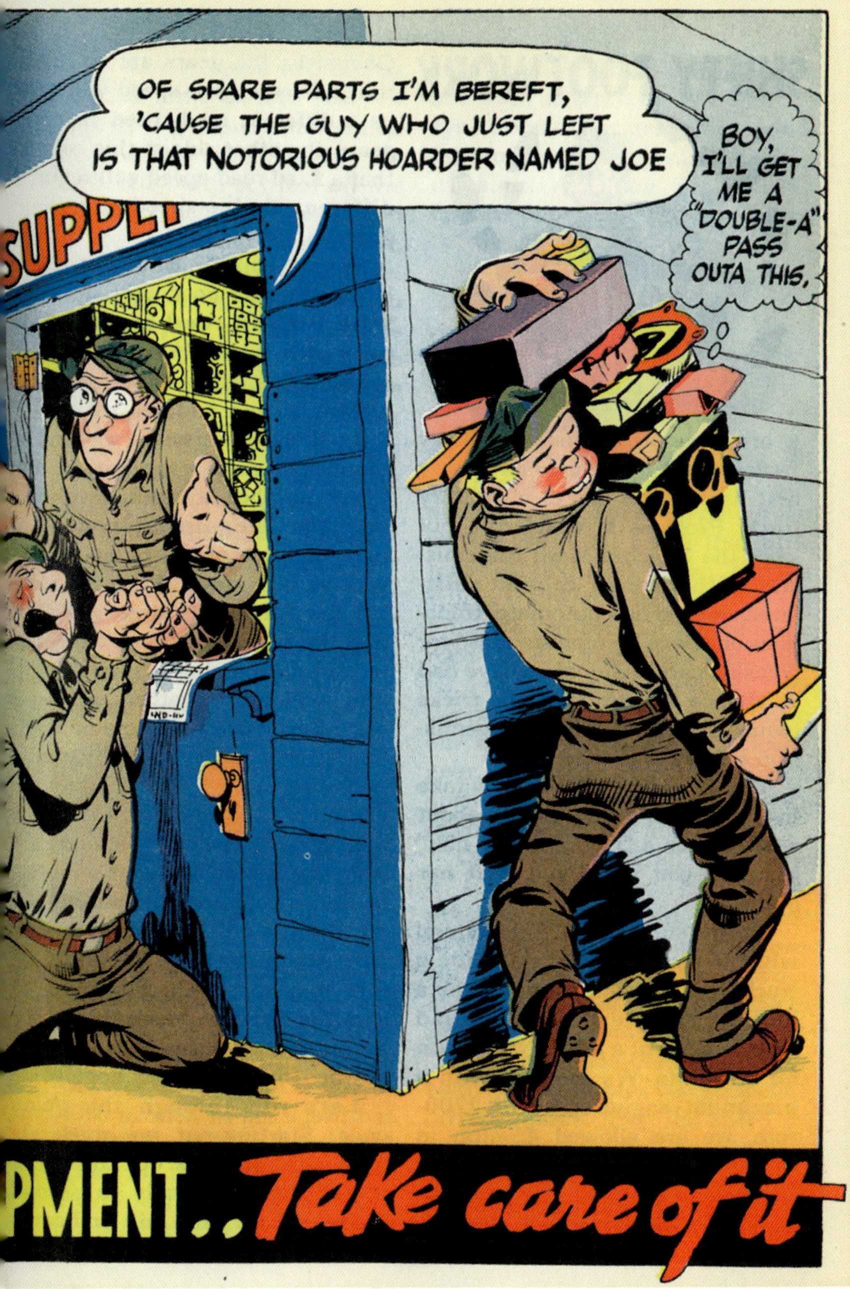
OF SPARE PARTS I'M BEREFT,
'CAUSE THE GUY WHO JUST LEFT
IS THAT NOTORIOUS HOARDER NAMED JOE
BOY, I'LL GET ME A "DOUBLE-A" PASS OUTA THIS.
SUPPL
PMENT.. Take care of it

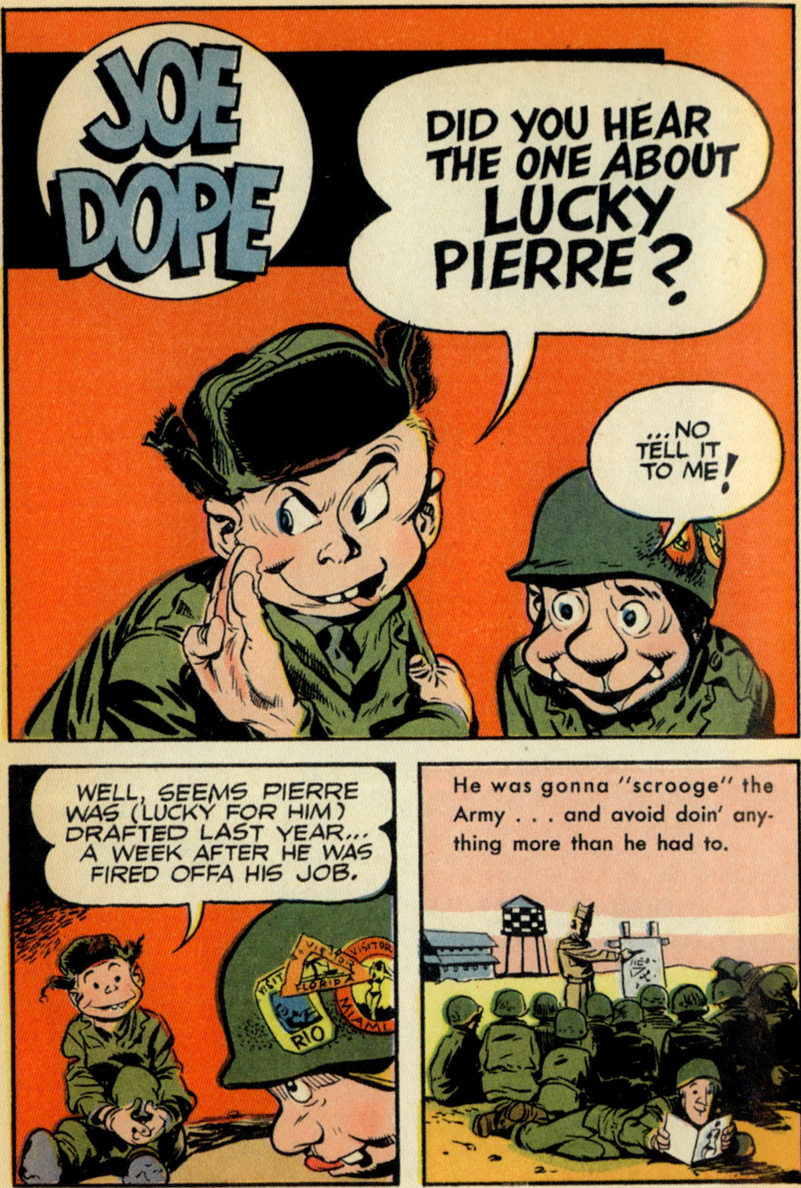
JOE DOPE
DID YOU HEAR THE ONE ABOUT LUCKY PIERRE?
...NO TELL IT TO ME!
WELL, SEEMS PIERRE WAS (LUCKY FOR HIM) DRAFTED LAST YEAR... A WEEK AFTER HE WAS FIRED OFFA HIS JOB.
VISIT FLORIDA
VISITOR
MIAMI
RIO
He was gonna "scrooge" the Army . . . and avoid doin' anything more than he had to.

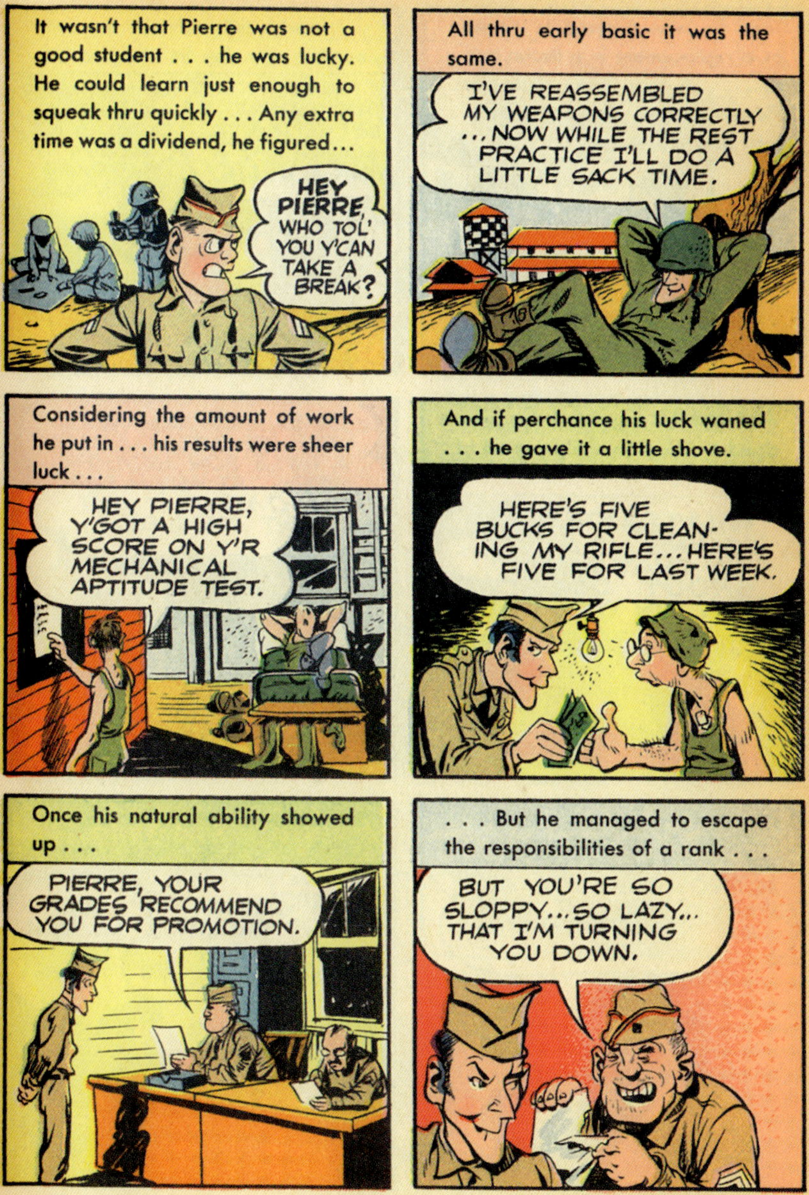
It wasn't that Pierre was not a good student . . . he was lucky. He could learn just enough to squeak thru quickly . . . Any extra time was a dividend, he figured . . .
HEY PIERRE, WHO TOL' YOU Y'CAN TAKE A BREAK?
All thru early basic it was the same.
I'VE REASSEMBLED MY WEAPONS CORRECTLY . . . NOW WHILE THE REST PRACTICE I'LL DO A LITTLE SACK TIME.
Considering the amount of work he put in . . . his results were sheer luck . . .
HEY PIERRE, Y'GOT A HIGH SCORE ON Y'R MECHANICAL APTITUDE TEST.
And if perchance his luck waned . . . he gave it a little shove.
HERE'S FIVE BUCKS FOR CLEANING MY RIFLE . . . HERE'S FIVE FOR LAST WEEK.
Once his natural ability showed up . . .
PIERRE, YOUR GRADES RECOMMEND YOU FOR PROMOTION.
. . . But he managed to escape the responsibilities of a rank . . .
BUT YOU'RE SO SLOPPY . . . SO LAZY . . . THAT I'M TURNING YOU DOWN.

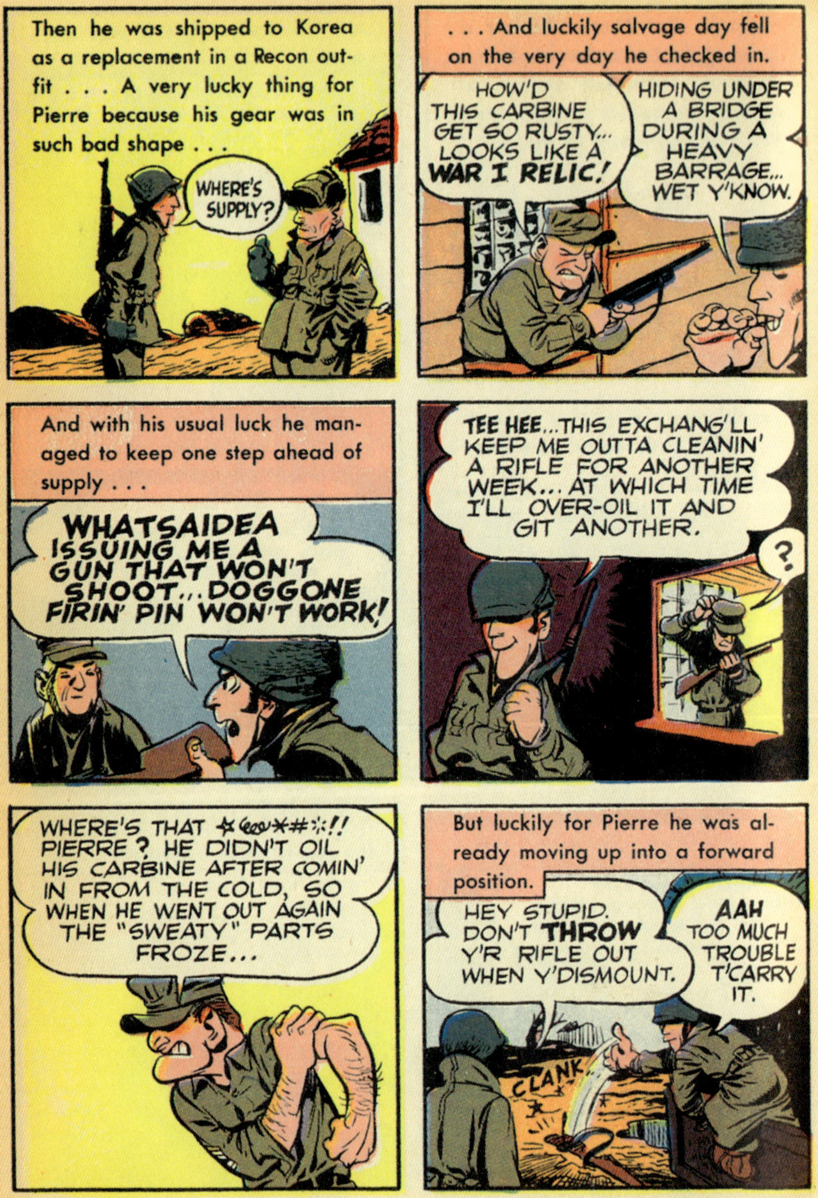
Then he was shipped to Korea as a replacement in a Recon outfit . . . A very lucky thing for Pierre because his gear was in such bad shape . . .
WHERE'S SUPPLY?
. . . And luckily salvage day fell on the very day he checked in.
HOW'D THIS CARBINE GET SO RUSTY... LOOKS LIKE A WAR I RELIC!
HIDING UNDER A BRIDGE DURING A HEAVY BARRAGE... WET Y'KNOW.
And with his usual luck he managed to keep one step ahead of supply . . .
WHATSAIDEA ISSUING ME A GUN THAT WON'T SHOOT... DOGGONE FIRIN' PIN WON'T WORK!
TEE HEE...THIS EXCHANG'LL KEEP ME OUTTA CLEANIN' A RIFLE FOR ANOTHER WEEK... AT WHICH TIME I'LL OVER-OIL IT AND GIT ANOTHER.
?
WHERE'S THAT *@*#*!! PIERRE? HE DIDN'T OIL HIS CARBINE AFTER COMIN' IN FROM THE COLD, SO WHEN HE WENT OUT AGAIN THE "SWEATY" PARTS FROZE...
But luckily for Pierre he was already moving up into a forward position.
HEY STUPID. DON'T THROW Y'R RIFLE OUT WHEN Y'DISMOUNT.
AAH TOO MUCH TROUBLE T'CARRY IT.
CLANK

Yesterday . . . the outfit went on a reconnoiter.

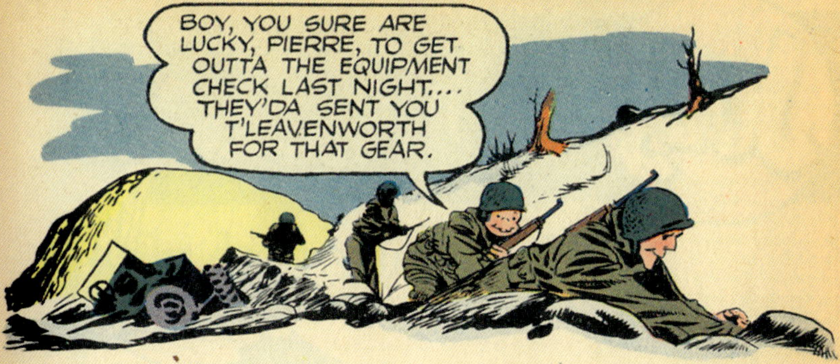
BOY, YOU SURE ARE LUCKY, PIERRE, TO GET OUTTA THE EQUIPMENT CHECK LAST NIGHT.... THEY'DA SENT YOU T'LEAVENWORTH FOR THAT GEAR.

Last night his patrol got cut off . . . After a night of rain and sleet, every man naturally dismantled his automatic weapons and oil-cleaned 'em . . . By dawn they were ready to run for it and shoot their way out . . .

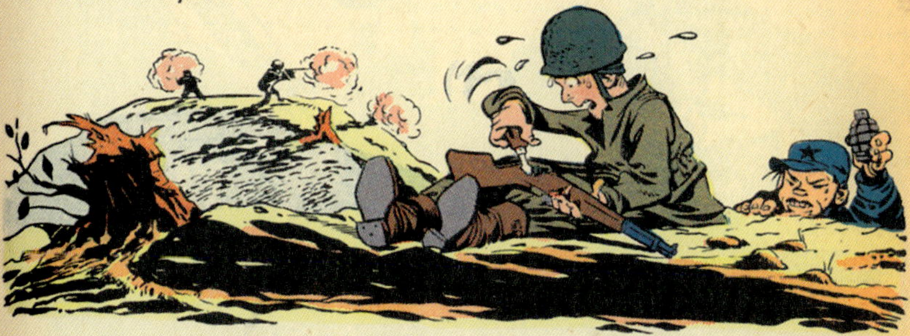

They all got out fine but Pierre. He had goofed off on the cleaning . . . (which wouldn't have helped since he had a two-week old mud cake in his barrel) and so he stayed there . . . Alas, ol' lucky Pierre . . . he sure scrooged the Army.

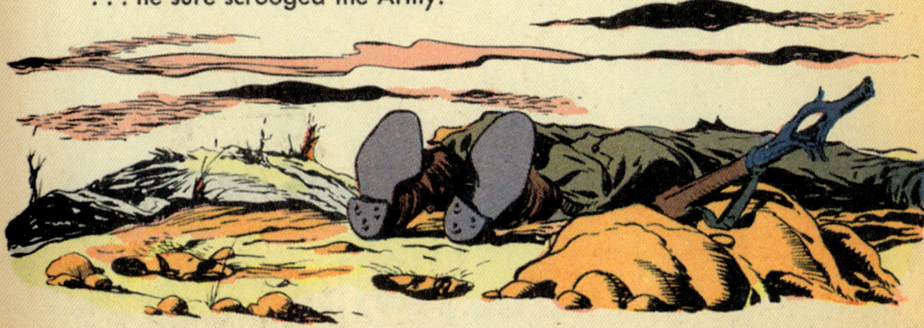

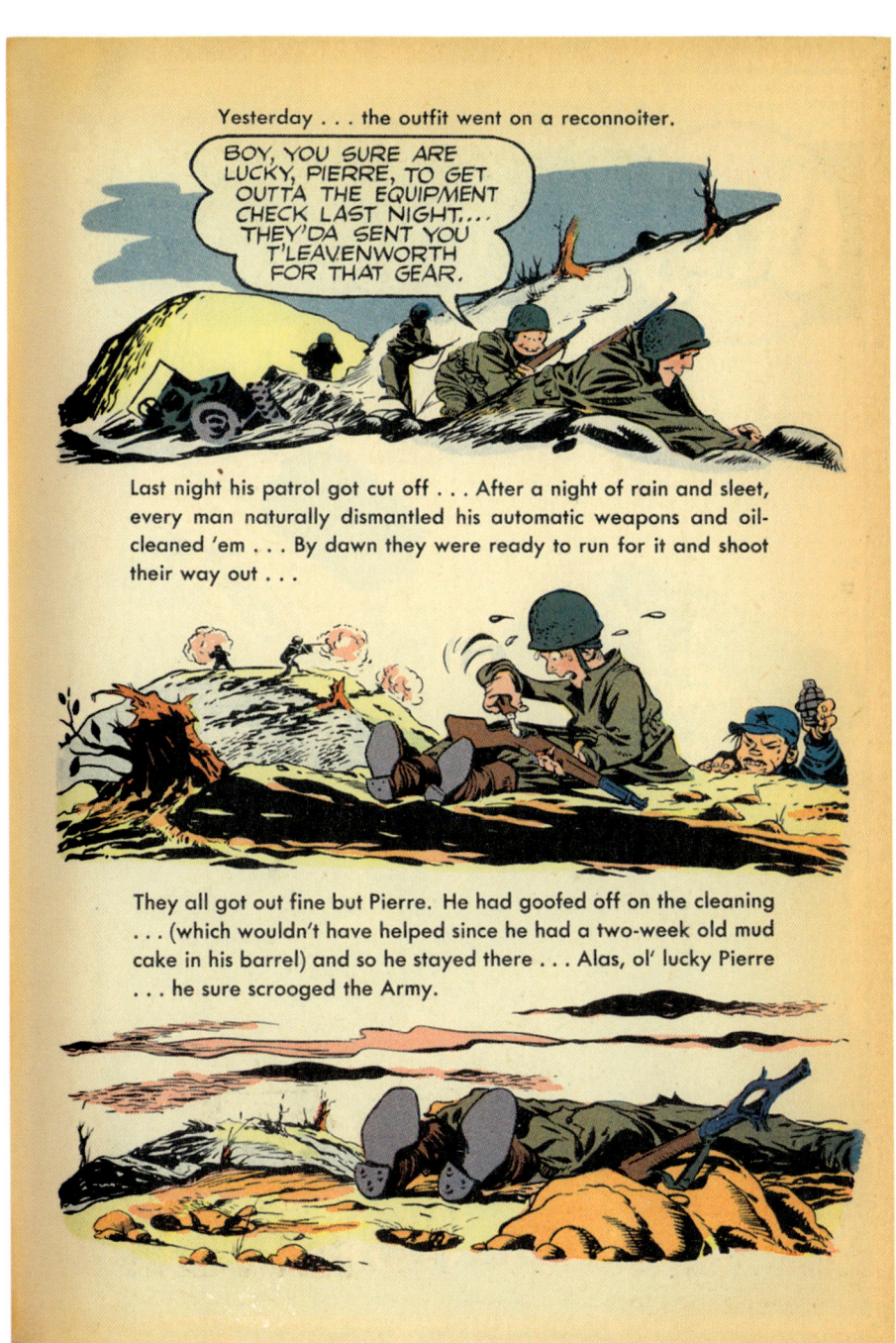

WHO GETS PS AND HOW

FIRST and foremost, there are no personal subscriptions (at any price) and there are no copies sent direct to individuals.

This is so the greatest number of individuals will get to see the copies that go to all using units. However, a plentitude of copies have been thoughtfully provided for the front office to hoard in its locked files for when your back-shop and front-line copies get tattered and smeared beyond legibility.

All copies are distributed through AG depots, to Publication Sections, then to your unit according to these authorized allowances (which appear in brief on the first page of each issue). Guard Units get copies from State Guard headquarters, and ORC Units from their Military District Hqrs.

If you need more than you're allowed for any certain reason, requisition your Pubs Section each month in advance. If you need copies of back issues, write direct to Editor, PS Magazine, Aberdeen Proving Ground, Maryland.

SYMBOL	UNIT, ORGANIZATION OR INSTALLATION	COPIES	SYMBOL	UNIT, ORGANIZATION OR INSTALLATION	COPIES
A (ORD OFF)	Hq of Armies	100	POE (ORD OFF)	Hq of POE's	3
AFF	Office, Chief, Army Field Forces	10	PRGR	Hq of proving grounds	5
Admin & Tech Svc Bd	Administrative and Technical Service Boards	10	PRGR 9	Hq of Proving Ground Ordnance	25
			Proc Dist	Hq of procurement districts	3
Ars	Hq of arsenals, plants, works & Army Installations of Mfg	25	REGT	Hq of regiments or groups	10
			Rct Sta	Hq of recruiting stations	3
BRIG	Hq of brigades	5	PMS & T	PMS & T's at ROTC units	5
Base Comd	Hq of base & isl. commands & hq, US Army Forces, except under "OS Maj Comd"	5	PMS & T 9	PMS & T's at ROTC Ordnance units	25
			RTC	Hq of Replacement Training centers	100
Bn	Hq of battalions	5	Sep Bn	Hq of separate battalions	10
Co	Hq of companies or similar units	12	Sch	Hq of general & special service schools	25
Co 9	except Ordnance, which get	20	Sch 9	Hq of general & special service Ordnance schools	50
Co 17	and Armored which get	20			
Co 55	and Transportation Corps which get	20	Sep Co	Hq of separate company or similar unit	15
CHQ	Hq of Corps	5	Tech Svc (Maint Br)	Off of the head of each Tech Serv	5
DIV (ORD OFF)	Hq of divisions (including Trng Div)	50	Tech Svc 9	except ORD	250
DIV 17 (ORD OFF)	Except Armored Division	100	Tng Div	Hq of training divisions	50
Dep	Hq of depots, incl. gen. depots, & sections of gen. depot	10	USMA w/schools	Hq of U.S. Military Academy	25
			Hosp	All Hospitals	15
Dspln Bks	Hq of disciplinary barracks	25	NG		Special
Dist	Hq of districts	3	ORC		None
Mil Dist	Hq of Mil Dists within Z1 (ea state)	100	Rct. Dist	Headquarters of recruiting districts	3
Div Engr	Division engineers (C1 2 installations)	5		**SPECIAL DISTRIBUTION**	
FT	Hq of Forts	5			
GH	Hq of general hospitals & centers	5	1. Preventive Maintenance Office — APG, (Editorial Staff & Preventive Maintenance Program functions)		2000
GH Library	General Hospital Library	25
MDW	Hq Military District of Washington	5	2. Ordnance Tank-Automotive center, Detroit, Michigan		250
OSD (ORD OFF)	Overseas supply divisions of POE's	2	3. Pentagon, as prescribed by TAG, except AC of S, G-4 Maint Br		10
OS Maj Comd (Ord Off)	Hq of overseas command directly under DA	100

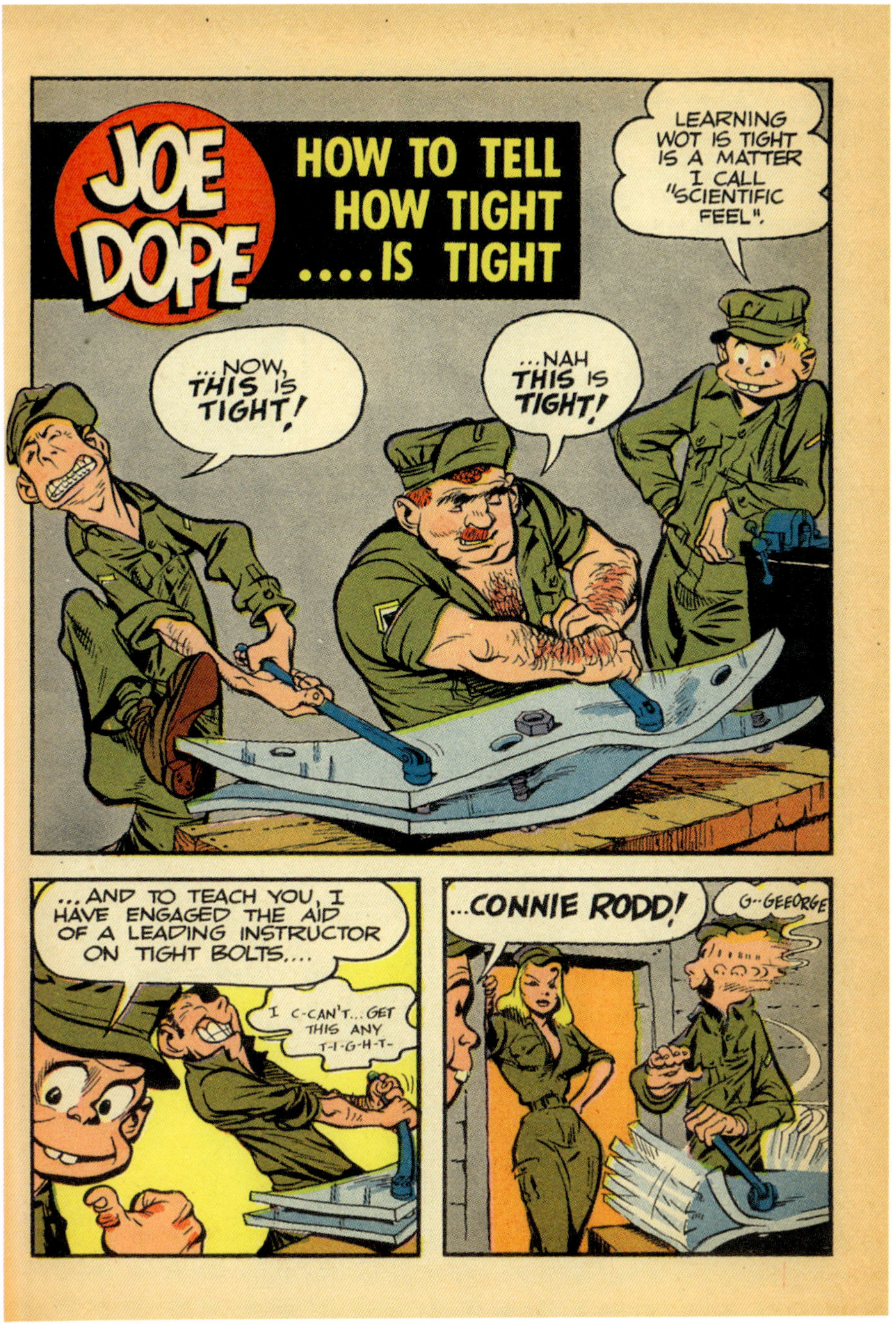
JOE DOPE
HOW TO TELL HOW TIGHT ....IS TIGHT
LEARNING WOT IS TIGHT IS A MATTER I CALL "SCIENTIFIC FEEL".
...NOW, THIS IS TIGHT!
...NAH THIS IS TIGHT!
...AND TO TEACH YOU, I HAVE ENGAGED THE AID OF A LEADING INSTRUCTOR ON TIGHT BOLTS....
I C-CAN'T...GET THIS ANY T-I-G-H-T-
...CONNIE RODD!
G--GEEORGE

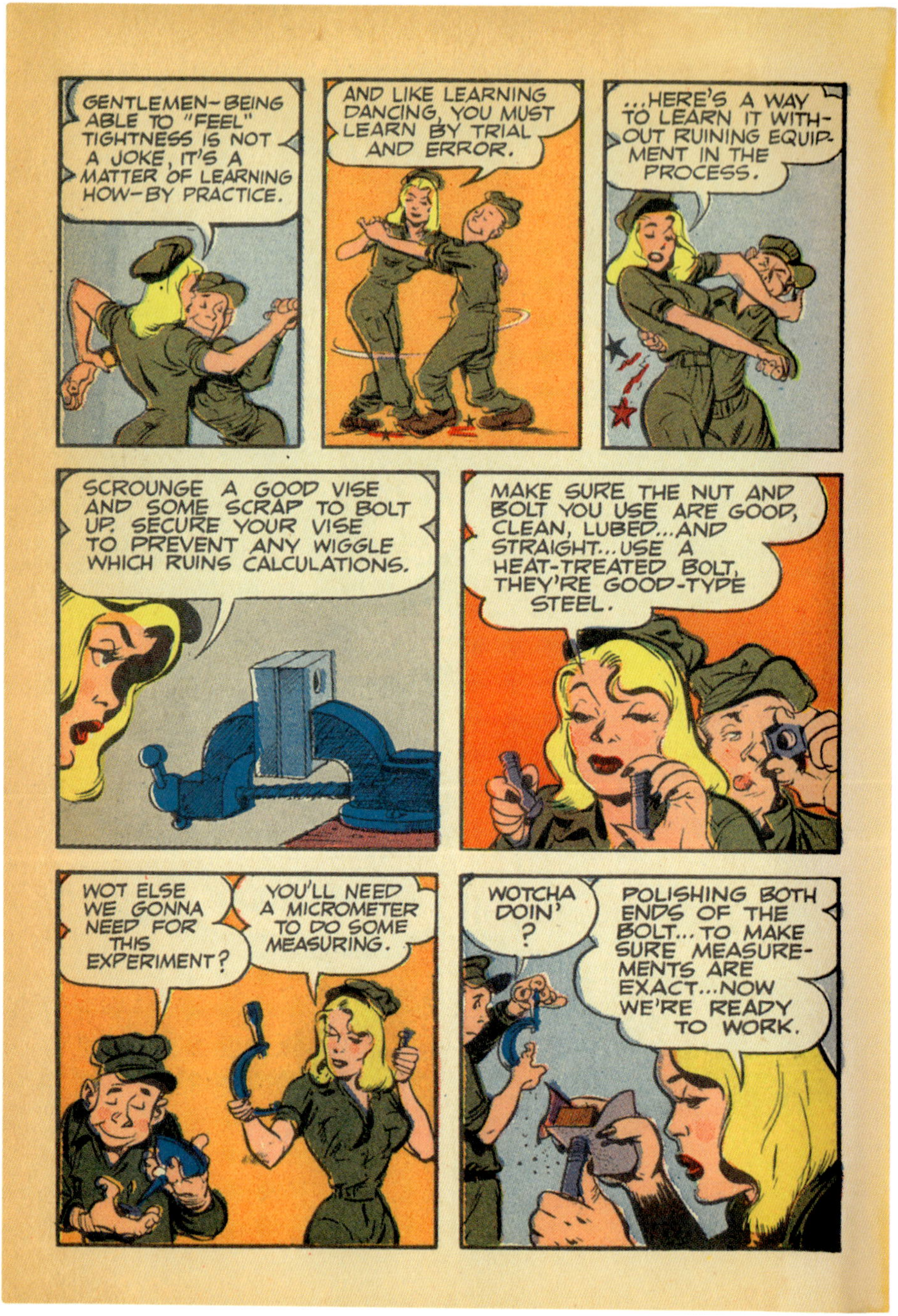
GENTLEMEN–BEING ABLE TO "FEEL" TIGHTNESS IS NOT A JOKE, IT'S A MATTER OF LEARNING HOW–BY PRACTICE.
AND LIKE LEARNING DANCING, YOU MUST LEARN BY TRIAL AND ERROR.
...HERE'S A WAY TO LEARN IT WITHOUT RUINING EQUIPMENT IN THE PROCESS.
SCROUNGE A GOOD VISE AND SOME SCRAP TO BOLT UP. SECURE YOUR VISE TO PREVENT ANY WIGGLE WHICH RUINS CALCULATIONS.
MAKE SURE THE NUT AND BOLT YOU USE ARE GOOD, CLEAN, LUBED...AND STRAIGHT...USE A HEAT-TREATED BOLT, THEY'RE GOOD-TYPE STEEL.
WOT ELSE WE GONNA NEED FOR THIS EXPERIMENT?
YOU'LL NEED A MICROMETER TO DO SOME MEASURING.
WOTCHA DOIN' ?
POLISHING BOTH ENDS OF THE BOLT... TO MAKE SURE MEASUREMENTS ARE EXACT...NOW WE'RE READY TO WORK.

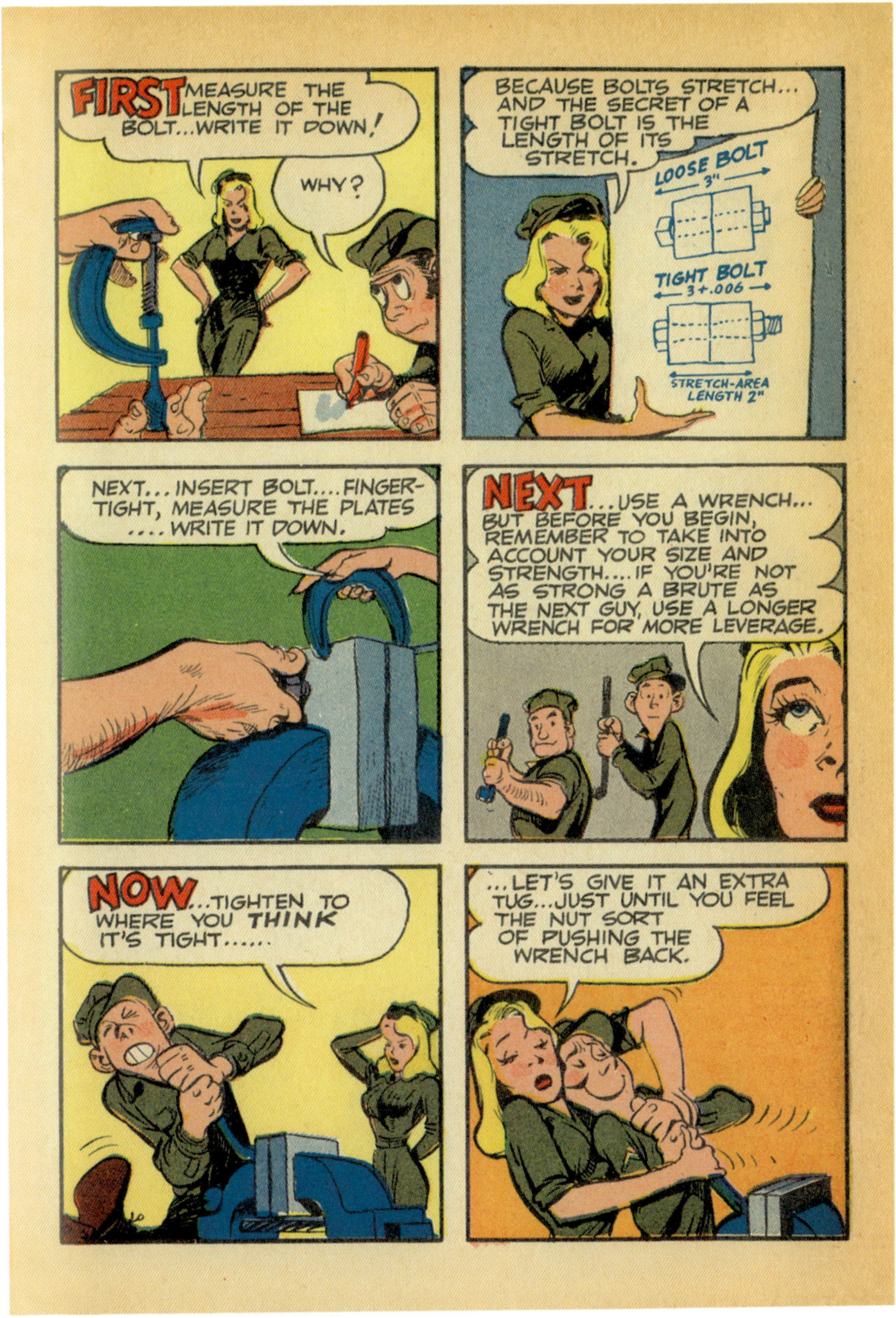
FIRST MEASURE THE LENGTH OF THE BOLT...WRITE IT DOWN!
WHY?
BECAUSE BOLTS STRETCH... AND THE SECRET OF A TIGHT BOLT IS THE LENGTH OF ITS STRETCH.
LOOSE BOLT
3"
TIGHT BOLT
3+.006
STRETCH-AREA LENGTH 2"
NEXT... INSERT BOLT.... FINGER-TIGHT, MEASURE THE PLATES .... WRITE IT DOWN.
NEXT...USE A WRENCH... BUT BEFORE YOU BEGIN, REMEMBER TO TAKE INTO ACCOUNT YOUR SIZE AND STRENGTH.... IF YOU'RE NOT AS STRONG A BRUTE AS THE NEXT GUY, USE A LONGER WRENCH FOR MORE LEVERAGE.
NOW...TIGHTEN TO WHERE YOU THINK IT'S TIGHT.....
...LET'S GIVE IT AN EXTRA TUG...JUST UNTIL YOU FEEL THE NUT SORT OF PUSHING THE WRENCH BACK.

NEXT TAKE YOUR "MIKE" AND MEASURE THE BOLT'S LENGTH.
NOTICE ...THE BOLT IS ANYWHERE FROM .002 TO .004 LONGER PER EACH INCH OF PLATE THICKNESS.
BOLT LENGTH... 3"
PLATE.......... 2"
BOLT NOW MEASURES 3.006"
PRESTO YOU HAVE A ...TIGHT BOLT... ANY QUESTIONS?
...YEAH HOW DO I REMEMBER THE "FEEL"?
MAN YOU PRACTICE- 'CAUSE ONCE YOU GET THAT FEEL IT STAYS WITH YOU....
BUT WONT THE BOLT STAY STRETCHED?
BOLTS ARE ELASTIC... NATURALLY CONSTANT TIGHTENING SOMEDAY WILL STRETCH YOUR BOLT TO USELESSNESS. SO THEN YOU REPLACE IT.... SO LONG BOYS.
TIME TO CHANGE BOLTS
MAN...THERE'S A GAL WOT IS, GEEORGE AND I MEAN GEEORGE!
YEAH AND NOW WILL YA LOOSEN THE BOLT, PLEASE!

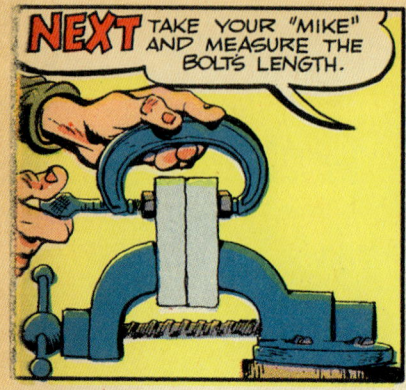

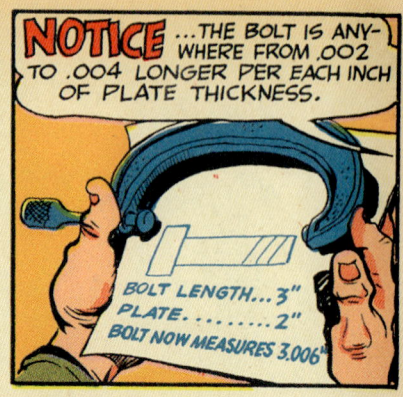

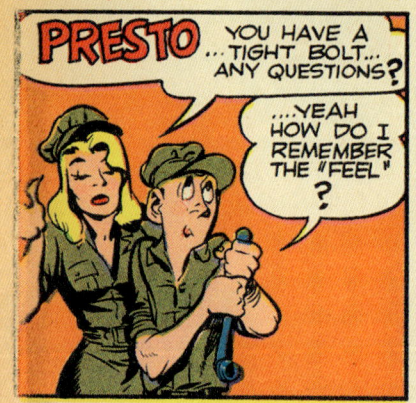

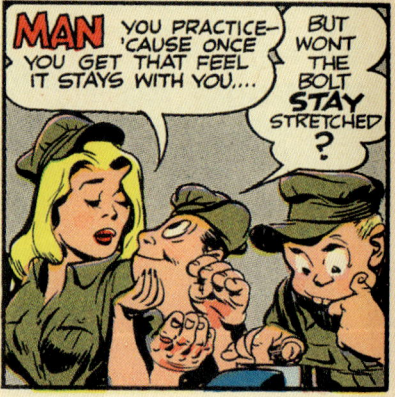

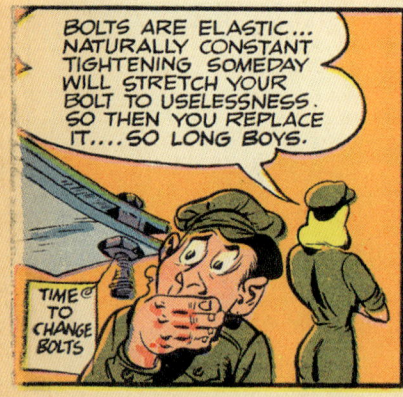

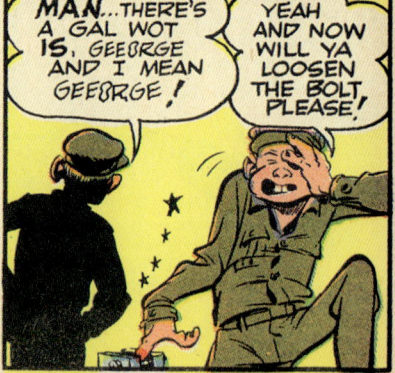

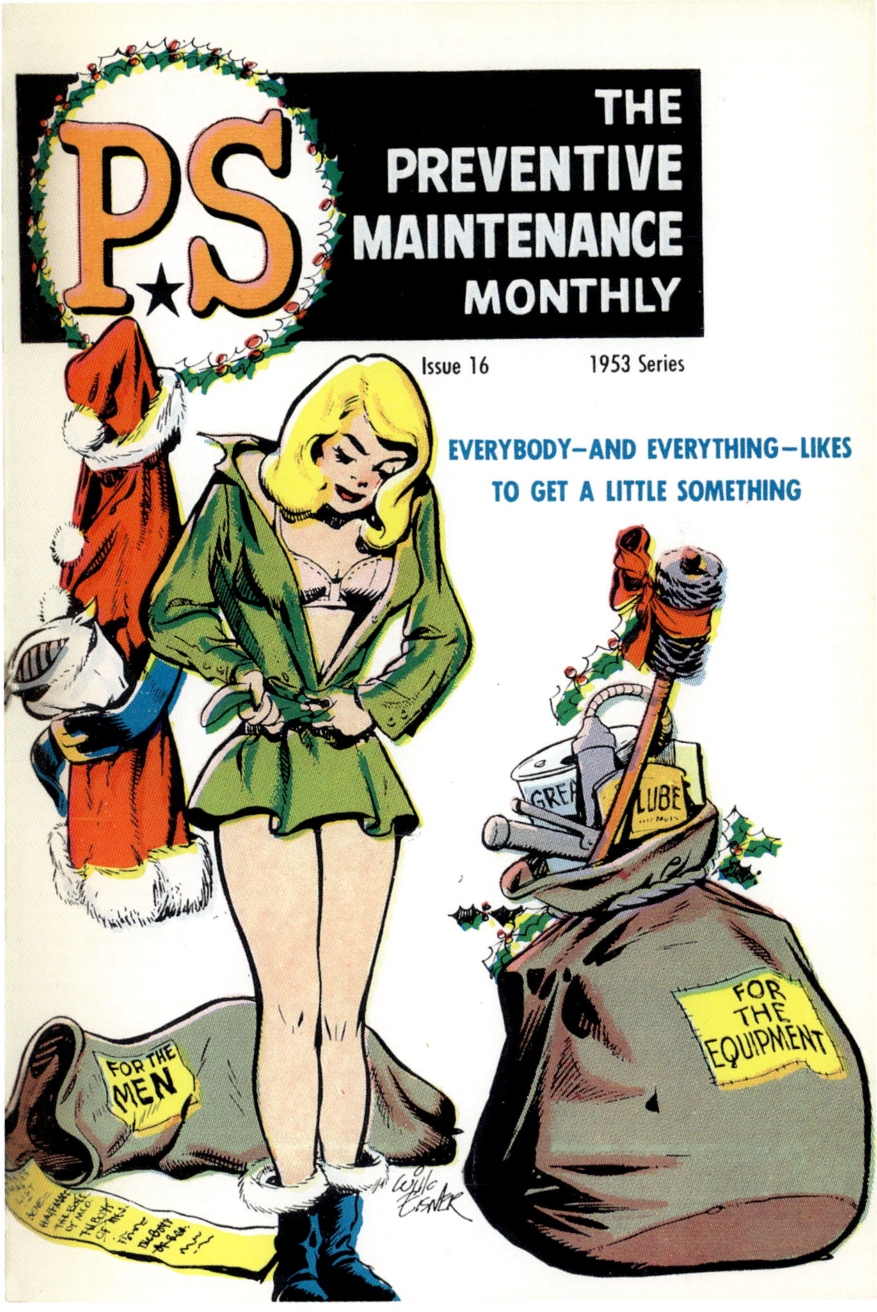
P.S
THE PREVENTIVE MAINTENANCE MONTHLY
Issue 16
1953 Series
EVERYBODY—AND EVERYTHING—LIKES TO GET A LITTLE SOMETHING
LUBE
FOR THE MEN
FOR THE EQUIPMENT

no. 16, 1953

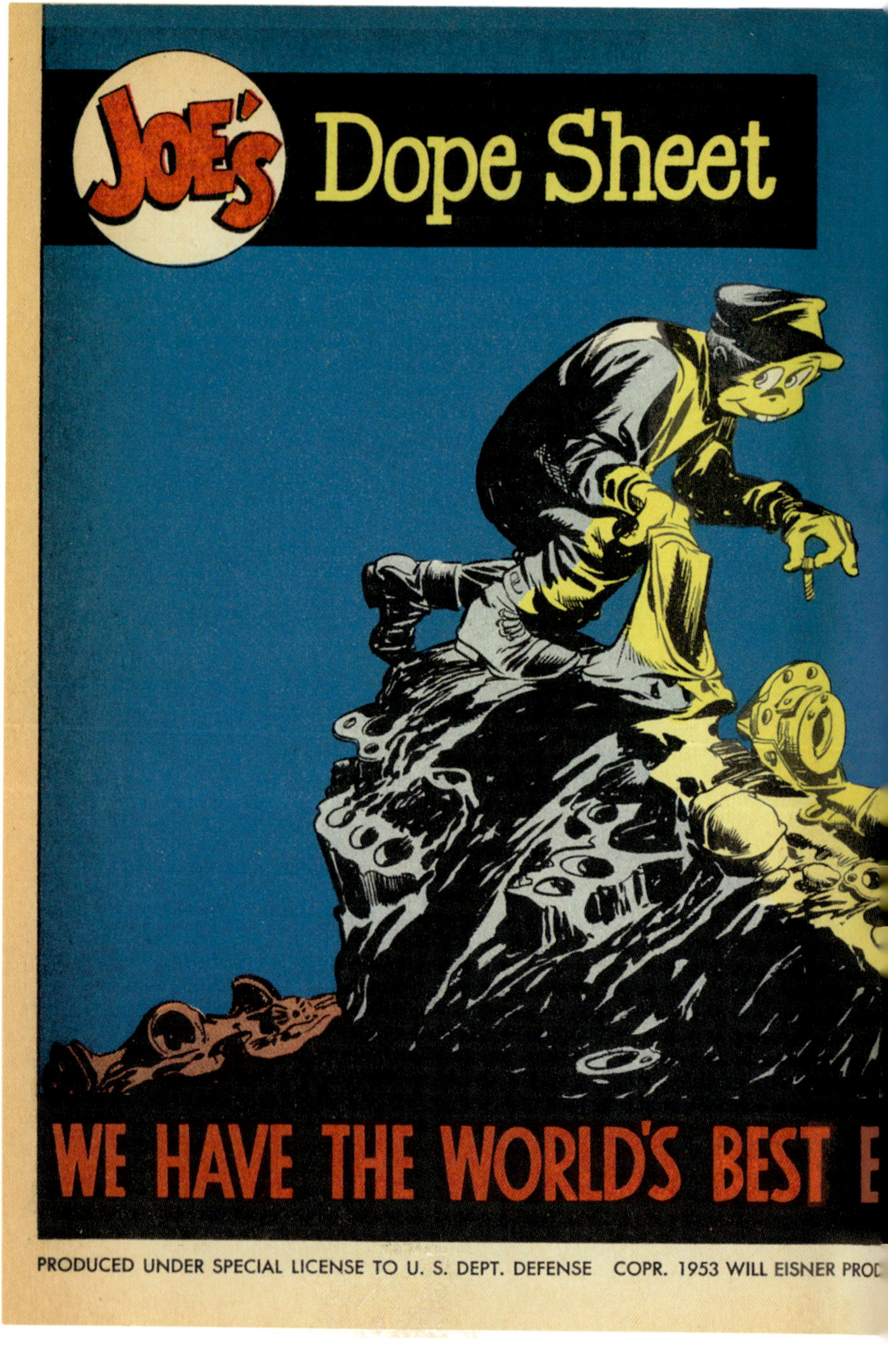
JOE'S Dope Sheet
WE HAVE THE WORLD'S BEST E
PRODUCED UNDER SPECIAL LICENSE TO U. S. DEPT. DEFENSE COPR. 1953 WILL EISNER PROD

no. 12, 1952

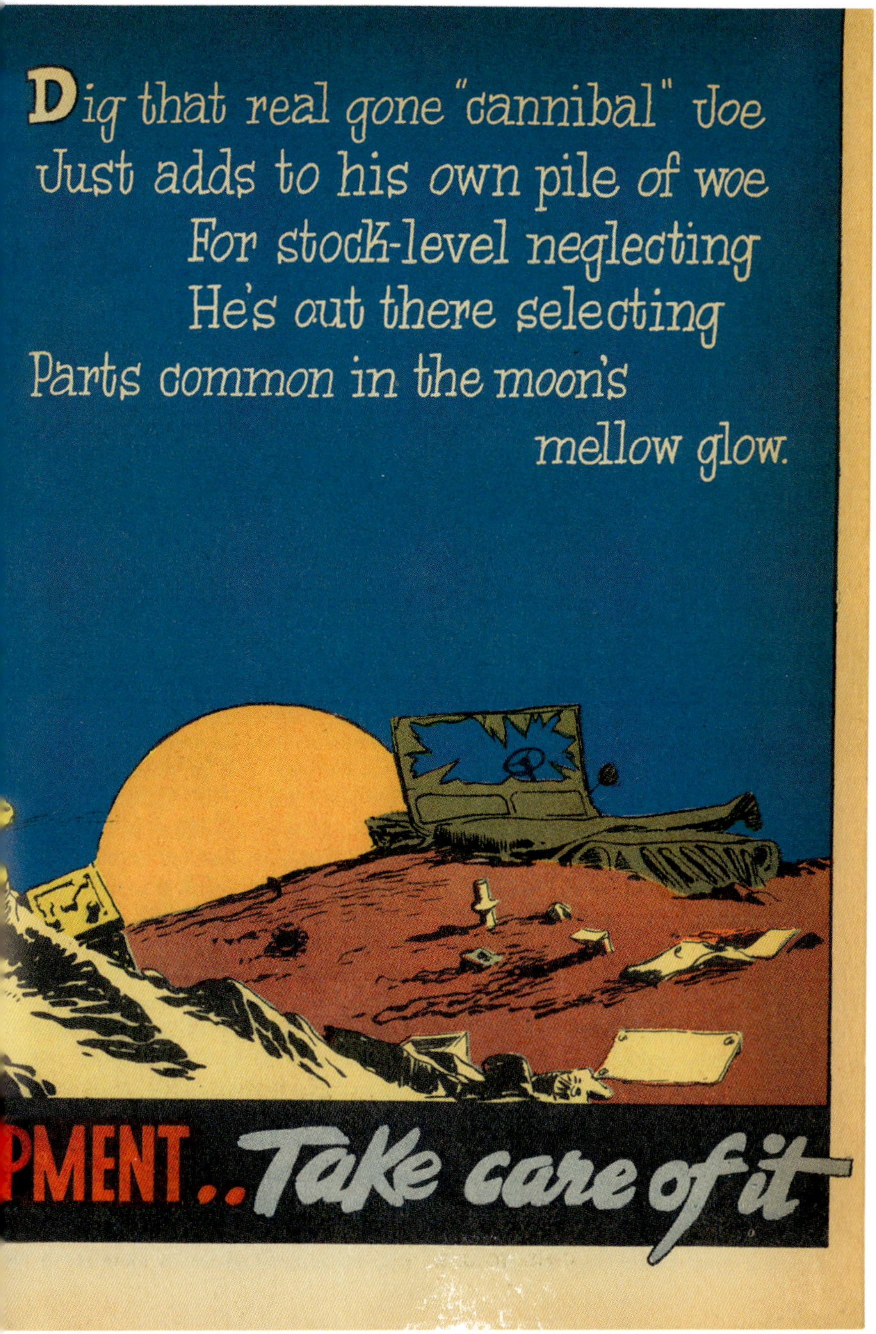
Dig that real gone "cannibal" Joe
Just adds to his own pile of woe
For stock-level neglecting
He's out there selecting
Parts common in the moon's
mellow glow.
PMENT.. Take care of it

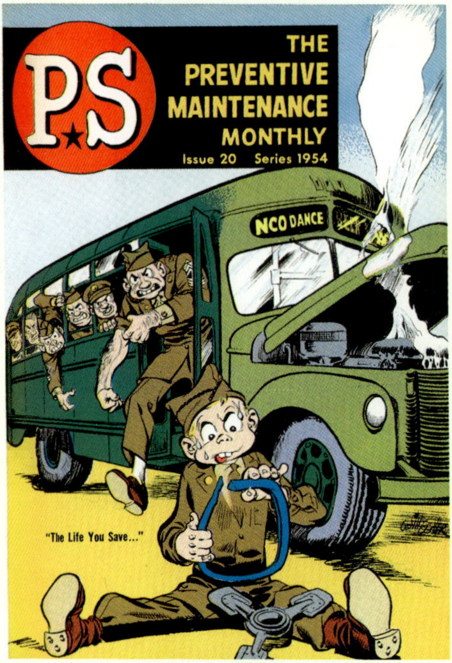
P★S
THE PREVENTIVE MAINTENANCE MONTHLY
Issue 20 Series 1954
NCO DANCE
"The Life You Save..."

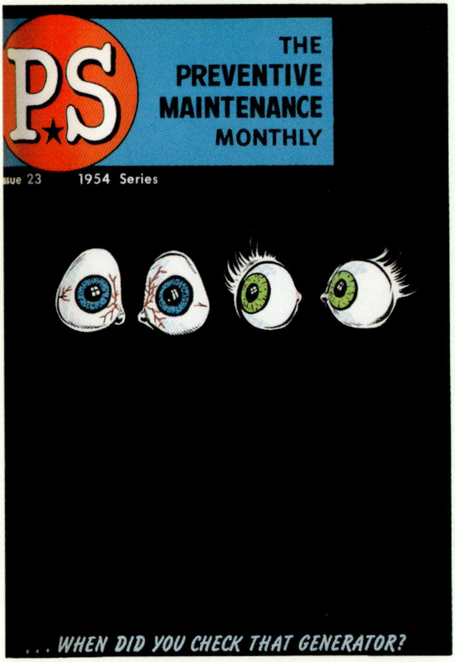
P★S
THE PREVENTIVE MAINTENANCE MONTHLY
sue 23 1954 Series
. . . WHEN DID YOU CHECK THAT GENERATOR?

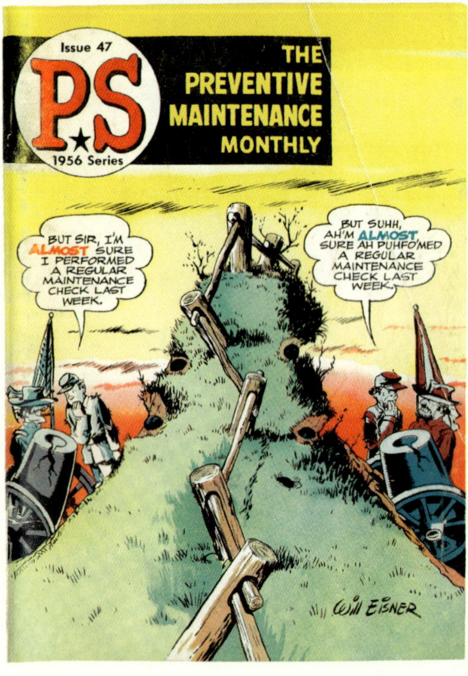
Issue 47
P★S
1956 Series
THE PREVENTIVE MAINTENANCE MONTHLY
BUT SIR, I'M ALMOST SURE I PERFORMED A REGULAR MAINTENANCE CHECK LAST WEEK.
BUT SUHH, AH'M ALMOST SURE AH PUHFO'MED A REGULAR MAINTENANCE CHECK LAST WEEK.
Will Eisner

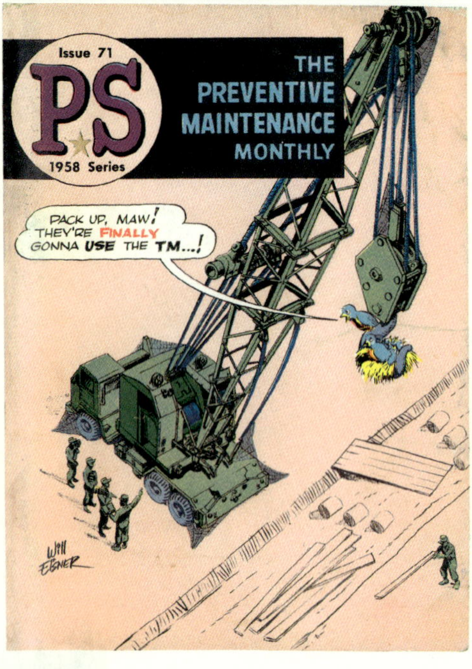
Issue 71
P★S
1958 Series
THE PREVENTIVE MAINTENANCE MONTHLY
PACK UP, MAW! THEY'RE FINALLY GONNA USE THE TM...!
Will Eisner

Issue 44
P.S
1956 Series
THE PREVENTIVE MAINTENANCE MONTHLY
BEAT THE HEAT with PREVENTIVE MAINTENANCE SEE PAGE 21
Will Eisner

Issue 84
P.S
1959 Series
THE PREVENTIVE MAINTENANCE MONTHLY
RATION COMBAT INDIVIDUAL C
FROZEN TURKEY
Will Eisner

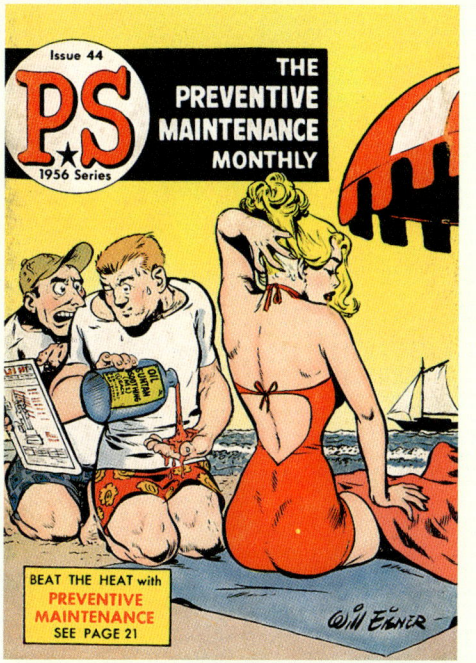

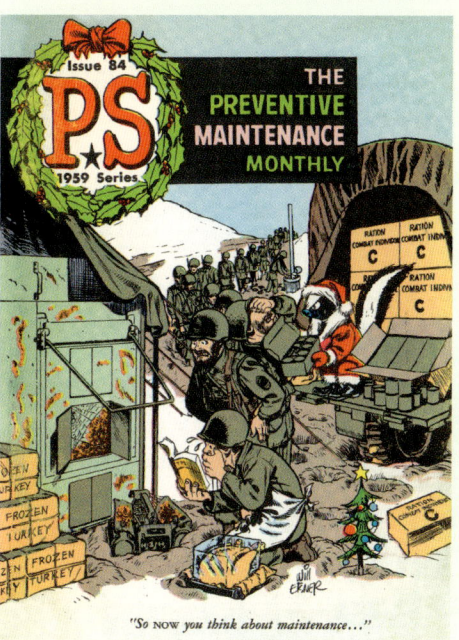

"So now you think about maintenance..."

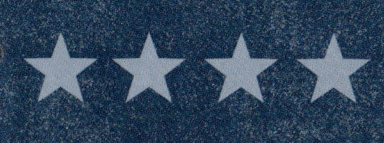

1954–1959

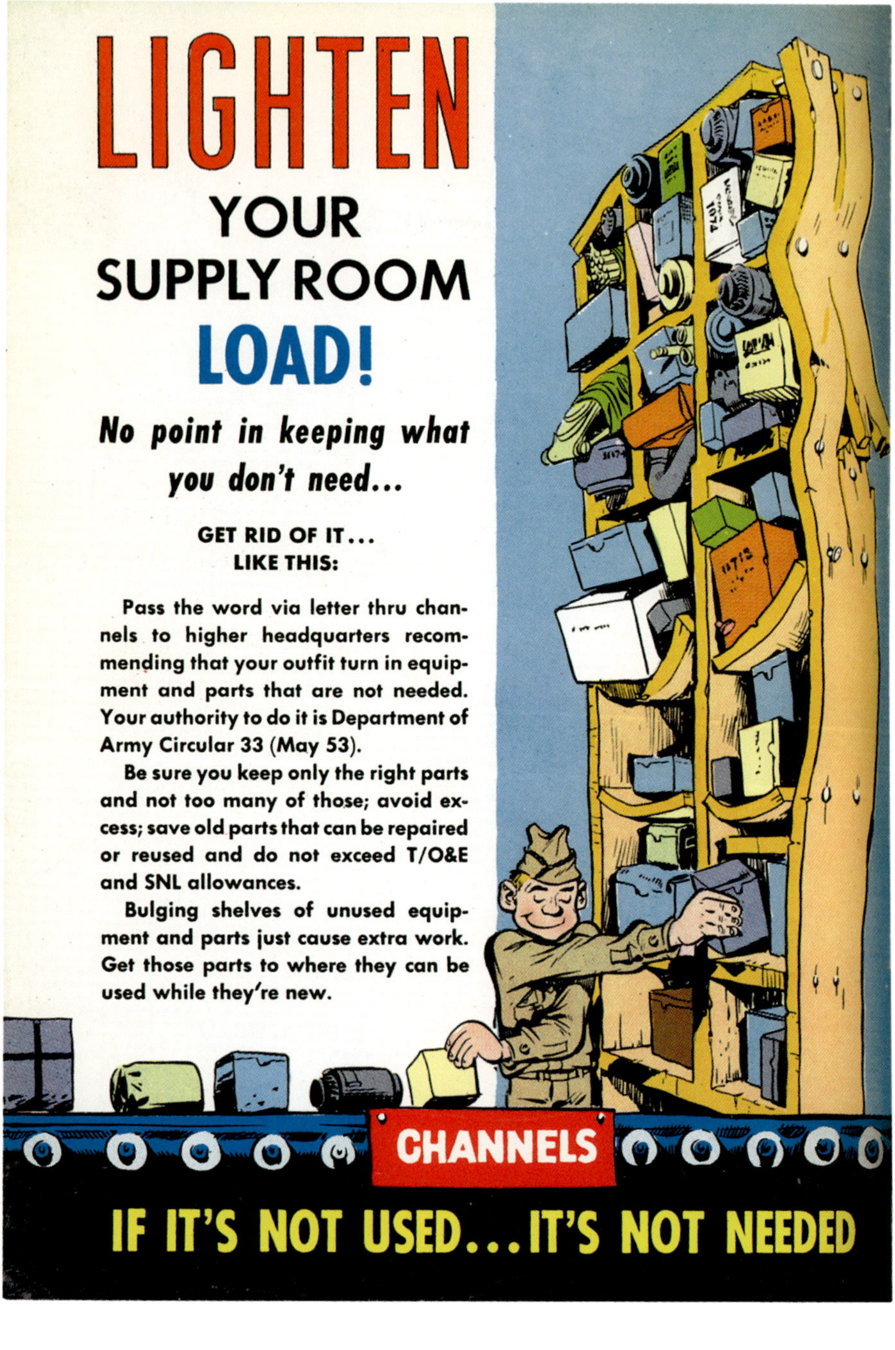
LIGHTEN
YOUR
SUPPLY ROOM
LOAD!
No point in keeping what you don't need...
GET RID OF IT...
LIKE THIS:
Pass the word via letter thru channels to higher headquarters recommending that your outfit turn in equipment and parts that are not needed. Your authority to do it is Department of Army Circular 33 (May 53).
Be sure you keep only the right parts and not too many of those; avoid excess; save old parts that can be repaired or reused and do not exceed T/O&E and SNL allowances.
Bulging shelves of unused equipment and parts just cause extra work. Get those parts to where they can be used while they're new.
CHANNELS
IF IT'S NOT USED...IT'S NOT NEEDED

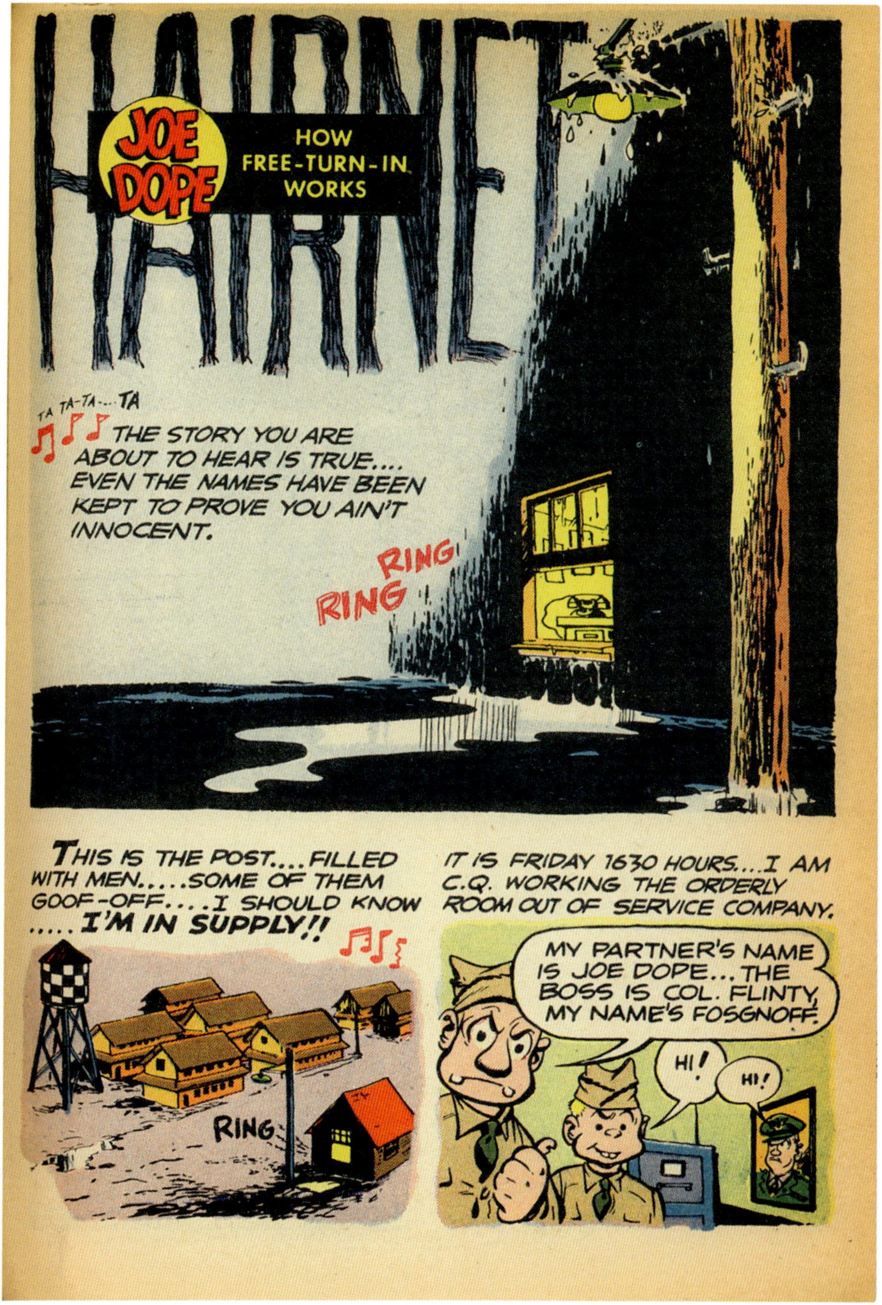
HAIRNET
JOE DOPE
HOW FREE-TURN-IN WORKS
TA TA-TA-...TA
THE STORY YOU ARE ABOUT TO HEAR IS TRUE.... EVEN THE NAMES HAVE BEEN KEPT TO PROVE YOU AIN'T INNOCENT.
RING
RING
THIS IS THE POST....FILLED WITH MEN.....SOME OF THEM GOOF-OFF....I SHOULD KNOW .....I'M IN SUPPLY!!
RING
IT IS FRIDAY 1630 HOURS...I AM C.Q. WORKING THE ORDERLY ROOM OUT OF SERVICE COMPANY.
MY PARTNER'S NAME IS JOE DOPE...THE BOSS IS COL. FLINTY, MY NAME'S FOSGNOFF.
HI!
HI!

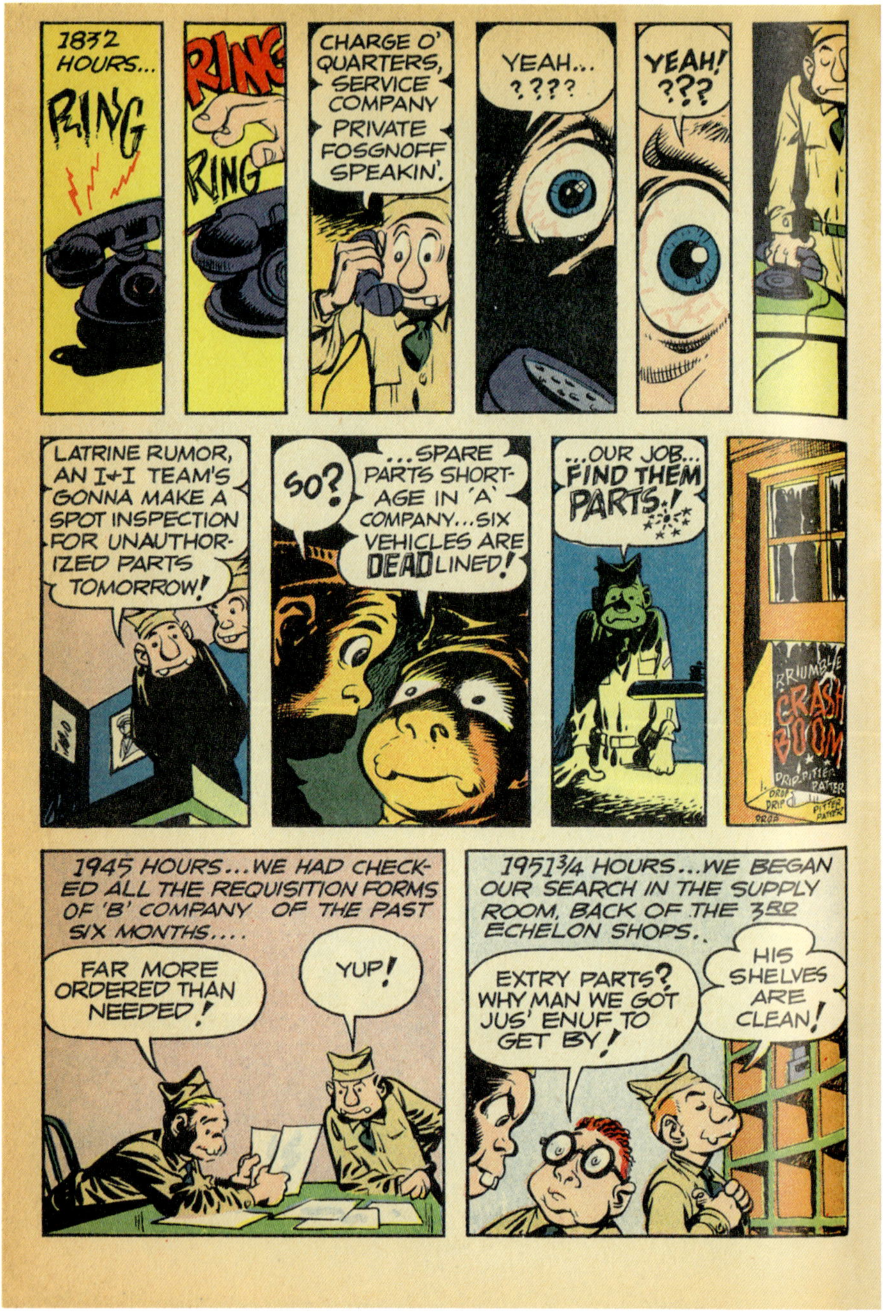

1832 HOURS...
RING
RING
RING
CHARGE O' QUARTERS, SERVICE COMPANY PRIVATE FOSGNOFF SPEAKIN'.
YEAH... ????
YEAH! ???
LATRINE RUMOR, AN I+I TEAM'S GONNA MAKE A SPOT INSPECTION FOR UNAUTHORIZED PARTS TOMORROW!
SO?
...SPARE PARTS SHORTAGE IN 'A' COMPANY...SIX VEHICLES ARE DEADLINED!
...OUR JOB... FIND THEM PARTS!
RRUMBLE
CRASH
BOOM
DRIP PITTER PATTER
1945 HOURS...WE HAD CHECKED ALL THE REQUISITION FORMS OF 'B' COMPANY OF THE PAST SIX MONTHS....
FAR MORE ORDERED THAN NEEDED!
YUP!
1951¾ HOURS...WE BEGAN OUR SEARCH IN THE SUPPLY ROOM, BACK OF THE 3RD ECHELON SHOPS..
EXTRY PARTS? WHY MAN WE GOT JUS' ENUF TO GET BY!
HIS SHELVES ARE CLEAN!

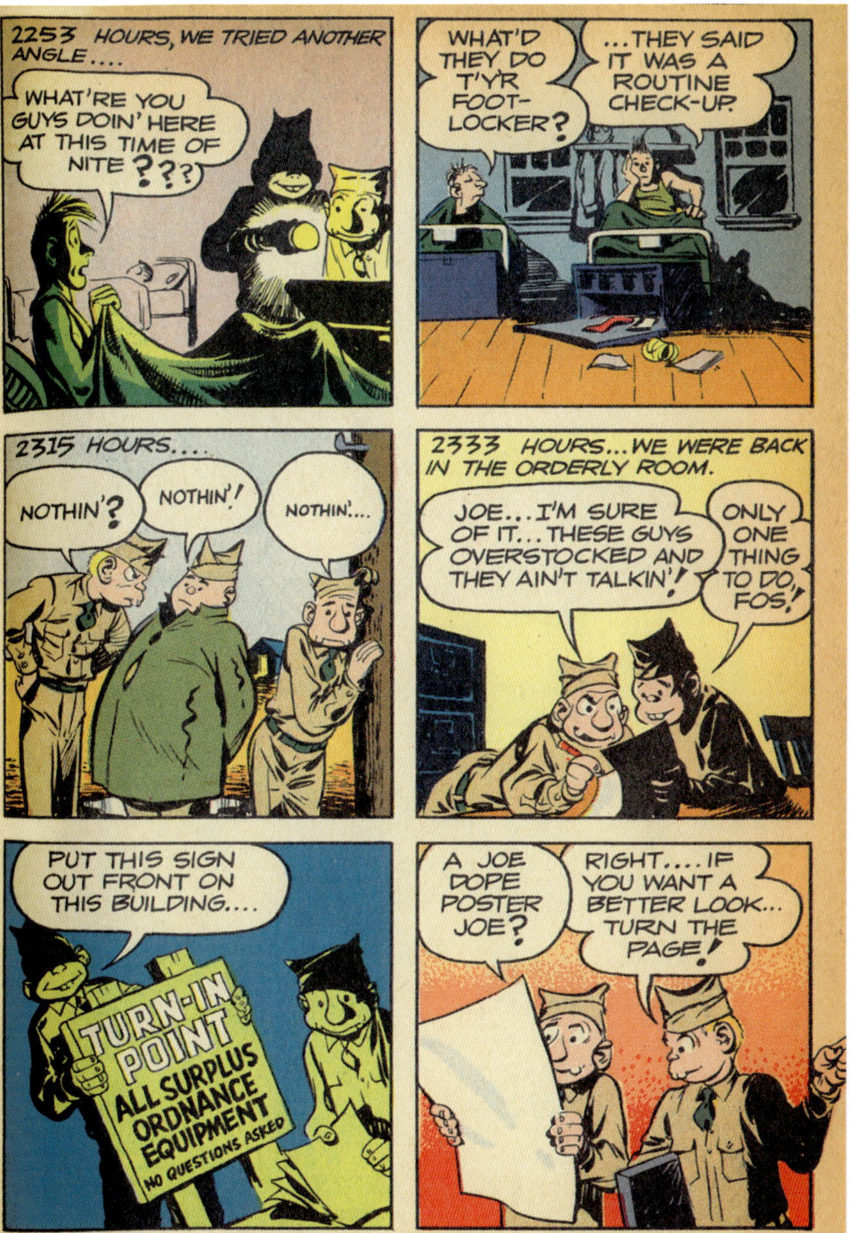
2253 HOURS, WE TRIED ANOTHER ANGLE....
WHAT'RE YOU GUYS DOIN' HERE AT THIS TIME OF NITE???
WHAT'D THEY DO T'YR FOOT-LOCKER?
...THEY SAID IT WAS A ROUTINE CHECK-UP.
2315 HOURS....
NOTHIN'?
NOTHIN'!
NOTHIN'....
2333 HOURS...WE WERE BACK IN THE ORDERLY ROOM.
JOE...I'M SURE OF IT...THESE GUYS OVERSTOCKED AND THEY AIN'T TALKIN'!
ONLY ONE THING TO DO, FOS!
PUT THIS SIGN OUT FRONT ON THIS BUILDING....
TURN-IN POINT
ALL SURPLUS ORDNANCE EQUIPMENT
NO QUESTIONS ASKED
A JOE DOPE POSTER JOE?
RIGHT.... IF YOU WANT A BETTER LOOK... TURN THE PAGE!

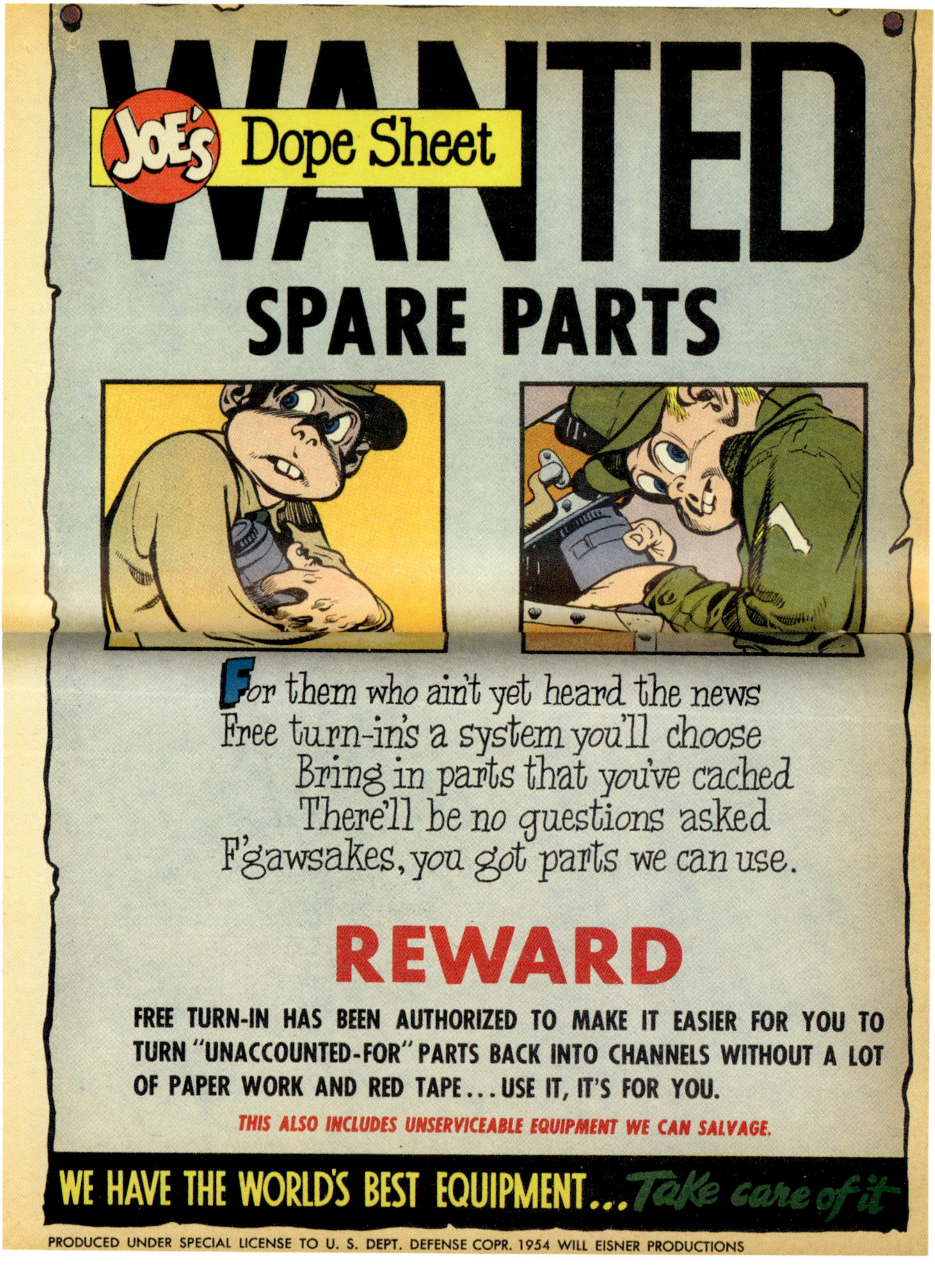
WANTED
JOE'S Dope Sheet
SPARE PARTS
For them who ain't yet heard the news
Free turn-in's a system you'll choose
Bring in parts that you've cached
There'll be no questions asked
F'gawsakes, you got parts we can use.
REWARD
FREE TURN-IN HAS BEEN AUTHORIZED TO MAKE IT EASIER FOR YOU TO TURN "UNACCOUNTED-FOR" PARTS BACK INTO CHANNELS WITHOUT A LOT OF PAPER WORK AND RED TAPE... USE IT, IT'S FOR YOU.
THIS ALSO INCLUDES UNSERVICEABLE EQUIPMENT WE CAN SALVAGE.
WE HAVE THE WORLD'S BEST EQUIPMENT... Take care of it
PRODUCED UNDER SPECIAL LICENSE TO U. S. DEPT. DEFENSE COPR. 1954 WILL EISNER PRODUCTIONS

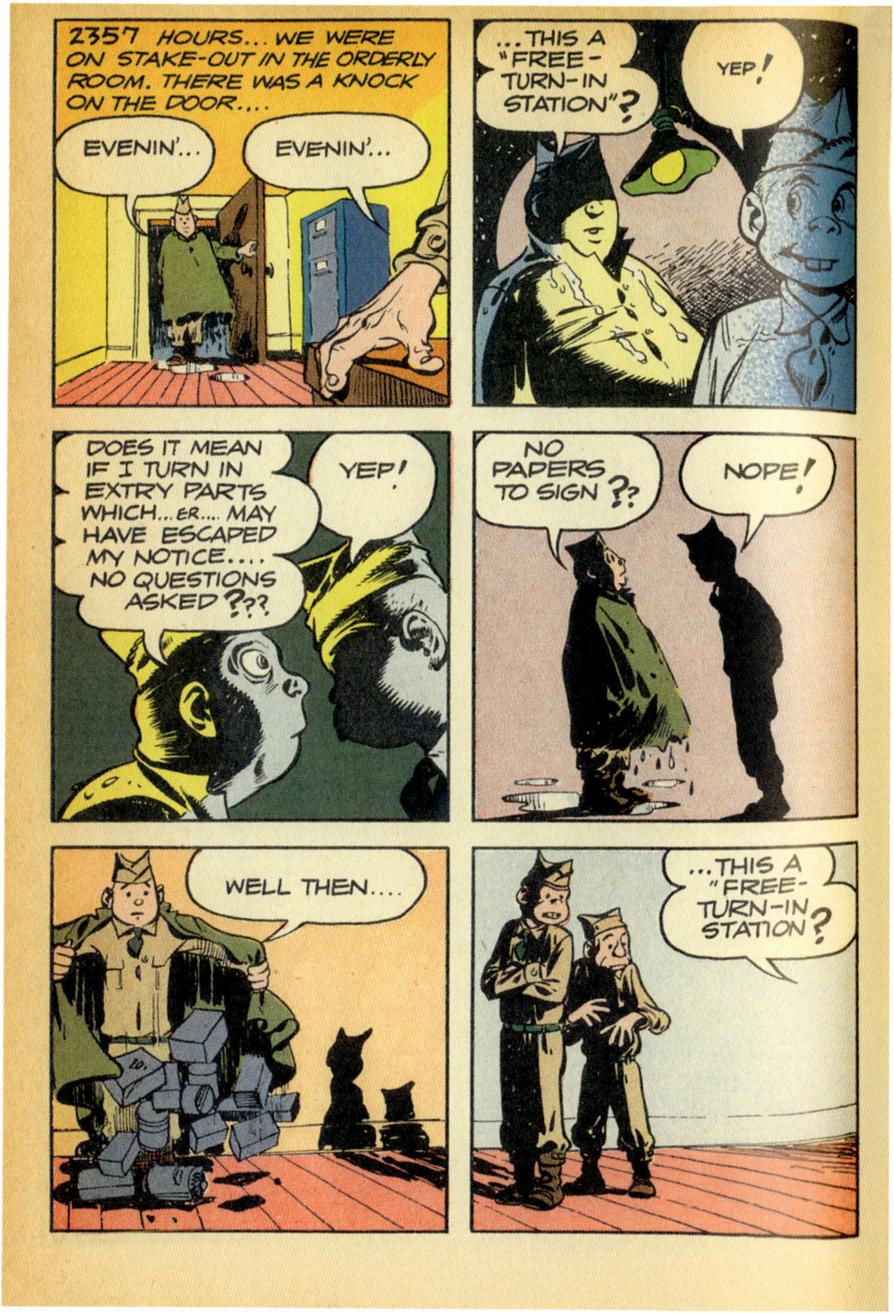
2357 HOURS... WE WERE ON STAKE-OUT IN THE ORDERLY ROOM. THERE WAS A KNOCK ON THE DOOR....
EVENIN'...
EVENIN'...
..THIS A "FREE-TURN-IN STATION"?
YEP!
DOES IT MEAN IF I TURN IN EXTRY PARTS WHICH...ER.... MAY HAVE ESCAPED MY NOTICE.... NO QUESTIONS ASKED???
YEP!
NO PAPERS TO SIGN ??
NOPE!
WELL THEN....
...THIS A "FREE-TURN-IN STATION?

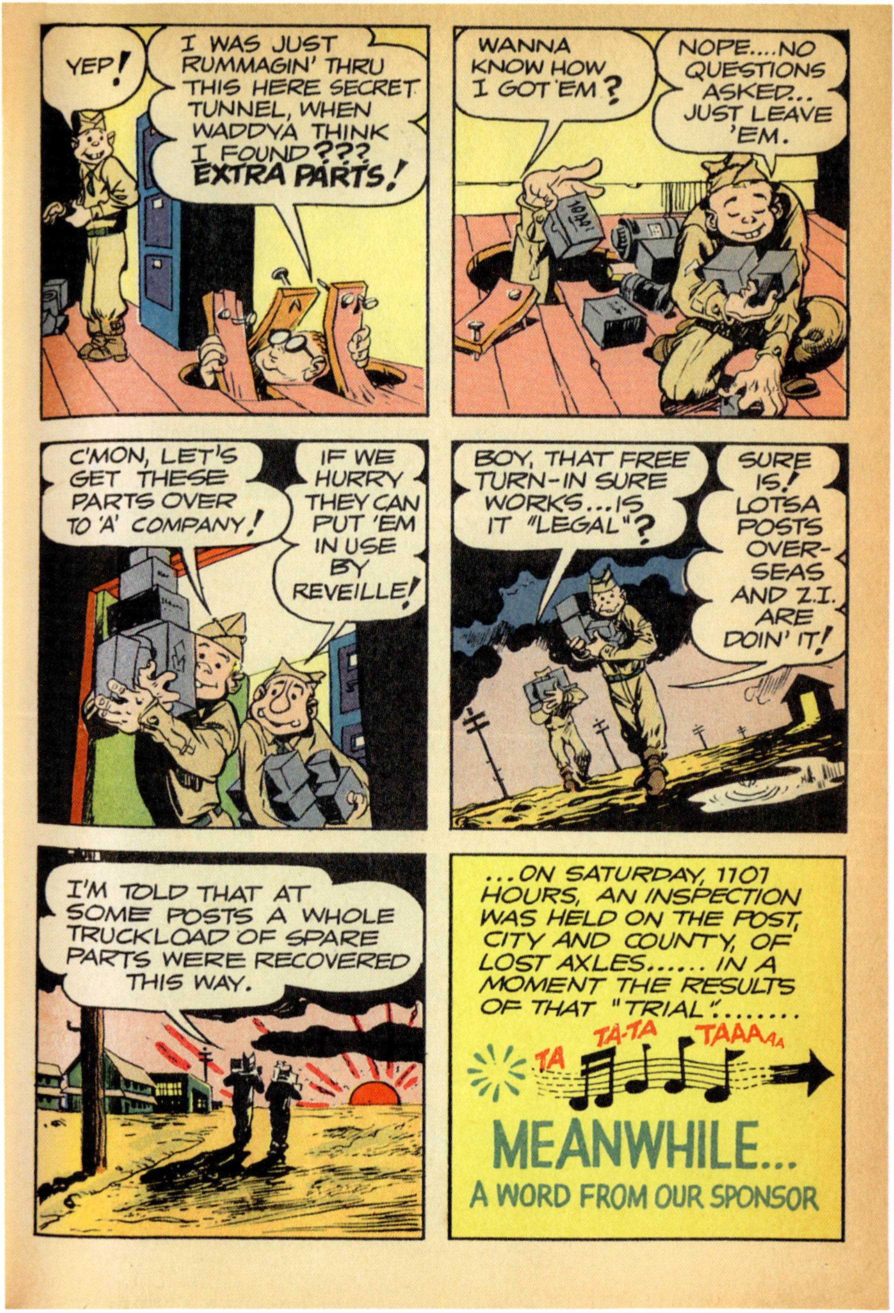
YEP!
I WAS JUST RUMMAGIN' THRU THIS HERE SECRET TUNNEL, WHEN WADDYA THINK I FOUND??? EXTRA PARTS!
WANNA KNOW HOW I GOT 'EM?
NOPE.... NO QUESTIONS ASKED... JUST LEAVE 'EM.
C'MON, LET'S GET THESE PARTS OVER TO 'A' COMPANY!
IF WE HURRY THEY CAN PUT 'EM IN USE BY REVEILLE!
BOY, THAT FREE TURN-IN SURE WORKS... IS IT "LEGAL"?
SURE IS! LOTSA POSTS OVER-SEAS AND Z.I. ARE DOIN' IT!
I'M TOLD THAT AT SOME POSTS A WHOLE TRUCKLOAD OF SPARE PARTS WERE RECOVERED THIS WAY.
...ON SATURDAY, 1107 HOURS, AN INSPECTION WAS HELD ON THE POST, CITY AND COUNTY, OF LOST AXLES...... IN A MOMENT THE RESULTS OF THAT "TRIAL"........
TA TA-TA TAAAAA
MEANWHILE...
A WORD FROM OUR SPONSOR

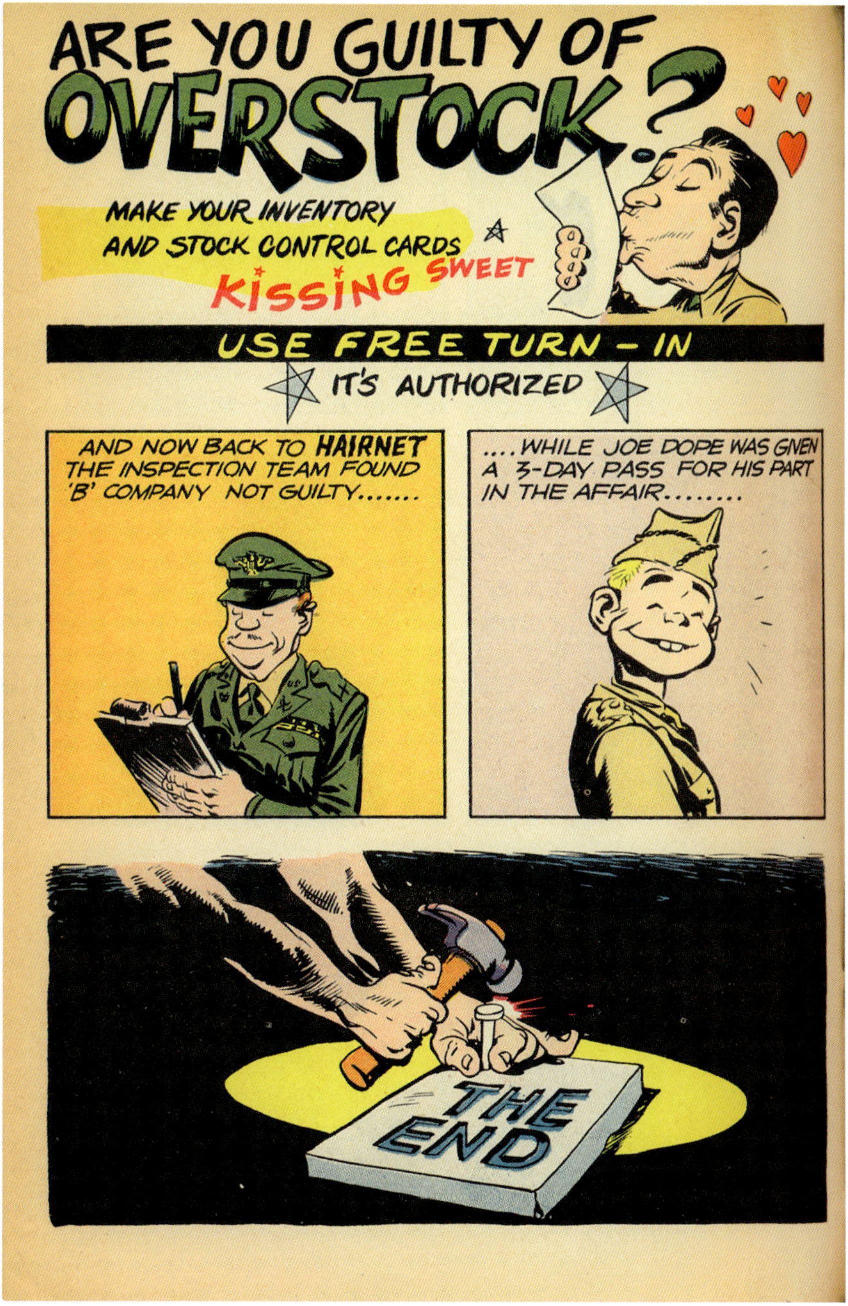
ARE YOU GUILTY OF OVERSTOCK?
MAKE YOUR INVENTORY AND STOCK CONTROL CARDS KISSING SWEET
USE FREE TURN-IN
IT'S AUTHORIZED
AND NOW BACK TO HAIRNET THE INSPECTION TEAM FOUND 'B' COMPANY NOT GUILTY......
....WHILE JOE DOPE WAS GIVEN A 3-DAY PASS FOR HIS PART IN THE AFFAIR........
THE END

DIRTY HEADS CAUSE TROUBLE

It's all in the head—keep it clean.

After you've used a grenade-launcher, take a look-see for dirt or carbon under the gas-cylinder lock-screw head of your M1 rifle. That head is a part of a valve in the lock-screw (Fig. 1). It seats itself like the valve in the head of an engine.

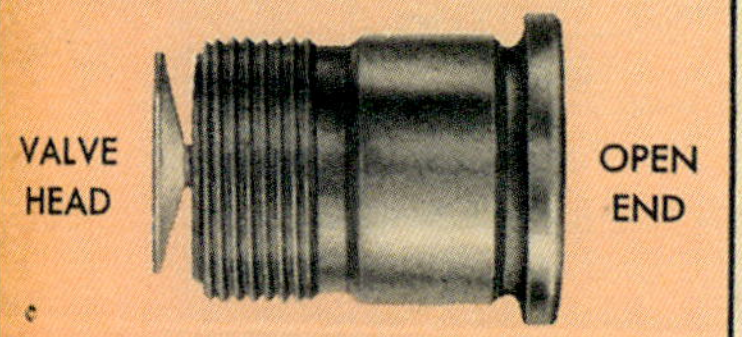

VALVE HEAD   **OPEN END**

Fig. 1—Here's a head that'll take a bit of pushing and holding to make sure it's clean.

When you stick a grenade launcher on your rifle, a stud on the launcher opens the valve in the lock-screw. This lets some of the gas escape from the front of the rifle when a grenade is fired.

Part of the gas escapes from the front of the rifle and prevents full recoil of the operating rod and gives you a single-shot weapon for grenade launching. It also prevents parts slamming back too hard in recoil and damaging them when you launch a grenade. But it does give dirt and carbon a chance to get under the valve-head.

Dirt or carbon under the head (Fig. 2) will distort the head and crack it. You've got a lotta gas pressure in there. Improper seating or cracks will give you a single-shot when you need a semi-automatic rifle.

To get at the head, stick the screw-driver end of your combination tool in the open end of the lock-screw and push against the valve stem. Then give it a going over with your old tooth brush and a little bore cleaner.

Fig. 2—A tooth brush moistened with rifle bore cleaner will move gook from the head.

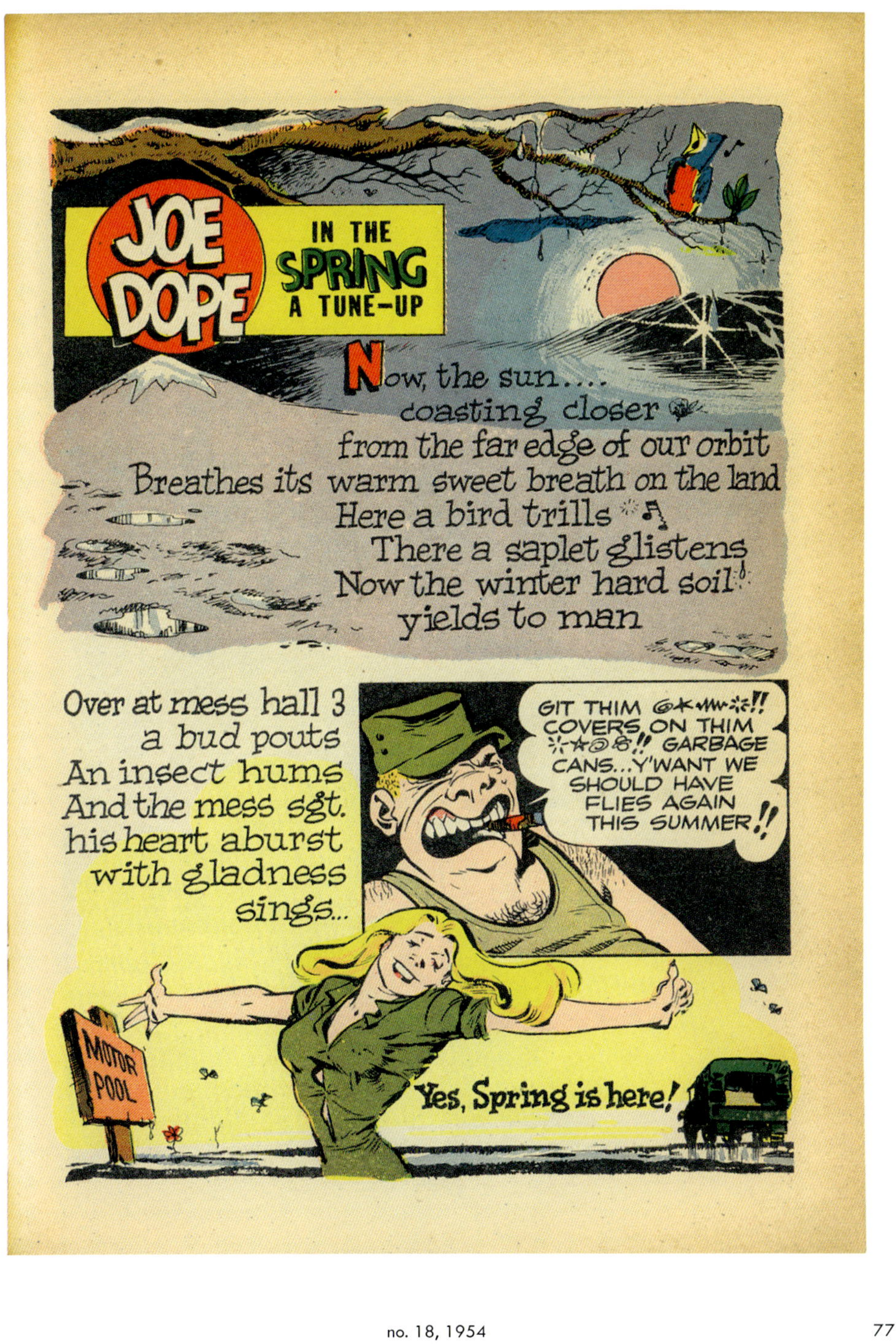
JOE DOPE
IN THE SPRING A TUNE-UP
Now, the sun.... coasting closer from the far edge of our orbit
Breathes its warm sweet breath on the land
Here a bird trills
There a saplet glistens
Now the winter hard soil yields to man
Over at mess hall 3 a bud pouts
An insect hums
And the mess sgt. his heart aburst with gladness sings...
GIT THIM @*!! COVERS ON THIM !! GARBAGE CANS...Y'WANT WE SHOULD HAVE FLIES AGAIN THIS SUMMER!!
MOTOR POOL
Yes, Spring is here!

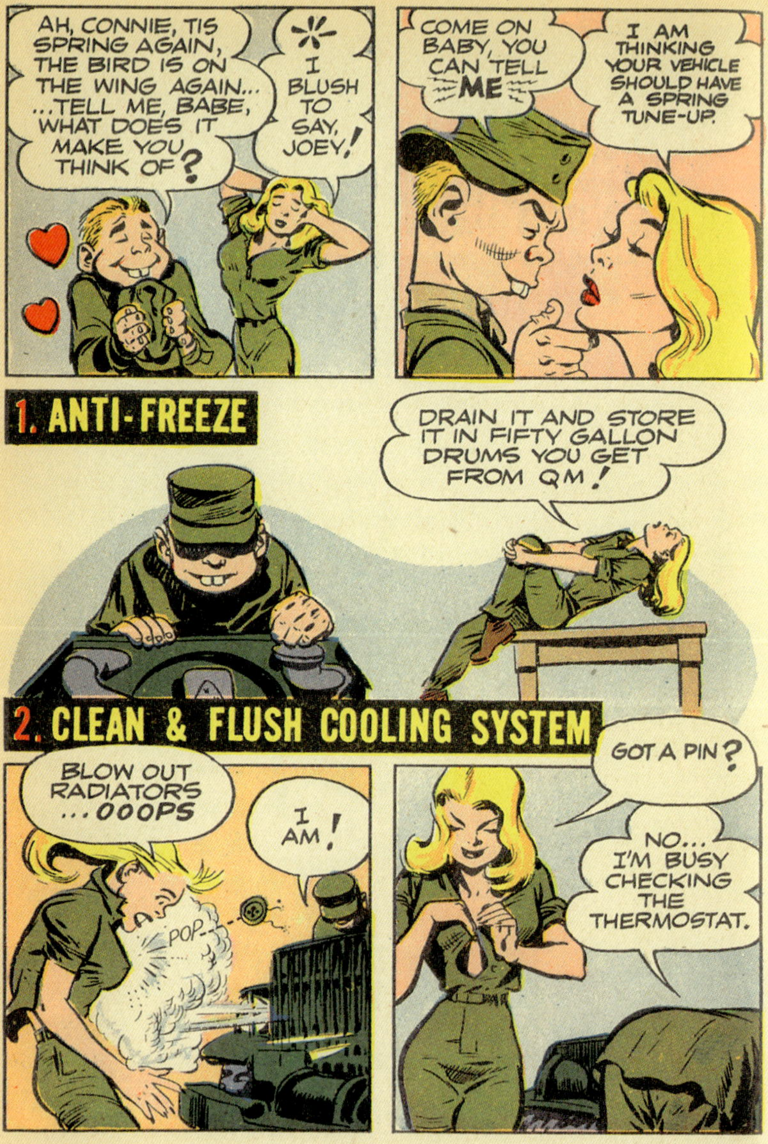
AH, CONNIE, TIS SPRING AGAIN, THE BIRD IS ON THE WING AGAIN... ...TELL ME, BABE, WHAT DOES IT MAKE YOU THINK OF?
I BLUSH TO SAY, JOEY!
COME ON BABY, YOU CAN TELL ME
I AM THINKING YOUR VEHICLE SHOULD HAVE A SPRING TUNE-UP.
1. ANTI-FREEZE
DRAIN IT AND STORE IT IN FIFTY GALLON DRUMS YOU GET FROM QM!
2. CLEAN & FLUSH COOLING SYSTEM
BLOW OUT RADIATORS ...OOOPS
I AM!
POP
GOT A PIN?
NO... I'M BUSY CHECKING THE THERMOSTAT.

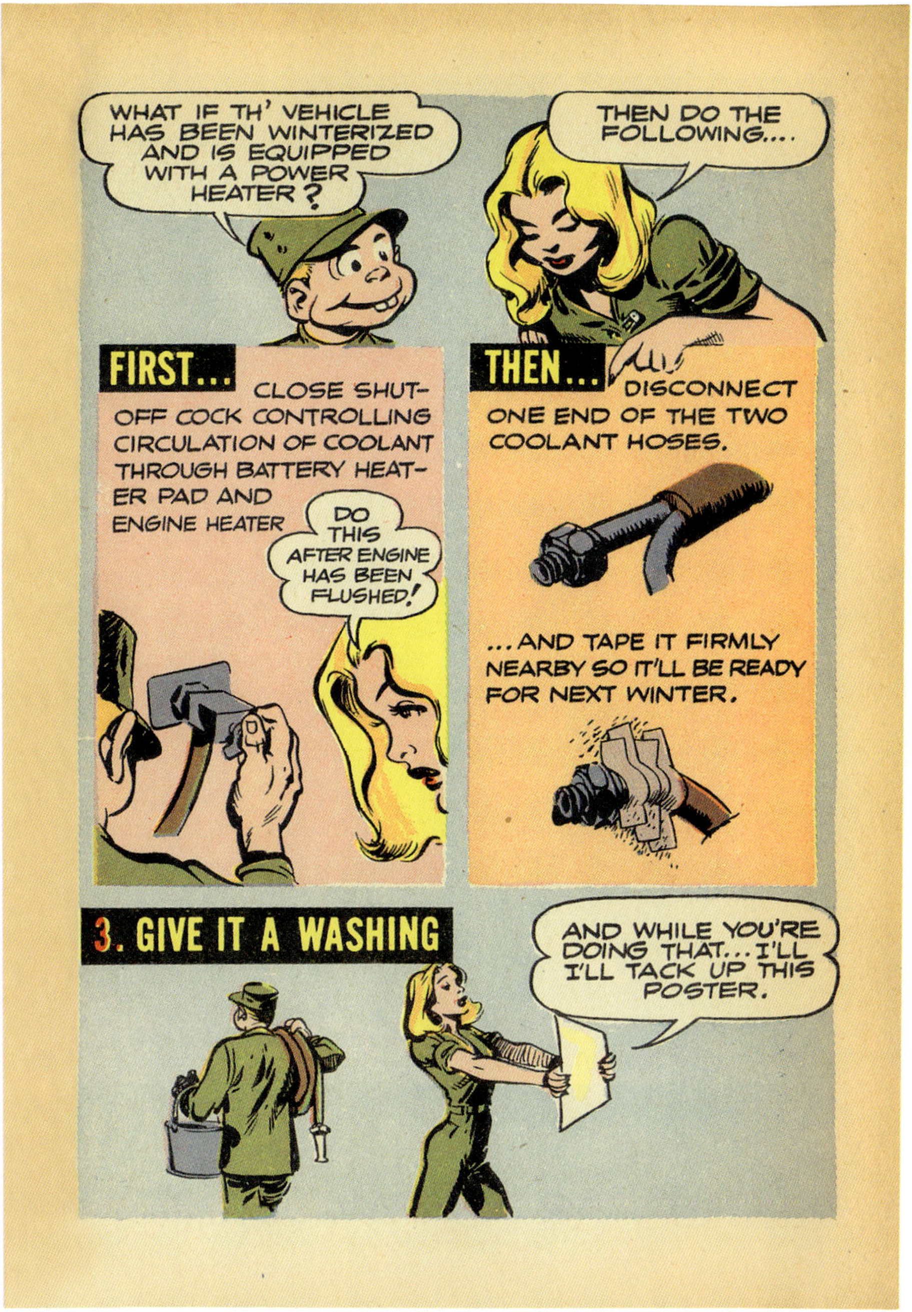

WHAT IF TH' VEHICLE HAS BEEN WINTERIZED AND IS EQUIPPED WITH A POWER HEATER?
THEN DO THE FOLLOWING....
FIRST...
CLOSE SHUT-OFF COCK CONTROLLING CIRCULATION OF COOLANT THROUGH BATTERY HEAT-ER PAD AND ENGINE HEATER
DO THIS AFTER ENGINE HAS BEEN FLUSHED!
THEN...
DISCONNECT ONE END OF THE TWO COOLANT HOSES.
...AND TAPE IT FIRMLY NEARBY SO IT'LL BE READY FOR NEXT WINTER.
3. GIVE IT A WASHING
AND WHILE YOU'RE DOING THAT... I'LL I'LL TACK UP THIS POSTER.

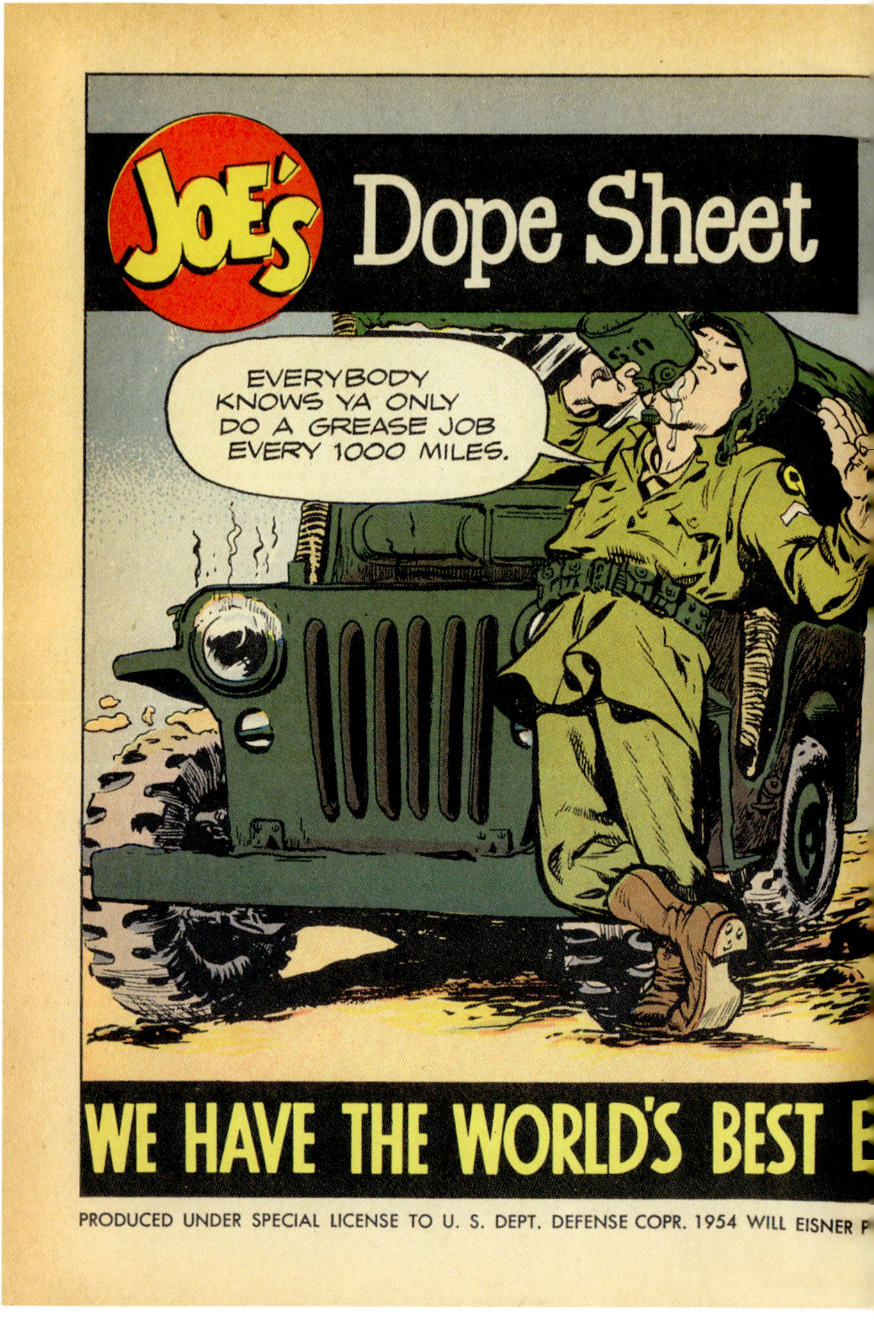
JOE'S Dope Sheet
EVERYBODY KNOWS YA ONLY DO A GREASE JOB EVERY 1000 MILES.
WE HAVE THE WORLD'S BEST E
PRODUCED UNDER SPECIAL LICENSE TO U. S. DEPT. DEFENSE COPR. 1954 WILL EISNER P

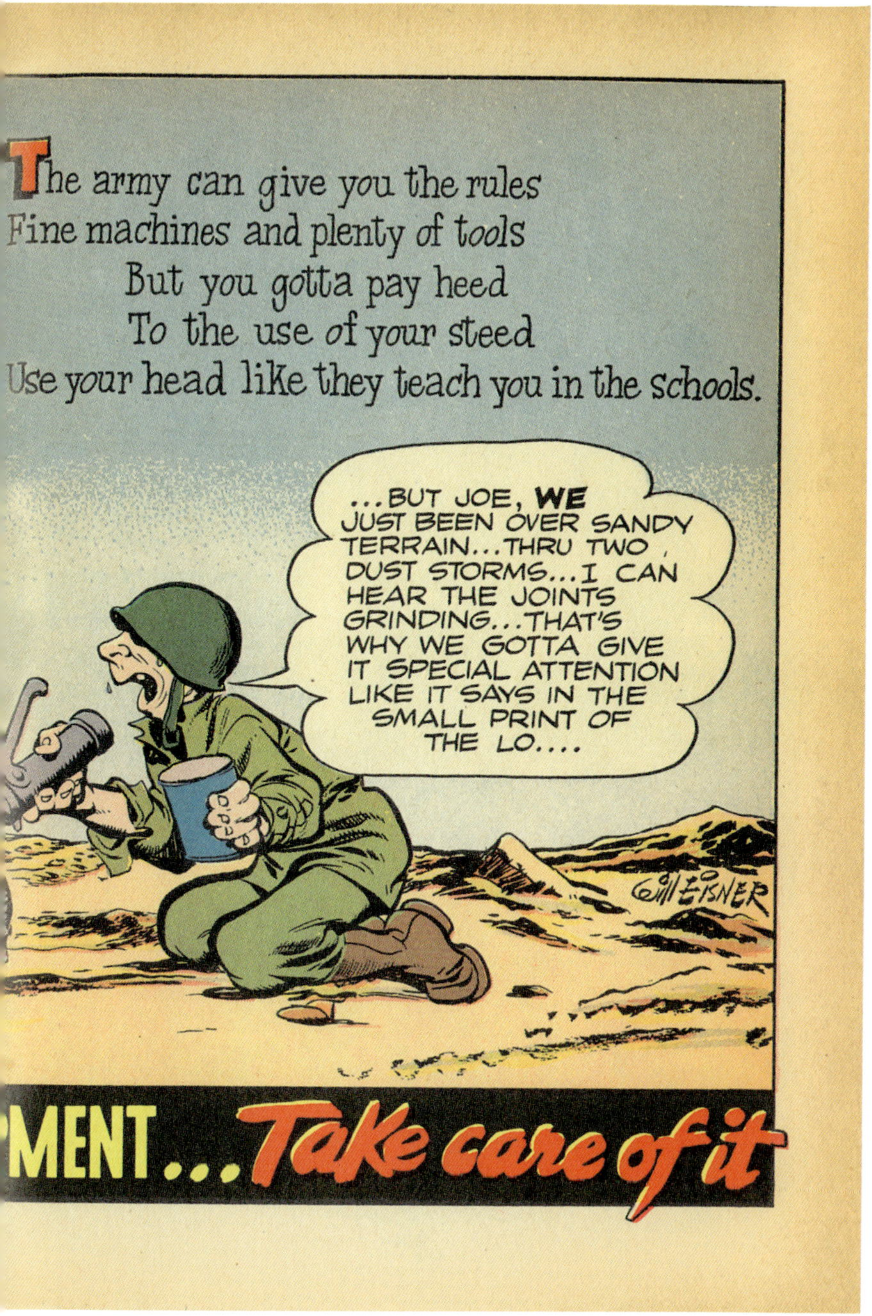
The army can give you the rules
Fine machines and plenty of tools
But you gotta pay heed
To the use of your steed
Use your head like they teach you in the schools.
...BUT JOE, WE JUST BEEN OVER SANDY TERRAIN...THRU TWO DUST STORMS...I CAN HEAR THE JOINTS GRINDING...THAT'S WHY WE GOTTA GIVE IT SPECIAL ATTENTION LIKE IT SAYS IN THE SMALL PRINT OF THE LO....
Will Eisner
MENT...Take care of it

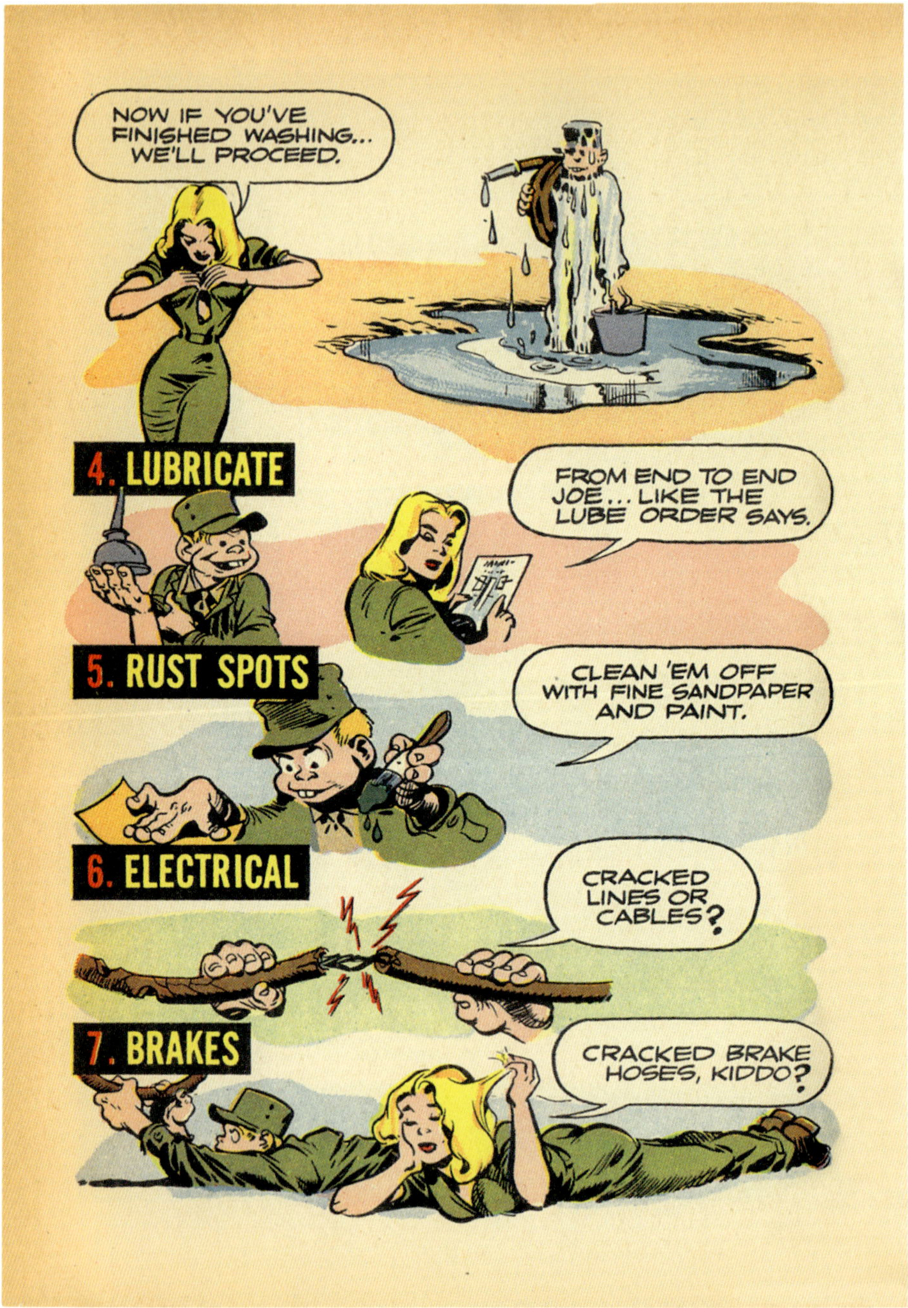
NOW IF YOU'VE FINISHED WASHING... WE'LL PROCEED.
4. LUBRICATE
FROM END TO END JOE... LIKE THE LUBE ORDER SAYS.
5. RUST SPOTS
CLEAN 'EM OFF WITH FINE SANDPAPER AND PAINT.
6. ELECTRICAL
CRACKED LINES OR CABLES?
7. BRAKES
CRACKED BRAKE HOSES, KIDDO?

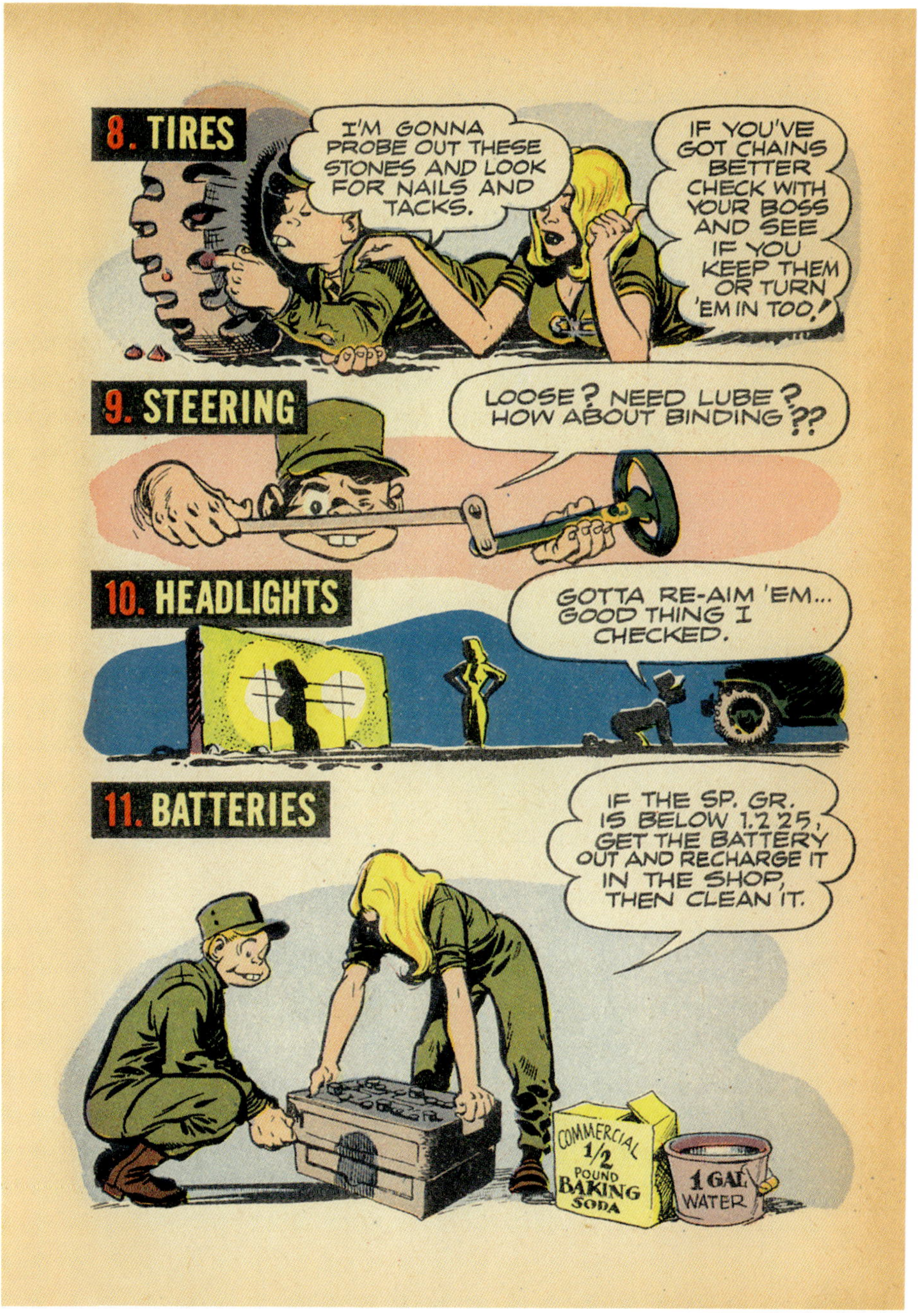
8. TIRES
I'M GONNA PROBE OUT THESE STONES AND LOOK FOR NAILS AND TACKS.
IF YOU'VE GOT CHAINS BETTER CHECK WITH YOUR BOSS AND SEE IF YOU KEEP THEM OR TURN 'EM IN TOO!
9. STEERING
LOOSE? NEED LUBE? HOW ABOUT BINDING??
10. HEADLIGHTS
GOTTA RE-AIM 'EM... GOOD THING I CHECKED.
11. BATTERIES
IF THE SP. GR. IS BELOW 1.225, GET THE BATTERY OUT AND RECHARGE IT IN THE SHOP, THEN CLEAN IT.
COMMERCIAL 1/2 POUND BAKING SODA
1 GAL WATER

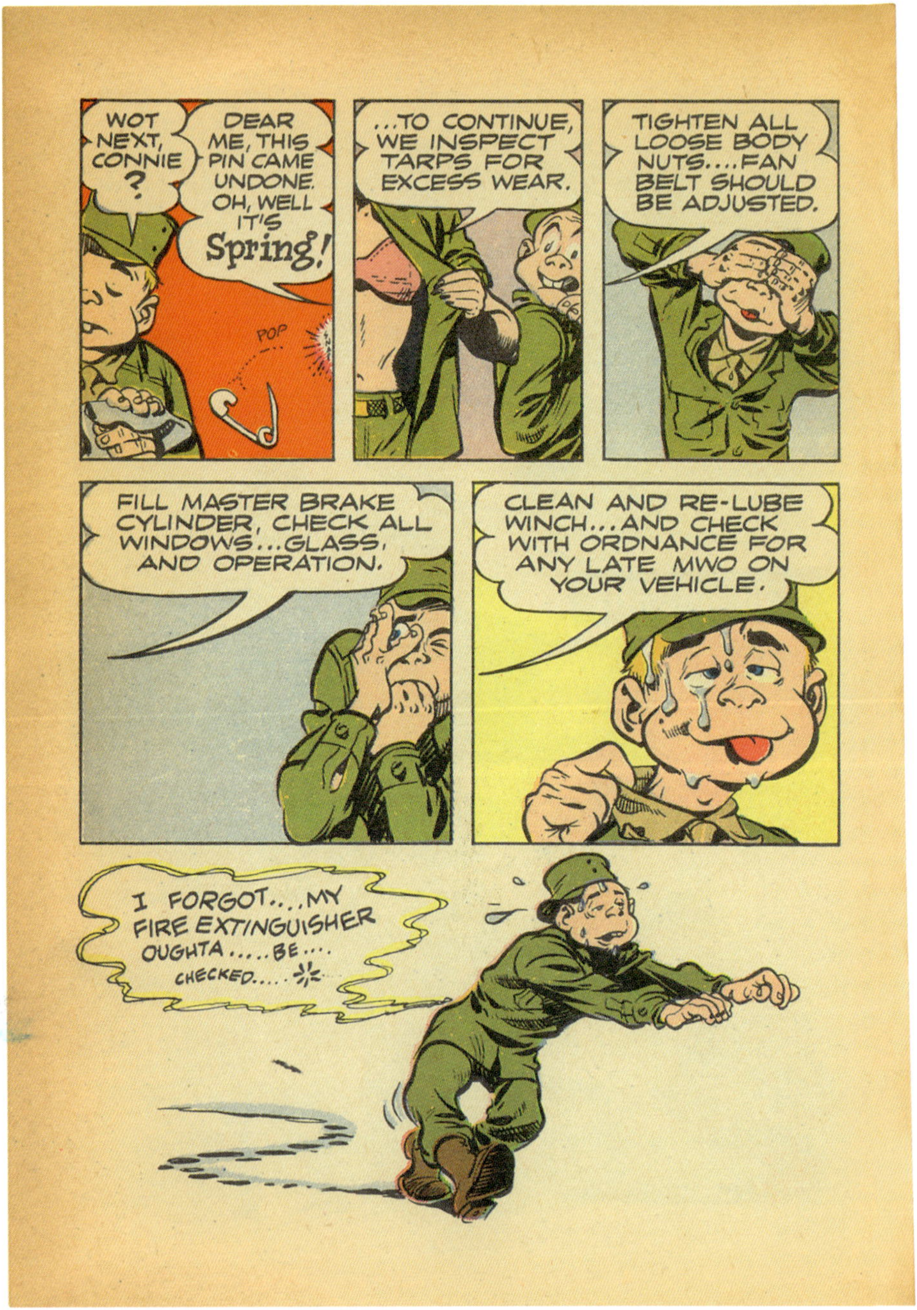
WOT NEXT, CONNIE ?
DEAR ME, THIS PIN CAME UNDONE. OH, WELL IT'S Spring!
POP
...TO CONTINUE, WE INSPECT TARPS FOR EXCESS WEAR.
TIGHTEN ALL LOOSE BODY NUTS....FAN BELT SHOULD BE ADJUSTED.
FILL MASTER BRAKE CYLINDER, CHECK ALL WINDOWS...GLASS, AND OPERATION.
CLEAN AND RE-LUBE WINCH...AND CHECK WITH ORDNANCE FOR ANY LATE MWO ON YOUR VEHICLE.
I FORGOT....MY FIRE EXTINGUISHER OUGHTA.....BE.... CHECKED....

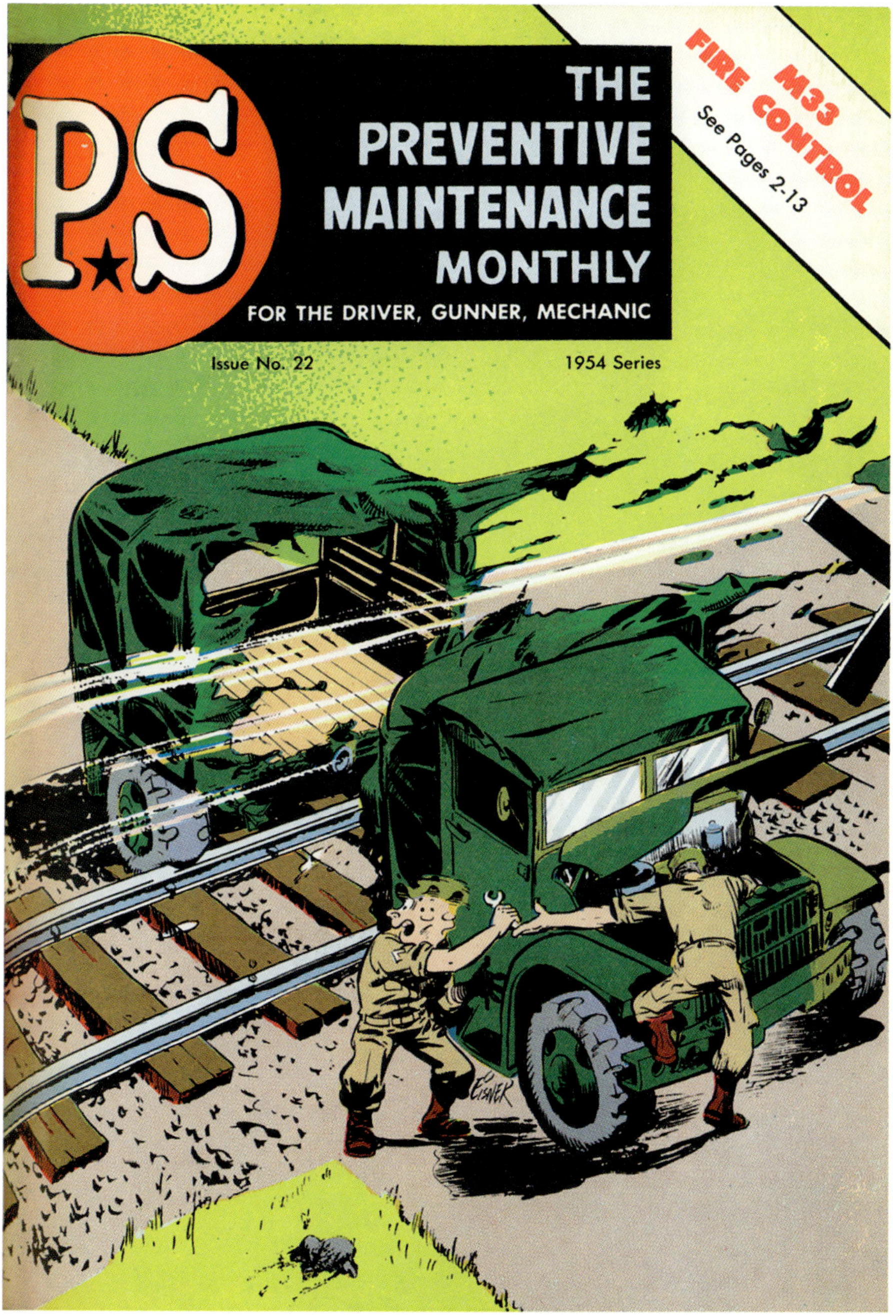
P.S
THE
PREVENTIVE
MAINTENANCE
MONTHLY
FOR THE DRIVER, GUNNER, MECHANIC
Issue No. 22
1954 Series
M33
FIRE CONTROL
See Pages 2-13
EISNER

no. 22, 1954

DON'T "BLIND-DATE" THE M34 AND M35 TRUCKS

(Be "from Missouri"...and see for yourself — even new stuff needs checking and adjusting.)

Say you've got a spanking new M34 or M35. Even though she's new, taking it for granted everything's in good order is like believing every sweater girl is real... sometimes they are and sometimes they stretch a point.

When you get a vehicle from the maker, you've got some work to do on it. You—the **driver** and the unit mechanic—you're the team that's so important to get and keep 'er rolling.

Here's a rundown on what the experts say ought to be done to it right off the bat (your truck, that is). Some of the things you do yourself, some of the things you just check to make sure they've been done before you got the truck. Remember: If something happens, it may have been someone else's boner, but it comes back on your weary feet if you have to leave your hack and walk home.

First, check the processing tag on the engine or vehicle, and if it says the engine contains preservative oil that is suitable for 500 miles of operation and it's the right seasonal grade, check it—but don't change it.

Check your buggy carefully to see that everything is in place. It'll also be well worth your time to give her a grease job and hit the hard-to-get-at fittings that might have been missed. If you get too much grease on any part, wipe off the excess.

Look for any possible missing grease fittings and keep your eyes open for loose or unsafetied bolts. The production boys do a good job, and the truck has had a complete inspection before you received her, but it's now **your** truck and if any trouble develops, it's **your** baby. So —go over her yourself with a fine-tooth comb. When you're satisfied that all's in good order, take her out on the job and give her every break.

The first 1000-mile inspection is the most important one the truck'll ever get. Any looseness or potential trouble is due to show then, and things you correct here are not likely to trouble you again.

Since you are particularly interested in catching leaks in the oil and hydraulic lines, pull this inspection on a dust-covered truck. Oil leaks and seeps show up better then. Look for signs of leaks around the oil filter, fuel pump, valve cover and pan. Check the air compressor for any leaks and check the compressor belt for adjustment according to page 247, TM 9-819 (Jan 52).

Examine the entire brake system for leakage from lines or cylinders. Check the level of the brake fluid in the master cylinder.

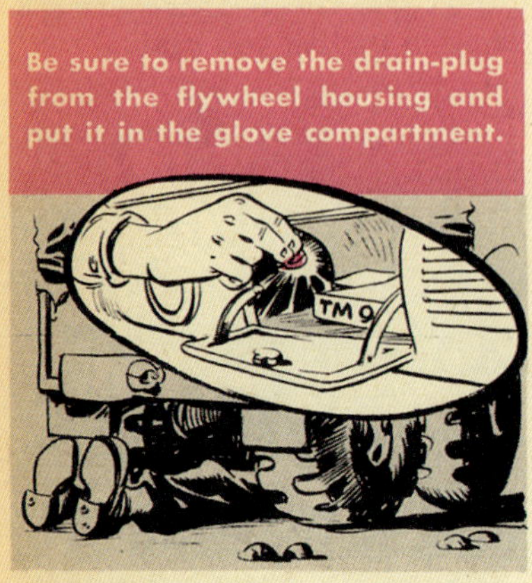
Be sure to remove the drain-plug from the flywheel housing and put it in the glove compartment.
TM 9

Effective with Vehicle Serial No. 127355 (15 Oct 53) a blind tapped boss was added to the flywheel housing for stowage of the drain plug. Later models have a threaded hole in the frame near the bell housing to screw in this gadget.

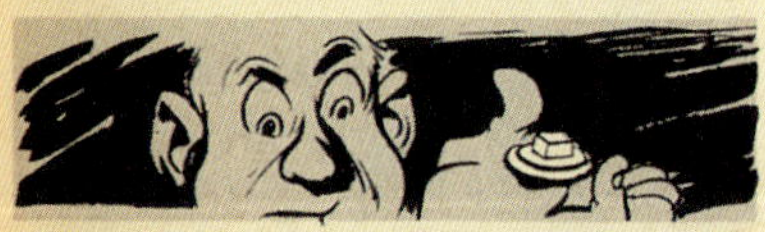

If you find oil dripping from the bottom of the flywheel housing, look for the leaks in either the oil filter, fuel pump, rocker-arm cover or air compressor, or an overfilled transmission.

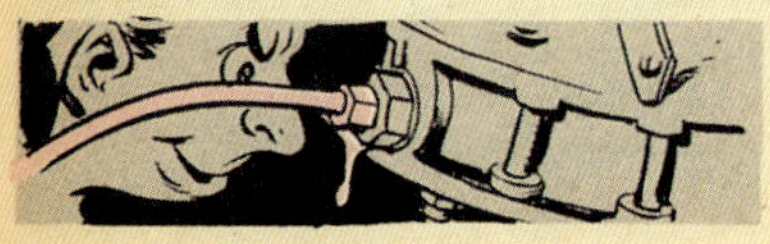

Tighten the wheel nuts and the axle-flange bolts. Check for loose nuts everywhere on the truck—steering gear and vibration damper attaching-bolts are most critical.

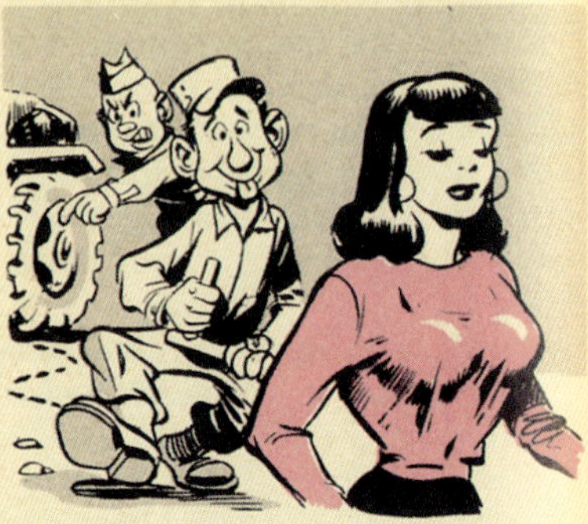

While thinking of steering, you mechanics should check the angle of the front wheels when fully turned, and toe-in. The angle shouldn't be over 28° (plus or minus 1°), and toe-in should be 1/16" to 1/8". Toe-in adjustment is your job, and the turning angle is handled by Ordnance.

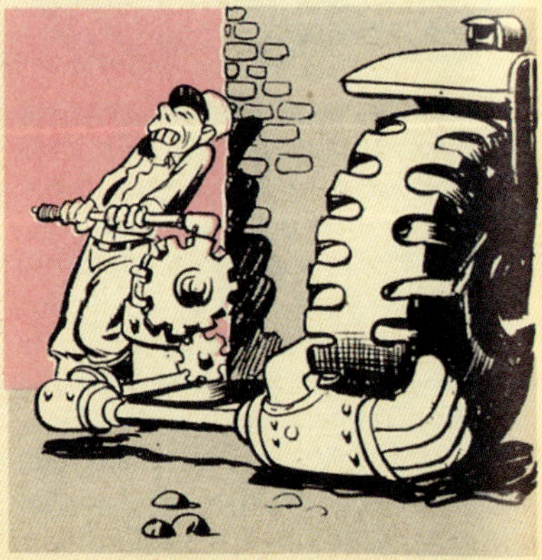

TM 9-819
PAGES 145-146

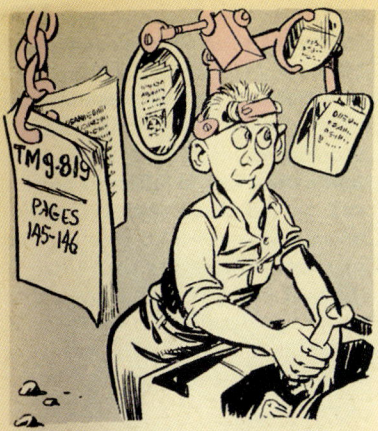

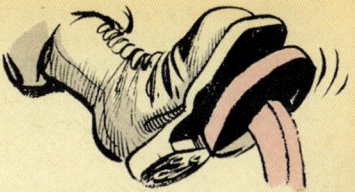

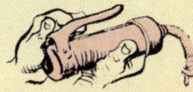

The mechanic resets valve tappets to 15-thousandths, with the engine at operating temperature, and sees that the cylinder-head bolts are torqued at 115 ft lbs—recheck valves after torquing heads. Then he looks at the fan and generator belts and adjusts, if needed (per pages 145-146, TM 9-819).

60
30
90
120
PRESSURE

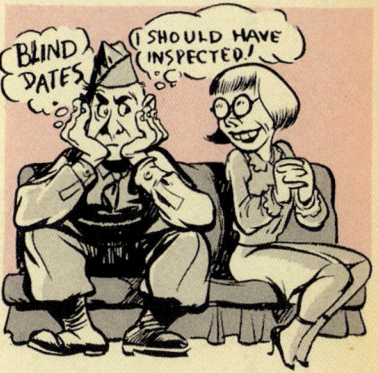

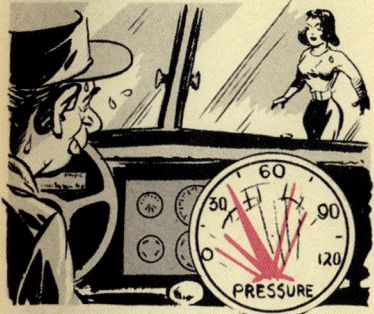

Check air-compressor governor. Air shouldn't build up past 110 lbs and there should be no leaks in the air system. Watch the gage—if pressure falls rapidly, you've got leaks.

Check the clutch pedal free-travel—it should be as per page 124, TM 9-819. Check the oil level in the engine air cleaner—bring it up to snuff.

Give the truck a complete lube job—yes, again—see LO 9-819.

BLIND DATES
I SHOULD HAVE INSPECTED!

It does sound kind of silly to be doing all this inspecting and adjusting on a brand-new truck, but believe it, the more you do now the less you'll have to do later. Besides, almost all of these items will be okay, but it's the ones that aren't just right that we're after. They're the jokers that cause headaches.

This inspection carries you up to the 1000-mile point. There you can have the throttle stop taken out of the carburetor and the governor checked for 3550 to 3600-

maximum-engine-rpm (no load). Be sure this is done by someone authorized to break the seals. An easy day-to-day check on the governor is to watch the speedometer when shifting. If you get more than 24-mph in third gear, high range, take it in to be checked.

These trucks are equipped with automatic front wheel drive, so there's a couple of precautions to take. If you ever have to let the truck drift or coast backward, make sure the transmission is shifted into

reverse. And if you ever let it coast forward, make sure it's not in reverse.

Since the transfer-case shift is linked to the main shift, the shift must agree with the truck's direction of motion or wind-up will result in the drive shafts. Forward wind-up causes hard steering and rearward wind-up causes the transmission shift-lever to jump out of reverse position if you try to use it. Too much wind-up will wear tires excessively and tear up the transfer case.

If you mechanics have to take a drive shaft out, jack up one of the wheels it serves first to get rid of wind-up. If you try removing a shaft when there's any wind-up in it, she'll clobber you—but good.

While all trucks below Serial No. 90475, which came out with the single-sprag clutch, are being modified to the double-sprag type, some are still in use. So—check the serial number (left frame rail, under the front fender, also on the dash) and then look at the transfer linkage. Compare it to the illustrations on pages 171-172 of TM 9-819 (Jan. 52).

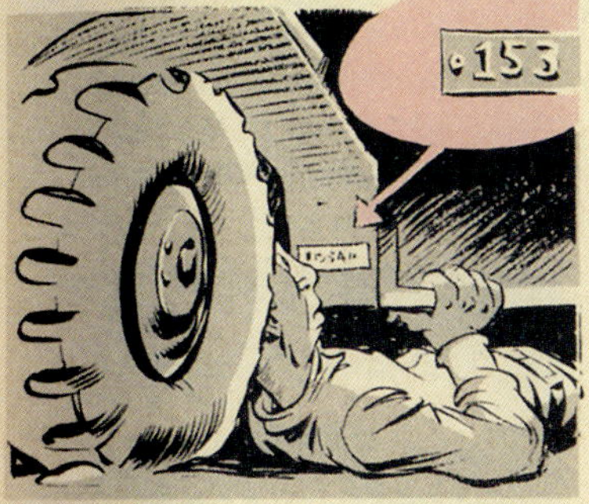
153

You need to have an old TM 9-819 (June 50), page 173, kicking around to tell you proper adjustment if you have a single-sprag type clutch. (That manual is out of supply now.)

The double-sprag adjustment is on 173-174 of TM 9-819 (Jan. 52). Or, preferably, get Ordnance

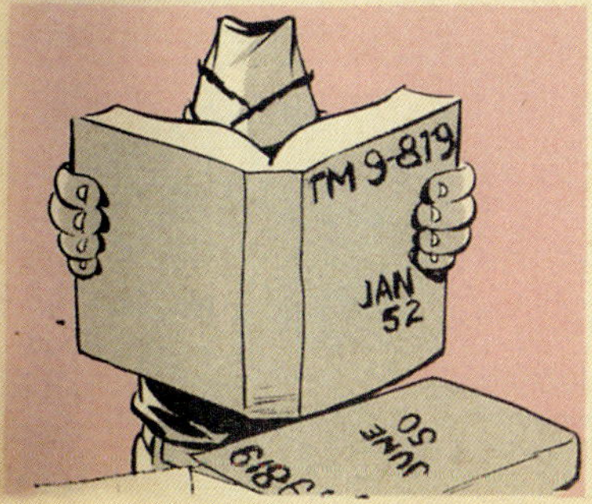
TM 9-819
JAN 52
JUNE 50

to install a double-sprag clutch and shift linkage as per MWO Ord G742-W3.

Now if you want to keep the brakes safe and sound, it's important to make an occasional check of the emergency brake to make sure the shoes are completely released and free. Check for grease on the shoes or drum. It might cause them to drag or even lock. Adjust them according to TM 9-819, pages 197-200 for the emergency brake, and pages 186-198 for the foot or service brake.

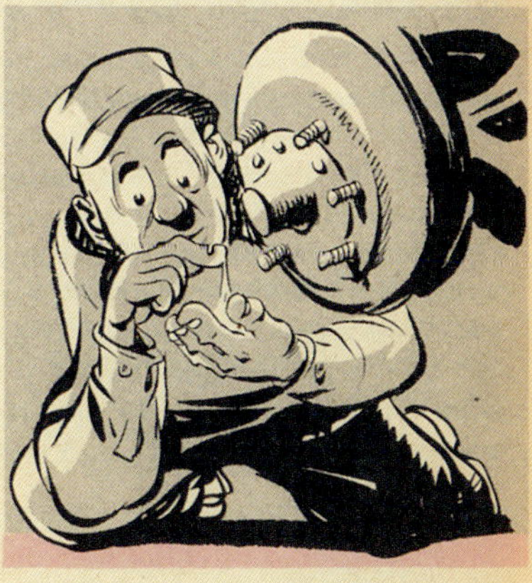

If you don't want to be shocked, disconnect the battery before you start playing around with the elec-

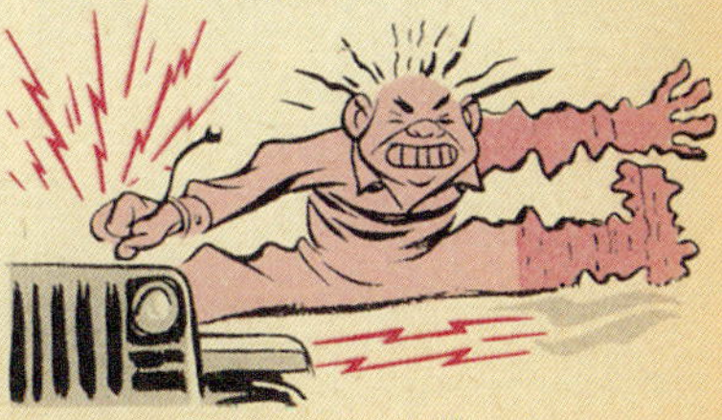

trical connections. Or, when you're using the slave battery receptacle (if you have one) to throw current into another vehicle, make sure you hook up positive to positive and negative to negative.

On the early model trucks, relocate the wiring harnesses leading to the blackout marker-lights before it rubs through its insulation and grounds out on the fender lip. Start on the right front fender and remove the 5/16″ nut and bolt from the fender support. Remove 1/4″ nut, bolt, and clip from where it's located and put it where you removed the 5/16″ nut and bolt. Same procedure goes for the left front fender. On later models this has already been done at the factory.

The "get-up-and-go" of your truck, in the long run, is pretty much up to you, depending on how well you look after it and how well you drive it. It's the old story of one hand washing the other. Even though everything's being done that can be done to make your truck operate as it should, it still can't do a thing without your care and direction.

REMOVE NUT & BOLT
BEFORE
AFTER
CLIP
CLIP
FENDER SUPPORT

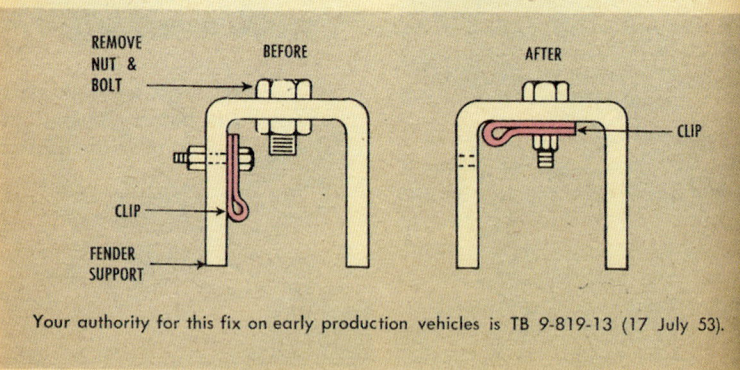

Your authority for this fix on early production vehicles is TB 9-819-13 (17 July 53).

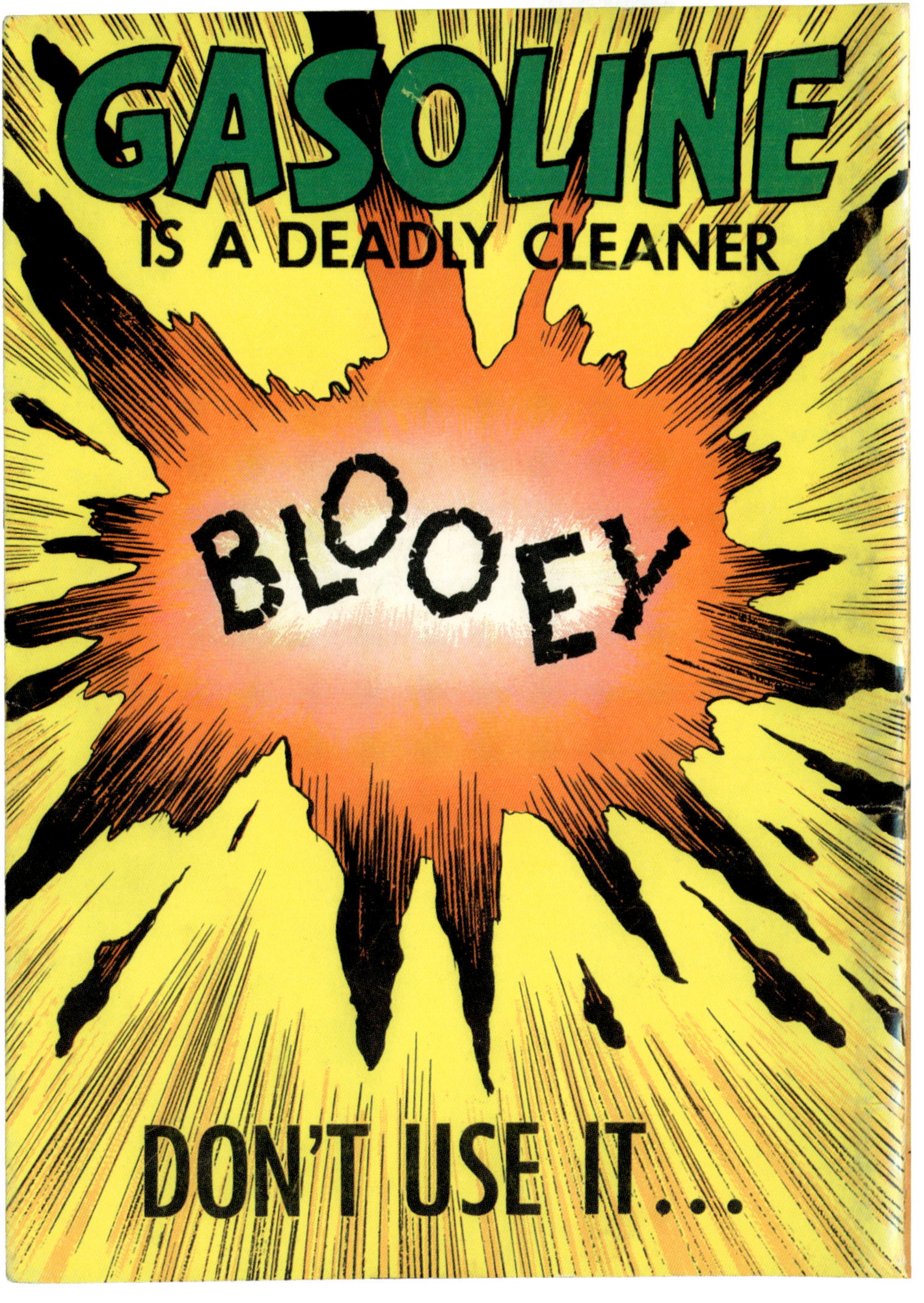
GASOLINE
IS A DEADLY CLEANER
BLOOEY
DON'T USE IT...

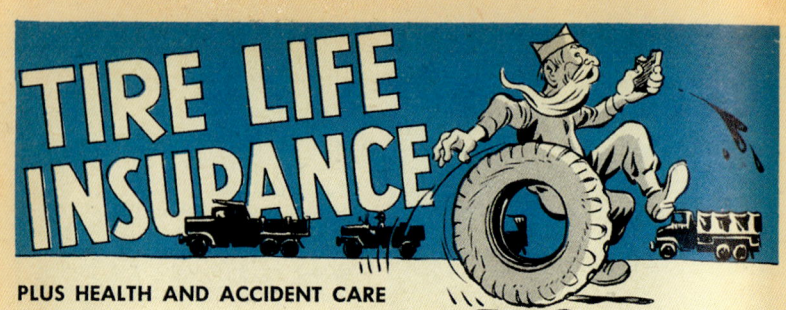

TIRE LIFE INSURANCE

PLUS HEALTH AND ACCIDENT CARE

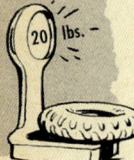

GOOD CARE IS THE BEST LIFE INSURANCE FOR TIRES. GOOD CARE KEEPS 'EM ROUND AND HAPPY AND ROLLING. BUT MANY A RUBBER ROLLER MEETS WITH BAD LUCK AND ACCIDENTS. SO THE BEST THING YOU CAN DO FOR A WOUNDED TIRE IS GET IT OFF THE WHEEL—BEFORE IT GETS SICKER AND DIES ON YOU. SO HERE WE ARE, GENTS—SOME TIPS ON TIRE CARE IN SICKNESS AND HEALTH TILL DEATH DO US PART.

IT'S A LIGHTWEIGHT... BUT IT'S TOUGH.

IT CAN HEAT UP HOTTER THAN BOILING WATER... RESIST 1 TON OF TEARING FORCE.

AN **INJURED** TIRE CAN'T TAKE IT... **TURN IT IN**

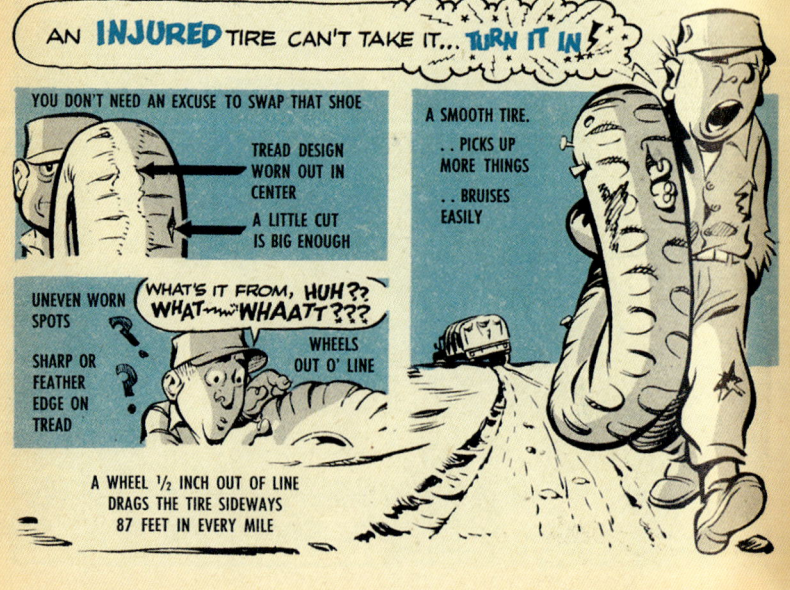

YOU DON'T NEED AN EXCUSE TO SWAP THAT SHOE
- TREAD DESIGN WORN OUT IN CENTER
- A LITTLE CUT IS BIG ENOUGH

A SMOOTH TIRE.
.. PICKS UP MORE THINGS
.. BRUISES EASILY

UNEVEN WORN SPOTS
SHARP OR FEATHER EDGE ON TREAD

WHAT'S IT FROM, HUH?? WHAT—WHAATT???

WHEELS OUT O' LINE

A WHEEL ½ INCH OUT OF LINE DRAGS THE TIRE SIDEWAYS 87 FEET IN EVERY MILE

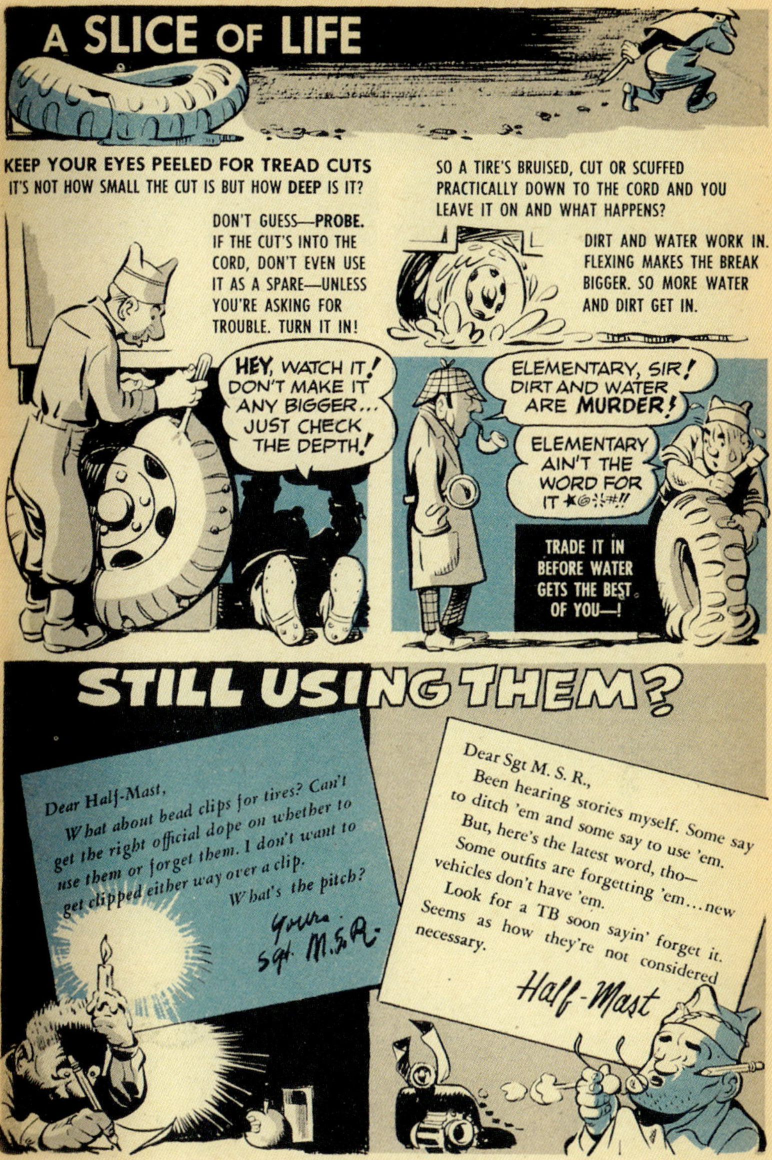
A SLICE OF LIFE
KEEP YOUR EYES PEELED FOR TREAD CUTS
IT'S NOT HOW SMALL THE CUT IS BUT HOW DEEP IS IT?
DON'T GUESS—PROBE. IF THE CUT'S INTO THE CORD, DON'T EVEN USE IT AS A SPARE—UNLESS YOU'RE ASKING FOR TROUBLE. TURN IT IN!
HEY, WATCH IT! DON'T MAKE IT ANY BIGGER... JUST CHECK THE DEPTH!
SO A TIRE'S BRUISED, CUT OR SCUFFED PRACTICALLY DOWN TO THE CORD AND YOU LEAVE IT ON AND WHAT HAPPENS?
DIRT AND WATER WORK IN. FLEXING MAKES THE BREAK BIGGER. SO MORE WATER AND DIRT GET IN.
ELEMENTARY, SIR! DIRT AND WATER ARE MURDER!
ELEMENTARY AIN'T THE WORD FOR IT ★@*#!!
TRADE IT IN BEFORE WATER GETS THE BEST OF YOU—!
STILL USING THEM?
Dear Half-Mast,
What about bead clips for tires? Can't get the right official dope on whether to use them or forget them. I don't want to get clipped either way over a clip.
What's the pitch?
Yours
Sgt. M.S.R.
Dear Sgt M. S. R.,
Been hearing stories myself. Some say to ditch 'em and some say to use 'em.
But, here's the latest word, tho—
Some outfits are forgetting 'em...new vehicles don't have 'em.
Look for a TB soon sayin' forget it. Seems as how they're not considered necessary.
Half-Mast

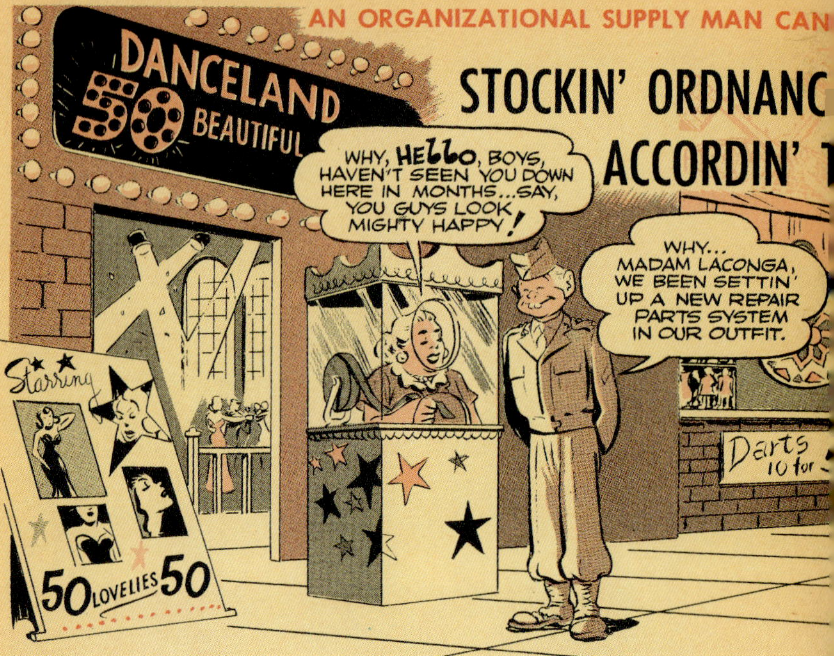
AN ORGANIZATIONAL SUPPLY MAN CAN
STOCKIN' ORDNANC
ACCORDIN' T
DANCELAND
50 BEAUTIFUL
WHY, HELLO, BOYS, HAVEN'T SEEN YOU DOWN HERE IN MONTHS...SAY, YOU GUYS LOOK MIGHTY HAPPY!
WHY... MADAM LACONGA, WE BEEN SETTIN' UP A NEW REPAIR PARTS SYSTEM IN OUR OUTFIT.
Starring
50 LOVELIES 50
Darts 10 for

That's right. You depend on Ord 7 allowances for your initial stock . . . you draw 'em to set yourself up in business . . . but after that you rely on ***Usage Experience** to tell you exactly how much of what you're to stock. You can either raise or lower the allowance quoted in Ord 7 . . . or you can even discontinue stocking an Ord 7 item altogether.

And anybody can do it . . . 'cause all it takes to readjust stock allowances, are stock records that prove exactly **how much** or **how little usage** your unit has for each item.

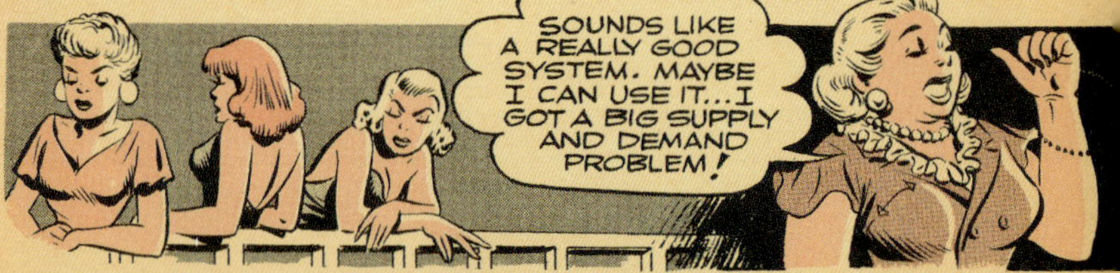
SOUNDS LIKE A REALLY GOOD SYSTEM. MAYBE I CAN USE IT...I GOT A BIG SUPPLY AND DEMAND PROBLEM!

***Usage Experience** (or Demand Experience) equals all the issues you make plus all the unfilled requests you have for any item during any given period.

…ED PROBLEMS LIKE SALLY RAND WHEN HE'S HEP TO…

…EPAIR PARTS …EMAND

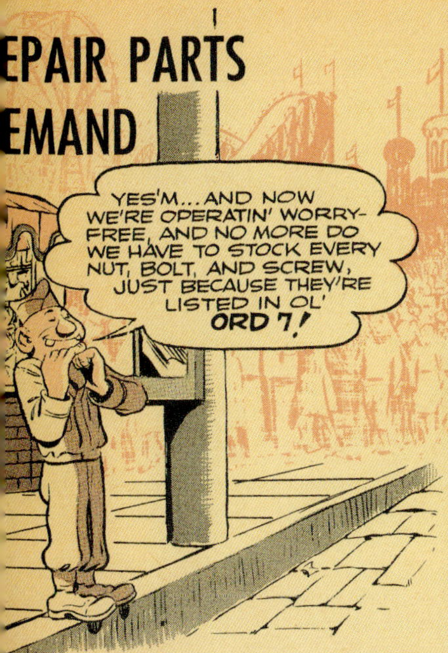
YES'M...AND NOW WE'RE OPERATIN' WORRY-FREE, AND NO MORE DO WE HAVE TO STOCK EVERY NUT, BOLT, AND SCREW, JUST BECAUSE THEY'RE LISTED IN OL' ORD 7!

Refreshing deal . . . no sweat, you say. OK, but before you get carried away shovin' stuff out the window, here's a warning note that should be painted in large letters all over the joint, and maybe even tattooed on your pointing finger: **"Don't cross yourself up with sloppy records."**

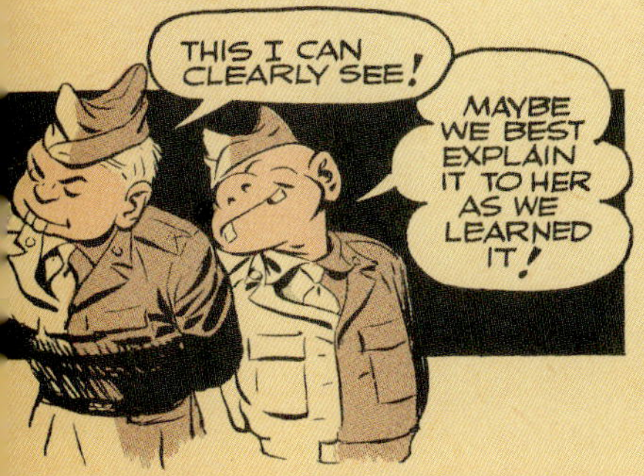
THIS I CAN CLEARLY SEE!
MAYBE WE BEST EXPLAIN IT TO HER AS WE LEARNED IT!

It's Legal

The authority that sez you can adjust stock levels according to usage experience is SR 711-15-5 (15 Jan 54).. para 34b states that "quantities of spare parts and equipment listed by Ord 7and Ord 8, Supply Manuals, are stock guides to be used in establishing initial operating levels by units, organizations and installation. Normally, allowances listed therein will not be required in the exact quantities specified after true usage factors become known. Allowances authorized therein do not necessarily have to be on hand with the exception of units that have been alerted or are on movement (overseas) orders. For such units the allowances indicated are minimum allowances and will be so carried by the units."

Remember—if you're alerted for overseas, make sure you have at least what Ord 7 SNL's require. You can hang on to your increased stock of any items, if your records show you had to raise the Ord allowances based on usage experience.

After you arrive overseas you can again start adjusting stock levels according to usage.

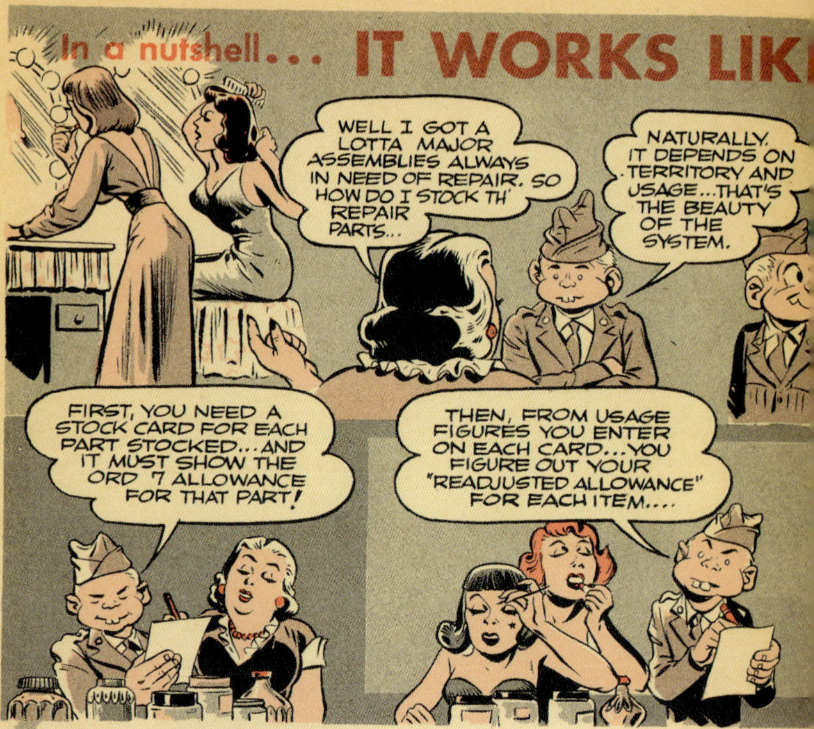
In a nutshell... IT WORKS LIK
WELL I GOT A LOTTA MAJOR ASSEMBLIES ALWAYS IN NEED OF REPAIR. SO HOW DO I STOCK TH' REPAIR PARTS...
NATURALLY, IT DEPENDS ON TERRITORY AND USAGE...THAT'S THE BEAUTY OF THE SYSTEM.
FIRST, YOU NEED A STOCK CARD FOR EACH PART STOCKED...AND IT MUST SHOW THE ORD 7 ALLOWANCE FOR THAT PART!
THEN, FROM USAGE FIGURES YOU ENTER ON EACH CARD...YOU FIGURE OUT YOUR "READJUSTED ALLOWANCE" FOR EACH ITEM....

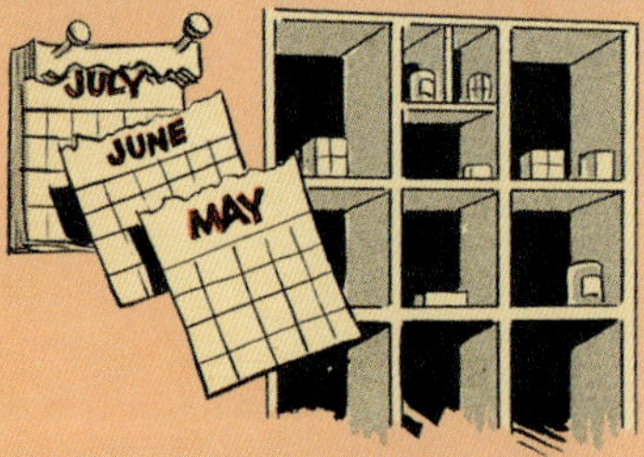
JULY
JUNE
MAY

READJUSTED ALLOWANCE...

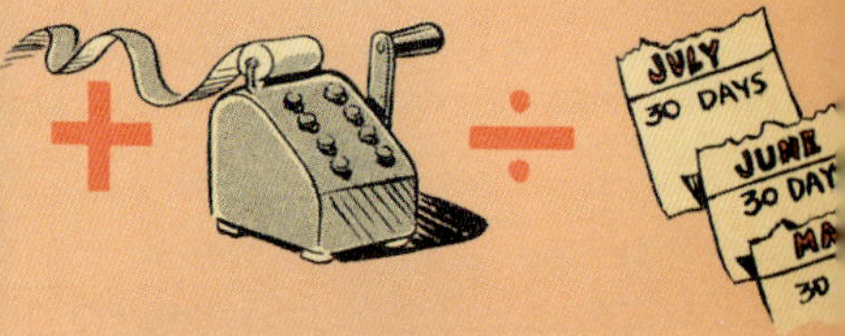
JULY
30 DAYS
JUNE
30 DAY

To get the Readjusted Allowance for any item for the first time, you **take an item's usage record for a specific period** (say, 45, 60 or 90 days).

Total up the issues and/or unfilled requests you had during that time. Then divide the answer by the number of 15-day periods included in the specific period of days that you are working with — since practically all units are authorized only a 15-day stock.

THIS
LOOKS LIKE A COMBAT ZONE TO ME!
BUT I DON'T SEE HOW...
MAYBE WE'D BETTER TELL YOU HOW WE DO IT IN THE ARMY... AND YOU CAN APPLY IT TO YOUR PROBLEM.

AND HOW TO FIGURE IT
=
READJUSTED ALLOWANCE
The figure you come up with is your new Readjusted Allowance.

HERE'S HOW WE WORK

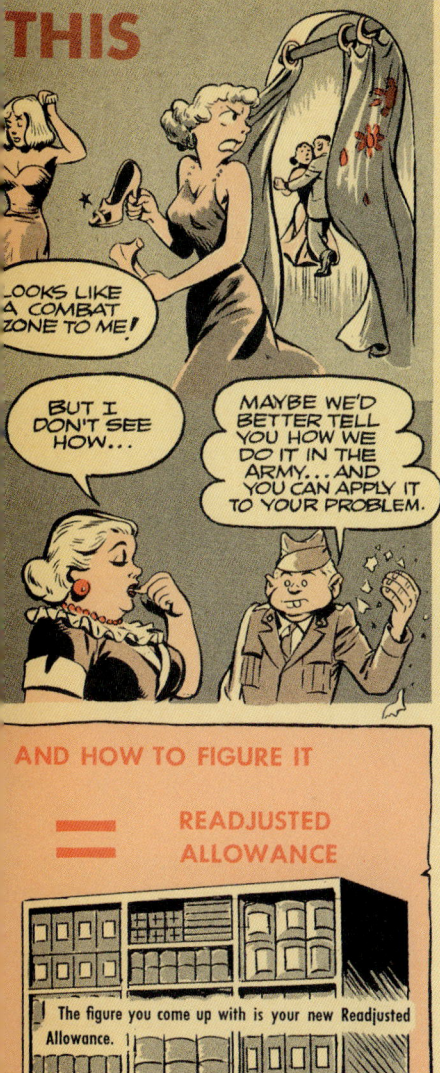

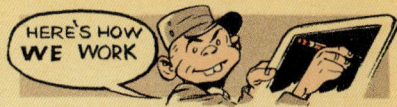

For example, if you total the issues and unfilled requests for 45 days you divide by 3 to get your new allowance. (The 3 represents three 15-day periods.)

MAY 1st TO JUNE 15th = 45 DAYS (OR 3 FIFTEEN DAY PERIODS)
XXXX← NEW ALLOWANCE
3) USAGE EXPERIENCE

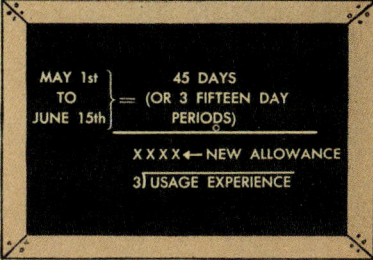

If you want to base your allowance on the usage figures of the past 60 days, then you divide by 4. And when you choose 90 days, you divide by 6.

MAY 1st TO JUNE 30th = 60 DAYS (OR 4 FIFTEEN DAY PERIODS)
XXXX← NEW ALLOWANCE
4) USAGE EXPERIENCE

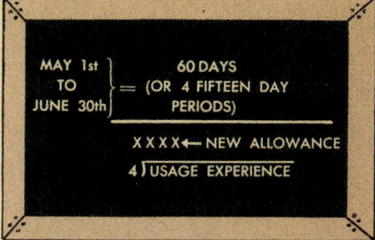

Then to keep your adjustment allowances running smooth, you readjust your allowances every time you requisition. If you are on a 15-day requisitioning schedule, you get your new readjusted figure by adding the issues and unfilled requests of the past 15 days to the last Readjusted Allowance figure, and dividing the total by 2.

That's it.

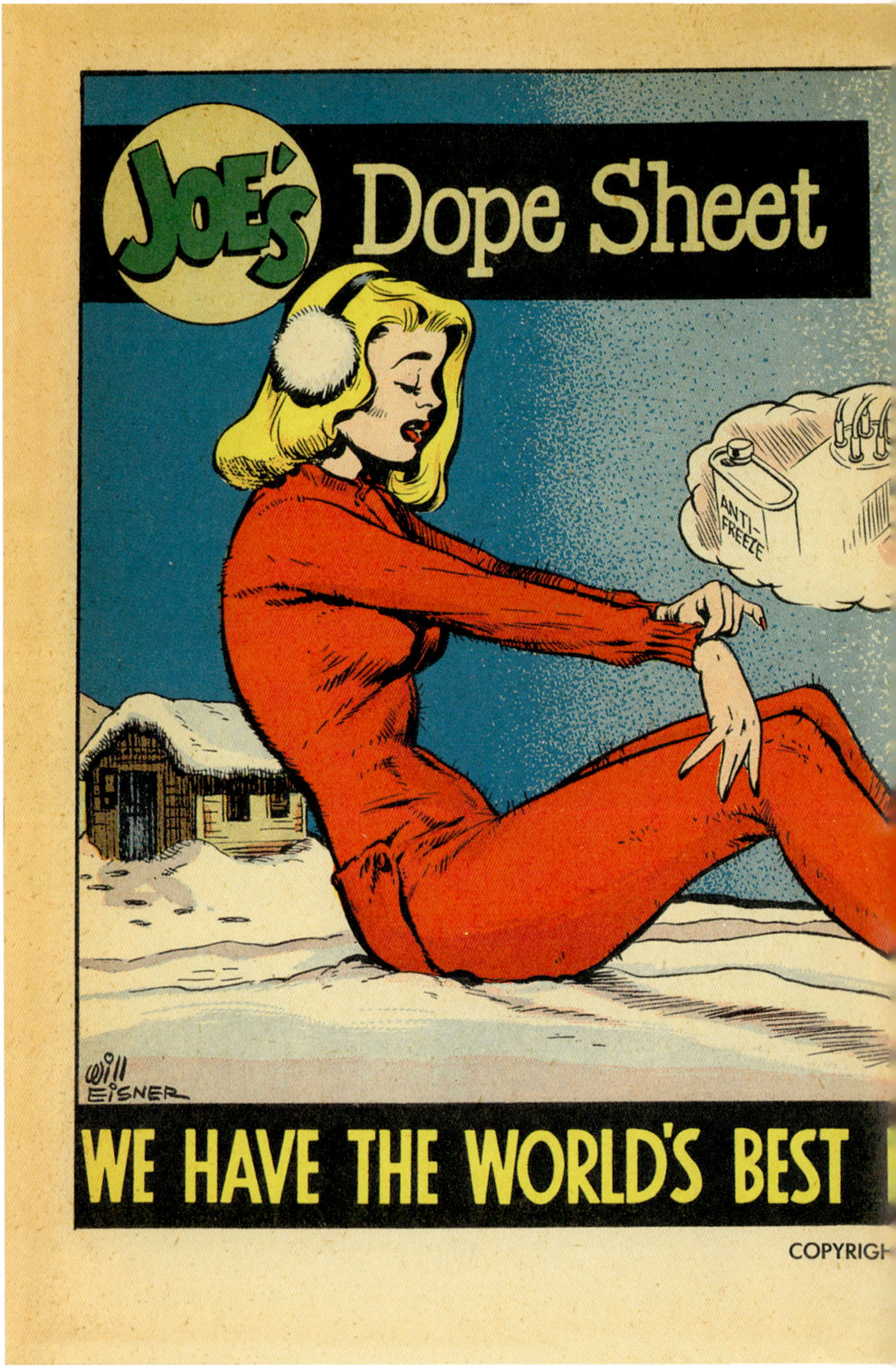
JOE'S Dope Sheet
ANTI-FREEZE
Will EISNER
WE HAVE THE WORLD'S BEST
COPYRIGH

no. 25, 1954

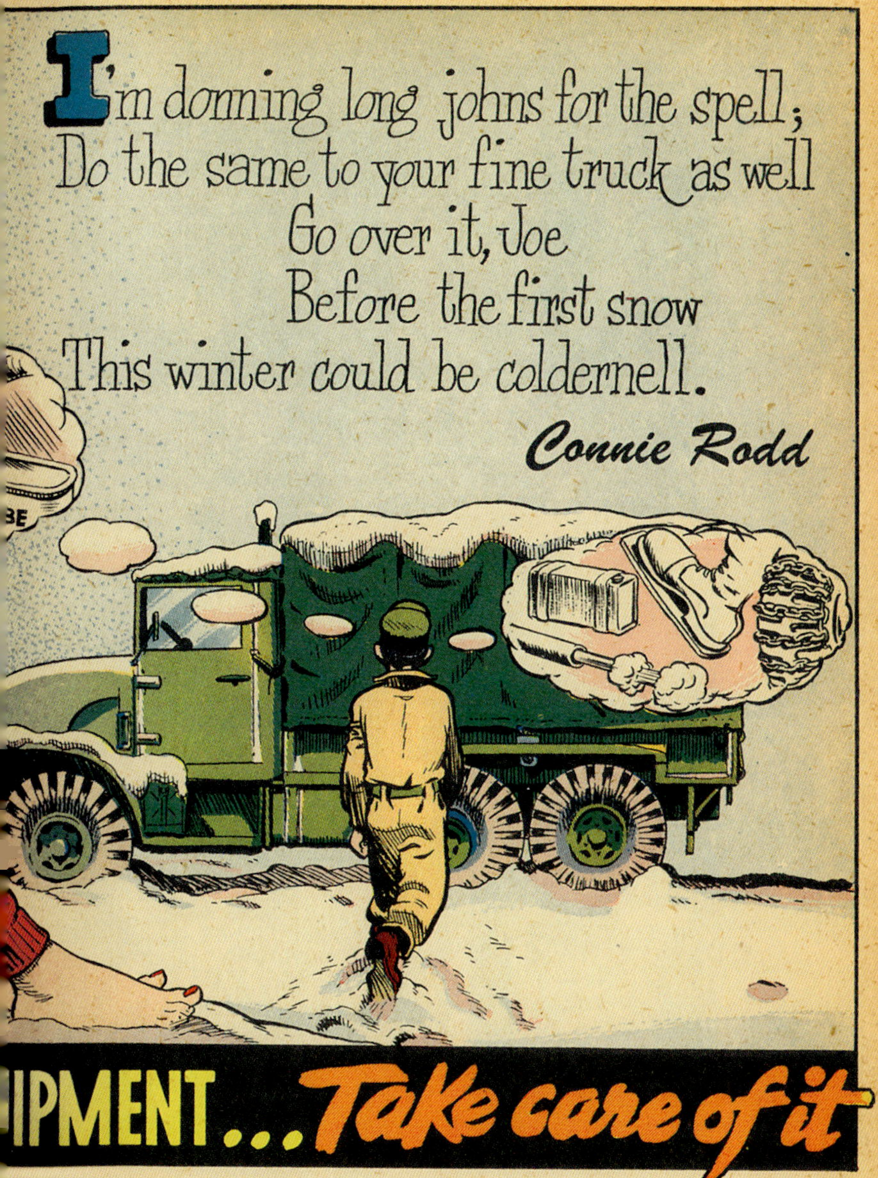
I'm donning long johns for the spell;
Do the same to your fine truck as well
Go over it, Joe
Before the first snow
This winter could be coldernell.
Connie Rodd
BE
IPMENT... Take care of it

WILL EISNER

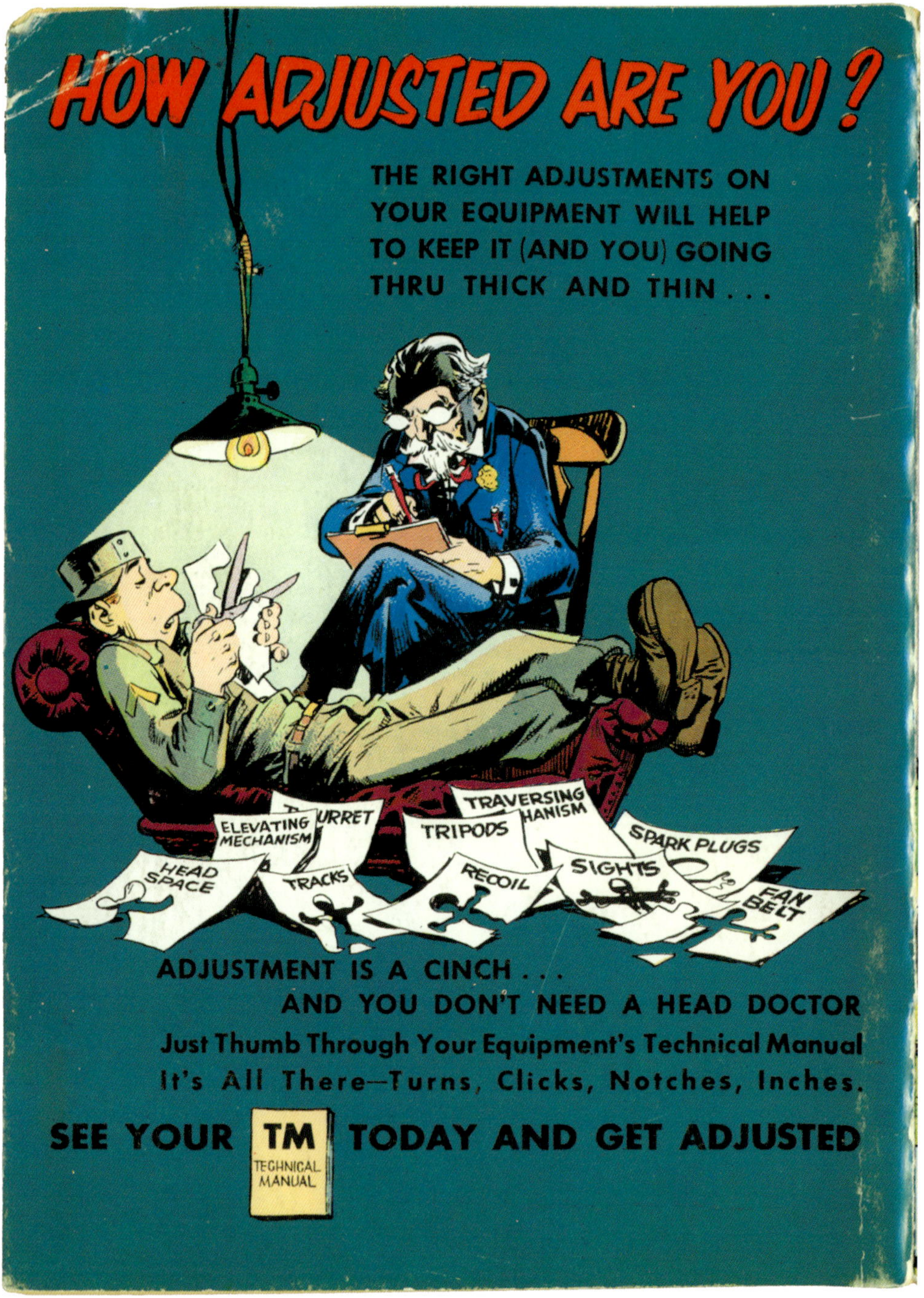
HOW ADJUSTED ARE YOU?
THE RIGHT ADJUSTMENTS ON YOUR EQUIPMENT WILL HELP TO KEEP IT (AND YOU) GOING THRU THICK AND THIN . . .
ELEVATING MECHANISM
URRET
TRAVERSING
HANISM
TRIPODS
SPARK PLUGS
HEAD SPACE
TRACKS
RECOIL
SIGHTS
FAN BELT
ADJUSTMENT IS A CINCH . . .
AND YOU DON'T NEED A HEAD DOCTOR
Just Thumb Through Your Equipment's Technical Manual
It's All There—Turns, Clicks, Notches, Inches.
SEE YOUR
TM
TECHNICAL MANUAL
TODAY AND GET ADJUSTED

no. 28, 1955

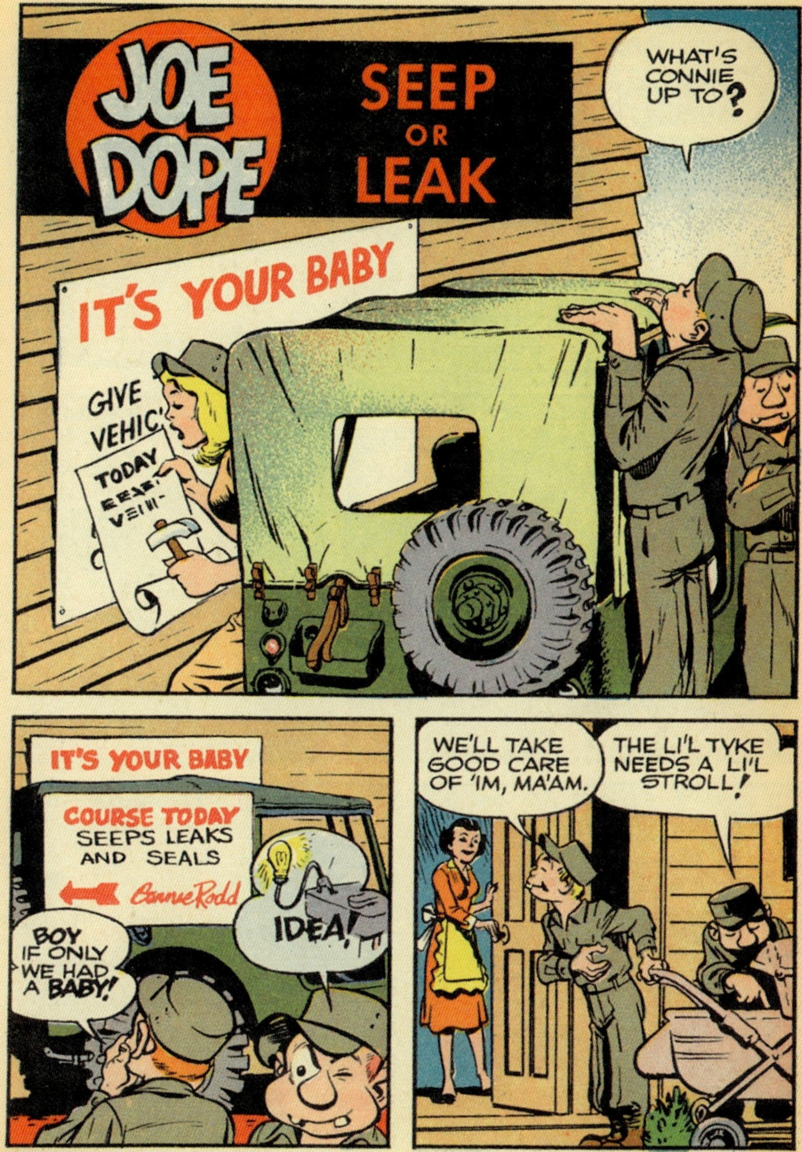
JOE DOPE
SEEP OR LEAK
WHAT'S CONNIE UP TO?
IT'S YOUR BABY
GIVE VEHIC
TODAY
IT'S YOUR BABY
COURSE TODAY SEEPS LEAKS AND SEALS
Connie Rodd
BOY IF ONLY WE HAD A BABY!
IDEA!
WE'LL TAKE GOOD CARE OF 'IM, MA'AM.
THE LI'L TYKE NEEDS A LI'L STROLL!

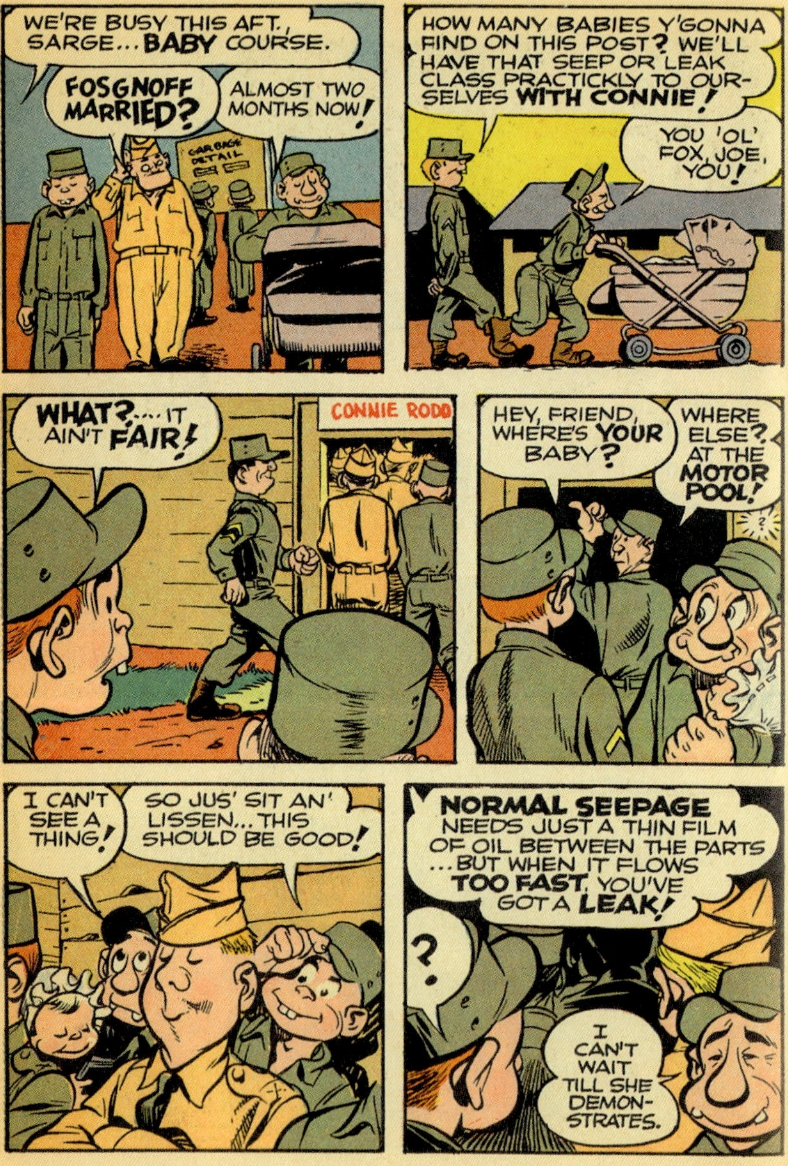
WE'RE BUSY THIS AFT., SARGE... BABY COURSE.
FOSGNOFF MARRIED?
ALMOST TWO MONTHS NOW!
GARBAGE DETAIL
HOW MANY BABIES Y'GONNA FIND ON THIS POST? WE'LL HAVE THAT SEEP OR LEAK CLASS PRACTICKLY TO OURSELVES WITH CONNIE!
YOU 'OL' FOX, JOE, YOU!
WHAT?... IT AIN'T FAIR!
CONNIE RODD
HEY, FRIEND, WHERE'S YOUR BABY?
WHERE ELSE? AT THE MOTOR POOL!
I CAN'T SEE A THING!
SO JUS' SIT AN' LISSEN... THIS SHOULD BE GOOD!
NORMAL SEEPAGE NEEDS JUST A THIN FILM OF OIL BETWEEN THE PARTS ...BUT WHEN IT FLOWS TOO FAST, YOU'VE GOT A LEAK!
?
I CAN'T WAIT TILL SHE DEMONSTRATES.

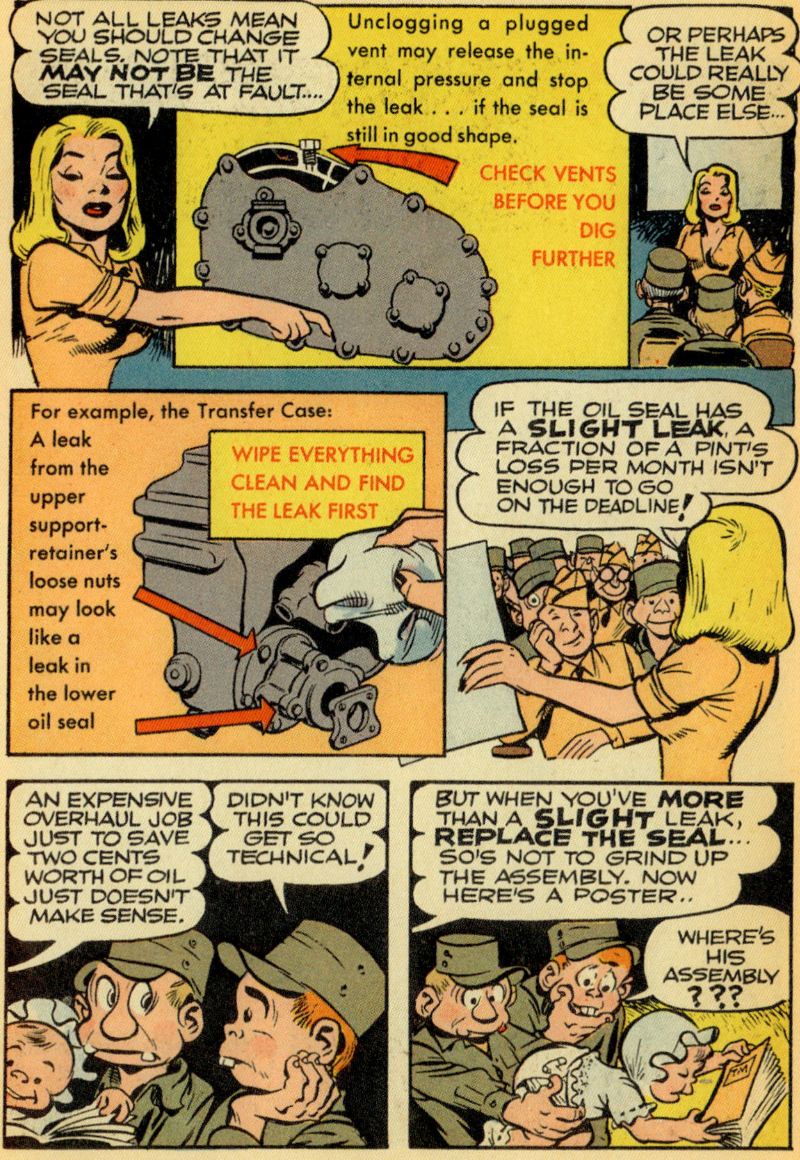
NOT ALL LEAKS MEAN YOU SHOULD CHANGE SEALS. NOTE THAT IT MAY NOT BE THE SEAL THAT'S AT FAULT....
Unclogging a plugged vent may release the internal pressure and stop the leak . . . if the seal is still in good shape.
CHECK VENTS BEFORE YOU DIG FURTHER
OR PERHAPS THE LEAK COULD REALLY BE SOME PLACE ELSE...
For example, the Transfer Case: A leak from the upper support-retainer's loose nuts may look like a leak in the lower oil seal
WIPE EVERYTHING CLEAN AND FIND THE LEAK FIRST
IF THE OIL SEAL HAS A SLIGHT LEAK, A FRACTION OF A PINT'S LOSS PER MONTH ISN'T ENOUGH TO GO ON THE DEADLINE!
AN EXPENSIVE OVERHAUL JOB JUST TO SAVE TWO CENTS WORTH OF OIL JUST DOESN'T MAKE SENSE.
DIDN'T KNOW THIS COULD GET SO TECHNICAL!
BUT WHEN YOU'VE MORE THAN A SLIGHT LEAK, REPLACE THE SEAL... SO'S NOT TO GRIND UP THE ASSEMBLY. NOW HERE'S A POSTER..
WHERE'S HIS ASSEMBLY ???

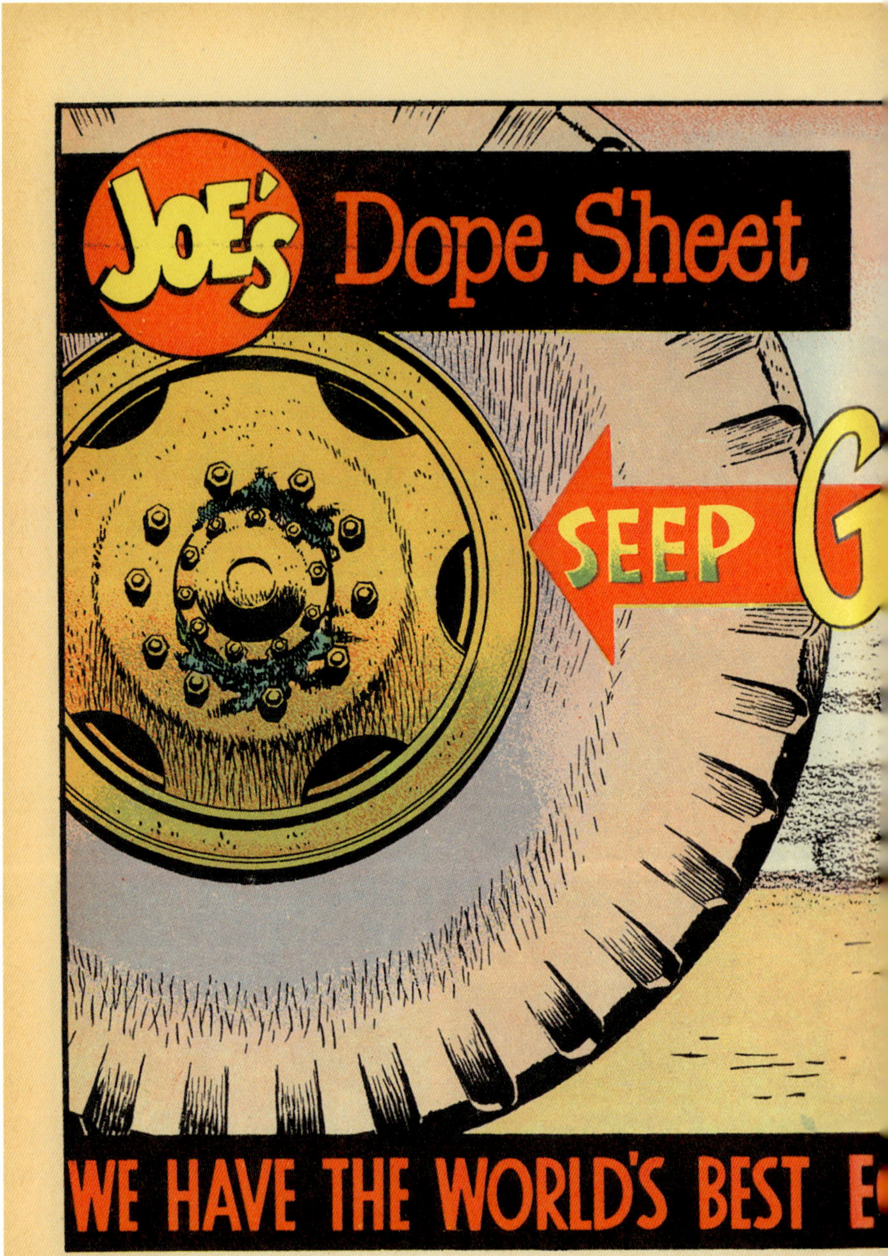
JOE'S Dope Sheet
SEEP
WE HAVE THE WORLD'S BEST

COPYRIGHT 1955

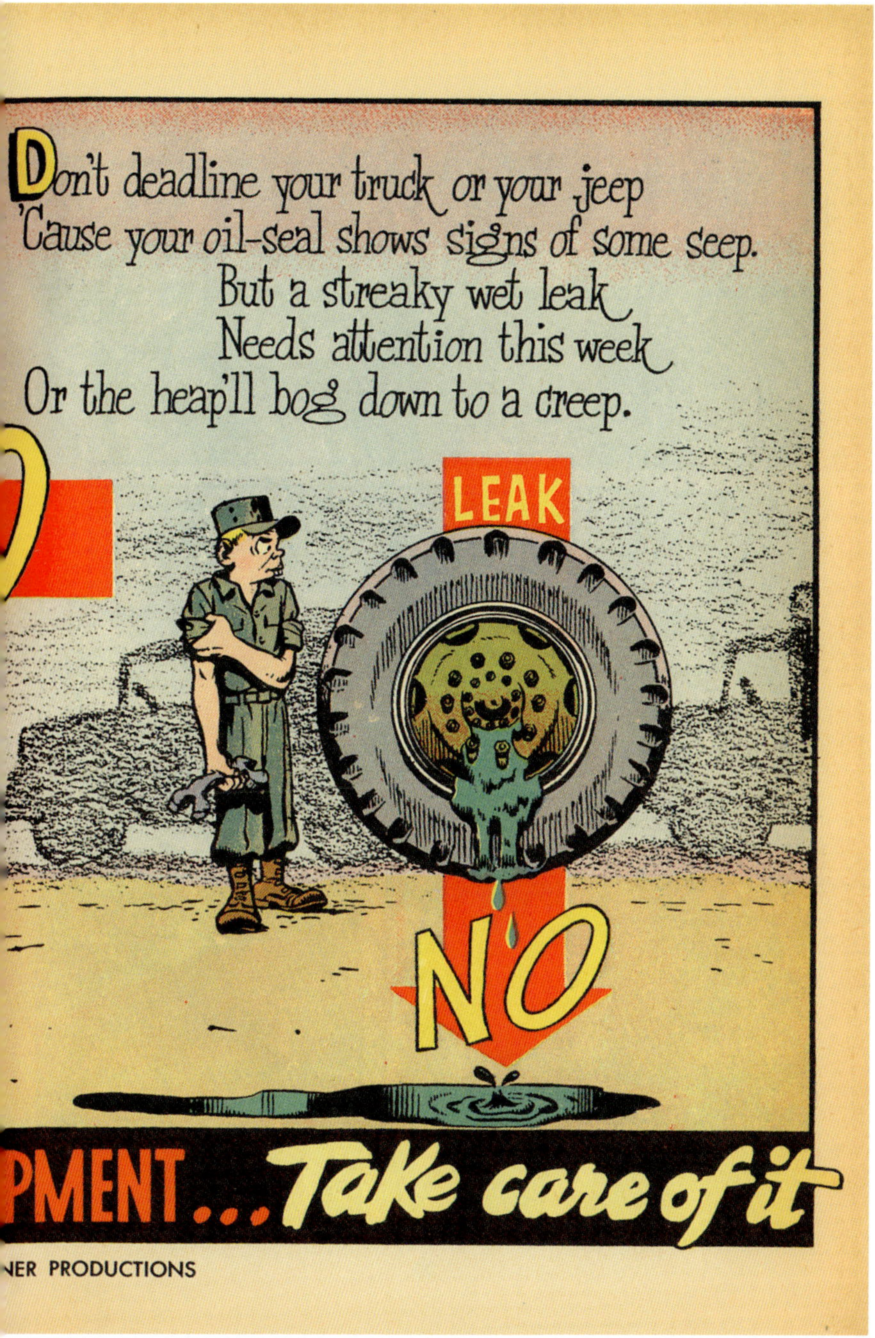

Don't deadline your truck or your jeep
'Cause your oil-seal shows signs of some seep.
But a streaky wet leak
Needs attention this week
Or the heap'll bog down to a creep.
LEAK
NO
PMENT... Take care of it
NER PRODUCTIONS

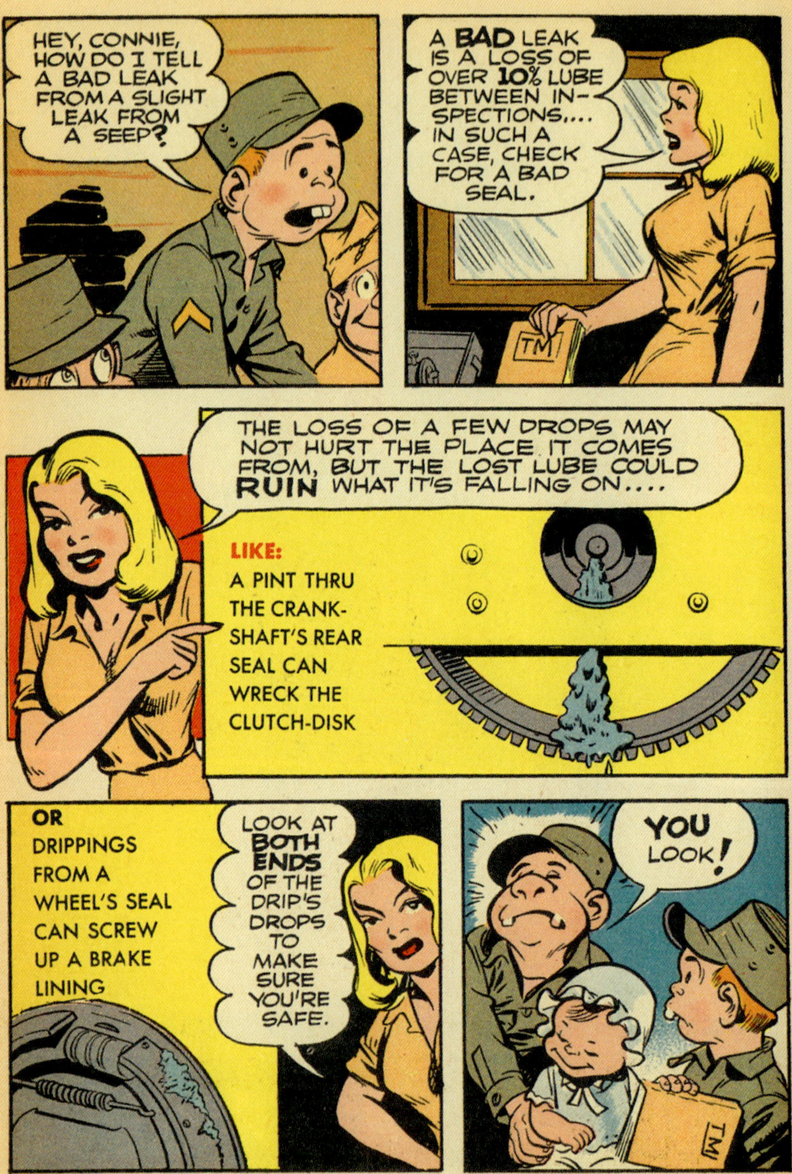
HEY, CONNIE, HOW DO I TELL A BAD LEAK FROM A SLIGHT LEAK FROM A SEEP?
A BAD LEAK IS A LOSS OF OVER 10% LUBE BETWEEN IN-SPECTIONS,... IN SUCH A CASE, CHECK FOR A BAD SEAL.
TM
THE LOSS OF A FEW DROPS MAY NOT HURT THE PLACE IT COMES FROM, BUT THE LOST LUBE COULD RUIN WHAT IT'S FALLING ON....
LIKE:
A PINT THRU THE CRANK-SHAFT'S REAR SEAL CAN WRECK THE CLUTCH-DISK
OR
DRIPPINGS FROM A WHEEL'S SEAL CAN SCREW UP A BRAKE LINING
LOOK AT BOTH ENDS OF THE DRIP'S DROPS TO MAKE SURE YOU'RE SAFE.
YOU LOOK!
TM

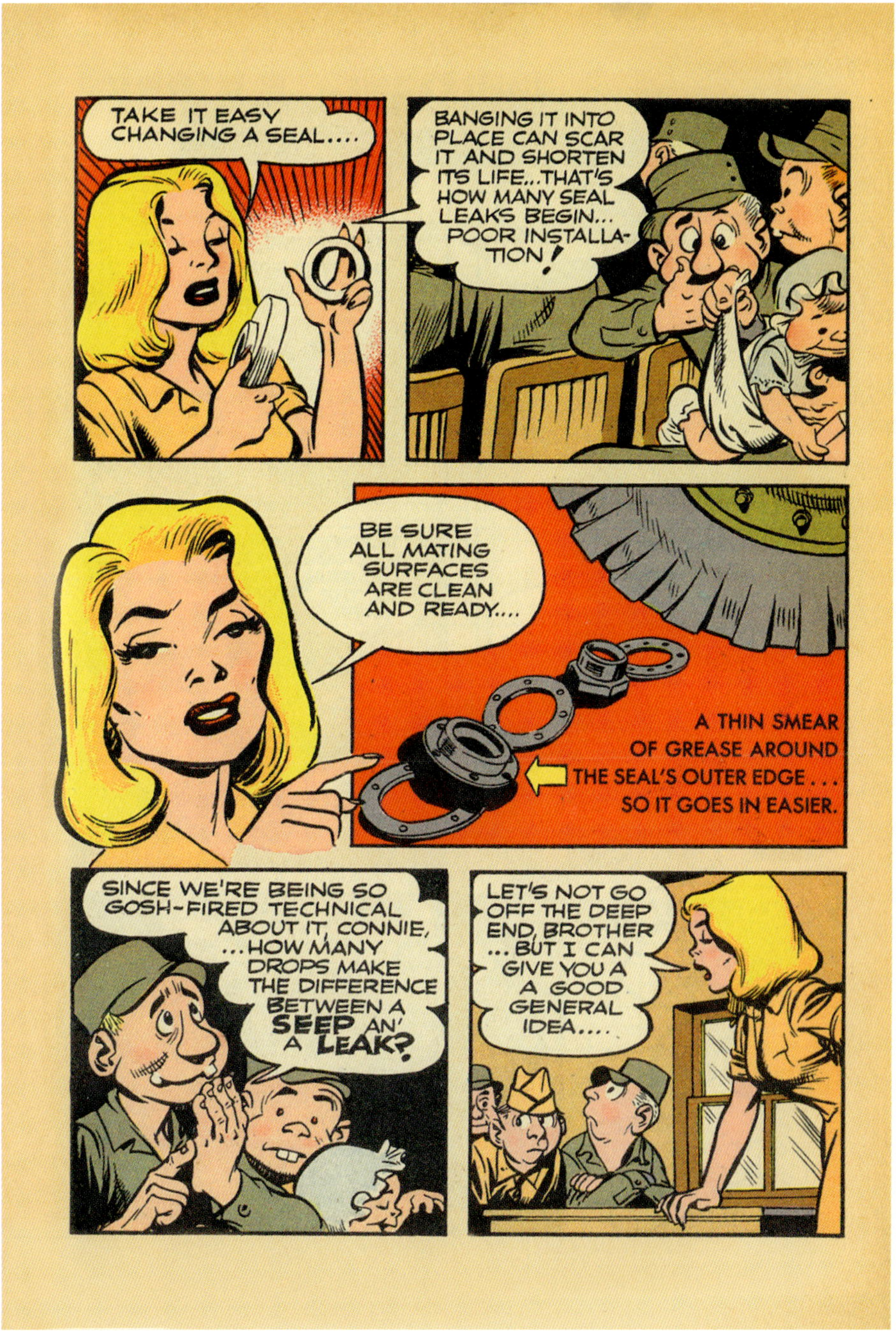
TAKE IT EASY CHANGING A SEAL....
BANGING IT INTO PLACE CAN SCAR IT AND SHORTEN ITS LIFE...THAT'S HOW MANY SEAL LEAKS BEGIN... POOR INSTALLA-TION!
BE SURE ALL MATING SURFACES ARE CLEAN AND READY....
A THIN SMEAR OF GREASE AROUND THE SEAL'S OUTER EDGE . . . SO IT GOES IN EASIER.
SINCE WE'RE BEING SO GOSH-FIRED TECHNICAL ABOUT IT, CONNIE, ...HOW MANY DROPS MAKE THE DIFFERENCE BETWEEN A SEEP AN' A LEAK?
LET'S NOT GO OFF THE DEEP END, BROTHER ...BUT I CAN GIVE YOU A A GOOD GENERAL IDEA....

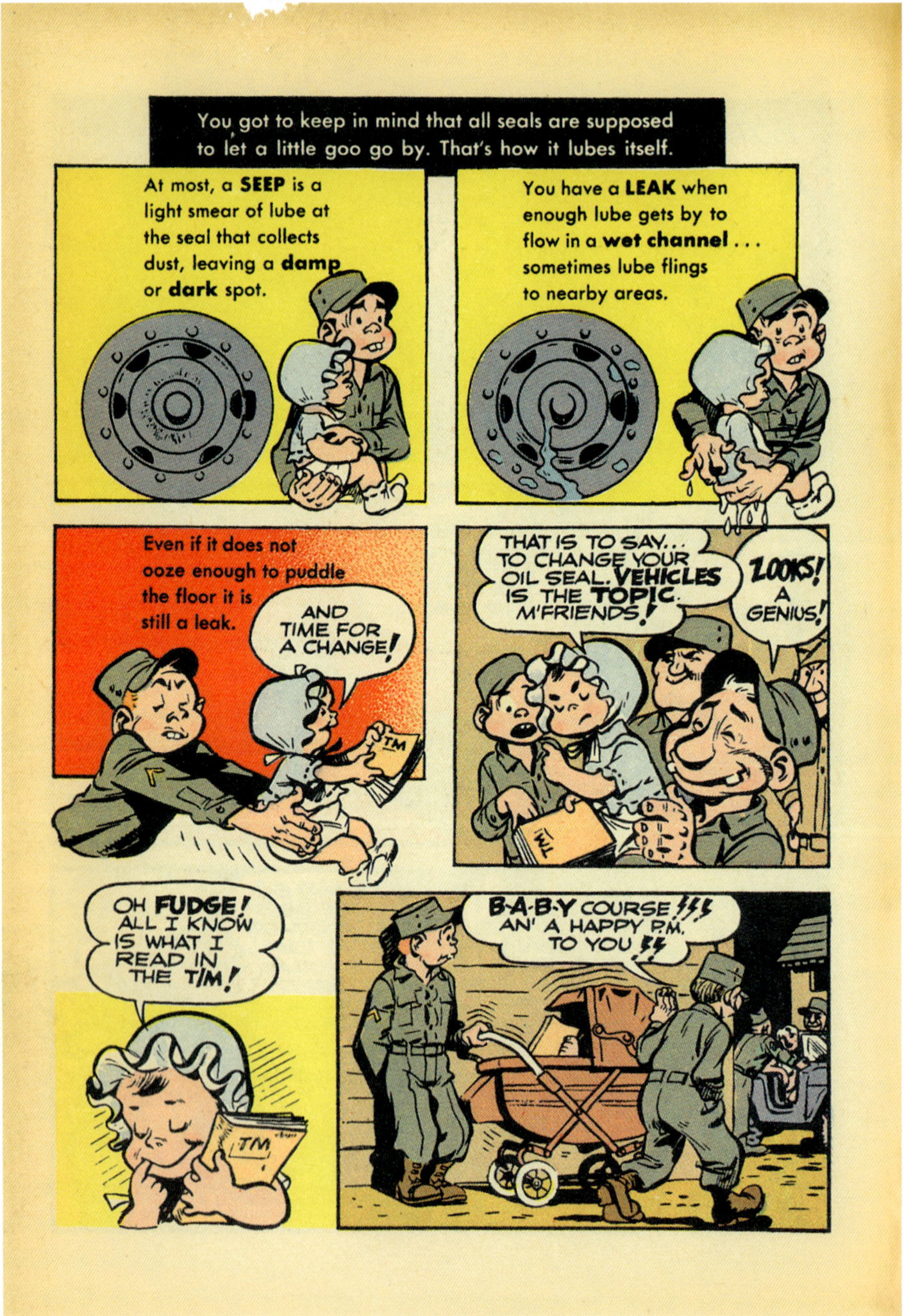
You got to keep in mind that all seals are supposed to let a little goo go by. That's how it lubes itself.
At most, a **SEEP** is a light smear of lube at the seal that collects dust, leaving a **damp** or **dark** spot.
You have a **LEAK** when enough lube gets by to flow in a **wet channel** . . . sometimes lube flings to nearby areas.
Even if it does not ooze enough to puddle the floor it is still a leak.
AND TIME FOR A CHANGE!
TM
THAT IS TO SAY... TO CHANGE YOUR OIL SEAL. VEHICLES IS THE TOPIC. M'FRIENDS!
LOOKS! A GENIUS!
TM
OH FUDGE! ALL I KNOW IS WHAT I READ IN THE T/M!
TM
B-A-B-Y COURSE!!! AN' A HAPPY P.M. TO YOU!!

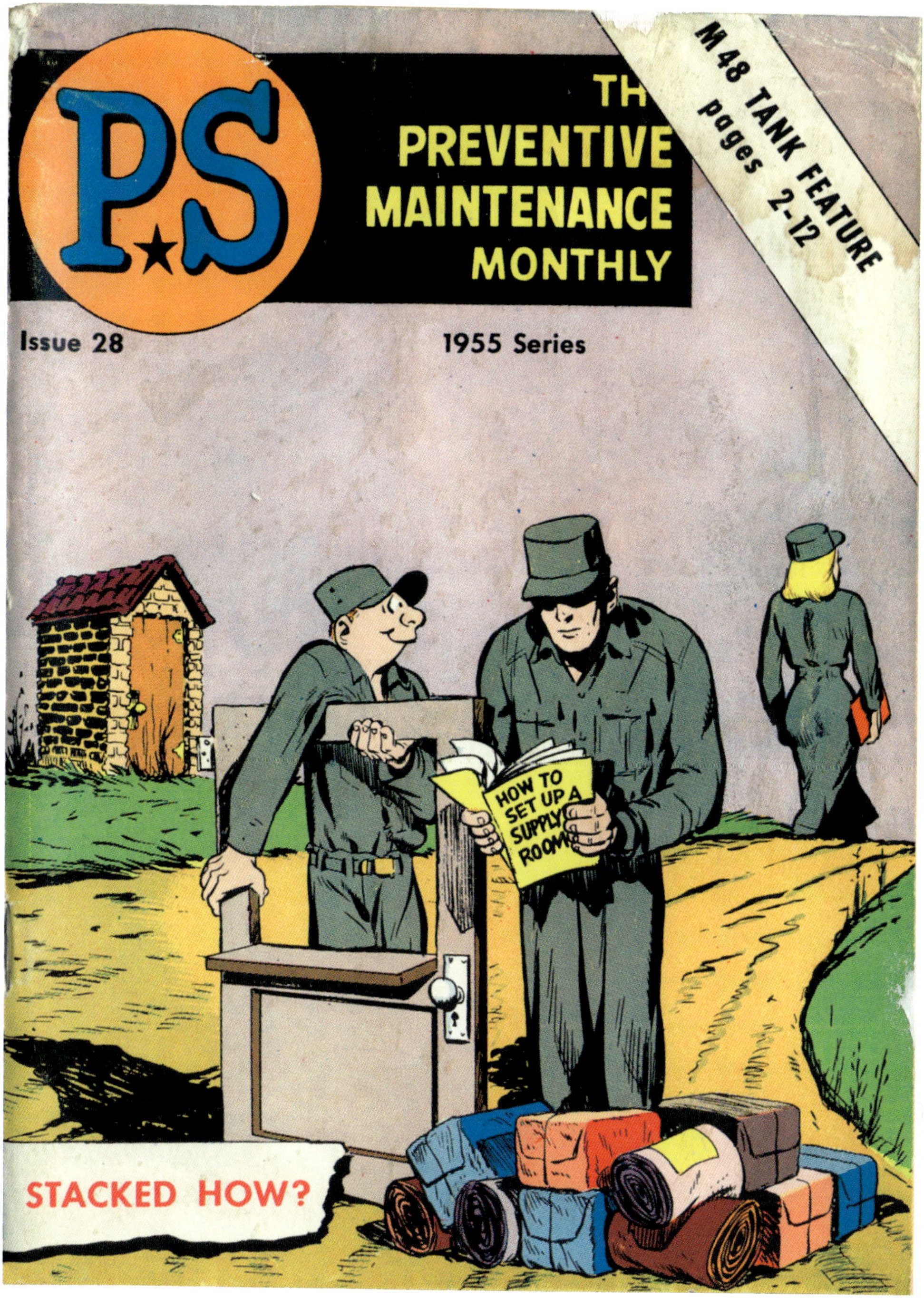
P.S
THE PREVENTIVE MAINTENANCE MONTHLY
M48 TANK FEATURE pages 2-12
Issue 28
1955 Series
HOW TO SET UP A SUPPLY ROOM
STACKED HOW?

no. 28, 1955

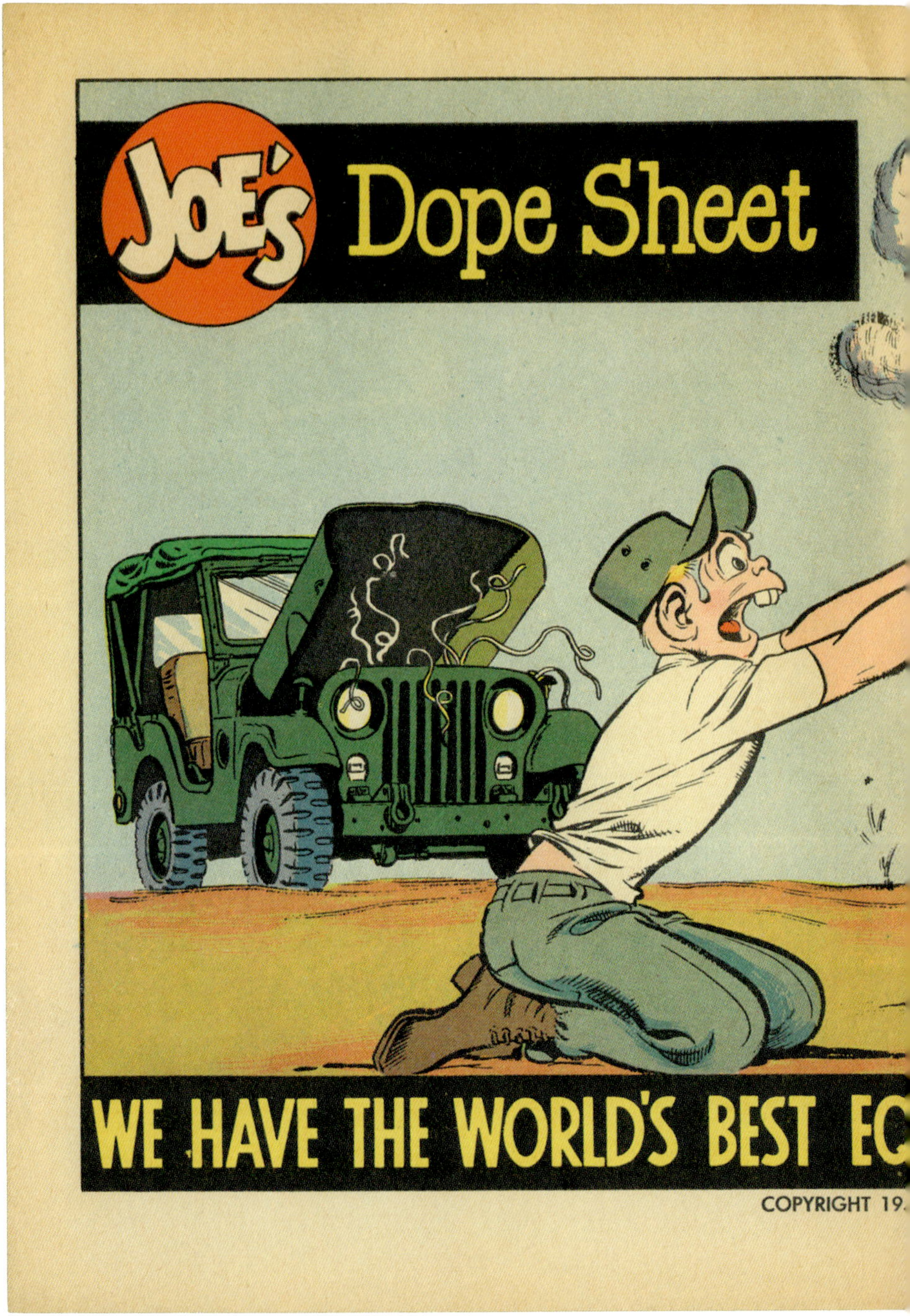
JOE'S
Dope Sheet
WE HAVE THE WORLD'S BEST EQ
COPYRIGHT 19.

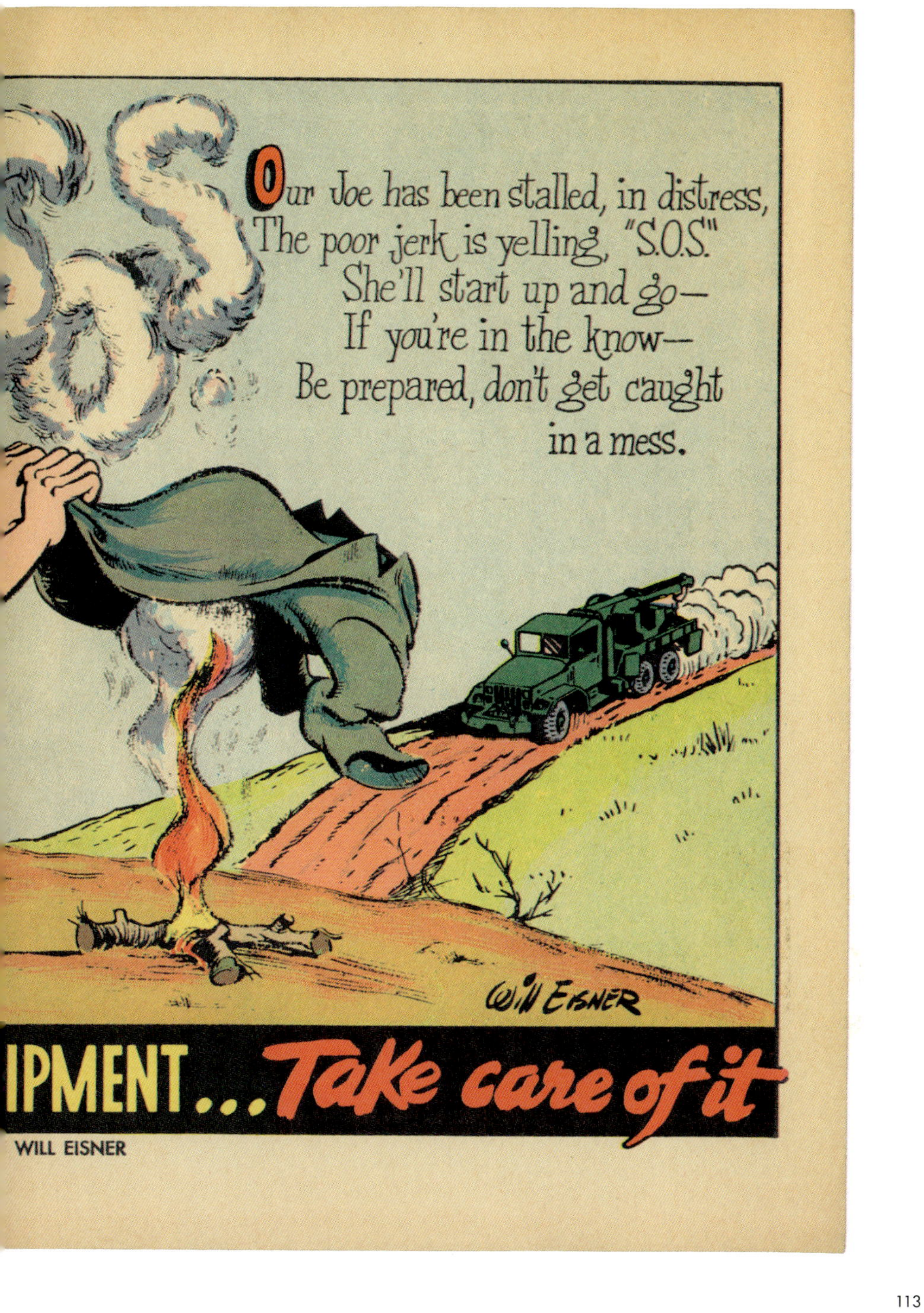
Our Joe has been stalled, in distress,
The poor jerk is yelling, "S.O.S."
She'll start up and go—
If you're in the know—
Be prepared, don't get caught in a mess.
Will Eisner
IPMENT... Take care of it

WILL EISNER

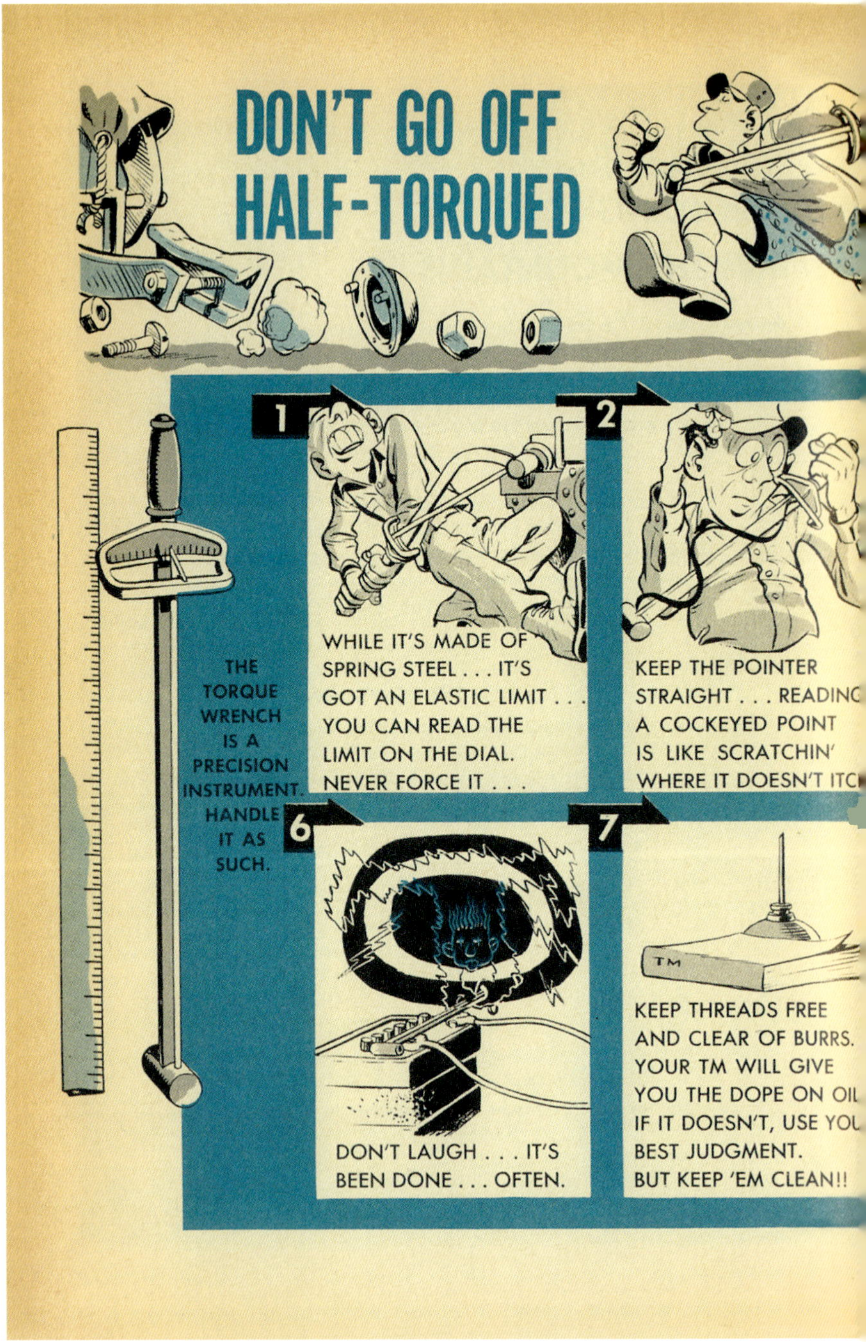
DON'T GO OFF HALF-TORQUED
THE TORQUE WRENCH IS A PRECISION INSTRUMENT. HANDLE IT AS SUCH.
1
WHILE IT'S MADE OF SPRING STEEL . . . IT'S GOT AN ELASTIC LIMIT . . . YOU CAN READ THE LIMIT ON THE DIAL. NEVER FORCE IT . . .
2
KEEP THE POINTER STRAIGHT . . . READIN A COCKEYED POINT IS LIKE SCRATCHIN' WHERE IT DOESN'T ITC
6
DON'T LAUGH . . . IT'S BEEN DONE . . . OFTEN.
7
TM
KEEP THREADS FREE AND CLEAR OF BURRS. YOUR TM WILL GIVE YOU THE DOPE ON OI IF IT DOESN'T, USE YOU BEST JUDGMENT. BUT KEEP 'EM CLEAN!!

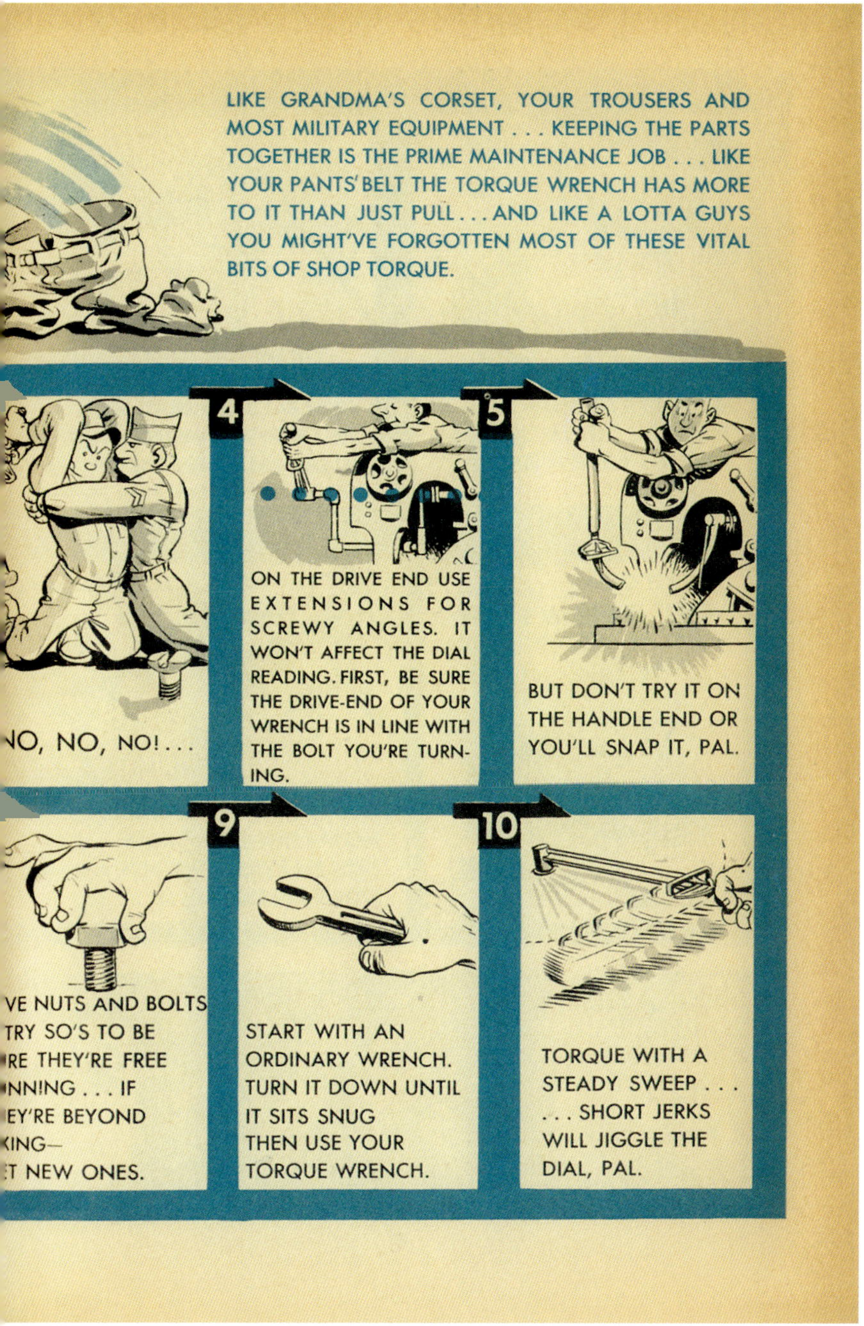
LIKE GRANDMA'S CORSET, YOUR TROUSERS AND MOST MILITARY EQUIPMENT . . . KEEPING THE PARTS TOGETHER IS THE PRIME MAINTENANCE JOB . . . LIKE YOUR PANTS' BELT THE TORQUE WRENCH HAS MORE TO IT THAN JUST PULL . . . AND LIKE A LOTTA GUYS YOU MIGHT'VE FORGOTTEN MOST OF THESE VITAL BITS OF SHOP TORQUE.
O, NO, NO! . . .
4
ON THE DRIVE END USE EXTENSIONS FOR SCREWY ANGLES. IT WON'T AFFECT THE DIAL READING. FIRST, BE SURE THE DRIVE-END OF YOUR WRENCH IS IN LINE WITH THE BOLT YOU'RE TURNING.
5
BUT DON'T TRY IT ON THE HANDLE END OR YOU'LL SNAP IT, PAL.
VE NUTS AND BOLTS
TRY SO'S TO BE
RE THEY'RE FREE
NNING . . . IF
EY'RE BEYOND
ING—
T NEW ONES.
9
START WITH AN ORDINARY WRENCH. TURN IT DOWN UNTIL IT SITS SNUG THEN USE YOUR TORQUE WRENCH.
10
TORQUE WITH A STEADY SWEEP . . . . . . SHORT JERKS WILL JIGGLE THE DIAL, PAL.

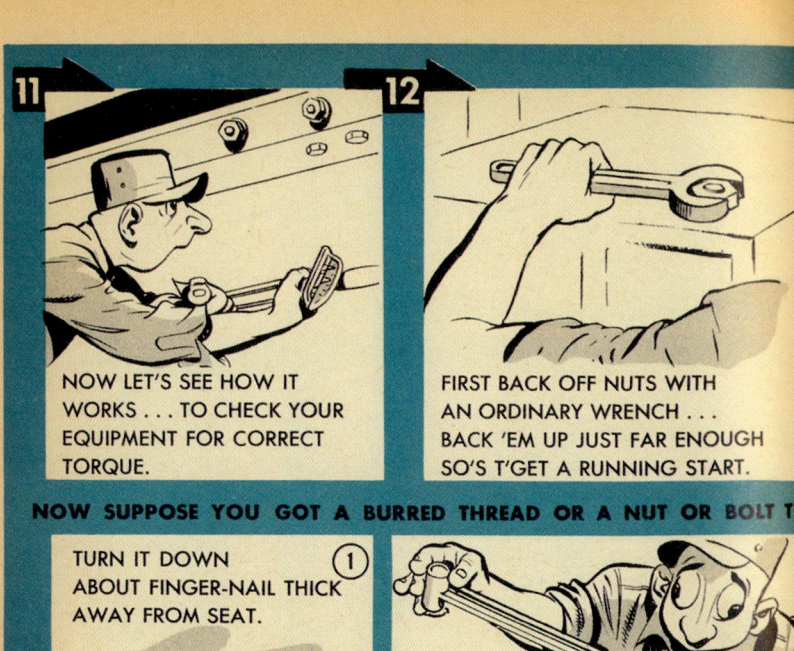

NOW LET'S SEE HOW IT WORKS . . . TO CHECK YOUR EQUIPMENT FOR CORRECT TORQUE.

FIRST BACK OFF NUTS WITH AN ORDINARY WRENCH . . . BACK 'EM UP JUST FAR ENOUGH SO'S T'GET A RUNNING START.

NOW SUPPOSE YOU GOT A BURRED THREAD OR A NUT OR BOLT T

TURN IT DOWN ABOUT FINGER-NAIL THICK AWAY FROM SEAT. ①

NOW APPLY THE TORQUE KEEP AN EYE ON THE NUT AND THE OTHER ON THE DIAL . . .

SPECIAL WORD ABOUT CYLINDER HEADS

BE SURE YOU FOLLOW THE MANUAL FOR SEQUENCE ON THIS OR YOU'LL CRACK THE HEAD.

FIRST TIME 'ROU

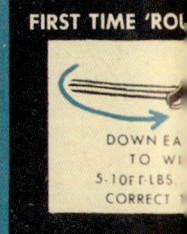

DOWN EA
TO WI
5-10 FT-LBS.
CORRECT 1

OW TIGHTEN . . . WITH A
CE EVEN SWEEPING
ROKE . . . LIKE CLOSING A DOOR.
14
NOW ALL YOU NEED IS PRACTICE... REMEMBER THIS IS A FINE INSTRUMENT!
CLAP
CLAP
CLAP
CLAP
TRA TIGHT FIT (WHICH YOU GOTTA USE FOR SOME GOOD REASON).
WHEN THE NUT BEGINS TO TURN . . . READ THE DIAL.
FT-LBS.
IE PUSH
RN THE
10 FT - LBS.
4
10 FT LBS
MAKE A NOTE
(MENTAL IF YOU GOT ROOM UP THERE).
NOW LET'S SAY THE CORRECT NORMAL TORQUE IS 100 FT-LBS.
5
NORMAL 100
EXTRA 10
110
E AROUND
OR THIRD
BRING 'EM
FF
EVERY ENGINE HEAD SEQUENCE IS DIFFERENT . . .
SO KEEP A TM HANDY. FOR EXAMPLE:
M 35
M 38A1

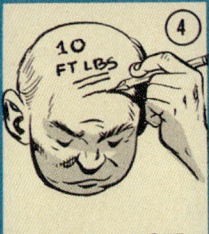

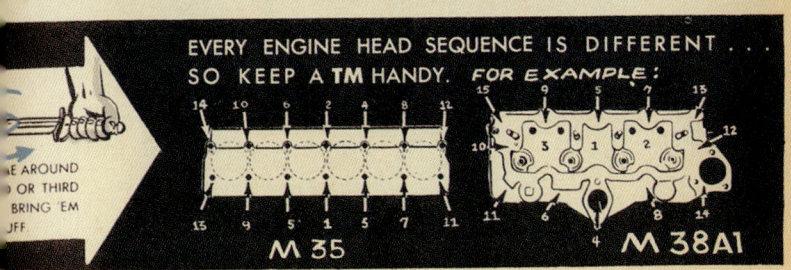

M1 Riflemen... THIS LITTLE GAME'LL MAK

CHECK YOUR M1 RIFLE FOR THE

Here's a little game you can play with your weapon that'll help make you a ready-teddy when the chips are down.

Suppose you've done everything to your weapon that you're supposed to do in the way of cleaning. There's no dirt, foreign matter or just plain muck left on it and you've got a right neat piece. Now give 'er the old eagle eye to see if she's going to come across the next time you give 'er a little squeeze. If she shows any of the following ailments, better turn 'er in for repair. Your armorer can repair some of the damage, and he'll send her on to Ordnance for the full treatment.

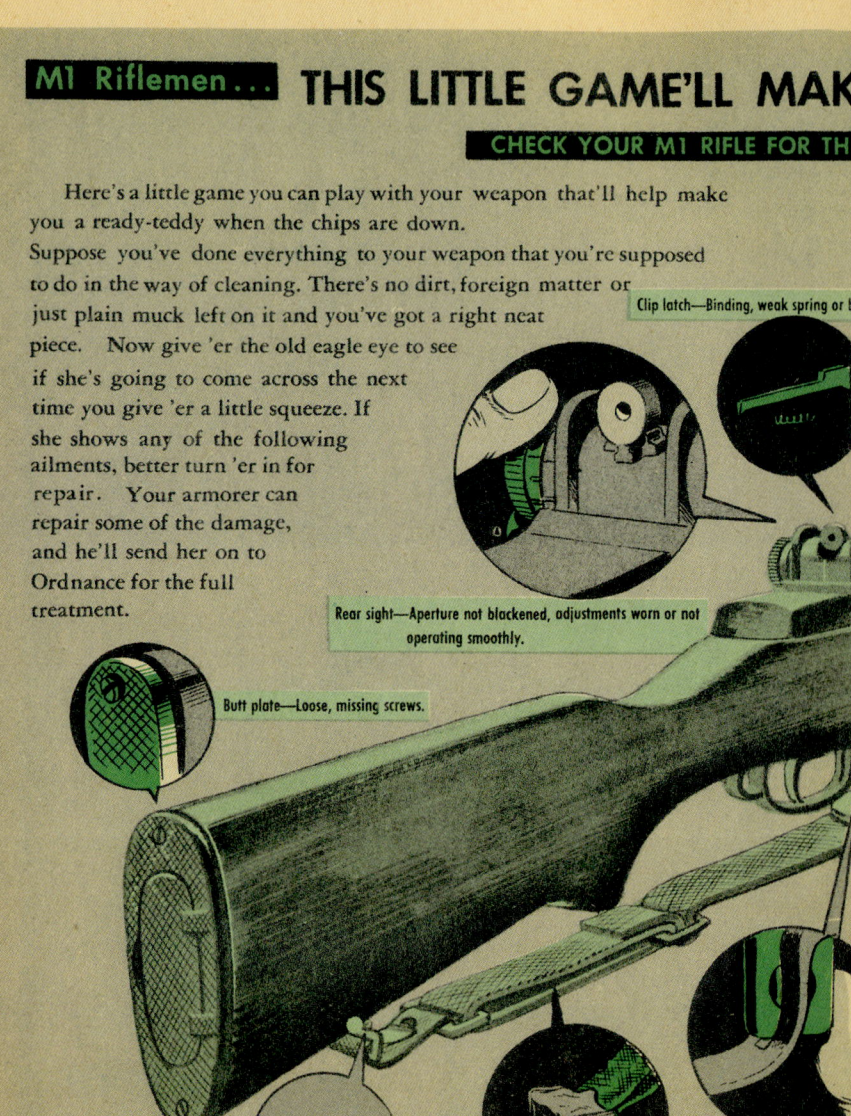

Clip latch—Binding, weak spring or br[oken]

Rear sight—Aperture not blackened, adjustments worn or not operating smoothly.

Butt plate—Loose, missing screws.

Swivels—Loose in stock.

Sling—Frayed or broken webbin[g], weak or faulty buckle

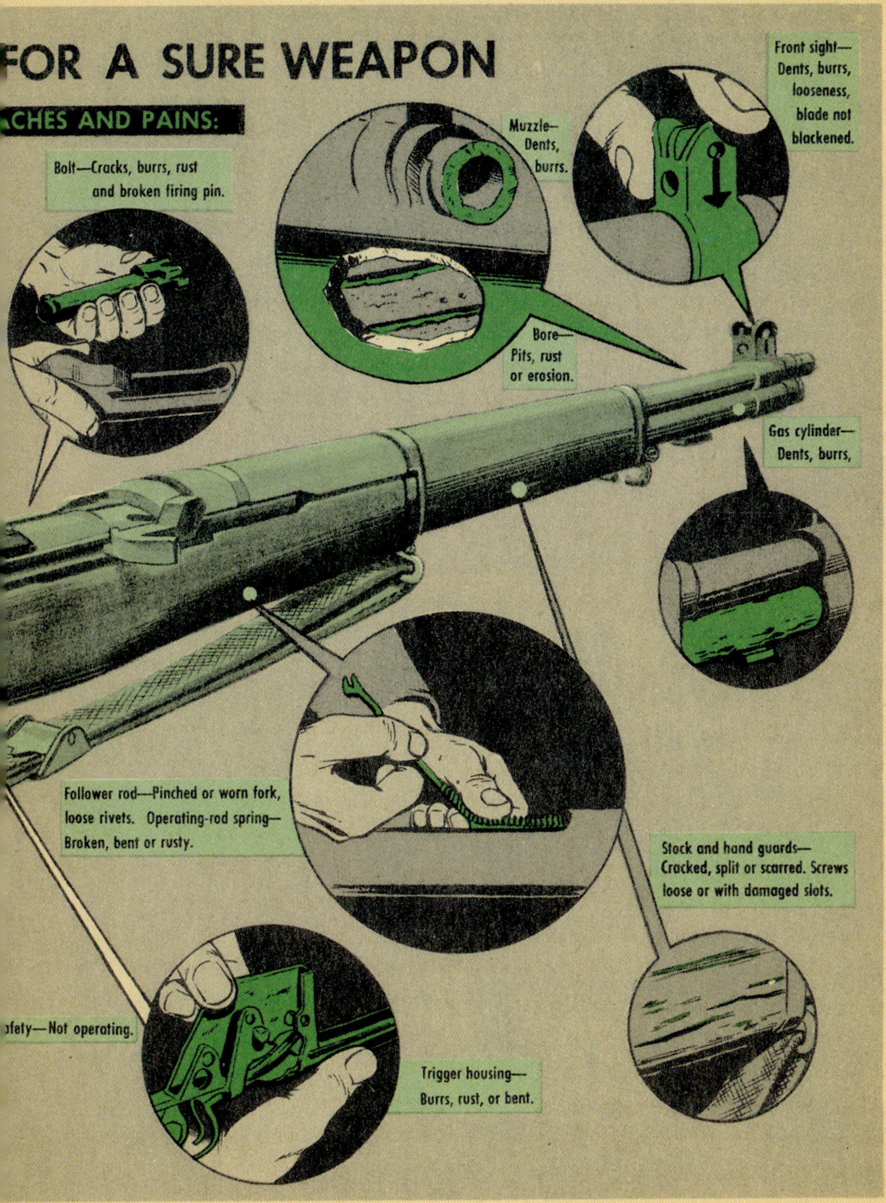
FOR A SURE WEAPON
CHES AND PAINS:
Bolt—Cracks, burrs, rust and broken firing pin.
Muzzle—Dents, burrs.
Front sight—Dents, burrs, looseness, blade not blackened.
Bore—Pits, rust or erosion.
Gas cylinder—Dents, burrs,
Follower rod—Pinched or worn fork, loose rivets. Operating-rod spring—Broken, bent or rusty.
Stock and hand guards—Cracked, split or scarred. Screws loose or with damaged slots.
afety—Not operating.
Trigger housing—Burrs, rust, or bent.

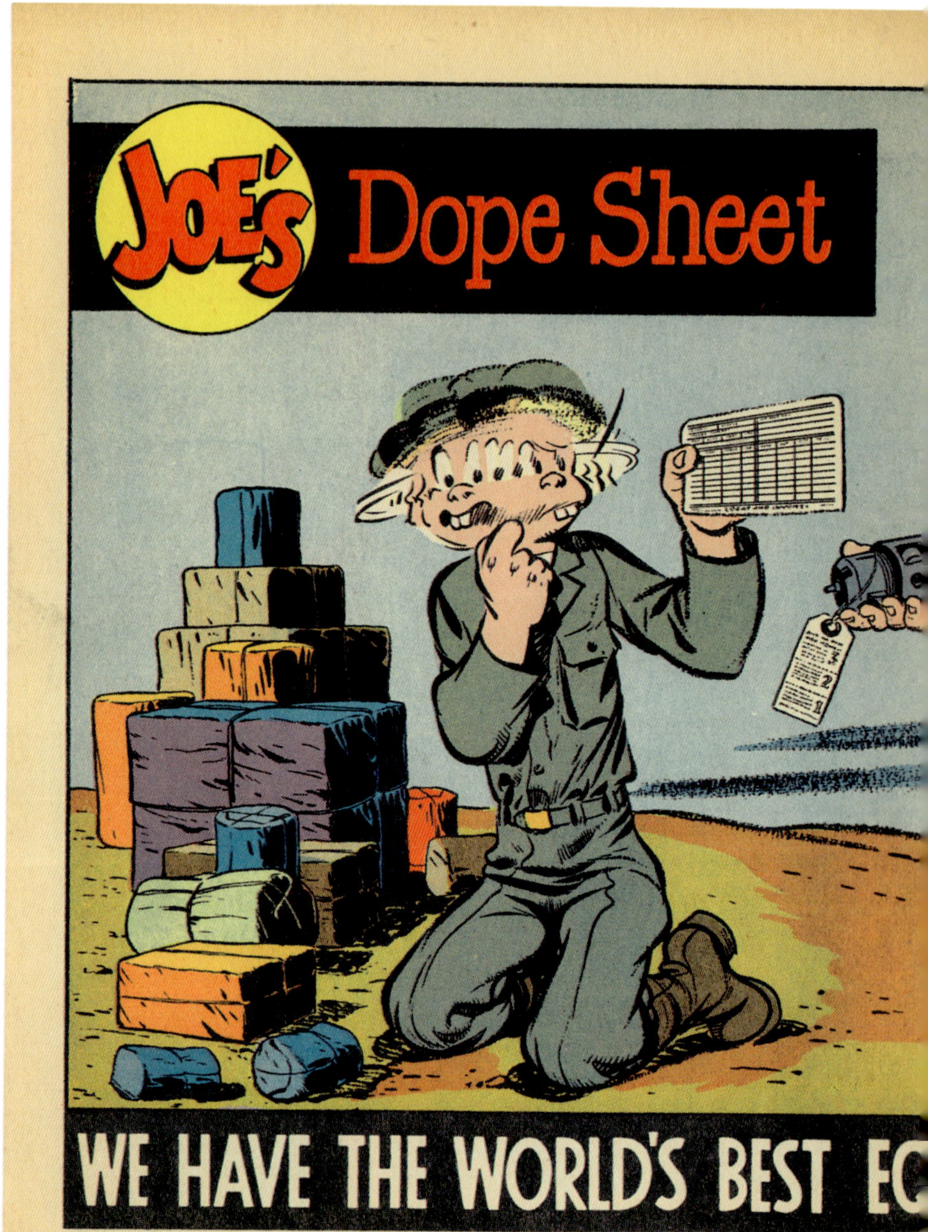
JOE'S Dope Sheet
WE HAVE THE WORLD'S BEST EQ

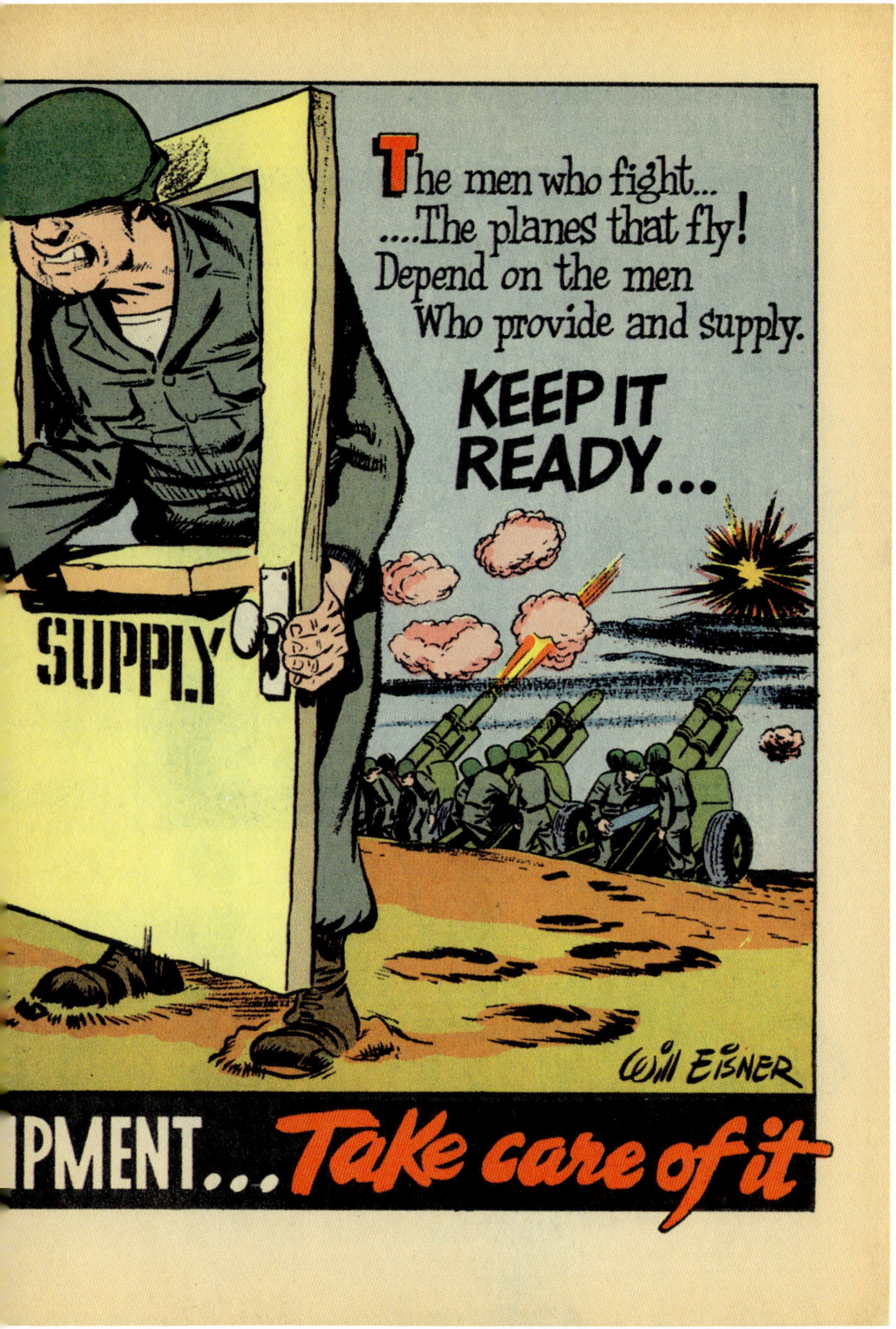
The men who fight...
....The planes that fly!
Depend on the men
Who provide and supply.
KEEP IT READY...
SUPPLY
Will Eisner
IPMENT... Take care of it

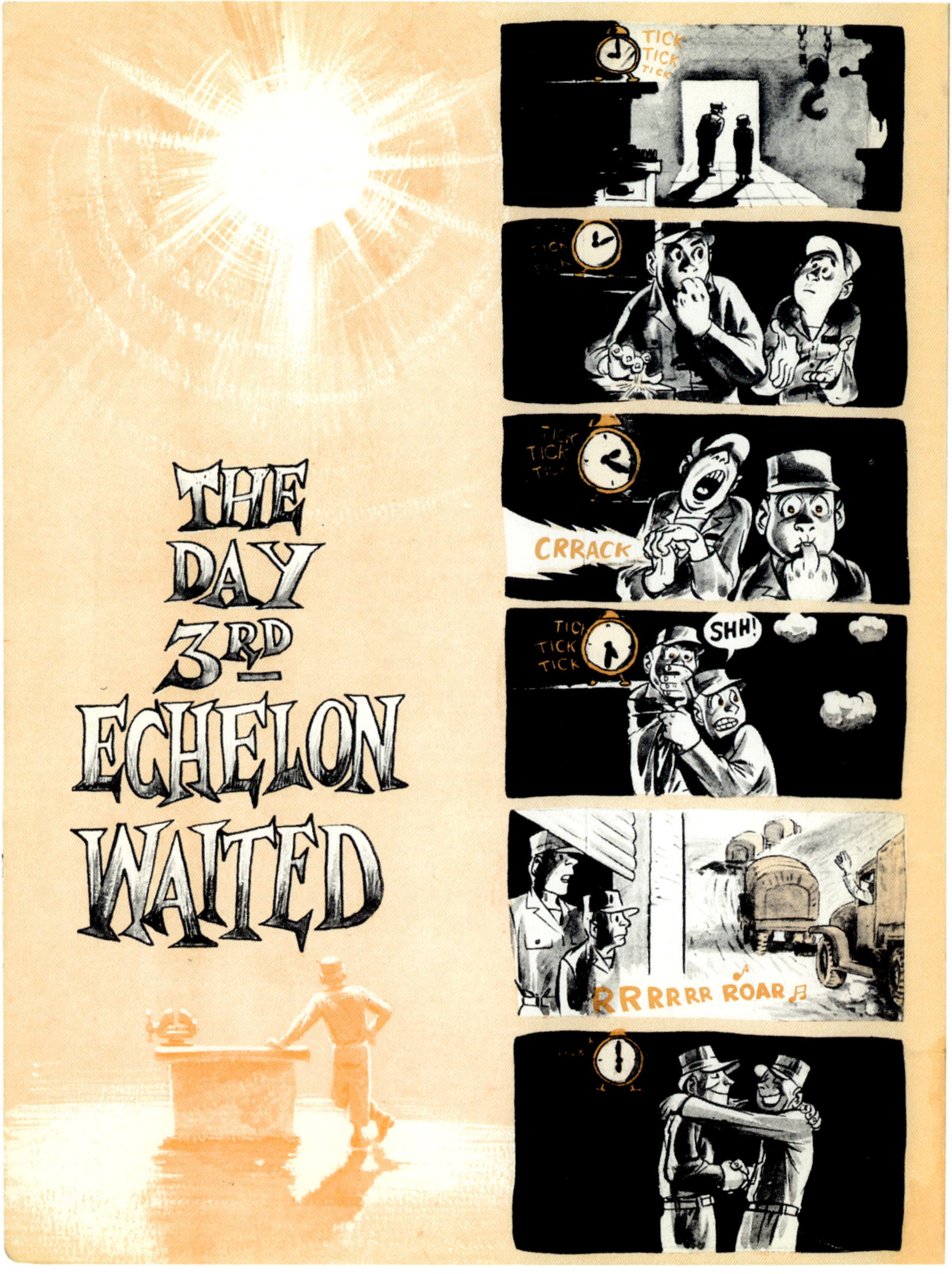
THE DAY 3RD ECHELON WAITED
TICK TICK TICK
TICK TICK
TICK TICK TICK
CRRACK
TICK TICK TICK
SHH!
RRRRRR ROAR

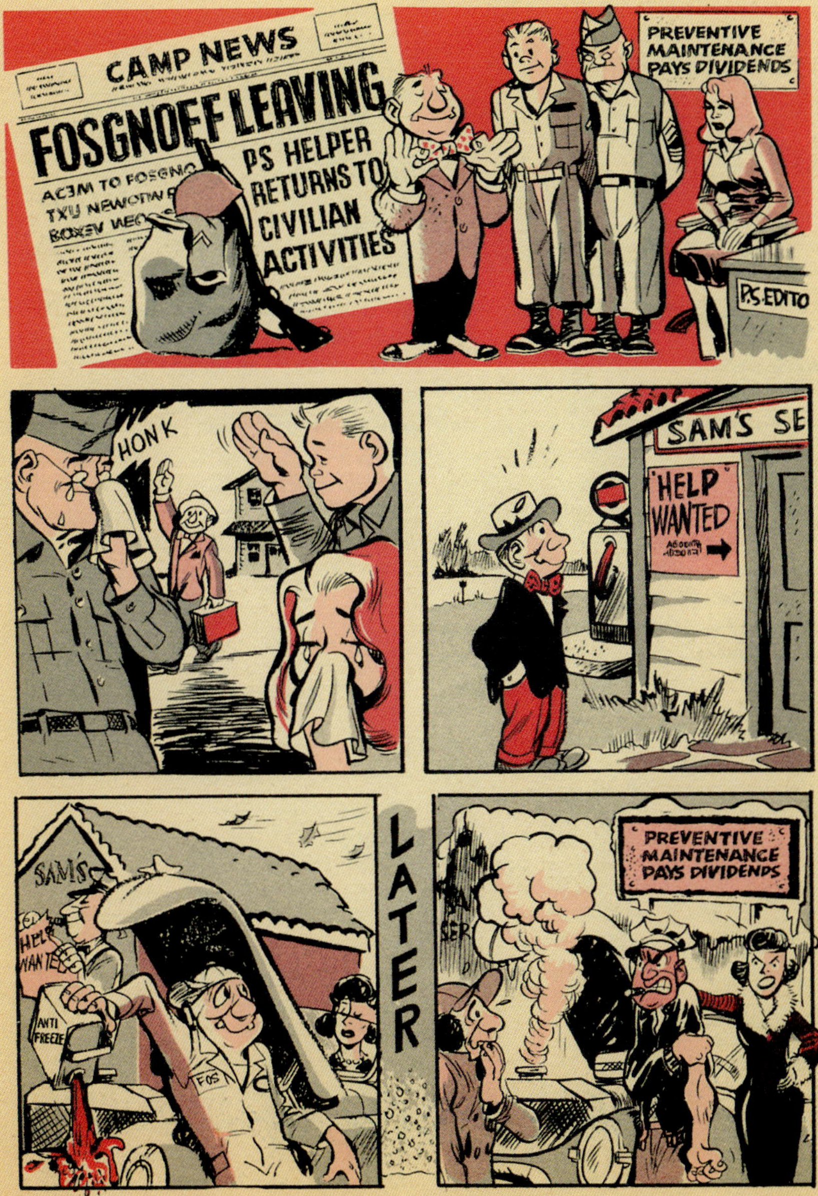
CAMP NEWS
FOSGNOFF LEAVING
PS HELPER RETURNS TO CIVILIAN ACTIVITIES
PREVENTIVE MAINTENANCE PAYS DIVIDENDS
P.S. EDITO
HONK
SAM'S SE
HELP WANTED
SAM'S
ANTI FREEZE
FOS
LATER
PREVENTIVE MAINTENANCE PAYS DIVIDENDS

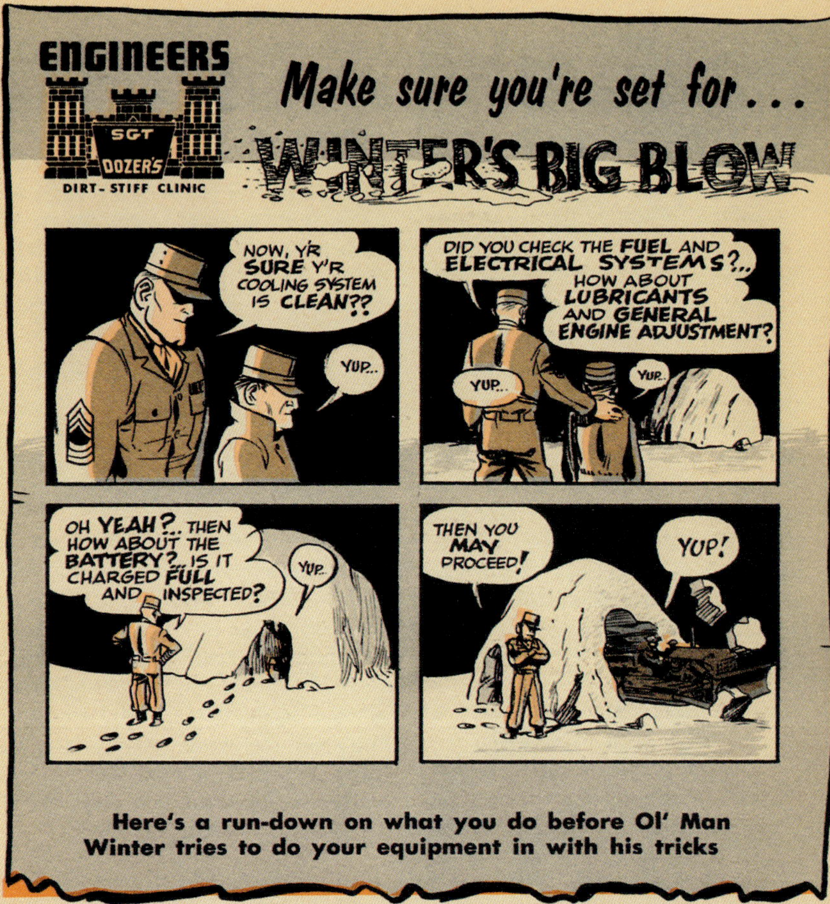
ENGINEERS
SGT DOZER'S
DIRT-STIFF CLINIC
Make sure you're set for...
WINTER'S BIG BLOW
NOW, Y'R SURE Y'R COOLING SYSTEM IS CLEAN??
YUP..
DID YOU CHECK THE FUEL AND ELECTRICAL SYSTEMS?..
HOW ABOUT LUBRICANTS AND GENERAL ENGINE ADJUSTMENT?
YUP..
YUP..
OH YEAH?.. THEN HOW ABOUT THE BATTERY?.. IS IT CHARGED FULL AND INSPECTED?
YUP..
THEN YOU MAY PROCEED!
YUP!
Here's a run-down on what you do before Ol' Man Winter tries to do your equipment in with his tricks

It'll soon be time for those brass monkeys to run for cover—with Old Man Winter just around the corner.

All of us know how important it is to have that Engineer equipment ready for winter's cold blasts.

There are cooling systems to clean and protect with anti-freeze; electrical and fuel systems to look over; batteries to pull, clean and inspect; engine adjustments to take care of; operator's controls to test; lubes to change or freshen up; tracks, wheels and tires to examine; power-control units to look after, and skillions of nuts, bolts, screws, gaskets and plugs to adjust and maybe replace.

Then there's a thorough scrub job for each piece of equipment, spot painting to be done, and preservative compound to be put on.

Connie Rodd's BRIEFS

Clean that well

Before you take a spark plug out of your vehicle's engine, be sure to clean out the plug well. If you've got any sand, dirt or trash in that well, it'll fall right down in the cylinder and really foul up your engine. So—clean that well.

Tight hatch? Natch!

Gotta be tight to be right. Any good tankman'll tell ya. A loose hatch-cover flapping around over rough terrain can bust a periscope—or somebody's skull. Y'got handy catch locks there, friend. So keep your hatch-covers tight—open or shut—but tight. Right?

Just a reminder

Next time you thumb through TM 9-767 (M26A1 truck-tractor), stick a note in on page 269 to remind the next guy that this vehicle uses an 18-mm spark plug (Ord Stock No. H004-0501002).

No rusty load

Here's a way to get rid of that rusty load you might be carryin' around. The next time you park your dump truck, elevate the dumper a little bit. That way water won't accumulate and the dumper'll stay free of rust. It only takes a few seconds to set a block between the dump body and the truck chassis... and the water'll run right out the back. It's just one of those little things that'll help your equipment last longer and do a better job.

Oughta be a law

Yeah, I'm against guys who play with fording-valve handles. Itchy hands could leave the valves partly closed, causing leaks all over the place. Better check the handle every day, at trip ticket set-up time, to make sure it's pushed in tight. And while you've got the hood up, see if the valves are wide open.

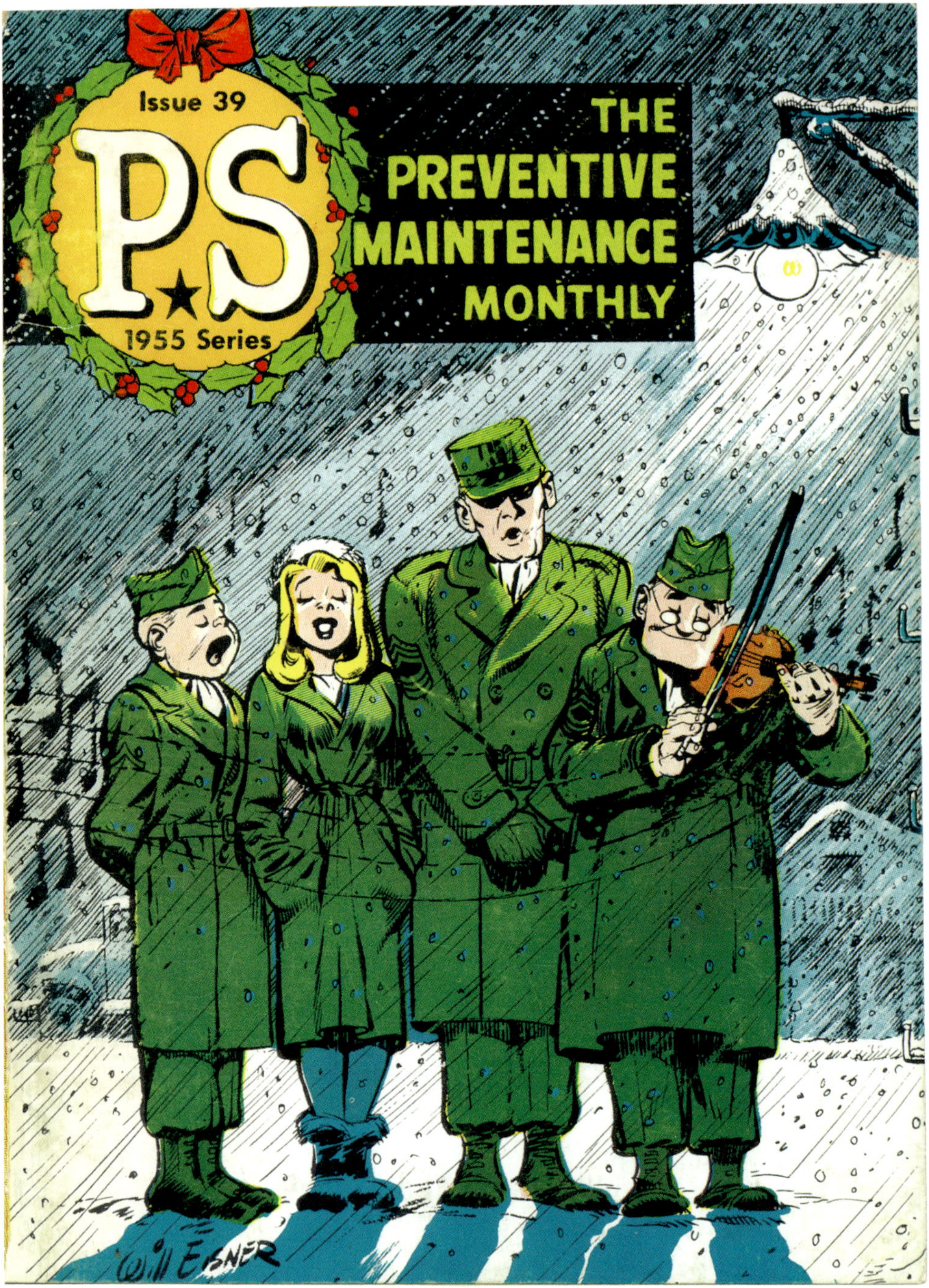
Issue 39
P.S
1955 Series
THE PREVENTIVE MAINTENANCE MONTHLY
Will Eisner

no. 39, 1955

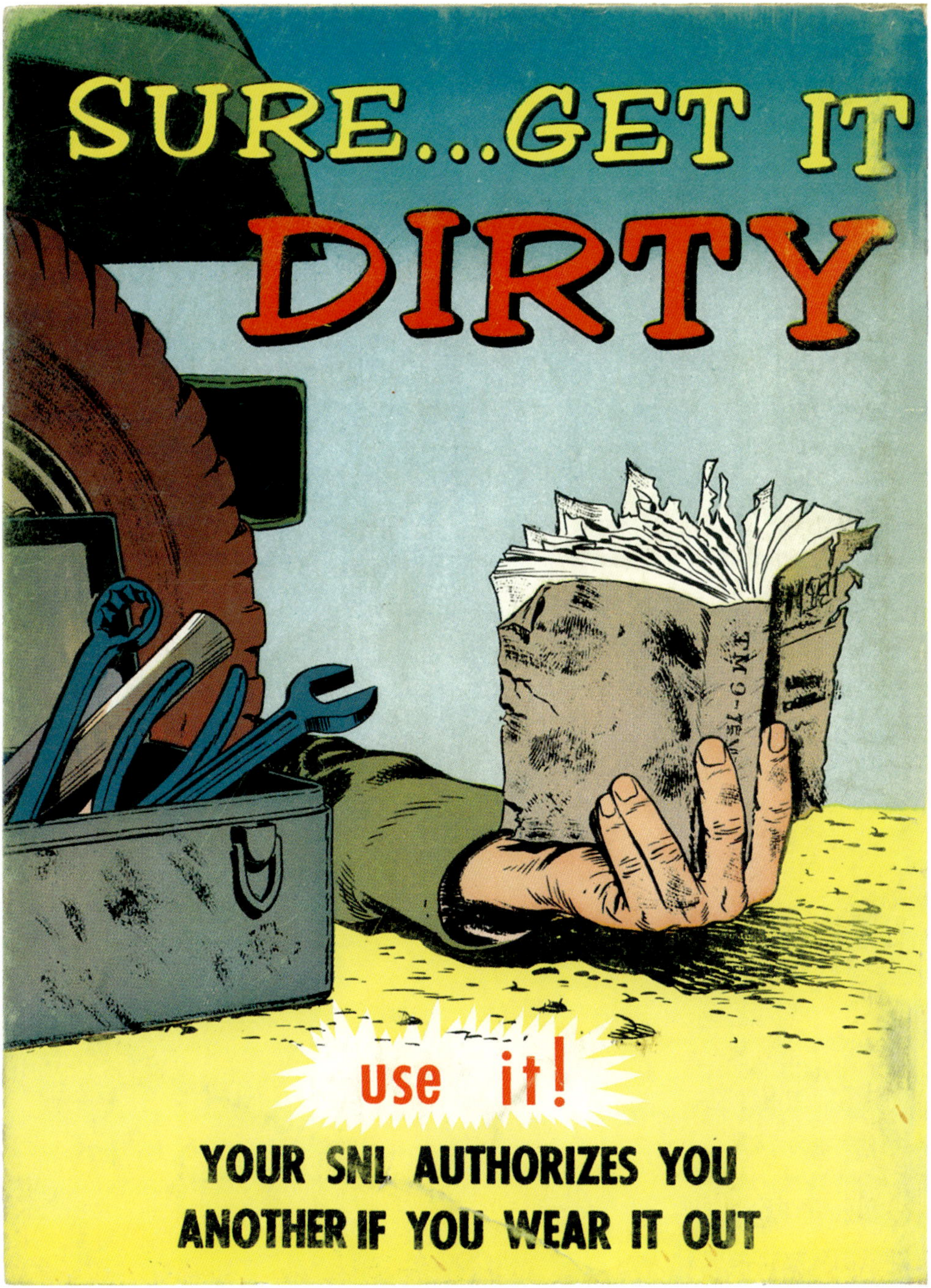
SURE...GET IT
DIRTY
TM 9-7
use it!
YOUR SNL AUTHORIZES YOU
ANOTHER IF YOU WEAR IT OUT

no. 40, 1956

NOT A KICK IN A CARLOAD

KNOW

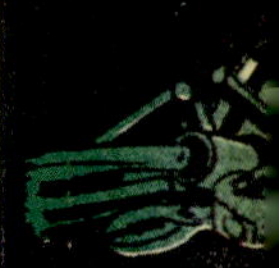

Your tools aren't going to kick back at you if you learn what they're used for and how to use them.

Of all the equipment you use, your common hand tools are the most useful and yet the most abused.

All the tools that are in your TOOL SET, Organizational Maintenance (2nd Echelon, Set No. 2 Common) are packed into this batch of pictures.

Mull over the pictures and get to know each by name, and what it's used for—sorta make friends with 'em—because they can be—friends, that is.

TOOL SET. Organizational Maintenance (2nd Echelon) Se

ADAPTER, quick acting air hose coupling, 1/4 in hose shk

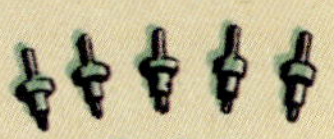

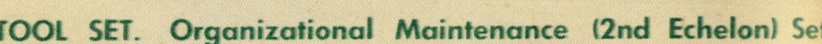

5 auth

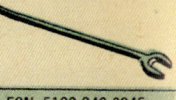

ENG 33-1000.100.050 | FSN............

ADAPTER SET, testing, 24 v-sealed elec systems (Delco-Remy and Auto-Lite for wheeled tactical vehicles), 7 adapters in mtl box.

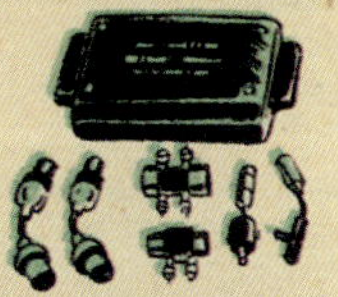

ORD 4910-356-7511 | FSN 4910-356-7511

ANVIL, BLACKSMITH'S: S face and horn, CI body wt 100 lb.

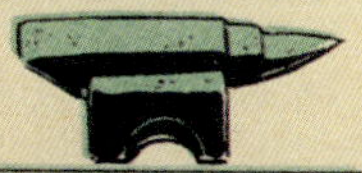

ORD 41-A-280-100 | FSN............

ATTACHING TOOL, SOLDERLESS TERMINAL: (crimping type) (formerly CRIMPER).

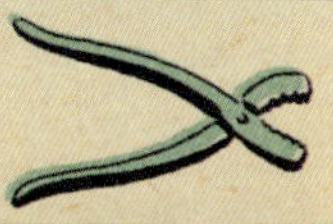

ORD 41-C-2765 | FSN 5120-224-9408

BAR, GREASE: sp shackle, solid (hex or oct) 30 3/16 lg.

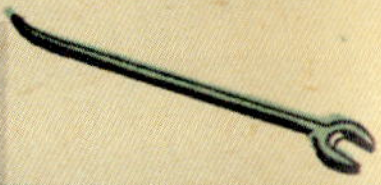

ORD 41-B-315 | FSN 5120-240-6045

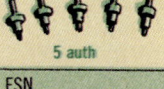

BAR, PINCH: jimmy, 3/4 in blade width, 24 in lg.

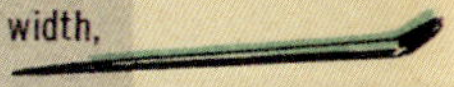

ORD 41-B-255 | FSN 5120-224-1388

BAR, WRECKING: gooseneck, claw and pinch pt, 3/4 in diam, 36 in lg.

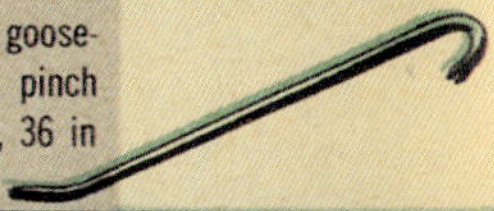

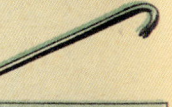

ORD 41-B-336 | FSN 5120-238-8589

BATTERY FILLER, GRAVITY: distilled water, unbreakable type, 1 gal cap (formerly FILLER).

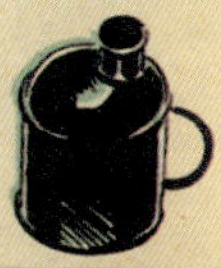

ORD 8-F-1000 | FSN 6140-234-7360

YOUR TOOLS
O NEED TO GIVE YOUR UPPLY A HARD TIME IF HE TOOLS YOU GET REN'T EXACTLY LIKE HE ONES LISTED. IT'S UST THAT DIFFERENT ANUFACTURERS HAVE ADE THE ITEM. BUT THEY'LL BOTH DO THE JOB!
YOU WANT TO KNOW IF YOU RATE THIS TOOL SET?..JUST TAKE A GANDER AT YOUR UNIT'S TOE. IT'LL BE THERE IF YOU'RE SUPPOSED TO HAVE IT!

. 2, Common. ORD 41-T-3538-855 FSN 5180-754-0650

BEAD LOOSENER, tire, tempered S w/S tu hdl, 35 in lg.

ORD 5120-00-17038 FSN............

BENDER SET, cop tu, spg wire type, set of six benders, 1/4, 5/16, 3/8, 7/16, 1/2, and 5/8 in (JAN-B-460).

ORD 41-B-530 FSN............

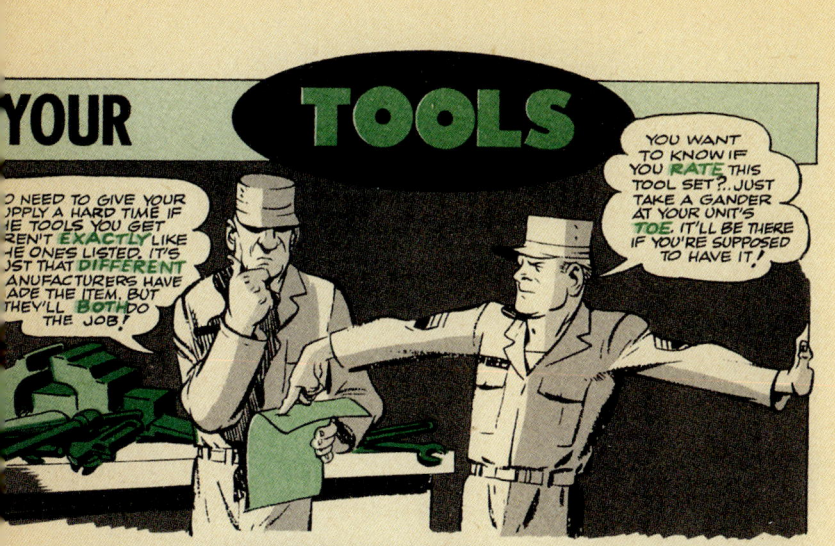

BENCH, cabinet, mtl frame w/drawers and dividers, Type VIII, Class A.

ORD 41-B-440 FSN............

24 auth

BLADE, HAND HACK-SAW: alloy, flex, 10 in lg, 1/2 in width, 0.025 in thk, 24 T per in.

ENG 41-1607.100-240 FSN 5110-228-3189

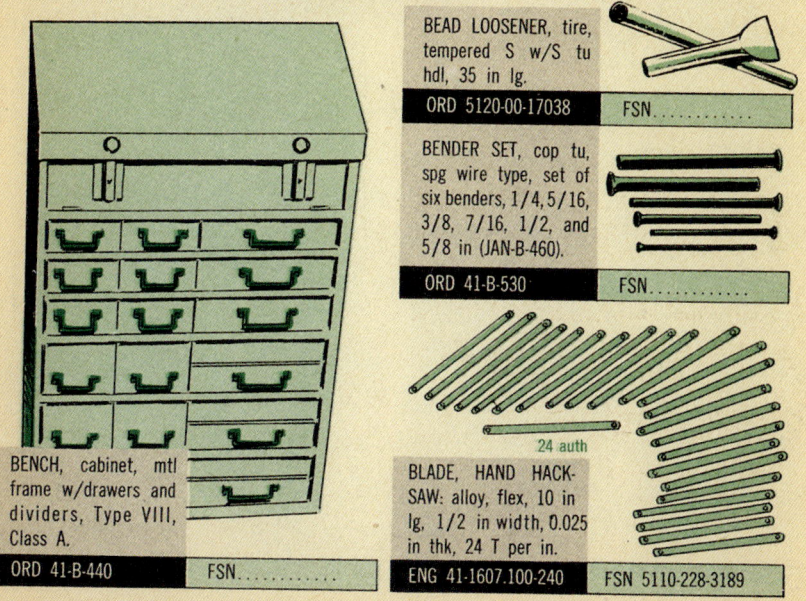

BLOWTORCH, GASOLINE: hand, rd tank, 1 qt cap (formerly TORCH).
ORD 5120-181-6746   FSN 5120-181-6746

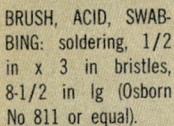

BRUSH, ACID, SWABBING: soldering, 1/2 in x 3 in bristles, 8-1/2 in lg (Osborn No 811 or equal).
ENG 38-2750.750-850   FSN 223-8002   24 auth

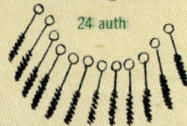

BRUSH, PAINT, SASH AND TRIM: oval, 1-7/16 x 1-1/16 in (FS H-B-490), size No 5.
ENG 38-4567.300-500   FSN 239-0959   5 auth

BRUSH, WIRE, SCRATCH: w/ wood hdl, 4x19 rows, 14 in lg, FS H-B-178, type II
ENG 38-5797.500-600   FSN ....   12 auth

2 auth

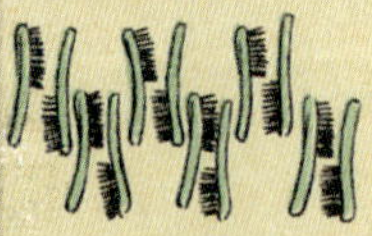

CABINET, tool, S, w/ drawers and bench top.
ORD 41-C-15   FSN 5140-357-5520

CABLE ASSEMBLY, POWER, ELECTRICAL: hand, ptbl w/ reflector guard and thumb switch, 25 ft all ru covered cord, and parallel blade plug connector (formerly LAMP).
ENG 17-3592.714-025   FSN 6150-265-6497   2 auth

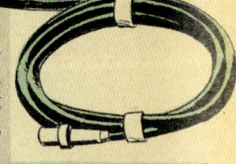

CABLE, extn, ru covered, 2 cond, stranded, w/ female plugs at both ends, No 1 AWG, 20 ft lg.
ORD 17-C-568   FSN 6145-474-9135

CAP, VISE JAW: br, 4 in (formerly JAW).
ORD 41-J-325   FSN 5120-221-1506   2 pairs auth

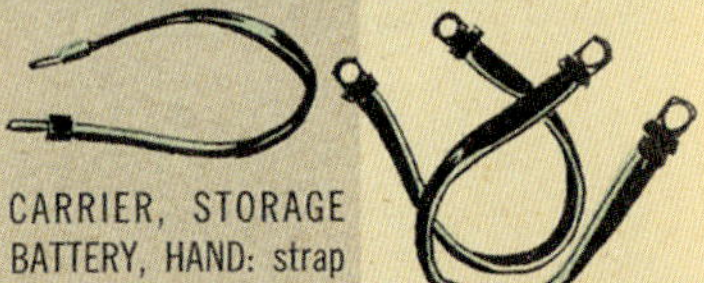

CARRIER, STORAGE BATTERY, HAND: strap type, 21 in lg.
ORD 41-C-445   FSN 5120-223-8454   3 auth

GOOD MAINTENANCE BEGINS WITH *PROPER* USAGE!

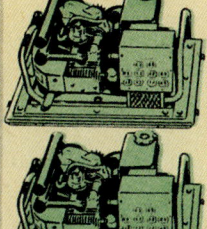
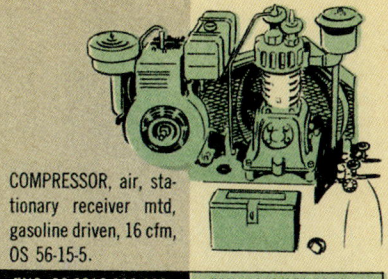

CHARGER, btry, ptbl, skid mtd, gasoline driven, 15 v, 2000 w/ carrying case.   3 auth
ENG 6130-473-6175   FSN 6130-473-6175

COMPRESSOR, air, stationary receiver mtd, gasoline driven, 16 cfm, OS 56-15-5.
ENG 66-3212.016-100   FSN 4310-351-9262

CHECK-UNIT, quick acting air hose coupling, swv, 1/4 in female pipe end.
5 auth
ORD H006-0538801   FSN............

KNOWING YOUR TOOL'S LIMITATIONS INCREASES ITS USEFULNESS

CLAMP "C": med service, 4 in cap.   2 auth
ORD 41-C-1730   FSN............

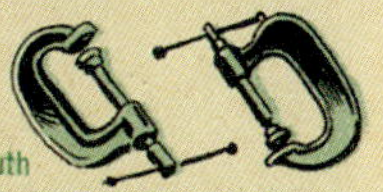

CLAMP "C": med service 6 in cap.   2 auth
ORD 41-C-1732   FSN............

CROWBAR: pinch pt, 1-1/4 in diam, 60 in lg (formerly BAR).   2 auth
ORD 41-B-175   FSN............

CLAMP, WHEEL CYLINDER, HYDRAULIC BRAKE: sliding arm type, 2-5/8 in min cyl lgh, 4-7/8 in max cyl lgh, 4 clamps per set.
4 sets auth
ORD 4910-244-4900   FSN 4910-244-4900

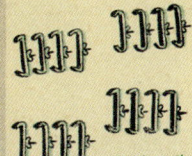

CUP, PAINT, SPRAY GUN: clamp type, w/ cover attachment, 1 qt cap.   2 auth
ORD 4940-190-5164   FSN 4940-190-5164

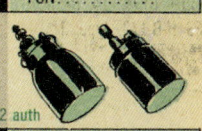

CUTTER, BOLT: rigid hd, clipper cut, 18 in lg, 1/4 in cap.
ORD 41-C-2280   FSN 5110-188-252

CLEANER AND TESTER, SPARK PLUG: bench mtd, 120 to 150 psi air pressure, dc, 12 v.
ORD 4910-261-5869   FSN 4910-261-5869

CUTTER, TUBE: 1/8 to 3/4 in cap w/reamer blade (for cop, br, tin, S and lead).
ORD 41-C-2825   FSN 5110-221-1052

TESTER, low voltage ckt, voltage R 0-1, 0-10, 0-50, 0-100, amp R 3-0-10, 15-0-50, 30-0-100, 150-0-500, 300-0-1000 (for testing gr, starter, regulators and wiring).
ORD 17-T-5575-50 FSN 6625-356-8269

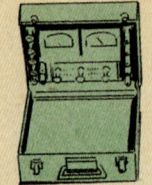

DELICATE TOOLS NEED EXTRA CAREFUL HANDLING!

THREADING SET, bolt and screw, NC, w/rd adjustable split dies, stocks, taps, and wrenches, 1/4-20NC to 1-8NC, 24 pc in case.
ORD 41-T-1895 FSN 5180-448-2362

THREADING SET, bolt and screw, NF, w/rd adjustable split dies, stocks, taps, wrenches, 1/4-28NF to 1-14NF, 24 pc in case. 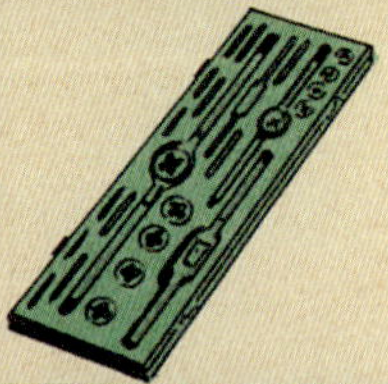
ORD 41-T-1925 FSN 5180-422-4975

THREADING SET, pipe, NPT, w/rect adjustable dies, stk, wrench, adjustable guide, and taps, 1/8-27 NPT to 1-11 1/2 NPT, 13 pc in case. 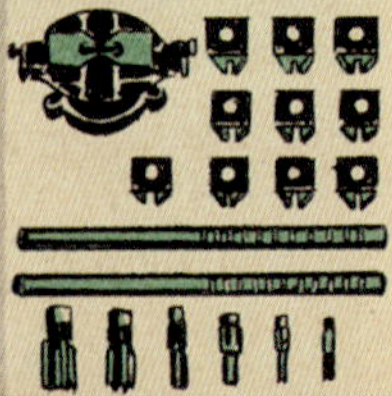
ORD 41-T-2023 FSN..........

TOOL, tire probing.
ORD 41-T-3374 FSN 5120-449-8047

TOOL, tire valve stem fishing.
ORD 41-T-3378 FSN 5120-423-2346

TOOL, valve repair.   2 auth
ORD 41-T-3382-20 FSN 5120-387-9642

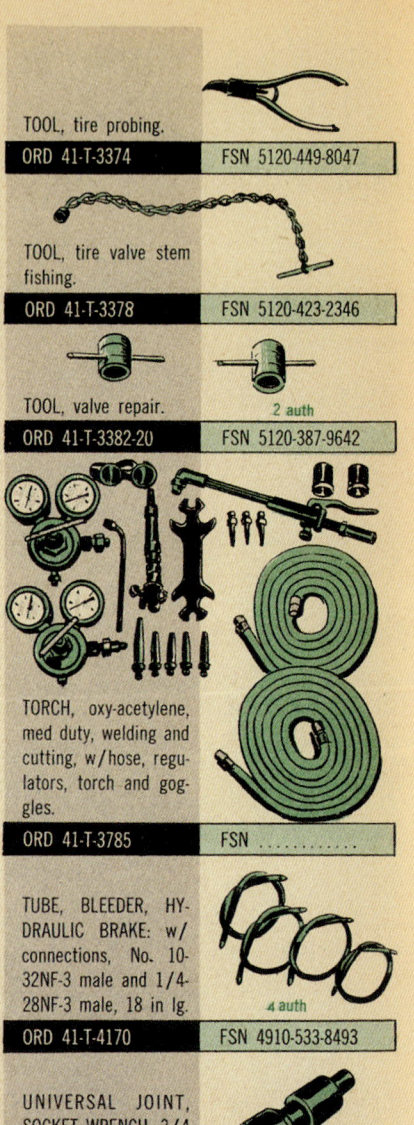

TORCH, oxy-acetylene, med duty, welding and cutting, w/hose, regulators, torch and goggles.
ORD 41-T-3785 FSN..........

TUBE, BLEEDER, HYDRAULIC BRAKE: w/ connections, No. 10-32NF-3 male and 1/4-28NF-3 male, 18 in lg.   4 auth
ORD 41-T-4170 FSN 4910-533-8493

UNIVERSAL JOINT, SOCKET WRENCH: 3/4 in sq-drive.
ORD 41-J-382 FSN 5120-228-9348

VISE, MACHINIST'S: bench, swv-base, stationary jaw, 4 in jaw wd, 5-1/2 in jaw opng.	
ORD 41-V-276	FSN 5120-243-1371

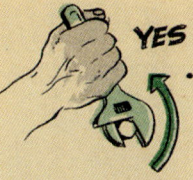 YES  ...NO

VULCANIZER, HOT PATCH: bench mtd, clamp type.	
ORD 4970-243-3130	FSN 4970-243-3130
WRENCH, OPEN END, ADJUSTABLE: sgle-hd, 1-1/2 in jaw opng, 10 in lg.	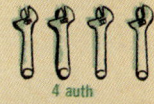 4 auth
ORD 41-W-487	FSN 5120-449-8083
WRENCH, adjustable, sgl open end, 1-5/16 in jaw opng, 12 in lg.	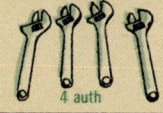 4 auth
ORD 41-W-488	FSN............
WRENCH, OPEN END, FIXED: tappet, dble-hd, 15 deg angle 7/16 and 1/2 in opngs.	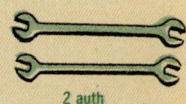 2 auth
ORD 41-W-3573	FSN 5120-184-8620
WRENCH, BOX: dble-hd, 12 pt, half moon, 9/16 and 5/8 in opngs.	
ORD 41-W-635	FSN 5120-222-1596
WRENCH, OPEN END, FIXED: tappet, dble-hd, 15 deg angle, 9/16 and 5/8 in opngs.	 2 auth
ORD 41-W-3579	FSN 5120-184-8221
WRENCH, BOX: dble-hd, 12 pt, half moon, 5/8 and 3/4 in opngs.	
ORD 41-W-636	FSN 5120-222-1597
WRENCH, BOX: dble-hd, 12 pt, lg, 15 deg offset, 1-1/16 and 1-1/8 in opngs.	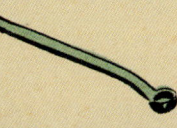
WRENCH, PIPE, ADJUSTABLE: hv-duty, 1/4 to 1 in pipe cap, 10 in lg.	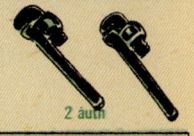 2 auth
ORD 41-W-1662	FSN 5120-240-5331
ORD 41-W-619-678	FSN 5120-184-8675
WRENCH BOX: dble-hd, 12 pt, lg, 15 deg offset, 1-1/4 and 1-3/8 in opngs.	
WRENCH, PIPE, ADJUSTABLE: hv-duty, 1 to 2 in pipe cap, 18 in lg.	
ORD 41-W-1664	FSN 5120-357-8711
ORD 41-W-619-698	FSN 5120-184-8677
WRENCH, DRAIN PLUG.	
WRENCH, SPANNER, HOOK: adjustable, 3/4 to 2 in circle diam.	
ORD 41-W-875	FSN 5120-222-1398
ORD 41-W-3249-900	FSN 5120-449-8235

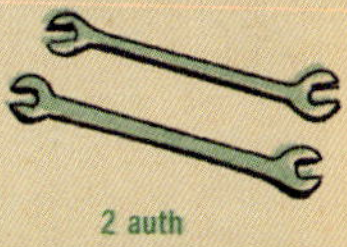

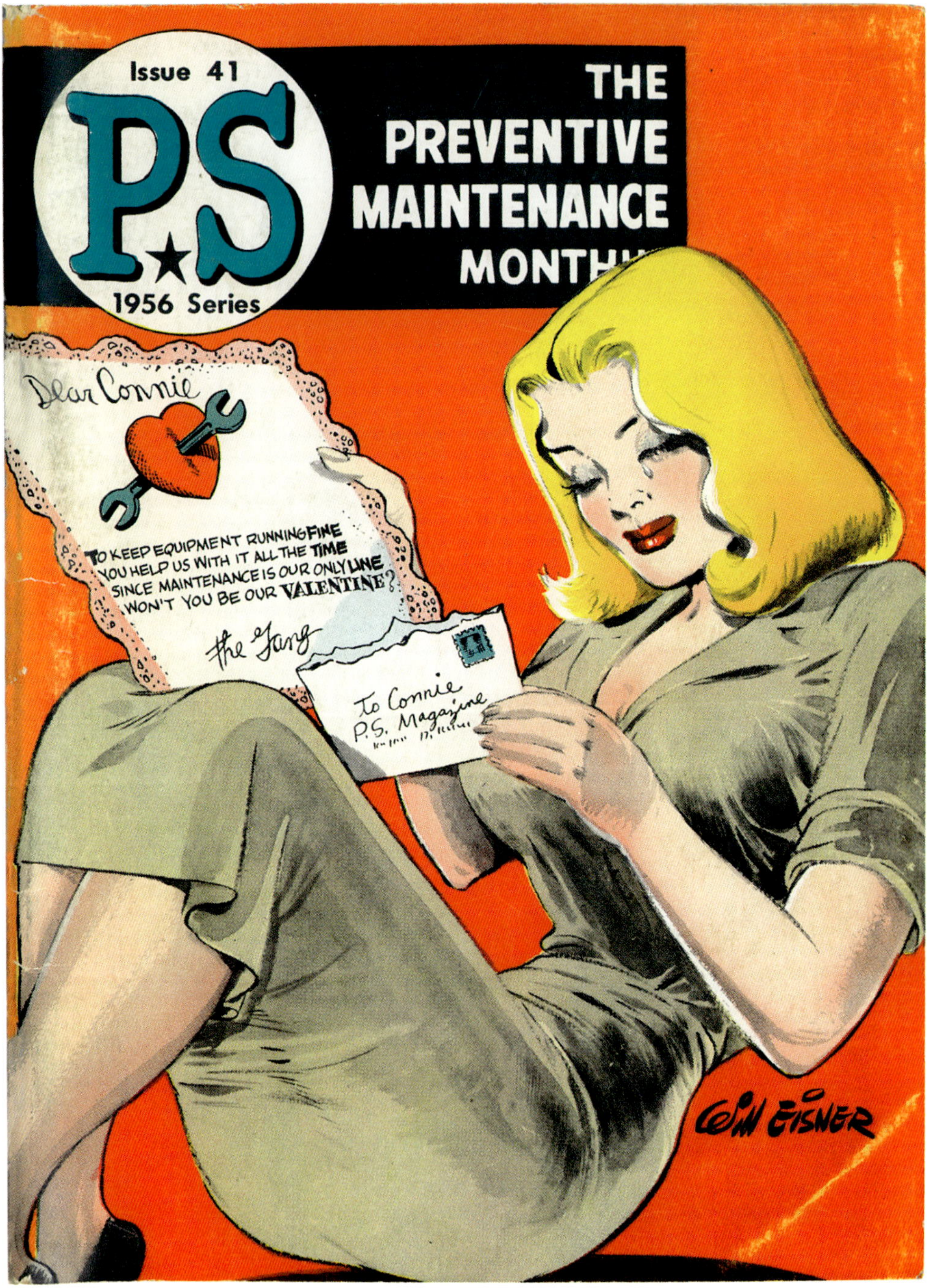
Issue 41
P.S
1956 Series
THE PREVENTIVE MAINTENANCE MONTHLY
Dear Connie
TO KEEP EQUIPMENT RUNNING FINE
YOU HELP US WITH IT ALL THE TIME
SINCE MAINTENANCE IS OUR ONLY LINE
WON'T YOU BE OUR VALENTINE?
the Gang
To Connie
P.S. Magazine
WILL EISNER

no. 41, 1956

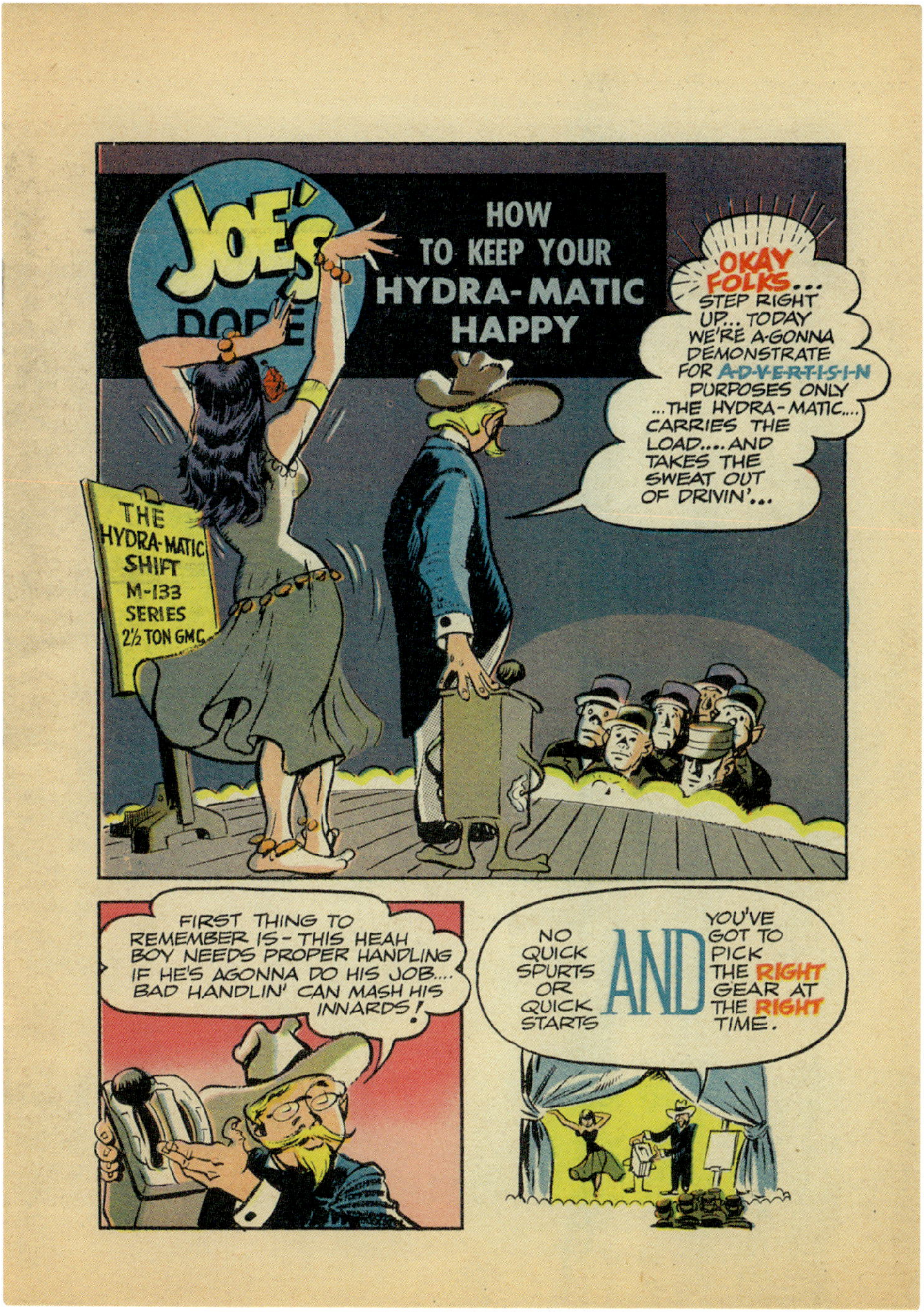
JOE'S
HOW TO KEEP YOUR HYDRA-MATIC HAPPY
OKAY FOLKS... STEP RIGHT UP... TODAY WE'RE A-GONNA DEMONSTRATE FOR A-D-V-E-R-T-I-S-I-N PURPOSES ONLY ...THE HYDRA-MATIC.... CARRIES THE LOAD.... AND TAKES THE SWEAT OUT OF DRIVIN'...
THE HYDRA-MATIC SHIFT M-133 SERIES 2½ TON GMC
FIRST THING TO REMEMBER IS - THIS HEAH BOY NEEDS PROPER HANDLING IF HE'S AGONNA DO HIS JOB.... BAD HANDLIN' CAN MASH HIS INNARDS!
NO QUICK SPURTS OR QUICK STARTS AND YOU'VE GOT TO PICK THE RIGHT GEAR AT THE RIGHT TIME.

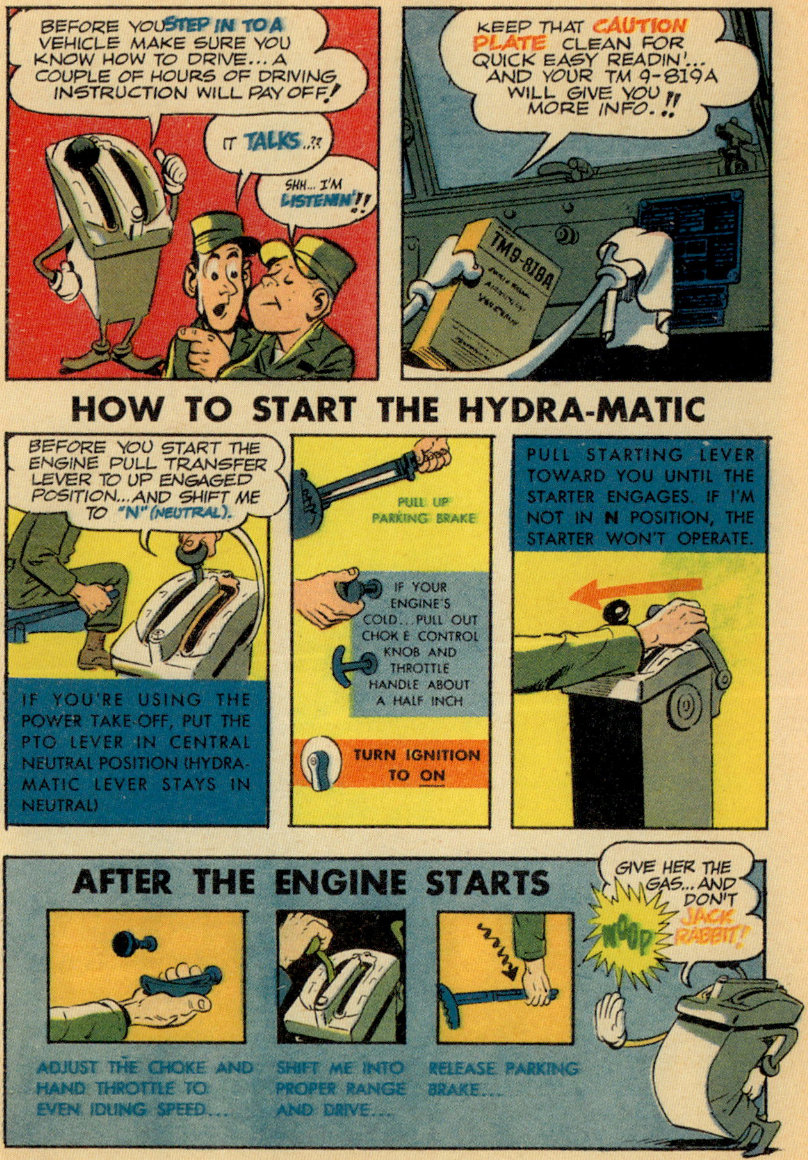
BEFORE YOU STEP IN TO A VEHICLE MAKE SURE YOU KNOW HOW TO DRIVE... A COUPLE OF HOURS OF DRIVING INSTRUCTION WILL PAY OFF!
IT TALKS..?!
SHH... I'M LISTENIN'!!
KEEP THAT CAUTION PLATE CLEAN FOR QUICK EASY READIN'... AND YOUR TM 9-819A WILL GIVE YOU MORE INFO.!!
TM9-819A
HOW TO START THE HYDRA-MATIC
BEFORE YOU START THE ENGINE PULL TRANSFER LEVER TO UP ENGAGED POSITION...AND SHIFT ME TO "N" (NEUTRAL).
IF YOU'RE USING THE POWER TAKE-OFF, PUT THE PTO LEVER IN CENTRAL NEUTRAL POSITION (HYDRA-MATIC LEVER STAYS IN NEUTRAL)
PULL UP PARKING BRAKE
IF YOUR ENGINE'S COLD...PULL OUT CHOK E CONTROL KNOB AND THROTTLE HANDLE ABOUT A HALF INCH
TURN IGNITION TO ON
PULL STARTING LEVER TOWARD YOU UNTIL THE STARTER ENGAGES. IF I'M NOT IN N POSITION, THE STARTER WON'T OPERATE.
AFTER THE ENGINE STARTS
ADJUST THE CHOKE AND HAND THROTTLE TO EVEN IDLING SPEED...
SHIFT ME INTO PROPER RANGE AND DRIVE...
RELEASE PARKING BRAKE...
GIVE HER THE GAS... AND DON'T JACK RABBIT!
WOOP

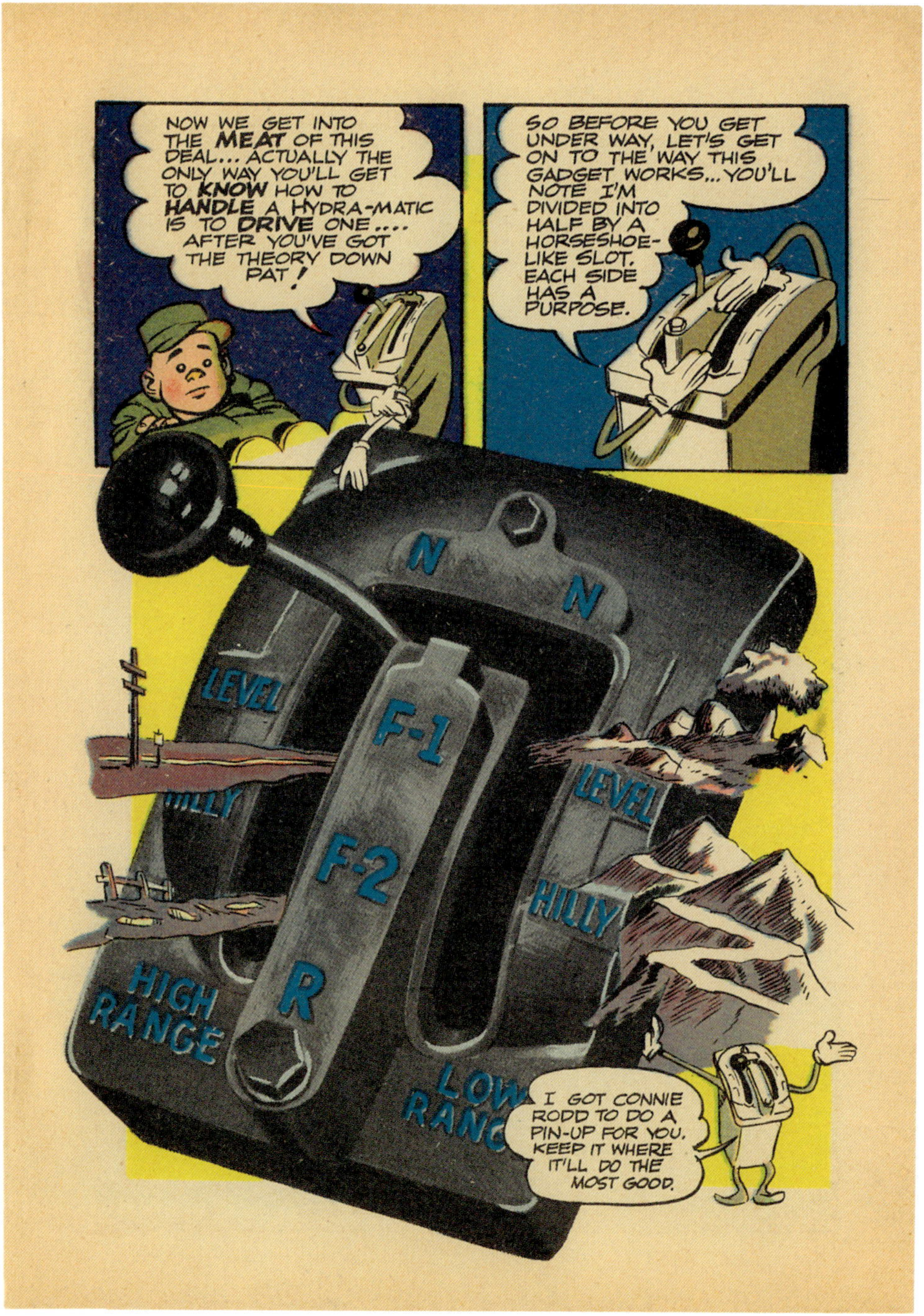
NOW WE GET INTO THE MEAT OF THIS DEAL... ACTUALLY THE ONLY WAY YOU'LL GET TO KNOW HOW TO HANDLE A HYDRA-MATIC IS TO DRIVE ONE.... AFTER YOU'VE GOT THE THEORY DOWN PAT!
SO BEFORE YOU GET UNDER WAY, LET'S GET ON TO THE WAY THIS GADGET WORKS... YOU'LL NOTE I'M DIVIDED INTO HALF BY A HORSESHOE-LIKE SLOT. EACH SIDE HAS A PURPOSE.
N
N
LEVEL
F-1
LEVEL
F-2
HILLY
HIGH RANGE
R
I GOT CONNIE RODD TO DO A PIN-UP FOR YOU. KEEP IT WHERE IT'LL DO THE MOST GOOD.

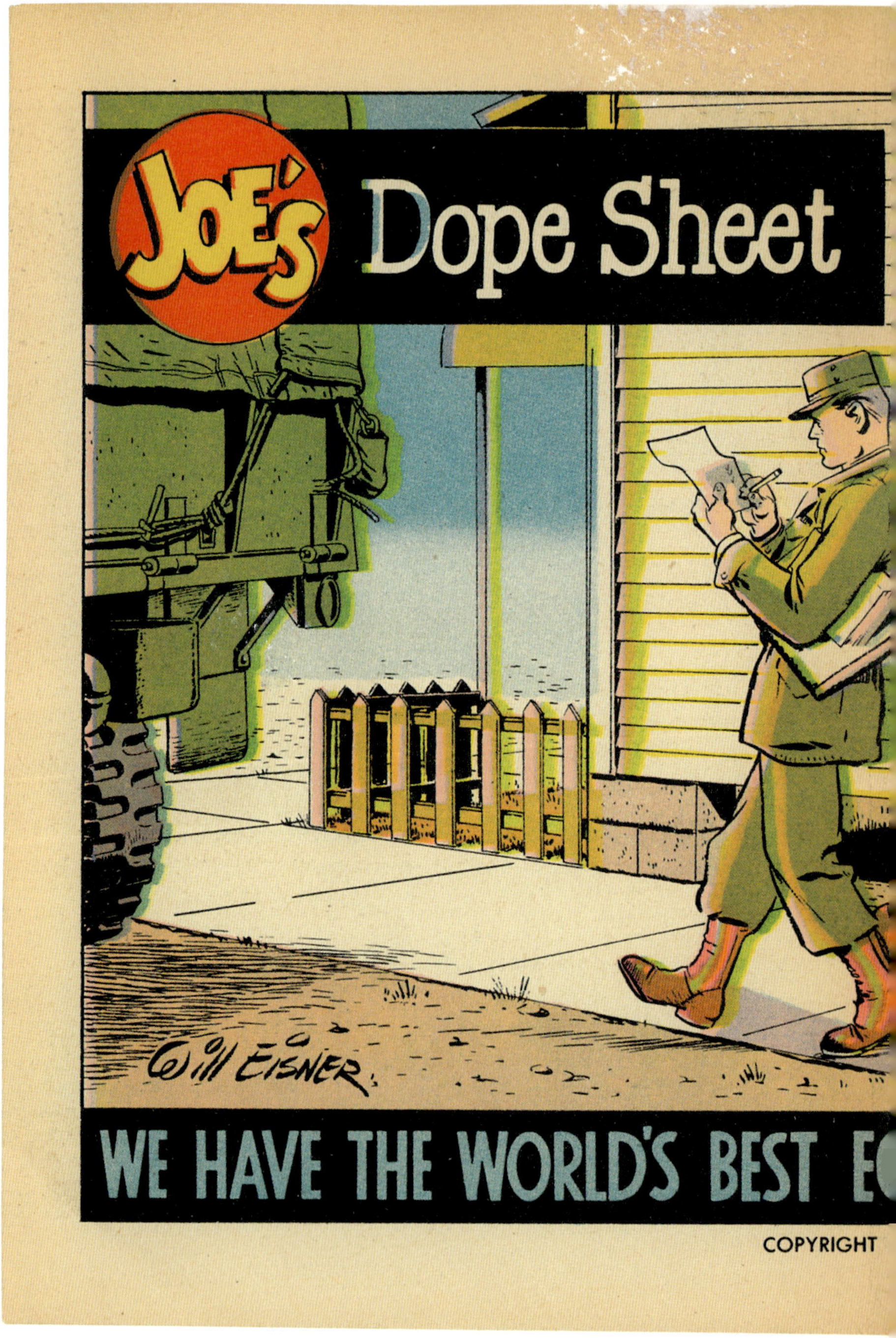
JOE'S Dope Sheet
WILL EISNER
WE HAVE THE WORLD'S BEST E
COPYRIGHT

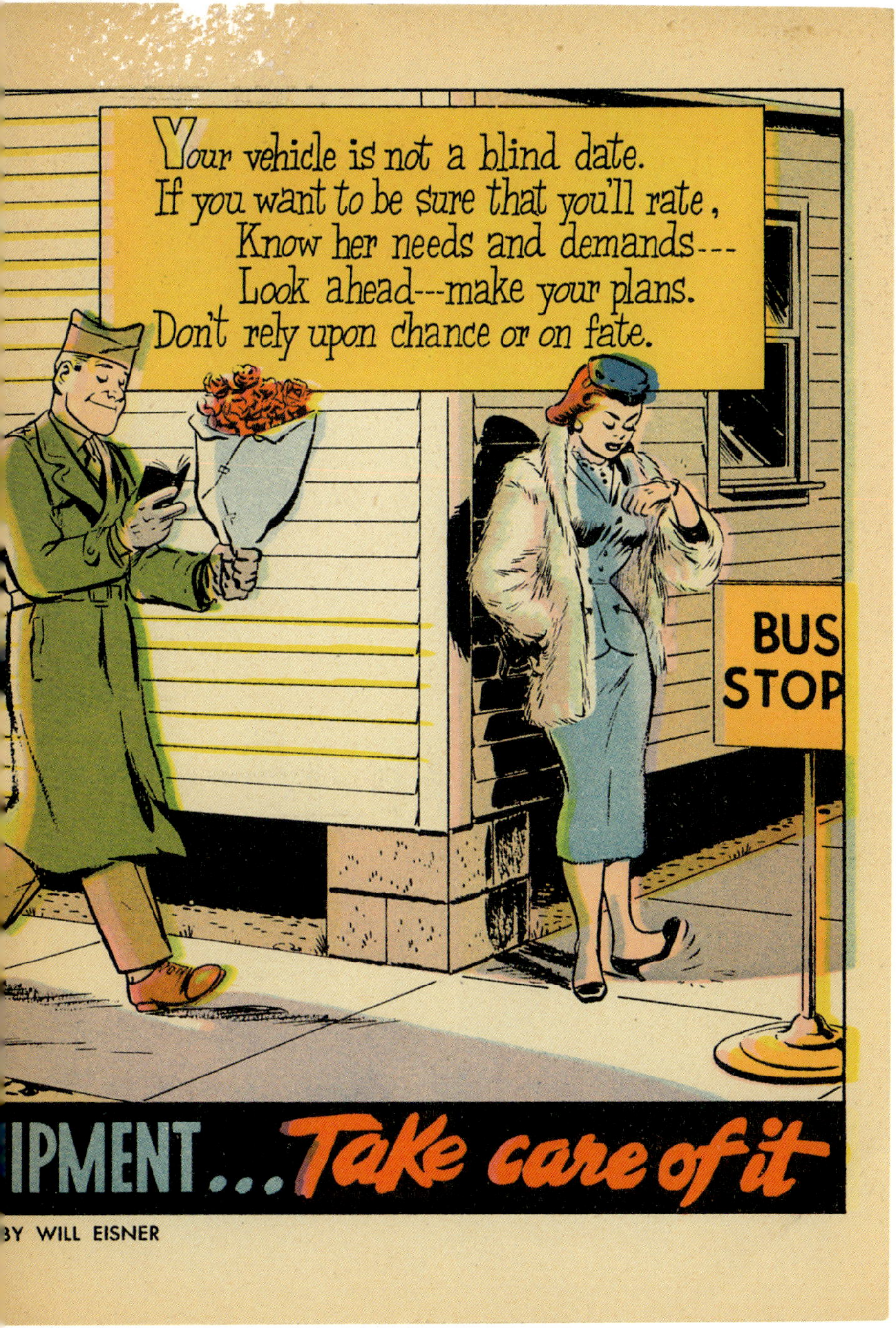
Your vehicle is not a blind date.
If you want to be sure that you'll rate,
Know her needs and demands---
Look ahead---make your plans.
Don't rely upon chance or on fate.
BUS STOP
IPMENT... Take care of it
BY WILL EISNER

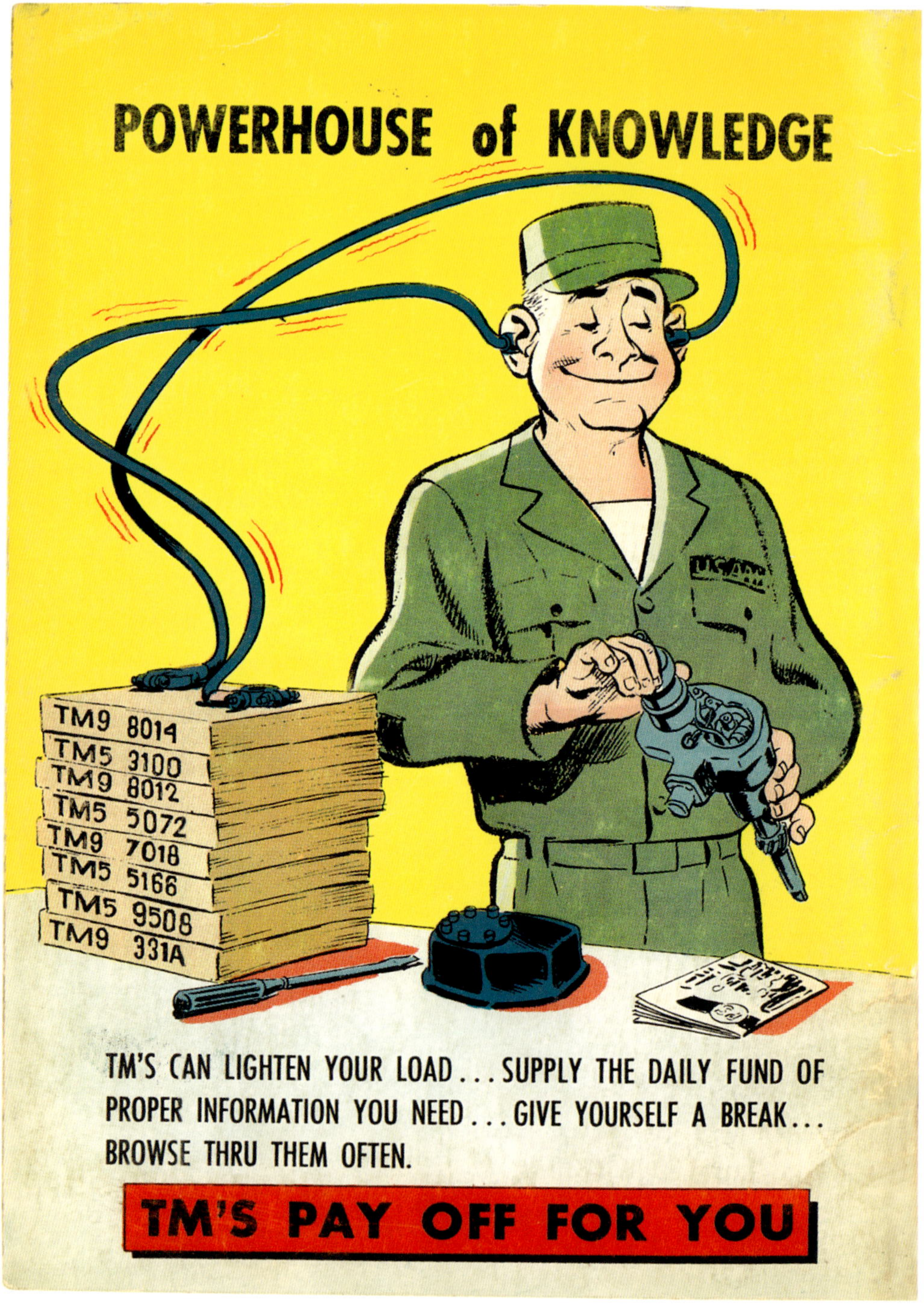
POWERHOUSE of KNOWLEDGE
TM9 8014
TM5 3100
TM9 8012
TM5 5072
TM9 7018
TM5 5166
TM5 9508
TM9 331A
TM'S CAN LIGHTEN YOUR LOAD . . . SUPPLY THE DAILY FUND OF PROPER INFORMATION YOU NEED . . . GIVE YOURSELF A BREAK . . . BROWSE THRU THEM OFTEN.
TM'S PAY OFF FOR YOU

no. 42, 1956

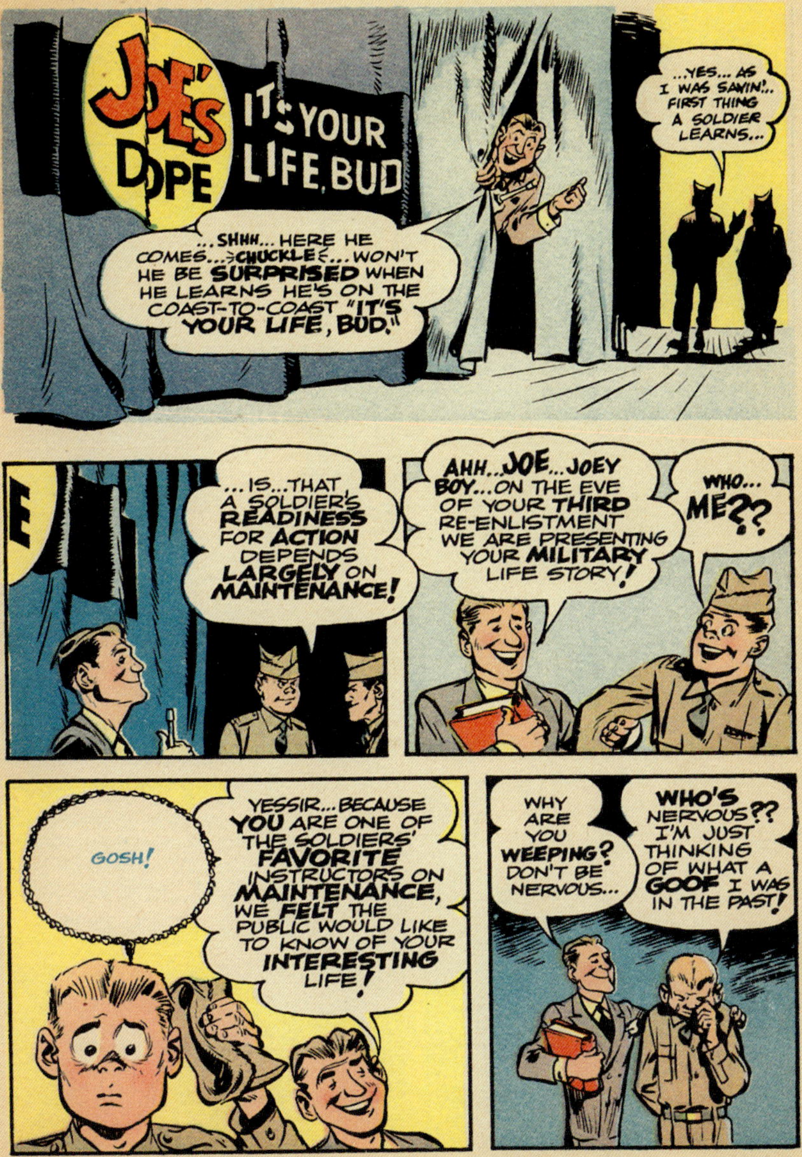
JOE'S DOPE
IT'S YOUR LIFE, BUD
...SHHH... HERE HE COMES...CHUCKLE... WON'T HE BE SURPRISED WHEN HE LEARNS HE'S ON THE COAST-TO-COAST "IT'S YOUR LIFE, BUD."
...YES... AS I WAS SAYIN'.. FIRST THING A SOLDIER LEARNS...
...IS...THAT A SOLDIER'S READINESS FOR ACTION DEPENDS LARGELY ON MAINTENANCE!
AHH...JOE...JOEY BOY...ON THE EVE OF YOUR THIRD RE-ENLISTMENT WE ARE PRESENTING YOUR MILITARY LIFE STORY!
WHO... ME??
GOSH!
YESSIR...BECAUSE YOU ARE ONE OF THE SOLDIERS' FAVORITE INSTRUCTORS ON MAINTENANCE, WE FELT THE PUBLIC WOULD LIKE TO KNOW OF YOUR INTERESTING LIFE!
WHY ARE YOU WEEPING? DON'T BE NERVOUS...
WHO'S NERVOUS?? I'M JUST THINKING OF WHAT A GOOF I WAS IN THE PAST!

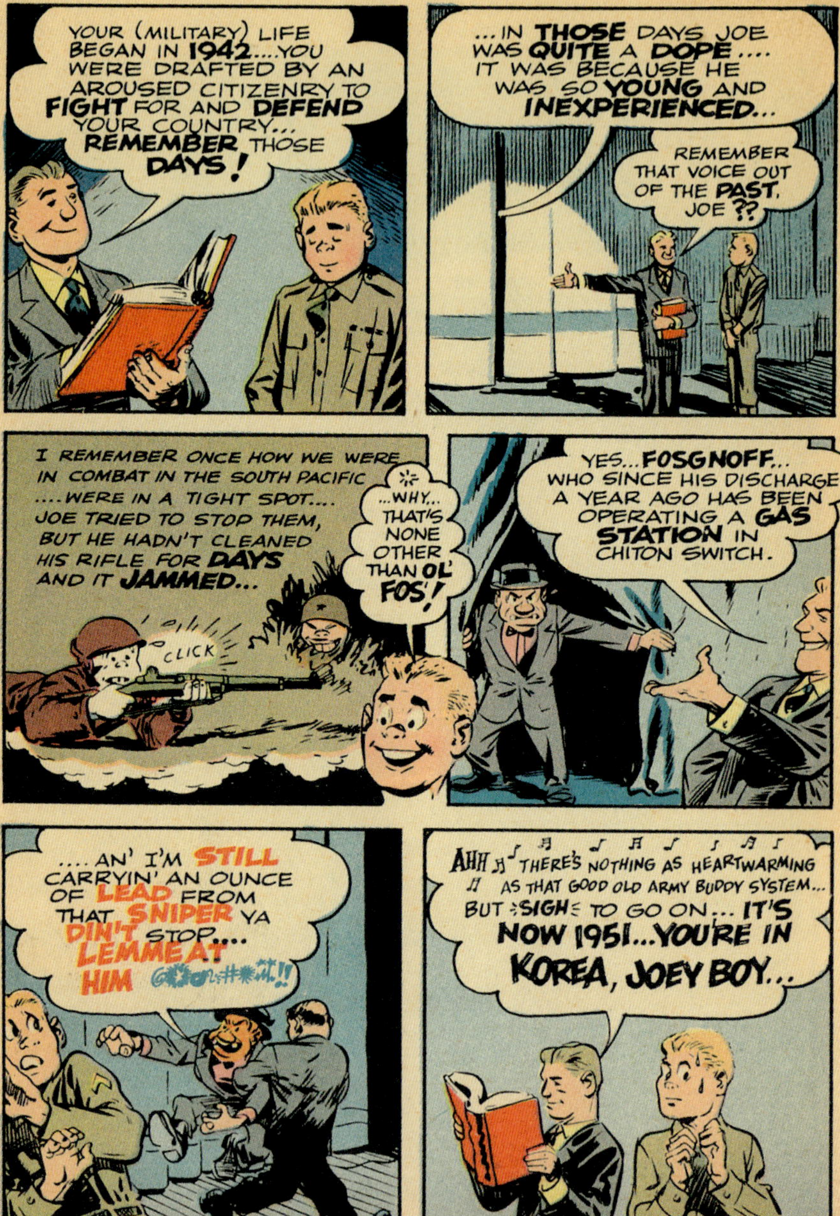
YOUR (MILITARY) LIFE BEGAN IN 1942....YOU WERE DRAFTED BY AN AROUSED CITIZENRY TO FIGHT FOR AND DEFEND YOUR COUNTRY... REMEMBER THOSE DAYS!
...IN THOSE DAYS JOE WAS QUITE A DOPE.... IT WAS BECAUSE HE WAS SO YOUNG AND INEXPERIENCED...
REMEMBER THAT VOICE OUT OF THE PAST, JOE ??
I REMEMBER ONCE HOW WE WERE IN COMBAT IN THE SOUTH PACIFIC ....WERE IN A TIGHT SPOT.... JOE TRIED TO STOP THEM, BUT HE HADN'T CLEANED HIS RIFLE FOR DAYS AND IT JAMMED...
CLICK
...WHY... THAT'S NONE OTHER THAN OL' FOS'!
YES...FOSGNOFF... WHO SINCE HIS DISCHARGE A YEAR AGO HAS BEEN OPERATING A GAS STATION IN CHITON SWITCH.
....AN' I'M STILL CARRYIN' AN OUNCE OF LEAD FROM THAT SNIPER YA DIN'T STOP.... LEMME AT HIM
AHH THERE'S NOTHING AS HEARTWARMING AS THAT GOOD OLD ARMY BUDDY SYSTEM... BUT SIGH TO GO ON... IT'S NOW 1951...YOU'RE IN KOREA, JOEY BOY...

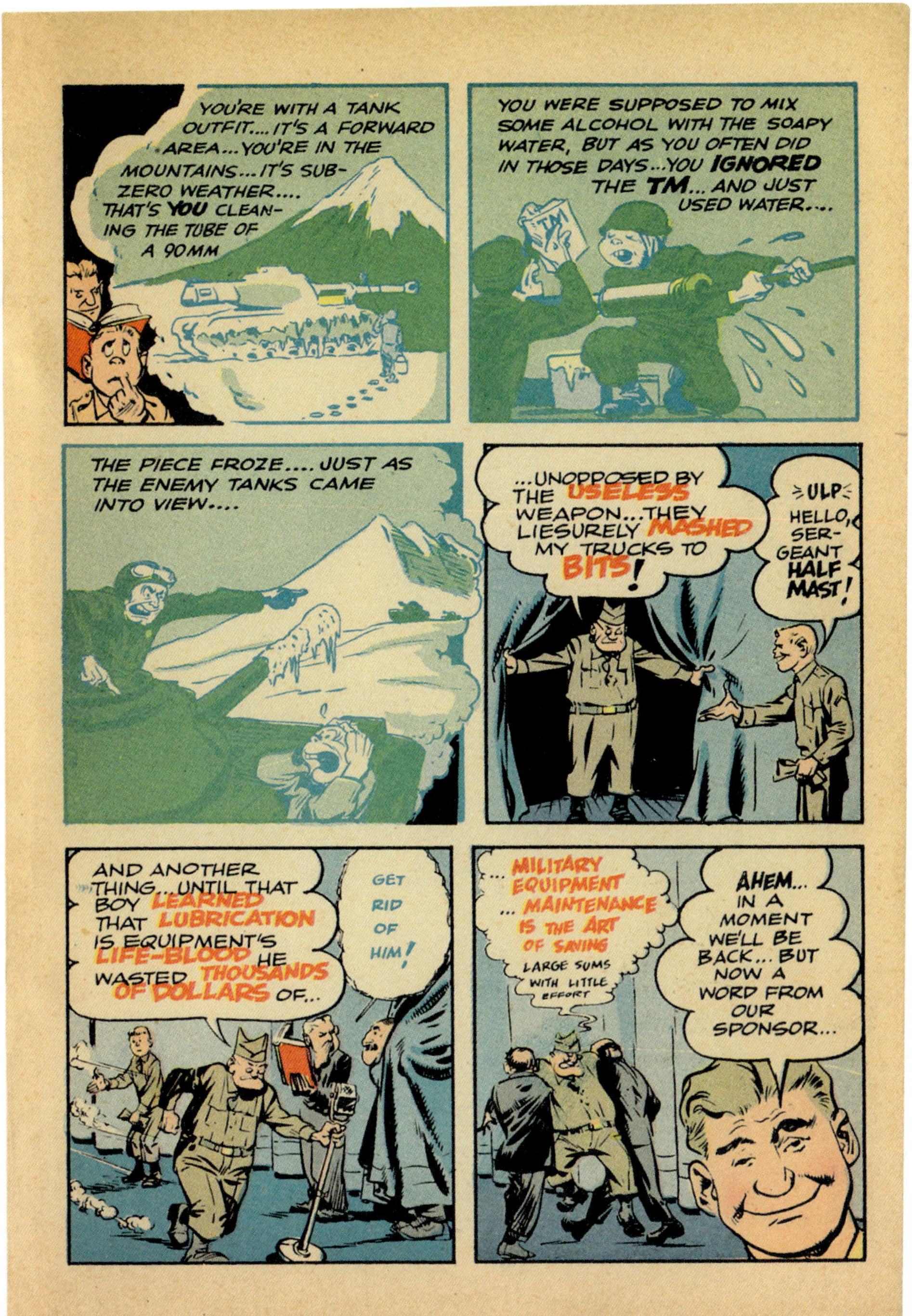
YOU'RE WITH A TANK OUTFIT... IT'S A FORWARD AREA... YOU'RE IN THE MOUNTAINS... IT'S SUB-ZERO WEATHER.... THAT'S YOU CLEANING THE TUBE OF A 90MM
YOU WERE SUPPOSED TO MIX SOME ALCOHOL WITH THE SOAPY WATER, BUT AS YOU OFTEN DID IN THOSE DAYS... YOU IGNORED THE TM... AND JUST USED WATER....
TM
THE PIECE FROZE.... JUST AS THE ENEMY TANKS CAME INTO VIEW....
...UNOPPOSED BY THE USELESS WEAPON... THEY LIESURELY MASHED MY TRUCKS TO BITS!
ULP HELLO, SER-GEANT HALF MAST!
AND ANOTHER THING... UNTIL THAT BOY LEARNED THAT LUBRICATION IS EQUIPMENT'S LIFE-BLOOD HE WASTED THOUSANDS OF DOLLARS OF...
GET RID OF HIM!
... MILITARY EQUIPMENT ... MAINTENANCE IS THE ART OF SAVING LARGE SUMS WITH LITTLE EFFORT
AHEM... IN A MOMENT WE'LL BE BACK... BUT NOW A WORD FROM OUR SPONSOR...

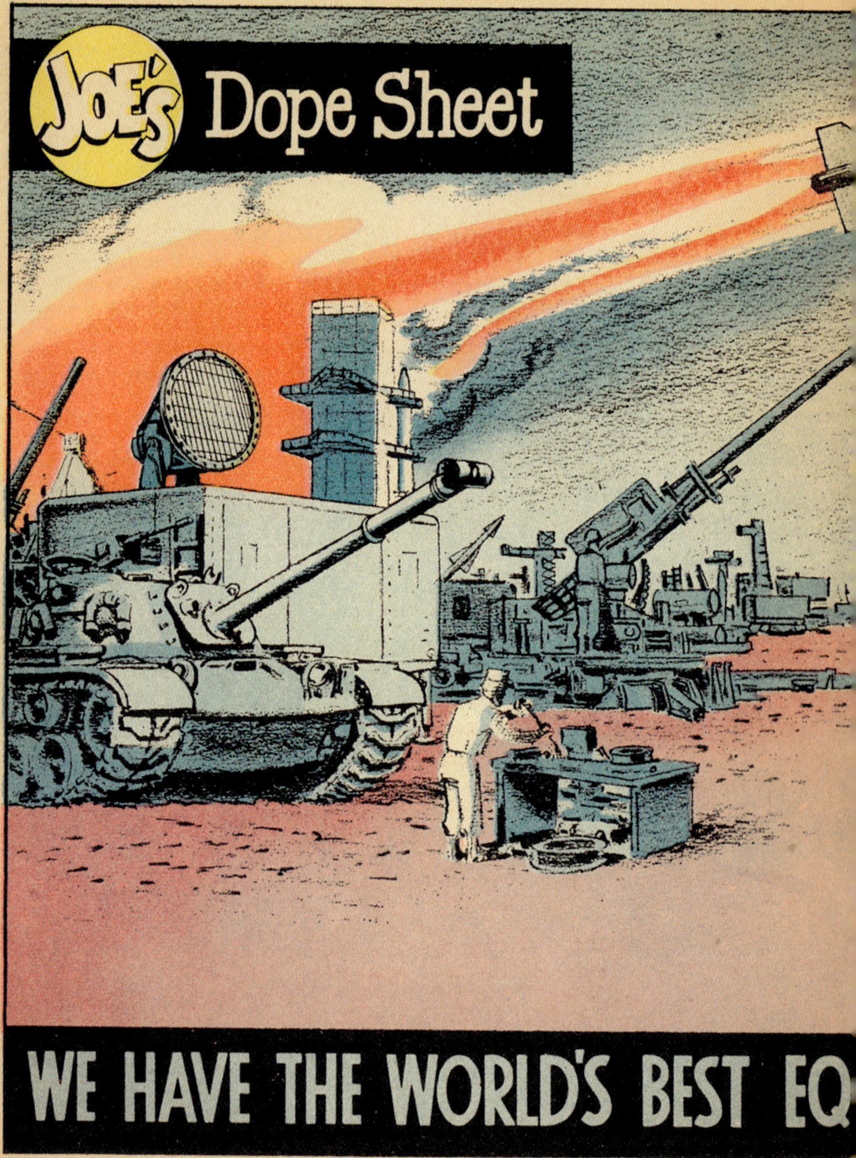
JOE'S Dope Sheet
WE HAVE THE WORLD'S BEST EQ

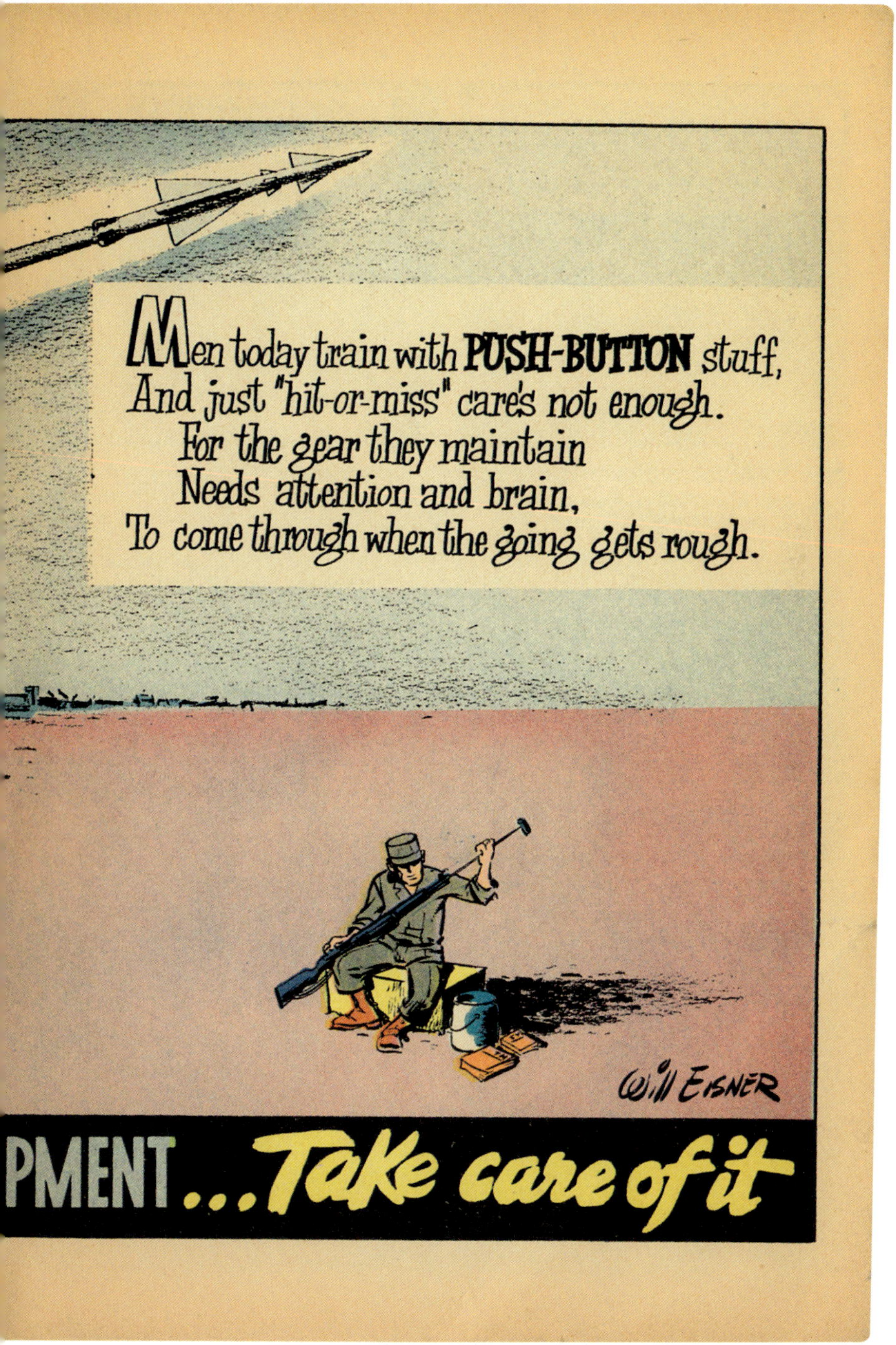
Men today train with PUSH-BUTTON stuff,
And just "hit-or-miss" care's not enough.
For the gear they maintain
Needs attention and brain,
To come through when the going gets rough.
Will Eisner
PMENT...Take care of it

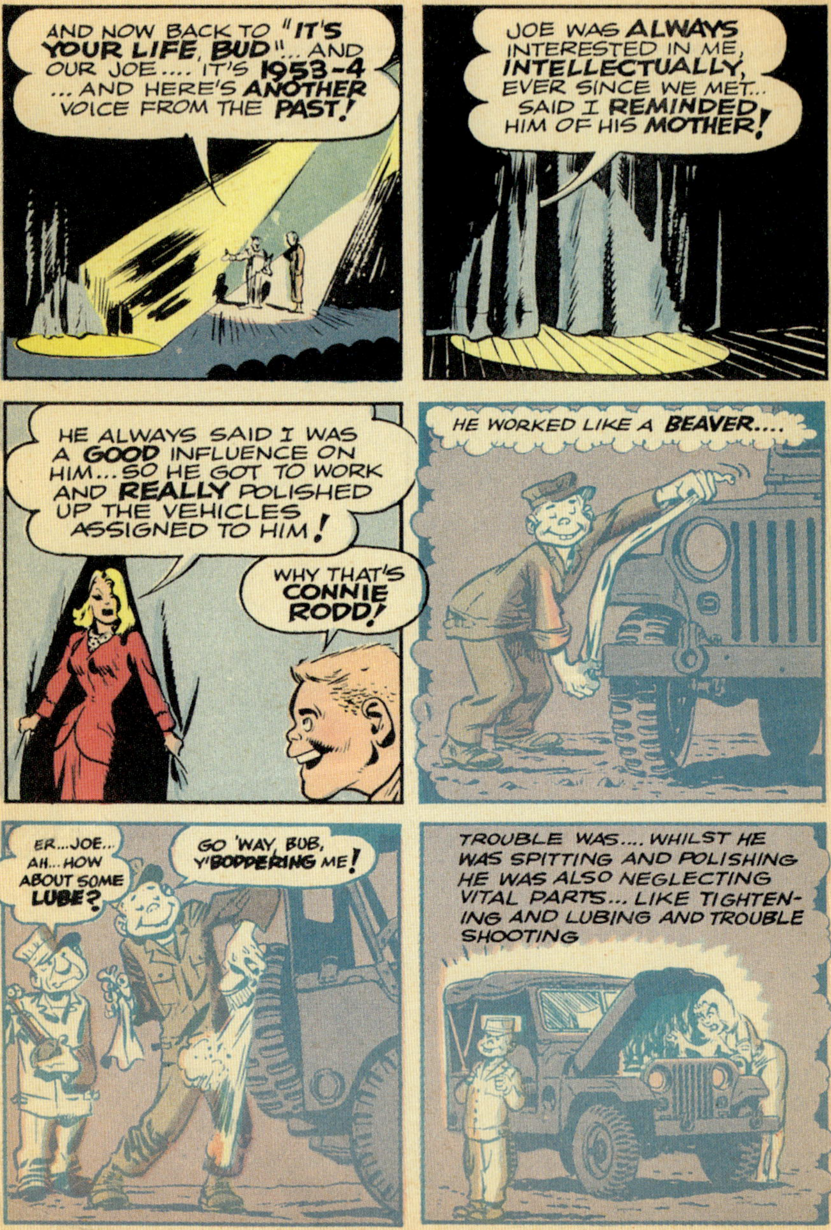
AND NOW BACK TO "IT'S YOUR LIFE, BUD"... AND OUR JOE.... IT'S 1953-4 ... AND HERE'S ANOTHER VOICE FROM THE PAST!
JOE WAS ALWAYS INTERESTED IN ME, INTELLECTUALLY, EVER SINCE WE MET... SAID I REMINDED HIM OF HIS MOTHER!
HE ALWAYS SAID I WAS A GOOD INFLUENCE ON HIM... SO HE GOT TO WORK AND REALLY POLISHED UP THE VEHICLES ASSIGNED TO HIM!
WHY THAT'S CONNIE RODD!
HE WORKED LIKE A BEAVER....
ER...JOE... AH... HOW ABOUT SOME LUBE?
GO 'WAY, BUB, Y'BODDERING ME!
TROUBLE WAS.... WHILST HE WAS SPITTING AND POLISHING HE WAS ALSO NEGLECTING VITAL PARTS... LIKE TIGHTENING AND LUBING AND TROUBLE SHOOTING

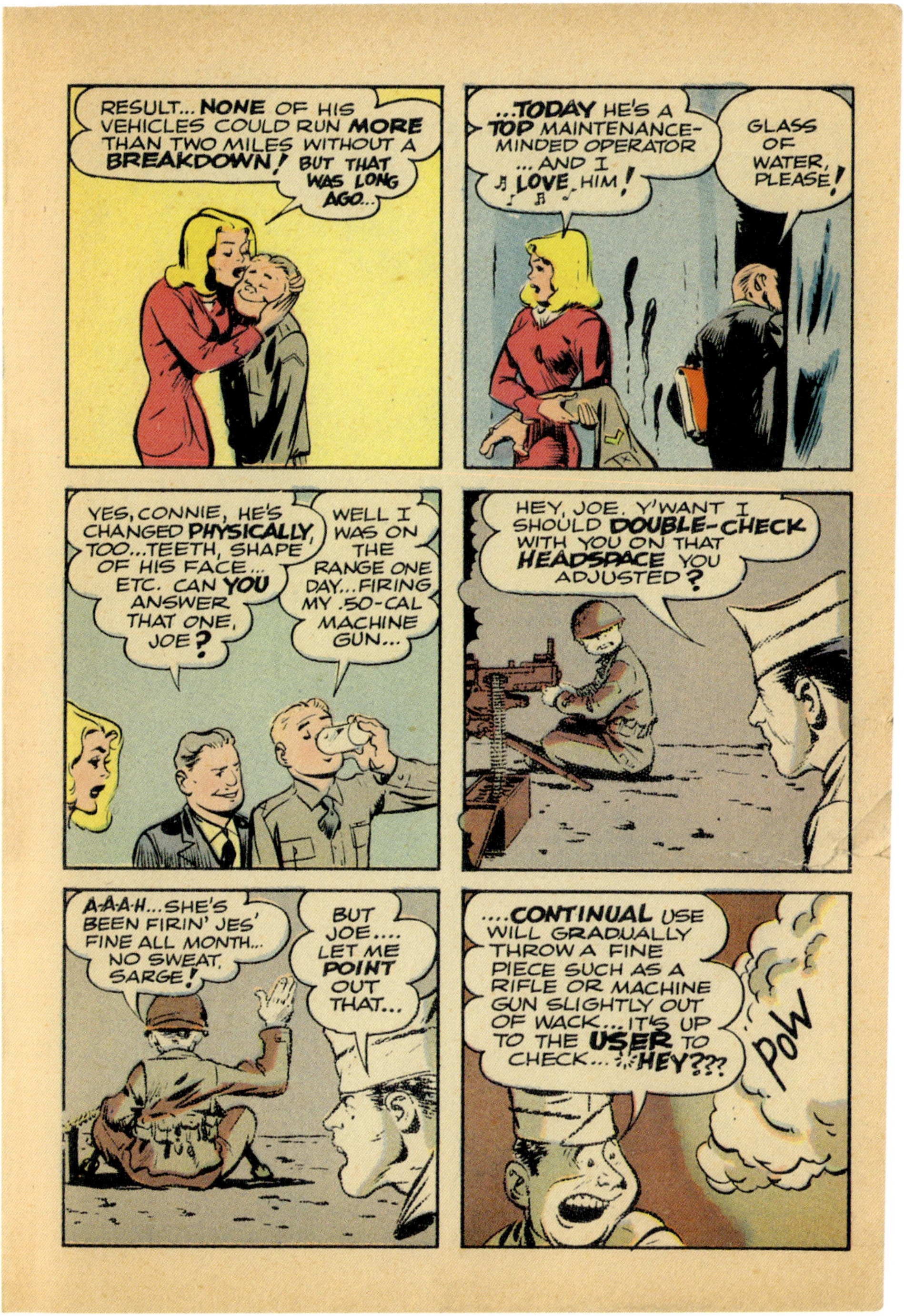
RESULT... NONE OF HIS VEHICLES COULD RUN MORE THAN TWO MILES WITHOUT A BREAKDOWN! BUT THAT WAS LONG AGO...
...TODAY HE'S A TOP MAINTENANCE-MINDED OPERATOR ...AND I LOVE HIM!
GLASS OF WATER, PLEASE!
YES, CONNIE, HE'S CHANGED PHYSICALLY, TOO...TEETH, SHAPE OF HIS FACE... ETC. CAN YOU ANSWER THAT ONE, JOE?
WELL I WAS ON THE RANGE ONE DAY...FIRING MY .50-CAL MACHINE GUN...
HEY, JOE. Y'WANT I SHOULD DOUBLE-CHECK WITH YOU ON THAT HEADSPACE YOU ADJUSTED?
A-A-A-H...SHE'S BEEN FIRIN' JES' FINE ALL MONTH... NO SWEAT, SARGE!
BUT JOE.... LET ME POINT OUT THAT...
....CONTINUAL USE WILL GRADUALLY THROW A FINE PIECE SUCH AS A RIFLE OR MACHINE GUN SLIGHTLY OUT OF WACK... IT'S UP TO THE USER TO CHECK... HEY???
POW

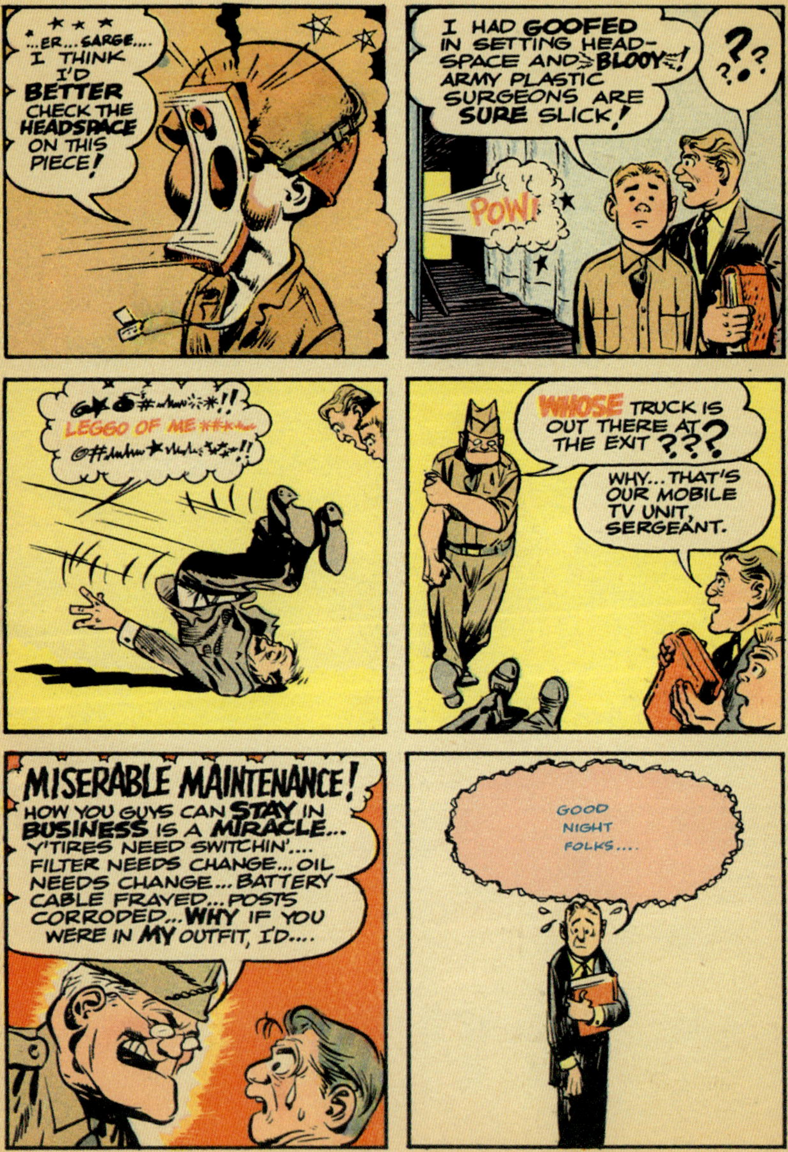
...ER... SARGE.... I THINK I'D BETTER CHECK THE HEADSPACE ON THIS PIECE!
I HAD GOOFED IN SETTING HEAD-SPACE AND BLOOY! ARMY PLASTIC SURGEONS ARE SURE SLICK!
POW!
LEGGO OF ME
WHOSE TRUCK IS OUT THERE AT THE EXIT ???
WHY... THAT'S OUR MOBILE TV UNIT, SERGEANT.
MISERABLE MAINTENANCE! HOW YOU GUYS CAN STAY IN BUSINESS IS A MIRACLE... Y'TIRES NEED SWITCHIN'.... FILTER NEEDS CHANGE... OIL NEEDS CHANGE... BATTERY CABLE FRAYED... POSTS CORRODED... WHY IF YOU WERE IN MY OUTFIT, I'D....
GOOD NIGHT FOLKS....

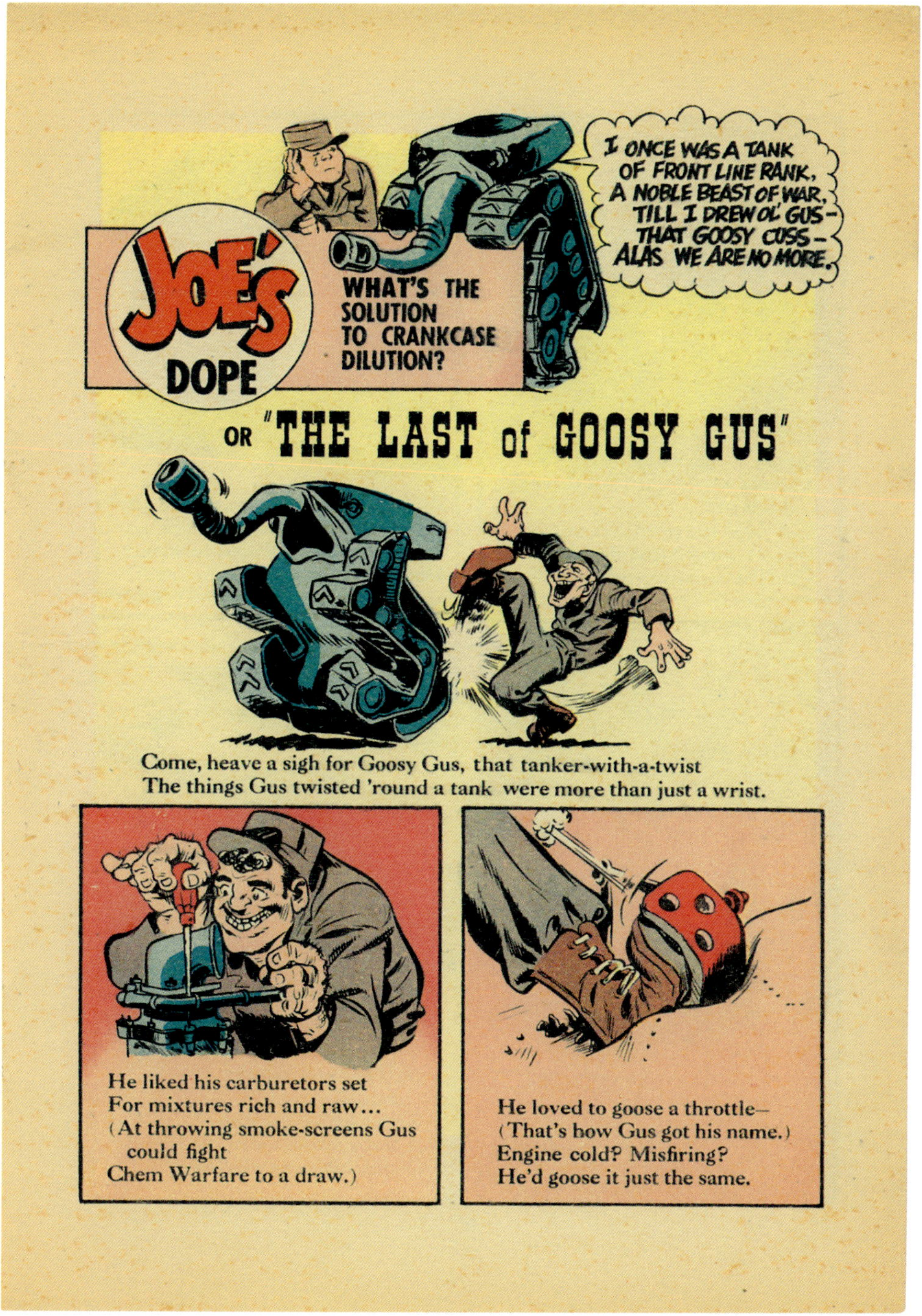
JOE'S DOPE
WHAT'S THE SOLUTION TO CRANKCASE DILUTION?
I ONCE WAS A TANK OF FRONT LINE RANK, A NOBLE BEAST OF WAR, TILL I DREW OL' GUS– THAT GOOSY CUSS– ALAS WE ARE NO MORE.
OR "THE LAST of GOOSY GUS"
Come, heave a sigh for Goosy Gus, that tanker-with-a-twist
The things Gus twisted 'round a tank were more than just a wrist.
He liked his carburetors set For mixtures rich and raw... (At throwing smoke-screens Gus could fight Chem Warfare to a draw.)
He loved to goose a throttle– (That's how Gus got his name.) Engine cold? Misfiring? He'd goose it just the same.

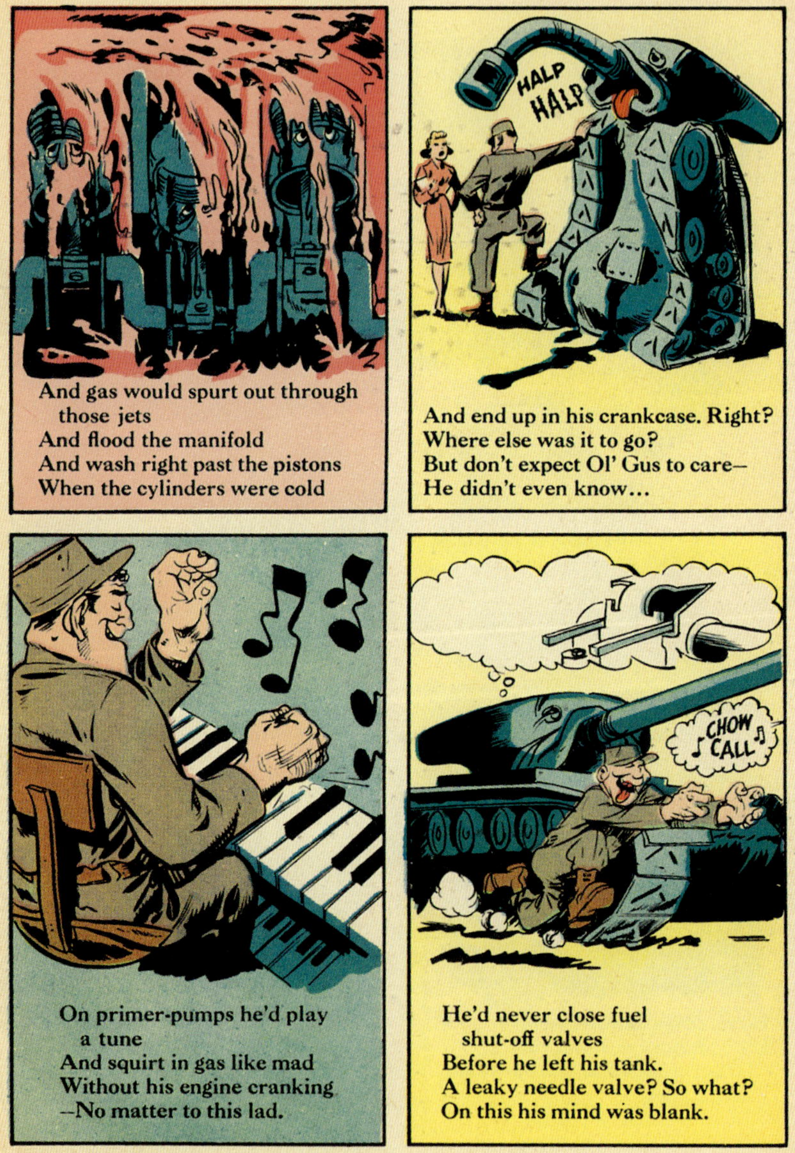
And gas would spurt out through
those jets
And flood the manifold
And wash right past the pistons
When the cylinders were cold
HALP
HALP
And end up in his crankcase. Right?
Where else was it to go?
But don't expect Ol' Gus to care—
He didn't even know...
On primer-pumps he'd play
a tune
And squirt in gas like mad
Without his engine cranking
—No matter to this lad.
CHOW CALL
He'd never close fuel
shut-off valves
Before he left his tank.
A leaky needle valve? So what?
On this his mind was blank.

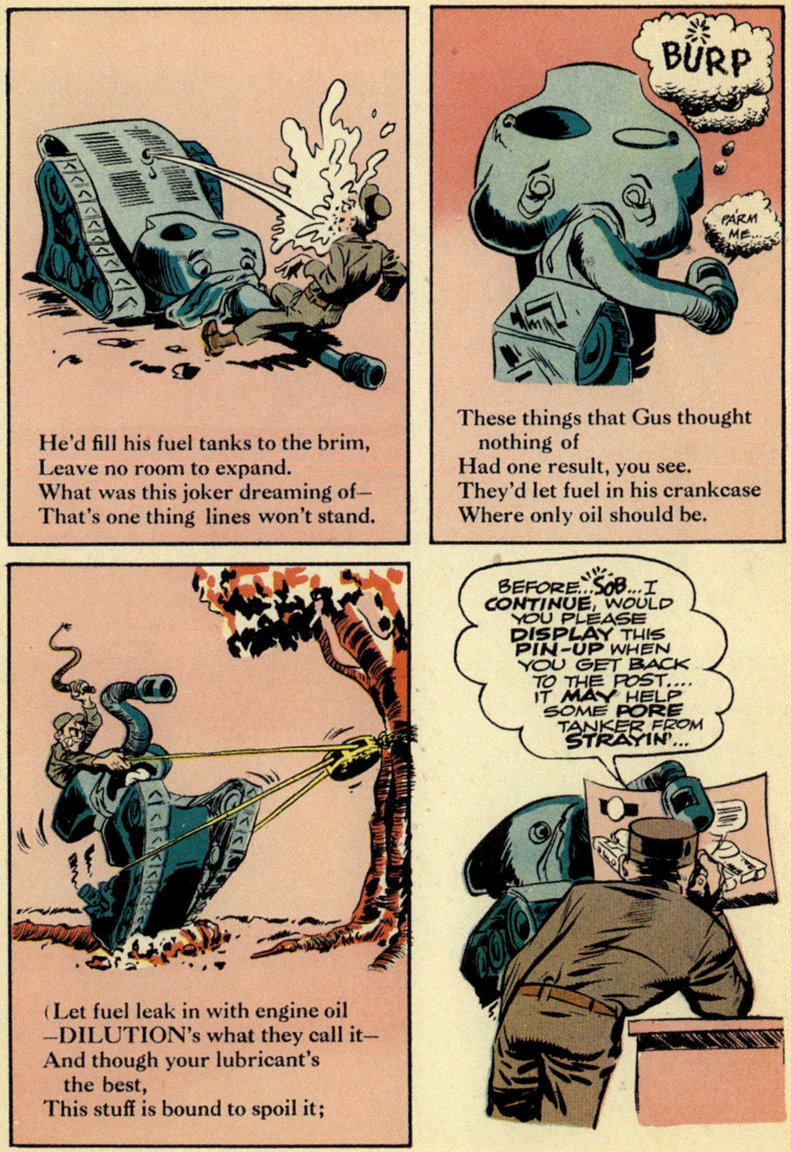
He'd fill his fuel tanks to the brim,
Leave no room to expand.
What was this joker dreaming of–
That's one thing lines won't stand.
BURP
PARM ME...
These things that Gus thought nothing of
Had one result, you see.
They'd let fuel in his crankcase
Where only oil should be.
(Let fuel leak in with engine oil
–DILUTION's what they call it–
And though your lubricant's the best,
This stuff is bound to spoil it;
BEFORE...SOB...I CONTINUE, WOULD YOU PLEASE DISPLAY THIS PIN-UP WHEN YOU GET BACK TO THE POST.... IT MAY HELP SOME PORE TANKER FROM STRAYIN'...

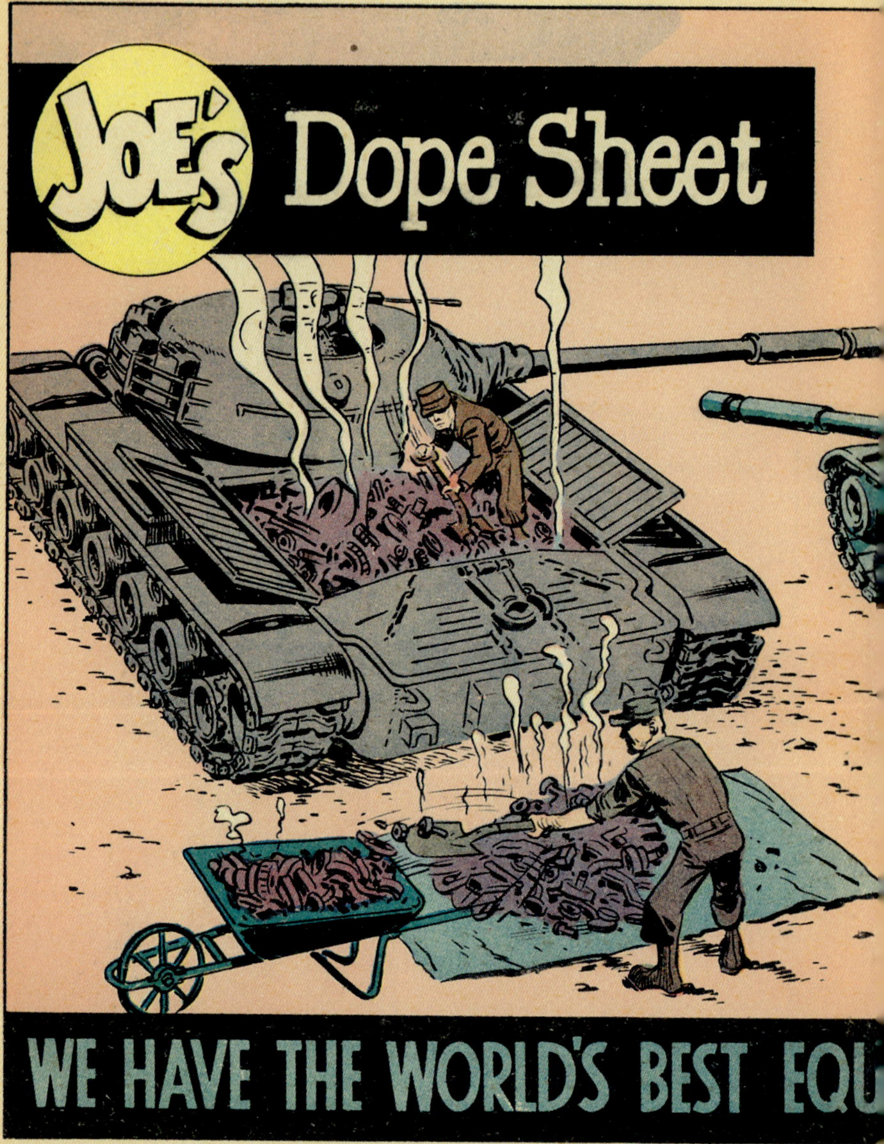
JOE'S Dope Sheet
WE HAVE THE WORLD'S BEST EQU

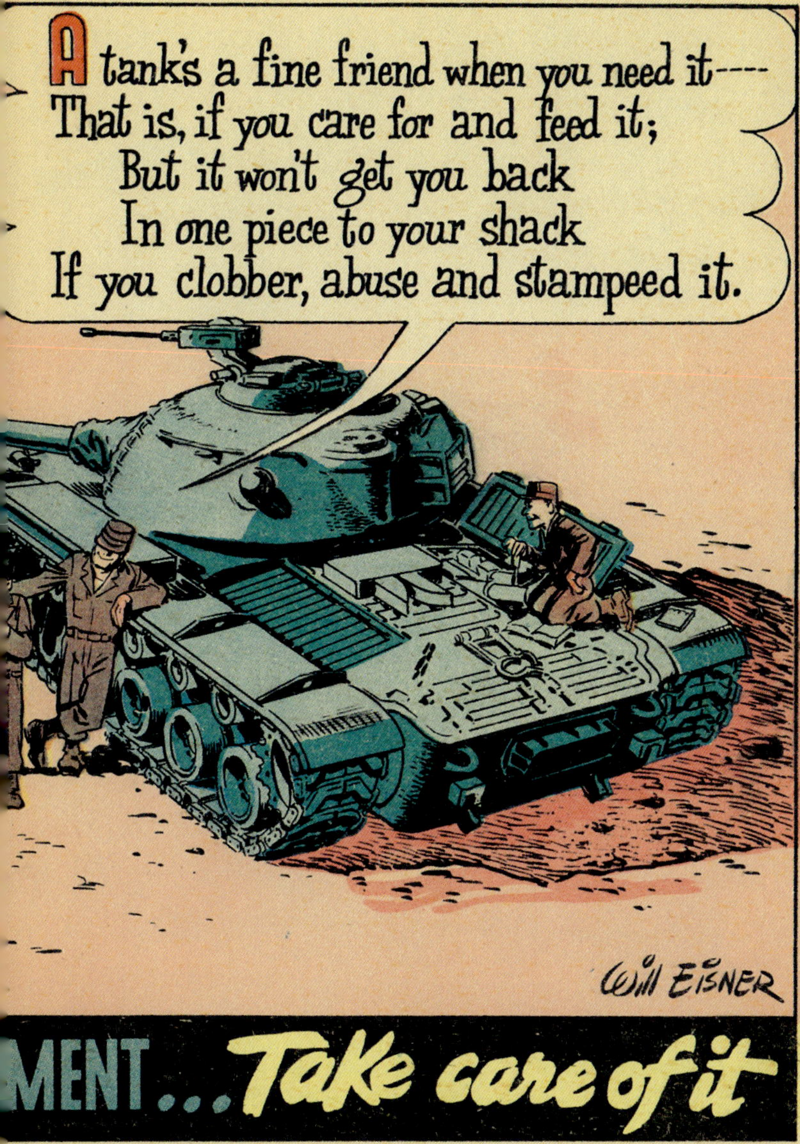
A tank's a fine friend when you need it----
That is, if you care for and feed it;
But it won't get you back
In one piece to your shack
If you clobber, abuse and stampeed it.
Will Eisner
MENT...Take care of it

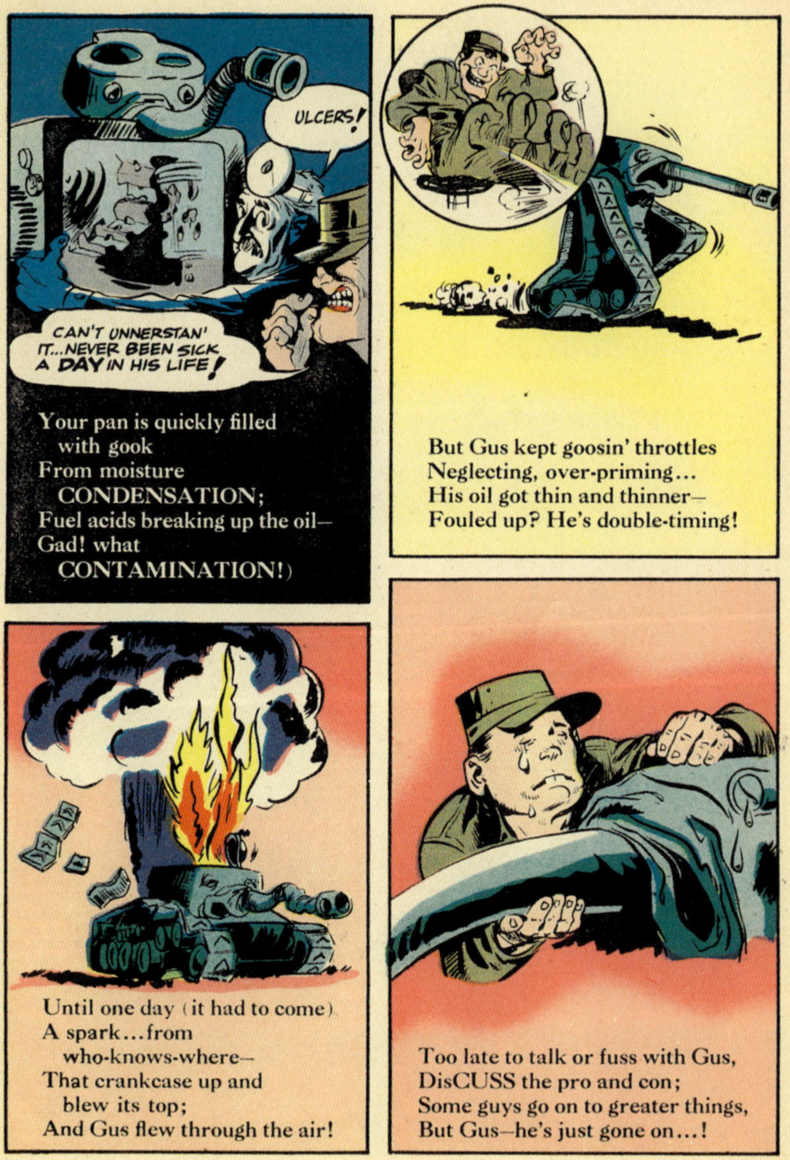
ULCERS!
CAN'T UNNERSTAN' IT...NEVER BEEN SICK A DAY IN HIS LIFE!
Your pan is quickly filled
with gook
From moisture
CONDENSATION;
Fuel acids breaking up the oil—
Gad! what
CONTAMINATION!)
But Gus kept goosin' throttles
Neglecting, over-priming...
His oil got thin and thinner—
Fouled up? He's double-timing!
Until one day (it had to come)
A spark...from
who-knows-where—
That crankcase up and
blew its top;
And Gus flew through the air!
Too late to talk or fuss with Gus,
DisCUSS the pro and con;
Some guys go on to greater things,
But Gus—he's just gone on...!

WELL, THAT WON'T EVER HAPPEN TO ME!
IT COULD HAPPEN TO ANY BODY ANY WHERE!
...WHEN, F'RINSTANCE, A FUEL PUMP DIAPHRAM GOES BUM AND LETS GAS ENTER THE ACCESSORY CASE AND ON INTO THE OIL PAN...
OIL PAN
OR...WHEN PRIMER PUMP CHECK BALL GETS OUTTA WHACK AND LETS ENGINE VACUUM PULL GAS FROM THE TANK INTO THE CYLINDERS AS YOU DECELERATE...
JUST KEEP A SHARP EYE OUT FOR TROUBLE SIGNS... LIKE OIL GETTING TOO THIN...
...OR IF THE OIL LEVEL STARTS TO RISE ON THE DIPSTICK...WHEN IT SHOULD BE FALLING... OKAY, OKAY... SO WHAT DOES THAT TELL YOU?
UNLESS YOU'VE BEEN MAKIN' LIKE GOOSY GUS... IT'S PUMP TROUBLE... GET 'EM CHECKED!
WELL, SO LONG, NOW...
ONE THING MORE ...IN SOME CASES THERE'S ANOTHER WAY Y'CAN GET A FOULED-UP FUEL MIXTURE AND DILUTED CRANCASE OIL....
HURRY UP!! I'M LATE.... GOTTA BREAK IN A NEW TANK DRIVER!
...AND THAT IS CARBURETOR ICING... DID YOU SEE P.S 40 PAGE 31??
P.S

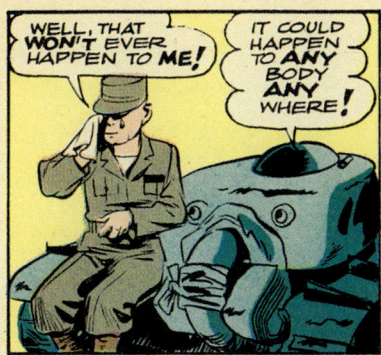

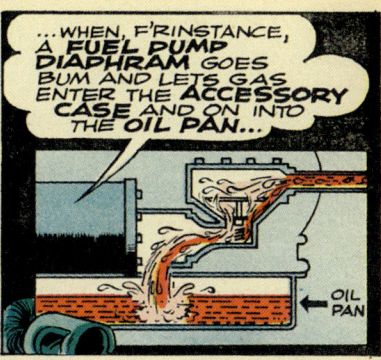

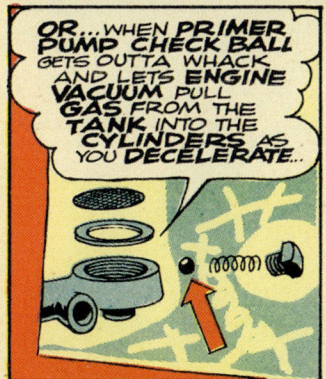

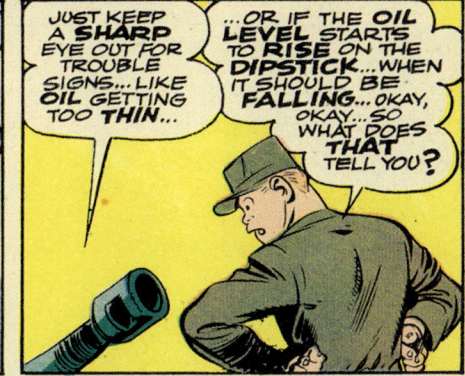

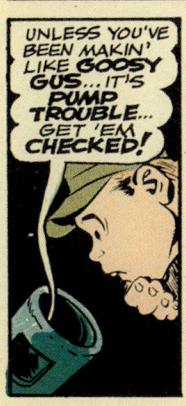

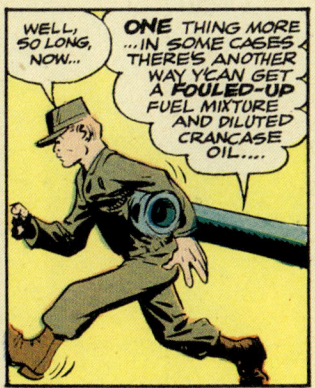

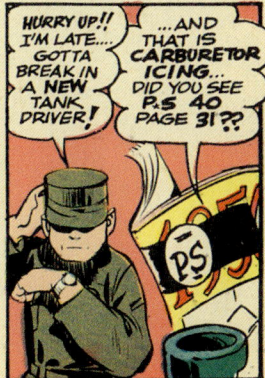

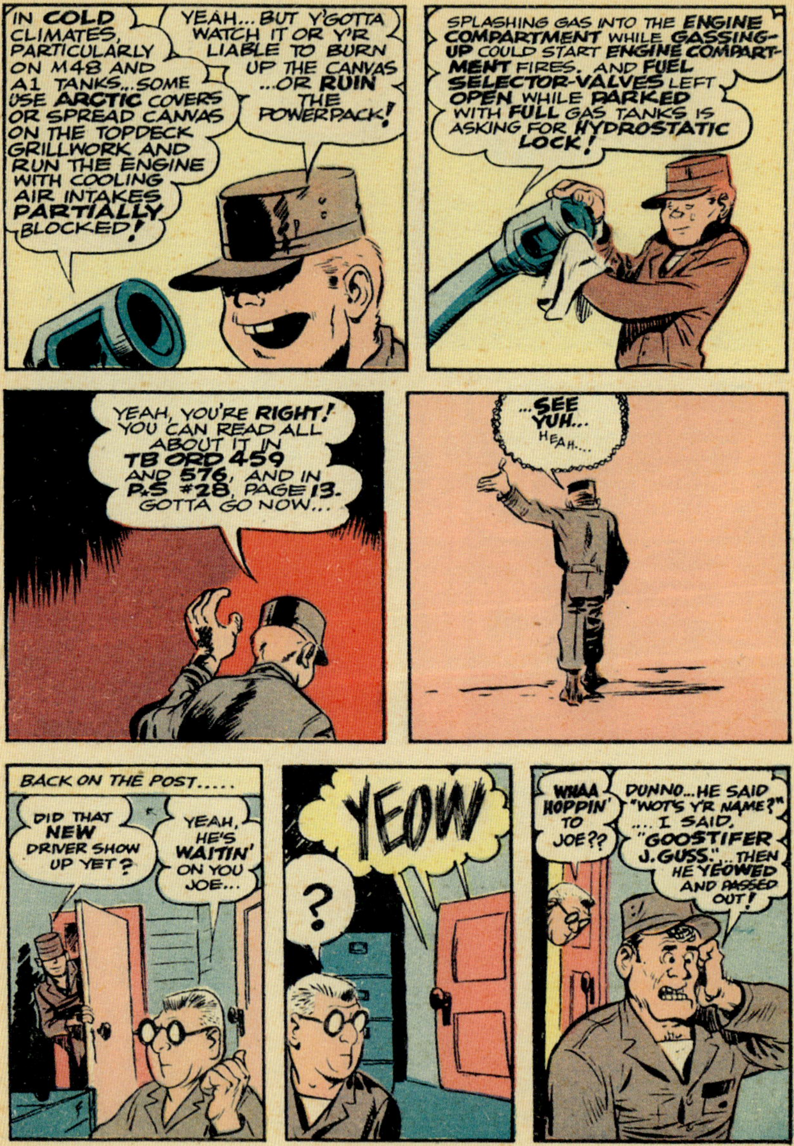
IN COLD CLIMATES, PARTICULARLY ON M48 AND A1 TANKS...SOME USE ARCTIC COVERS OR SPREAD CANVAS ON THE TOPDECK GRILLWORK AND RUN THE ENGINE WITH COOLING AIR INTAKES PARTIALLY BLOCKED!
YEAH... BUT Y'GOTTA WATCH IT OR Y'R LIABLE TO BURN UP THE CANVAS ...OR RUIN THE POWERPACK!
SPLASHING GAS INTO THE ENGINE COMPARTMENT WHILE GASSING-UP COULD START ENGINE COMPARTMENT FIRES. AND FUEL SELECTOR-VALVES LEFT OPEN WHILE PARKED WITH FULL GAS TANKS IS ASKING FOR HYDROSTATIC LOCK!
YEAH, YOU'RE RIGHT! YOU CAN READ ALL ABOUT IT IN TB ORD 459 AND 576, AND IN P.S #28, PAGE 13. GOTTA GO NOW...
...SEE YUH... HEAH...
BACK ON THE POST.....
DID THAT NEW DRIVER SHOW UP YET?
YEAH, HE'S WAITIN' ON YOU JOE...
YEOW
?
WHAA HOPPIN' TO JOE??
DUNNO...HE SAID "WOT'S Y'R NAME?" ... I SAID, "GOOSTIFER J. GUSS."... THEN HE YEOWED AND PASSED OUT!

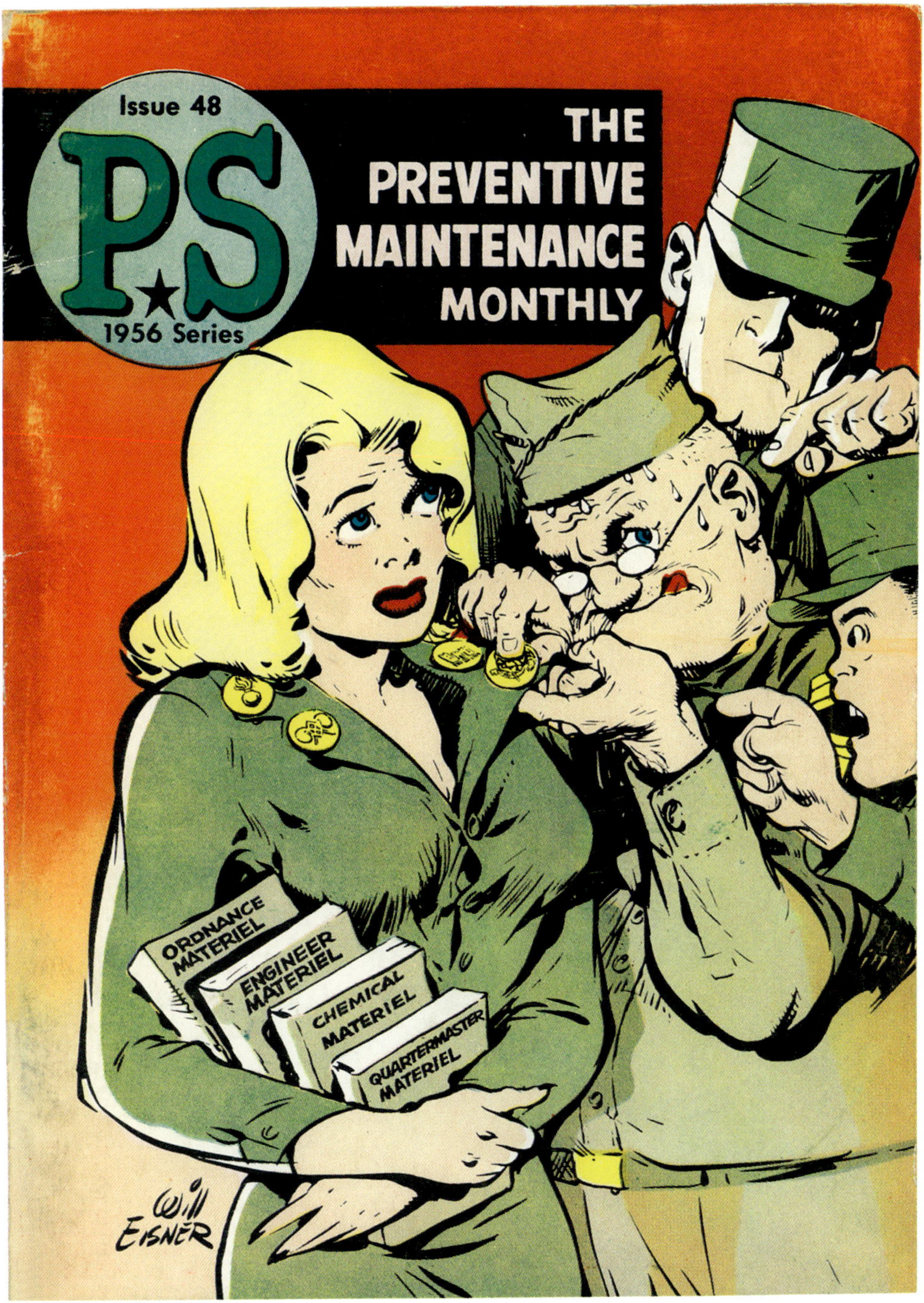
Issue 48
P.S
1956 Series
THE
PREVENTIVE
MAINTENANCE
MONTHLY
ORDNANCE MATERIEL
ENGINEER MATERIEL
CHEMICAL MATERIEL
QUARTERMASTER MATERIEL
Will EISNER

no. 48, 1956

IS YOUR HONEYMOON OVER WIT

Are you forgetting those little things that count? The boys are saying— and it's not a latent rumor—that some fire control mechanics on the M33 fire control systems are taking little maintenance procedures for granted. They've been at the business a long time, doing the same things over and over. Maybe it gets a little monotonous. After a while, somebody takes shortcuts or figures there's an easier way to do things, or just plain forgets.

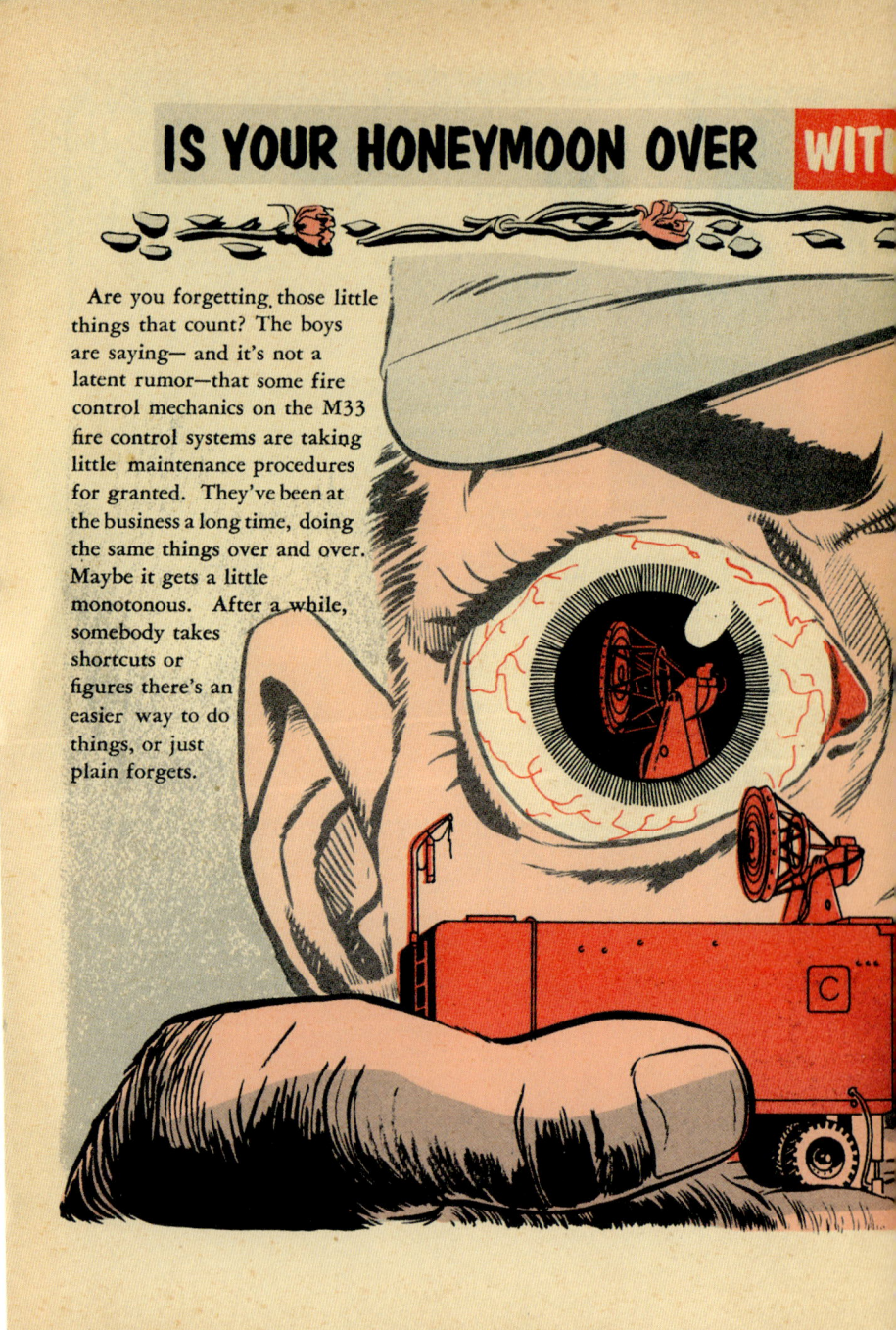

HE M33 FIRE CONTROL SYSTEM?

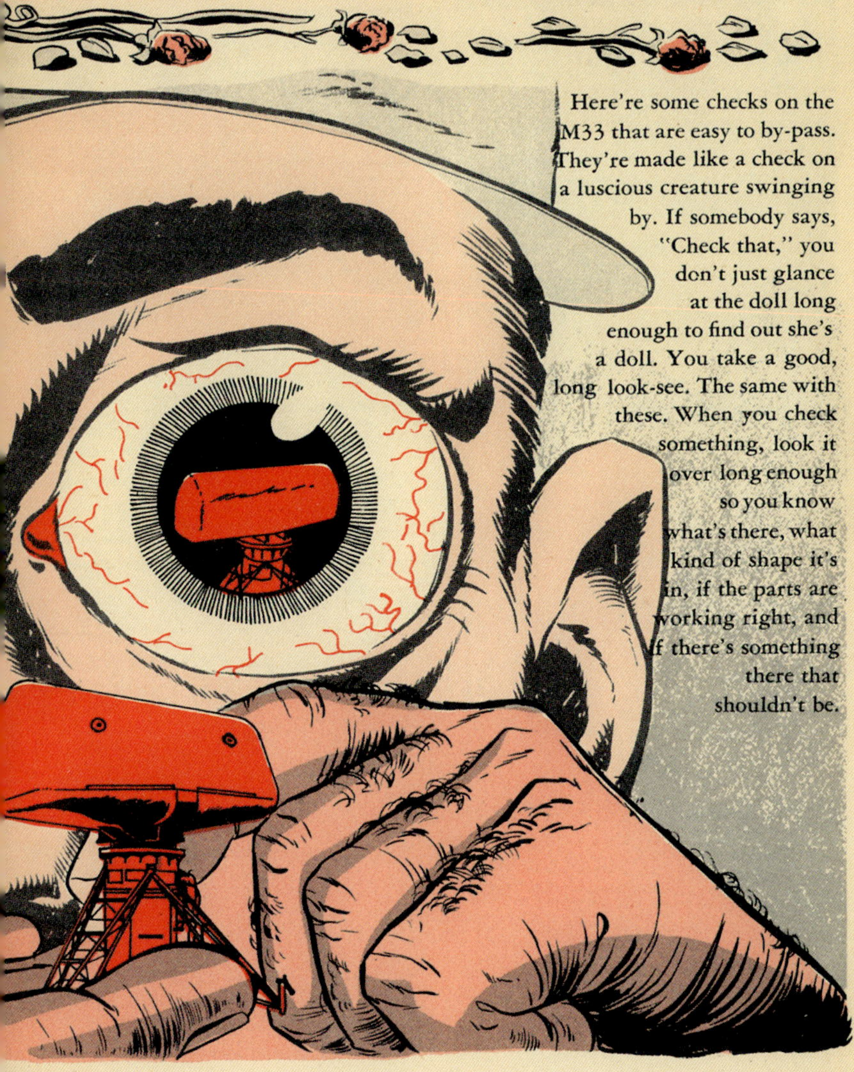

Here're some checks on the M33 that are easy to by-pass. They're made like a check on a luscious creature swinging by. If somebody says, "Check that," you don't just glance at the doll long enough to find out she's a doll. You take a good, long look-see. The same with these. When you check something, look it over long enough so you know what's there, what kind of shape it's in, if the parts are working right, and if there's something there that shouldn't be.

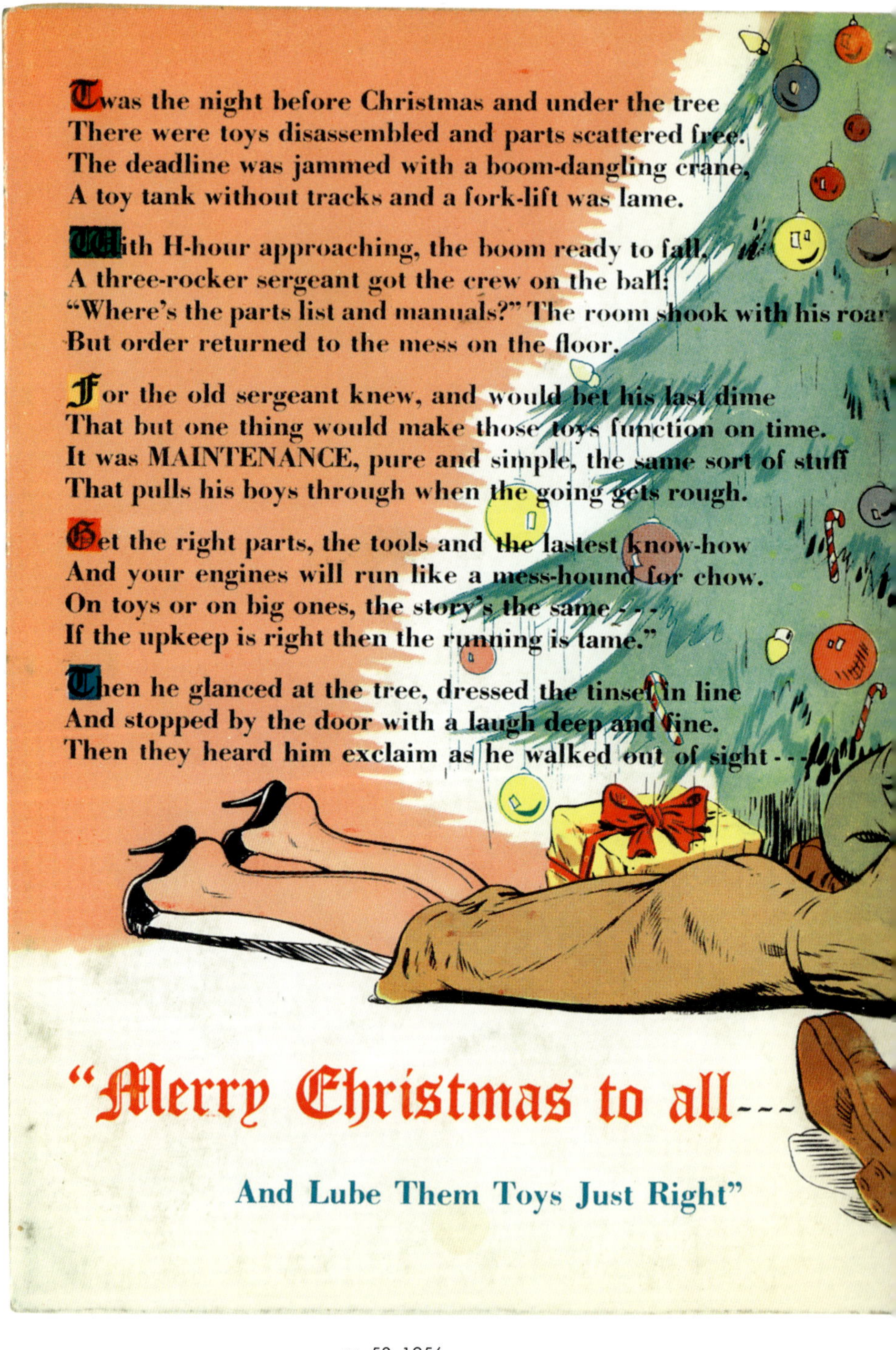

Twas the night before Christmas and under the tree
There were toys disassembled and parts scattered free.
The deadline was jammed with a boom-dangling crane,
A toy tank without tracks and a fork-lift was lame.

With H-hour approaching, the boom ready to fall,
A three-rocker sergeant got the crew on the ball:
"Where's the parts list and manuals?" The room shook with his roar
But order returned to the mess on the floor.

For the old sergeant knew, and would bet his last dime
That but one thing would make those toys function on time.
It was MAINTENANCE, pure and simple, the same sort of stuff
That pulls his boys through when the going gets rough.

Get the right parts, the tools and the lastest know-how
And your engines will run like a mess-hound for chow.
On toys or on big ones, the story's the same - - -
If the upkeep is right then the running is tame."

Then he glanced at the tree, dressed the tinsel in line
And stopped by the door with a laugh deep and fine.
Then they heard him exclaim as he walked out of sight - - -

"Merry Christmas to all - - -

And Lube Them Toys Just Right"

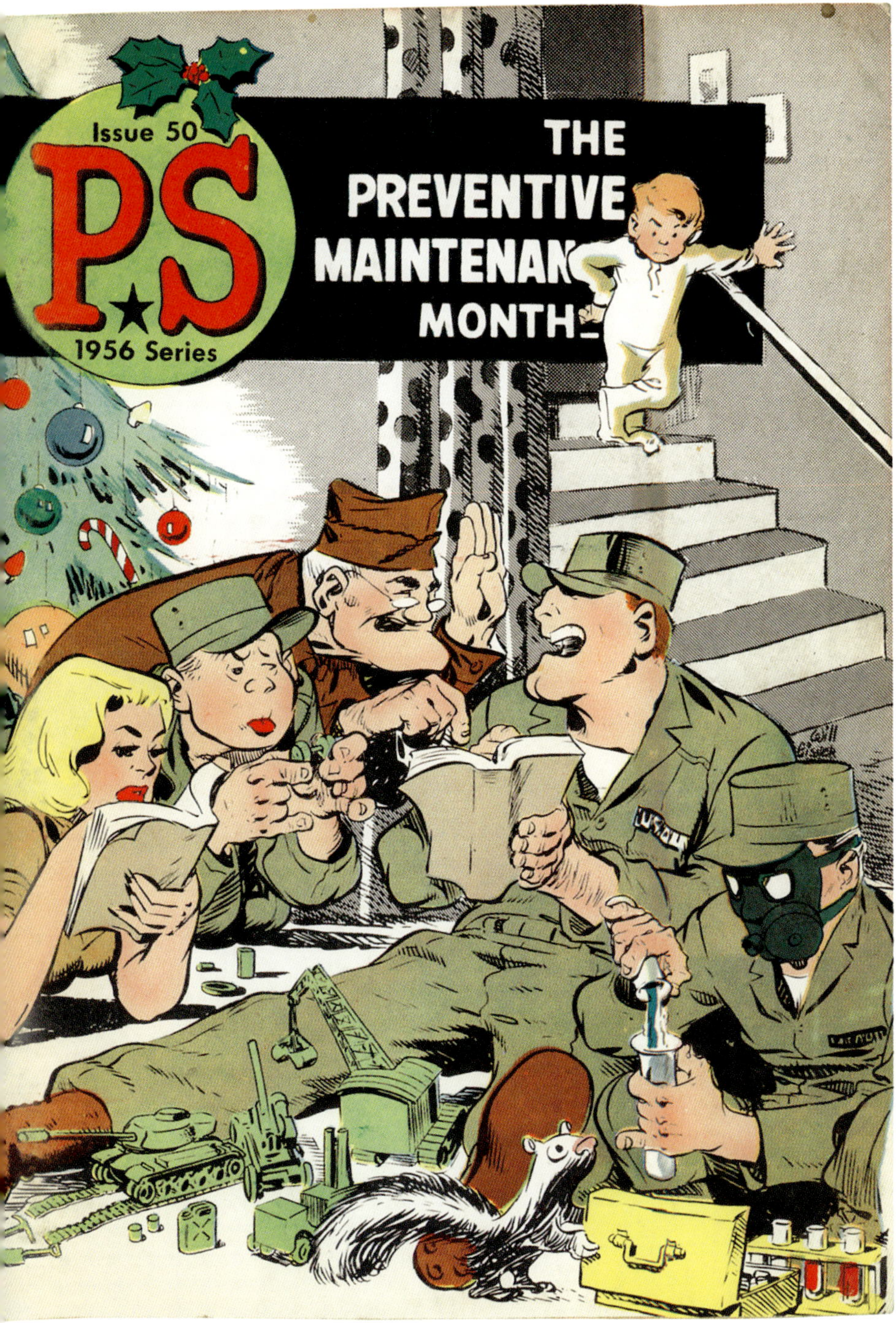
Issue 50
P.S
1956 Series
THE
PREVENTIVE
MAINTENAN
MONTH

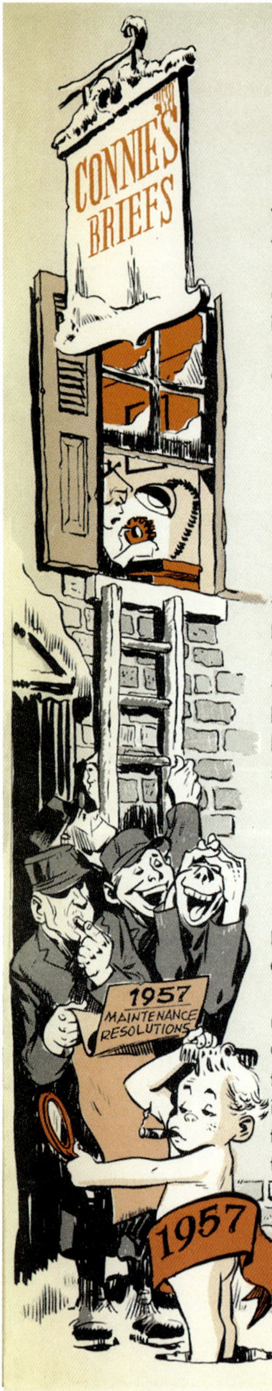
CONNIE'S BRIEFS
1957 MAINTENANCE RESOLUTIONS
1957

T34E1 storage story

The T34E1 sighting system with the Skysweeper is seldom—if ever—used. But that doesn't mean to leave her in a box like Christmas tree trimmings. Take it out to perform preventive maintenance services like TM 9-361, Section XV says.

No wind

In spite of what you may've read on page 484 of TM 9-8022 keep compressed air away from those wheel bearings. Heed the caution on page 199. When you think you're doing those bearings a favor by blowin' 'em dry, you may just be sending 'em to salvage in short order.

Lights out

You'd better hang on to Light, head, service, assy G251-7765212 if you've got a 155-mm SP howitzer M44 (T194). It won't exhaust to G260-7419686 light. Due to the size and location of mounting, the light and connectors hit the light guard and won't position right.

OK O-rings

Any trouble with the O-rings in Nike missile? Could be you're not zeroed in on removing, installing and lubing. The right scoop is in Nike Handbook No. 11.1 (revised Feb 56). For OK O-rings, that's the method for you.

For damp RCATs

RCATs OQ-19B and OQ-19D used on over-water flights need insulation on the waterproof seals of the J-1 controller, servos, receivers, and junction boxes. Use Electrical insulating compound paste (FSN 5970-224-5276 formerly FSN 5790-251-9149 as listed in Ord 3 SNL K-1). It'll be put in a revision of Ord 7 SNL Y-32.

No drips wanted

You got drips dropping into your Fire Control (M244, M244E1, M258, M259 or M262) trailers? If so, there's a TB out that'll tell you how to keep the roofs of these trailers from leaking. The publication is TB 9-8224-1 (19 Oct 55), and it tells you how to apply and maintain sealant material on those roofs. Why not get yourself a copy?

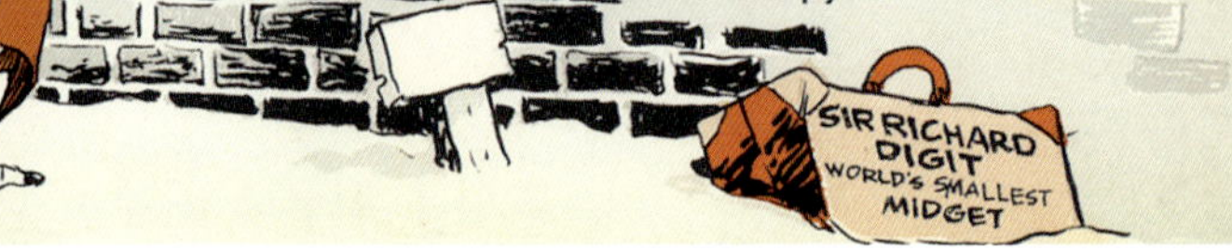
SIR RICHARD DIGIT
WORLD'S SMALLEST MIDGET

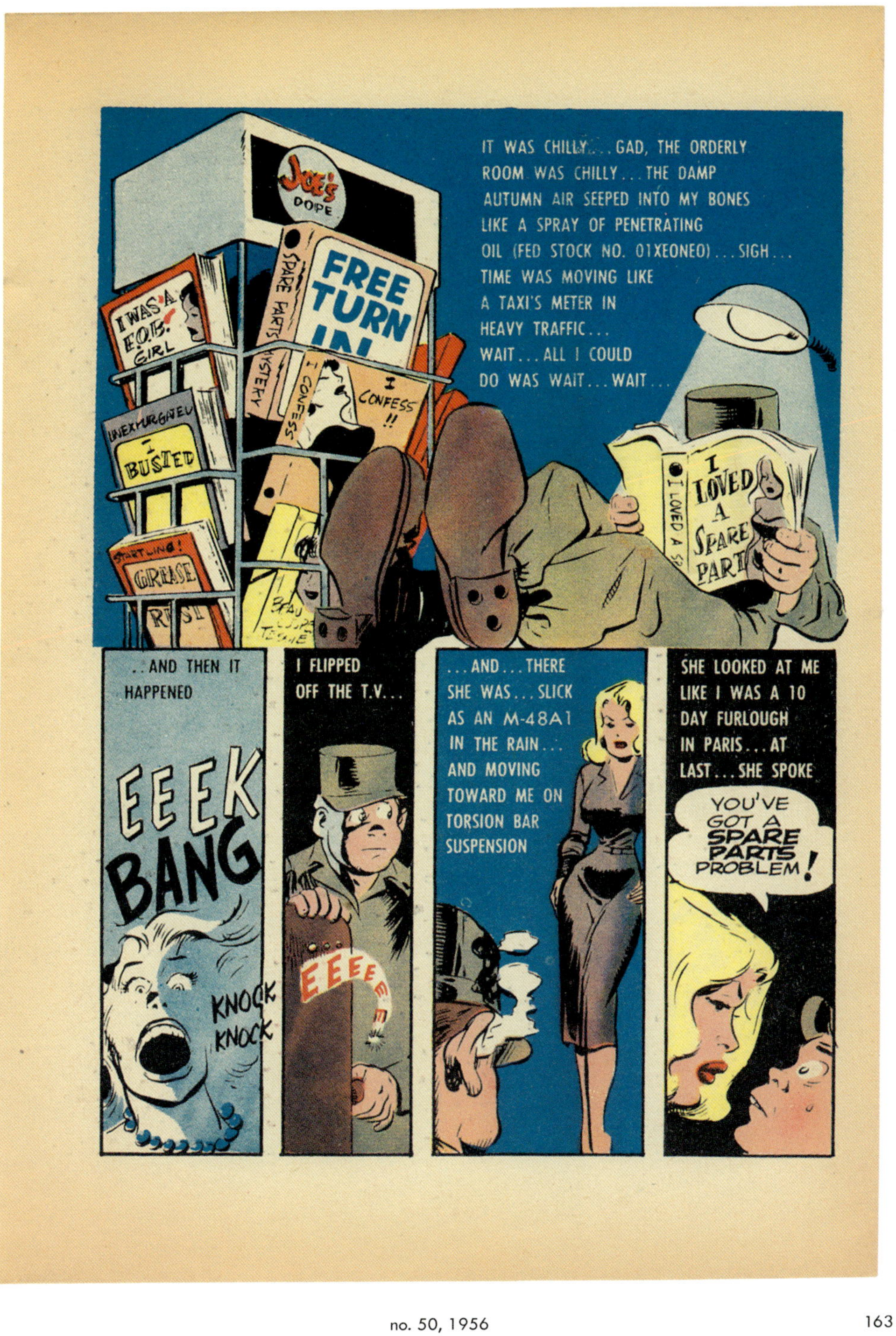

IT WAS CHILLY . . . GAD, THE ORDERLY ROOM WAS CHILLY . . . THE DAMP AUTUMN AIR SEEPED INTO MY BONES LIKE A SPRAY OF PENETRATING OIL (FED STOCK NO. 01XEONEO) . . . SIGH . . . TIME WAS MOVING LIKE A TAXI'S METER IN HEAVY TRAFFIC . . . WAIT . . . ALL I COULD DO WAS WAIT . . . WAIT . . .
JOE'S DOPE
FREE TURN IN
SPARE PARTS MYSTERY
I WAS A F.O.B. GIRL
I CONFESS
I CONFESS !!
UNEXPURGATED
I BUSTED
STARTLING!
GREASE
I LOVED A SPARE PART
. . AND THEN IT HAPPENED
EEEK
BANG
KNOCK KNOCK
I FLIPPED OFF THE T.V. . .
EEEEEE
. . . AND . . . THERE SHE WAS . . . SLICK AS AN M-48A1 IN THE RAIN . . . AND MOVING TOWARD ME ON TORSION BAR SUSPENSION
SHE LOOKED AT ME LIKE I WAS A 10 DAY FURLOUGH IN PARIS . . . AT LAST . . . SHE SPOKE
YOU'VE GOT A SPARE PARTS PROBLEM!

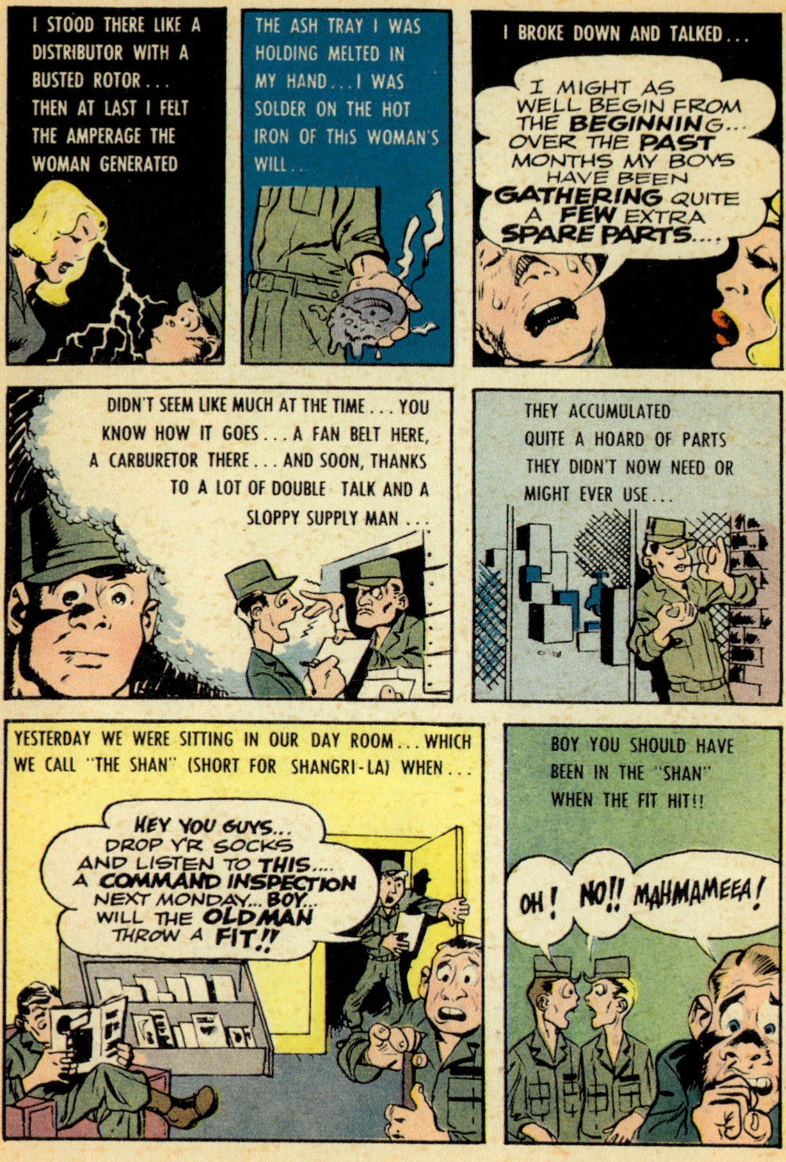
I STOOD THERE LIKE A DISTRIBUTOR WITH A BUSTED ROTOR... THEN AT LAST I FELT THE AMPERAGE THE WOMAN GENERATED
THE ASH TRAY I WAS HOLDING MELTED IN MY HAND... I WAS SOLDER ON THE HOT IRON OF THIS WOMAN'S WILL...
I BROKE DOWN AND TALKED...
I MIGHT AS WELL BEGIN FROM THE BEGINNING... OVER THE PAST MONTHS MY BOYS HAVE BEEN GATHERING QUITE A FEW EXTRA SPARE PARTS....
DIDN'T SEEM LIKE MUCH AT THE TIME... YOU KNOW HOW IT GOES... A FAN BELT HERE, A CARBURETOR THERE... AND SOON, THANKS TO A LOT OF DOUBLE TALK AND A SLOPPY SUPPLY MAN...
THEY ACCUMULATED QUITE A HOARD OF PARTS THEY DIDN'T NOW NEED OR MIGHT EVER USE...
YESTERDAY WE WERE SITTING IN OUR DAY ROOM... WHICH WE CALL "THE SHAN" (SHORT FOR SHANGRI-LA) WHEN...
HEY YOU GUYS... DROP Y'R SOCKS AND LISTEN TO THIS.... A COMMAND INSPECTION NEXT MONDAY... BOY... WILL THE OLDMAN THROW A FIT!!
BOY YOU SHOULD HAVE BEEN IN THE "SHAN" WHEN THE FIT HIT!!
OH!
NO!!
MAHMAMEEA!

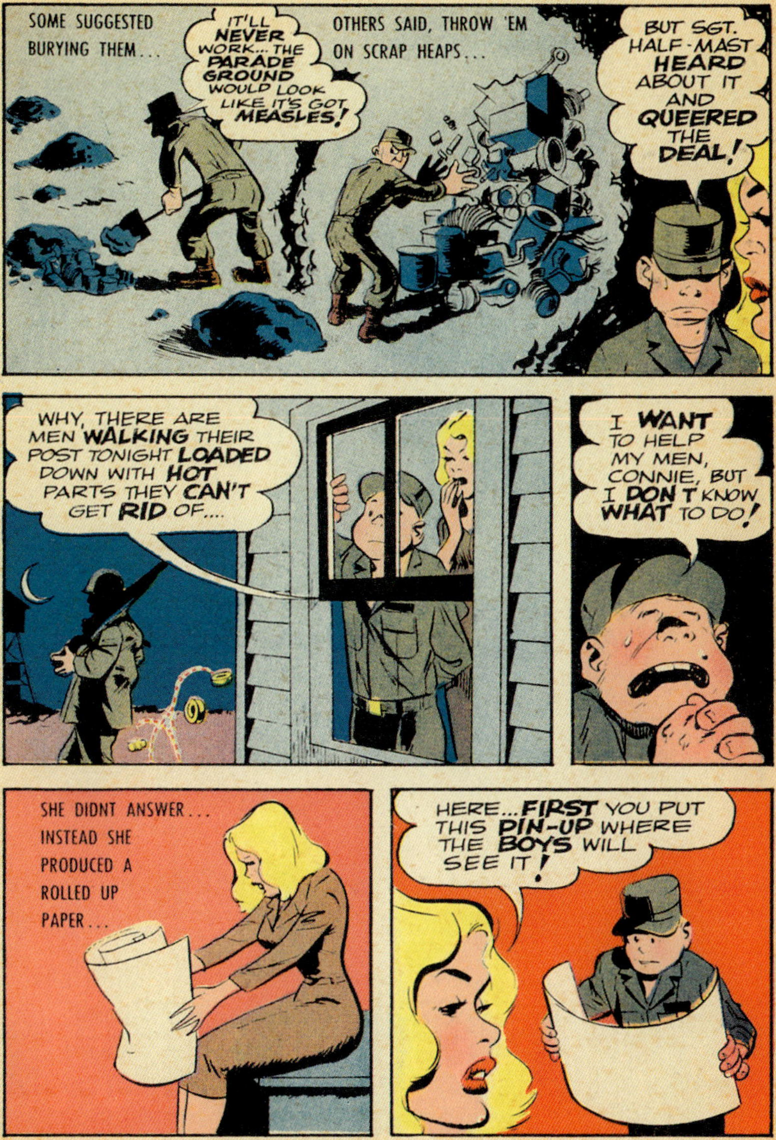
SOME SUGGESTED BURYING THEM...
IT'LL NEVER WORK... THE PARADE GROUND WOULD LOOK LIKE IT'S GOT MEASLES!
OTHERS SAID, THROW 'EM ON SCRAP HEAPS...
BUT SGT. HALF-MAST HEARD ABOUT IT AND QUEERED THE DEAL!
WHY, THERE ARE MEN WALKING THEIR POST TONIGHT LOADED DOWN WITH HOT PARTS THEY CAN'T GET RID OF....
I WANT TO HELP MY MEN, CONNIE, BUT I DON'T KNOW WHAT TO DO!
SHE DIDNT ANSWER... INSTEAD SHE PRODUCED A ROLLED UP PAPER...
HERE... FIRST YOU PUT THIS PIN-UP WHERE THE BOYS WILL SEE IT!

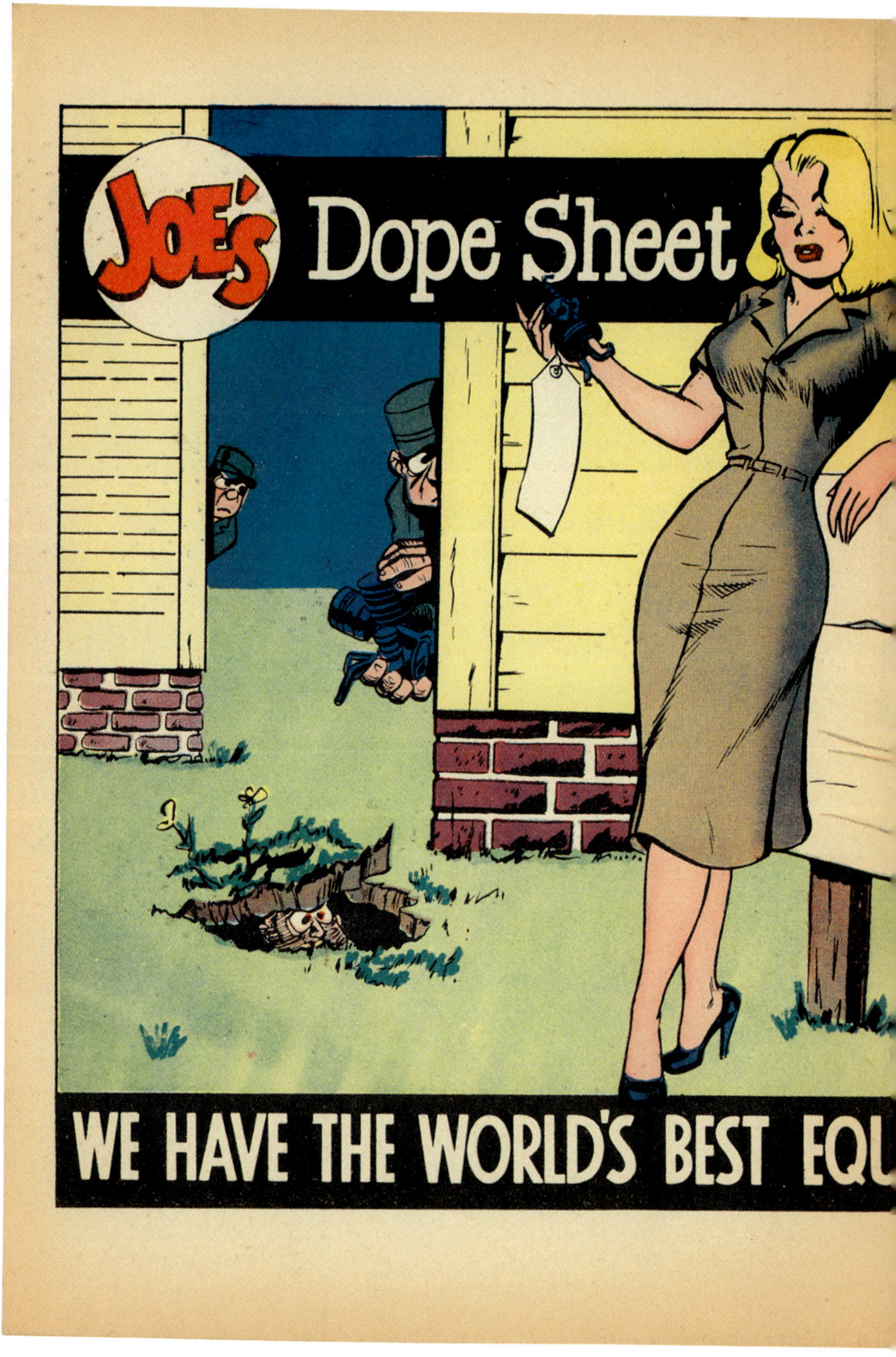
JOE'S Dope Sheet
WE HAVE THE WORLD'S BEST EQU

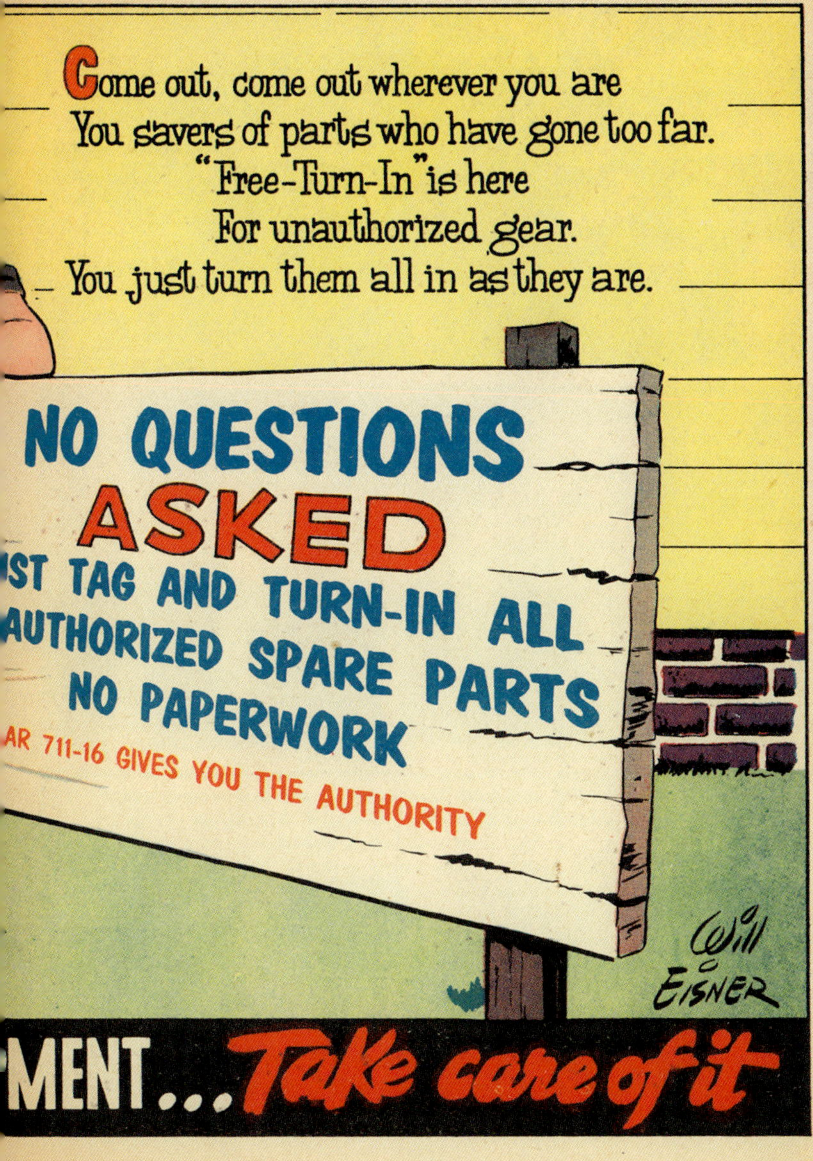
Come out, come out wherever you are
You savers of parts who have gone too far.
"Free-Turn-In" is here
For unauthorized gear.
You just turn them all in as they are.
NO QUESTIONS
ASKED
ST TAG AND TURN-IN ALL
AUTHORIZED SPARE PARTS
NO PAPERWORK
AR 711-16 GIVES YOU THE AUTHORITY
Will Eisner
MENT... Take care of it

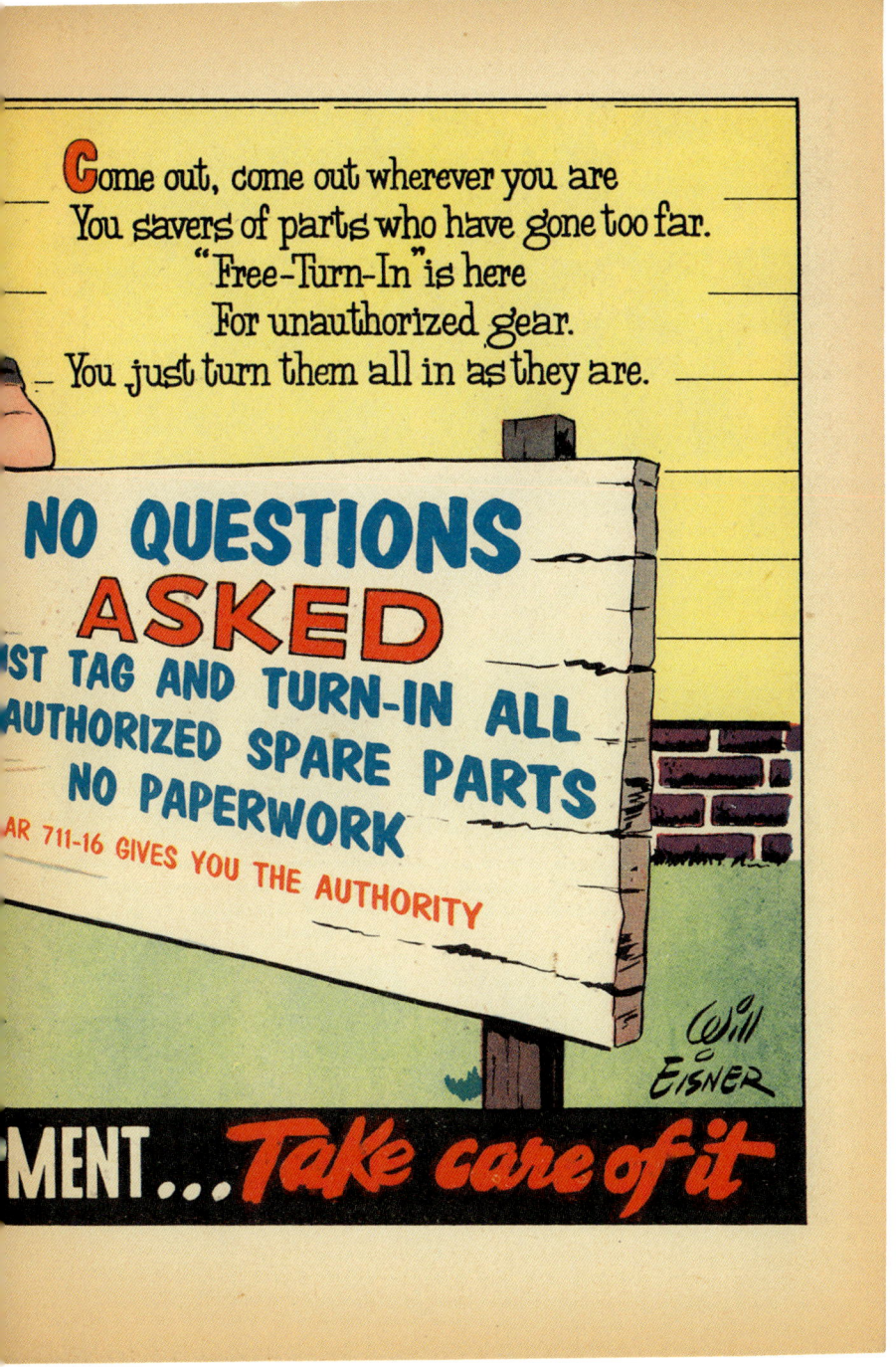

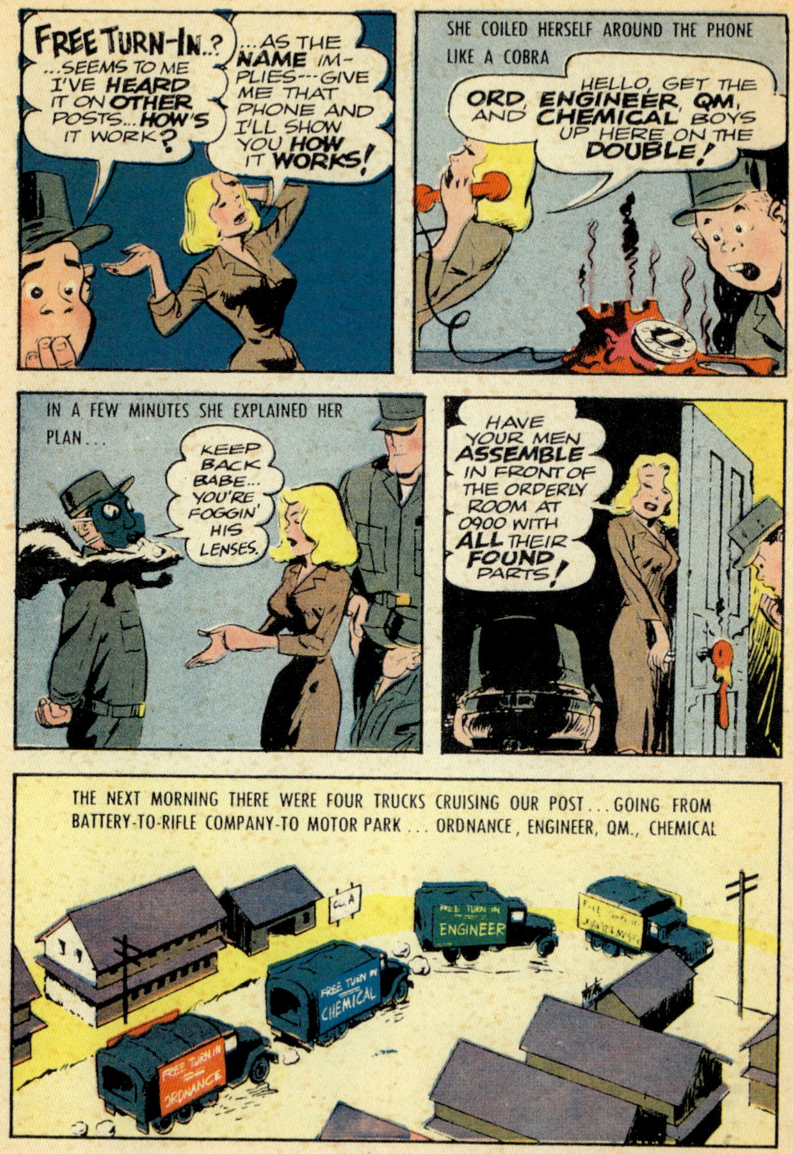
FREE TURN-IN..? ...SEEMS TO ME I'VE HEARD IT ON OTHER POSTS... HOW'S IT WORK?
...AS THE NAME IMPLIES---GIVE ME THAT PHONE AND I'LL SHOW YOU HOW IT WORKS!
SHE COILED HERSELF AROUND THE PHONE LIKE A COBRA
HELLO, GET THE ORD, ENGINEER, QM, AND CHEMICAL BOYS UP HERE ON THE DOUBLE!
IN A FEW MINUTES SHE EXPLAINED HER PLAN...
KEEP BACK BABE... YOU'RE FOGGIN' HIS LENSES.
HAVE YOUR MEN ASSEMBLE IN FRONT OF THE ORDERLY ROOM AT 0900 WITH ALL THEIR FOUND PARTS!
THE NEXT MORNING THERE WERE FOUR TRUCKS CRUISING OUR POST... GOING FROM BATTERY-TO-RIFLE COMPANY-TO MOTOR PARK ... ORDNANCE, ENGINEER, QM., CHEMICAL
FREE TURN IN ENGINEER
FREE TURN IN CHEMICAL
FREE TURN IN ORDNANCE

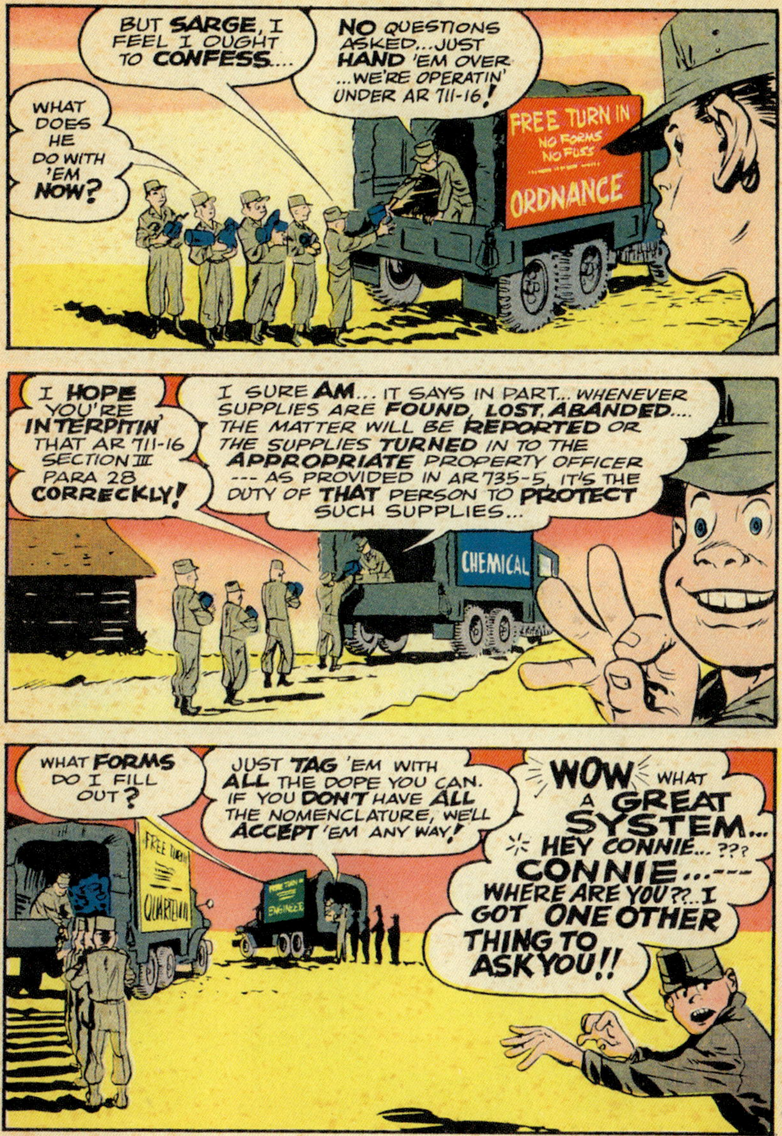
BUT SARGE, I FEEL I OUGHT TO CONFESS....
WHAT DOES HE DO WITH 'EM NOW?
NO QUESTIONS ASKED...JUST HAND 'EM OVER ...WE'RE OPERATIN' UNDER AR 711-16!
FREE TURN IN
NO FORMS NO FUSS
ORDNANCE
I HOPE YOU'RE INTERPITIN' THAT AR 711-16 SECTION III PARA 28 CORRECKLY!
I SURE AM... IT SAYS IN PART... WHENEVER SUPPLIES ARE FOUND, LOST, ABANDED.... THE MATTER WILL BE REPORTED OR THE SUPPLIES TURNED IN TO THE APPROPRIATE PROPERTY OFFICER --- AS PROVIDED IN AR 735-5, IT'S THE DUTY OF THAT PERSON TO PROTECT SUCH SUPPLIES...
CHEMICAL
WHAT FORMS DO I FILL OUT?
JUST TAG 'EM WITH ALL THE DOPE YOU CAN. IF YOU DON'T HAVE ALL THE NOMENCLATURE, WE'LL ACCEPT 'EM ANY WAY!
WOW WHAT A GREAT SYSTEM... HEY CONNIE... ??? CONNIE...--- WHERE ARE YOU??..I GOT ONE OTHER THING TO ASK YOU!!

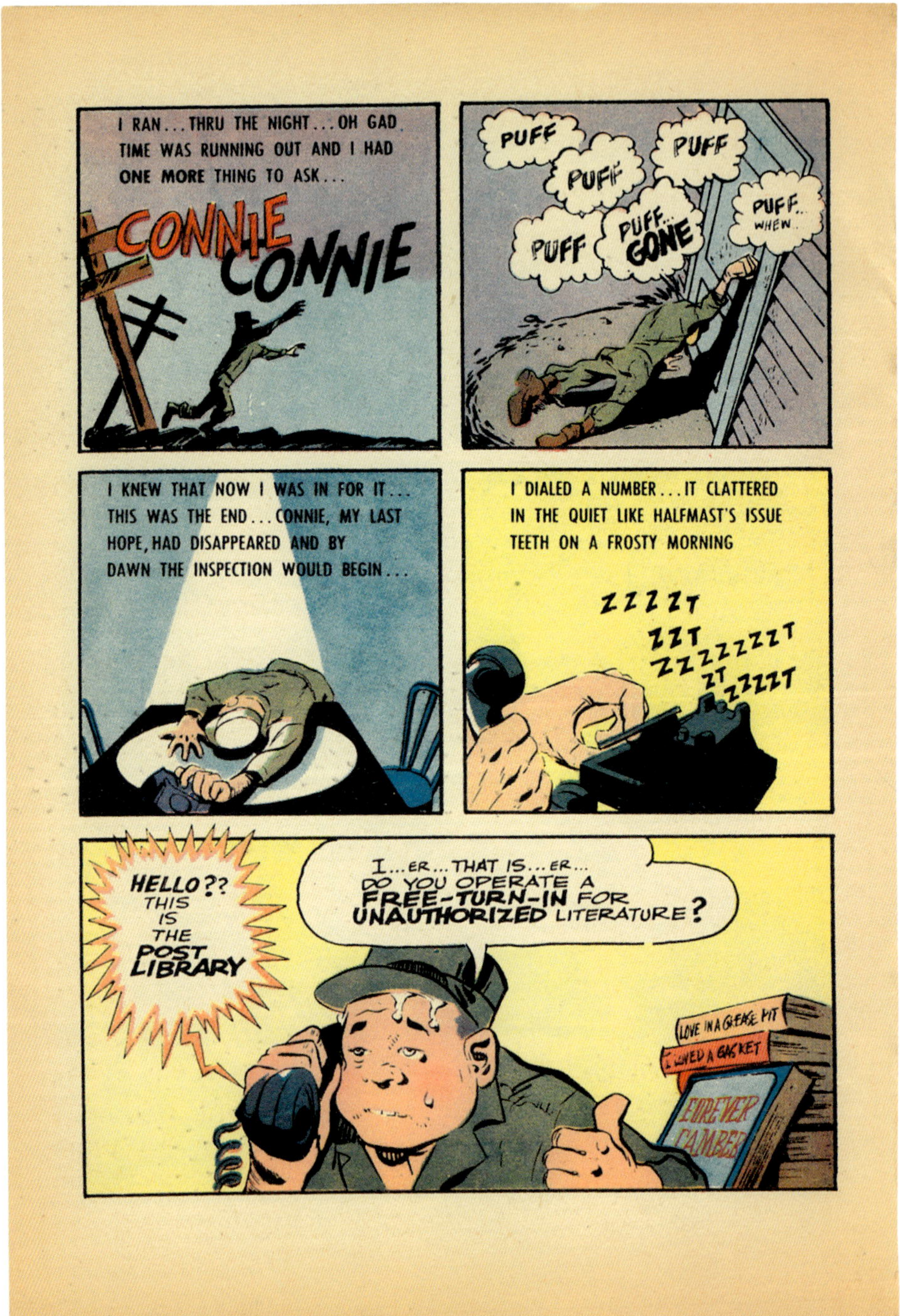

I RAN... THRU THE NIGHT... OH GAD TIME WAS RUNNING OUT AND I HAD ONE MORE THING TO ASK...
CONNIE
CONNIE
PUFF
PUFF
PUFF
PUFF
PUFF... GONE
PUFF... WHEW...
I KNEW THAT NOW I WAS IN FOR IT... THIS WAS THE END... CONNIE, MY LAST HOPE, HAD DISAPPEARED AND BY DAWN THE INSPECTION WOULD BEGIN...
I DIALED A NUMBER... IT CLATTERED IN THE QUIET LIKE HALFMAST'S ISSUE TEETH ON A FROSTY MORNING
ZZZZT ZZT ZZZZZZZT ZT ZZZZT
HELLO?? THIS IS THE POST LIBRARY
I... ER... THAT IS... ER... DO YOU OPERATE A FREE-TURN-IN FOR UNAUTHORIZED LITERATURE?
LOVE IN A GREASE PIT
I LOVED A GASKET
FOREVER CAMBER

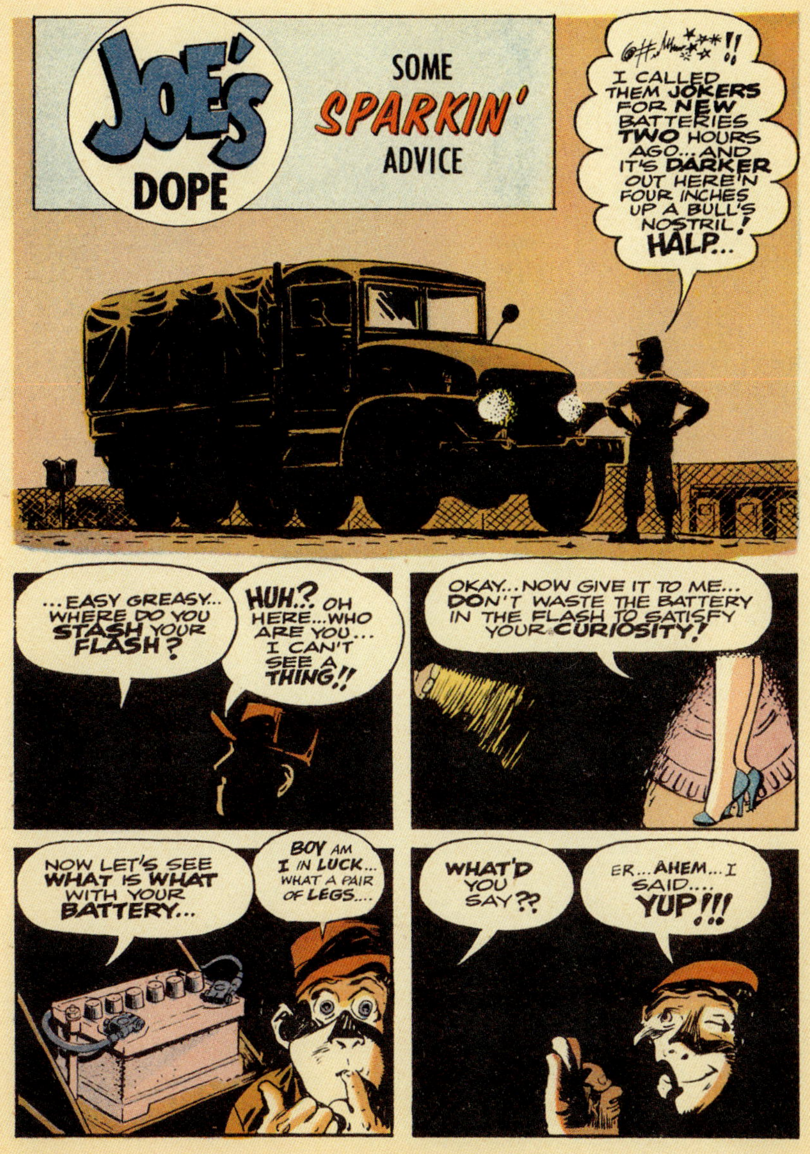
JOE'S DOPE
SOME SPARKIN' ADVICE
I CALLED THEM JOKERS FOR NEW BATTERIES TWO HOURS AGO...AND IT'S DARKER OUT HERE'N FOUR INCHES UP A BULL'S NOSTRIL! HALP...
...EASY GREASY... WHERE DO YOU STASH YOUR FLASH?
HUH?. OH HERE...WHO ARE YOU... I CAN'T SEE A THING!!
OKAY...NOW GIVE IT TO ME... DON'T WASTE THE BATTERY IN THE FLASH TO SATISFY YOUR CURIOSITY!
NOW LET'S SEE WHAT IS WHAT WITH YOUR BATTERY...
BOY AM I IN LUCK... WHAT A PAIR OF LEGS....
WHAT'D YOU SAY??
ER...AHEM...I SAID.... YUP!!!

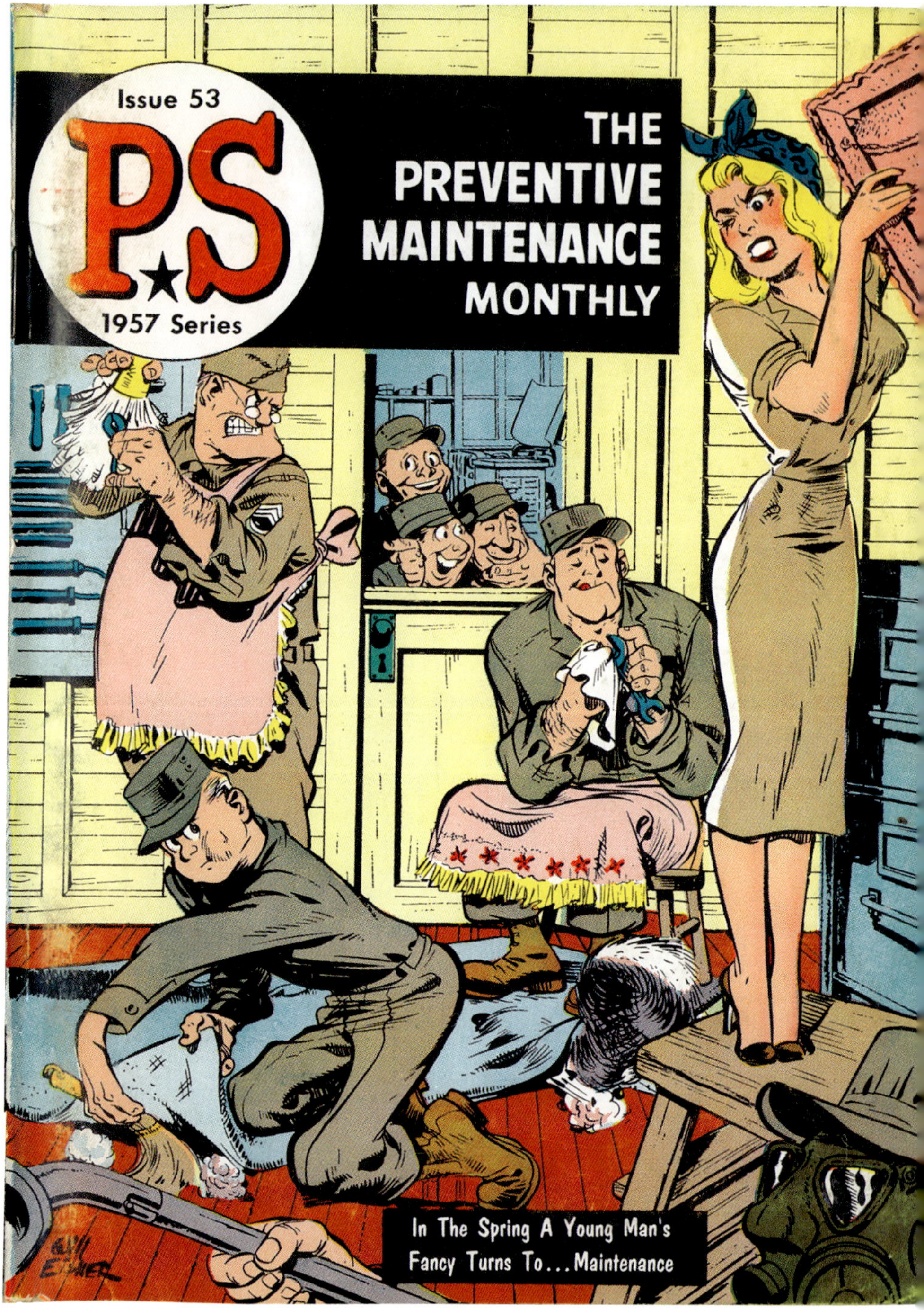
Issue 53
P.S
1957 Series
THE
PREVENTIVE
MAINTENANCE
MONTHLY
In The Spring A Young Man's
Fancy Turns To... Maintenance

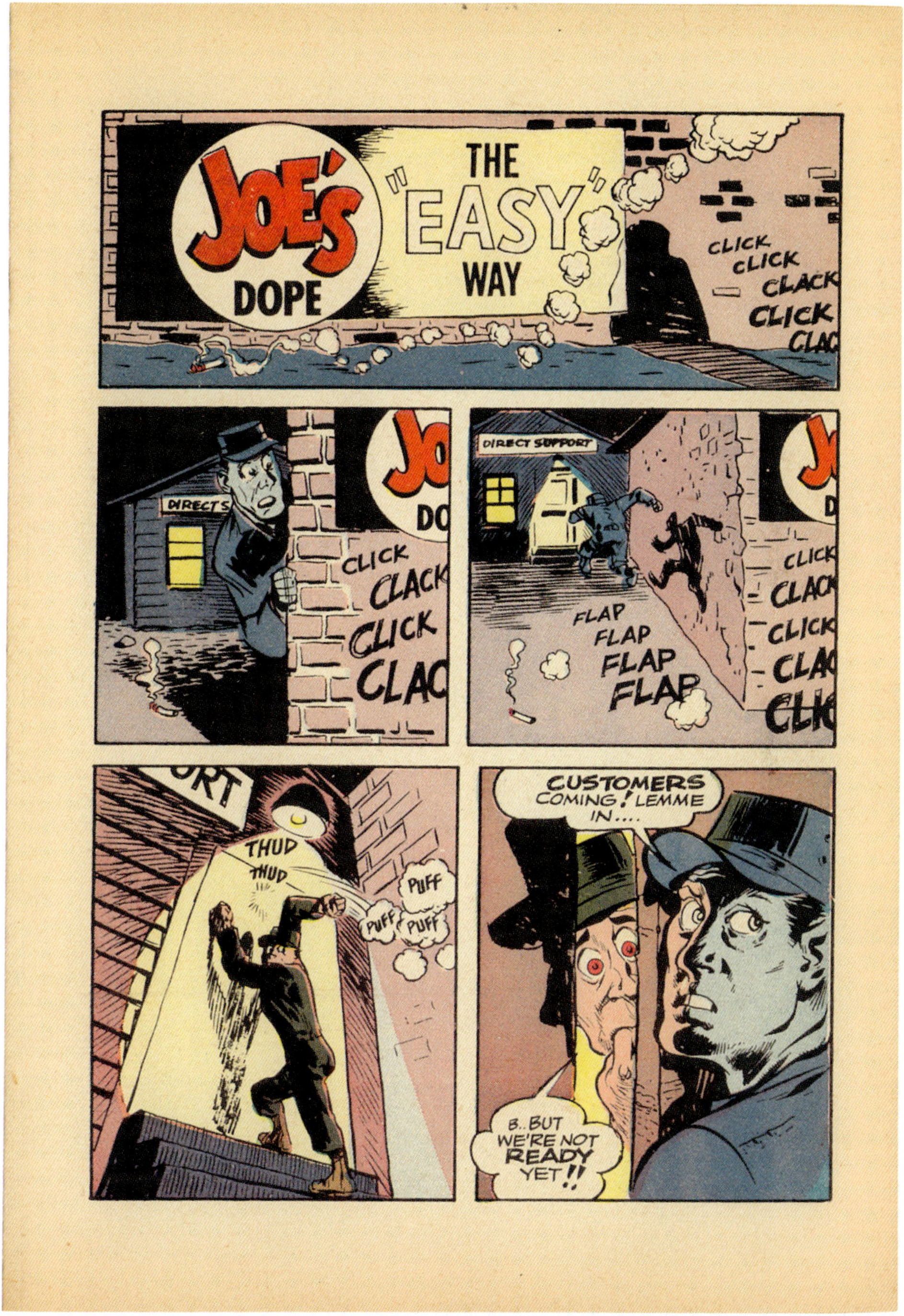
JOE'S DOPE
THE "EASY" WAY
CLICK CLICK CLACK CLICK CLAC
DIRECT S
CLICK CLACK CLICK CLAC
DIRECT SUPPORT
FLAP FLAP FLAP FLAP
CLICK CLACK CLICK CLAC CLIC
THUD THUD
PUFF PUFF PUFF
CUSTOMERS COMING! LEMME IN....
B..BUT WE'RE NOT READY YET!!

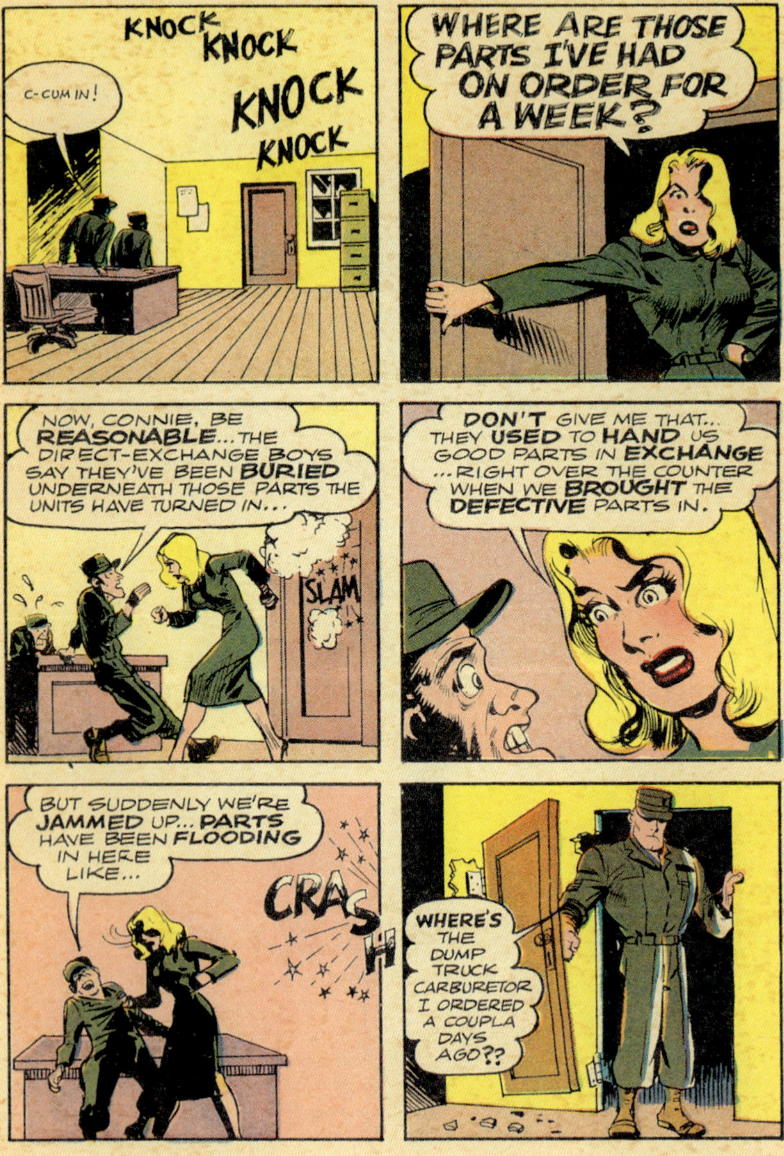
KNOCK KNOCK
C-CUM IN!
KNOCK
KNOCK
WHERE ARE THOSE PARTS I'VE HAD ON ORDER FOR A WEEK?
NOW, CONNIE, BE REASONABLE... THE DIRECT-EXCHANGE BOYS SAY THEY'VE BEEN BURIED UNDERNEATH THOSE PARTS THE UNITS HAVE TURNED IN...
SLAM
DON'T GIVE ME THAT.. THEY USED TO HAND US GOOD PARTS IN EXCHANGE ...RIGHT OVER THE COUNTER WHEN WE BROUGHT THE DEFECTIVE PARTS IN.
BUT SUDDENLY WE'RE JAMMED UP... PARTS HAVE BEEN FLOODING IN HERE LIKE...
CRASH
WHERE'S THE DUMP TRUCK CARBURETOR I ORDERED A COUPLA DAYS AGO??

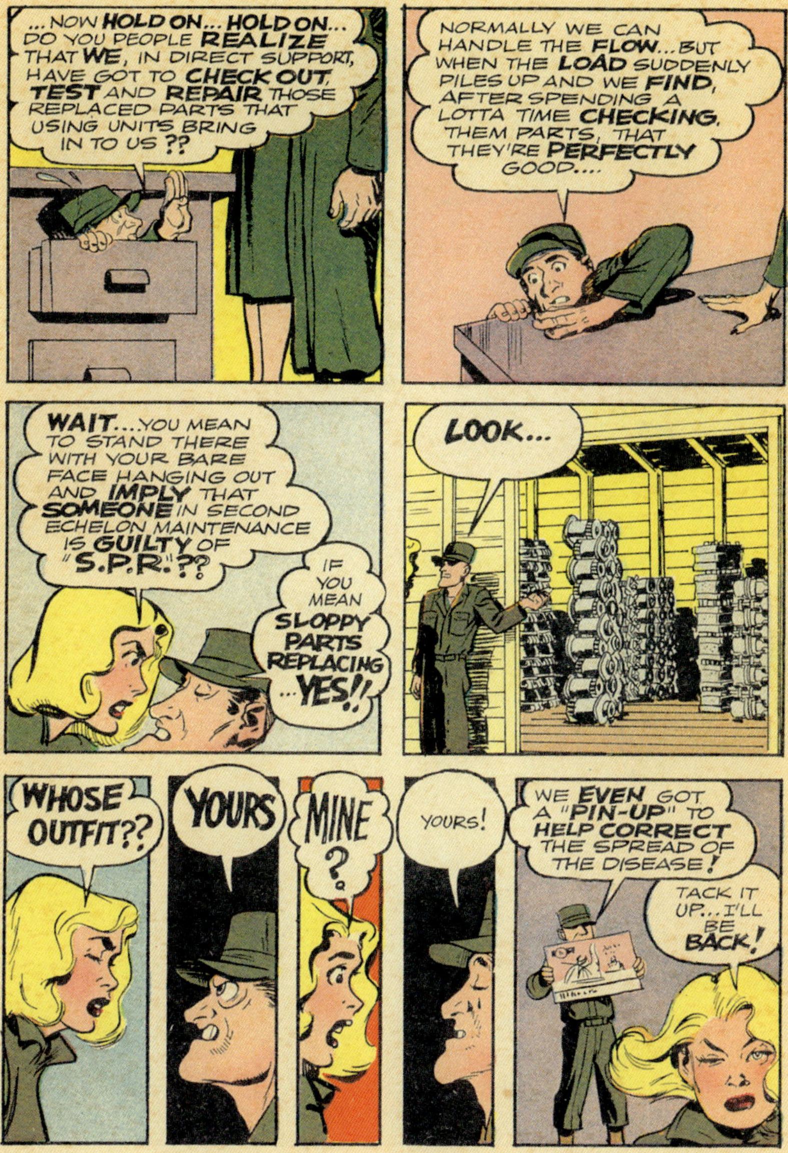
...NOW HOLD ON... HOLD ON... DO YOU PEOPLE REALIZE THAT WE, IN DIRECT SUPPORT, HAVE GOT TO CHECK OUT, TEST AND REPAIR THOSE REPLACED PARTS THAT USING UNITS BRING IN TO US??
NORMALLY WE CAN HANDLE THE FLOW... BUT WHEN THE LOAD SUDDENLY PILES UP AND WE FIND, AFTER SPENDING A LOTTA TIME CHECKING THEM PARTS, THAT THEY'RE PERFECTLY GOOD....
WAIT....YOU MEAN TO STAND THERE WITH YOUR BARE FACE HANGING OUT AND IMPLY THAT SOMEONE IN SECOND ECHELON MAINTENANCE IS GUILTY OF "S.P.R."??
IF YOU MEAN SLOPPY PARTS REPLACING ...YES!!
LOOK...
WHOSE OUTFIT??
YOURS
MINE ?
YOURS!
WE EVEN GOT A "PIN-UP" TO HELP CORRECT THE SPREAD OF THE DISEASE!
TACK IT UP...I'LL BE BACK!

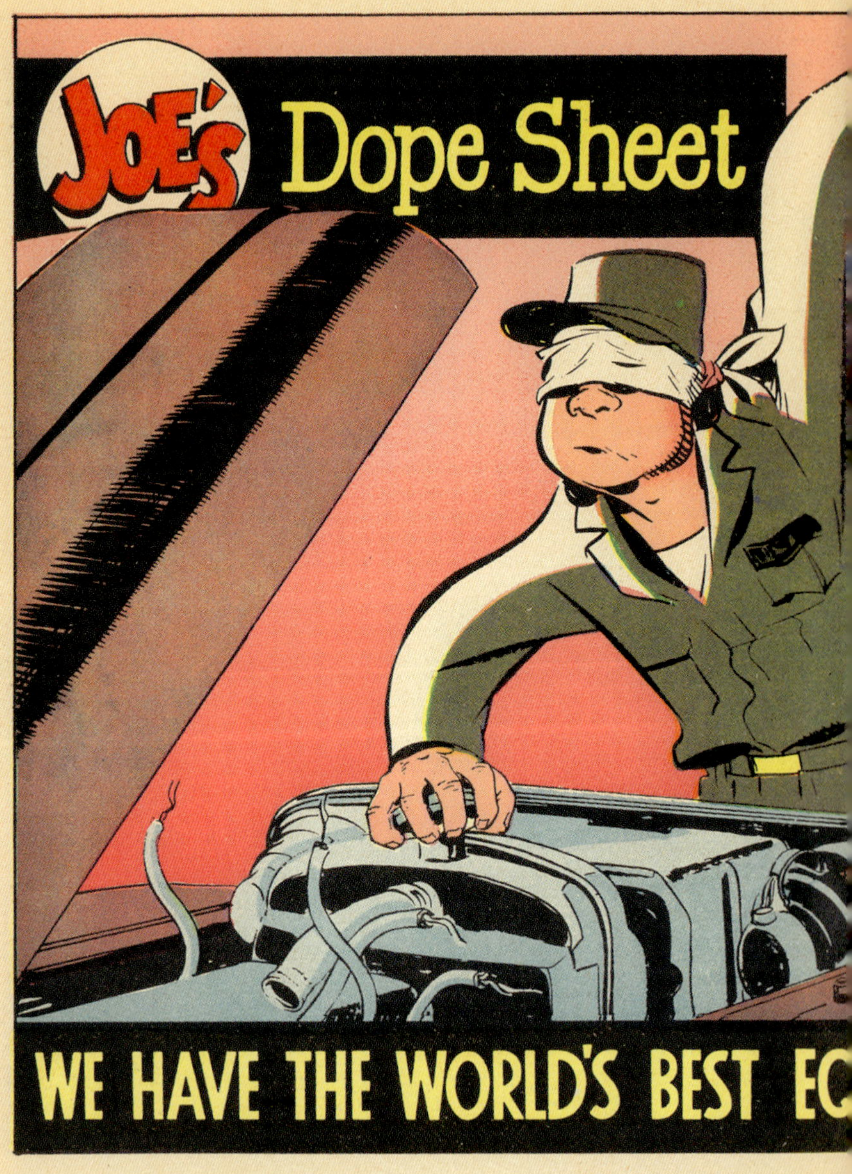
JOE'S Dope Sheet
WE HAVE THE WORLD'S BEST EQ

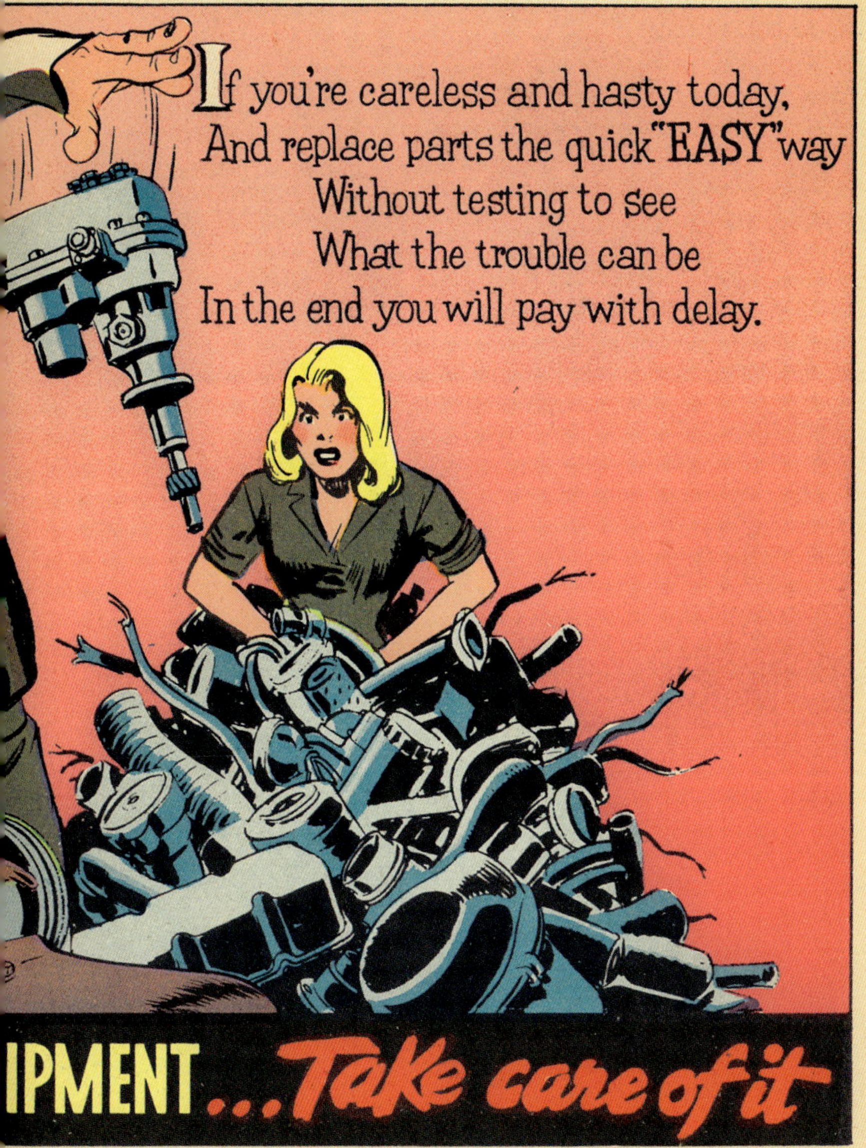
If you're careless and hasty today,
And replace parts the quick "EASY" way
Without testing to see
What the trouble can be
In the end you will pay with delay.
IPMENT ... Take care of it

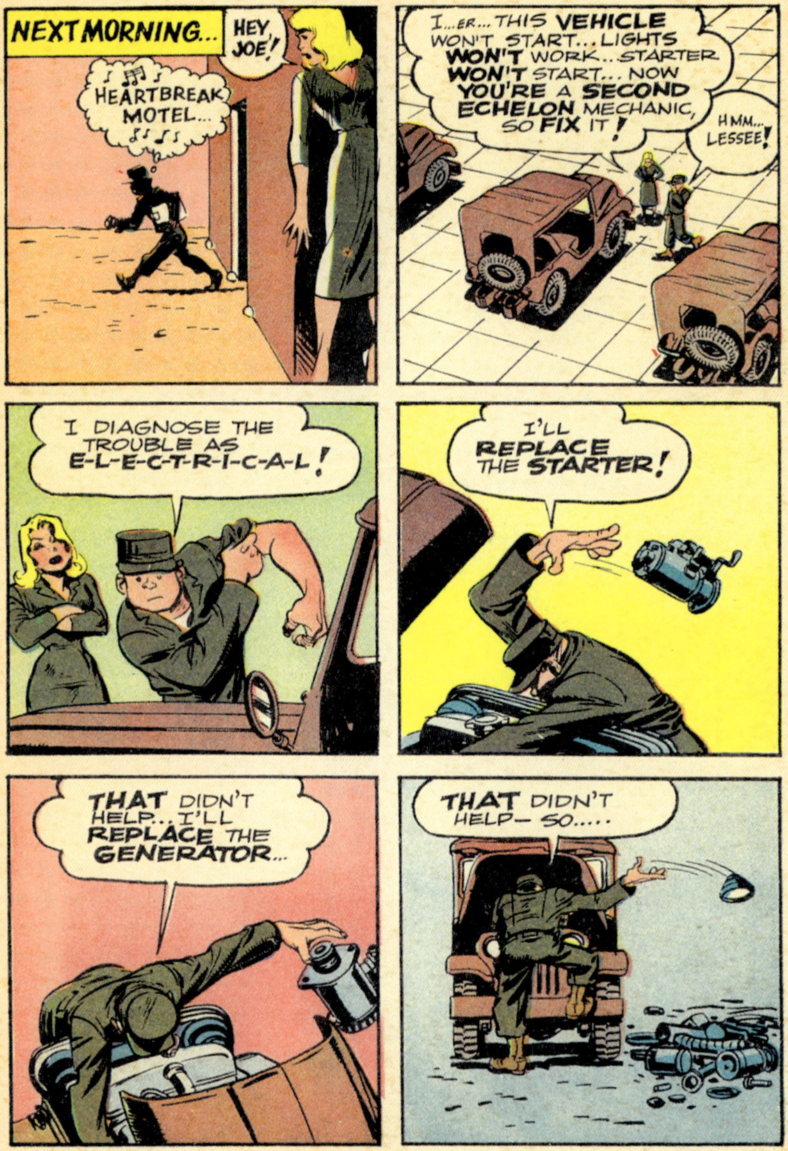
NEXT MORNING...
HEY, JOE!
HEARTBREAK MOTEL...
I...ER...THIS VEHICLE WON'T START... LIGHTS WON'T WORK...STARTER WON'T START... NOW YOU'RE A SECOND ECHELON MECHANIC, SO FIX IT!
HMM... LESSEE!
I DIAGNOSE THE TROUBLE AS E-L-E-C-T-R-I-C-A-L!
I'LL REPLACE THE STARTER!
THAT DIDN'T HELP... I'LL REPLACE THE GENERATOR...
THAT DIDN'T HELP— SO.....

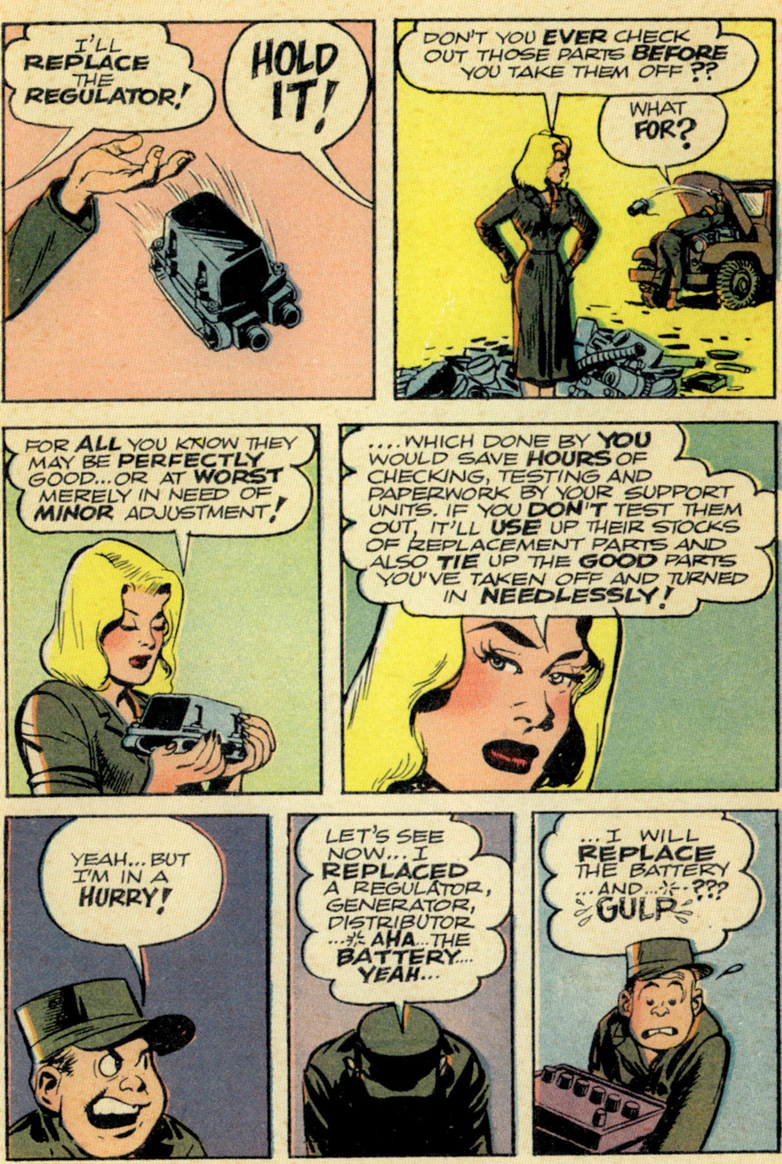
I'LL REPLACE THE REGULATOR!
HOLD IT!
DON'T YOU EVER CHECK OUT THOSE PARTS BEFORE YOU TAKE THEM OFF??
WHAT FOR?
FOR ALL YOU KNOW THEY MAY BE PERFECTLY GOOD...OR AT WORST MERELY IN NEED OF MINOR ADJUSTMENT!
....WHICH DONE BY YOU WOULD SAVE HOURS OF CHECKING, TESTING AND PAPERWORK BY YOUR SUPPORT UNITS. IF YOU DON'T TEST THEM OUT, IT'LL USE UP THEIR STOCKS OF REPLACEMENT PARTS AND ALSO TIE UP THE GOOD PARTS YOU'VE TAKEN OFF AND TURNED IN NEEDLESSLY!
YEAH... BUT I'M IN A HURRY!
LET'S SEE NOW... I REPLACED A REGULATOR, GENERATOR, DISTRIBUTOR ... AHA... THE BATTERY... YEAH...
... I WILL REPLACE THE BATTERY ... AND... ??? GULP

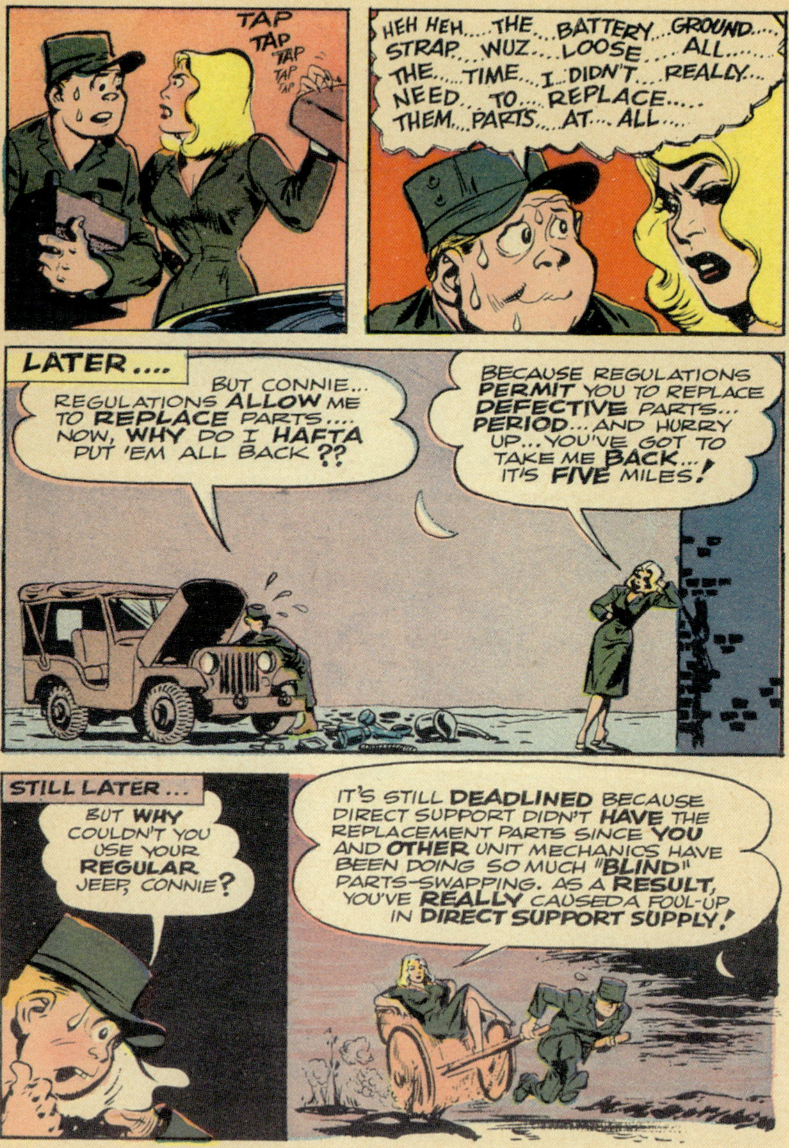
TAP TAP TAP TAP TAP
HEH HEH.... THE... BATTERY... GROUND.... STRAP... WUZ... LOOSE.... ALL..... THE..... TIME... I... DIDN'T.... REALLY.... NEED... TO.... REPLACE..... THEM.... PARTS.... AT.... ALL....
LATER ....
BUT CONNIE... REGULATIONS ALLOW ME TO REPLACE PARTS.... NOW, WHY DO I HAFTA PUT 'EM ALL BACK??
BECAUSE REGULATIONS PERMIT YOU TO REPLACE DEFECTIVE PARTS... PERIOD...AND HURRY UP...YOU'VE GOT TO TAKE ME BACK... IT'S FIVE MILES!
STILL LATER ...
BUT WHY COULDN'T YOU USE YOUR REGULAR JEEP, CONNIE?
IT'S STILL DEADLINED BECAUSE DIRECT SUPPORT DIDN'T HAVE THE REPLACEMENT PARTS SINCE YOU AND OTHER UNIT MECHANICS HAVE BEEN DOING SO MUCH "BLIND" PARTS-SWAPPING. AS A RESULT, YOU'VE REALLY CAUSED A FOUL-UP IN DIRECT SUPPORT SUPPLY!

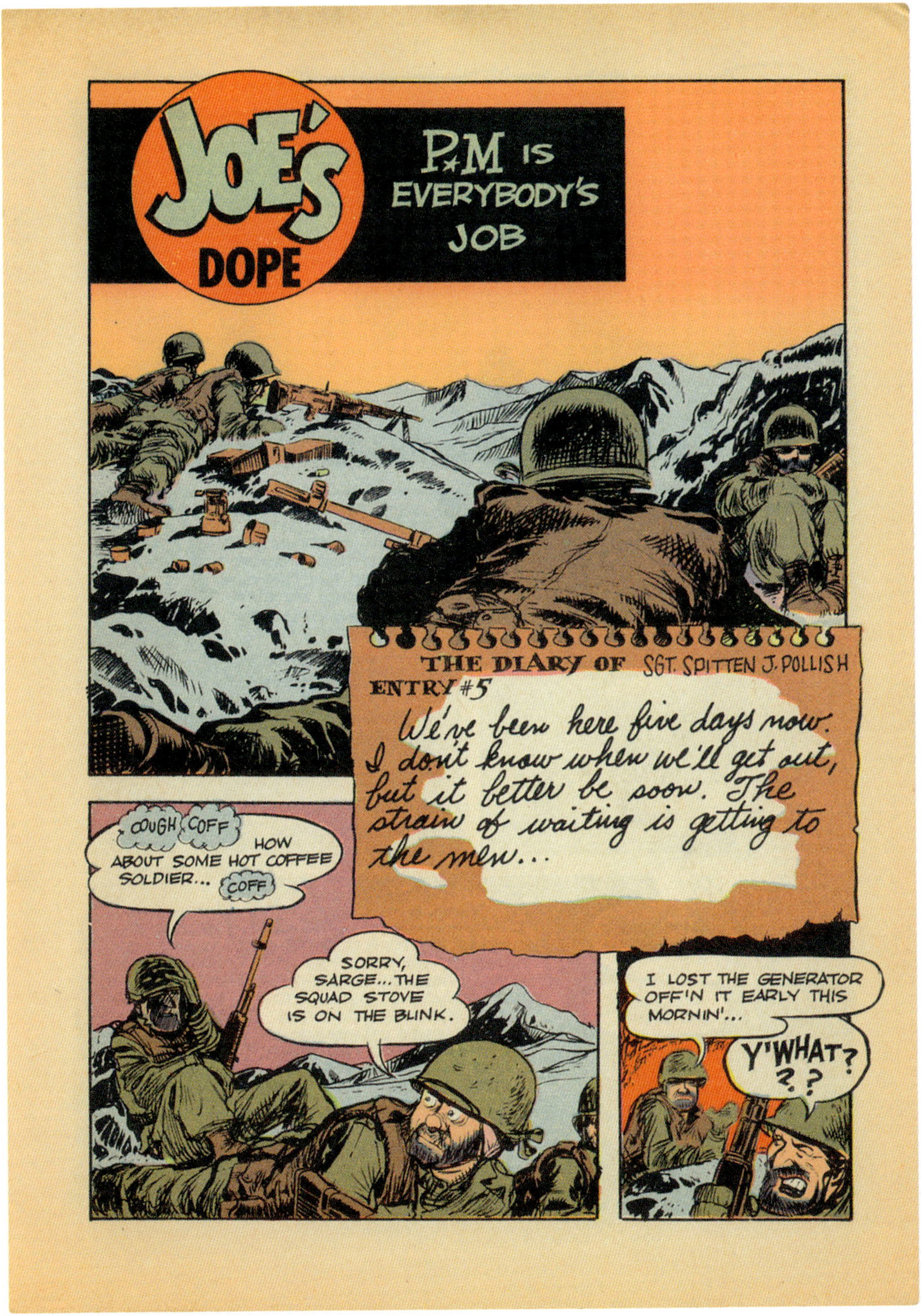
JOE'S DOPE
P★M IS EVERYBODY'S JOB
THE DIARY OF SGT. SPITTEN J. POLLISH
ENTRY #5
We've been here five days now. I don't know when we'll get out, but it better be soon. The strain of waiting is getting to the men...
COUGH COFF HOW ABOUT SOME HOT COFFEE SOLDIER... COFF
SORRY, SARGE... THE SQUAD STOVE IS ON THE BLINK.
I LOST THE GENERATOR OFF'N IT EARLY THIS MORNIN'...
Y'WHAT? ??

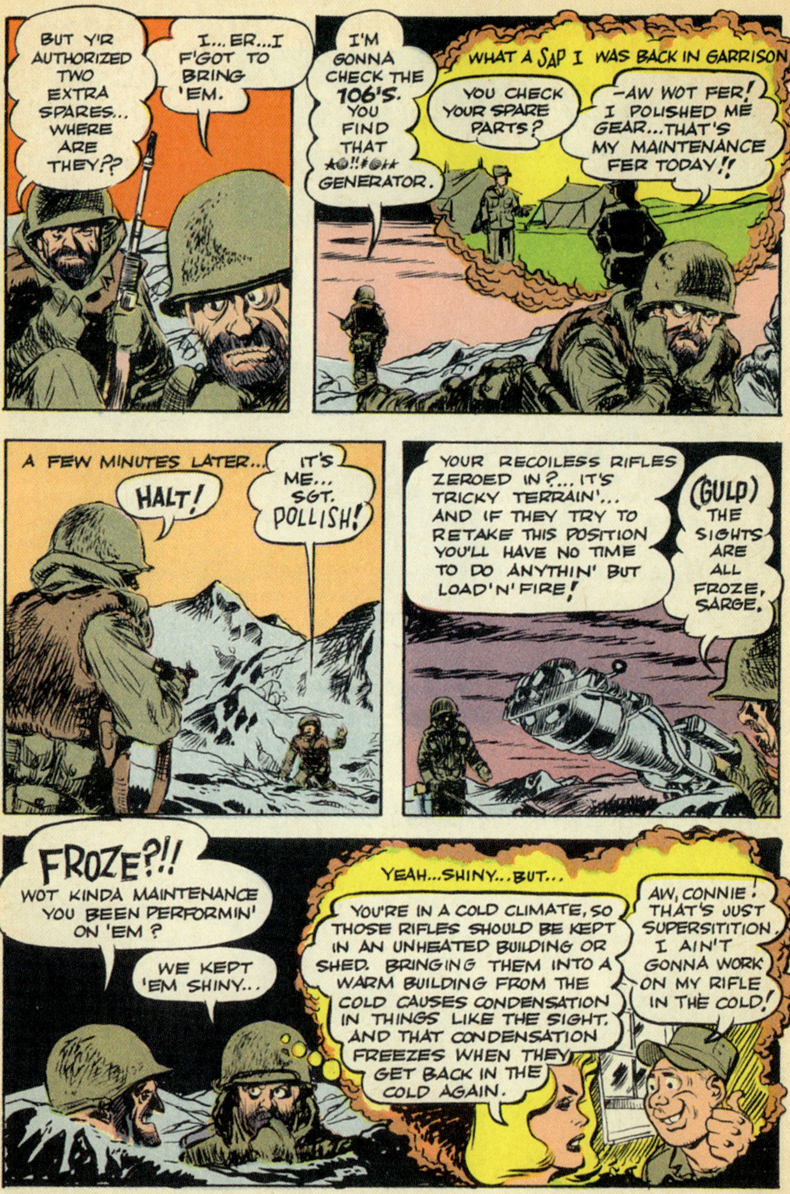

BUT Y'R AUTHORIZED TWO EXTRA SPARES... WHERE ARE THEY??
I... ER... I F'GOT TO BRING 'EM.
I'M GONNA CHECK THE 106'S. YOU FIND THAT *@!!#@** GENERATOR.
WHAT A SAP I WAS BACK IN GARRISON
YOU CHECK YOUR SPARE PARTS?
—AW WOT FER! I POLISHED ME GEAR... THAT'S MY MAINTENANCE FER TODAY!!
A FEW MINUTES LATER...
HALT!
IT'S ME... SGT. POLLISH!
YOUR RECOILESS RIFLES ZEROED IN?... IT'S TRICKY TERRAIN'... AND IF THEY TRY TO RETAKE THIS POSITION YOU'LL HAVE NO TIME TO DO ANYTHIN' BUT LOAD'N'FIRE!
(GULP) THE SIGHTS ARE ALL FROZE, SARGE.
FROZE?!! WOT KINDA MAINTENANCE YOU BEEN PERFORMIN' ON 'EM?
WE KEPT 'EM SHINY...
YEAH...SHINY...BUT...
YOU'RE IN A COLD CLIMATE, SO THOSE RIFLES SHOULD BE KEPT IN AN UNHEATED BUILDING OR SHED. BRINGING THEM INTO A WARM BUILDING FROM THE COLD CAUSES CONDENSATION IN THINGS LIKE THE SIGHT. AND THAT CONDENSATION FREEZES WHEN THEY GET BACK IN THE COLD AGAIN.
AW, CONNIE! THAT'S JUST SUPERSITITION. I AIN'T GONNA WORK ON MY RIFLE IN THE COLD!

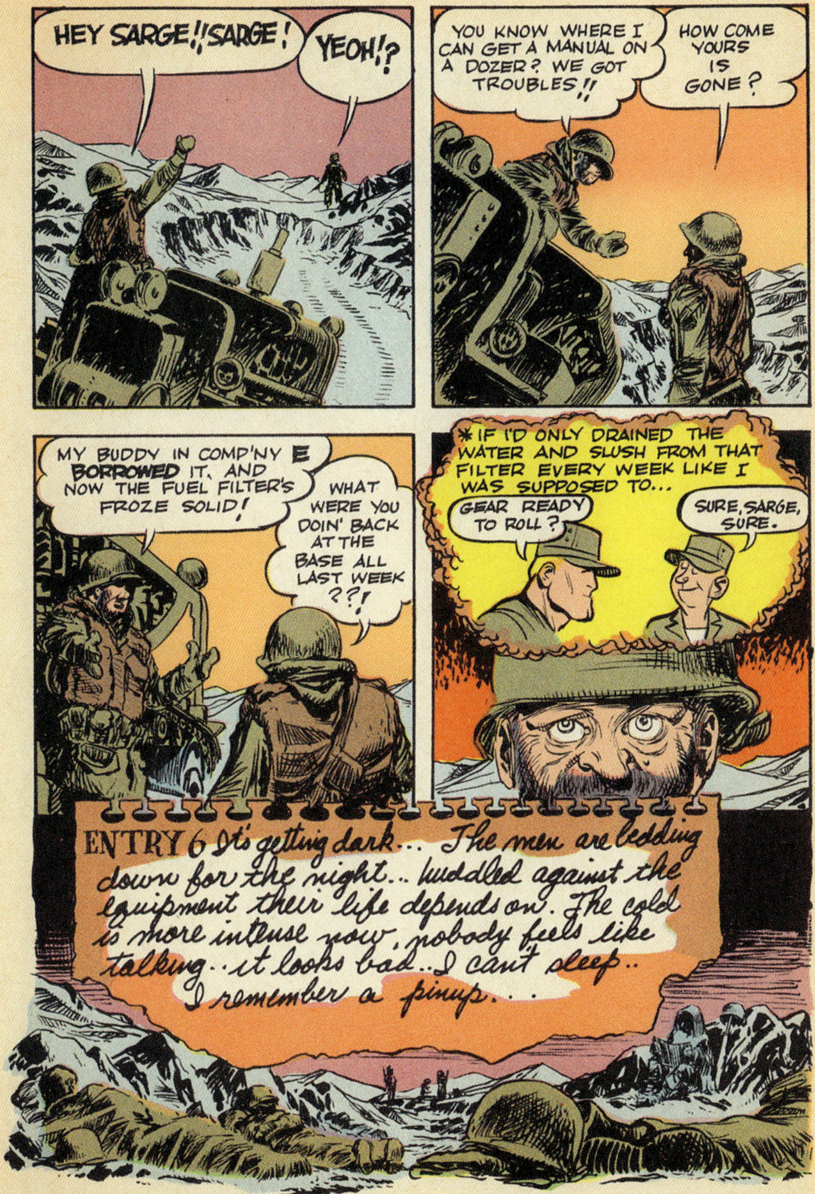
HEY SARGE!! SARGE!
YEOH!?
YOU KNOW WHERE I CAN GET A MANUAL ON A DOZER? WE GOT TROUBLES!!
HOW COME YOURS IS GONE?
MY BUDDY IN COMP'NY E BORROWED IT, AND NOW THE FUEL FILTER'S FROZE SOLID!
WHAT WERE YOU DOIN' BACK AT THE BASE ALL LAST WEEK ??!
*IF I'D ONLY DRAINED THE WATER AND SLUSH FROM THAT FILTER EVERY WEEK LIKE I WAS SUPPOSED TO...
GEAR READY TO ROLL?
SURE, SARGE, SURE.
ENTRY 6 It's getting dark... The men are bedding down for the night... huddled against the equipment their life depends on. The cold is more intense now, nobody feels like talking.. it looks bad.. I can't sleep.. I remember a pinup...

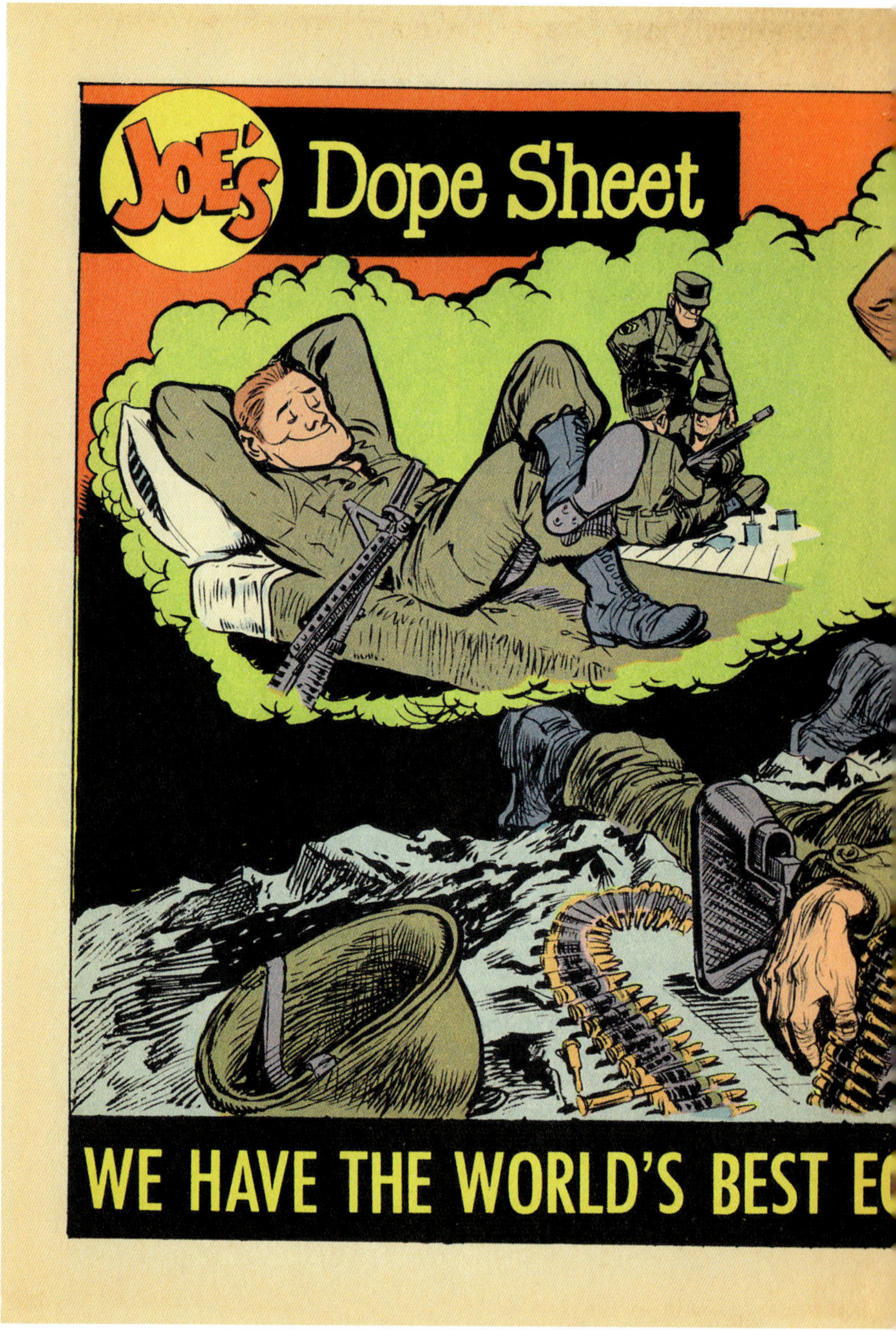
JOE'S Dope Sheet
WE HAVE THE WORLD'S BEST E

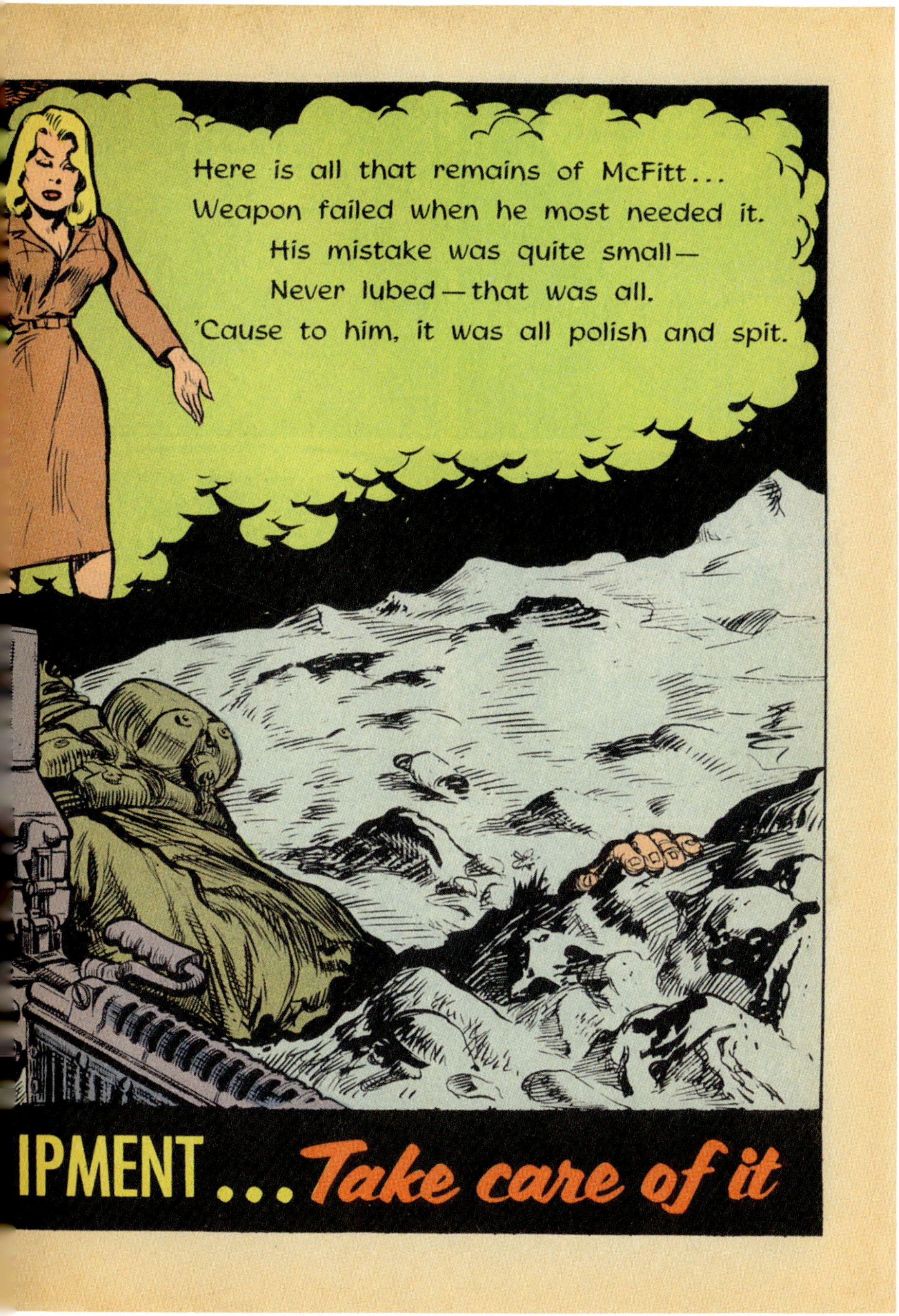
Here is all that remains of McFitt...
Weapon failed when he most needed it.
His mistake was quite small—
Never lubed—that was all.
'Cause to him, it was all polish and spit.
IPMENT...Take care of it

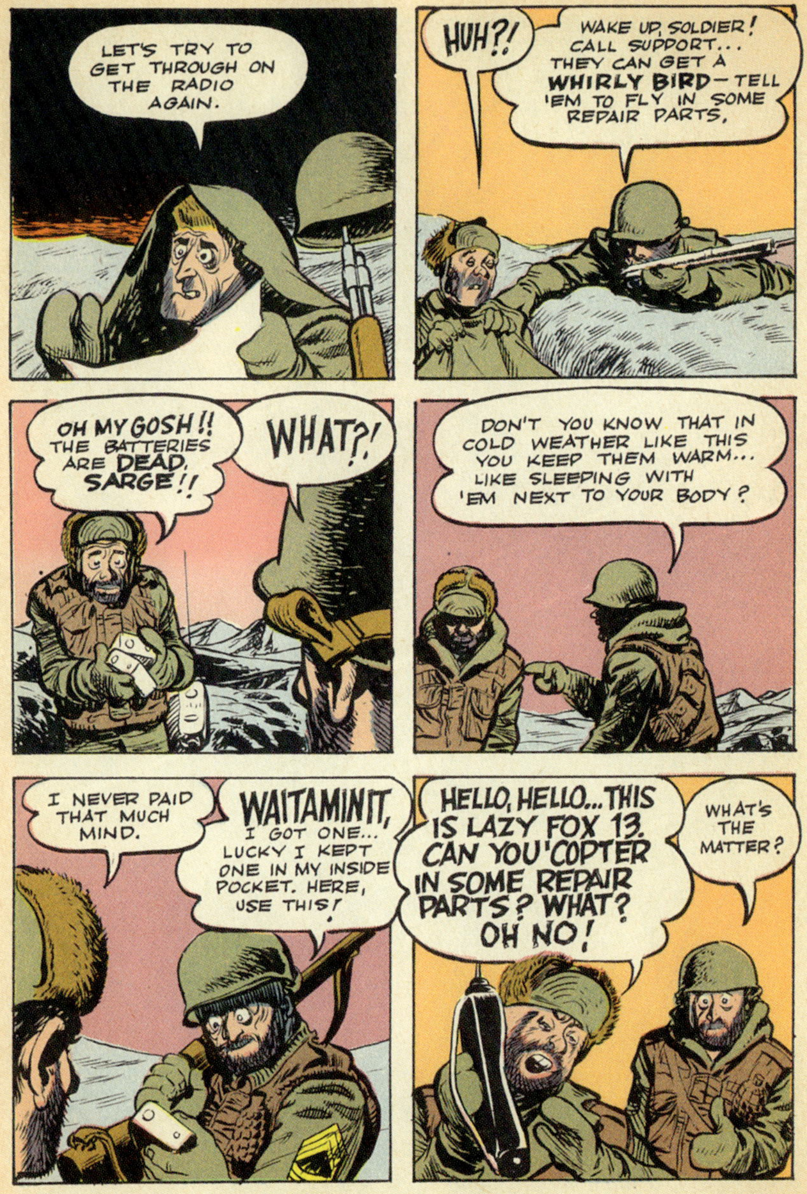
LET'S TRY TO GET THROUGH ON THE RADIO AGAIN.
HUH?!
WAKE UP, SOLDIER! CALL SUPPORT... THEY CAN GET A WHIRLY BIRD—TELL 'EM TO FLY IN SOME REPAIR PARTS,
OH MY GOSH!! THE BATTERIES ARE DEAD, SARGE!!
WHAT?!
DON'T YOU KNOW THAT IN COLD WEATHER LIKE THIS YOU KEEP THEM WARM... LIKE SLEEPING WITH 'EM NEXT TO YOUR BODY?
I NEVER PAID THAT MUCH MIND.
WAITAMINIT, I GOT ONE... LUCKY I KEPT ONE IN MY INSIDE POCKET. HERE, USE THIS!
HELLO, HELLO... THIS IS LAZY FOX 13. CAN YOU 'COPTER IN SOME REPAIR PARTS? WHAT? OH NO!
WHAT'S THE MATTER?

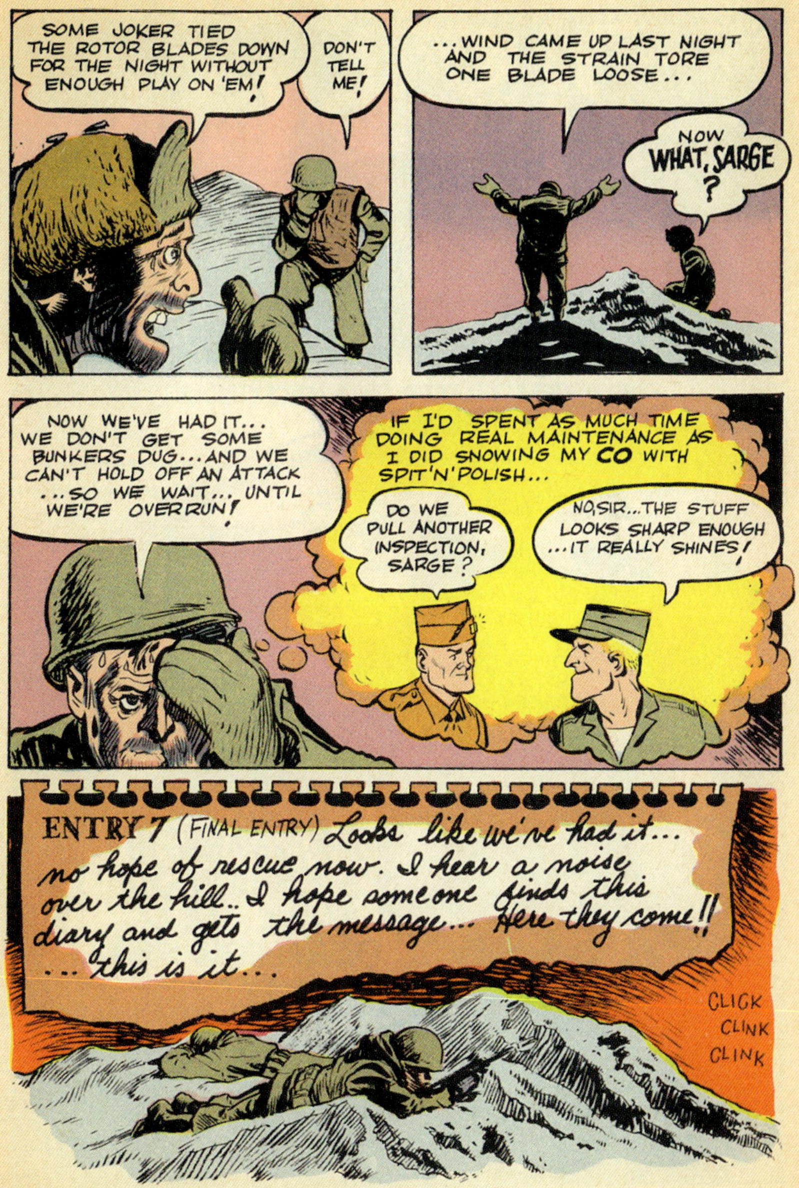
SOME JOKER TIED THE ROTOR BLADES DOWN FOR THE NIGHT WITHOUT ENOUGH PLAY ON 'EM!
DON'T TELL ME!
...WIND CAME UP LAST NIGHT AND THE STRAIN TORE ONE BLADE LOOSE...
NOW WHAT, SARGE?
NOW WE'VE HAD IT... WE DON'T GET SOME BUNKERS DUG...AND WE CAN'T HOLD OFF AN ATTACK ...SO WE WAIT... UNTIL WE'RE OVERRUN!
IF I'D SPENT AS MUCH TIME DOING REAL MAINTENANCE AS I DID SNOWING MY CO WITH SPIT'N'POLISH...
DO WE PULL ANOTHER INSPECTION, SARGE?
NO,SIR...THE STUFF LOOKS SHARP ENOUGH ...IT REALLY SHINES!
ENTRY 7 (FINAL ENTRY) Looks like we've had it... no hope of rescue now. I hear a noise over the hill.. I hope someone finds this diary and gets the message... Here they come!! ... this is it...
CLICK
CLINK
CLINK

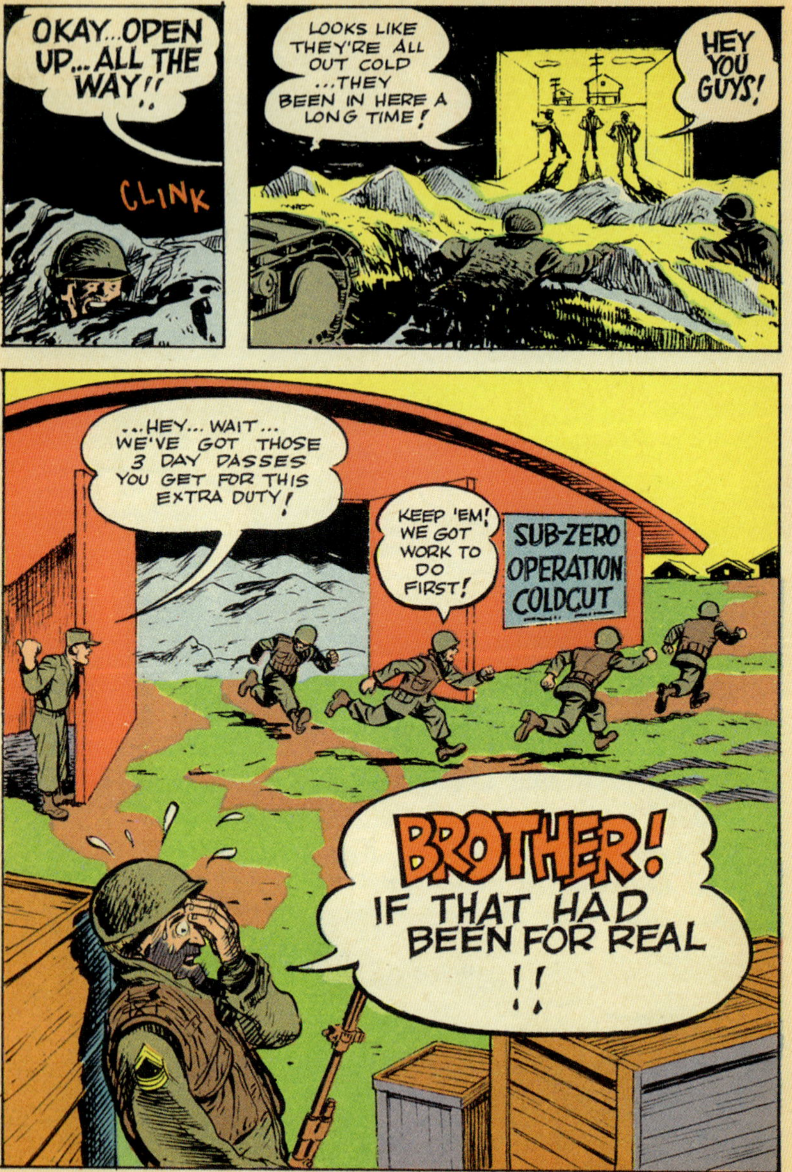
OKAY...OPEN UP...ALL THE WAY!!
CLINK
LOOKS LIKE THEY'RE ALL OUT COLD ...THEY BEEN IN HERE A LONG TIME!
HEY YOU GUYS!
...HEY... WAIT... WE'VE GOT THOSE 3 DAY PASSES YOU GET FOR THIS EXTRA DUTY!
KEEP 'EM! WE GOT WORK TO DO FIRST!
SUB-ZERO OPERATION COLDCUT
BROTHER! IF THAT HAD BEEN FOR REAL !!

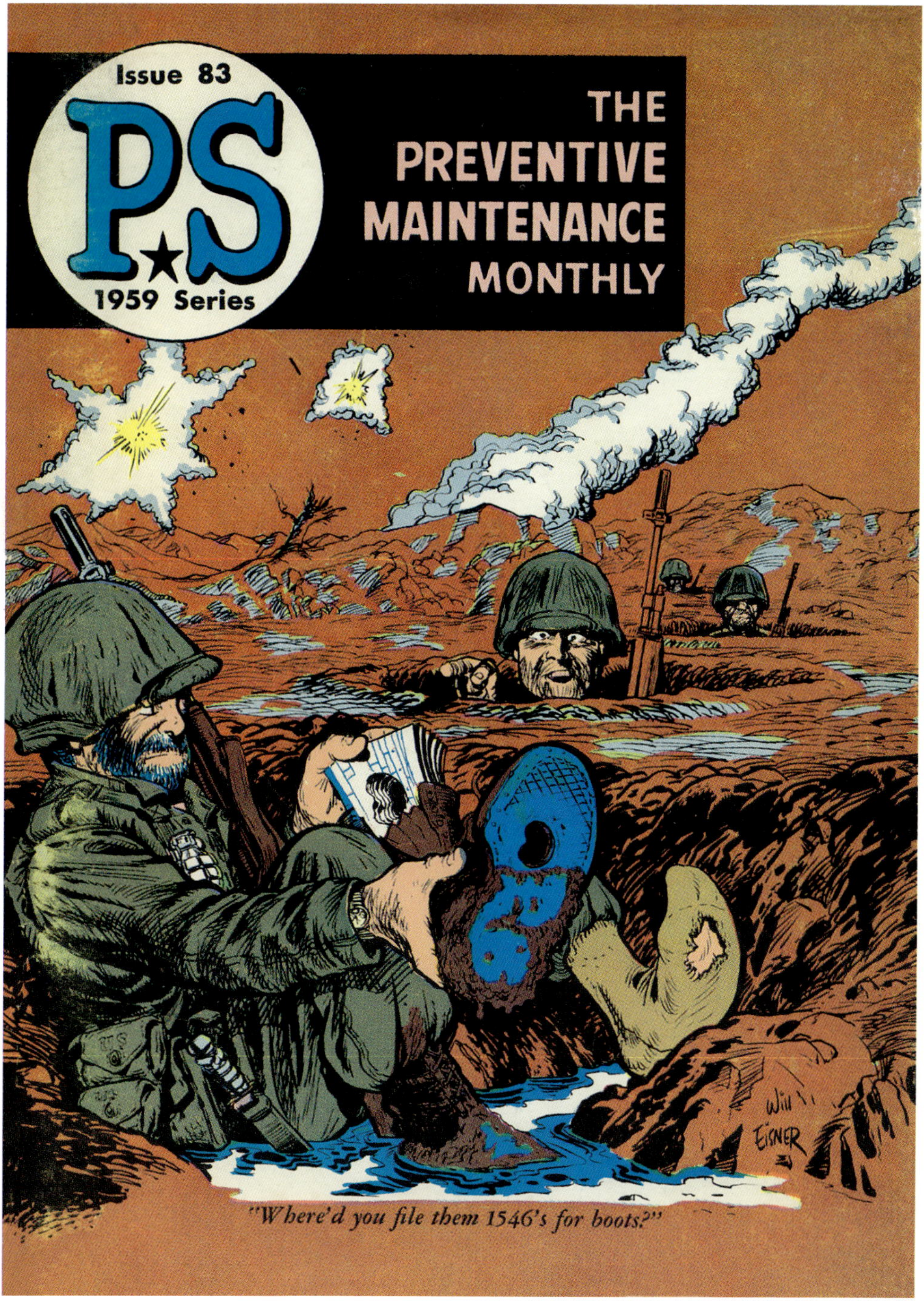
Issue 83
PS
1959 Series
THE PREVENTIVE MAINTENANCE MONTHLY
Will Eisner
"Where'd you file them 1546's for boots?"

no. 83, 1959

WHO'S IN CHARGE

That can be a real ticklish question under certain conditions.

Real embarrassing (and dangerous) . . . if the situation's not right.

When it comes to Preventive Maintenance, tho, there's no if, why or but. AR 750-5, para 9, pins PM down so you don't have to guess about who's in charge. Here's what it says:

> a. Command responsibility.
> Commanders are required to insure that all equipment issued or assigned to their command is maintained in a serviceable condition and is properly cared for and used, and that personnel under their command comply with technical instructions.

'Course, that one hits your CO. But, everybody's not a commander . . . how about you?

The next paragraph pulls no punches:

> b. Direct responsibility.
> Direct responsibility is defined as responsibility of individuals for equipment entrusted to them for their individual use or for use by subordinates.

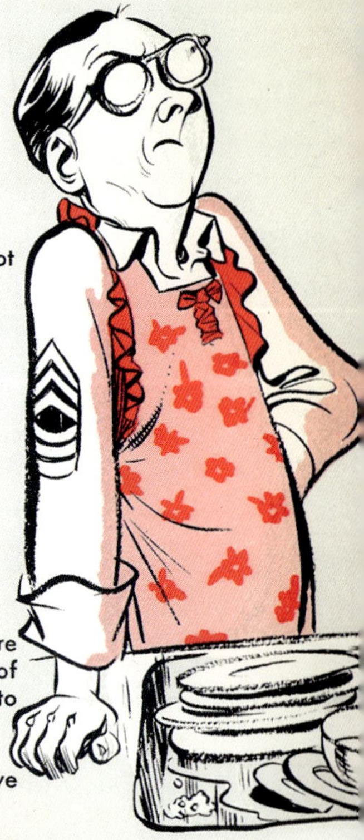

That takes care of **everybody** . . . whether you're an individual soldier issued equipment to take care of and use right, or a man like your sergeant who has to see that his men take care of their equipment.

So, it's all pinned down—

You are in charge when it comes to Preventive Maintenance.

Issue No. 75   **1959 Series**

Published by the Department of the Army for the information of organizational maintenance and supply personnel. Distribution is made through normal publication channels. Within limits of availability, older issues may be obtained direct from Preventive Maintenance Agency, Raritan Arsenal, Metuchen, New Jersey.

IN THIS ISSUE

ARTICLES

Cold Weather Operation	2
Nike-Ajax Tools	13
106-MM Rifle Tools	16
Radios, PRC 8, 9, 10	20
Spiral 4 Connectors	24
Tracked Vehicles	28, 38
Wheeled Vehicles	25-28, 39, 56, 62-64
G744 Carburetors	26
ENG Equipment Inventory	40
How to Read Pubs	51
Smoke Generators	54
M3A2 Decons	55
Stopping On Ice	56

DEPARTMENTS

Connie Rodd	25
Question and Answer	37
Contributions	62
Connie Briefs	65

PS wants your ideas and contributions, and is glad to answer your questions. Just write to: **Sgt Half-Mast, PS, Raritan Arsenal, Metuchen, New Jersey.** Names and addresses are kept in confidence.

The printing of this publication has been approved by the Director of the Bureau of the Budget (27 Apr 56). DISTRIBUTION: Active Army, DCSPER (2); ACSI (1); DCSOPS (1); DCSLOG (10); ACSRC (1); CAMG (1); CoA (1); CUSARROTC (1); CofF (1); CINFO (1); TIG (1); TJAG (1); CLL (1); CMH (1); CNGB (1); Dir of SpWarfare (1); Technical Stf, DA (5) except CofEngrs (75); CofOrd (275); TQMG (25); Chaplain Bd (5); CAMG Bd, (5); TAG Bd, USA (5); USA Intl Bd (5); Technical Stf Bd (5); USCONARC (10); OS Maj Comd (5); MDW (5); Armies (50); Corps (3); Div (2), except Armor Div (100); Brig (3); Regt/Gp (3); Bn (5); Co, Btry (15) except Med Co (5); Ft & Camps (6); Svc Colleges (5); Br Svc Sch (5); except USAES (100); USA Ord Sch (25); USA QM Sch (25); USMA (25); Joint Sch (5); Specialist Sch (5); PMST Sr Div Units (3) except PMST Sr Div Ord Units (25); PMST Jr Div Units (3); PMST Mil Sch Div Units (3); Gen Depots (5); Sup. Sec. Gen Depots (5); Depots (5); Ord Tk Autmv Comd (100); AH (5); USATC (100); Fld Comd, AFSWP (10); Ports of Emb (05) (3); Trans Terminal Comd (3); Army Terminals (3); OS Sup Agcy (2); PG (5); Arsenals (25); CmlCMatCom (25); DB (25); Engr Maint Cen (270); RMS (3); Div Engr (2), except New England Div Engr (20); Engr Dist (10); NG: State AG Special List. USAR: Mil Dist Special List. For explanation of abbreviations used, see AR 320-50.

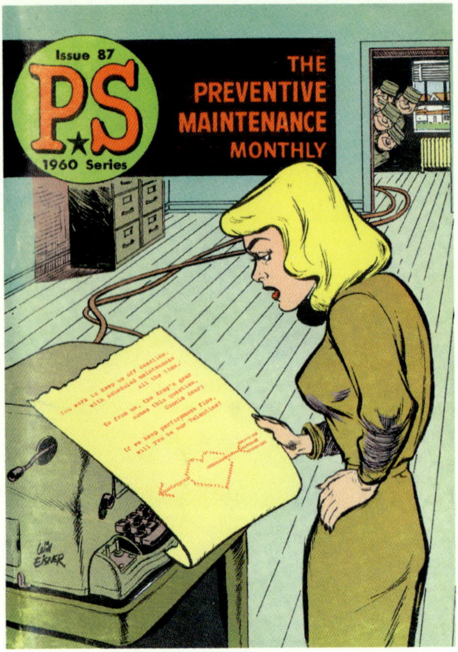
Issue 87
P★S
1960 Series
THE PREVENTIVE MAINTENANCE MONTHLY
Will Eisner

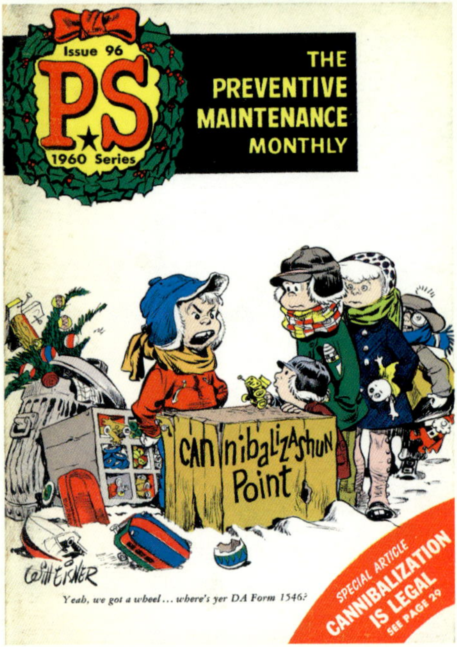
Issue 96
P★S
1960 Series
THE PREVENTIVE MAINTENANCE MONTHLY
Cannibalizashun Point
Will Eisner
Yeah, we got a wheel... where's yer DA Form 1546?
SPECIAL ARTICLE
CANNIBALIZATION IS LEGAL
SEE PAGE 29

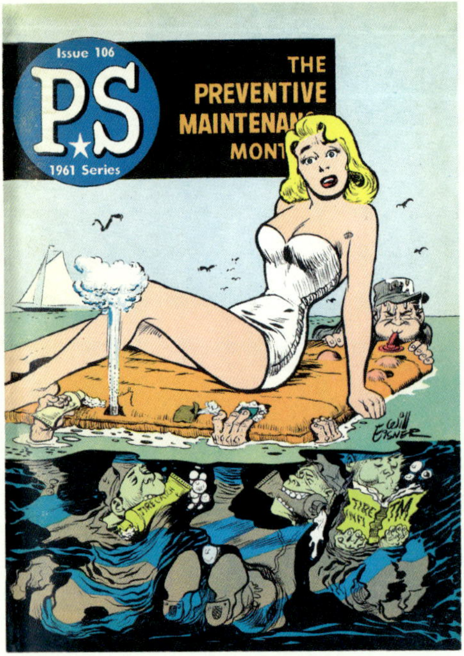
Issue 106
P★S
1961 Series
THE PREVENTIVE MAINTENAN MONT
Will Eisner

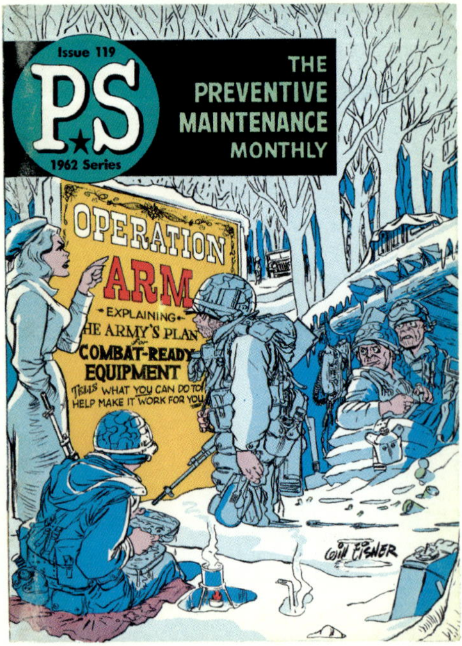
Issue 119
P★S
1962 Series
THE PREVENTIVE MAINTENANCE MONTHLY
OPERATION ARM
EXPLAINING
HE ARMY'S PLAN for COMBAT-READY EQUIPMENT
TELLS WHAT YOU CAN DO TO HELP MAKE IT WORK FOR YOU
Will Eisner

Issue 100
P.S
1961 Series
THE PREVENTIVE MAINTENANCE MONTHLY
30 40
Will Eisner

Issue 174
P.S
1967 Series
THE PREVENTIVE MAINTENANCE MONTHLY
WHAT'S SO UNUSUAL ABOUT THESE CONDITIONS?
YES, THESE NORMAL ALLA TIME, JOE!
THINK IT'S BAD NOW... WAIT TILL THE DRY SEASON STARTS!
VIETNAM ENTIRE ISSUE
Will Eisner

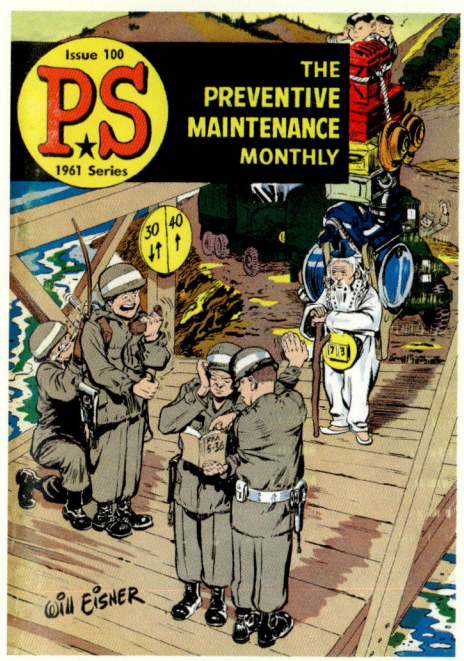

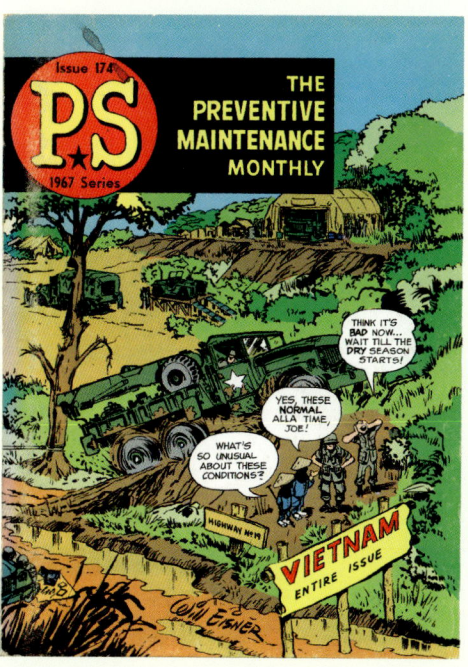

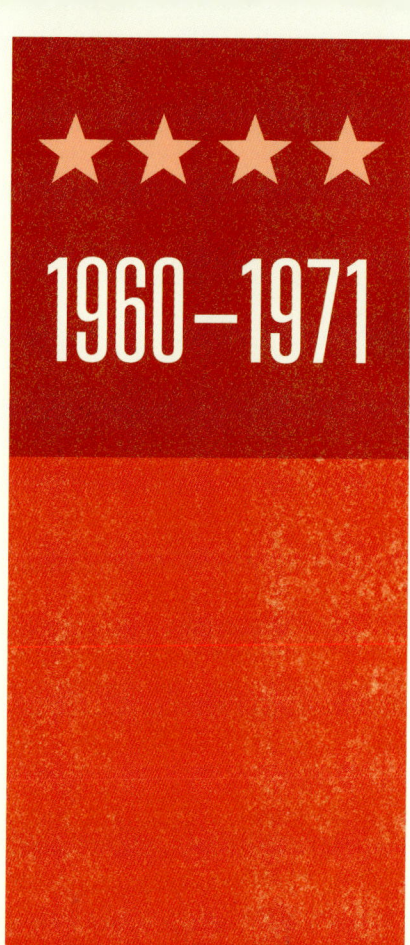

1960–1971

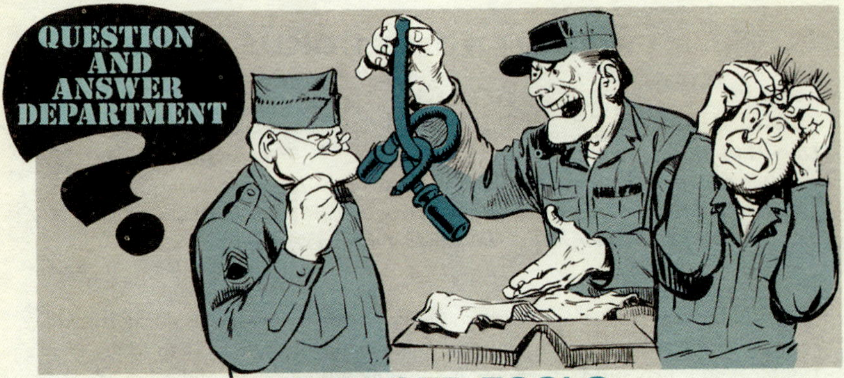
QUESTION AND ANSWER DEPARTMENT

DAMAGED TOOLS

Dear Half-Mast,

We had a few surprises when we unwrapped some tools in the assembly building at our Nike site. We got them on requisition.

The threads on a grease gun extension were chewed up and the blade on a cross tip screwdriver was all burred.

What gives?

WO L. R.

Dear WO L. R.,

H-m-m-m. That's one of those deals that shouldn't happen but did. And the tech service—in this case, Ordnance—wants to track down the situation and that's for sure.

Tell you what I'd do—send the tools back to my support unit. AR 711-16 gives the support people the scoop on accepting the bum tools.

Now . . . finding out you have bad tools after you've started to use them is a different story. When this happens, you want to fire off a UER (DA Form 468) right quick. AR 700-38 gives the go-ahead on sending in the UER.

Just make sure your UER mentions the shipping order number you got the tools under, the name of your support unit and the name of your outfit. And, of course, the UER goes to the tech service responsible for the tool.

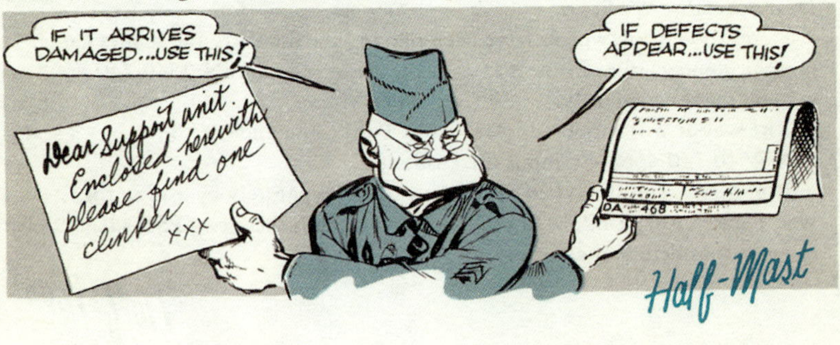
IF IT ARRIVES DAMAGED...USE THIS!
IF DEFECTS APPEAR...USE THIS!
Dear Support unit. Enclosed herewith please find one clinker xxx
DA 468
Half-Mast

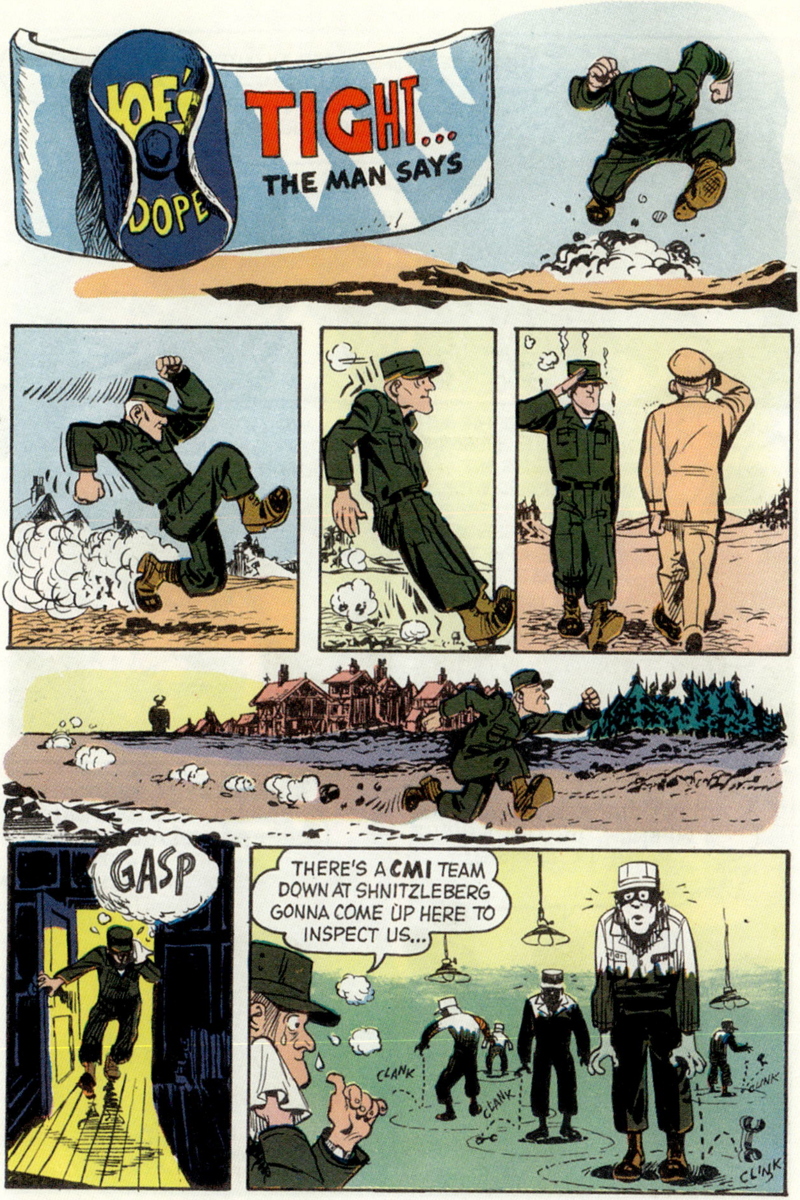
JOE'S DOPE
TIGHT...
THE MAN SAYS
GASP
THERE'S A CMI TEAM DOWN AT SHNITZLEBERG GONNA COME UP HERE TO INSPECT US...
CLANK
CLANK
CLINK
CLINK

no. 90, 1960

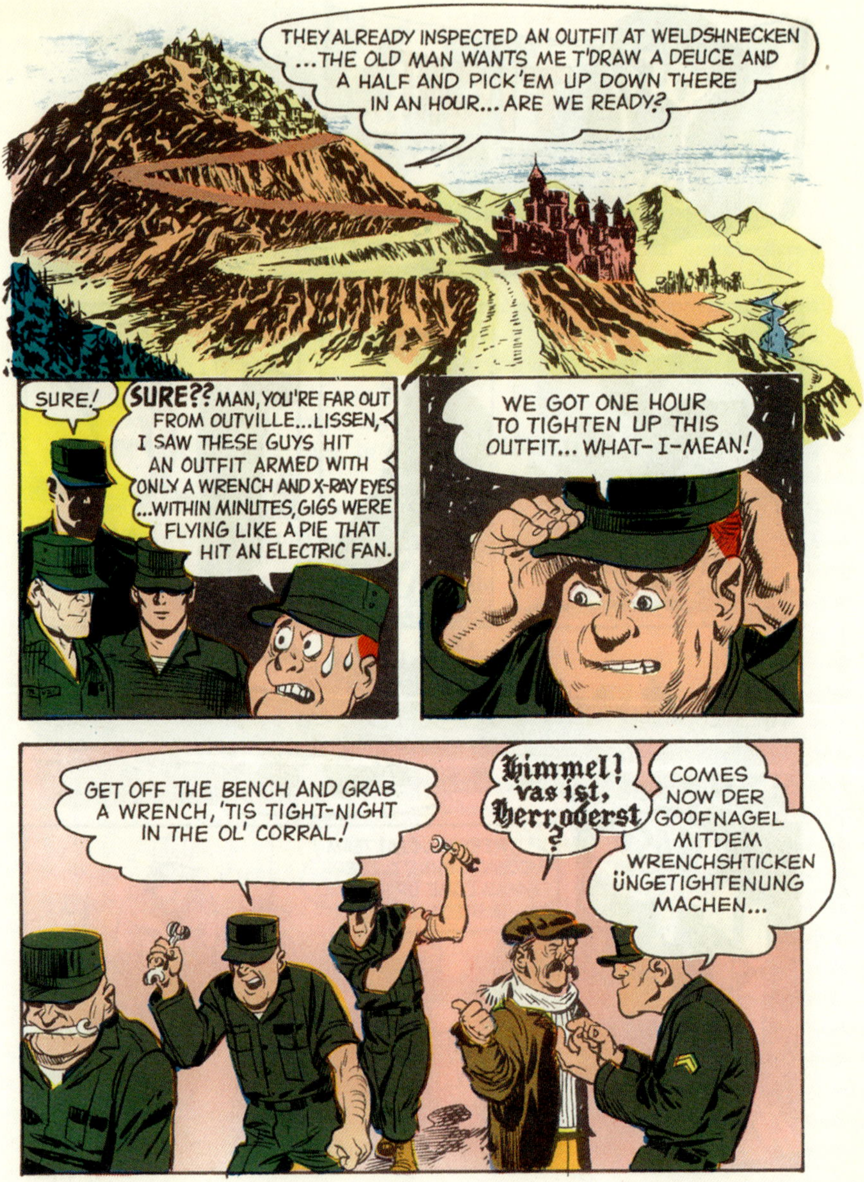
THEY ALREADY INSPECTED AN OUTFIT AT WELDSHNECKEN ...THE OLD MAN WANTS ME T'DRAW A DEUCE AND A HALF AND PICK'EM UP DOWN THERE IN AN HOUR... ARE WE READY?
SURE!
SURE?? MAN, YOU'RE FAR OUT FROM OUTVILLE...LISSEN, I SAW THESE GUYS HIT AN OUTFIT ARMED WITH ONLY A WRENCH AND X-RAY EYES ...WITHIN MINUTES, GIGS WERE FLYING LIKE A PIE THAT HIT AN ELECTRIC FAN.
WE GOT ONE HOUR TO TIGHTEN UP THIS OUTFIT... WHAT-I-MEAN!
GET OFF THE BENCH AND GRAB A WRENCH, 'TIS TIGHT-NIGHT IN THE OL' CORRAL!
Himmel! vas ist, Herr oberst?
COMES NOW DER GOOFNAGEL MITDEM WRENCHSHTICKEN ÜNGETIGHTENUNG MACHEN...

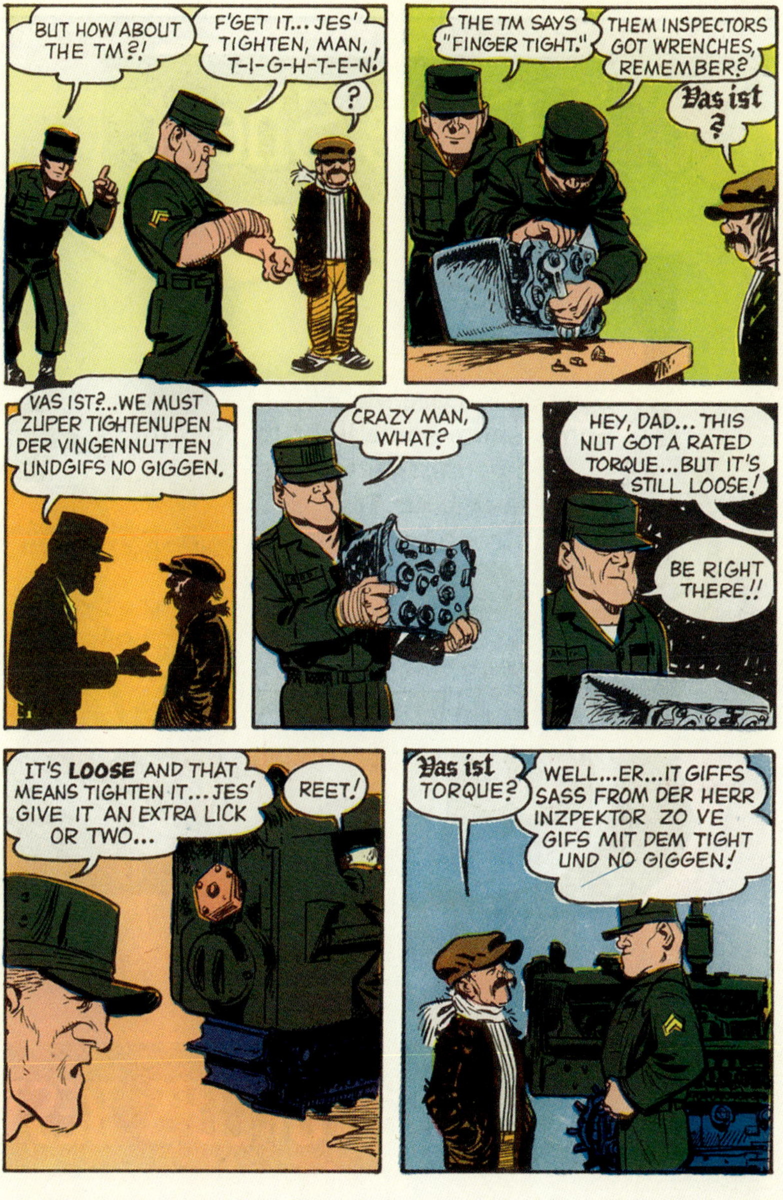
BUT HOW ABOUT THE TM?!
F'GET IT... JES' TIGHTEN, MAN, T-I-G-H-T-E-N!
?
THE TM SAYS "FINGER TIGHT."
THEM INSPECTORS GOT WRENCHES, REMEMBER?
Vas ist ?
VAS IST?...WE MUST ZUPER TIGHTENUPEN DER VINGENNUTTEN UNDGIFS NO GIGGEN.
CRAZY MAN, WHAT?
HEY, DAD... THIS NUT GOT A RATED TORQUE...BUT IT'S STILL LOOSE!
BE RIGHT THERE!!
IT'S LOOSE AND THAT MEANS TIGHTEN IT...JES' GIVE IT AN EXTRA LICK OR TWO...
REET!
Vas ist TORQUE?
WELL...ER...IT GIFFS SASS FROM DER HERR INZPEKTOR ZO VE GIFS MIT DEM TIGHT UND NO GIGGEN!

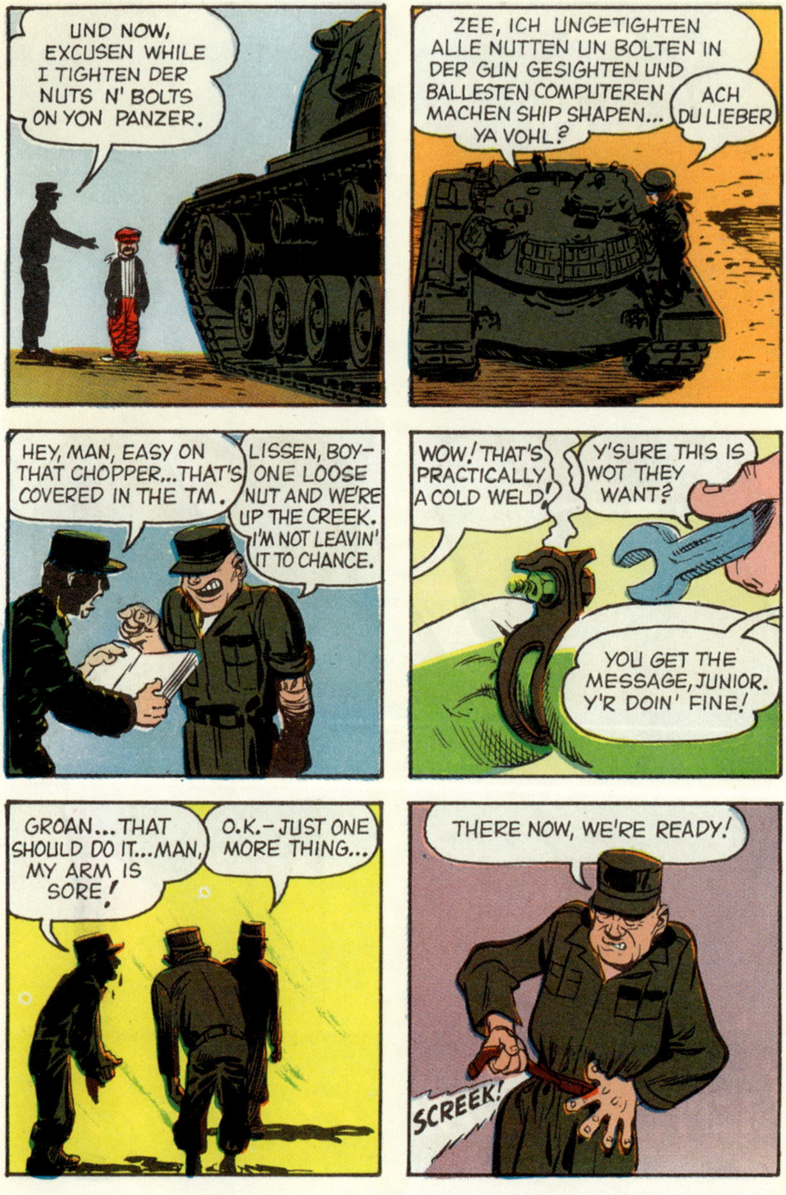
UND NOW, EXCUSEN WHILE I TIGHTEN DER NUTS N' BOLTS ON YON PANZER.
ZEE, ICH UNGETIGHTEN ALLE NUTTEN UN BOLTEN IN DER GUN GESIGHTEN UND BALLESTEN COMPUTEREN MACHEN SHIP SHAPEN... YA VOHL?
ACH DU LIEBER
HEY, MAN, EASY ON THAT CHOPPER...THAT'S COVERED IN THE TM.
LISSEN, BOY–ONE LOOSE NUT AND WE'RE UP THE CREEK. I'M NOT LEAVIN' IT TO CHANCE.
WOW! THAT'S PRACTICALLY A COLD WELD!
Y'SURE THIS IS WOT THEY WANT?
YOU GET THE MESSAGE, JUNIOR. Y'R DOIN' FINE!
GROAN... THAT SHOULD DO IT...MAN, MY ARM IS SORE!
O.K.–JUST ONE MORE THING...
THERE NOW, WE'RE READY!
SCREEK!

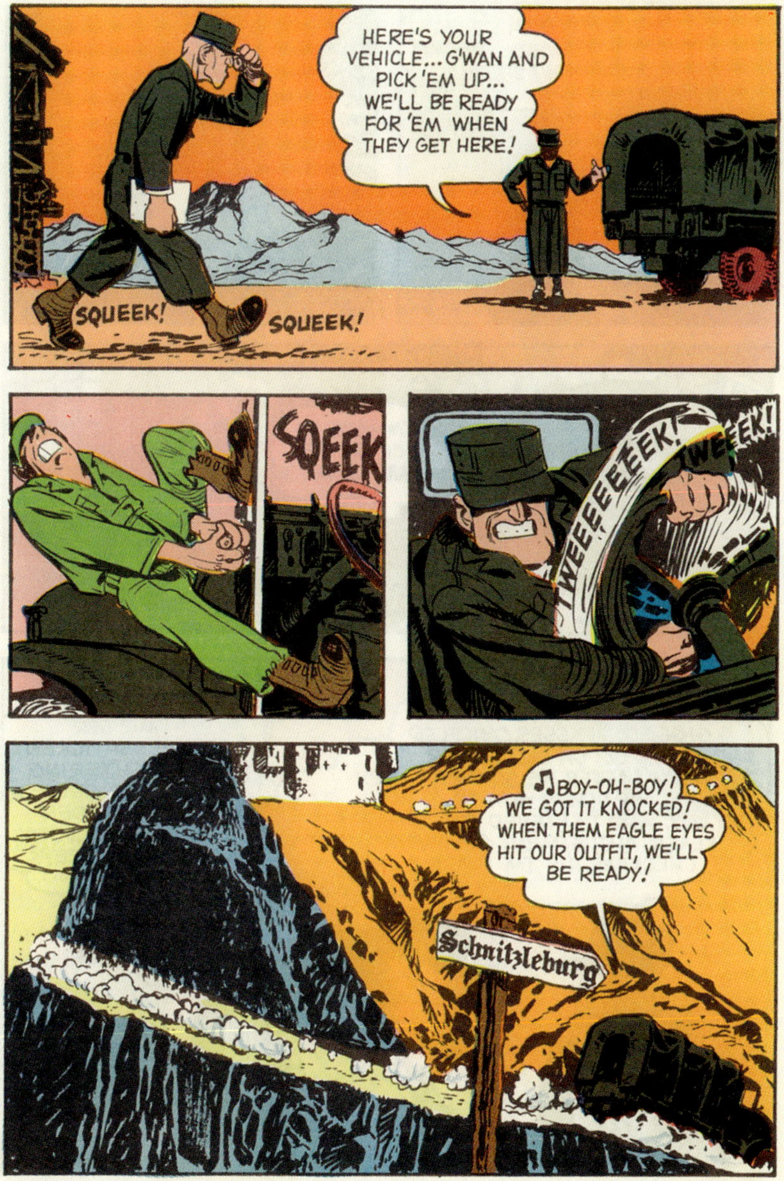
HERE'S YOUR VEHICLE... G'WAN AND PICK 'EM UP... WE'LL BE READY FOR 'EM WHEN THEY GET HERE!
SQUEEK!
SQUEEK!
SQEEK
TWEEEEEEEK!
TWEEEK!
♫ BOY-OH-BOY! WE GOT IT KNOCKED! WHEN THEM EAGLE EYES HIT OUR OUTFIT, WE'LL BE READY!
Schnitzleburg

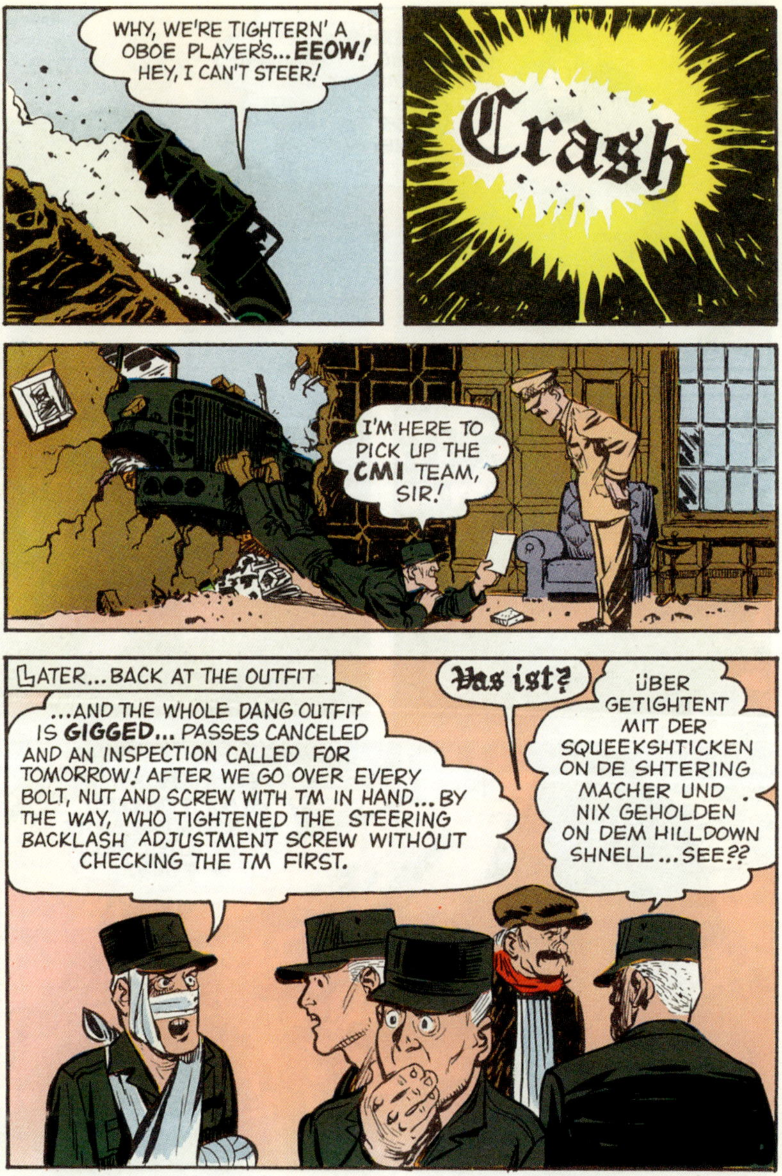

WHY, WE'RE TIGHTERN' A OBOE PLAYER'S... EEOW! HEY, I CAN'T STEER!
Crash
I'M HERE TO PICK UP THE CMI TEAM, SIR!
LATER... BACK AT THE OUTFIT
...AND THE WHOLE DANG OUTFIT IS GIGGED... PASSES CANCELED AND AN INSPECTION CALLED FOR TOMORROW! AFTER WE GO OVER EVERY BOLT, NUT AND SCREW WITH TM IN HAND... BY THE WAY, WHO TIGHTENED THE STEERING BACKLASH ADJUSTMENT SCREW WITHOUT CHECKING THE TM FIRST.
Vas ist?
ÜBER GETIGHTENT MIT DER SQUEEKSHTICKEN ON DE SHTERING MACHER UND NIX GEHOLDEN ON DEM HILLDOWN SHNELL... SEE??

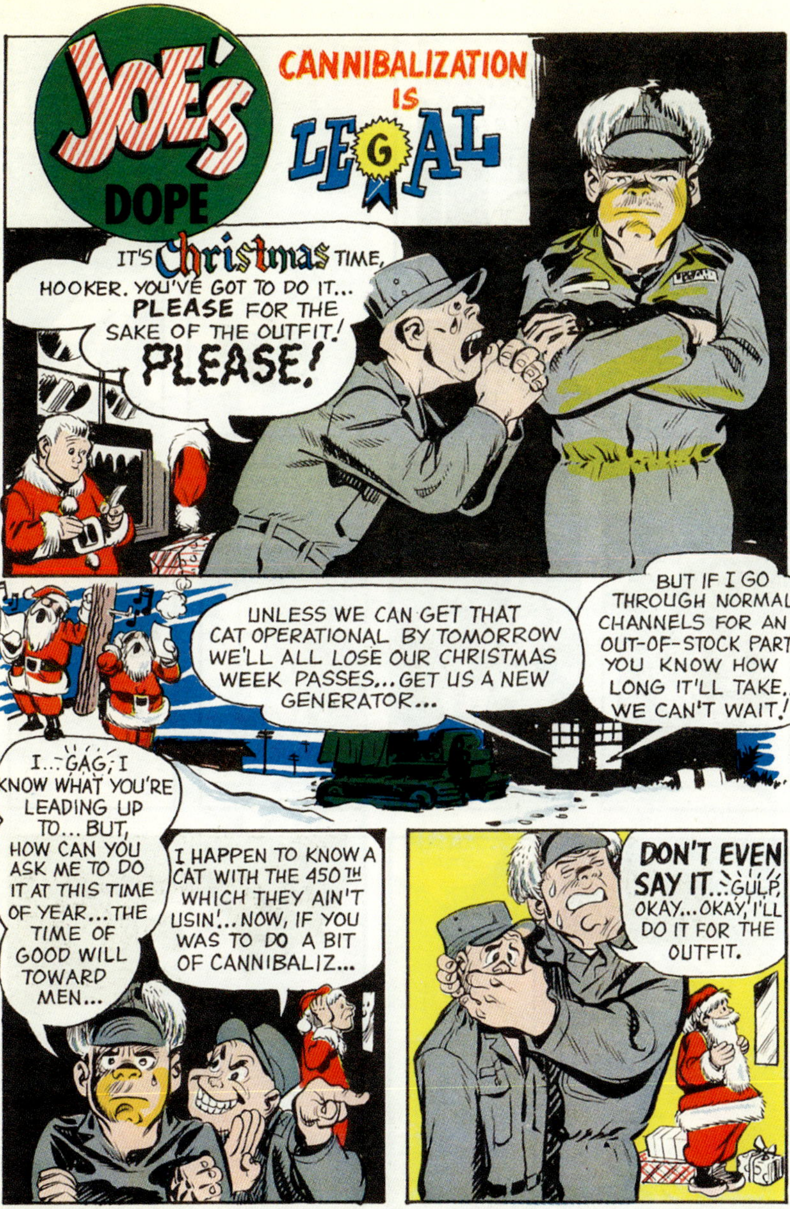
JOE'S DOPE
CANNIBALIZATION IS LEGAL
IT'S Christmas TIME, HOOKER. YOU'VE GOT TO DO IT... PLEASE FOR THE SAKE OF THE OUTFIT! PLEASE!
UNLESS WE CAN GET THAT CAT OPERATIONAL BY TOMORROW WE'LL ALL LOSE OUR CHRISTMAS WEEK PASSES... GET US A NEW GENERATOR...
BUT IF I GO THROUGH NORMAL CHANNELS FOR AN OUT-OF-STOCK PART, YOU KNOW HOW LONG IT'LL TAKE... WE CAN'T WAIT!
I... GAG, I KNOW WHAT YOU'RE LEADING UP TO... BUT, HOW CAN YOU ASK ME TO DO IT AT THIS TIME OF YEAR... THE TIME OF GOOD WILL TOWARD MEN...
I HAPPEN TO KNOW A CAT WITH THE 450TH WHICH THEY AIN'T USIN'... NOW, IF YOU WAS TO DO A BIT OF CANNIBALIZ...
DON'T EVEN SAY IT... GULP, OKAY... OKAY, I'LL DO IT FOR THE OUTFIT.

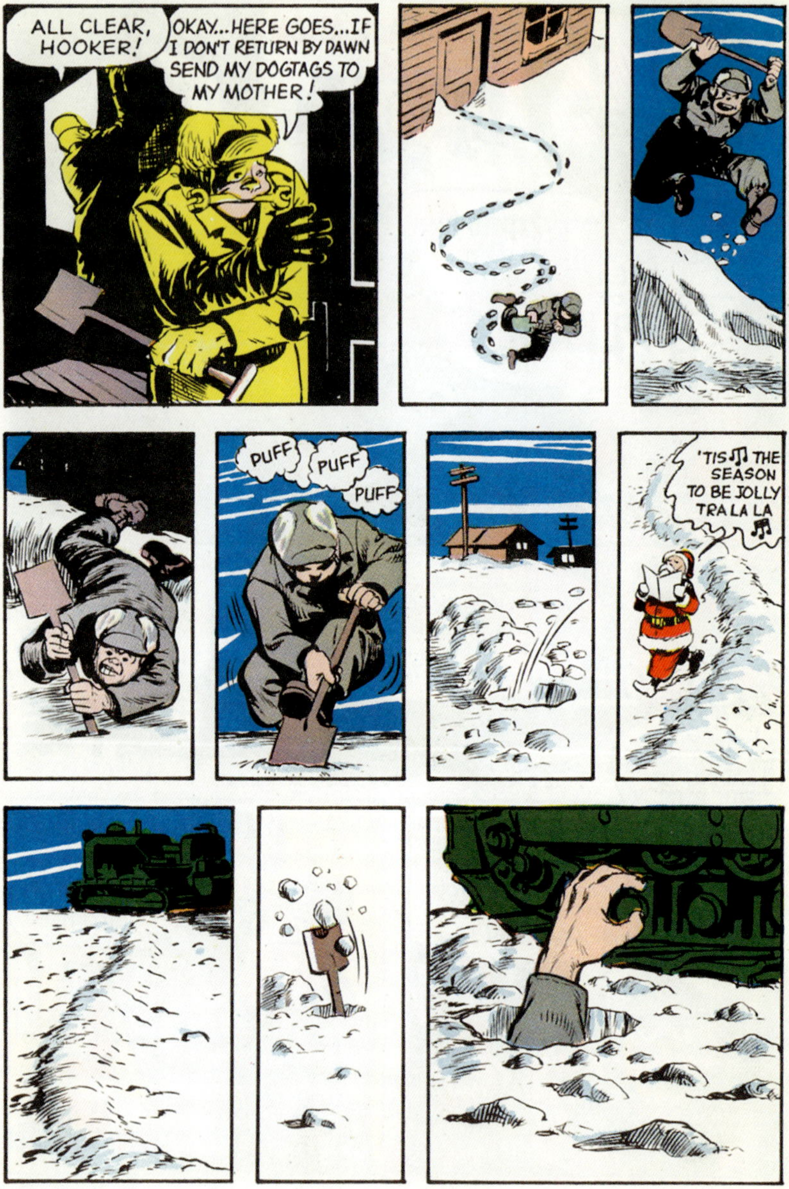
ALL CLEAR, HOOKER!
OKAY...HERE GOES...IF I DON'T RETURN BY DAWN SEND MY DOGTAGS TO MY MOTHER!
PUFF
PUFF
PUFF
'TIS THE SEASON TO BE JOLLY TRA LA LA

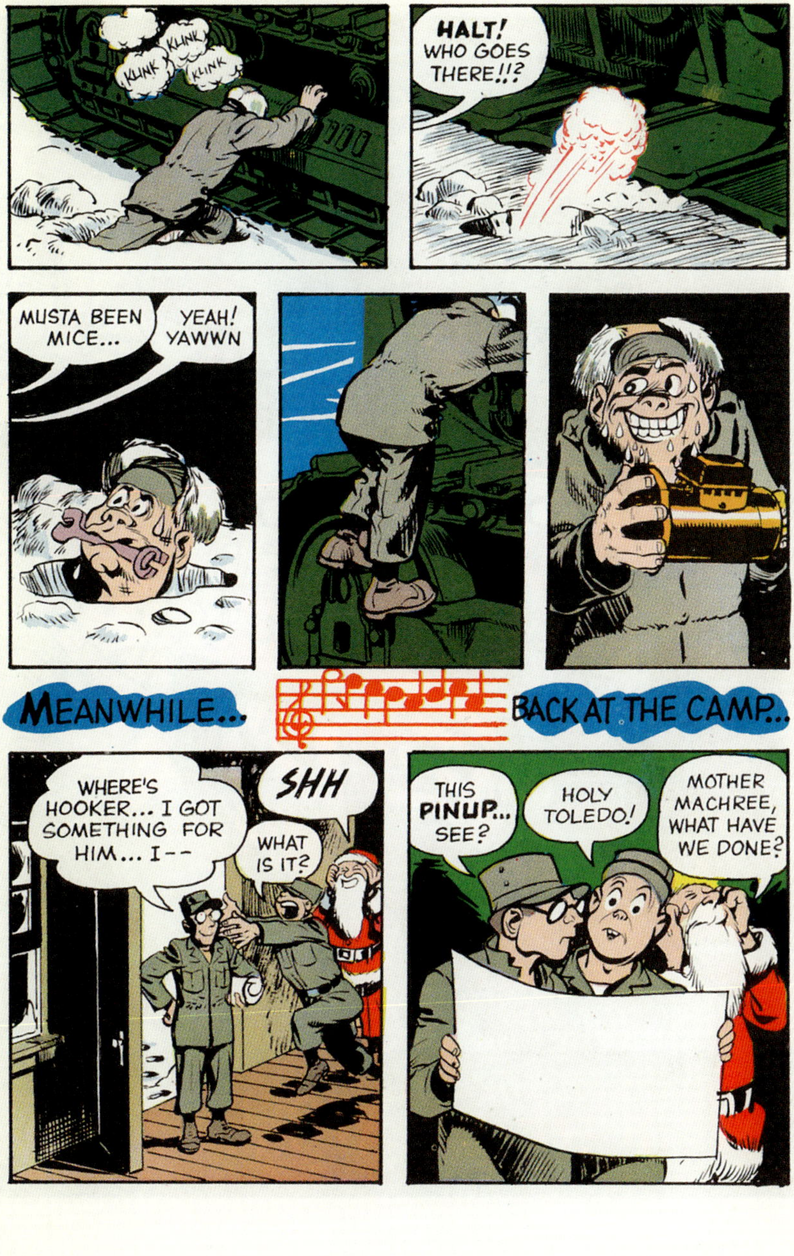
KLINK
KLINK
KLINK
HALT! WHO GOES THERE!!?
MUSTA BEEN MICE...
YEAH! YAWWN
MEANWHILE...
BACK AT THE CAMP...
WHERE'S HOOKER... I GOT SOMETHING FOR HIM... I--
SHH
WHAT IS IT?
THIS PINUP... SEE?
HOLY TOLEDO!
MOTHER MACHREE, WHAT HAVE WE DONE?

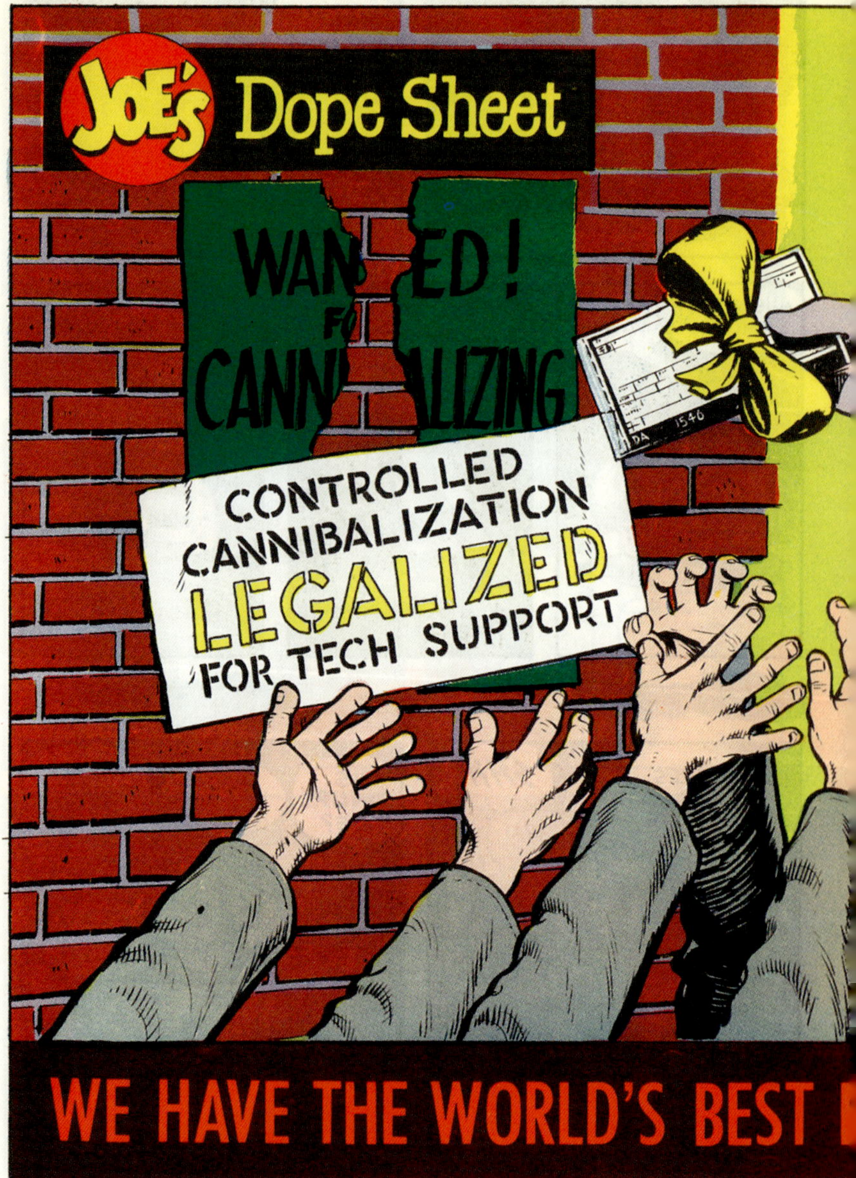
JOE'S Dope Sheet
WAN ED!
F
CANN ALIZING
CONTROLLED
CANNIBALIZATION
LEGALIZED
FOR TECH SUPPORT
WE HAVE THE WORLD'S BEST

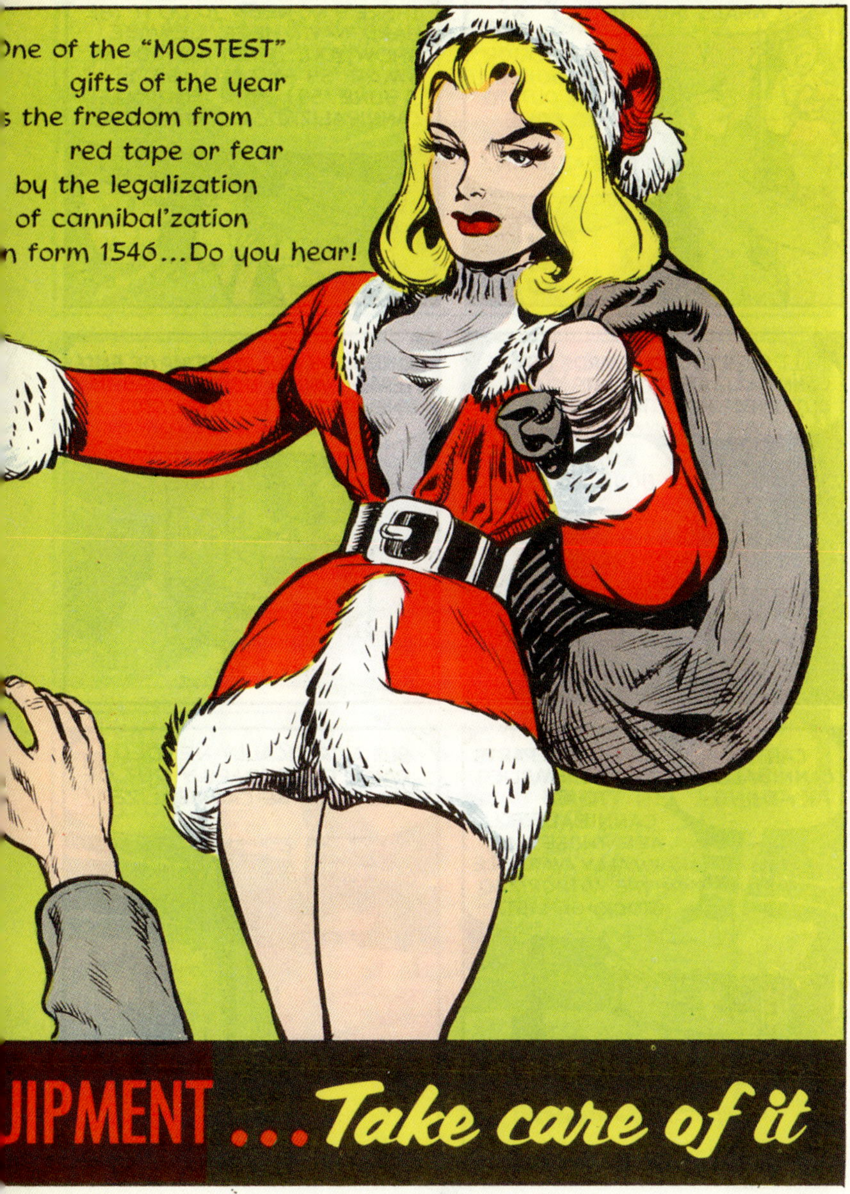
One of the "MOSTEST"
gifts of the year
s the freedom from
red tape or fear
by the legalization
of cannibal'zation
n form 1546...Do you hear!
JIPMENT ...Take care of it

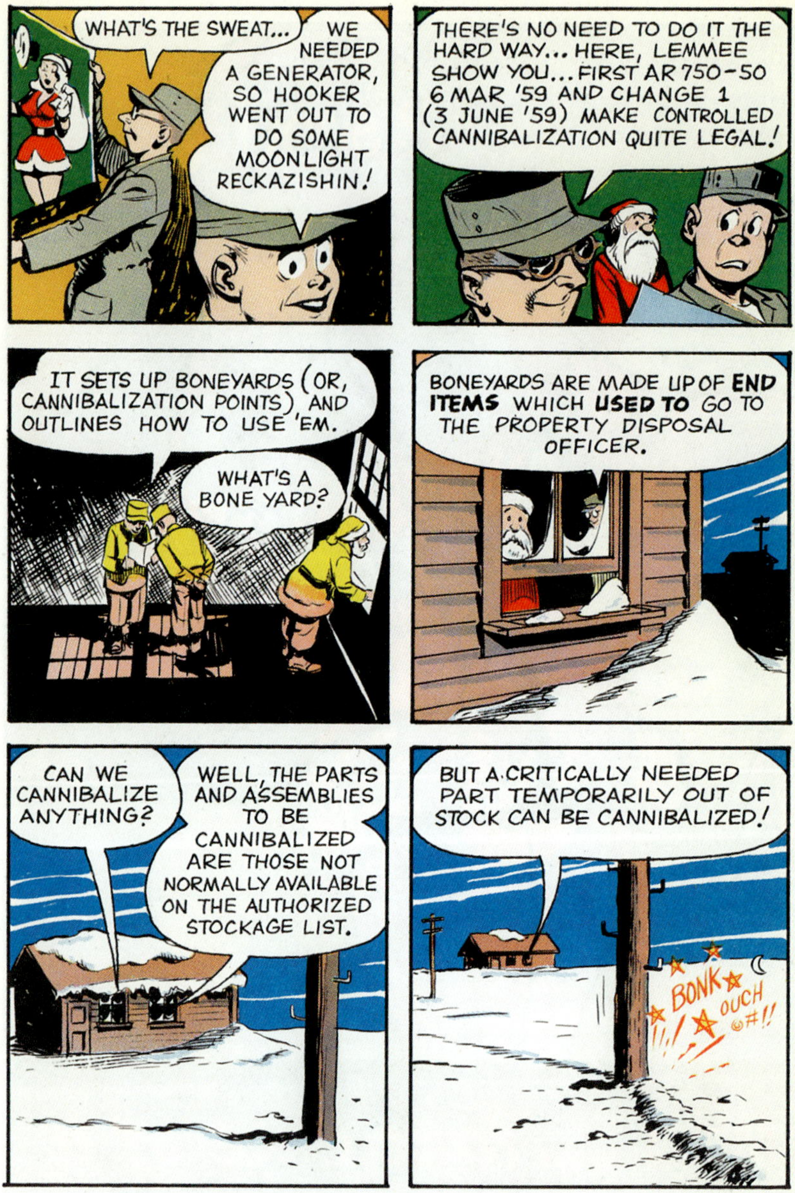

WHAT'S THE SWEAT... WE NEEDED A GENERATOR, SO HOOKER WENT OUT TO DO SOME MOONLIGHT RECKAZIZHIN!
THERE'S NO NEED TO DO IT THE HARD WAY... HERE, LEMMEE SHOW YOU... FIRST AR 750-50 6 MAR '59 AND CHANGE 1 (3 JUNE '59) MAKE CONTROLLED CANNIBALIZATION QUITE LEGAL!
IT SETS UP BONEYARDS (OR, CANNIBALIZATION POINTS) AND OUTLINES HOW TO USE 'EM.
WHAT'S A BONE YARD?
BONEYARDS ARE MADE UP OF END ITEMS WHICH USED TO GO TO THE PROPERTY DISPOSAL OFFICER.
CAN WE CANNIBALIZE ANYTHING?
WELL, THE PARTS AND ASSEMBLIES TO BE CANNIBALIZED ARE THOSE NOT NORMALLY AVAILABLE ON THE AUTHORIZED STOCKAGE LIST.
BUT A CRITICALLY NEEDED PART TEMPORARILY OUT OF STOCK CAN BE CANNIBALIZED!
BONK
OUCH
!!,!
@#!!

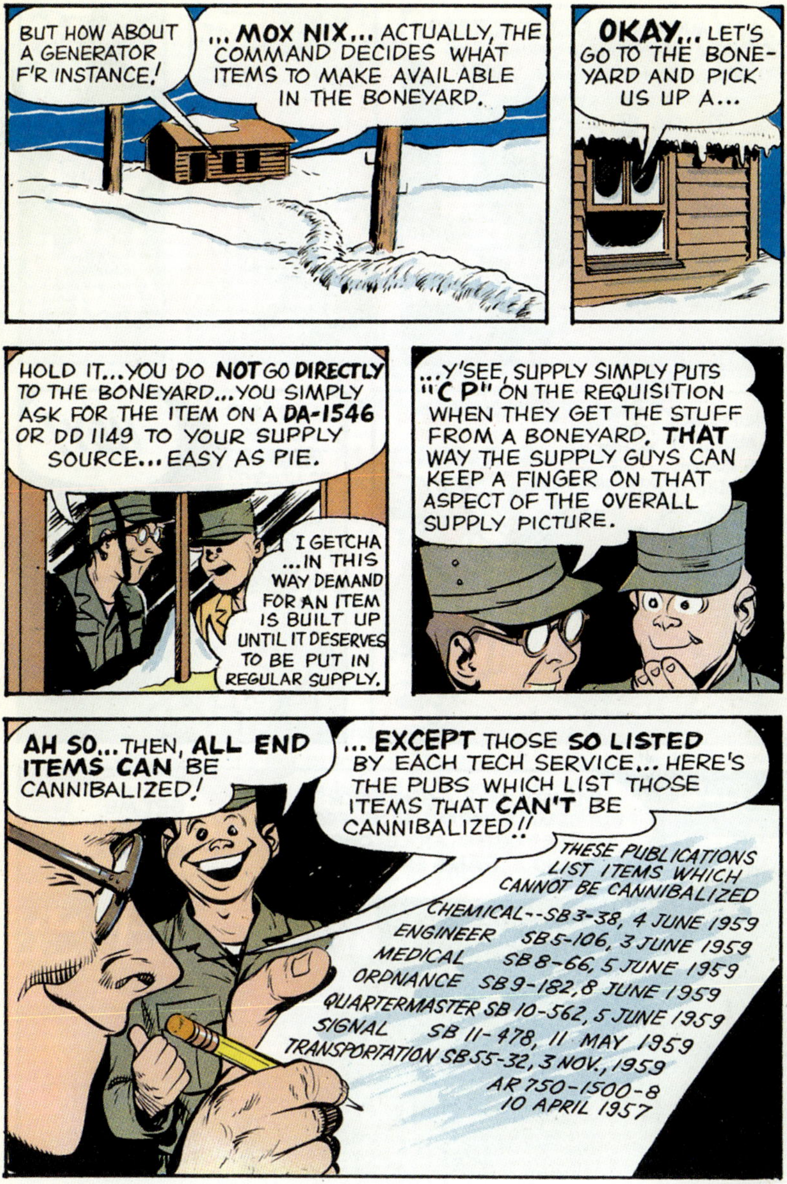

BUT HOW ABOUT A GENERATOR F'R INSTANCE!
... MOX NIX... ACTUALLY, THE COMMAND DECIDES WHAT ITEMS TO MAKE AVAILABLE IN THE BONEYARD.
OKAY... LET'S GO TO THE BONEYARD AND PICK US UP A...
HOLD IT... YOU DO NOT GO DIRECTLY TO THE BONEYARD... YOU SIMPLY ASK FOR THE ITEM ON A DA-1546 OR DD 1149 TO YOUR SUPPLY SOURCE... EASY AS PIE.
I GETCHA ...IN THIS WAY DEMAND FOR AN ITEM IS BUILT UP UNTIL IT DESERVES TO BE PUT IN REGULAR SUPPLY.
...Y'SEE, SUPPLY SIMPLY PUTS "C P" ON THE REQUISITION WHEN THEY GET THE STUFF FROM A BONEYARD. THAT WAY THE SUPPLY GUYS CAN KEEP A FINGER ON THAT ASPECT OF THE OVERALL SUPPLY PICTURE.
AH SO... THEN, ALL END ITEMS CAN BE CANNIBALIZED!
... EXCEPT THOSE SO LISTED BY EACH TECH SERVICE... HERE'S THE PUBS WHICH LIST THOSE ITEMS THAT CAN'T BE CANNIBALIZED!!
THESE PUBLICATIONS LIST ITEMS WHICH CANNOT BE CANNIBALIZED
CHEMICAL--SB 3-38, 4 JUNE 1959
ENGINEER SB 5-106, 3 JUNE 1959
MEDICAL SB 8-66, 5 JUNE 1959
ORDNANCE SB 9-182, 8 JUNE 1959
QUARTERMASTER SB 10-562, 5 JUNE 1959
SIGNAL SB 11-478, 11 MAY 1959
TRANSPORTATION SB 55-32, 3 NOV., 1959
AR 750-1500-8
10 APRIL 1957

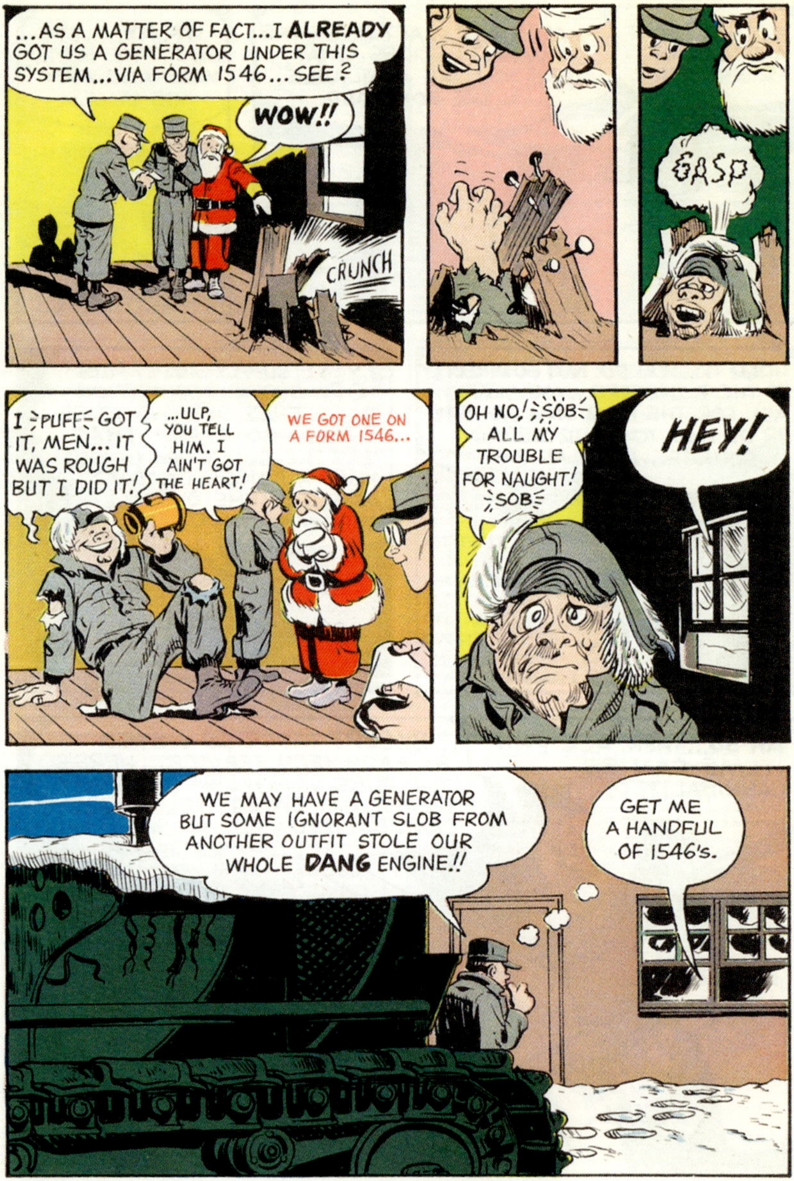

...AS A MATTER OF FACT...I ALREADY GOT US A GENERATOR UNDER THIS SYSTEM...VIA FORM 1546...SEE?
WOW!!
CRUNCH
GASP
I PUFF GOT IT, MEN... IT WAS ROUGH BUT I DID IT!
...ULP, YOU TELL HIM. I AIN'T GOT THE HEART!
WE GOT ONE ON A FORM 1546...
OH NO! SOB ALL MY TROUBLE FOR NAUGHT! SOB
HEY!
WE MAY HAVE A GENERATOR BUT SOME IGNORANT SLOB FROM ANOTHER OUTFIT STOLE OUR WHOLE DANG ENGINE!!
GET ME A HANDFUL OF 1546's.

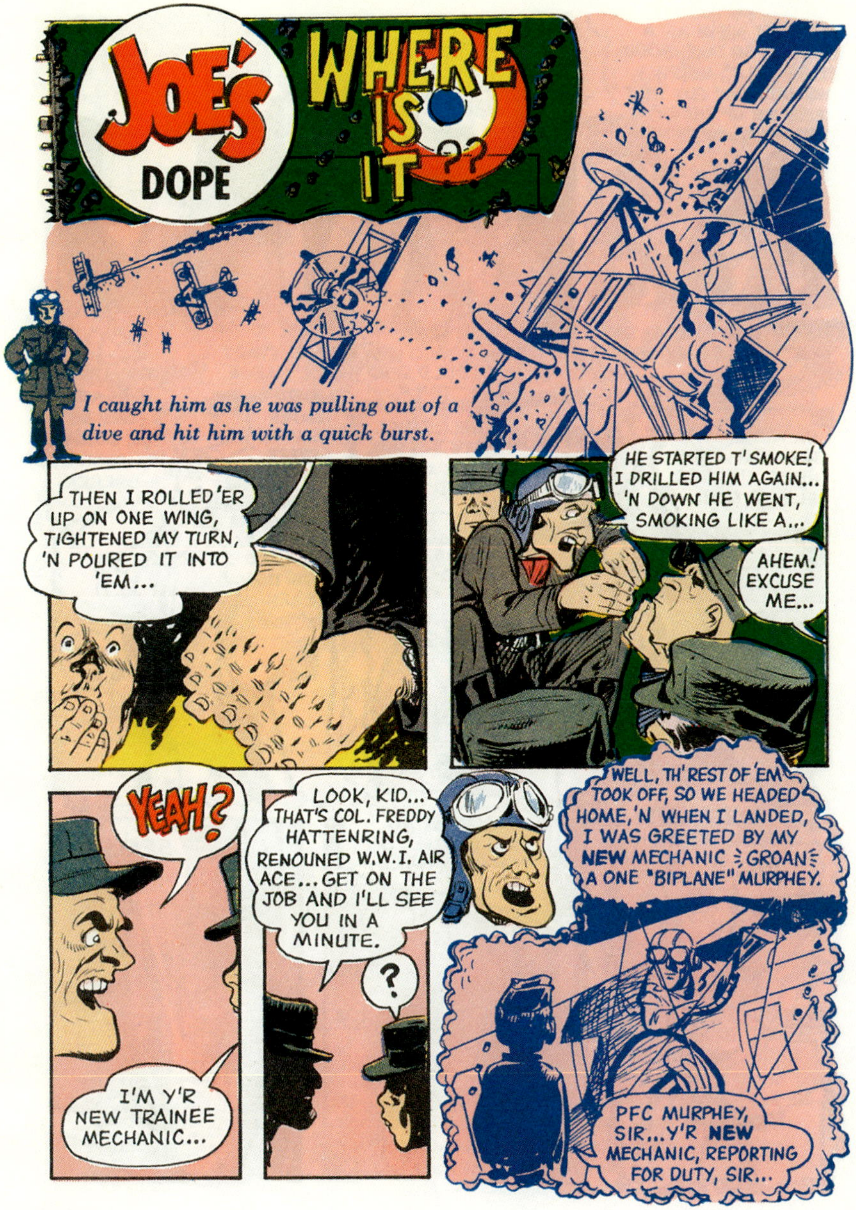
JOE'S DOPE
WHERE IS IT??
I caught him as he was pulling out of a dive and hit him with a quick burst.
THEN I ROLLED 'ER UP ON ONE WING, TIGHTENED MY TURN, 'N POURED IT INTO 'EM...
HE STARTED T' SMOKE! I DRILLED HIM AGAIN... 'N DOWN HE WENT, SMOKING LIKE A...
AHEM! EXCUSE ME...
YEAH?
I'M Y'R NEW TRAINEE MECHANIC...
LOOK, KID... THAT'S COL. FREDDY HATTENRING, RENOUNED W.W.I. AIR ACE... GET ON THE JOB AND I'LL SEE YOU IN A MINUTE.
?
WELL, TH' REST OF 'EM TOOK OFF, SO WE HEADED HOME, 'N WHEN I LANDED, I WAS GREETED BY MY NEW MECHANIC ≡GROAN≡ A ONE "BIPLANE" MURPHEY.
PFC MURPHEY, SIR... Y'R NEW MECHANIC, REPORTING FOR DUTY, SIR...

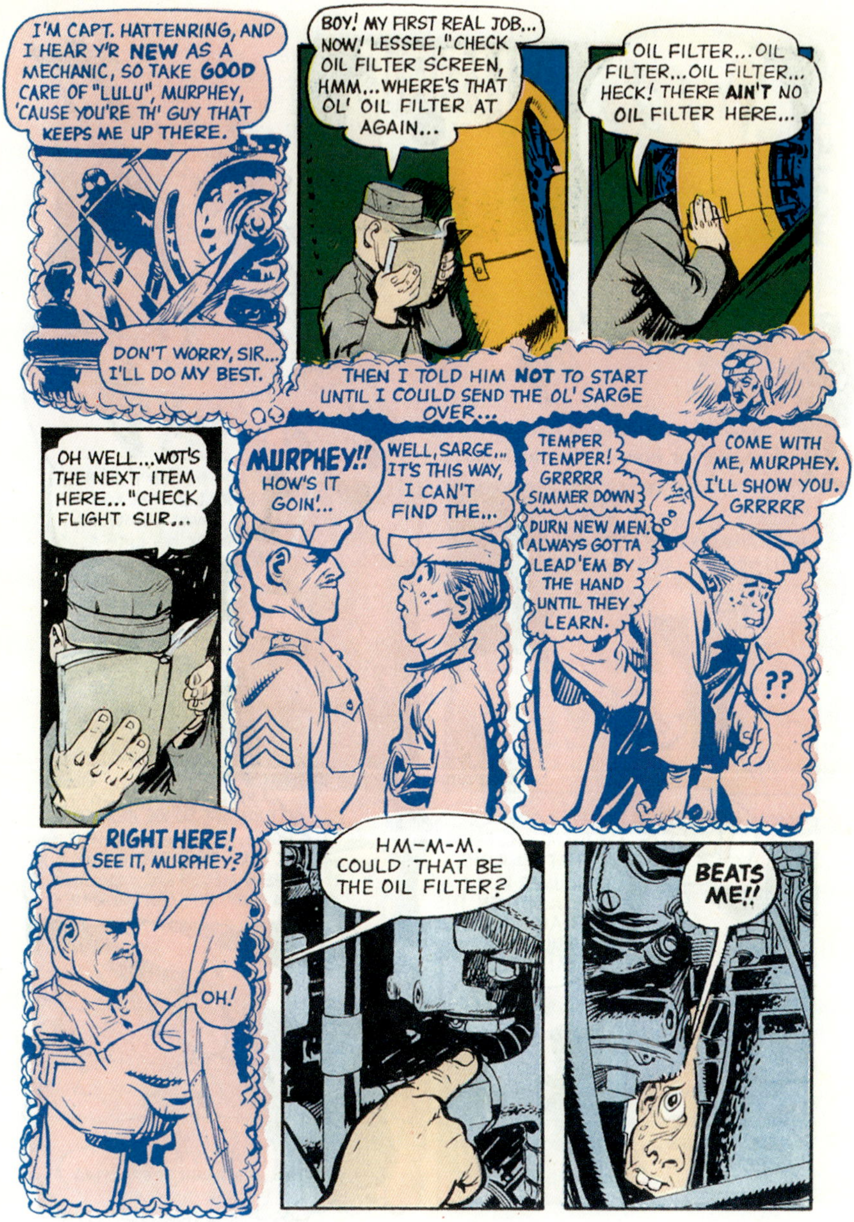

I'M CAPT. HATTENRING, AND I HEAR Y'R NEW AS A MECHANIC, SO TAKE GOOD CARE OF "LULU", MURPHEY, 'CAUSE YOU'RE TH' GUY THAT KEEPS ME UP THERE.
DON'T WORRY, SIR... I'LL DO MY BEST.
BOY! MY FIRST REAL JOB... NOW! LESSEE, "CHECK OIL FILTER SCREEN, HMM... WHERE'S THAT OL' OIL FILTER AT AGAIN...
OIL FILTER... OIL FILTER... OIL FILTER... HECK! THERE AIN'T NO OIL FILTER HERE...
THEN I TOLD HIM NOT TO START UNTIL I COULD SEND THE OL' SARGE OVER...
OH WELL... WOT'S THE NEXT ITEM HERE... "CHECK FLIGHT SUR...
MURPHEY!! HOW'S IT GOIN'...
WELL, SARGE... IT'S THIS WAY, I CAN'T FIND THE...
TEMPER TEMPER! GRRRRR SIMMER DOWN
DURN NEW MEN. ALWAYS GOTTA LEAD 'EM BY THE HAND UNTIL THEY LEARN.
COME WITH ME, MURPHEY. I'LL SHOW YOU. GRRRRR
??
RIGHT HERE! SEE IT, MURPHEY?
OH!
HM-M-M. COULD THAT BE THE OIL FILTER?
BEATS ME!!

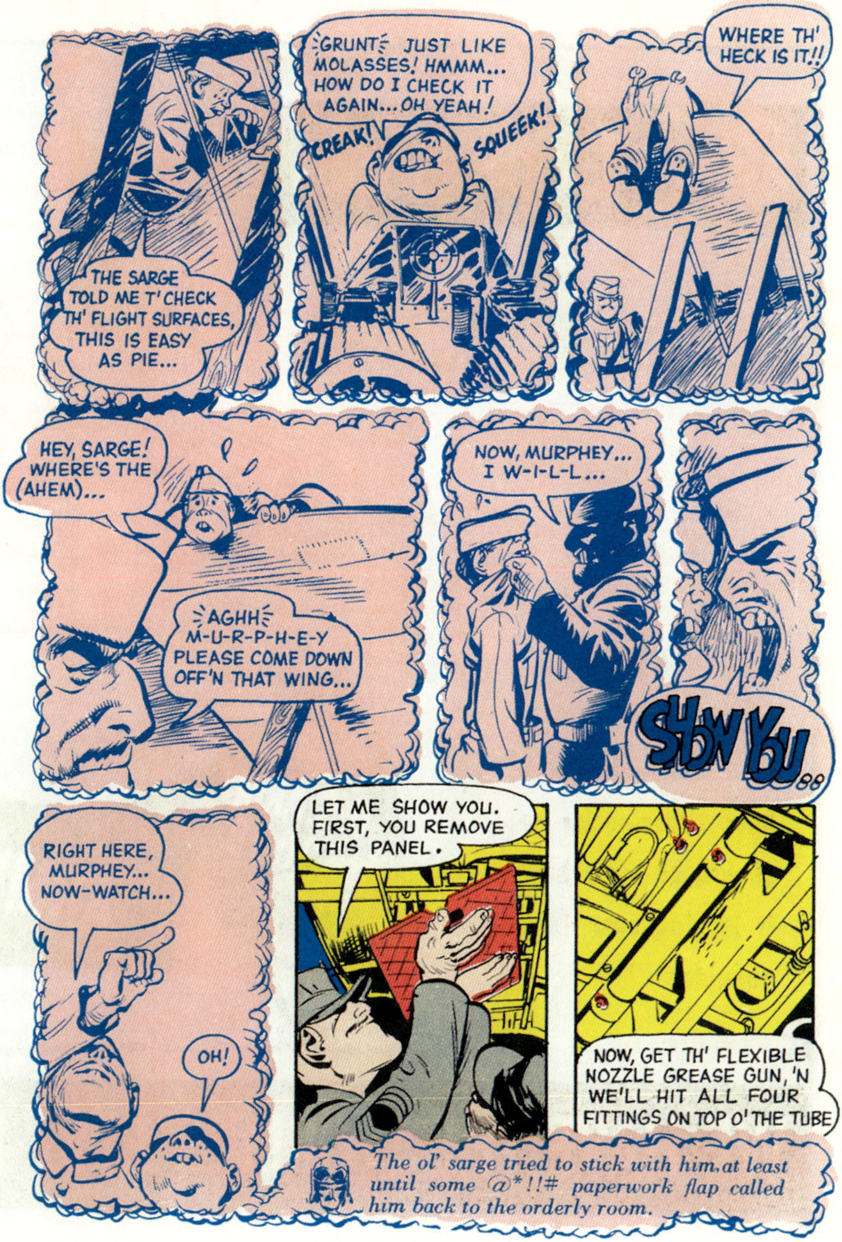
THE SARGE TOLD ME T' CHECK TH' FLIGHT SURFACES, THIS IS EASY AS PIE...
≡GRUNT≡ JUST LIKE MOLASSES! HMMM... HOW DO I CHECK IT AGAIN... OH YEAH!
CREAK!
SQUEEK!
WHERE TH' HECK IS IT!!
HEY, SARGE! WHERE'S THE (AHEM)...
≡AGHH≡ M-U-R-P-H-E-Y PLEASE COME DOWN OFF'N THAT WING...
NOW, MURPHEY... I W-I-L-L...
SHOW YOU
RIGHT HERE, MURPHEY... NOW-WATCH...
OH!
LET ME SHOW YOU. FIRST, YOU REMOVE THIS PANEL.
NOW, GET TH' FLEXIBLE NOZZLE GREASE GUN, 'N WE'LL HIT ALL FOUR FITTINGS ON TOP O' THE TUBE
The ol' sarge tried to stick with him, at least until some @*!!# paperwork flap called him back to the orderly room.

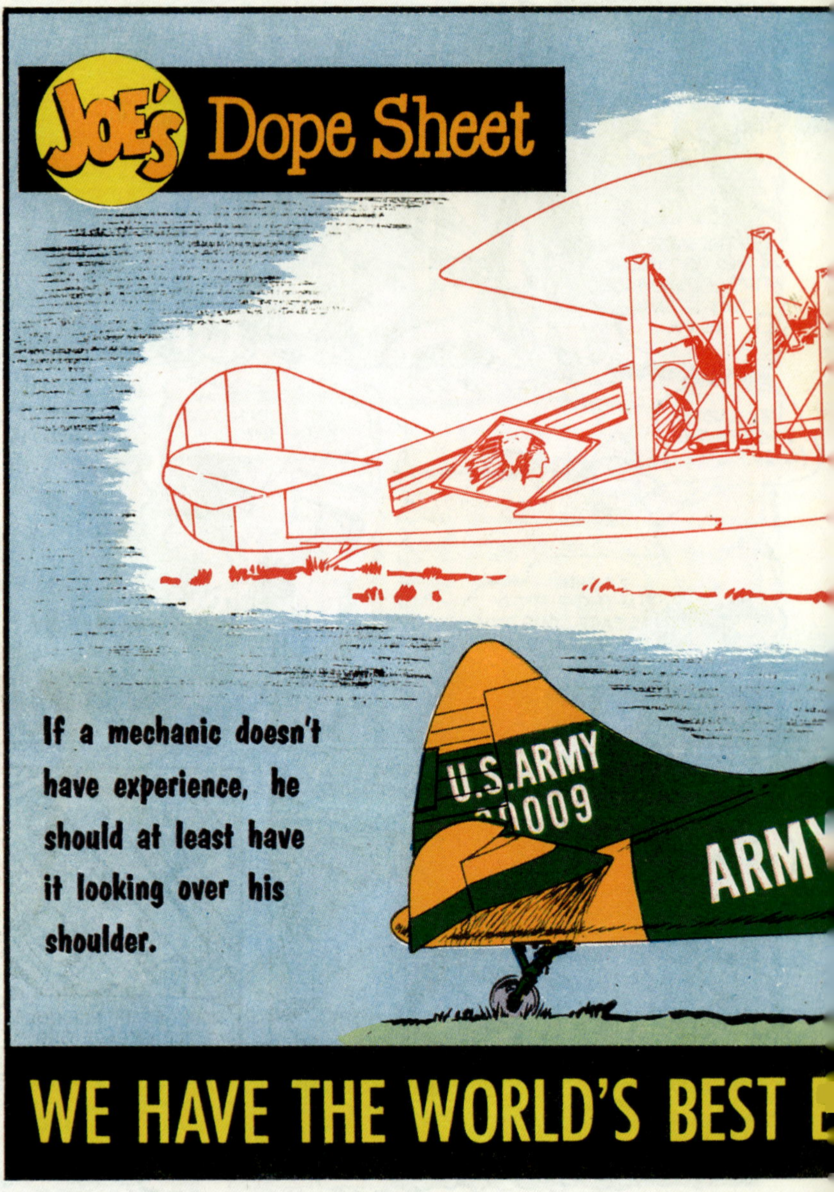
JOE'S Dope Sheet
If a mechanic doesn't have experience, he should at least have it looking over his shoulder.
U.S.ARMY
ARMY
WE HAVE THE WORLD'S BEST

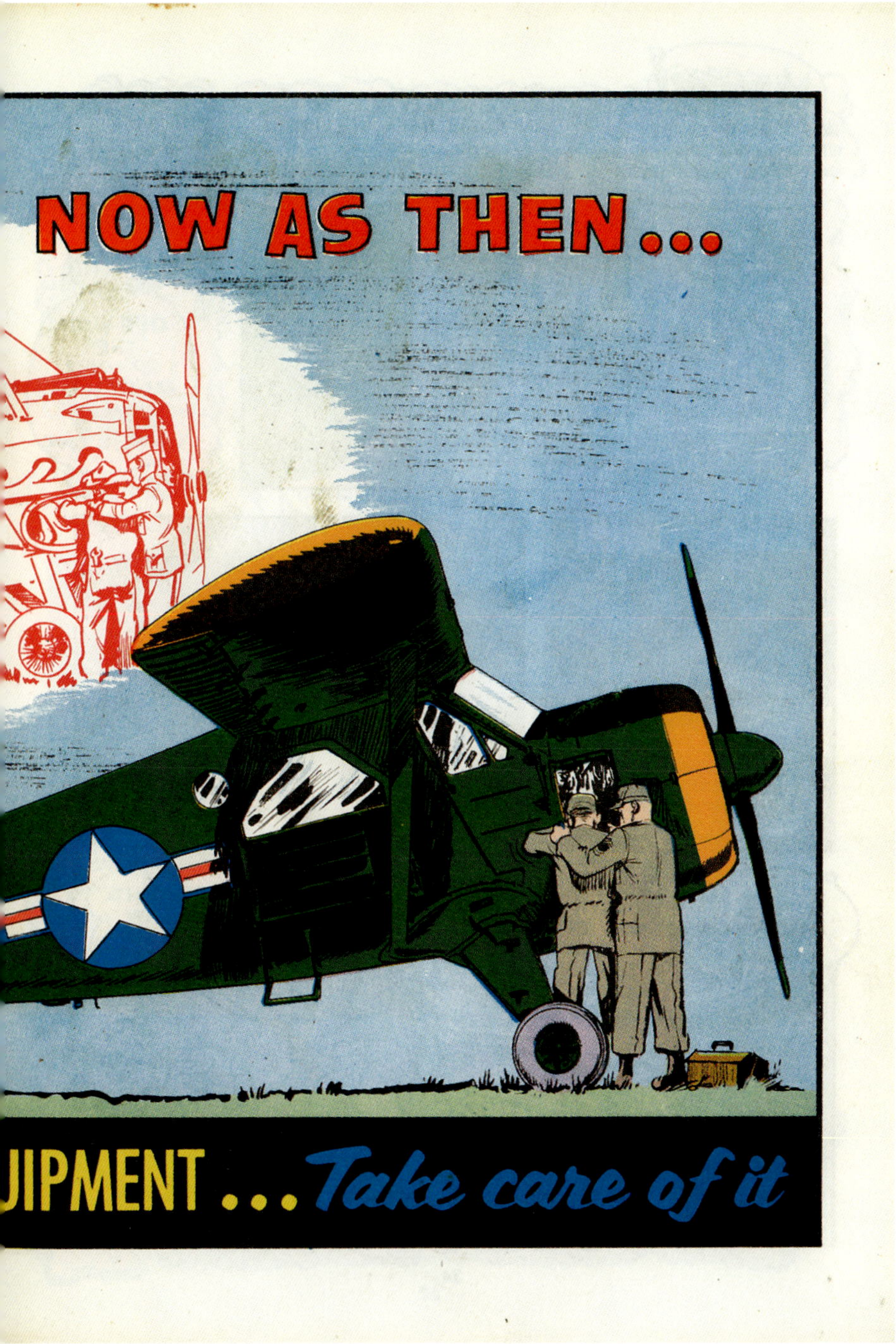

NOW AS THEN...
UIPMENT ... Take care of it

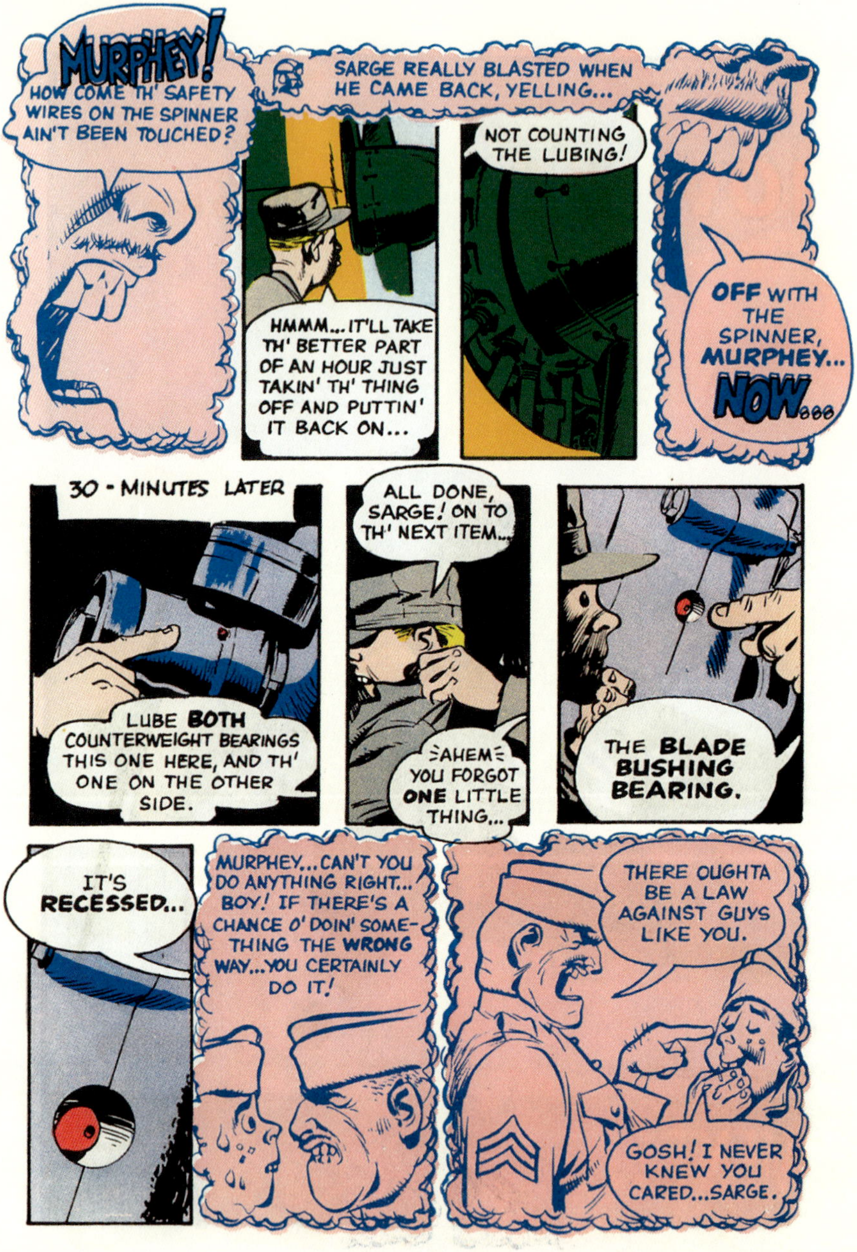
MURPHEY! HOW COME TH' SAFETY WIRES ON THE SPINNER AIN'T BEEN TOUCHED?
SARGE REALLY BLASTED WHEN HE CAME BACK, YELLING...
HMMM... IT'LL TAKE TH' BETTER PART OF AN HOUR JUST TAKIN' TH' THING OFF AND PUTTIN' IT BACK ON...
NOT COUNTING THE LUBING!
OFF WITH THE SPINNER, MURPHEY... NOW...
30 - MINUTES LATER
LUBE BOTH COUNTERWEIGHT BEARINGS THIS ONE HERE, AND TH' ONE ON THE OTHER SIDE.
ALL DONE, SARGE! ON TO TH' NEXT ITEM...
AHEM YOU FORGOT ONE LITTLE THING...
THE BLADE BUSHING BEARING.
IT'S RECESSED...
MURPHEY... CAN'T YOU DO ANYTHING RIGHT... BOY! IF THERE'S A CHANCE O' DOIN' SOMETHING THE WRONG WAY... YOU CERTAINLY DO IT!
THERE OUGHTA BE A LAW AGAINST GUYS LIKE YOU.
GOSH! I NEVER KNEW YOU CARED... SARGE.

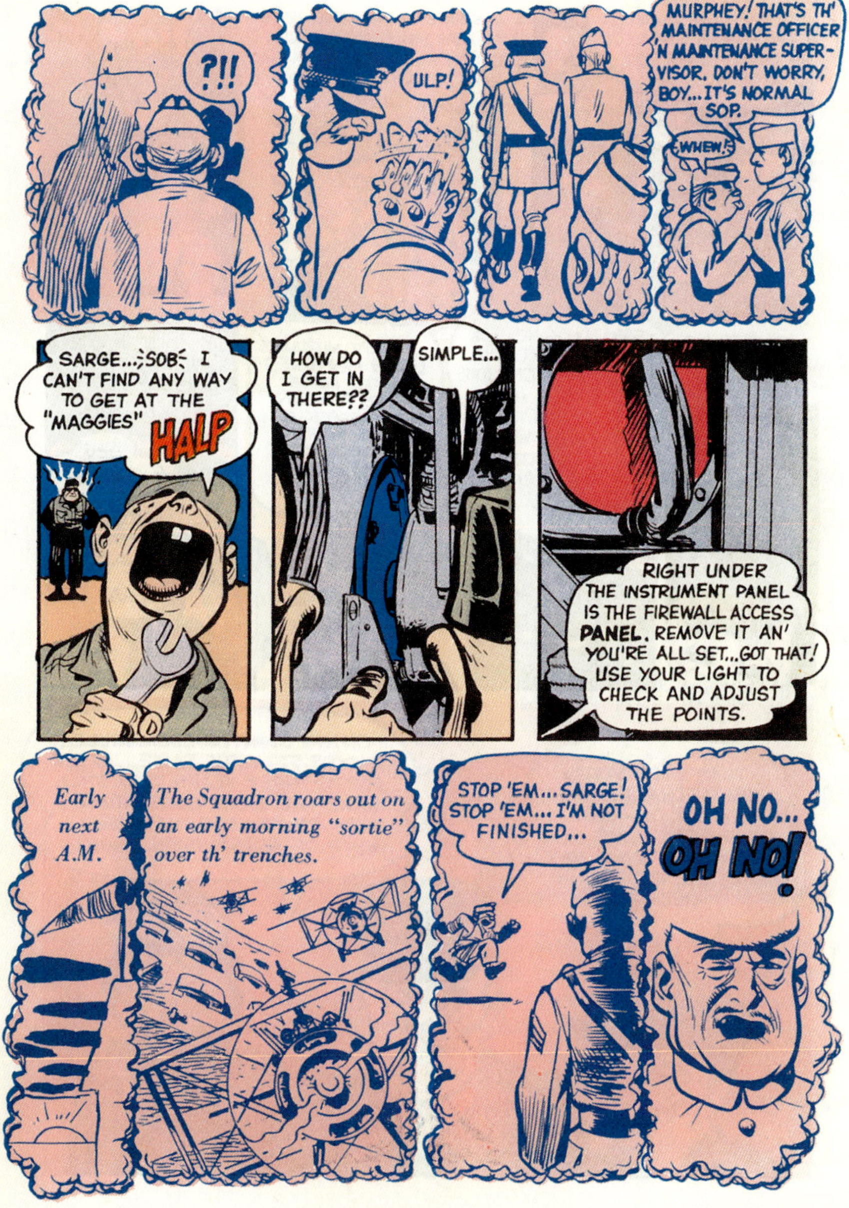
?!!
ULP!
MURPHEY! THAT'S TH' MAINTENANCE OFFICER 'N MAINTENANCE SUPER-VISOR. DON'T WORRY, BOY... IT'S NORMAL SOP.
WHEW!
SARGE...SOB I CAN'T FIND ANY WAY TO GET AT THE "MAGGIES"
HALP
HOW DO I GET IN THERE??
SIMPLE...
RIGHT UNDER THE INSTRUMENT PANEL IS THE FIREWALL ACCESS PANEL. REMOVE IT AN' YOU'RE ALL SET...GOT THAT! USE YOUR LIGHT TO CHECK AND ADJUST THE POINTS.
Early next A.M.
The Squadron roars out on an early morning "sortie" over th' trenches.
STOP 'EM... SARGE! STOP 'EM... I'M NOT FINISHED...
OH NO...
OH NO!

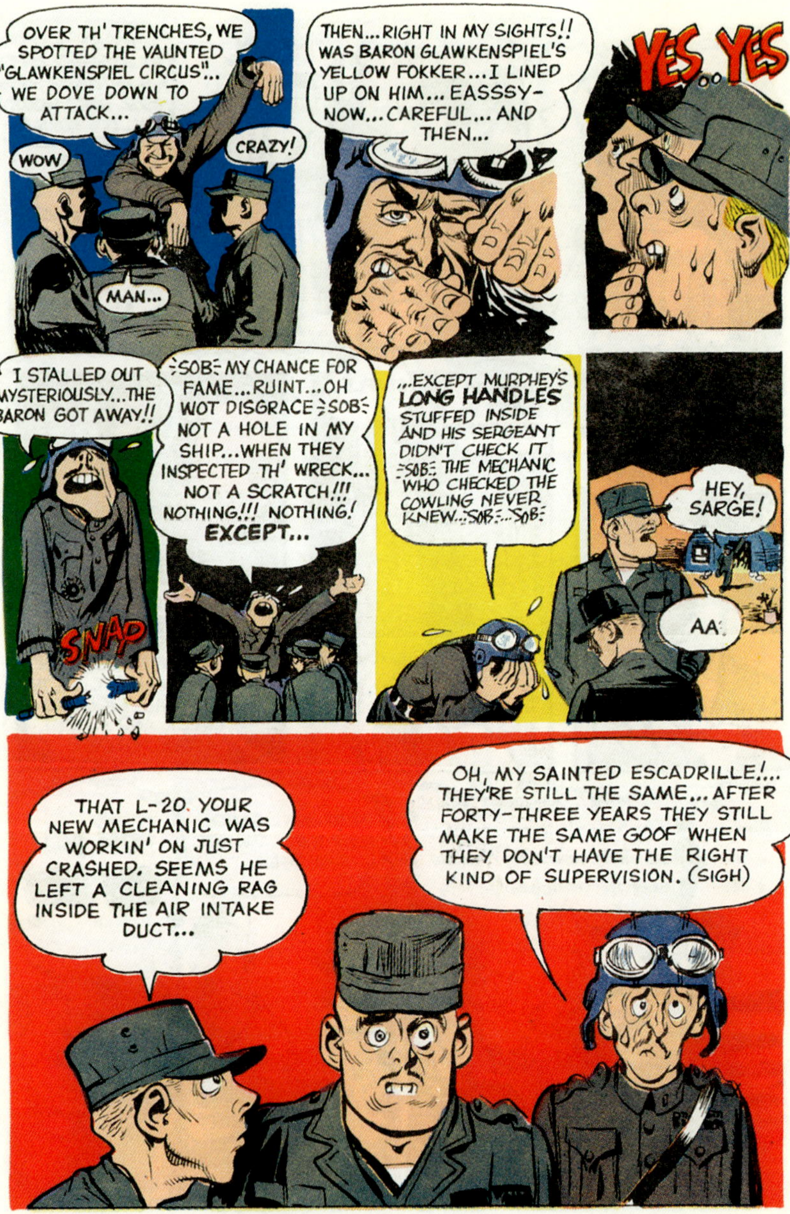

OVER TH' TRENCHES, WE SPOTTED THE VAUNTED "GLAWKENSPIEL CIRCUS"... WE DOVE DOWN TO ATTACK...
WOW
CRAZY!
MAN...
THEN... RIGHT IN MY SIGHTS!! WAS BARON GLAWKENSPIEL'S YELLOW FOKKER... I LINED UP ON HIM... EASSSY- NOW... CAREFUL... AND THEN...
YES.. YES
I STALLED OUT MYSTERIOUSLY... THE BARON GOT AWAY!!
SNAP
SOB MY CHANCE FOR FAME... RUINT... OH WOT DISGRACE SOB NOT A HOLE IN MY SHIP... WHEN THEY INSPECTED TH' WRECK... NOT A SCRATCH!!! NOTHING!!! NOTHING! EXCEPT...
...EXCEPT MURPHEY'S LONG HANDLES STUFFED INSIDE AND HIS SERGEANT DIDN'T CHECK IT SOB THE MECHANIC WHO CHECKED THE COWLING NEVER KNEW... SOB SOB
HEY, SARGE!
AA
THAT L-20 YOUR NEW MECHANIC WAS WORKIN' ON JUST CRASHED. SEEMS HE LEFT A CLEANING RAG INSIDE THE AIR INTAKE DUCT...
OH, MY SAINTED ESCADRILLE!... THEY'RE STILL THE SAME... AFTER FORTY-THREE YEARS THEY STILL MAKE THE SAME GOOF WHEN THEY DON'T HAVE THE RIGHT KIND OF SUPERVISION. (SIGH)

NO GO TOW

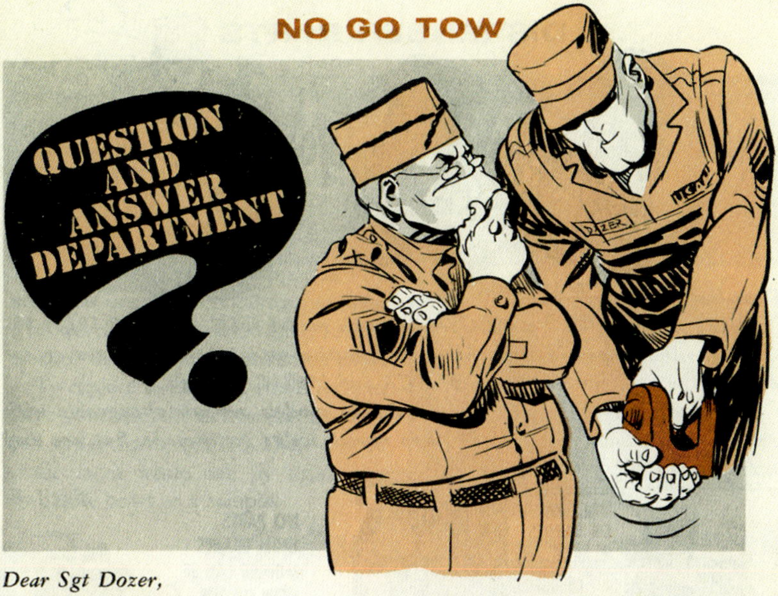
QUESTION AND ANSWER DEPARTMENT
DOZER

Dear Sgt Dozer,

We sure were glad to get these new 9A Series D-8 tractors for our heavy equipment section. We've got troubles, though. The drawbar pin is too big to fit the tongue hole in some of our towed equipment.

What can we do? — *CWO K. E. K.*

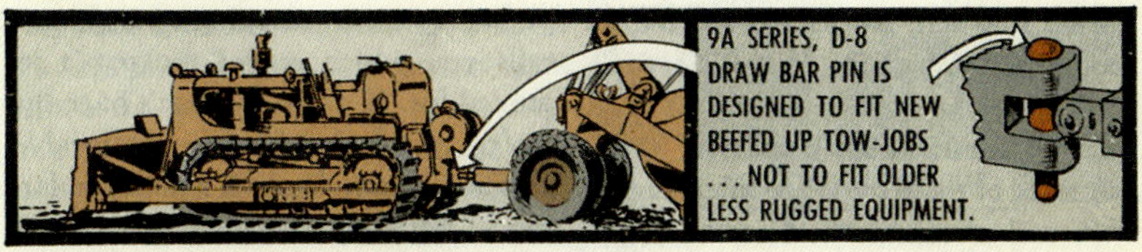
9A SERIES, D-8 DRAW BAR PIN IS DESIGNED TO FIT NEW BEEFED UP TOW-JOBS ... NOT TO FIT OLDER LESS RUGGED EQUIPMENT.

Dear Mr. K. E. K.,

Nothing.

That drawbar pin is different for a reason. Your 9A Series D-8 is strong enough to jerk the guts right out of some of your older towed equipment. Its drawbar pin is designed so it will fit right—with tow-jobs that are beefed to take the gaff. On others, it won't.

If you go modifying the drawbar pin to pull anything else, you're asking for trouble. Of course, if you're in a spot where you only have the old-type scrapers and stuff, with only 9A D-8's to pull it, you're really in a bind.

In that case, talk with support people. If they can't rig a swap for you, the only answer is to **take it easy.** Watch your drawbar pull, and use a pusher to ease the strain.

Sgt Dozer

WHAT'S WITH

Every time Half-Mast or Connie goes out to see how maintenance in the units is going, there's one question that hits them every time:

"How official is PS?"

The guys really mean to ask: "Is PS an order?"

The answer is "No."

Here's the story in a nutshell:

PS is published by the Department of the Army for information ...as it says on the opposite page: "for the information of organizational maintenance and supply personnel."

That does not make PS a directive.

The information in PS becomes directive and you've got to do what it says only when your major unit commander says it will be followed. (Some commanders have put out their word on just how PS is to be used in their own commands.)

You see, PS is published for information so that any outfit can use it to best fit its own needs to keep their equipment ready for combat. AR 750-5 says that every commander is responsible for keeping his equipment in top condition. So, if your major unit CO thinks that the info in PS will help his unit keep combat-ready,

PS — THE PREVENTIVE MAINTENANCE MONTHLY

Issue No. 96   1960 Series

Published by the Department of the Army for the information of organizational maintenance and supply personnel. Distribution is made through normal publication channels. Within limits of availability, older issues may be obtained direct from PS Magazine, Raritan Arsenal, Metuchen, New Jersey.

IN THIS ISSUE

ARTICLES

	Page
Missile	
Nike Trailers	28
Nike Tool Sets	64
Armament	
M14 Rifle	2
.30 & .50-cal Machine Guns	3
M1 Rifle	3
Communications Equipment	
Radiacmeter	50
RT-66/GRC Receiver-Transmitter	51
Plugs	51
AN/GRC-9 Radios: Be Your Own Inspector	52-57
Mast Sections	58
AN/PRC-8	58
Publications	
Office Machines	37
TB IG 2	39
TB QM 32 Info	41
Aircraft	
Otter (U-1A)	59
Batteries	62
Wheeled Vehicles	
5-ton Truck: Be Your Own Inspector	4-18
M38A1 Jeep	19
G742 & 749 Trucks	20
Jeeps	38
G742 Trucks	63
Tail-Light Bulbs	64
General	
Felt & Leather Seals	20
Protective Mask	25
M3A3 Smoke Generator	26
Inspection Gigs	42
Battery Charger: Be Your Own Inspector	44-49

DEPARTMENTS

Connie Rodd	19
Joe's Dope	29
Question and Answer	37
Contributions	63
Connie Rodd's Briefs	Inside Back Cover

PS wants your ideas and contributions, and is glad to answer your questions. Names and addresses are kept in confidence. Just write to:

Sgt Half-Mast,
PS Magazine,
Raritan Arsenal,
Metuchen, New Jersey.

DISTRIBUTION:
In accordance with requirements submitted on DA Form 12-4.

---

maybe he'll give the PS articles his support—by directive.

It might be helpful for you to know that every bit of information in PS is checked over by the heads of the Army's technical services or by the wheels in the Pentagon before it's printed. Every effort is made to be sure the dope is accurate and practical for your use.

It's all aimed at giving you a helping hand at getting your maintenance job done so your equipment will be ready to fight —any time.

M60

Dear Half-Mast,

Getting the safety out of the M60 trigger housing is a trying chore. After a few torn finger nails, skinned knuckles, and lost safety springs one of the instructors here introduced us to a simple tool.

It does the job safely, easily and quickly.

The tool can be made out of any short 6-inch piece of tough steel rod, or an old screw driver blade.

FILE NOTCH SO TOOL WILL FIT UNDER HOUSING RETAINING PIN

A six-inch length of strong steel rod with its front end ground to a flat edge. Center of flat edge is filed out to form a pronged (U) end. Prongs are ¼-inch deep and ⅛-inch apart.

(NOTE: length of prongs is not important. But opening between points must be just wide enough to sit on the shoulders of the plunger).

It's used like this:

1. Rotate the safety up (this gives you a gap underneath to insert the tool).
2. Slip the tool under the trigger housing retaining pin and place the tool's tiny prongs on the shoulders of the safety plunger.
3. Press down on the handle of the tool. Now with the spring and plunger pressure released (as you press down) the safety pulls out easily. The tool gives you the needed leverage to break the spring's tight hold and also keeps the spring and plunger from flying wild when the safety's pulled out.

TO REPLACE THE SAFETY:
1. Put the safety spring and plunger in the housing and grip the plunger shoulders with the tool point as before.
2. Press down on the tool handle and at the same time replace the safety in the trigger house.

Now remove the tool and rotate the safety down, and that's it.

The tool makes a pesky job very easy.

SFC R. A.

Safety Tool
3
PRESS DOWN
1
2
PULL SAFETY OUT

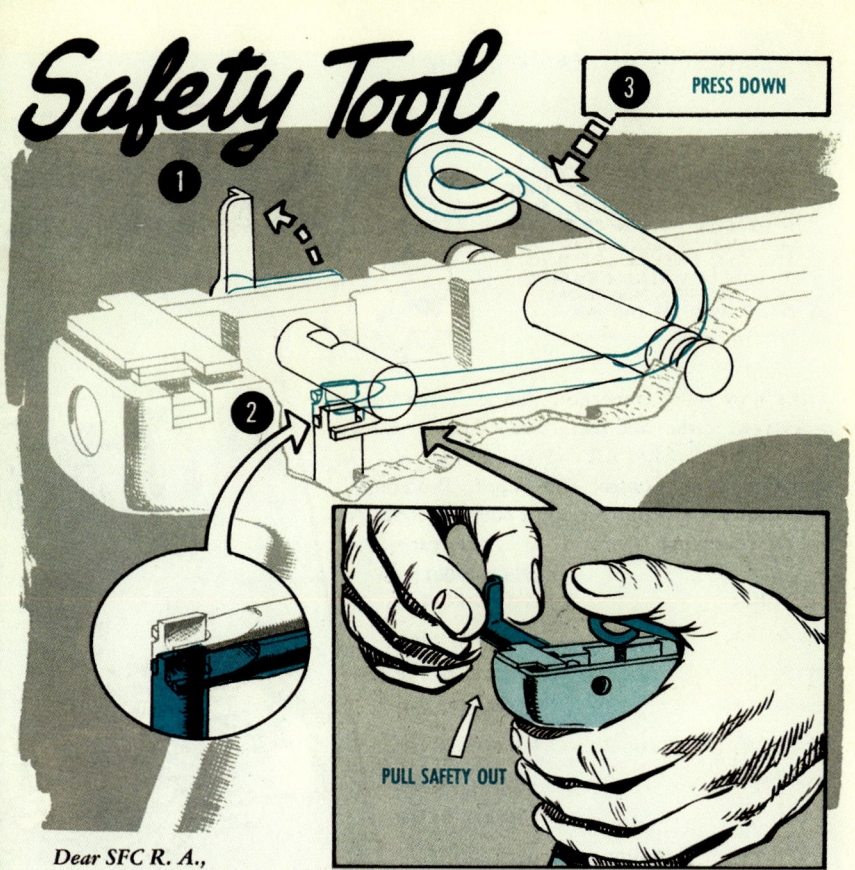

Dear SFC R. A.,

OK, but did you ever try it with the buffer yoke?

Pull out on the safety as you work it back and forth. Slip yoke prong in space between the housing and the end of the safety, and hold plunger down as you pull safety all the way out.

To replace: Insert plunger and spring into housing. Push safety into housing until it butts up against plunger. Now, as you press plunger with yoke, push safety in with your thumb.

As the end of the safety clears the top of the plunger, you can guide the safety all the way into its recess with the yoke. Rotate the safety forward, and it's done.

Half-Mast

THE ARMY'S BRAND NEW . . .

EQUIPMENT RECORD SYSTEM . . .

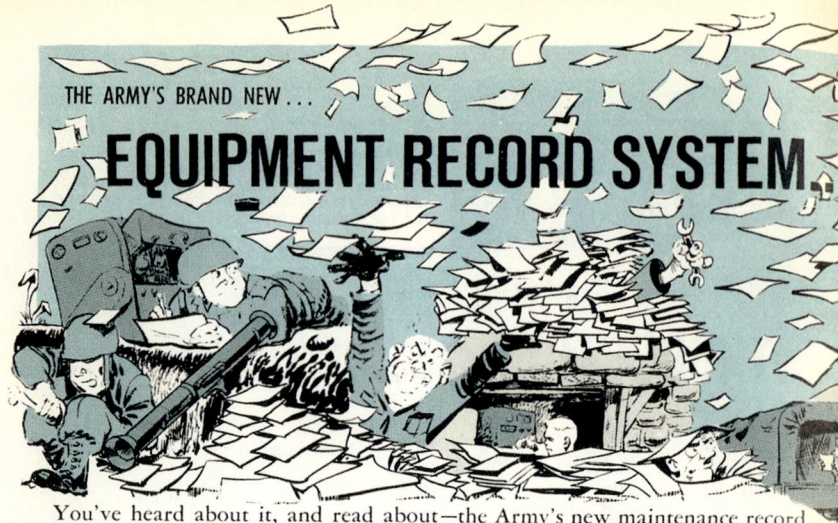

You've heard about it, and read about—the Army's new maintenance record system (it was called "Operation TAPER" while it was under test in 1961), and any day now you'll be meeting it face-to-face. It's covered by Change 2 to AR 750-5, "Maintenance of Supplies and Equipment" (Apr 62). And, it's being set up world-wide per the schedule in DA Circular 700-15, "Instructions for Implementation of the New Equipment Record System" (Apr 62).

Since it's to be your new maintenance-way of life, here's your chance to stand back a little ways and take a thoughtful look at how this important change stacks up.

Its official name is "Army Equipment Record System and Procedures." It applies to **all** categories of Army equipment (trucks, tanks, bulldozers, generators, flamethrowers, artillery, aircraft, guided missiles, x-ray machines, materiel handling equipment, etc., etc.), except some marine rail, and all nuclear items.

The book that gets the new system rolling is TM 38-750, May 62, which supersedes instructions on maintenance forms and procedures in old standbys like TM 9-2810, TM 5-505, TM 3-313, TM 10-1400, and TM 10-1600.

TM 38-750
DEPARTMENT OF THE ARMY TECHNICAL MANUAL
THE ARMY EQUIPMENT RECORD SYSTEM AND PROCEDURES
DEPARTMENT OF THE ARMY
MAY 1962

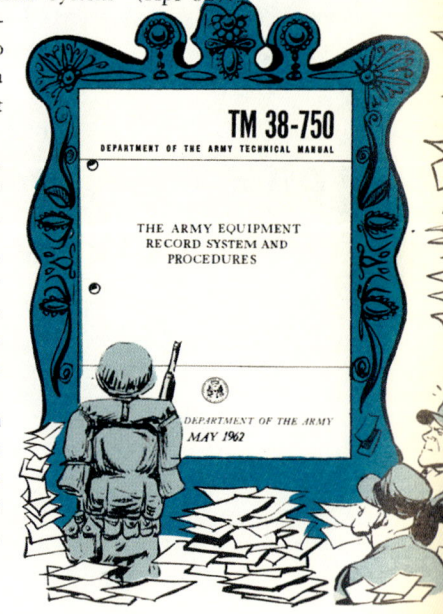

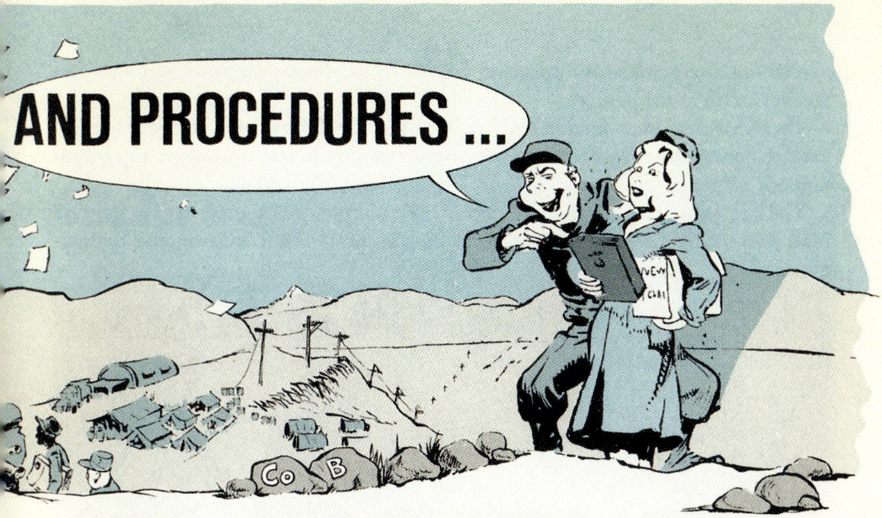
AND PROCEDURES ...

In case you don't take too kindly to changes, it might help you to get started off on the right foot if you realize that the new system consolidates many directives and whacks off a bunch of forms. This should make your job easier and simpler and gives management info to commanders all up the line.

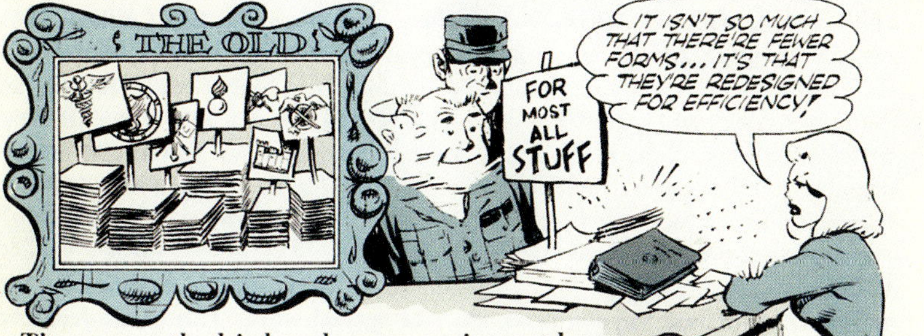
THE OLD
FOR MOST ALL STUFF
IT ISN'T SO MUCH THAT THERE'RE FEWER FORMS... IT'S THAT THEY'RE REDESIGNED FOR EFFICIENCY!

The new method is based on an equipment log.

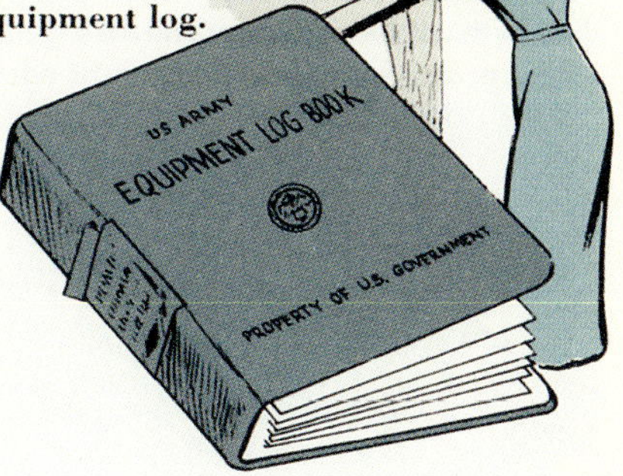
US ARMY
EQUIPMENT LOG BOOK
PROPERTY OF U.S. GOVERNMENT

A piece of equipment will get its log at the very beginning—when the item's brought into the Army supply system. From then on the log remains a permanent and vital part of the equipment. It'll contain the equipment's complete maintenance and service history—from its acceptance into the Army to its retirement.

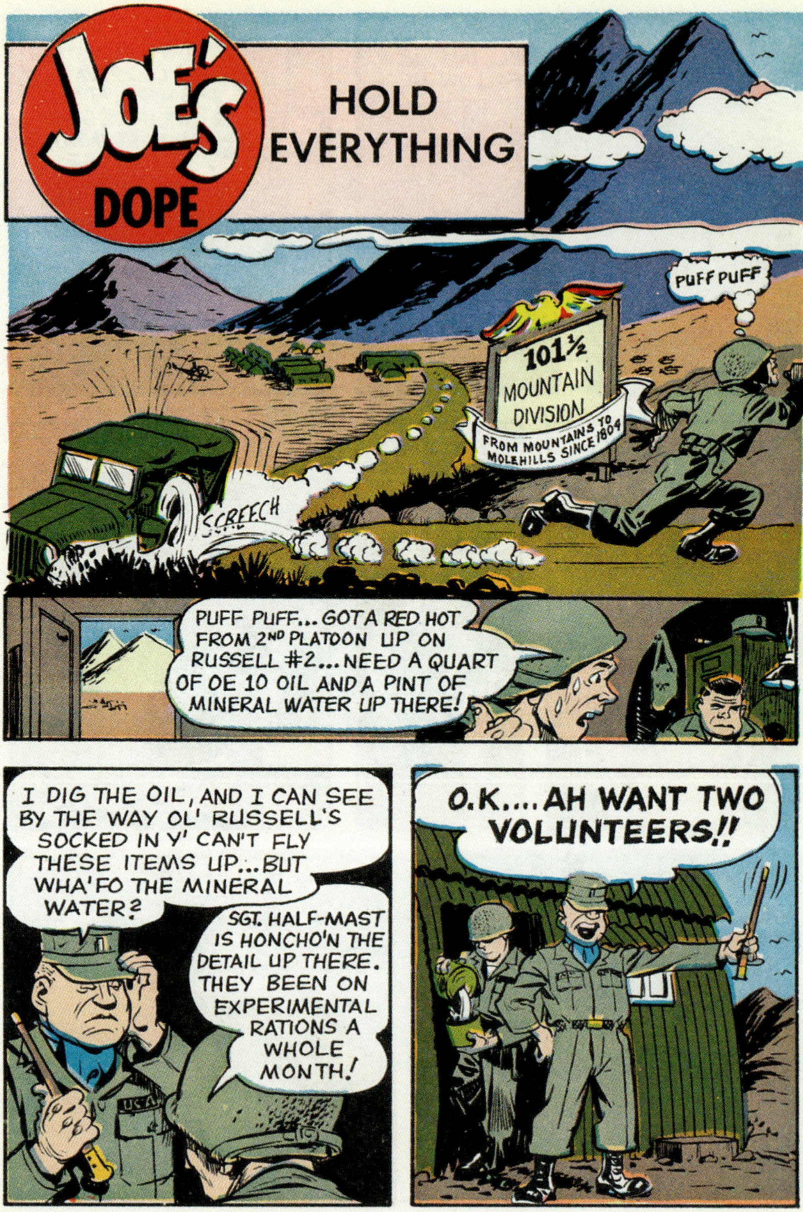
JOE'S DOPE
HOLD EVERYTHING
PUFF PUFF
101½ MOUNTAIN DIVISION
FROM MOUNTAINS TO MOLEHILLS SINCE 1804
SCREECH
PUFF PUFF... GOT A RED HOT FROM 2ND PLATOON UP ON RUSSELL #2... NEED A QUART OF OE 10 OIL AND A PINT OF MINERAL WATER UP THERE!
I DIG THE OIL, AND I CAN SEE BY THE WAY OL' RUSSELL'S SOCKED IN Y' CAN'T FLY THESE ITEMS UP... BUT WHA'FO THE MINERAL WATER?
SGT. HALF-MAST IS HONCHO'N THE DETAIL UP THERE. THEY BEEN ON EXPERIMENTAL RATIONS A WHOLE MONTH!
O.K.... AH WANT TWO VOLUNTEERS!!

no. 106, 1961

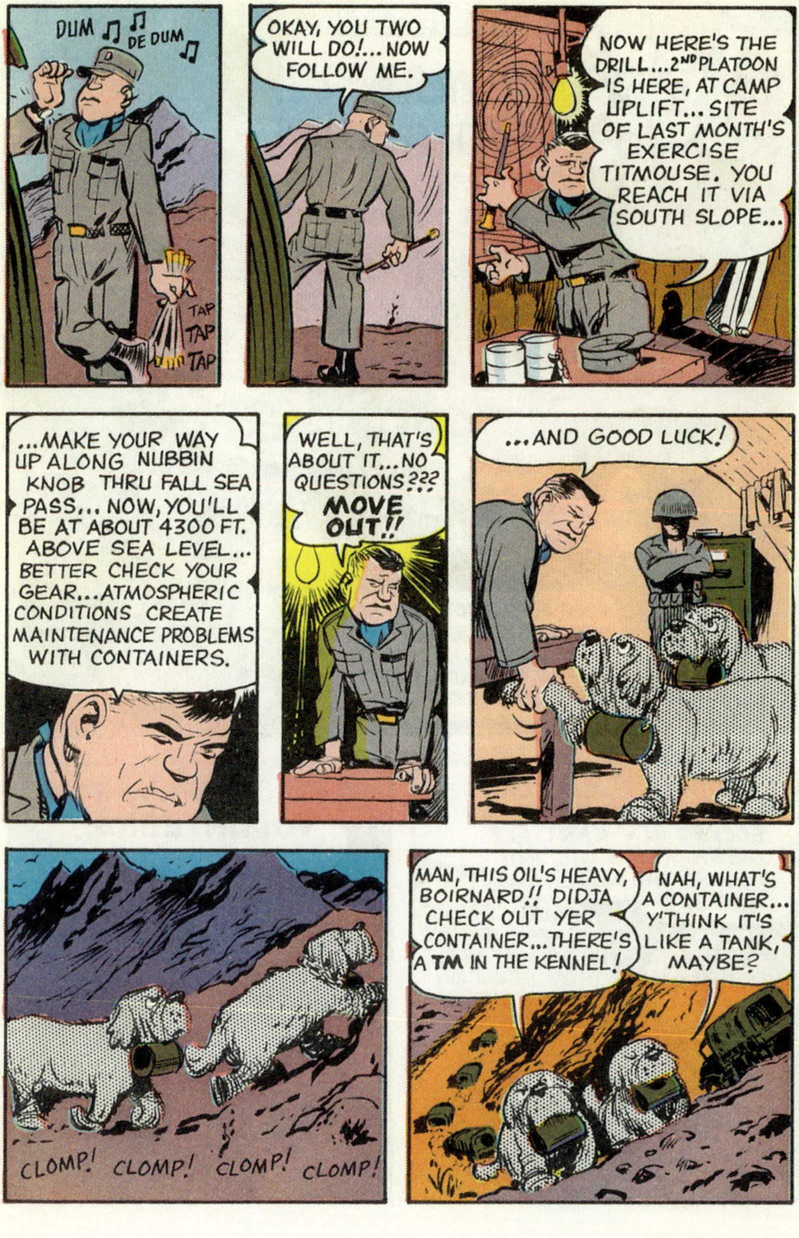
DUM ♫ ♫ DE DUM ♫
TAP TAP TAP
OKAY, YOU TWO WILL DO!... NOW FOLLOW ME.
NOW HERE'S THE DRILL...2ND PLATOON IS HERE, AT CAMP UPLIFT... SITE OF LAST MONTH'S EXERCISE TITMOUSE. YOU REACH IT VIA SOUTH SLOPE...
...MAKE YOUR WAY UP ALONG NUBBIN KNOB THRU FALL SEA PASS... NOW, YOU'LL BE AT ABOUT 4300 FT. ABOVE SEA LEVEL... BETTER CHECK YOUR GEAR...ATMOSPHERIC CONDITIONS CREATE MAINTENANCE PROBLEMS WITH CONTAINERS.
WELL, THAT'S ABOUT IT...NO QUESTIONS??? MOVE OUT!!
...AND GOOD LUCK!
CLOMP! CLOMP! CLOMP! CLOMP!
MAN, THIS OIL'S HEAVY, BOIRNARD!! DIDJA CHECK OUT YER CONTAINER...THERE'S A TM IN THE KENNEL!
NAH, WHAT'S A CONTAINER... Y'THINK IT'S LIKE A TANK, MAYBE?

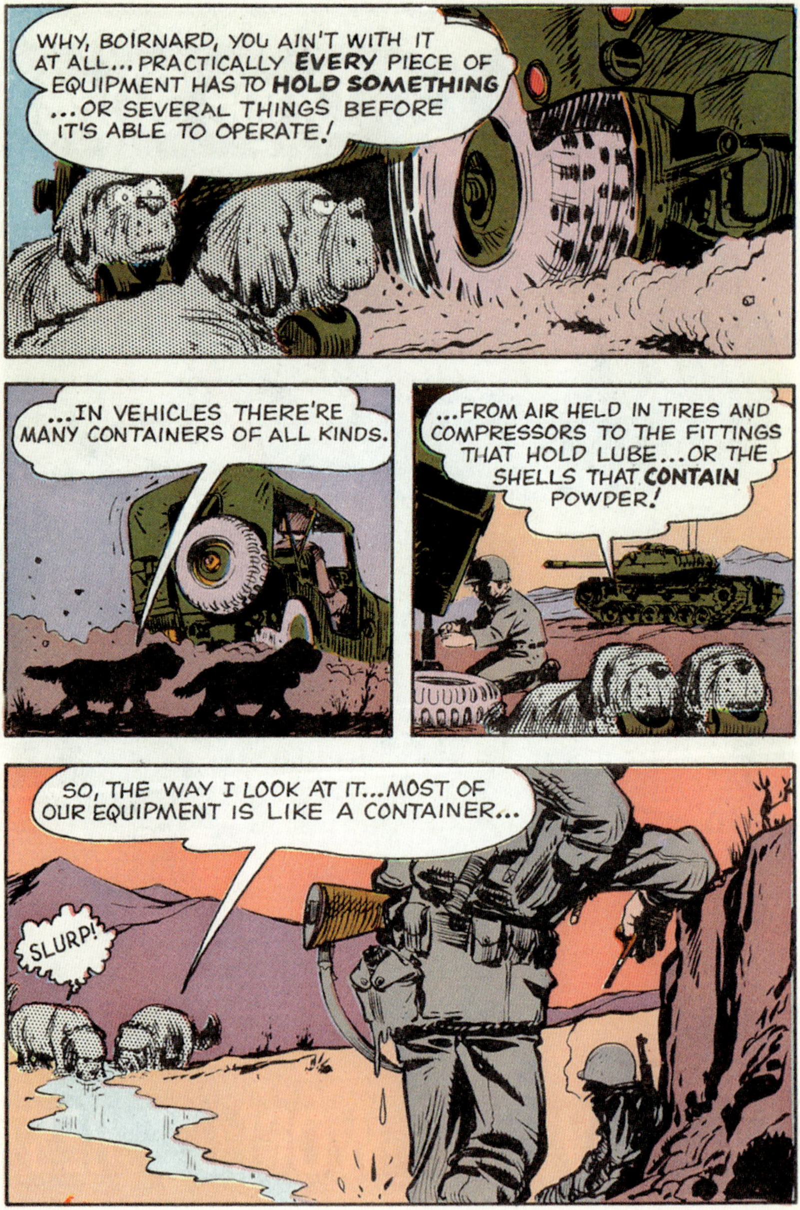
WHY, BOIRNARD, YOU AIN'T WITH IT AT ALL... PRACTICALLY **EVERY** PIECE OF EQUIPMENT HAS TO **HOLD SOMETHING** ...OR SEVERAL THINGS BEFORE IT'S ABLE TO OPERATE!
...IN VEHICLES THERE'RE MANY CONTAINERS OF ALL KINDS.
...FROM AIR HELD IN TIRES AND COMPRESSORS TO THE FITTINGS THAT HOLD LUBE...OR THE SHELLS THAT **CONTAIN** POWDER!
SO, THE WAY I LOOK AT IT...MOST OF OUR EQUIPMENT IS LIKE A CONTAINER...
SLURP!

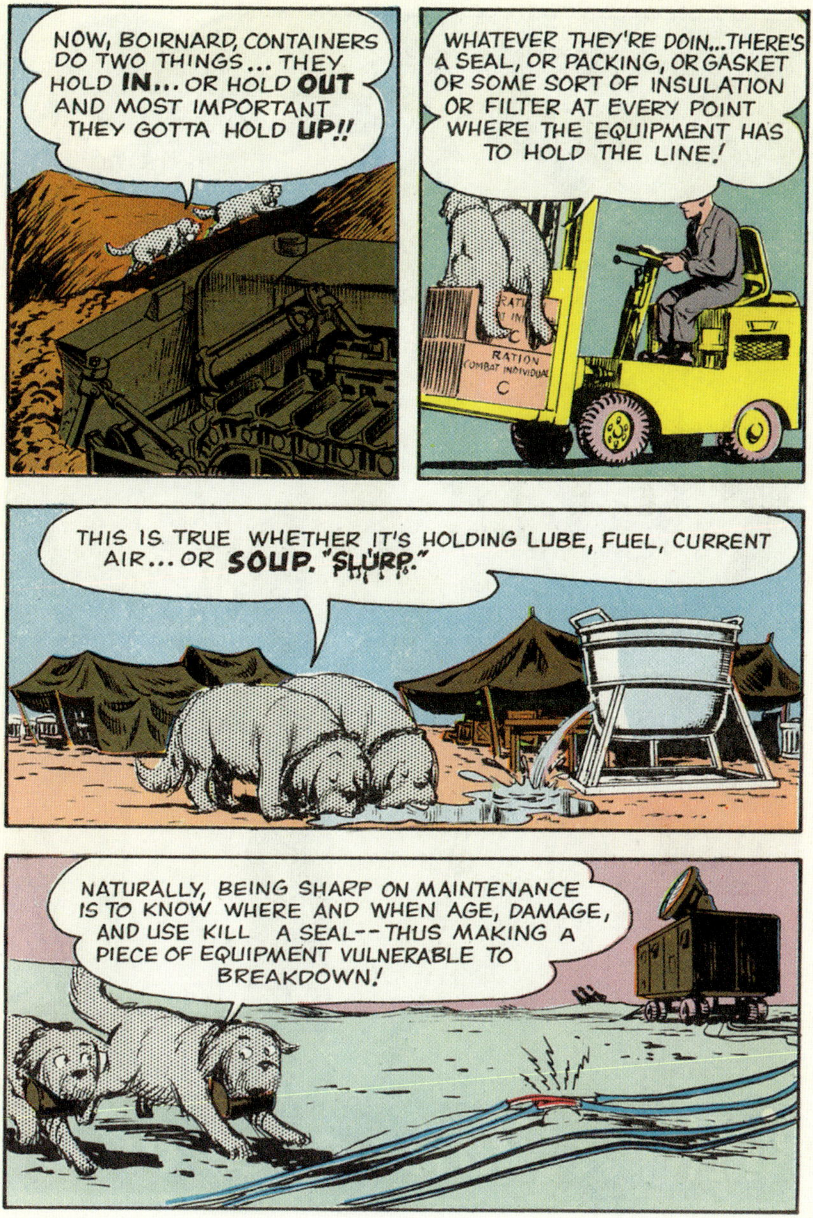
NOW, BOIRNARD, CONTAINERS DO TWO THINGS... THEY HOLD IN... OR HOLD OUT AND MOST IMPORTANT THEY GOTTA HOLD UP!!
WHATEVER THEY'RE DOIN...THERE'S A SEAL, OR PACKING, OR GASKET OR SOME SORT OF INSULATION OR FILTER AT EVERY POINT WHERE THE EQUIPMENT HAS TO HOLD THE LINE!
RATION COMBAT INDIVIDUAL C
THIS IS TRUE WHETHER IT'S HOLDING LUBE, FUEL, CURRENT AIR... OR SOUP. "SLURP."
NATURALLY, BEING SHARP ON MAINTENANCE IS TO KNOW WHERE AND WHEN AGE, DAMAGE, AND USE KILL A SEAL--THUS MAKING A PIECE OF EQUIPMENT VULNERABLE TO BREAKDOWN!

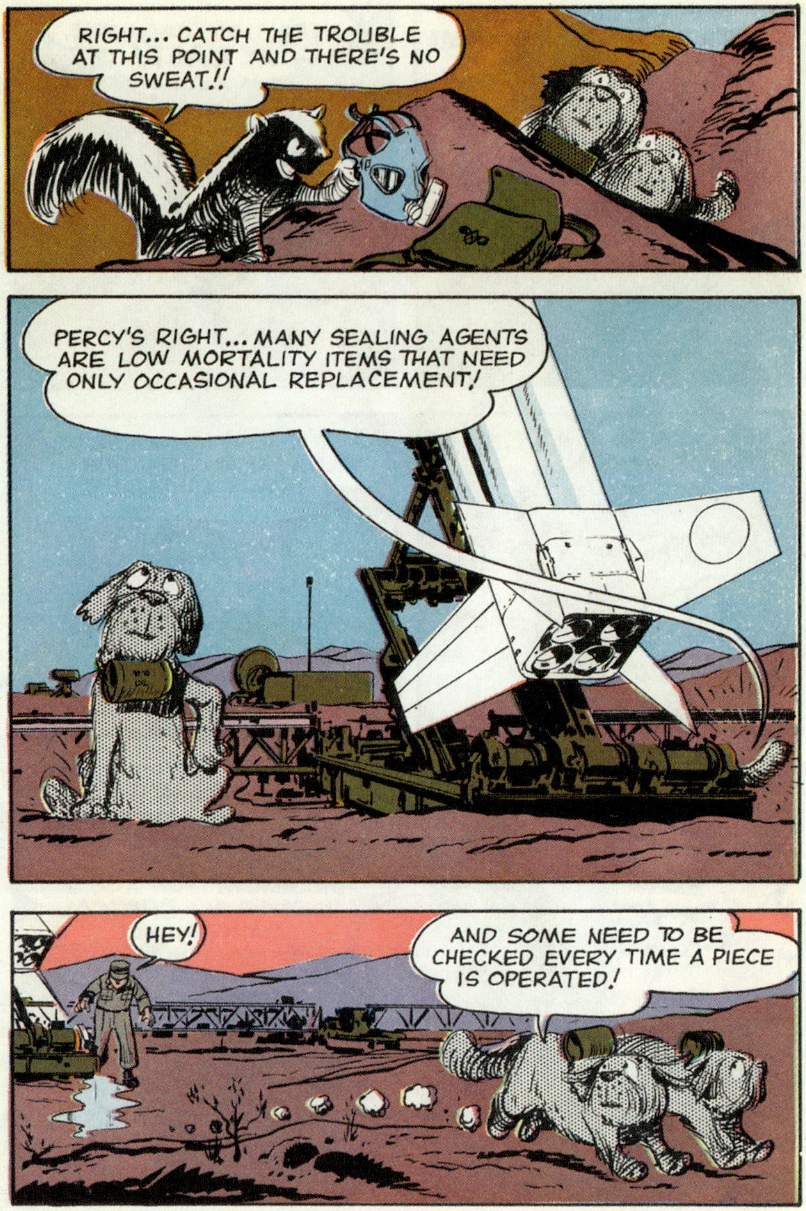
RIGHT... CATCH THE TROUBLE AT THIS POINT AND THERE'S NO SWEAT!!
PERCY'S RIGHT... MANY SEALING AGENTS ARE LOW MORTALITY ITEMS THAT NEED ONLY OCCASIONAL REPLACEMENT!
HEY!
AND SOME NEED TO BE CHECKED EVERY TIME A PIECE IS OPERATED!

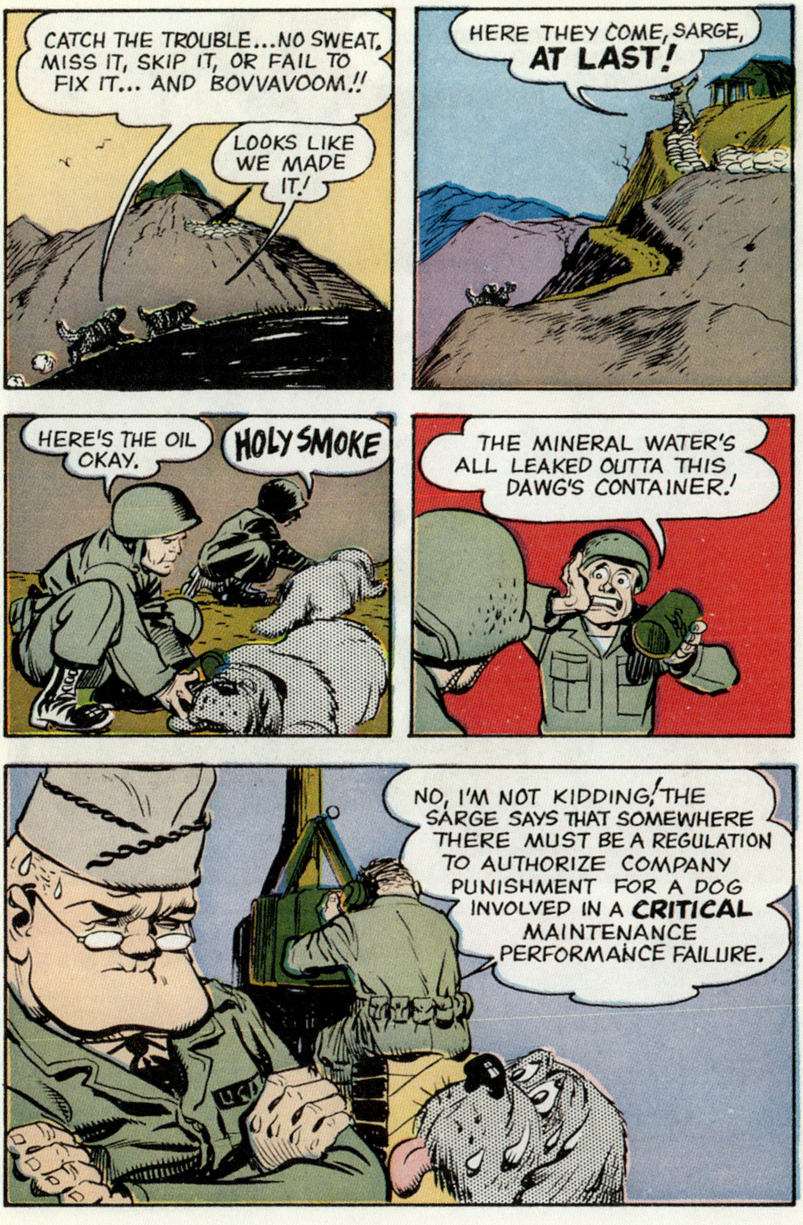
CATCH THE TROUBLE...NO SWEAT. MISS IT, SKIP IT, OR FAIL TO FIX IT... AND BOVVAVOOM!!
LOOKS LIKE WE MADE IT!
HERE THEY COME, SARGE, AT LAST!
HERE'S THE OIL OKAY.
HOLY SMOKE
THE MINERAL WATER'S ALL LEAKED OUTTA THIS DAWG'S CONTAINER!
NO, I'M NOT KIDDING! THE SARGE SAYS THAT SOMEWHERE THERE MUST BE A REGULATION TO AUTHORIZE COMPANY PUNISHMENT FOR A DOG INVOLVED IN A CRITICAL MAINTENANCE PERFORMANCE FAILURE.

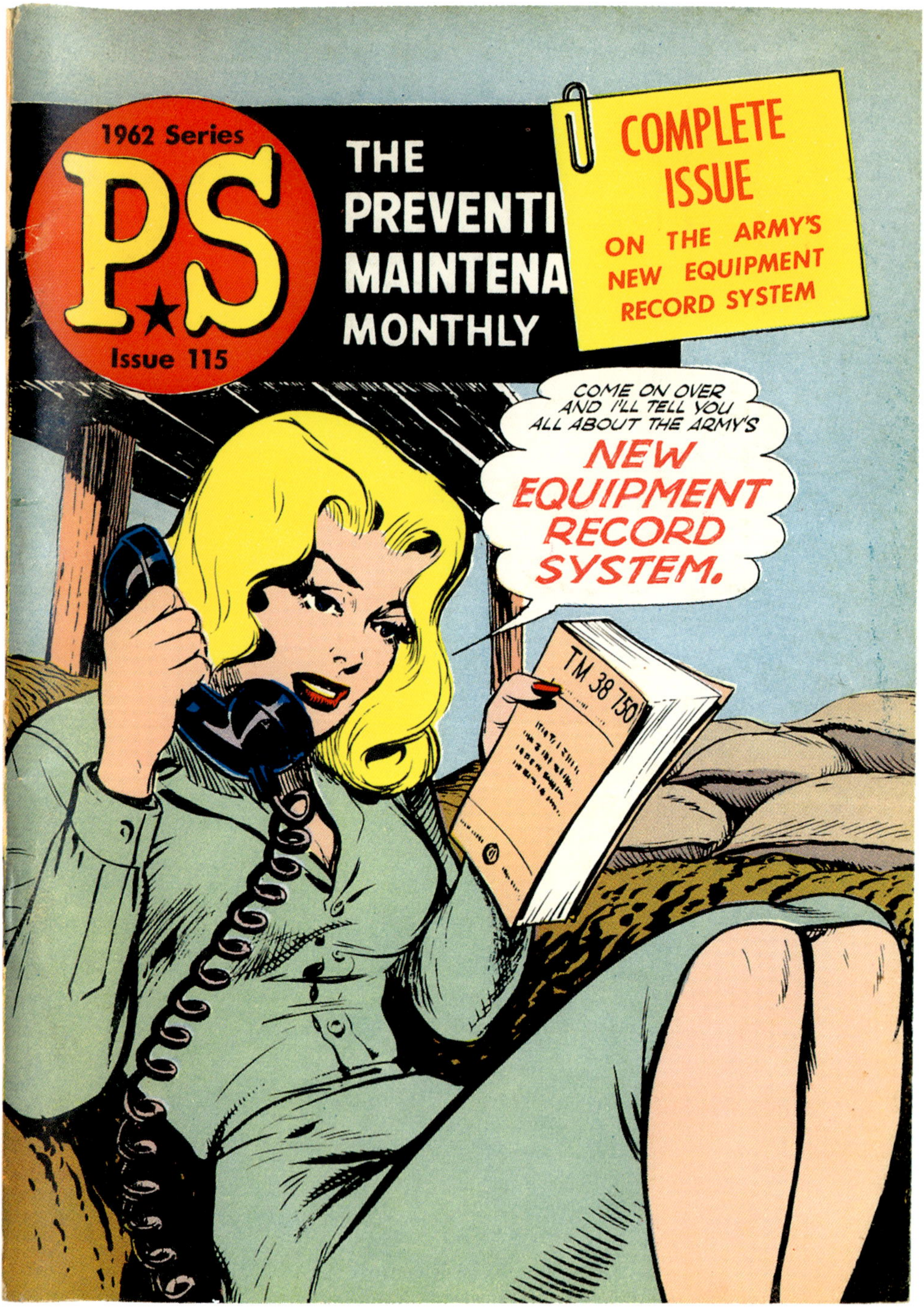
1962 Series
P.S
Issue 115
THE
PREVENTI
MAINTENA
MONTHLY
COMPLETE
ISSUE
ON THE ARMY'S
NEW EQUIPMENT
RECORD SYSTEM
COME ON OVER AND I'LL TELL YOU ALL ABOUT THE ARMY'S NEW EQUIPMENT RECORD SYSTEM.
TM 38 750

no. 115, 1962

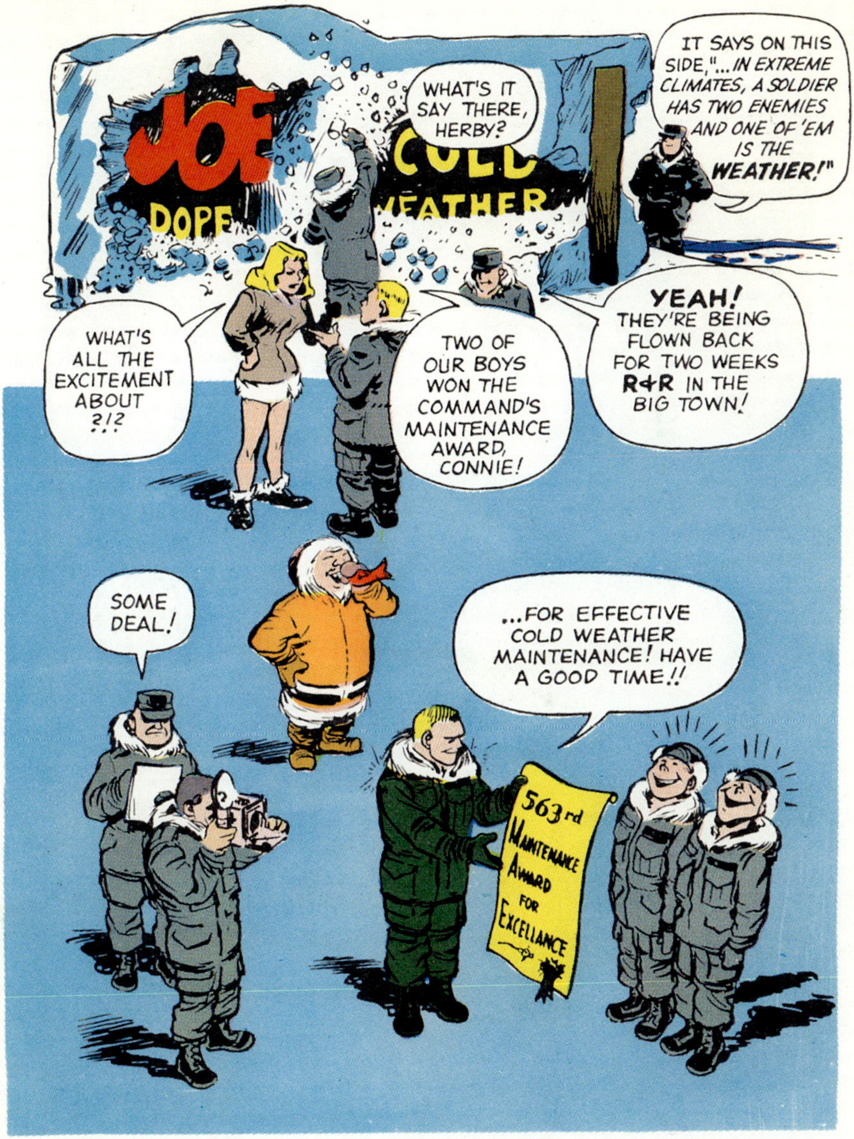
JOE
DOPE
COLD
WEATHER
WHAT'S IT SAY THERE, HERBY?
IT SAYS ON THIS SIDE, "...IN EXTREME CLIMATES, A SOLDIER HAS TWO ENEMIES AND ONE OF 'EM IS THE WEATHER!"
WHAT'S ALL THE EXCITEMENT ABOUT ?!?
TWO OF OUR BOYS WON THE COMMAND'S MAINTENANCE AWARD, CONNIE!
YEAH! THEY'RE BEING FLOWN BACK FOR TWO WEEKS R&R IN THE BIG TOWN!
SOME DEAL!
...FOR EFFECTIVE COLD WEATHER MAINTENANCE! HAVE A GOOD TIME!!
563rd MAINTENANCE AWARD FOR EXCELLIANCE

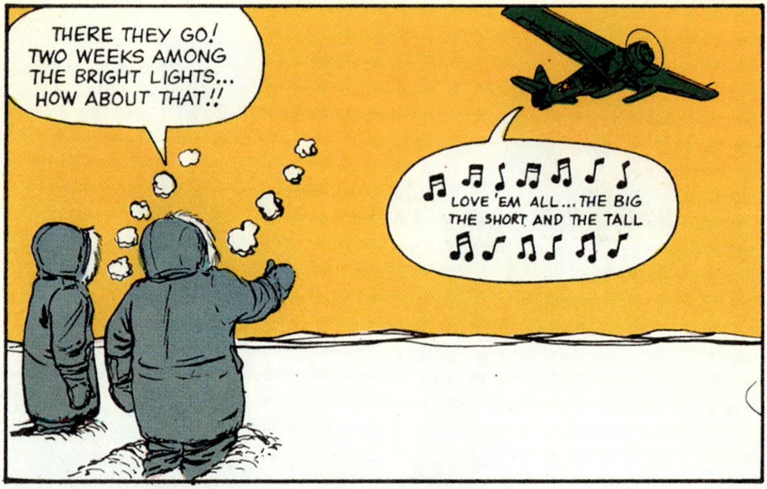
THERE THEY GO! TWO WEEKS AMONG THE BRIGHT LIGHTS... HOW ABOUT THAT!!
LOVE 'EM ALL... THE BIG THE SHORT AND THE TALL

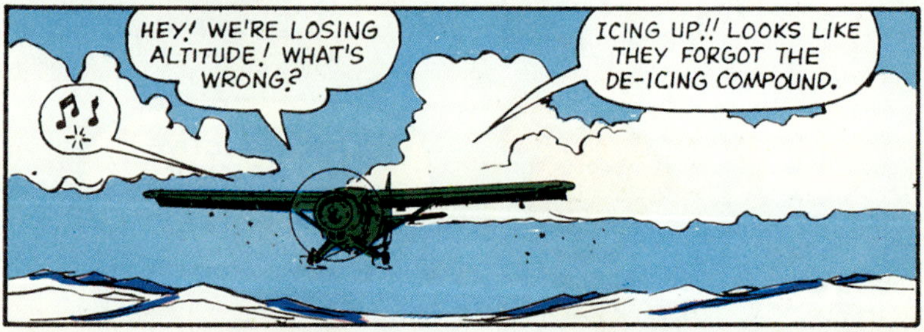
HEY! WE'RE LOSING ALTITUDE! WHAT'S WRONG?
ICING UP!! LOOKS LIKE THEY FORGOT THE DE-ICING COMPOUND.

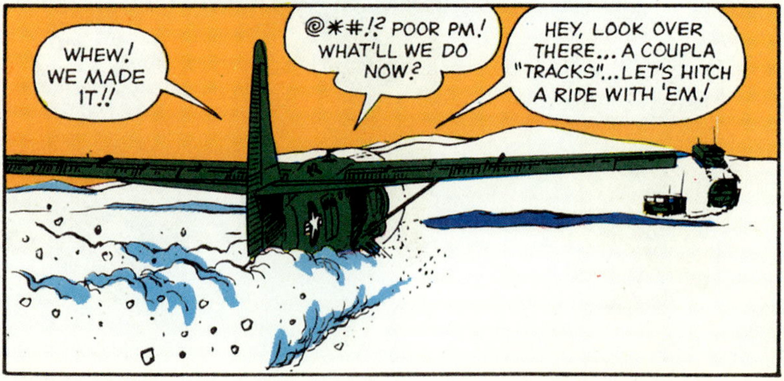
WHEW! WE MADE IT!!
@*#!? POOR PM! WHAT'LL WE DO NOW?
HEY, LOOK OVER THERE... A COUPLA "TRACKS"... LET'S HITCH A RIDE WITH 'EM!

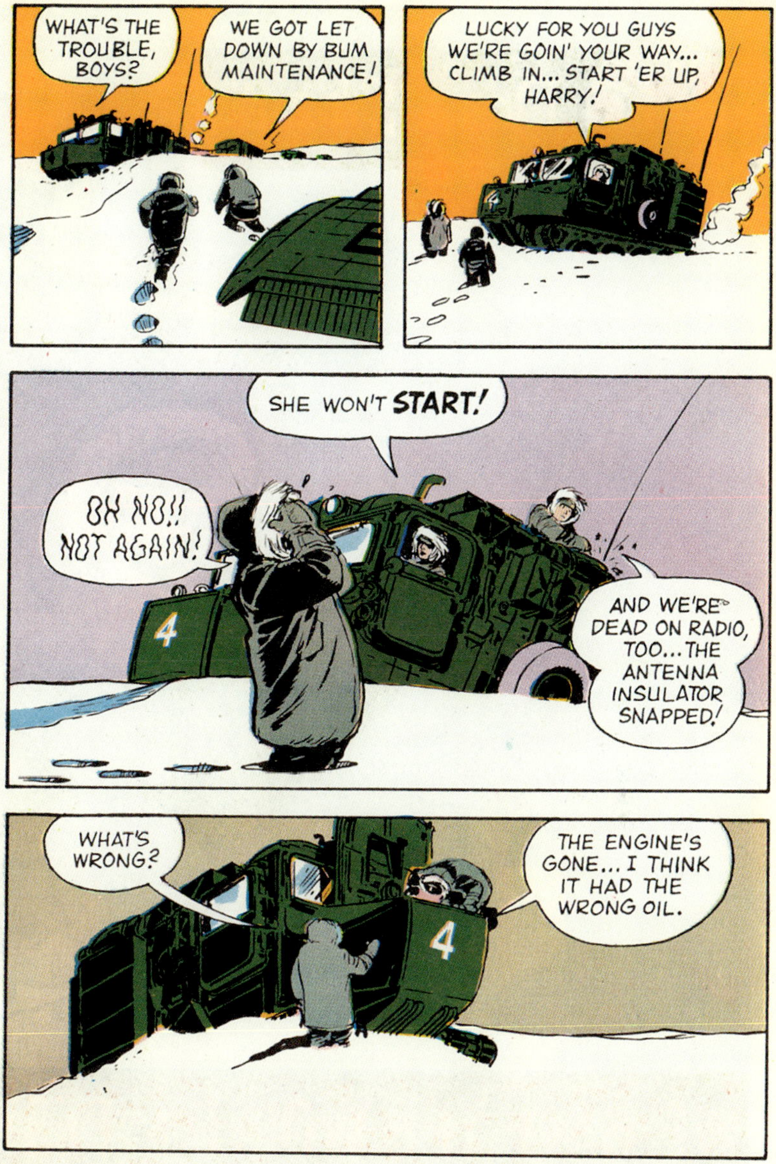
WHAT'S THE TROUBLE, BOYS?
WE GOT LET DOWN BY BUM MAINTENANCE!
LUCKY FOR YOU GUYS WE'RE GOIN' YOUR WAY... CLIMB IN... START 'ER UP, HARRY!
SHE WON'T START!
OH NO!! NOT AGAIN!
AND WE'RE DEAD ON RADIO, TOO... THE ANTENNA INSULATOR SNAPPED!
WHAT'S WRONG?
THE ENGINE'S GONE... I THINK IT HAD THE WRONG OIL.
4
4

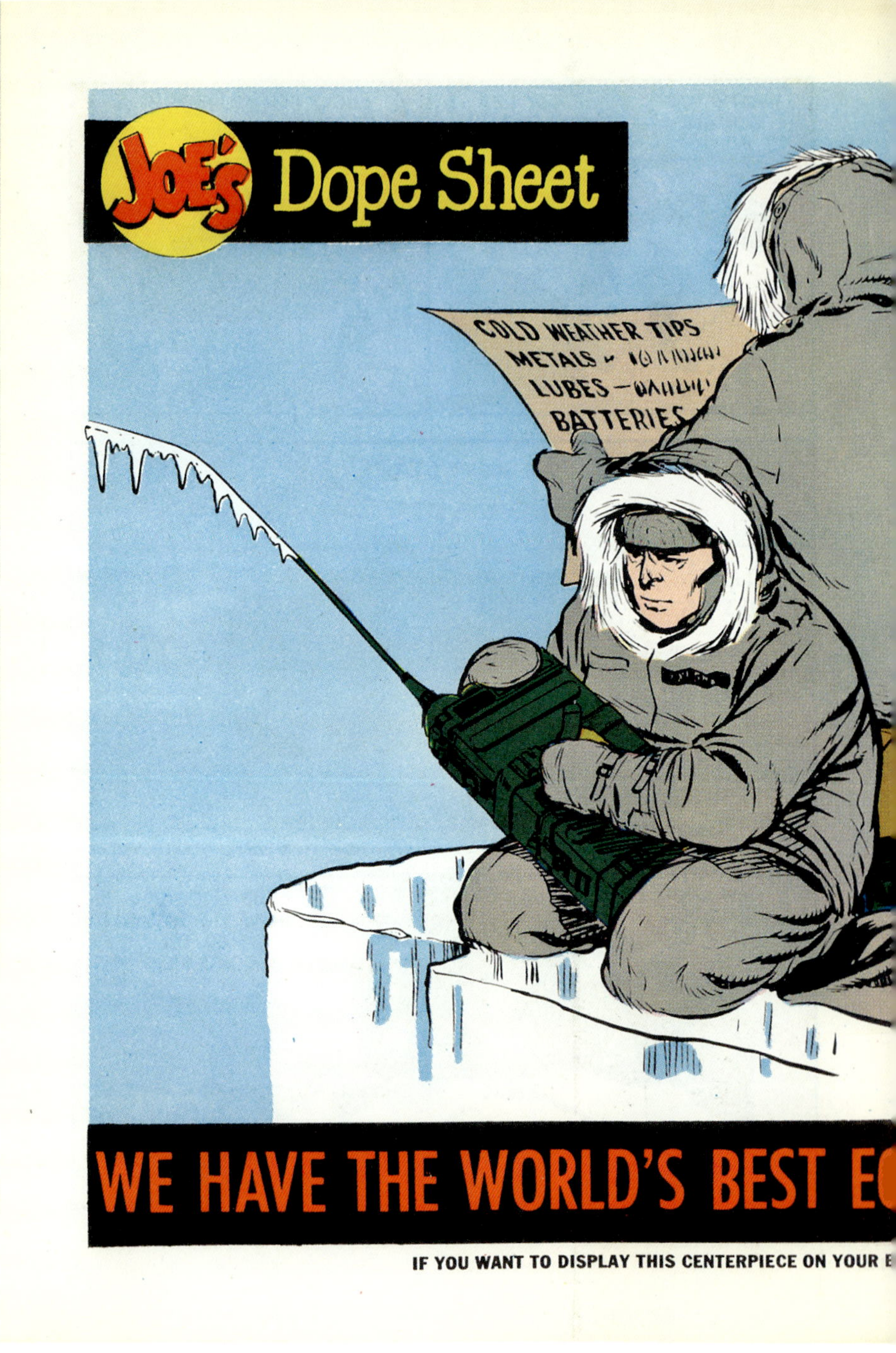
JOE'S Dope Sheet
COLD WEATHER TIPS
METALS
LUBES
BATTERIES
WE HAVE THE WORLD'S BEST E
IF YOU WANT TO DISPLAY THIS CENTERPIECE ON YOUR

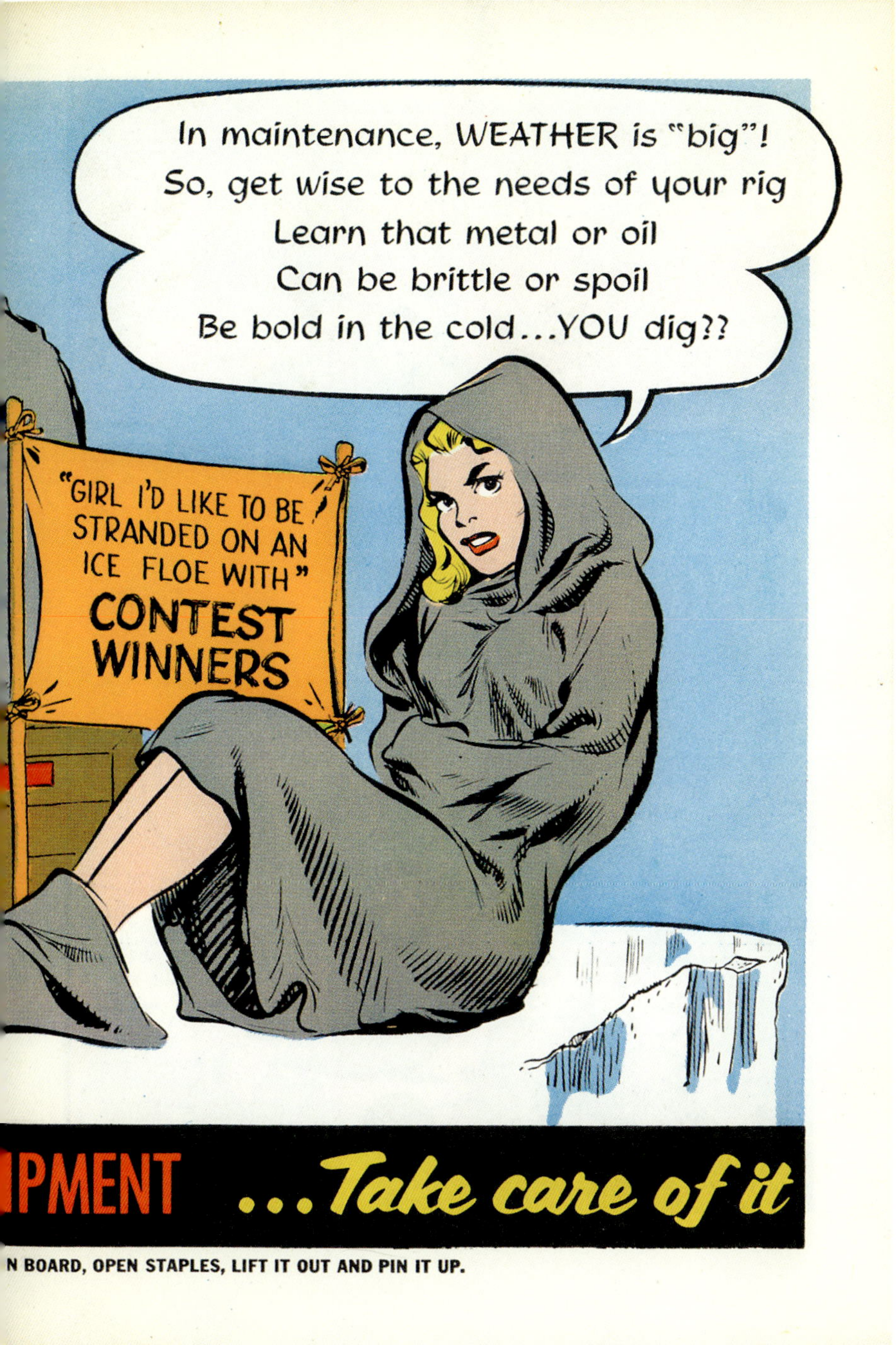
In maintenance, WEATHER is "big"!
So, get wise to the needs of your rig
Learn that metal or oil
Can be brittle or spoil
Be bold in the cold...YOU dig??
"GIRL I'D LIKE TO BE STRANDED ON AN ICE FLOE WITH"
CONTEST WINNERS
PMENT ...Take care of it
N BOARD, OPEN STAPLES, LIFT IT OUT AND PIN IT UP.

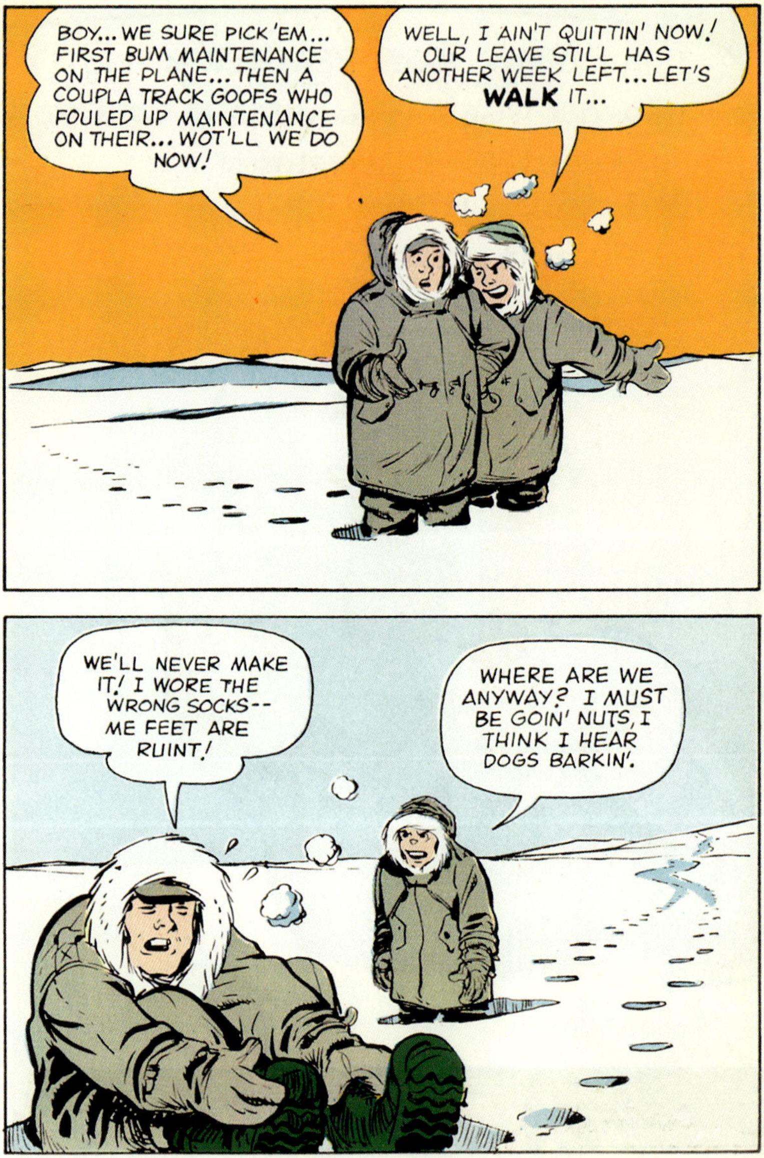
BOY... WE SURE PICK 'EM... FIRST BUM MAINTENANCE ON THE PLANE... THEN A COUPLA TRACK GOOFS WHO FOULED UP MAINTENANCE ON THEIR... WOT'LL WE DO NOW!
WELL, I AIN'T QUITTIN' NOW! OUR LEAVE STILL HAS ANOTHER WEEK LEFT... LET'S **WALK** IT...
WE'LL NEVER MAKE IT! I WORE THE WRONG SOCKS-- ME FEET ARE RUINT!
WHERE ARE WE ANYWAY? I MUST BE GOIN' NUTS, I THINK I HEAR DOGS BARKIN'.

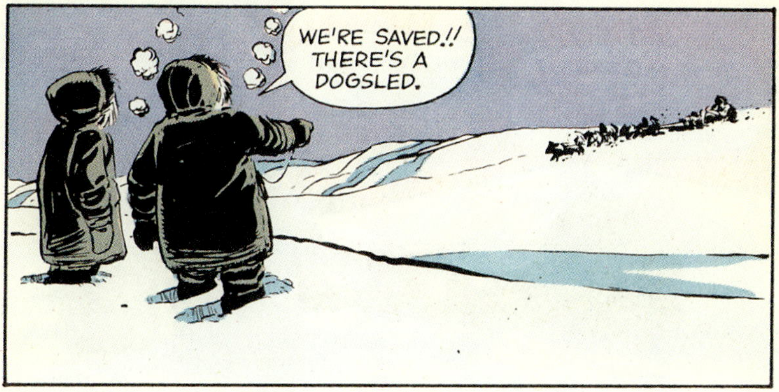
WE'RE SAVED!! THERE'S A DOGSLED.

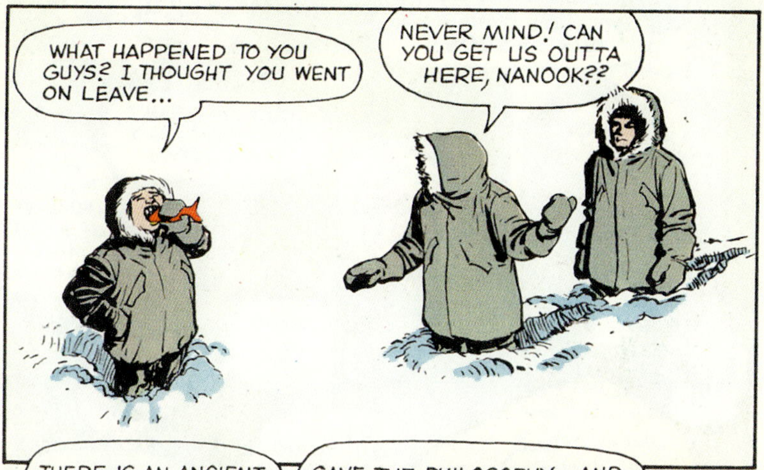
WHAT HAPPENED TO YOU GUYS? I THOUGHT YOU WENT ON LEAVE...
NEVER MIND! CAN YOU GET US OUTTA HERE, NANOOK??

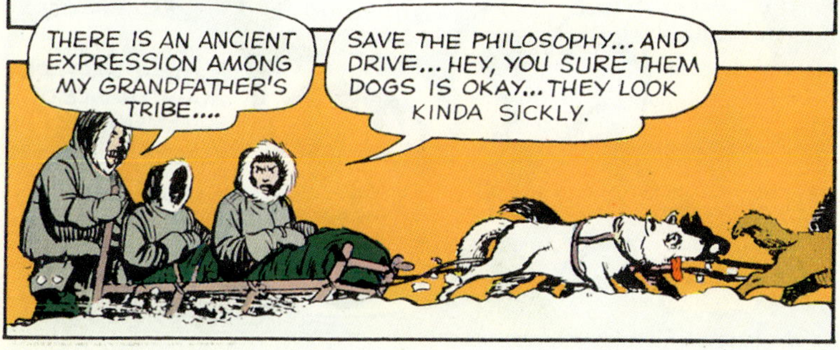
THERE IS AN ANCIENT EXPRESSION AMONG MY GRANDFATHER'S TRIBE....
SAVE THE PHILOSOPHY... AND DRIVE... HEY, YOU SURE THEM DOGS IS OKAY... THEY LOOK KINDA SICKLY.

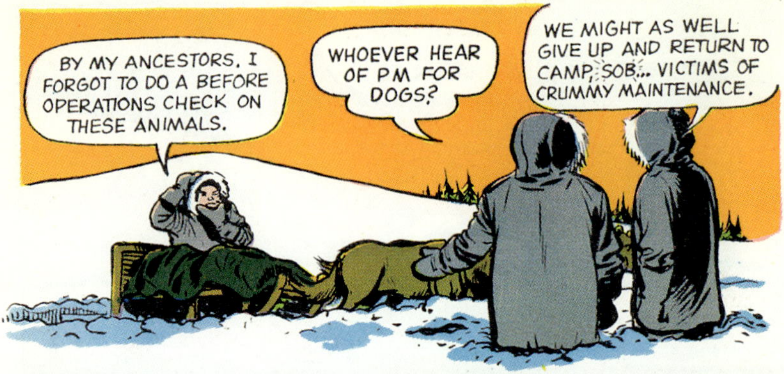
BY MY ANCESTORS, I FORGOT TO DO A BEFORE OPERATIONS CHECK ON THESE ANIMALS.
WHOEVER HEAR OF PM FOR DOGS?
WE MIGHT AS WELL GIVE UP AND RETURN TO CAMP, SOB... VICTIMS OF CRUMMY MAINTENANCE.

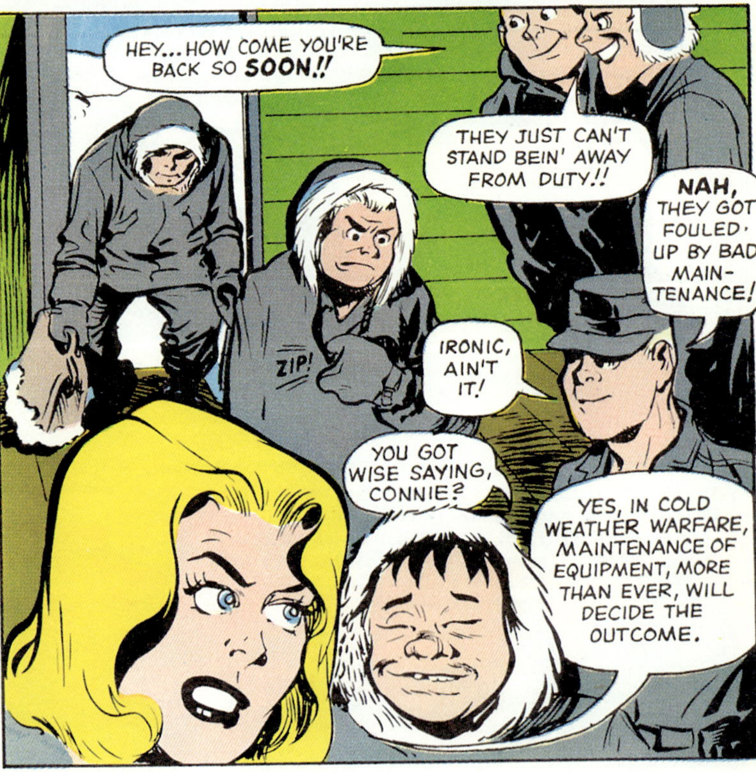
HEY...HOW COME YOU'RE BACK SO **SOON!!**
THEY JUST CAN'T STAND BEIN' AWAY FROM DUTY!!
NAH, THEY GOT FOULED UP BY BAD MAIN-TENANCE!
ZIP!
IRONIC, AIN'T IT!
YOU GOT WISE SAYING, CONNIE?
YES, IN COLD WEATHER WARFARE, MAINTENANCE OF EQUIPMENT, MORE THAN EVER, WILL DECIDE THE OUTCOME.

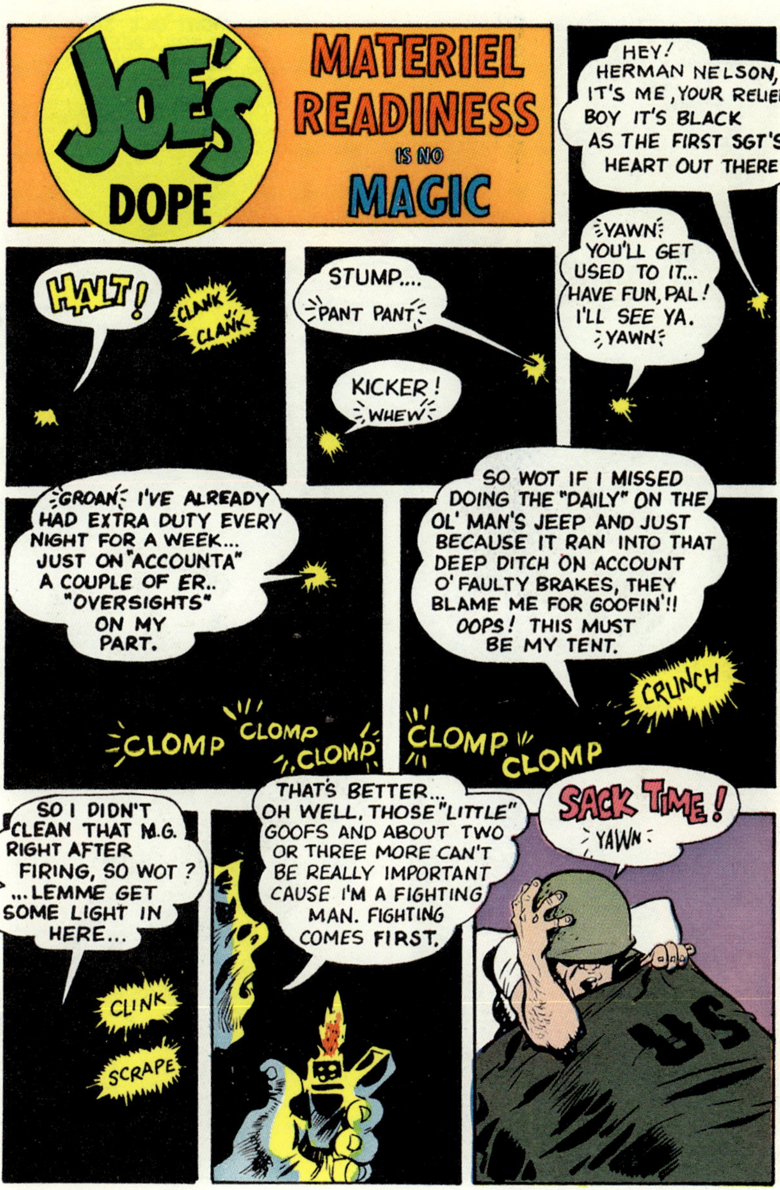
JOE'S DOPE
MATERIEL READINESS IS NO MAGIC
HEY! HERMAN NELSON, IT'S ME, YOUR RELIEF. BOY IT'S BLACK AS THE FIRST SGT'S HEART OUT THERE!
YAWN YOU'LL GET USED TO IT... HAVE FUN, PAL! I'LL SEE YA. YAWN
HALT!
CLANK CLANK
STUMP.... PANT PANT
KICKER! WHEW
GROAN I'VE ALREADY HAD EXTRA DUTY EVERY NIGHT FOR A WEEK... JUST ON "ACCOUNTA" A COUPLE OF ER.. "OVERSIGHTS" ON MY PART.
CLOMP CLOMP CLOMP
SO WOT IF I MISSED DOING THE "DAILY" ON THE OL' MAN'S JEEP AND JUST BECAUSE IT RAN INTO THAT DEEP DITCH ON ACCOUNT O' FAULTY BRAKES, THEY BLAME ME FOR GOOFIN'!! OOPS! THIS MUST BE MY TENT.
CRUNCH
CLOMP CLOMP
SO I DIDN'T CLEAN THAT M.G. RIGHT AFTER FIRING, SO WOT? ...LEMME GET SOME LIGHT IN HERE...
CLINK
SCRAPE
THAT'S BETTER... OH WELL, THOSE "LITTLE" GOOFS AND ABOUT TWO OR THREE MORE CAN'T BE REALLY IMPORTANT CAUSE I'M A FIGHTING MAN. FIGHTING COMES FIRST.
SACK TIME! YAWN
US

no. 128, 1963

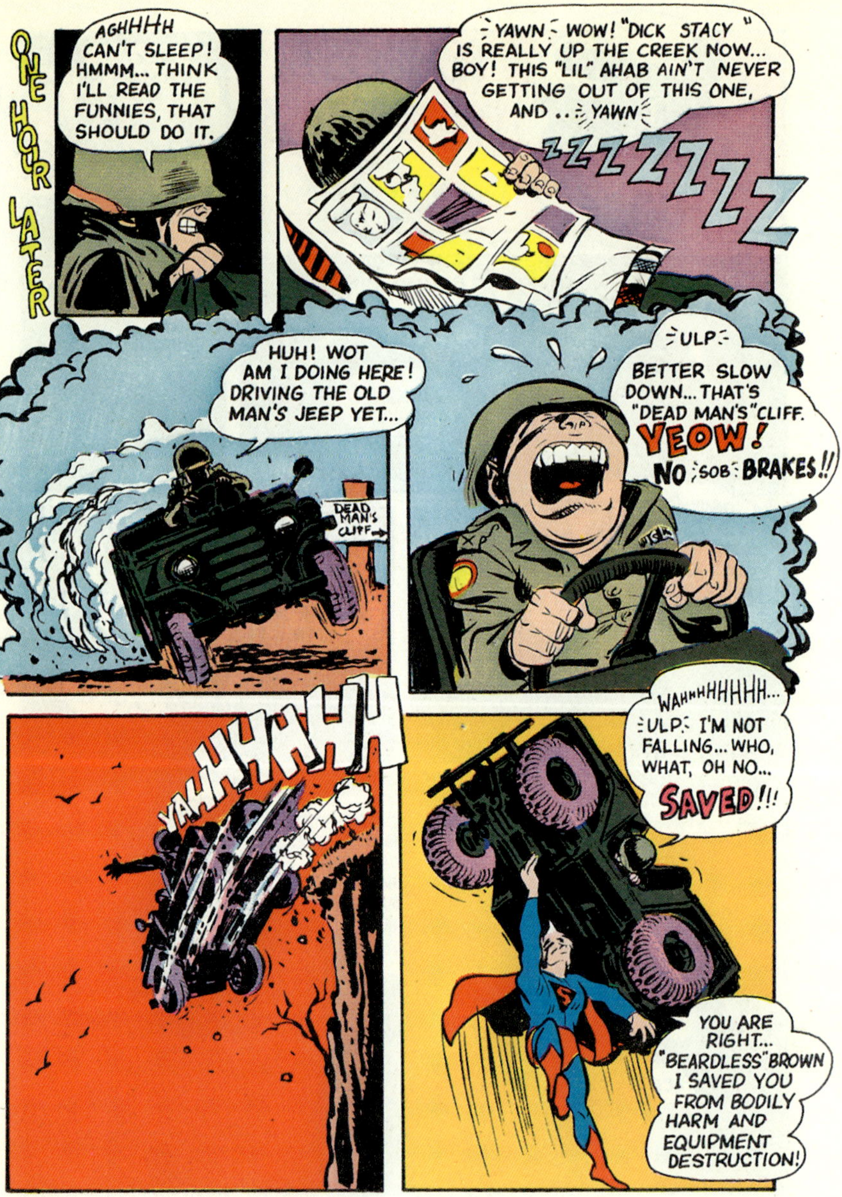
ONE HOUR LATER
AGHHHH CAN'T SLEEP! HMMM... THINK I'LL READ THE FUNNIES, THAT SHOULD DO IT.
YAWN WOW! "DICK STACY" IS REALLY UP THE CREEK NOW... BOY! THIS "LIL" AHAB AIN'T NEVER GETTING OUT OF THIS ONE, AND .. YAWN
ZZZZZZZZ
HUH! WOT AM I DOING HERE! DRIVING THE OLD MAN'S JEEP YET...
DEAD MAN'S CLIFF
ULP BETTER SLOW DOWN... THAT'S "DEAD MAN'S" CLIFF. YEOW! NO SOB BRAKES!!
YAHHHHHHH
WAHHHHHHHH... ULP I'M NOT FALLING... WHO, WHAT, OH NO... SAVED!!!
YOU ARE RIGHT... "BEARDLESS" BROWN I SAVED YOU FROM BODILY HARM AND EQUIPMENT DESTRUCTION!

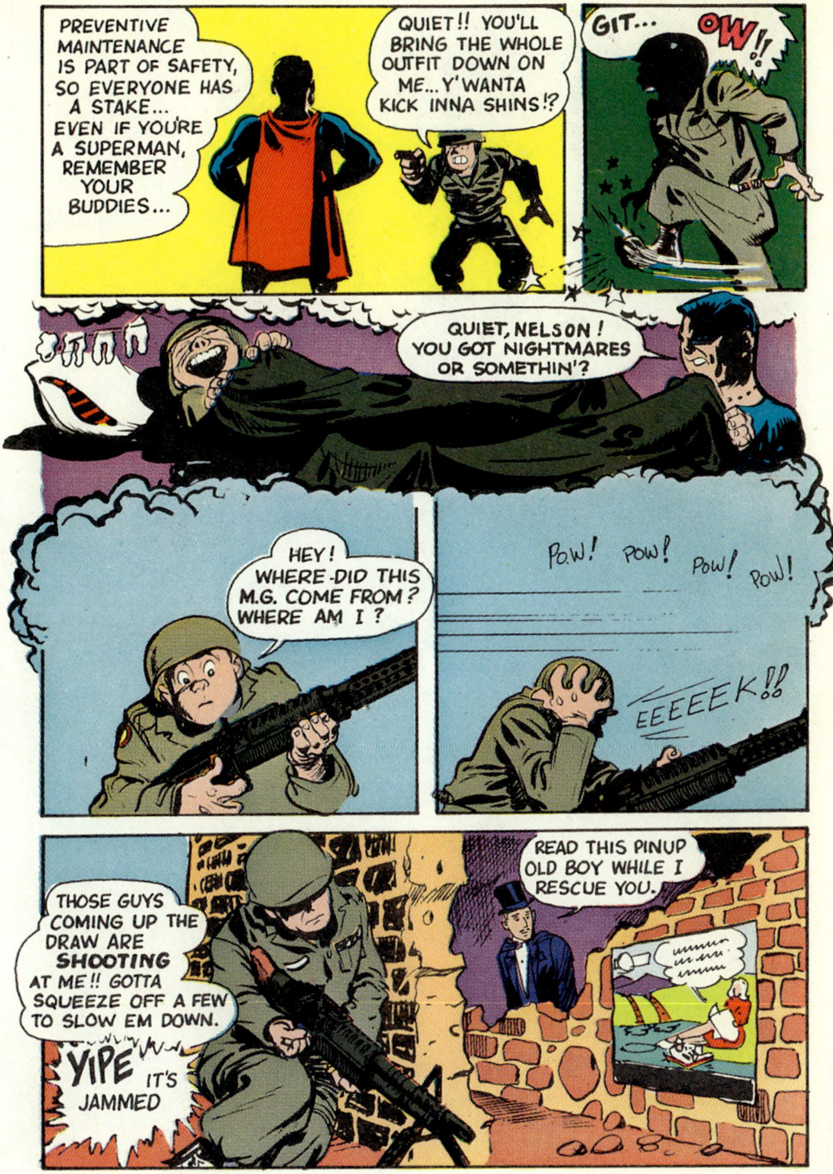
PREVENTIVE MAINTENANCE IS PART OF SAFETY, SO EVERYONE HAS A STAKE... EVEN IF YOU'RE A SUPERMAN, REMEMBER YOUR BUDDIES...
QUIET!! YOU'LL BRING THE WHOLE OUTFIT DOWN ON ME... Y'WANTA KICK INNA SHINS!?
GIT... OW!!
QUIET, NELSON! YOU GOT NIGHTMARES OR SOMETHIN'?
HEY! WHERE DID THIS M.G. COME FROM? WHERE AM I?
POW! POW! POW! POW!
EEEEEK!!
THOSE GUYS COMING UP THE DRAW ARE SHOOTING AT ME!! GOTTA SQUEEZE OFF A FEW TO SLOW EM DOWN.
YIPE IT'S JAMMED
READ THIS PINUP OLD BOY WHILE I RESCUE YOU.

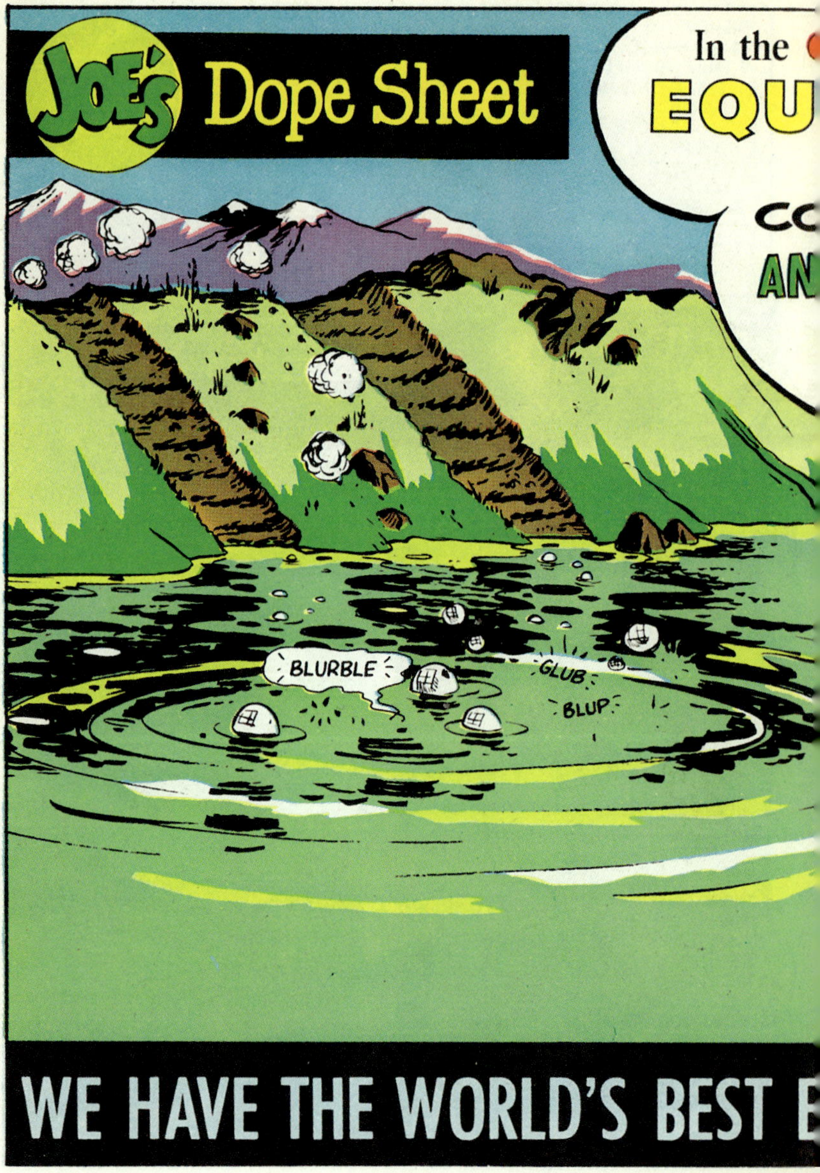
JOE'S
Dope Sheet
In the
BLURBLE
GLUB
BLUP
WE HAVE THE WORLD'S BEST

IF YOU WANT TO DISPLAY THIS CENTERPIECE ON YOU

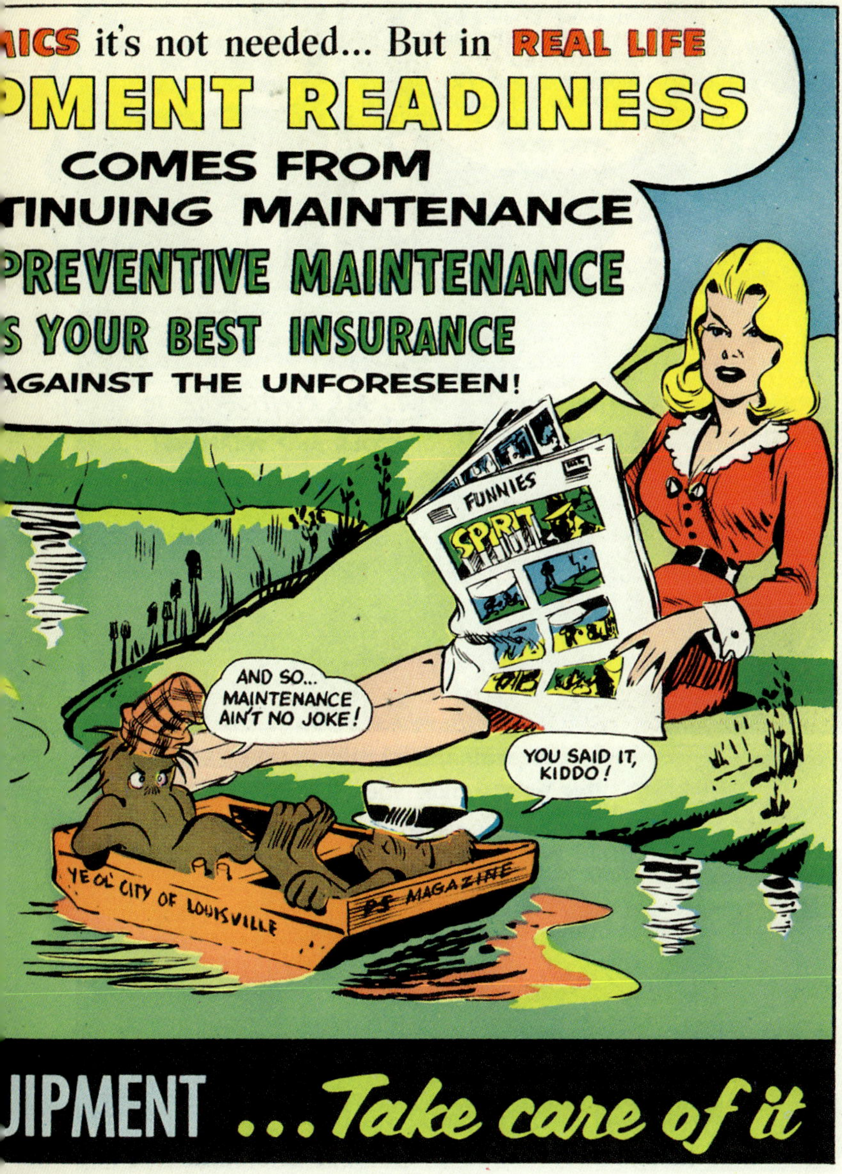
ICS it's not needed... But in REAL LIFE
PMENT READINESS
COMES FROM
TINUING MAINTENANCE
PREVENTIVE MAINTENANCE
S YOUR BEST INSURANCE
AGAINST THE UNFORESEEN!
FUNNIES
SPRT
AND SO... MAINTENANCE AIN'T NO JOKE!
YOU SAID IT, KIDDO!
YE OL' CITY OF LOUISVILLE
PS MAGAZINE
JIPMENT ...Take care of it

ETIN BOARD, OPEN STAPLES, LIFT IT OUT AND PIN IT UP.

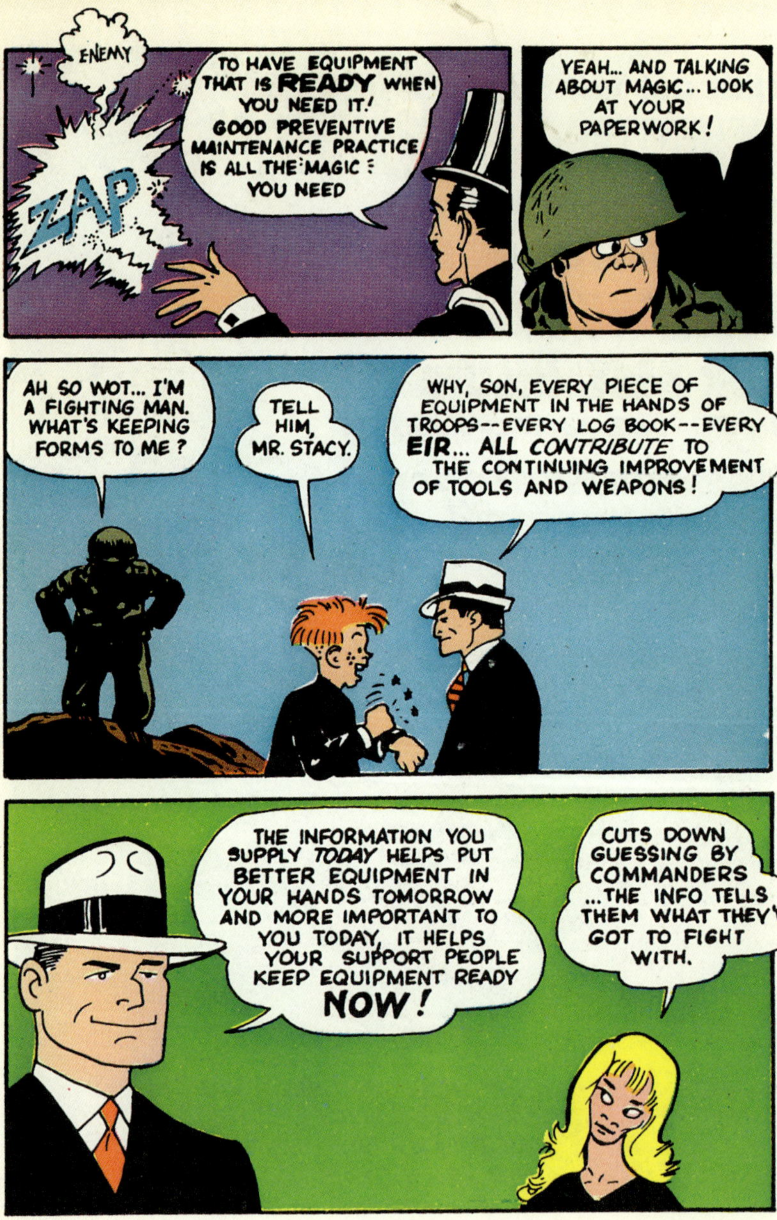
ENEMY
TO HAVE EQUIPMENT THAT IS READY WHEN YOU NEED IT! GOOD PREVENTIVE MAINTENANCE PRACTICE IS ALL THE MAGIC YOU NEED
ZAP
YEAH... AND TALKING ABOUT MAGIC... LOOK AT YOUR PAPERWORK!
AH SO WOT... I'M A FIGHTING MAN. WHAT'S KEEPING FORMS TO ME?
TELL HIM, MR. STACY.
WHY, SON, EVERY PIECE OF EQUIPMENT IN THE HANDS OF TROOPS--EVERY LOG BOOK--EVERY EIR... ALL CONTRIBUTE TO THE CONTINUING IMPROVEMENT OF TOOLS AND WEAPONS!
THE INFORMATION YOU SUPPLY TODAY HELPS PUT BETTER EQUIPMENT IN YOUR HANDS TOMORROW AND MORE IMPORTANT TO YOU TODAY, IT HELPS YOUR SUPPORT PEOPLE KEEP EQUIPMENT READY NOW!
CUTS DOWN GUESSING BY COMMANDERS ...THE INFO TELLS THEM WHAT THEY'VE GOT TO FIGHT WITH.

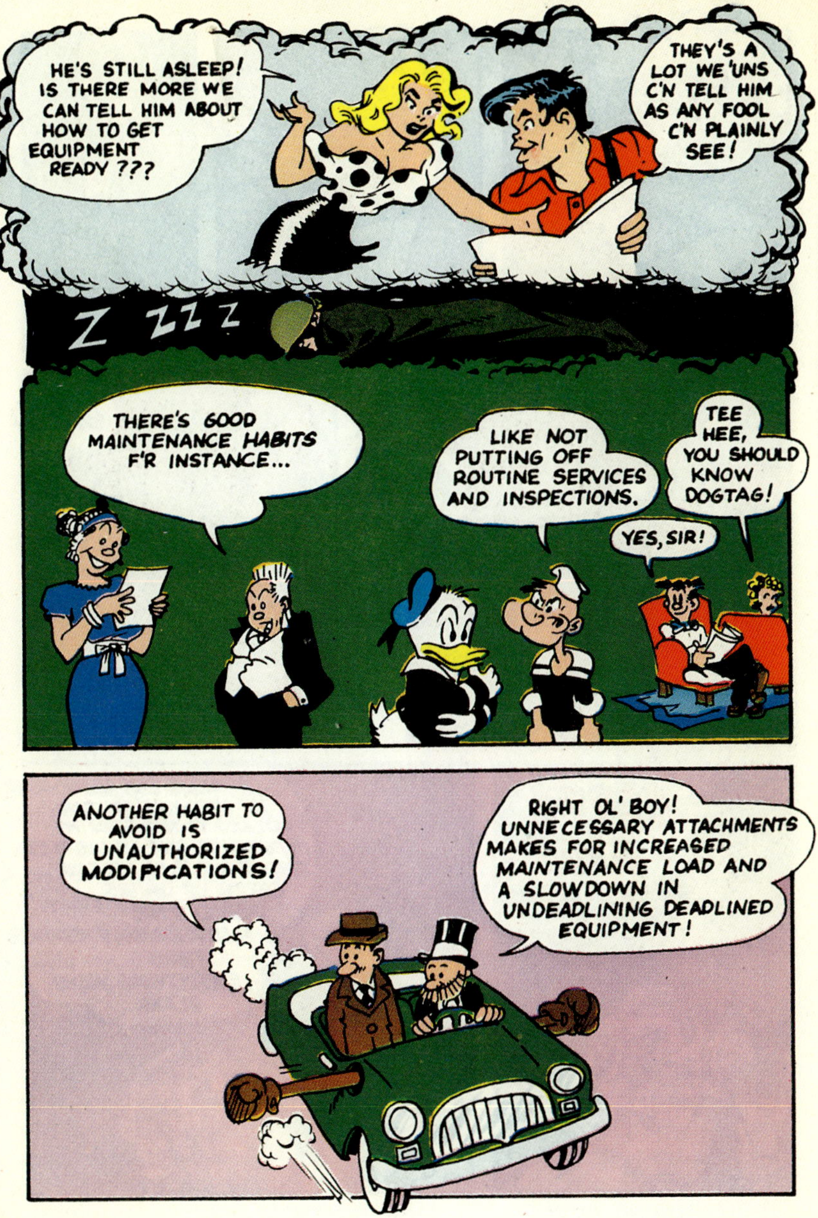
HE'S STILL ASLEEP! IS THERE MORE WE CAN TELL HIM ABOUT HOW TO GET EQUIPMENT READY ???
THEY'S A LOT WE 'UNS C'N TELL HIM AS ANY FOOL C'N PLAINLY SEE!
Z ZZZ
THERE'S GOOD MAINTENANCE HABITS F'R INSTANCE...
LIKE NOT PUTTING OFF ROUTINE SERVICES AND INSPECTIONS.
TEE HEE, YOU SHOULD KNOW DOGTAG!
YES, SIR!
ANOTHER HABIT TO AVOID IS UNAUTHORIZED MODIFICATIONS!
RIGHT OL' BOY! UNNECESSARY ATTACHMENTS MAKES FOR INCREASED MAINTENANCE LOAD AND A SLOWDOWN IN UNDEADLINING DEADLINED EQUIPMENT!

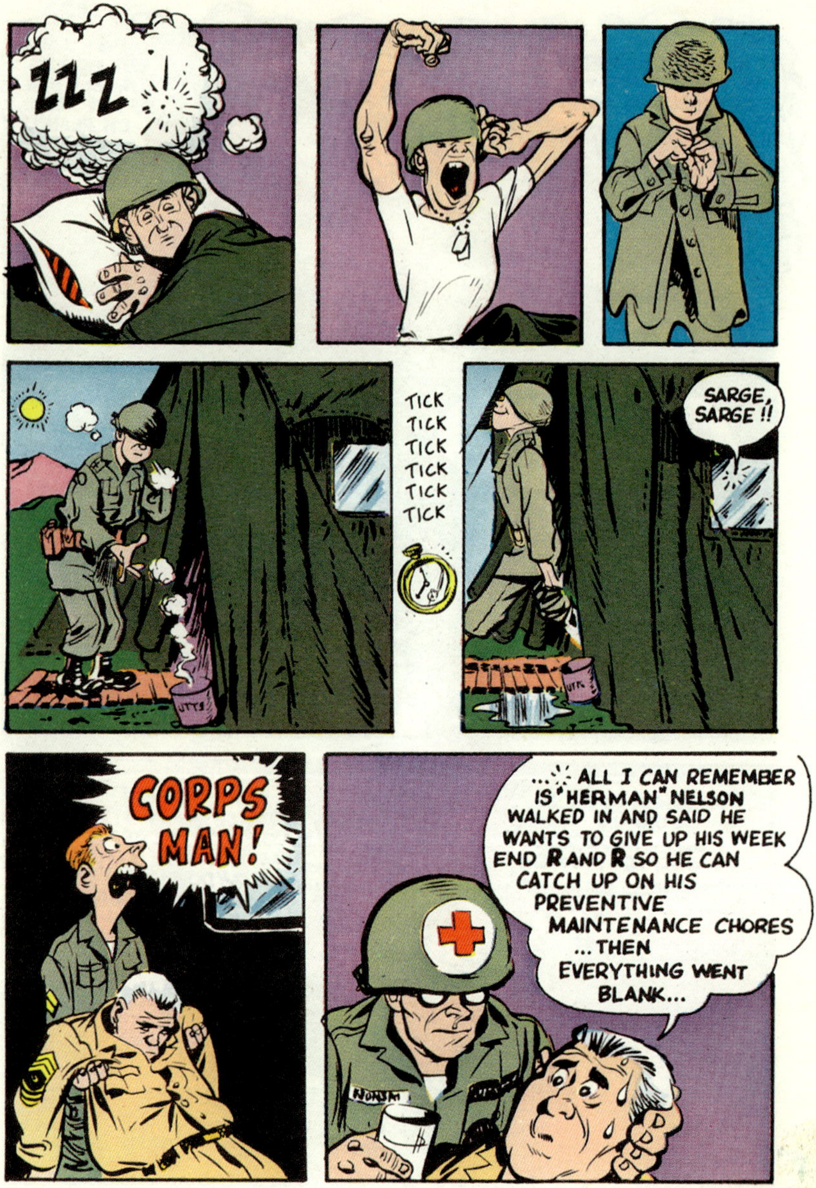
ZZZ
TICK
TICK
TICK
TICK
TICK
TICK
SARGE, SARGE !!
CORPS MAN!
...ALL I CAN REMEMBER IS "HERMAN" NELSON WALKED IN AND SAID HE WANTS TO GIVE UP HIS WEEK END R AND R SO HE CAN CATCH UP ON HIS PREVENTIVE MAINTENANCE CHORES ...THEN EVERYTHING WENT BLANK...

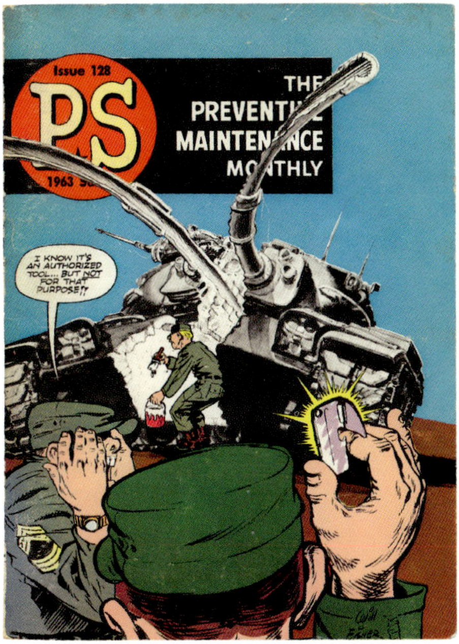
Issue 128
P★S
1963 Series
THE PREVENTIVE MAINTENANCE MONTHLY
I KNOW IT'S AN AUTHORIZED TOOL... BUT NOT FOR THAT PURPOSE!!

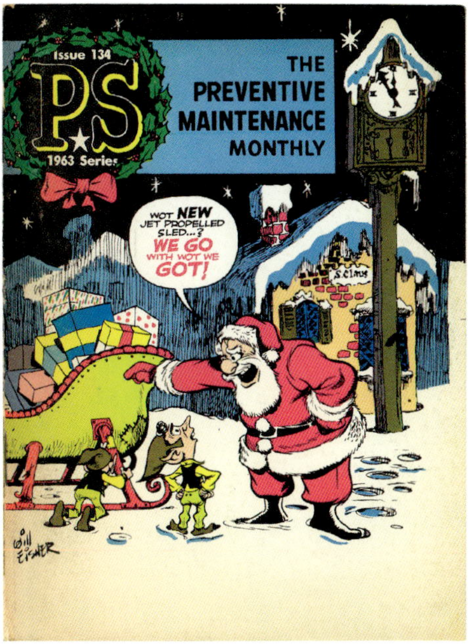
Issue 134
P★S
1963 Series
THE PREVENTIVE MAINTENANCE MONTHLY
WOT NEW JET PROPELLED SLED...? WE GO WITH WOT WE GOT!
Will Eisner

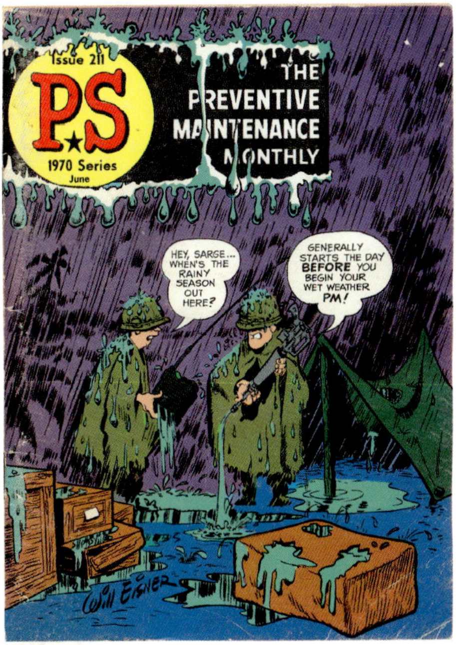
Issue 211
P★S
1970 Series
June
THE PREVENTIVE MAINTENANCE MONTHLY
HEY, SARGE... WHEN'S THE RAINY SEASON OUT HERE?
GENERALLY STARTS THE DAY BEFORE YOU BEGIN YOUR WET WEATHER PM!
Will Eisner

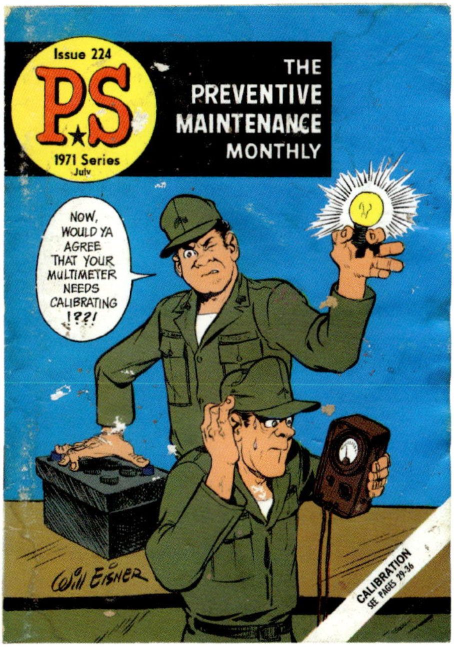
Issue 224
P★S
1971 Series
July
THE PREVENTIVE MAINTENANCE MONTHLY
NOW, WOULD YA AGREE THAT YOUR MULTIMETER NEEDS CALIBRATING !??!
Will Eisner
CALIBRATION SEE PAGES 29-36

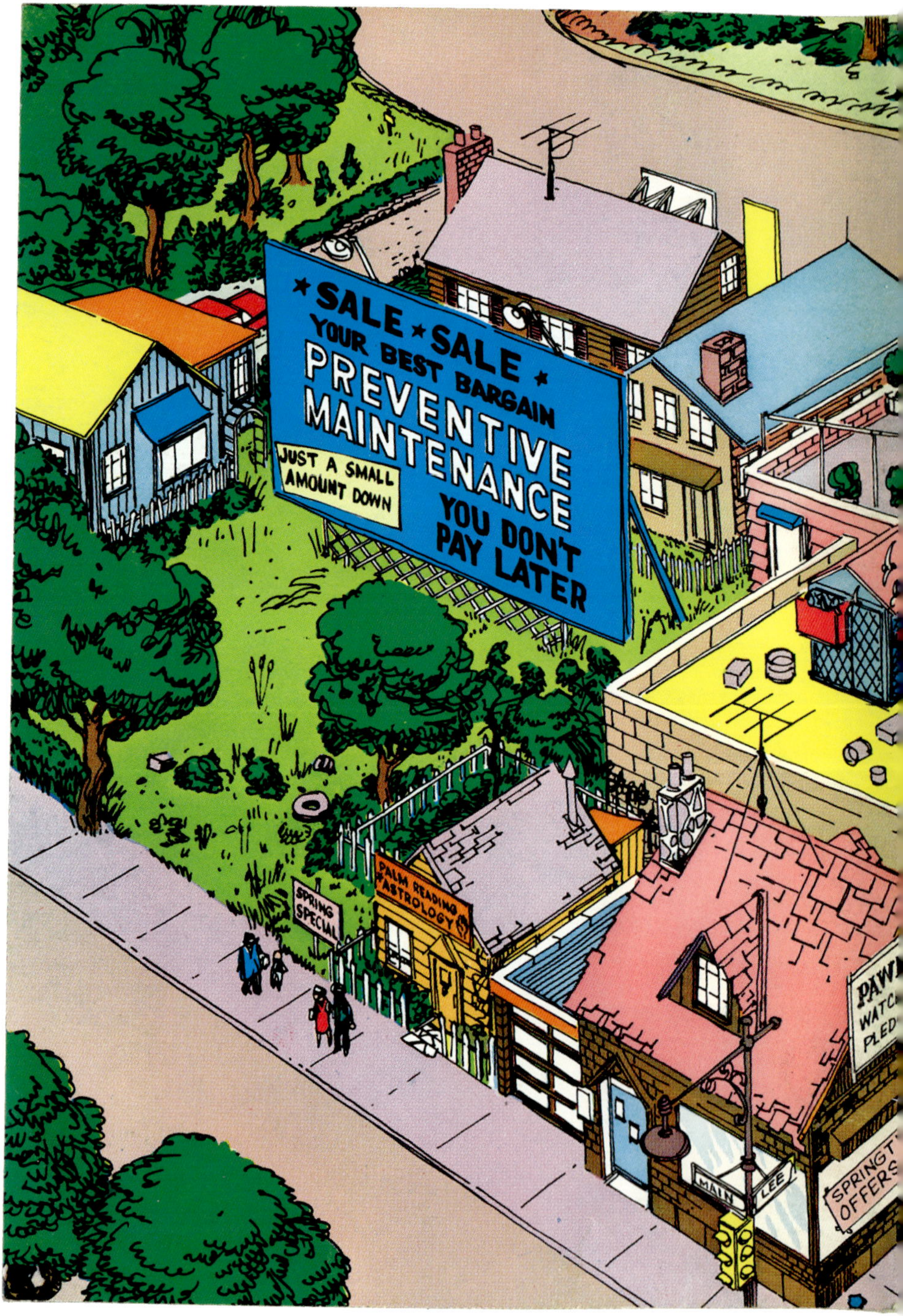
★SALE★SALE★
YOUR BEST BARGAIN
PREVENTIVE
MAINTENANCE
JUST A SMALL
AMOUNT DOWN
YOU DON'T
PAY LATER
PALM READING
ASTROLOGY
SPRING
SPECIAL
MAIN
LEE

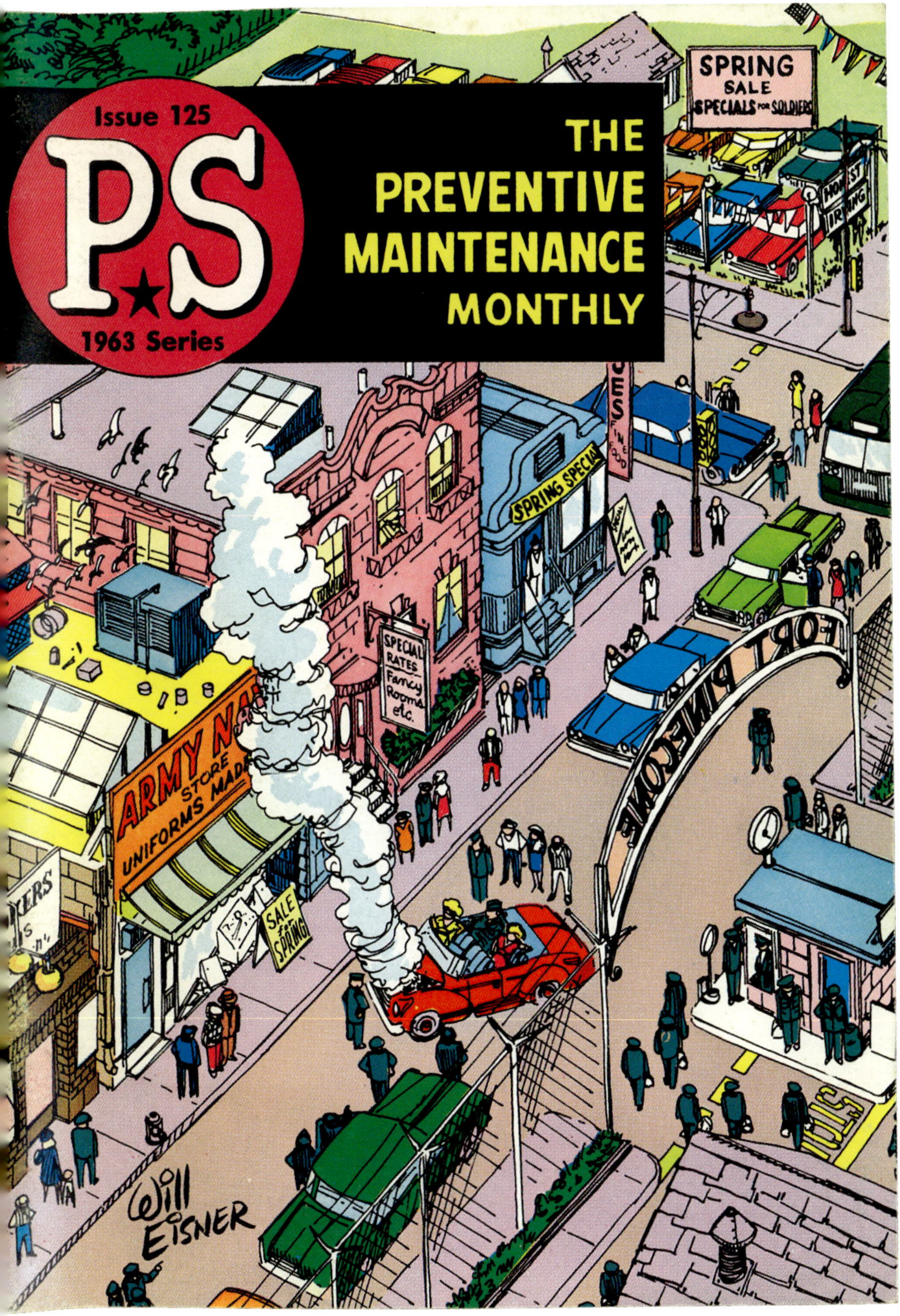
Issue 125
P.S
1963 Series
THE
PREVENTIVE
MAINTENANCE
MONTHLY
SPRING
SALE
SPECIALS FOR SOLDIERS
SPRING SPECIAL
FINE FOOD
SPECIAL
RATES
Fancy
Rooms
etc.
ARMY NA
STORE
UNIFORMS MAD
SALE
for
SPRING
FORT PINECONE
Will
EISNER

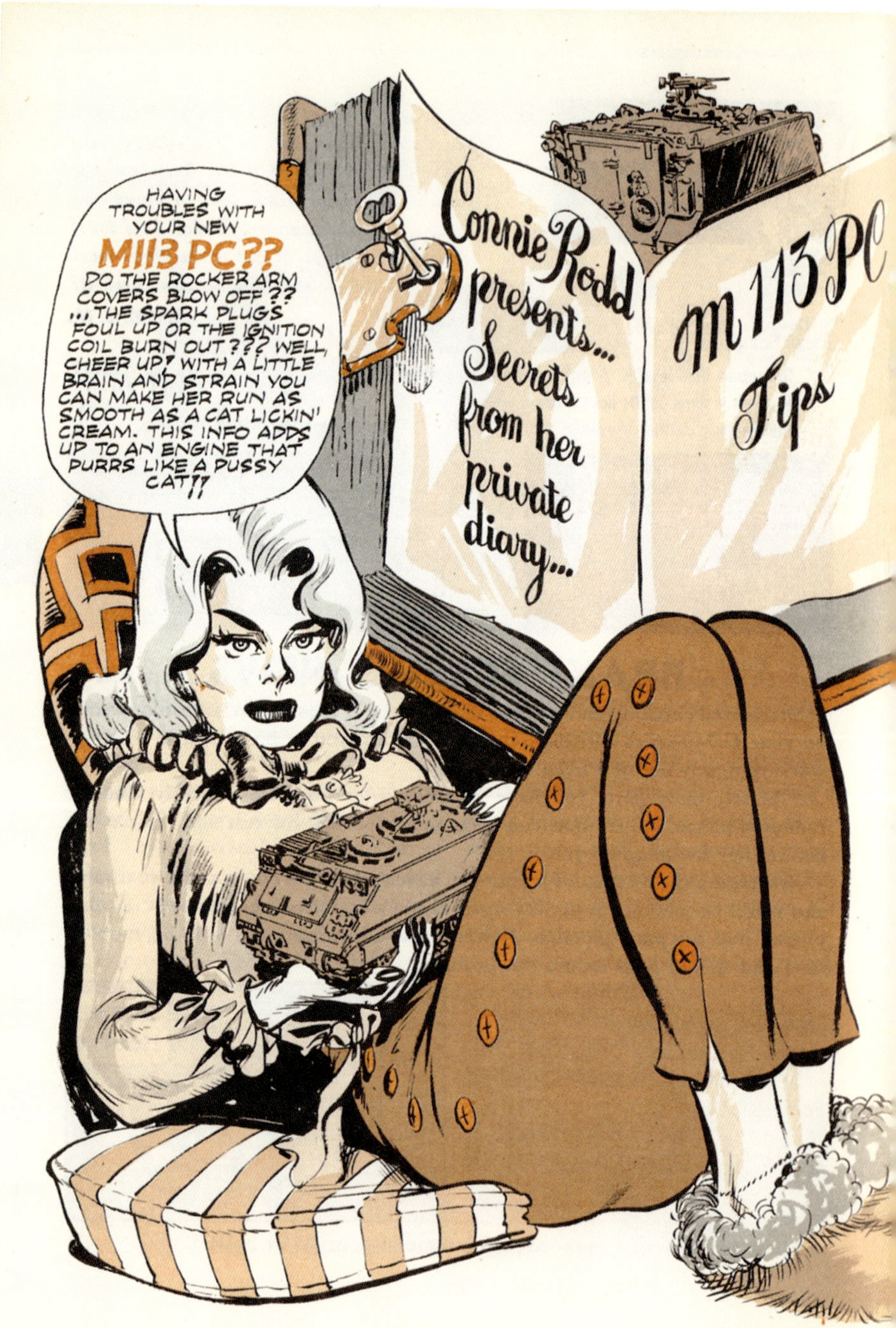
HAVING TROUBLES WITH YOUR NEW
M113 PC??
DO THE ROCKER ARM COVERS BLOW OFF ?? .. THE SPARK PLUGS FOUL UP OR THE IGNITION COIL BURN OUT ??? WELL, CHEER UP! WITH A LITTLE BRAIN AND STRAIN YOU CAN MAKE HER RUN AS SMOOTH AS A CAT LICKIN' CREAM. THIS INFO ADDS UP TO AN ENGINE THAT PURRS LIKE A PUSSY CAT!!
Connie Rodd presents... Secrets from her private diary...
M 113 PC Tips

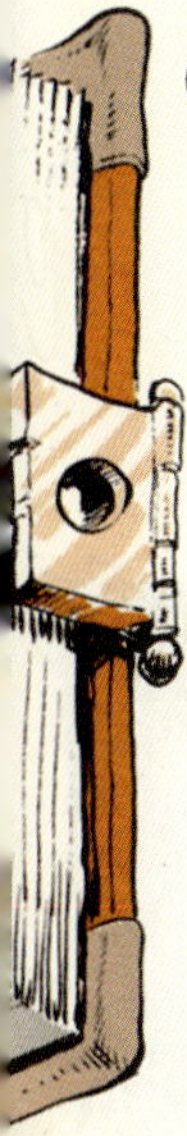

Ignition Timing

.64IN ±
.03

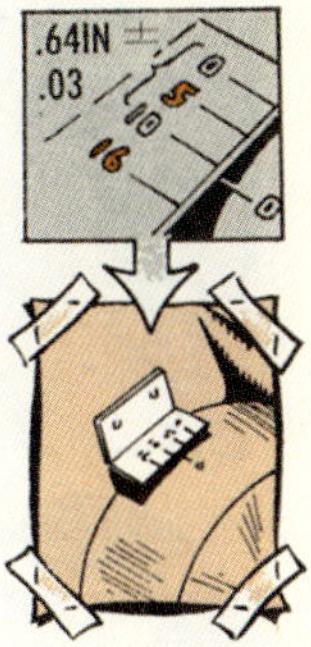

Set the ignition timing like it says in TM 9-2300-224-20 (Dec 61) on pages 130-131. Make sure the ignition timing arrow lines up with the 10° mark on the timing plate. A lot of the older M113's were issued with the setting at 16° BTDC. In fact, there may not even be a 10° mark on the ignition timing plate.

If there is no 10° mark, have your support scribe a mark .64 inch down from the 0 mark. Once the mark is scribed—it'll be about half-way between the 5° and the 16° marks—get your timing arrow set on it. This'll stop a lot of trouble.

Spark Plug Cables

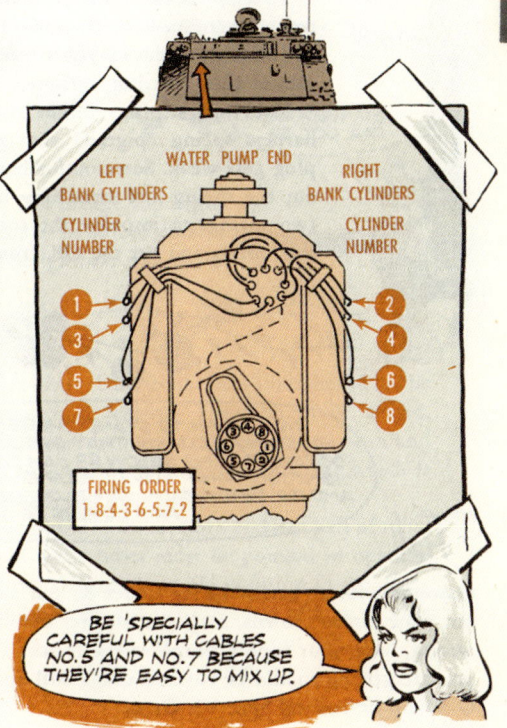

Do the spark plug cables on your M113 PC cross you up?

If they get hooked to the wrong spark plugs, your engine will make with a lot of backfiring when you start up. You'll also get crankcase explosions that can knock off the rocker-arm covers. To be sure each cable is where it belongs, check its identification tag number on the cable and connect it to the right spark plug like you see in Fig 117, page 130, and Fig 120B, page 132 of TM 9-2300-224-20 (Dec 61).

WATER PUMP END
LEFT BANK CYLINDERS
RIGHT BANK CYLINDERS
CYLINDER NUMBER
CYLINDER NUMBER
1
3
5
7
2
4
6
8
FIRING ORDER 1-8-4-3-6-5-7-2
BE 'SPECIALLY CAREFUL WITH CABLES NO.5 AND NO.7 BECAUSE THEY'RE EASY TO MIX UP.

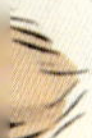

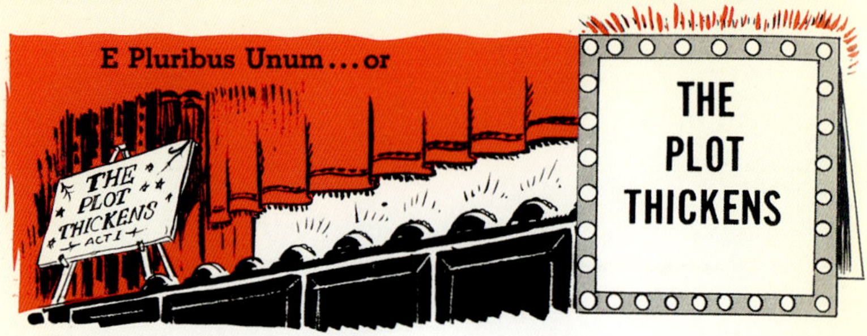
E Pluribus Unum . . . or
THE PLOT THICKENS
THE PLOT THICKENS ACT I

The people who put out the telephone directories for the posts, camps and stations have been doing some mighty peculiar things recently

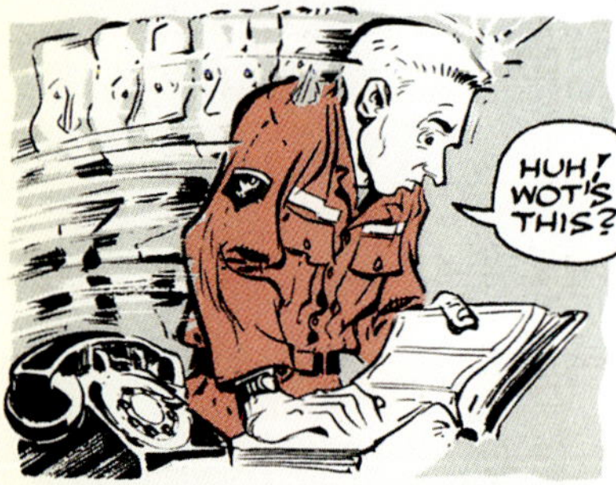
HUH! WOT'S THIS?

as you can see by thumbing through the maintenance section of your post directory, where more than likely you'll find the post maintenance activities lumped together under a general term such as "Consolidated Field Maintenance" or "Combined Field Maintenance,"

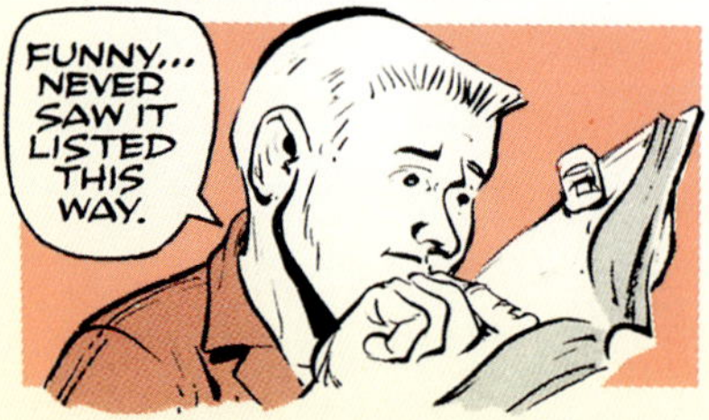
FUNNY... NEVER SAW IT LISTED THIS WAY.

and further broken down under such functional sections as Armament, Tracked Vehicles, Wheel Vehicles, General Purpose, Avionics, Electronics, Aircraft and such, instead of being listed under the old technical service breakout;

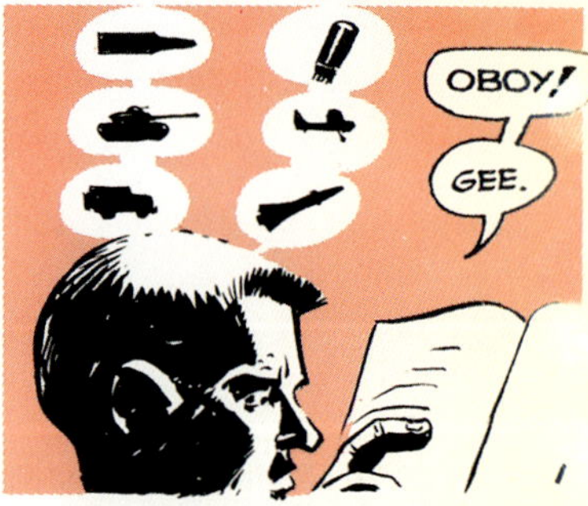
OBOY!
GEE.

and when you start looking real close you may discover that a number of these functional sections have the same building number or address,

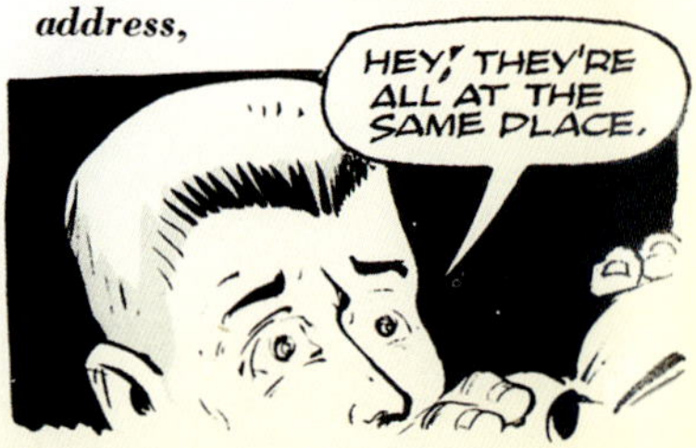
HEY! THEY'RE ALL AT THE SAME PLACE.

AHHHHH
WHO ME!
I JUST MAKE
'EM BUDDY.
TELEPHONE
SERVICE

which should send shivers of gladness through your heart since there's nothing more convenient than having a one-building or one-area service center where your tank, for example, can get its engine, guns, radio, searchlight and filter unit, gas particulate, up-snuffed pretty much in one fell swoop instead of having to be shuttled around from one specialty shop to another at a considerable waste of time and effort,

and why didn't somebody think of this before!

YEAH!
WHY
DIDN'T
THEY?

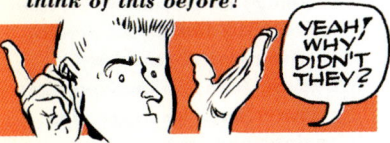

But as you continue to ponder the unearthly delights of such a system it suddenly dawns on you that

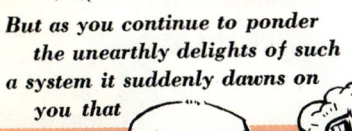

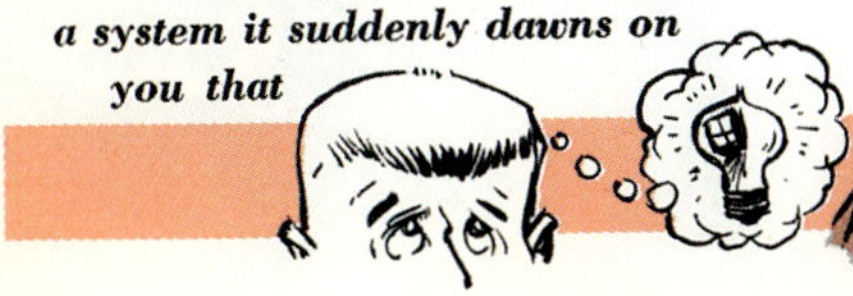

gee, the authority and responsibility for combining and consolidating these important maintenance functions doesn't generally rest on the shoulders of people who compile telephone directories

MUST BE
BIG STUFF!

so there must be some really big stick *behind this idea*

WOW!

and the directory people just carried it through in their neat and orderly fashion,

YEAH...
THAT'S ALL.

so you start looking further and sure enough, you start running across such titles as "Director of Field Maintenance," and "Superintendent of Field Maintenance," and other awesome positions

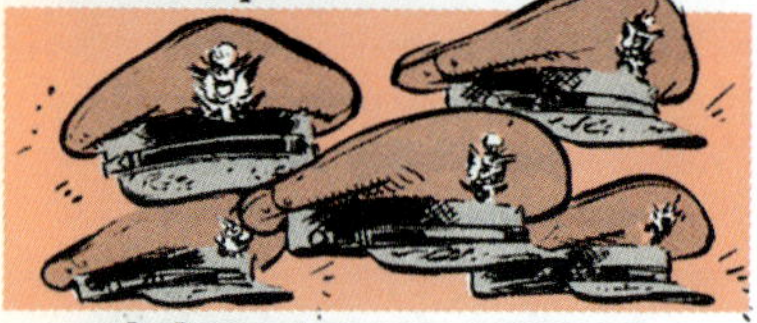

and there no longer seems to be any doubt as to "who's in charge here,"

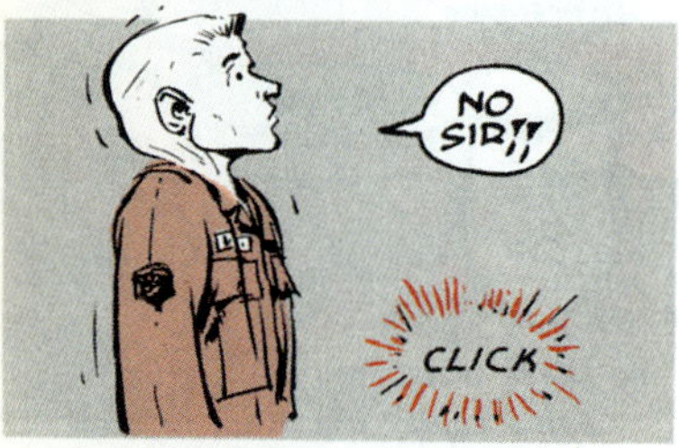
NO SIR!!
CLICK

which is sure going to make it easy for your "Old Man" to conduct his maintenance business since he always felt that under the old system he wasn't being "supported" so much by maintenance as he was "surrounded" by it,

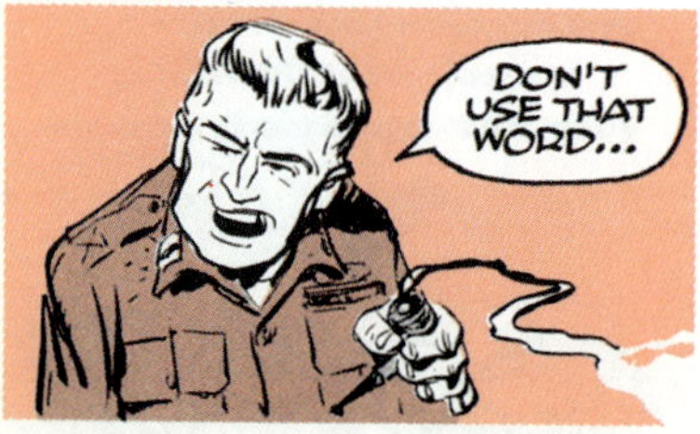
DON'T USE THAT WORD...

and CO's for some strange reason take a mighty dim view of being "surrounded."

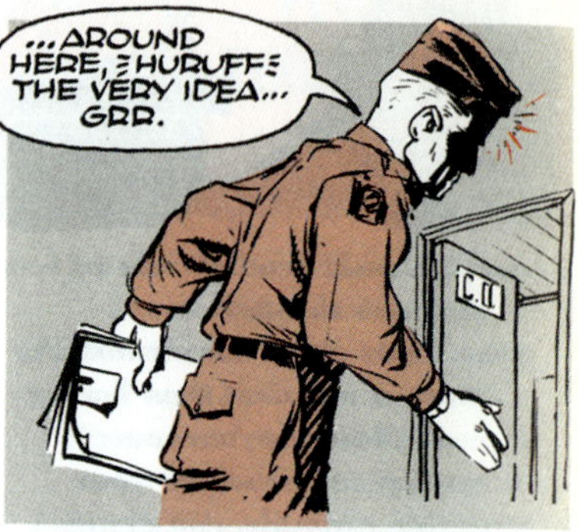
...AROUND HERE, =HURUFF= THE VERY IDEA... GRR.
C.O.

Well, any ol' how, the more you study the directory the more intriguing it becomes and

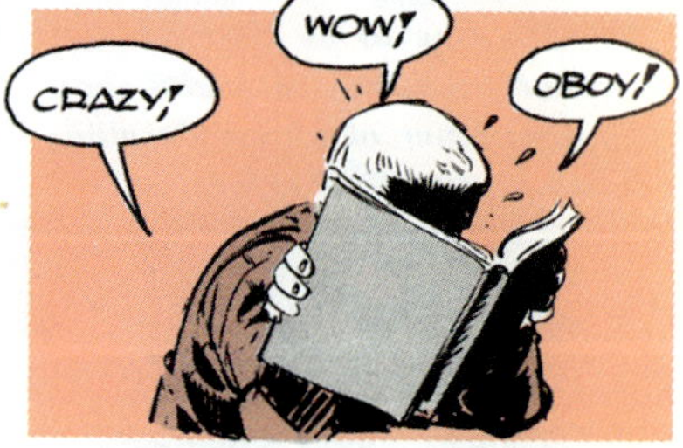
CRAZY!
WOW!
OBOY!

and you go on to think of all kinds of benefits that could develop from this consolidated system, both for the equipment users and the supporting maintenance personnel,

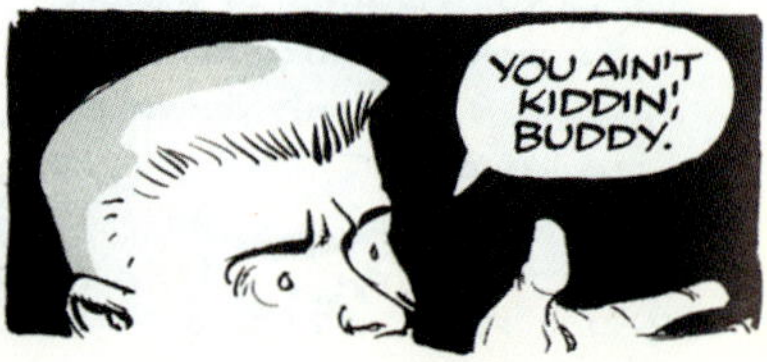
YOU AIN'T KIDDIN', BUDDY.

and you suddenly remember the old joke about the telephone directory being reviewed by a literary critic who said it has a marvelous list of characters but not much of a plot,

YECH! I'M HYSTERICAL.

and you get to thinking that maybe there's a heap sight more plot and action involved here than the critic ever dreamed of

Y'R RIGHT... HMM.

and it just could be that this on-post, off-Broadway drama may turn out to be one of the outstanding performances of the season.

ALL STAR-CAST... TOO...

At any rate, it's well worth waiting for the final curtain, wouldn't you say?

R-ROGER OL-BEAN.

Published by the Department of the Army for the Information of organizational maintenance and supply personnel. Distribution is made through normal publication channels. Within limits of availability, older issues may be obtained direct from U. S. Army Maintenance Board, Attn. PS Magazine, Fort Knox, Kentucky 40121.

THE **PREVENTIVE MAINTENANCE** MONTHLY
Issue No. 134 1963 Series

IN THIS ISSUE

GROUND MOBILITY 4-14

TRACKS		WHEELS	
M113	4-5, 6	5 Ton Trucks	10
M60	6-7, 8	Tankers	11
M41	8	M151	12-13
M42	9	M62	14
M88, M51	9		

FIREPOWER 16-25

105 Howitzer	16-17	Nike-Hercules	20-23
M73	18	Hawk	22-25
M37C	19		

AIR MOBILITY 37-49

Mojave (CH-37)	37, 44-45	Exhaust Valve	46-47
Choctaw (CH-34)	38-41	Castellated	
MWO Problem	42-43	Nuts	46-47
Gasket Board	43	Huey (UH-1A)	48
Safety Belt	45	Avionics Help	48-49

COMMUNICATIONS 50-58

RT-77	50-51	AN/TCC-7	55
AN/GGC-3	52	RL-172/G	56
PP-34/MSM	53	Cable Care	57
T-302	54	Report Damage	58

GENERAL AND SUPPLY

Due-Outs	26	Food Container	59
TB 9-30	26	Immersion Heater	60-61
DA Form 2408-3	27	Medical Kit Care	62-63
DA Form 2062	28	Tent Poles	64
New Pubs	15	Supply	4, 7, 8, 9, 11, 23, 46, 48

Use of funds for printing of this publication has been approved by Headquarters, Department of the Army, 4 April 1962. DISTRIBUTION: In accordance with requirements submitted on DA Form 12-4.

PS wants your ideas and contributions, and is glad to answer your questions. Name and address are kept in confidence. Just write to:

Sgt. Half-Mast,
PS Magazine,
Fort Knox, Ky.
40121

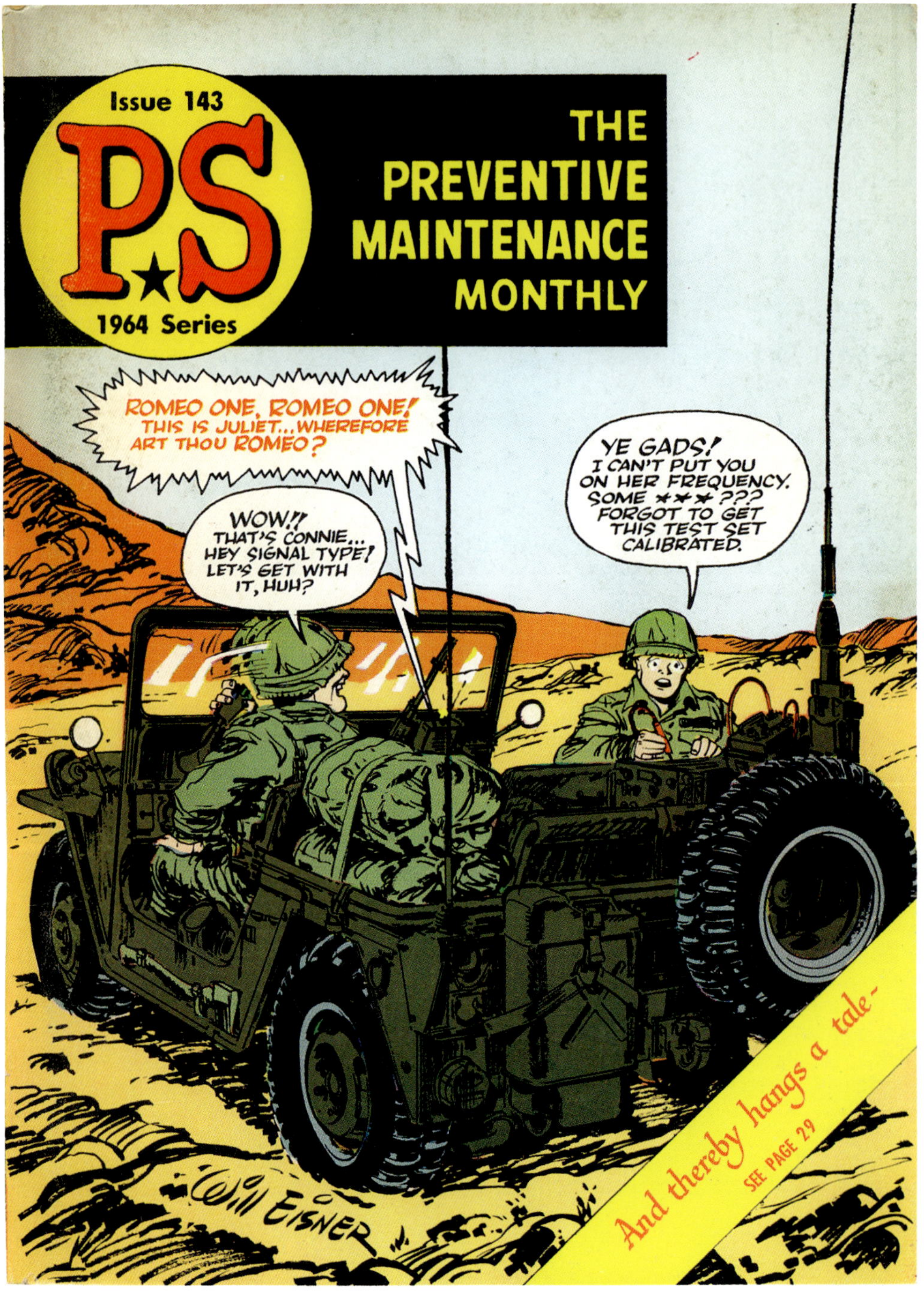
Issue 143
P.S
1964 Series
THE PREVENTIVE MAINTENANCE MONTHLY
ROMEO ONE, ROMEO ONE! THIS IS JULIET...WHEREFORE ART THOU ROMEO?
WOW!! THAT'S CONNIE... HEY SIGNAL TYPE! LET'S GET WITH IT, HUH?
YE GADS! I CAN'T PUT YOU ON HER FREQUENCY. SOME ***??? FORGOT TO GET THIS TEST SET CALIBRATED.
Will Eisner
And thereby hangs a tale-
SEE PAGE 29

no. 143, 1964

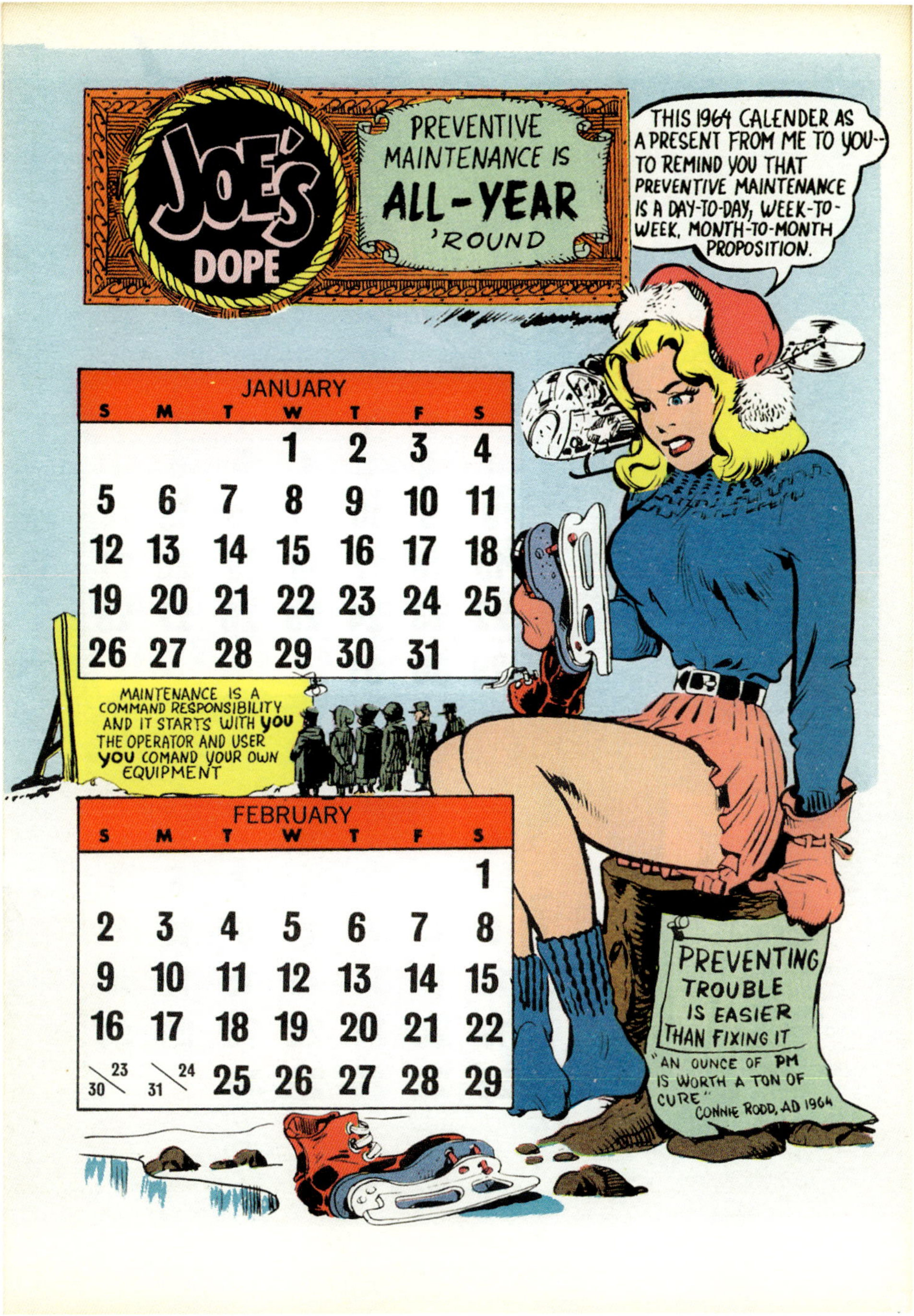

JOE'S DOPE
PREVENTIVE MAINTENANCE IS ALL-YEAR 'ROUND
THIS 1964 CALENDER AS A PRESENT FROM ME TO YOU-- TO REMIND YOU THAT PREVENTIVE MAINTENANCE IS A DAY-TO-DAY, WEEK-TO-WEEK, MONTH-TO-MONTH PROPOSITION.
JANUARY
S M T W T F S
1 2 3 4
5 6 7 8 9 10 11
12 13 14 15 16 17 18
19 20 21 22 23 24 25
26 27 28 29 30 31
MAINTENANCE IS A COMMAND RESPONSIBILITY AND IT STARTS WITH YOU THE OPERATOR AND USER YOU COMAND YOUR OWN EQUIPMENT
FEBRUARY
S M T W T F S
1
2 3 4 5 6 7 8
9 10 11 12 13 14 15
16 17 18 19 20 21 22
23/30 24/31 25 26 27 28 29
PREVENTING TROUBLE IS EASIER THAN FIXING IT
"AN OUNCE OF PM IS WORTH A TON OF CURE" CONNIE RODD, AD 1964

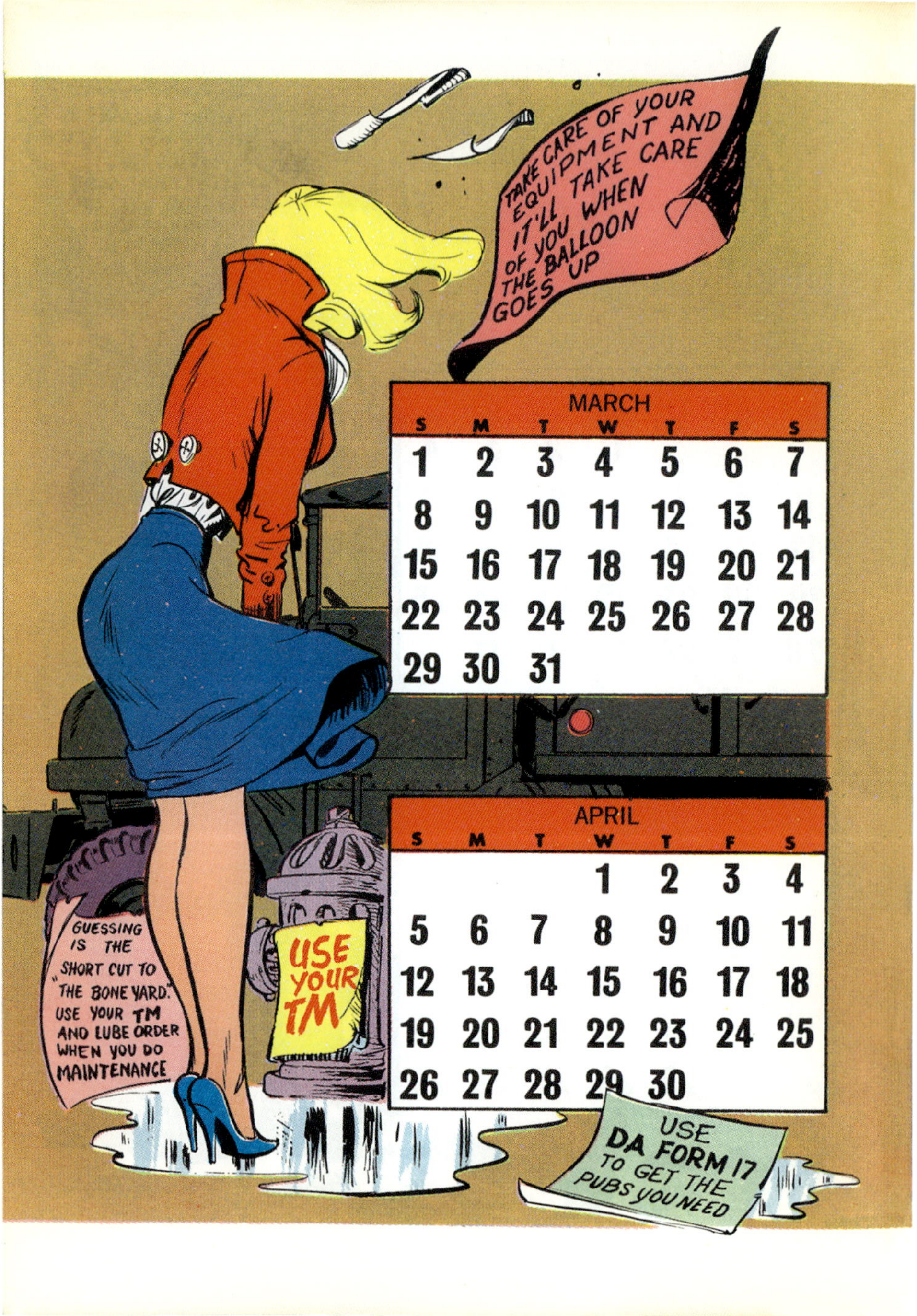
TAKE CARE OF YOUR EQUIPMENT AND IT'LL TAKE CARE OF YOU WHEN THE BALLOON GOES UP
MARCH
S M T W T F S
1 2 3 4 5 6 7
8 9 10 11 12 13 14
15 16 17 18 19 20 21
22 23 24 25 26 27 28
29 30 31
APRIL
S M T W T F S
1 2 3 4
5 6 7 8 9 10 11
12 13 14 15 16 17 18
19 20 21 22 23 24 25
26 27 28 29 30
GUESSING IS THE SHORT CUT TO "THE BONE YARD." USE YOUR TM AND LUBE ORDER WHEN YOU DO MAINTENANCE
USE YOUR TM
USE DA FORM 17 TO GET THE PUBS YOU NEED

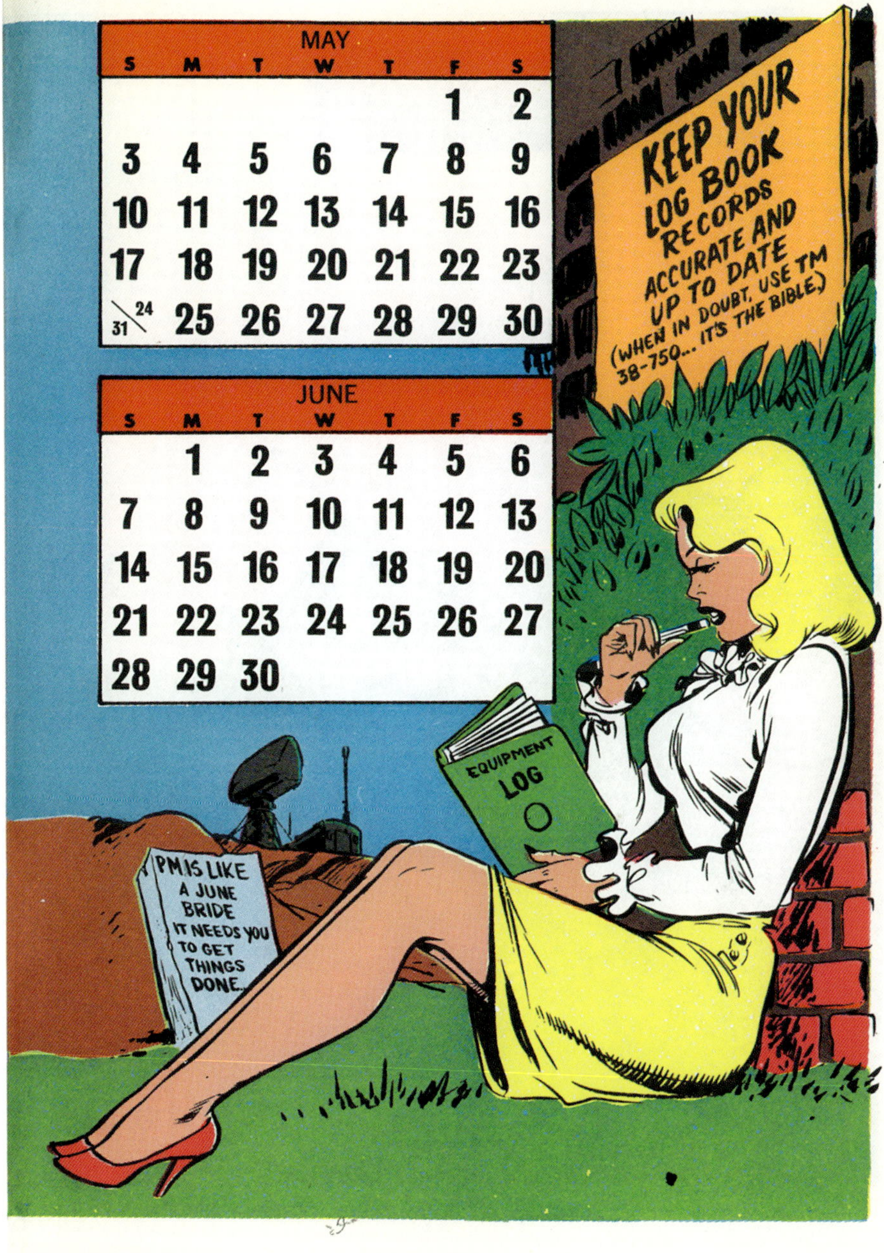
MAY
S M T W T F S
1 2
3 4 5 6 7 8 9
10 11 12 13 14 15 16
17 18 19 20 21 22 23
24/31 25 26 27 28 29 30
JUNE
S M T W T F S
1 2 3 4 5 6
7 8 9 10 11 12 13
14 15 16 17 18 19 20
21 22 23 24 25 26 27
28 29 30
KEEP YOUR LOG BOOK RECORDS ACCURATE AND UP TO DATE
(WHEN IN DOUBT, USE TM 38-750... IT'S THE BIBLE.)
EQUIPMENT LOG
PM IS LIKE A JUNE BRIDE IT NEEDS YOU TO GET THINGS DONE.

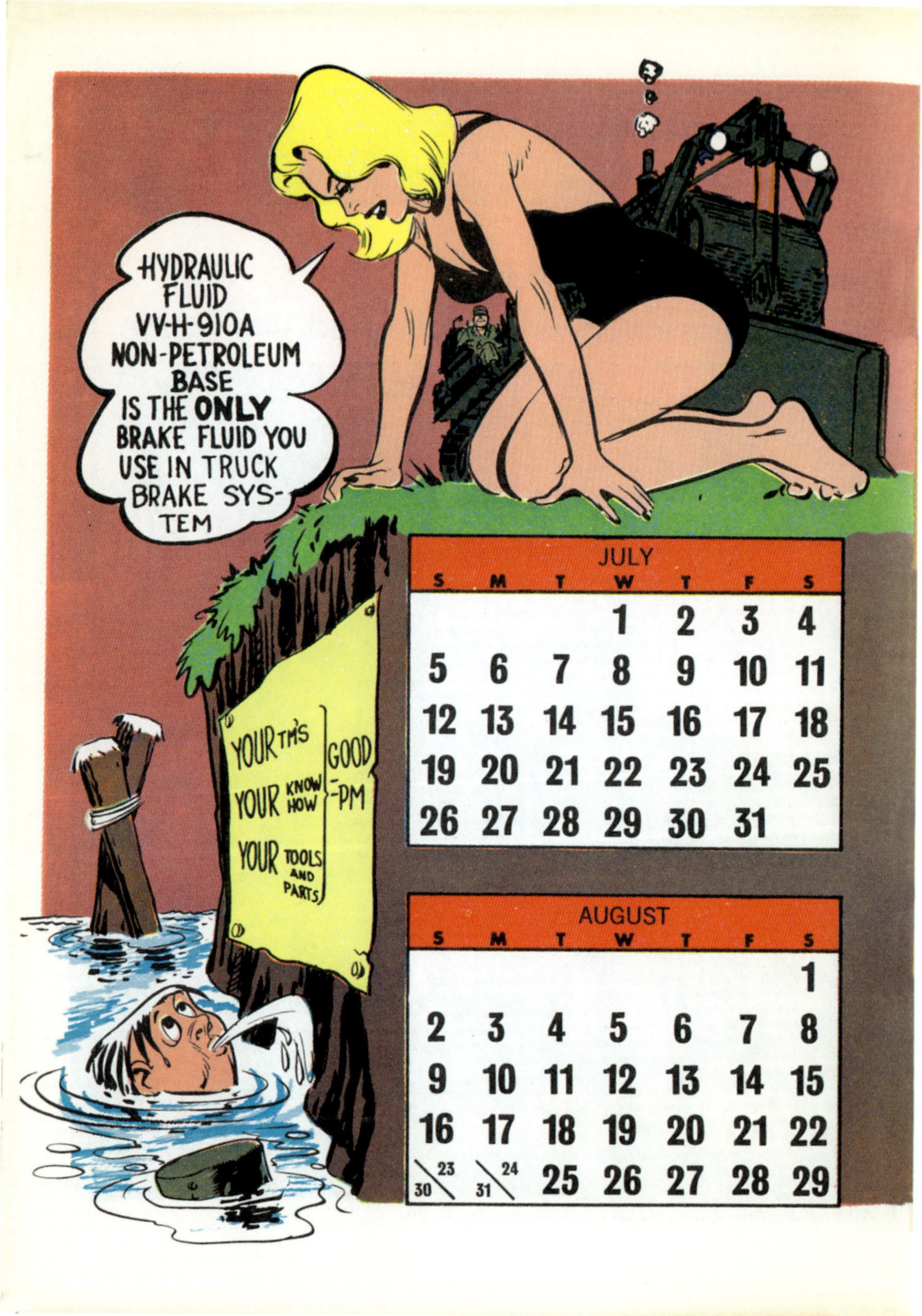
HYDRAULIC FLUID VV-H-910A NON-PETROLEUM BASE IS THE **ONLY** BRAKE FLUID YOU USE IN TRUCK BRAKE SYS-TEM
YOUR TM'S
YOUR KNOW HOW
YOUR TOOLS AND PARTS
GOOD -PM
JULY
S M T W T F S
1 2 3 4
5 6 7 8 9 10 11
12 13 14 15 16 17 18
19 20 21 22 23 24 25
26 27 28 29 30 31
AUGUST
S M T W T F S
1
2 3 4 5 6 7 8
9 10 11 12 13 14 15
16 17 18 19 20 21 22
23/30 24/31 25 26 27 28 29

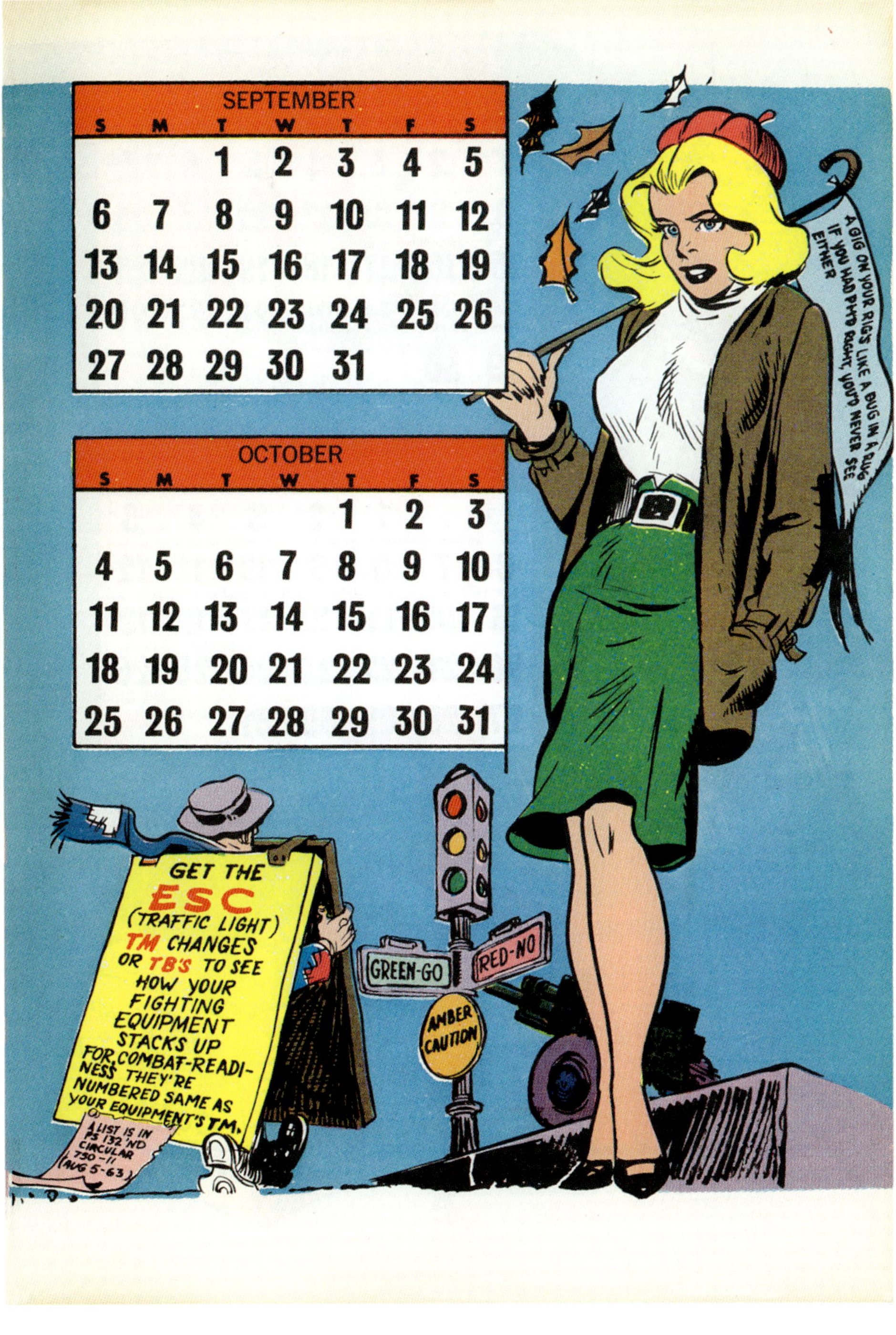
SEPTEMBER
S M T W T F S
1 2 3 4 5
6 7 8 9 10 11 12
13 14 15 16 17 18 19
20 21 22 23 24 25 26
27 28 29 30 31
OCTOBER
S M T W T F S
1 2 3
4 5 6 7 8 9 10
11 12 13 14 15 16 17
18 19 20 21 22 23 24
25 26 27 28 29 30 31
A GIG ON YOUR RIG'S LIKE A BUG IN A RUG IF YOU HAD PM'D RIGHT, YOU'D NEVER SEE EITHER
GET THE ESC (TRAFFIC LIGHT) TM CHANGES OR TB'S TO SEE HOW YOUR FIGHTING EQUIPMENT STACKS UP FOR COMBAT-READINESS THEY'RE NUMBERED SAME AS YOUR EQUIPMENT'S TM.
A LIST IS IN PS 132 'ND CIRCULAR 750-11 (AUG 5-63)
GREEN-GO
RED-NO
AMBER CAUTION

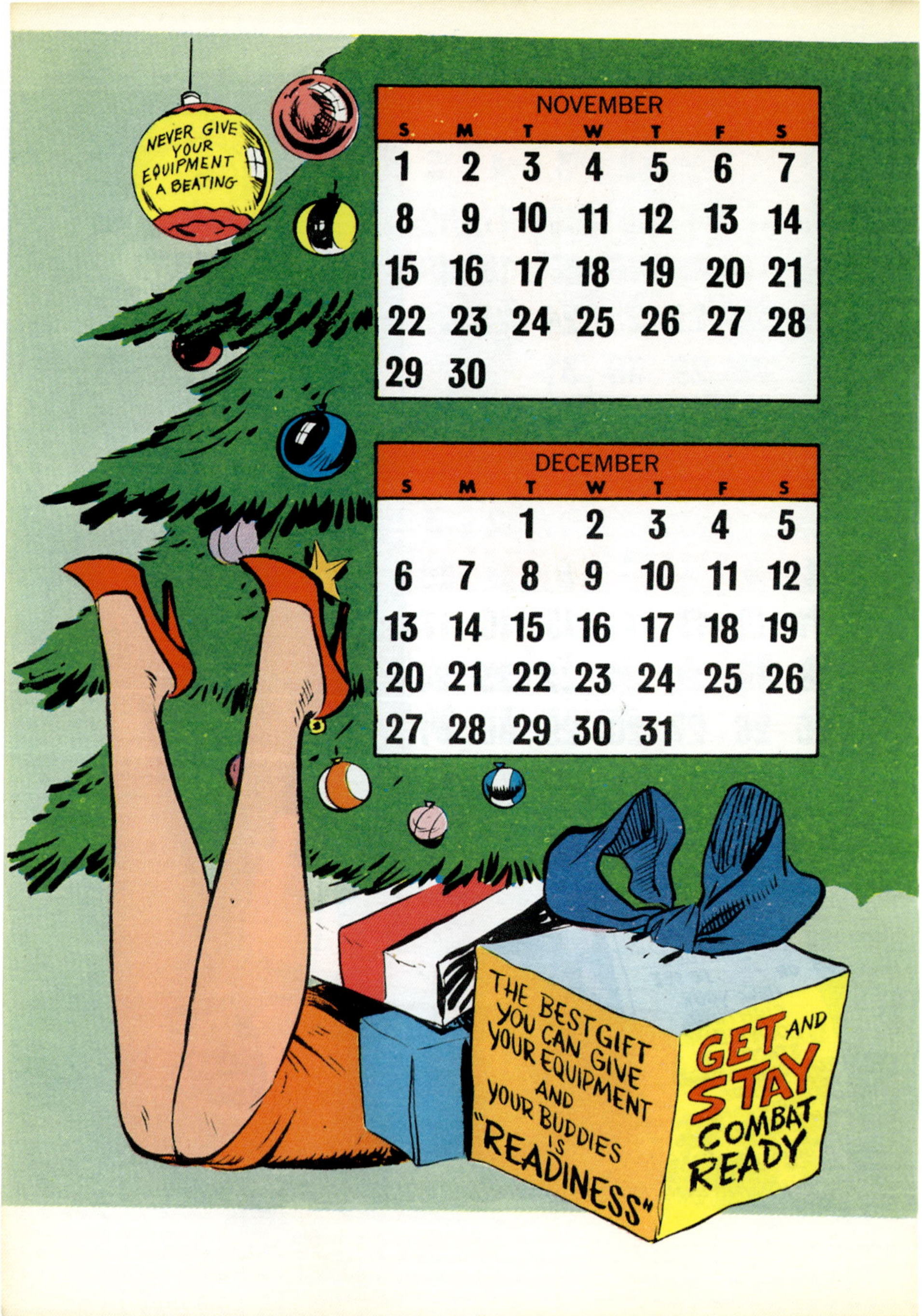
NEVER GIVE YOUR EQUIPMENT A BEATING
NOVEMBER
S M T W T F S
1 2 3 4 5 6 7
8 9 10 11 12 13 14
15 16 17 18 19 20 21
22 23 24 25 26 27 28
29 30
DECEMBER
S M T W T F S
1 2 3 4 5
6 7 8 9 10 11 12
13 14 15 16 17 18 19
20 21 22 23 24 25 26
27 28 29 30 31
THE BEST GIFT YOU CAN GIVE YOUR EQUIPMENT AND YOUR BUDDIES IS "READINESS"
GET AND STAY COMBAT READY

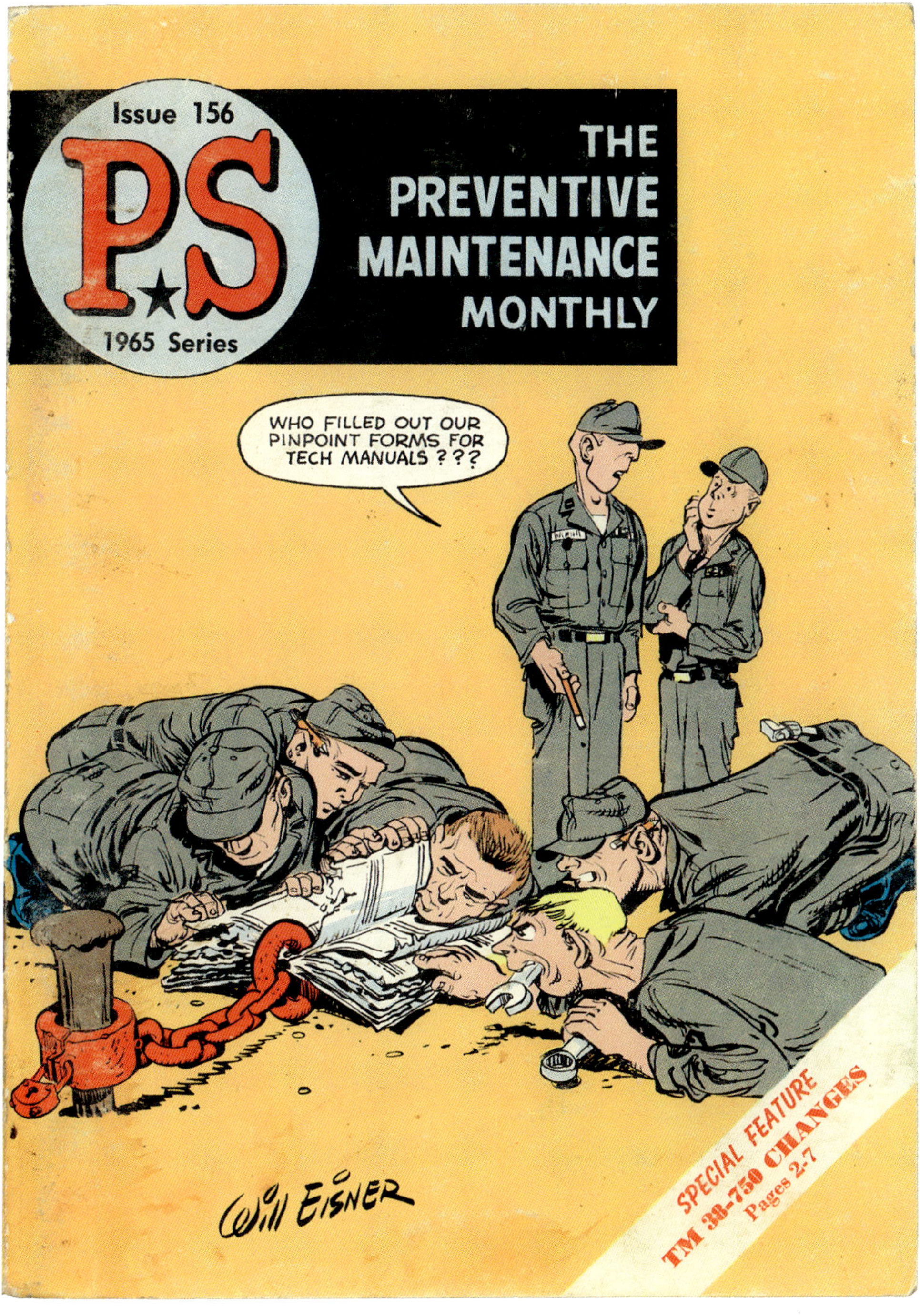
Issue 156
PS
1965 Series
THE PREVENTIVE MAINTENANCE MONTHLY
WHO FILLED OUT OUR PINPOINT FORMS FOR TECH MANUALS ???
Will Eisner
SPECIAL FEATURE
TM 38-750 CHANGES
Pages 2-7

no. 156, 1965

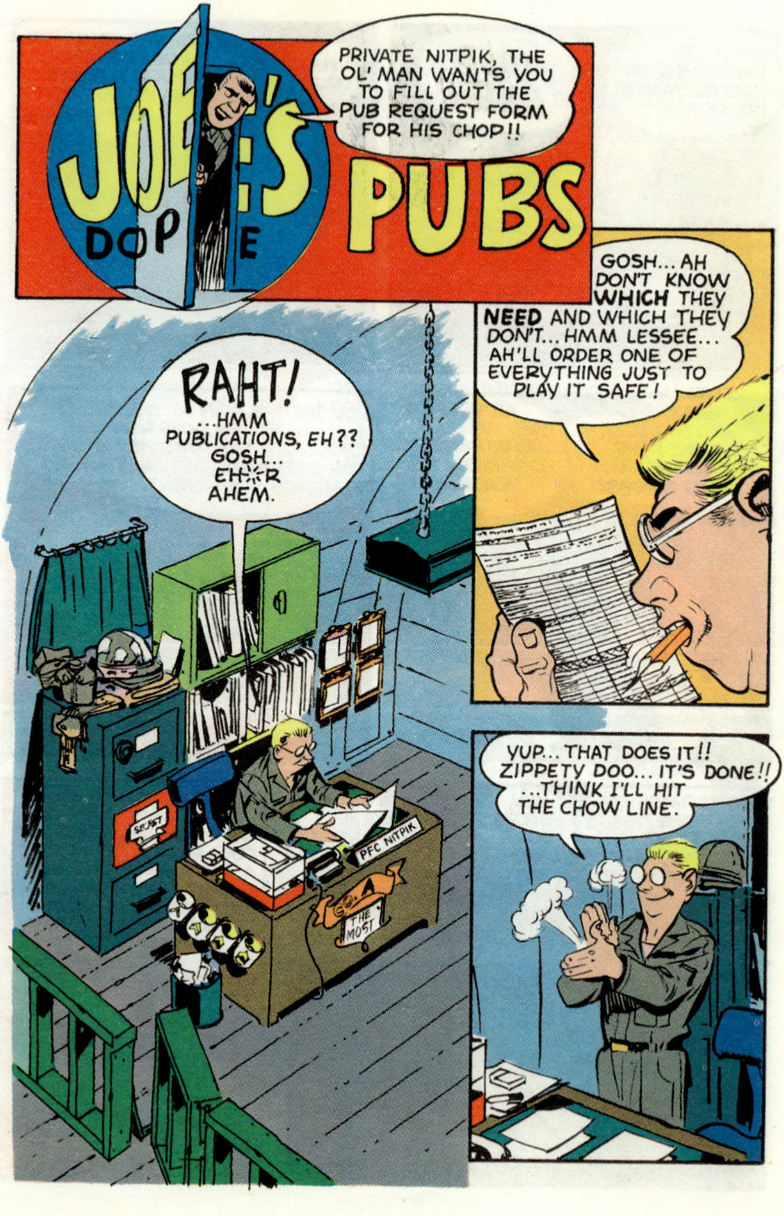
JOE'S DOPE
PUBS
PRIVATE NITPIK, THE OL' MAN WANTS YOU TO FILL OUT THE PUB REQUEST FORM FOR HIS CHOP!!
RAHT! ...HMM PUBLICATIONS, EH?? GOSH... EH*R AHEM.
GOSH... AH DON'T KNOW WHICH THEY NEED AND WHICH THEY DON'T... HMM LESSEE... AH'LL ORDER ONE OF EVERYTHING JUST TO PLAY IT SAFE!
PFC NITPIK
THE MOST
YUP... THAT DOES IT!! ZIPPETY DOO... IT'S DONE!! ...THINK I'LL HIT THE CHOW LINE.

no. 156, 1965

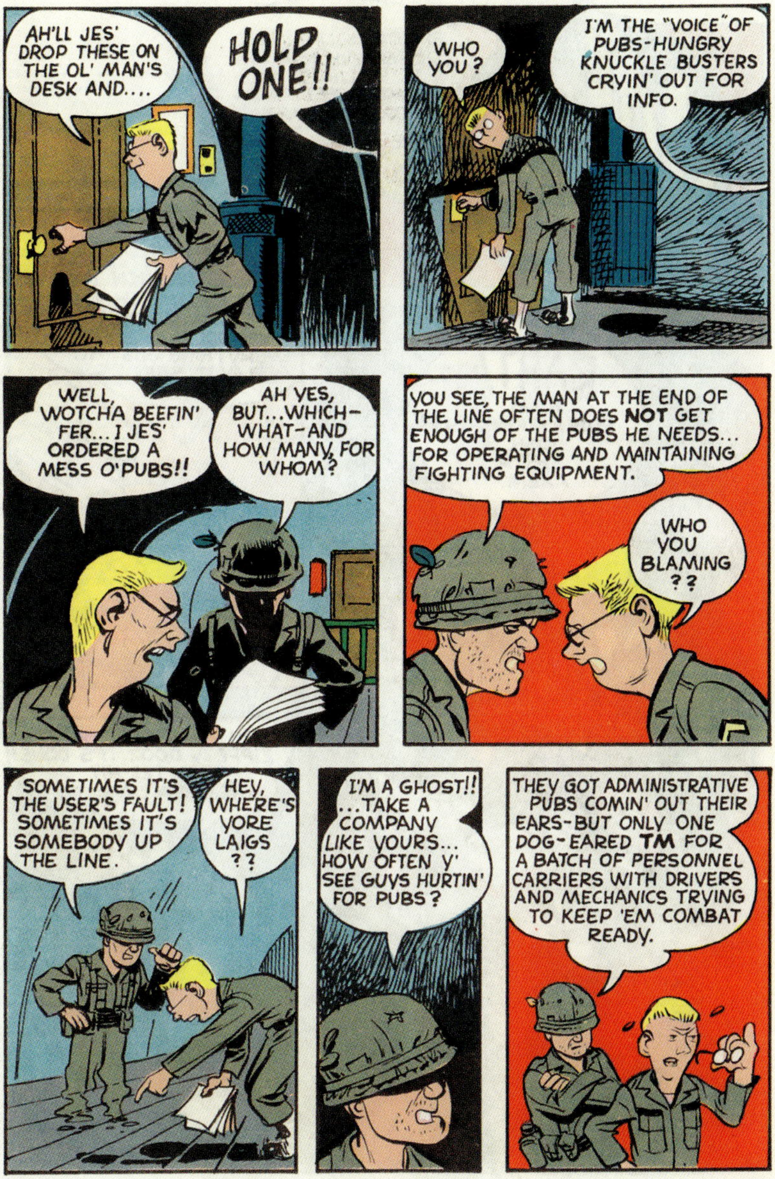
AH'LL JES' DROP THESE ON THE OL' MAN'S DESK AND....
HOLD ONE!!
WHO YOU?
I'M THE "VOICE" OF PUBS-HUNGRY KNUCKLE BUSTERS CRYIN' OUT FOR INFO.
WELL, WOTCHA BEEFIN' FER... I JES' ORDERED A MESS O'PUBS!!
AH YES, BUT...WHICH-WHAT-AND HOW MANY, FOR WHOM?
YOU SEE, THE MAN AT THE END OF THE LINE OFTEN DOES NOT GET ENOUGH OF THE PUBS HE NEEDS... FOR OPERATING AND MAINTAINING FIGHTING EQUIPMENT.
WHO YOU BLAMING ??
SOMETIMES IT'S THE USER'S FAULT! SOMETIMES IT'S SOMEBODY UP THE LINE.
HEY, WHERE'S YORE LAIGS ??
I'M A GHOST!! ...TAKE A COMPANY LIKE YOURS... HOW OFTEN Y' SEE GUYS HURTIN' FOR PUBS?
THEY GOT ADMINISTRATIVE PUBS COMIN' OUT THEIR EARS-BUT ONLY ONE DOG-EARED TM FOR A BATCH OF PERSONNEL CARRIERS WITH DRIVERS AND MECHANICS TRYING TO KEEP 'EM COMBAT READY.

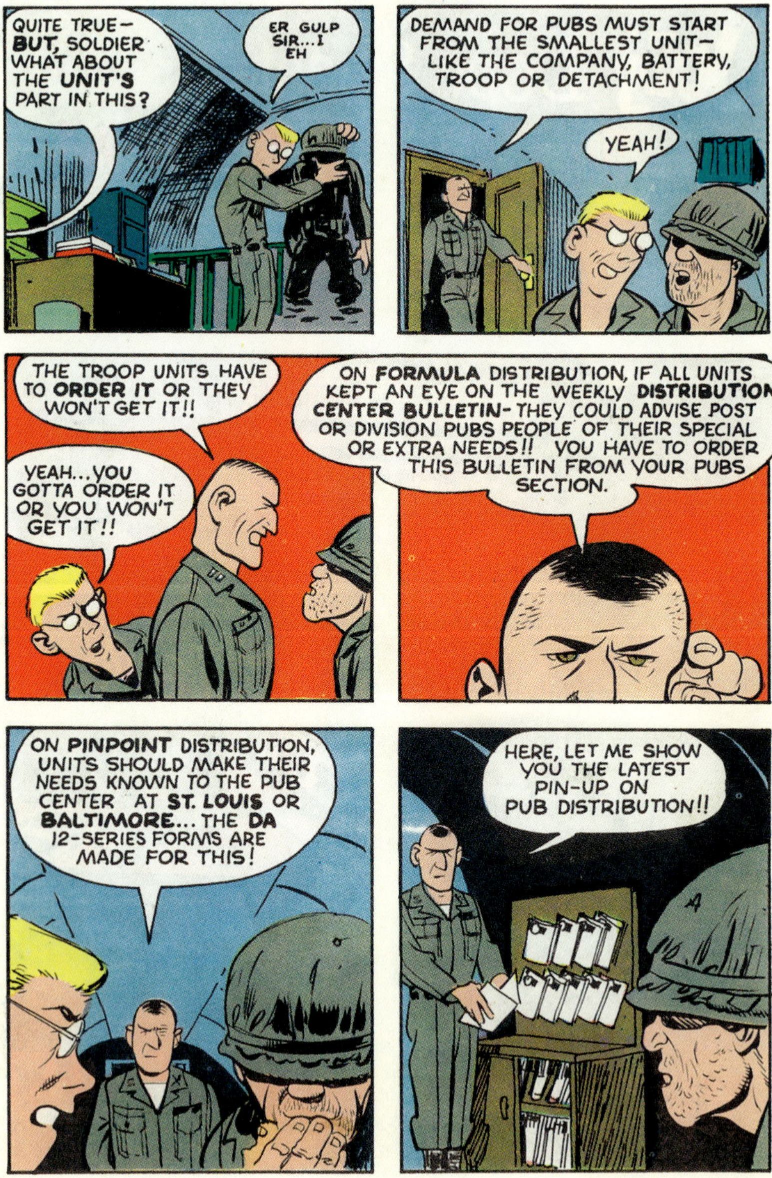
QUITE TRUE—
BUT, SOLDIER
WHAT ABOUT
THE UNIT'S
PART IN THIS?
ER GULP
SIR...I
EH
DEMAND FOR PUBS MUST START
FROM THE SMALLEST UNIT—
LIKE THE COMPANY, BATTERY,
TROOP OR DETACHMENT!
YEAH!
THE TROOP UNITS HAVE
TO ORDER IT OR THEY
WON'T GET IT!!
YEAH...YOU
GOTTA ORDER IT
OR YOU WON'T
GET IT!!
ON FORMULA DISTRIBUTION, IF ALL UNITS
KEPT AN EYE ON THE WEEKLY DISTRIBUTION
CENTER BULLETIN- THEY COULD ADVISE POST
OR DIVISION PUBS PEOPLE OF THEIR SPECIAL
OR EXTRA NEEDS!! YOU HAVE TO ORDER
THIS BULLETIN FROM YOUR PUBS
SECTION.
ON PINPOINT DISTRIBUTION,
UNITS SHOULD MAKE THEIR
NEEDS KNOWN TO THE PUB
CENTER AT ST. LOUIS OR
BALTIMORE... THE DA
12-SERIES FORMS ARE
MADE FOR THIS!
HERE, LET ME SHOW
YOU THE LATEST
PIN-UP ON
PUB DISTRIBUTION!!

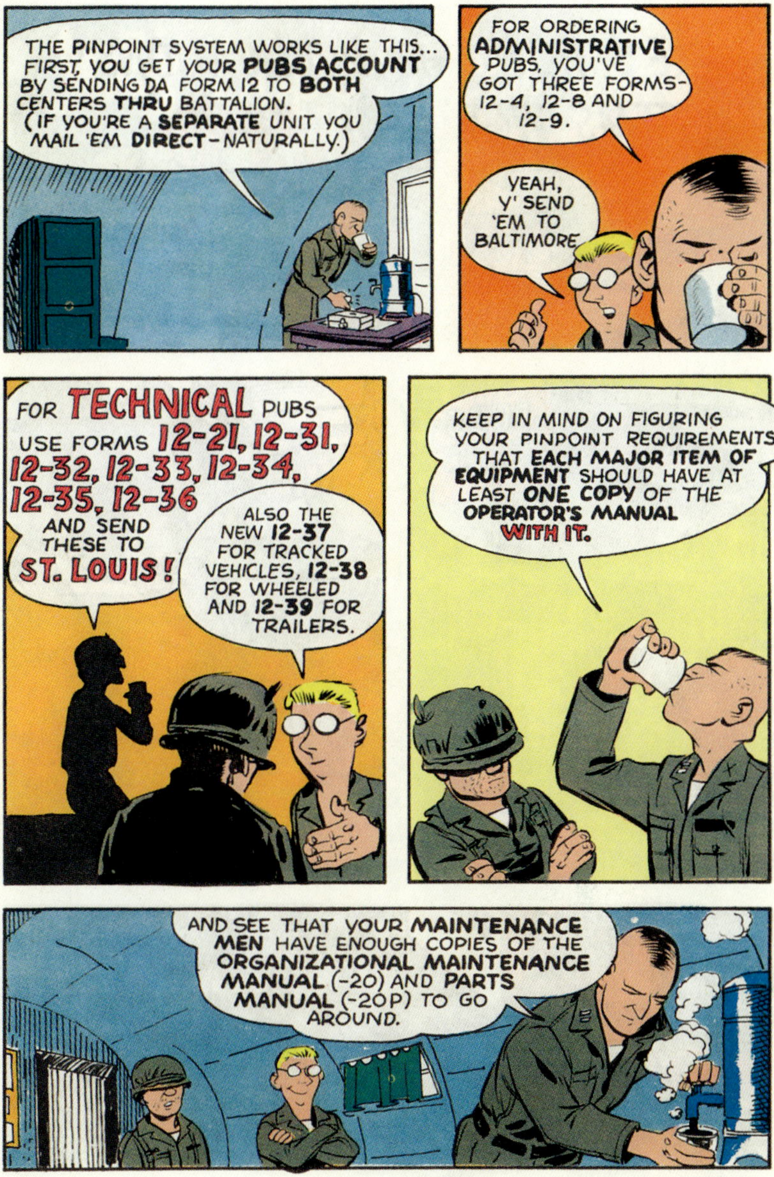
THE PINPOINT SYSTEM WORKS LIKE THIS... FIRST, YOU GET YOUR PUBS ACCOUNT BY SENDING DA FORM 12 TO BOTH CENTERS THRU BATTALION. (IF YOU'RE A SEPARATE UNIT YOU MAIL 'EM DIRECT–NATURALLY.)
FOR ORDERING ADMINISTRATIVE PUBS, YOU'VE GOT THREE FORMS- 12-4, 12-8 AND 12-9.
YEAH, Y' SEND 'EM TO BALTIMORE
FOR TECHNICAL PUBS USE FORMS 12-21, 12-31, 12-32, 12-33, 12-34, 12-35, 12-36 AND SEND THESE TO ST. LOUIS!
ALSO THE NEW 12-37 FOR TRACKED VEHICLES, 12-38 FOR WHEELED AND 12-39 FOR TRAILERS.
KEEP IN MIND ON FIGURING YOUR PINPOINT REQUIREMENTS THAT EACH MAJOR ITEM OF EQUIPMENT SHOULD HAVE AT LEAST ONE COPY OF THE OPERATOR'S MANUAL WITH IT.
AND SEE THAT YOUR MAINTENANCE MEN HAVE ENOUGH COPIES OF THE ORGANIZATIONAL MAINTENANCE MANUAL (-20) AND PARTS MANUAL (-20P) TO GO AROUND.

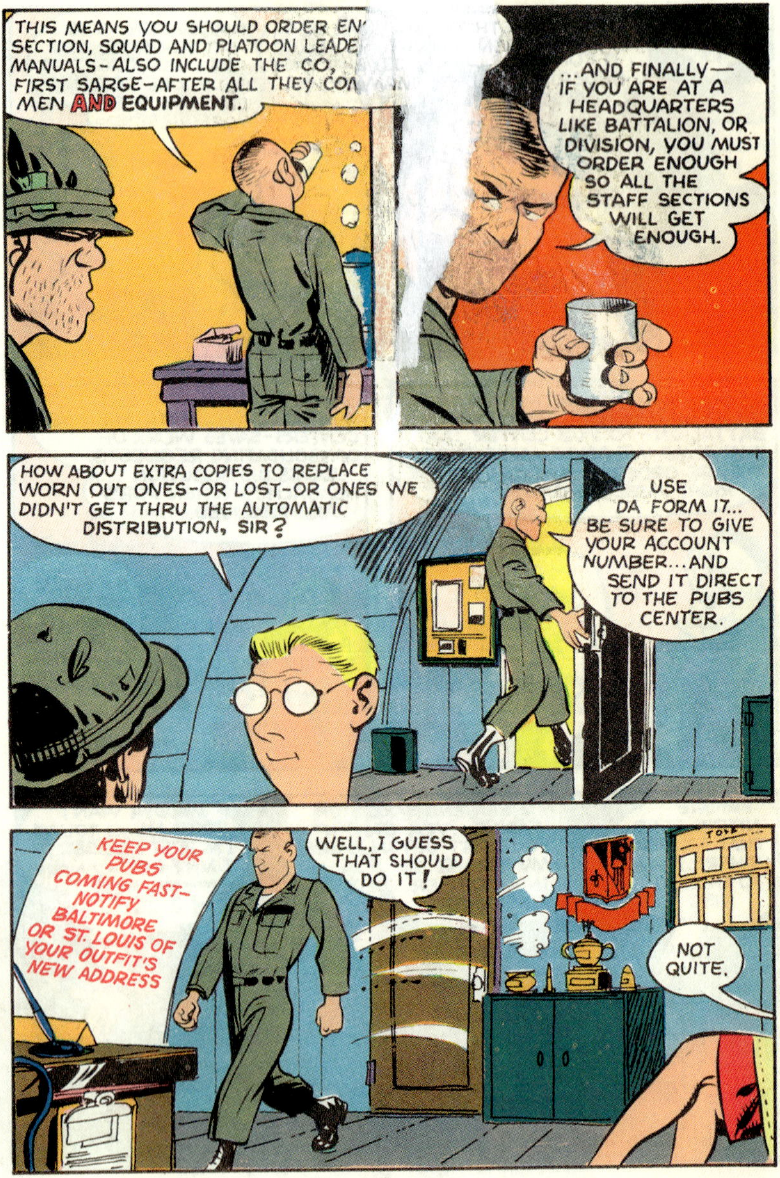
THIS MEANS YOU SHOULD ORDER EN
SECTION, SQUAD AND PLATOON LEADE
MANUALS-ALSO INCLUDE THE CO,
FIRST SARGE-AFTER ALL THEY COM
MEN AND EQUIPMENT.
...AND FINALLY— IF YOU ARE AT A HEADQUARTERS LIKE BATTALION, OR DIVISION, YOU MUST ORDER ENOUGH SO ALL THE STAFF SECTIONS WILL GET ENOUGH.
HOW ABOUT EXTRA COPIES TO REPLACE WORN OUT ONES-OR LOST-OR ONES WE DIDN'T GET THRU THE AUTOMATIC DISTRIBUTION, SIR?
USE DA FORM 17... BE SURE TO GIVE YOUR ACCOUNT NUMBER...AND SEND IT DIRECT TO THE PUBS CENTER.
KEEP YOUR PUBS COMING FAST-NOTIFY BALTIMORE OR ST. LOUIS OF YOUR OUTFIT'S NEW ADDRESS
WELL, I GUESS THAT SHOULD DO IT!
NOT QUITE.

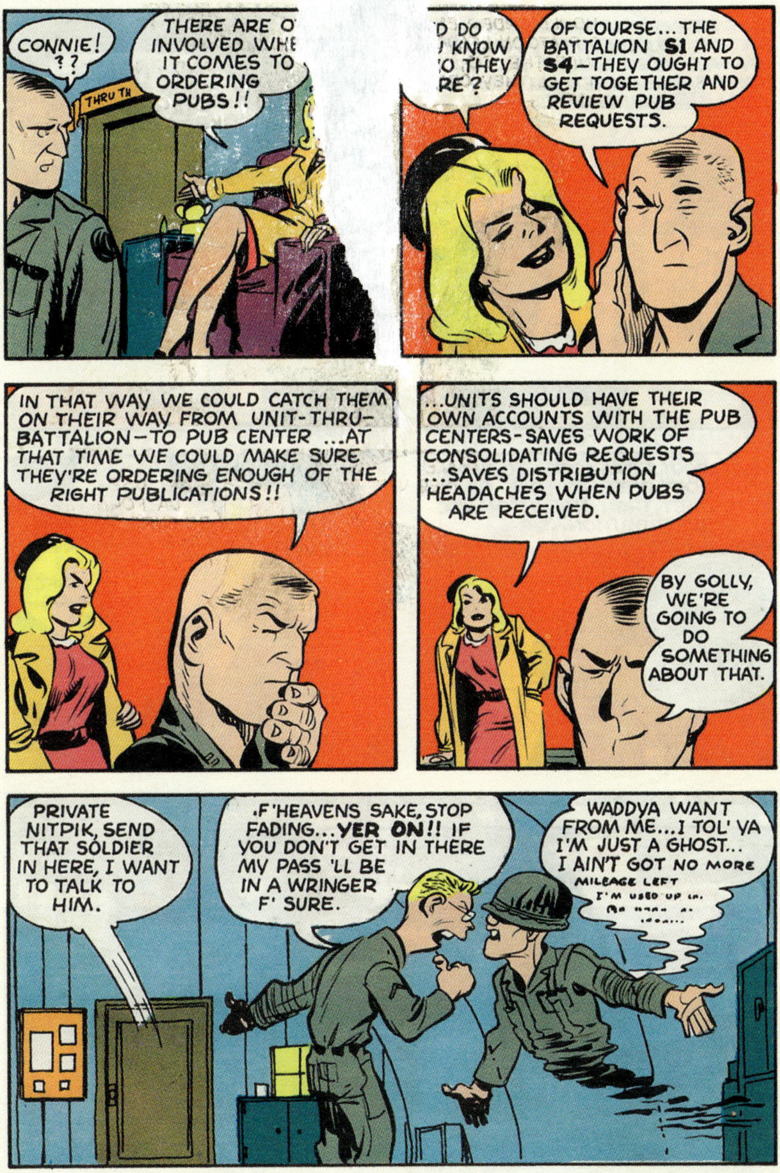
CONNIE! ??
THERE ARE O
INVOLVED WHE
IT COMES TO
ORDERING
PUBS!!
'D DO
J KNOW
O THEY
RE ?
OF COURSE... THE BATTALION S1 AND S4—THEY OUGHT TO GET TOGETHER AND REVIEW PUB REQUESTS.
THRU TH
IN THAT WAY WE COULD CATCH THEM ON THEIR WAY FROM UNIT-THRU-BATTALION—TO PUB CENTER ...AT THAT TIME WE COULD MAKE SURE THEY'RE ORDERING ENOUGH OF THE RIGHT PUBLICATIONS!!
...UNITS SHOULD HAVE THEIR OWN ACCOUNTS WITH THE PUB CENTERS-SAVES WORK OF CONSOLIDATING REQUESTS ...SAVES DISTRIBUTION HEADACHES WHEN PUBS ARE RECEIVED.
BY GOLLY, WE'RE GOING TO DO SOMETHING ABOUT THAT.
PRIVATE NITPIK, SEND THAT SOLDIER IN HERE, I WANT TO TALK TO HIM.
.F'HEAVENS SAKE, STOP FADING...YER ON!! IF YOU DON'T GET IN THERE MY PASS 'LL BE IN A WRINGER F' SURE.
WADDYA WANT FROM ME...I TOL' YA I'M JUST A GHOST... I AIN'T GOT NO MORE MILEAGE LEFT
I'M USED UP IN.

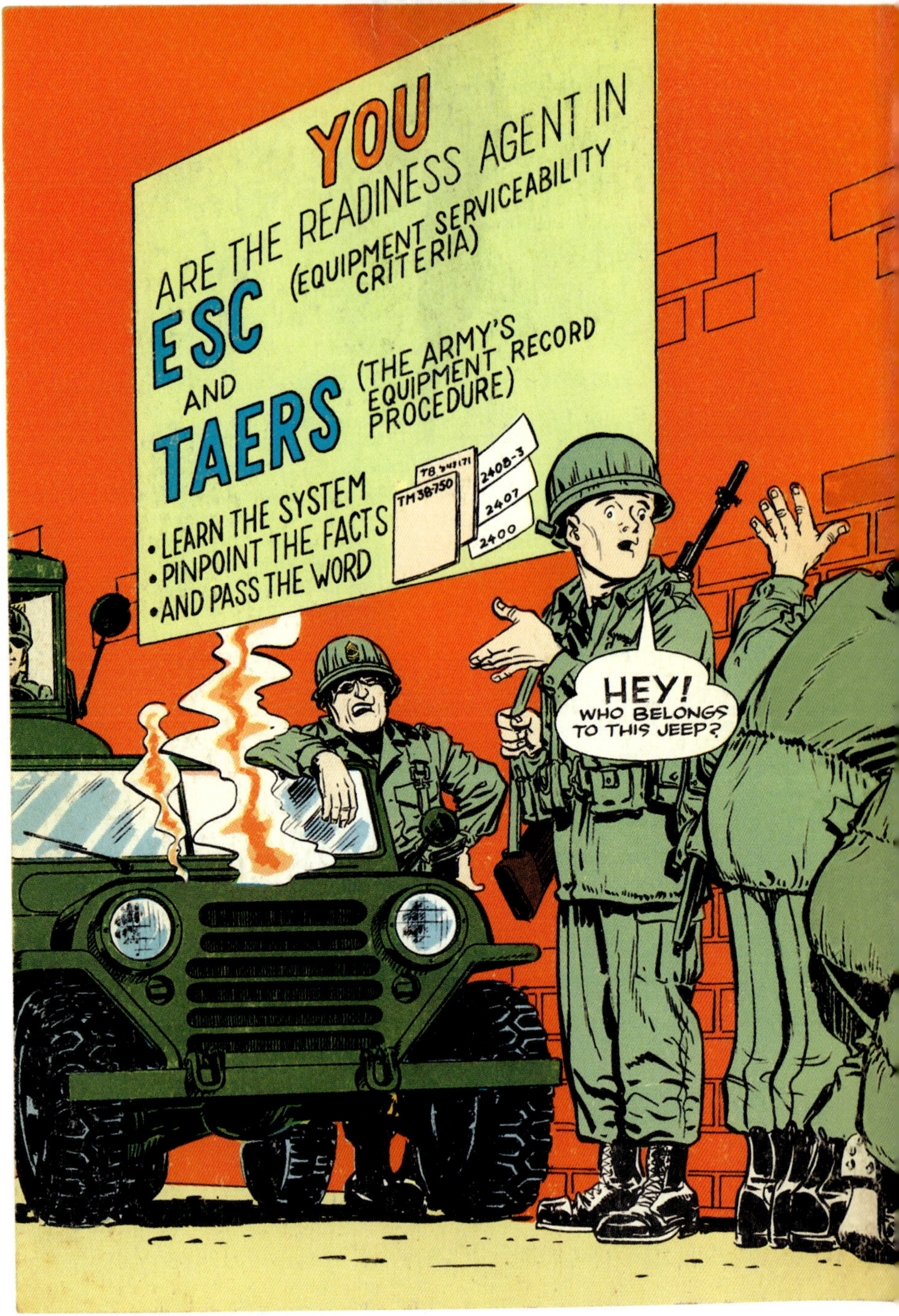
YOU
ARE THE READINESS AGENT IN
ESC (EQUIPMENT SERVICEABILITY CRITERIA)
AND
TAERS (THE ARMY'S EQUIPMENT RECORD PROCEDURE)
• LEARN THE SYSTEM
• PINPOINT THE FACTS
• AND PASS THE WORD
TM 38-750
2408-3
2407
2400
HEY! WHO BELONGS TO THIS JEEP?

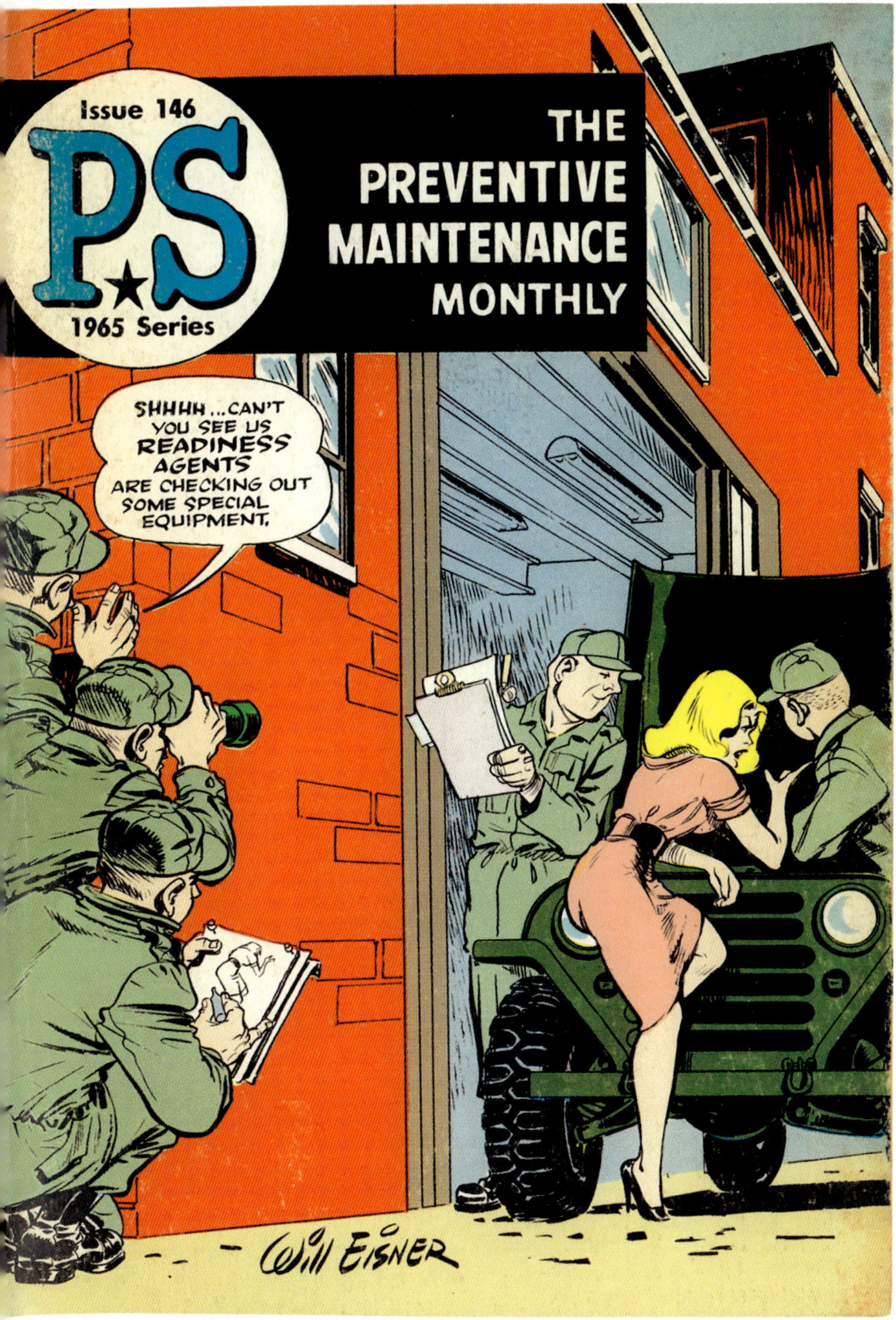
Issue 146
P★S
1965 Series
THE PREVENTIVE MAINTENANCE MONTHLY
SHHHH...CAN'T YOU SEE US READINESS AGENTS ARE CHECKING OUT SOME SPECIAL EQUIPMENT.
Will Eisner

FOR THE FIRST 21 YEARS OF OUR EXISTENCE, 1951-1971, MOST OF THE CREATIVE IMAGES THAT OUR READERS SAW WERE DRAWN BY ***WILL EISNER.***

ALTHOUGH OTHER ARTISTS WORKED FOR HIM, IT WAS HIS STYLE, HIS CREATIVITY AND HIS SHEER ARTISTIC GENIUS THAT DEFINED THE LOOK OF P*S MAGAZINE AND THE CHARACTERS THAT THE SOLDIERS CAME TO KNOW AND LOVE... GRANITE-JAWED SERGEANT HALF-MAST, VIVACIOUS CONNIE RODD, GOOFY PVT. JOE DOPE AND MANY OTHERS.

EVERY PERSON THAT HAS EVER WORKED AT P*S HAS BEEN AFFECTED BY HIS LEGACY AND THE STANDARDS THAT HE SET.

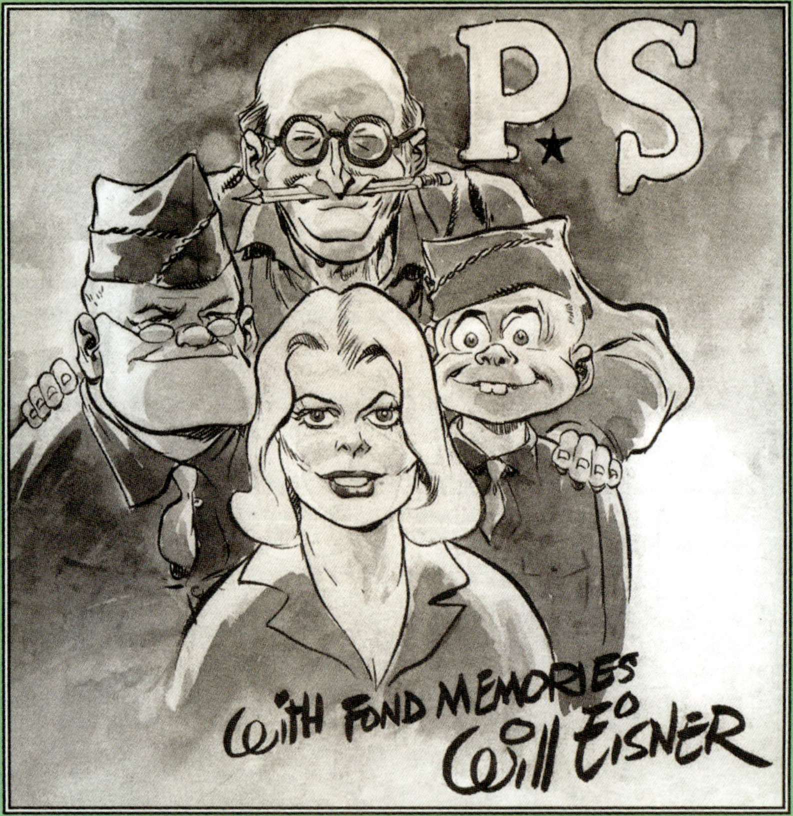
P*S
With Fond Memories
Will Eisner

IN MEMORY OF WILL EISNER, 1917-2005...

THE FOND MEMORIES ARE ALL OURS! THE STAFF OF P*S MAGAZINE

DISTRIBUTION: To be distributed in accordance with the initial distribution number (IDN) 340312, requirements for TB 43-PS-Series.

☆ U.S. GOVERNMENT PRINTING OFFICE: 20035 — 750-113/80028

For Sale by the Superintendent of Documents, U.S. Government Printing Office
Internet: bookstore.gpo.gov Phone: toll free (866) 512-1800; DC area (202) 512-1800
Fax: (202) 512-2250 Mail: Stop SSOP, Washington DC 20402-0001

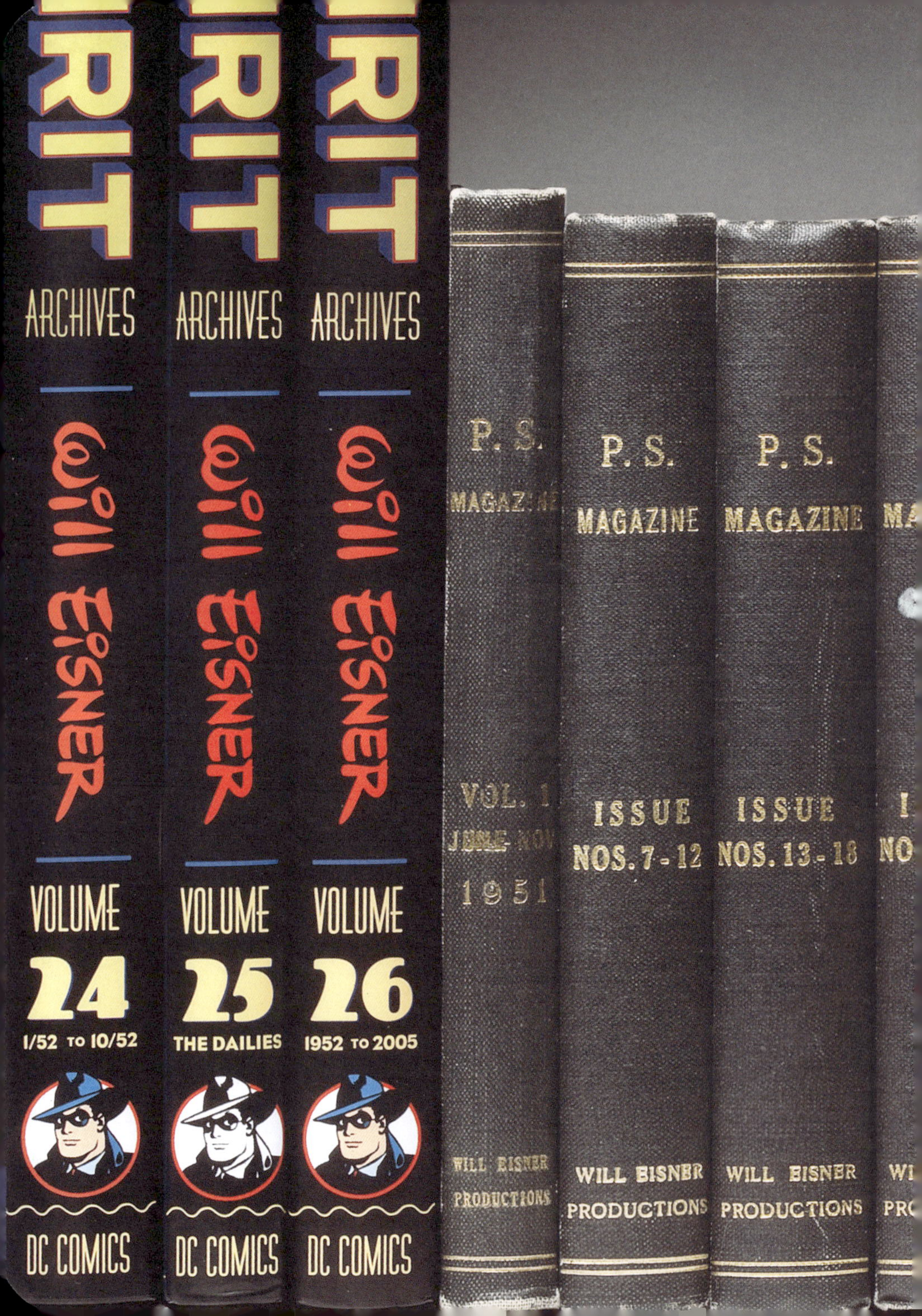
ARCHIVES
Will Eisner
VOLUME
24
1/52 TO 10/52
DC COMICS
ARCHIVES
Will Eisner
VOLUME
25
THE DAILIES
DC COMICS
ARCHIVES
Will Eisner
VOLUME
26
1952 TO 2005
DC COMICS
P. S.
VOL. 1
1951
WILL EISNER
PRODUCTIONS
P. S.
MAGAZINE
ISSUE
NOS. 7 - 12
WILL EISNER
PRODUCTIONS
P. S.
MAGAZINE
ISSUE
NOS. 13 - 18
WILL EISNER
PRODUCTIONS